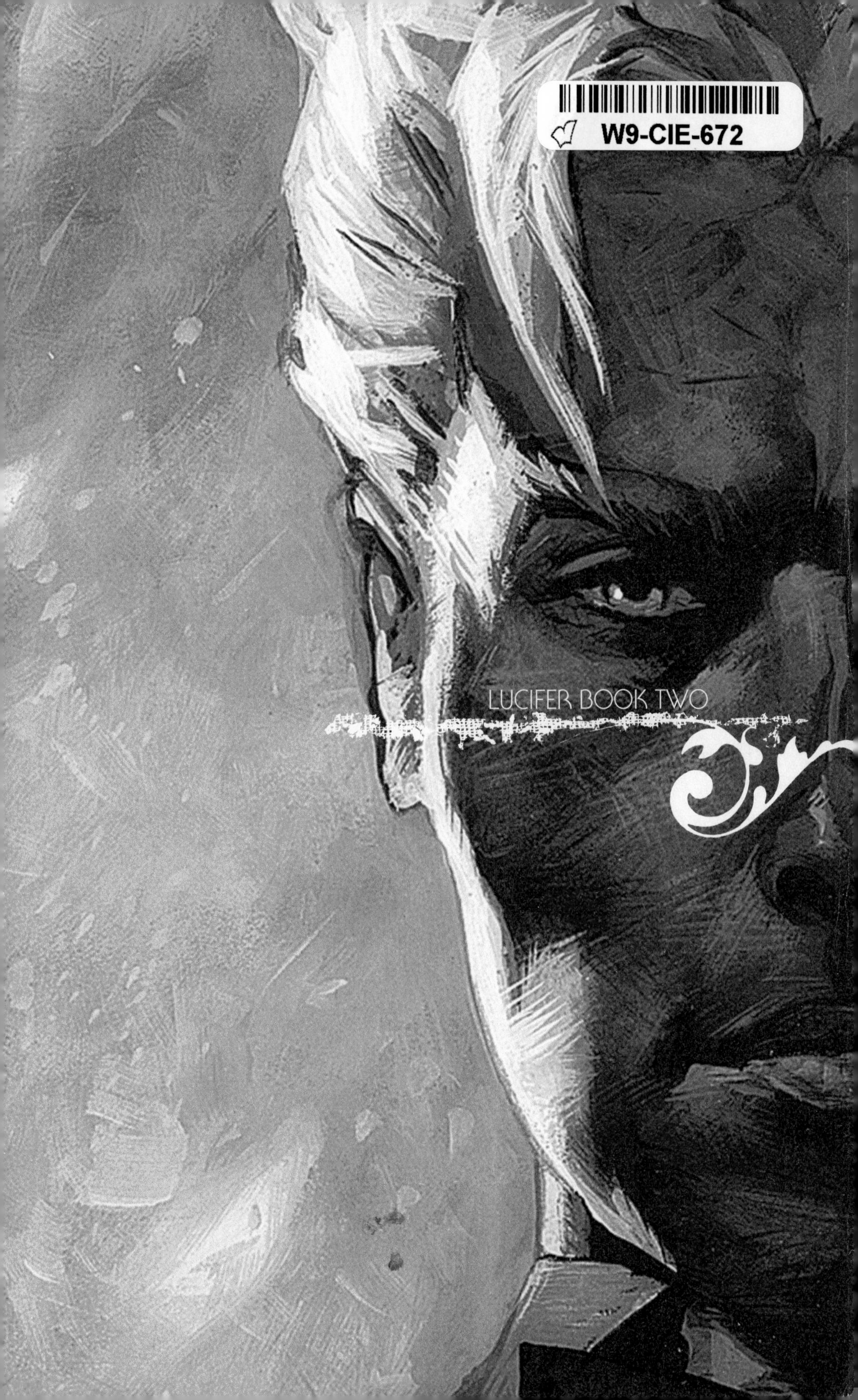
LUCIFER BOOK TWO

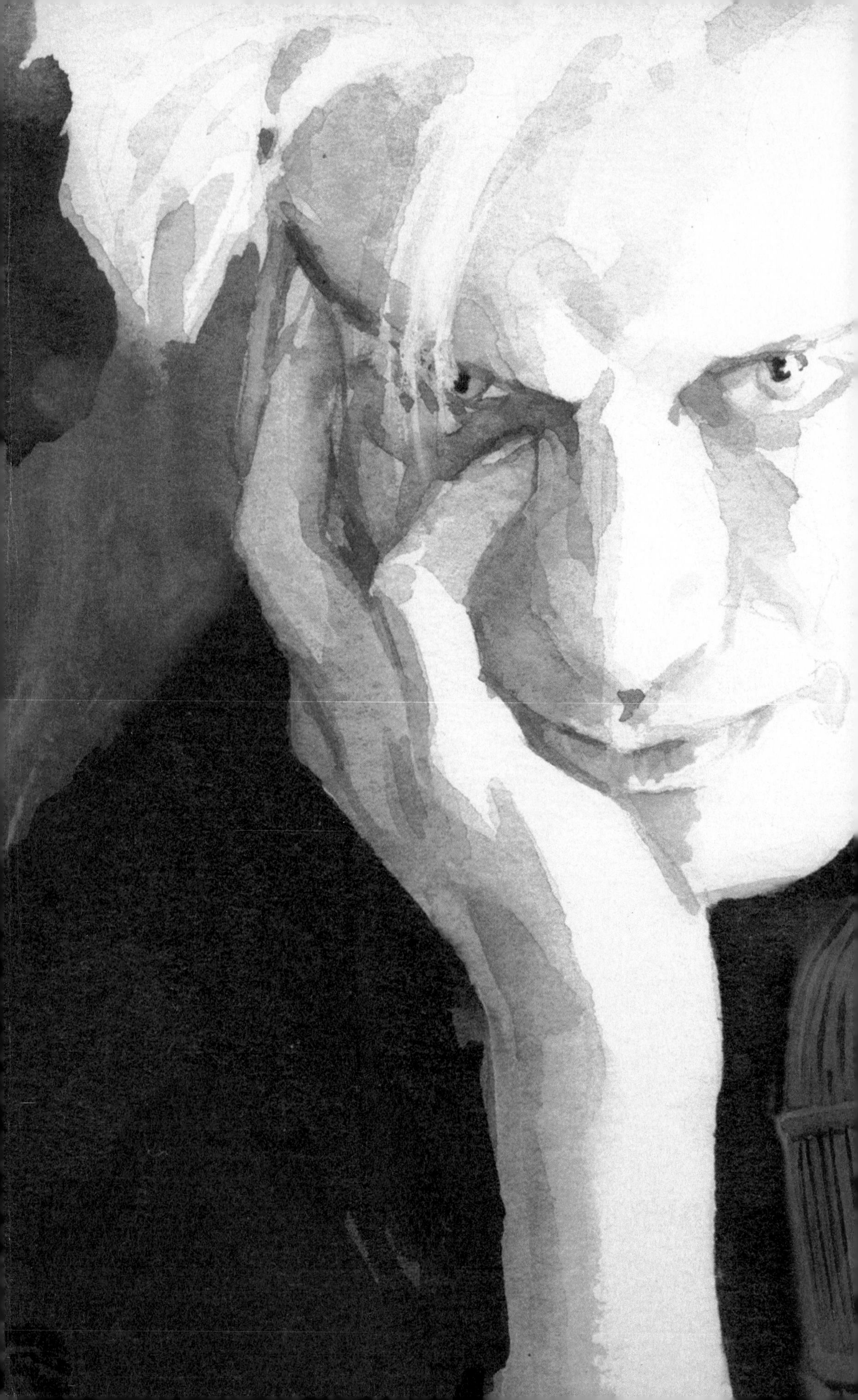

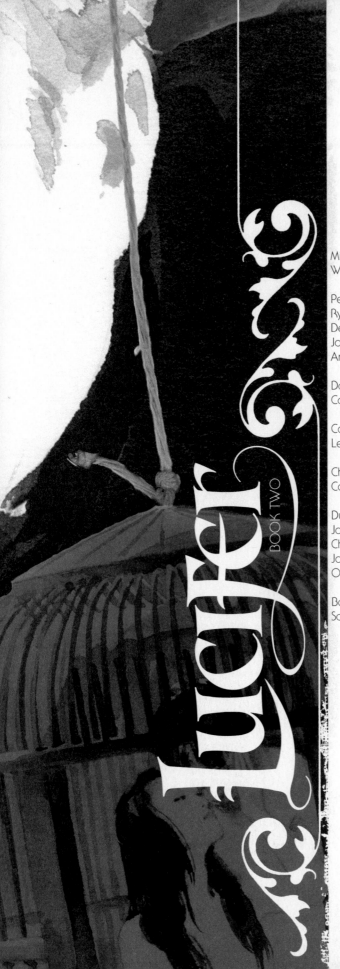

Lucifer

BOOK TWO

Mike Carey
Writer

Peter Gross
Ryan Kelly
Dean Ormston
Jon J Muth
Artists

Daniel Vozzo
Colorist

Comicraft
Letterer

Christopher Moeller
Cover Art

Duncan Fegredo
John Van Fleet
Christopher Moeller
Jon J Muth
Original Series Covers

Based on characters created by Neil Gaiman,
Sam Kieth and Mike Dringenberg.

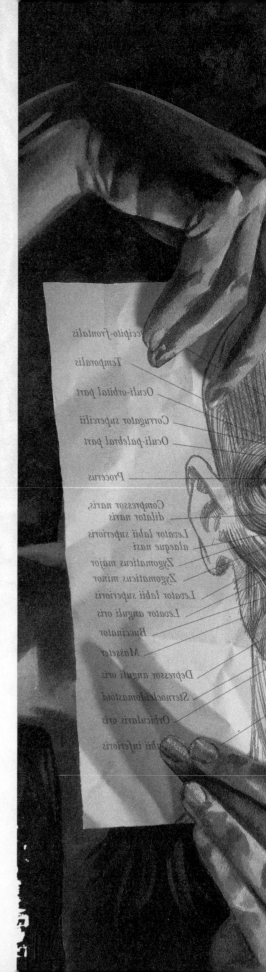

Shelly Bond Editor – Original Series

Will Dennis Associate Editor – Original Series

Mariah Huehner Assistant Editor – Original Series

Jeb Woodard Group Editor – Collected Editions

Scott Nybakken Editor – Collected Edition

Steve Cook Design Director – Books

Louis Prandi Publication Design

Shelly Bond VP & Executive Editor – Vertigo

Diane Nelson President

Dan DiDio and Jim Lee Co-Publishers

Geoff Johns Chief Creative Officer

Amit Desai Senior VP – Marketing & Global Franchise Management

Nairi Gardiner Senior VP – Finance

Sam Ades VP – Digital Marketing

Bobbie Chase VP – Talent Development

Mark Chiarello Senior VP – Art, Design & Collected Editions

John Cunningham VP – Content Strategy

Anne DePies VP – Strategy Planning & Reporting

Don Falletti VP – Manufacturing Operations

Lawrence Ganem VP – Editorial Administration & Talent Relations

Alison Gill Senior VP – Manufacturing & Operations

Hank Kanalz Senior VP – Editorial Strategy & Administration

Jay Kogan VP – Legal Affairs

Derek Maddalena Senior VP – Sales & Business Development

Jack Mahan VP – Business Affairs

Dan Miron VP – Sales Planning & Trade Development

Nick Napolitano VP – Manufacturing Administration

Carol Roeder VP – Marketing

Eddie Scannell VP – Mass Account & Digital Sales

Courtney Simmons Senior VP. – Publicity & Communications

Jim (Ski) Sokolowski VP – Comic Book Specialty & Newsstand Sales

Sandy Yi Senior VP – Global Franchise Management

LUCIFER BOOK TWO

Published by DC Comics. Copyright © 2013 DC Comics.
All Rights Reserved.

DC Comics, 2900 W. Alameda Avenue, Burbank, CA 91505
Printed by RR Donnelley, Salem, VA, USA. Third Printing.
ISBN: 978-1-4012-4260-2

Library of Congress Cataloging-in-Publication Data

Carey, Mike, 1959- author.
  Lucifer Book Two / Mike Carey, Peter Gross.
     pages cm
  "Originally published in single magazine form as LUCIFER 14-28,
LUCIFER: NIRVANA."
  ISBN 978-1-4012-4260-2
  1. Graphic novels. I. Gross, Peter, 1958- illustrator. II. Title.
PN6728.L79C39 2013
741.5'973—dc23
                                                    2013021260

Table of Contents

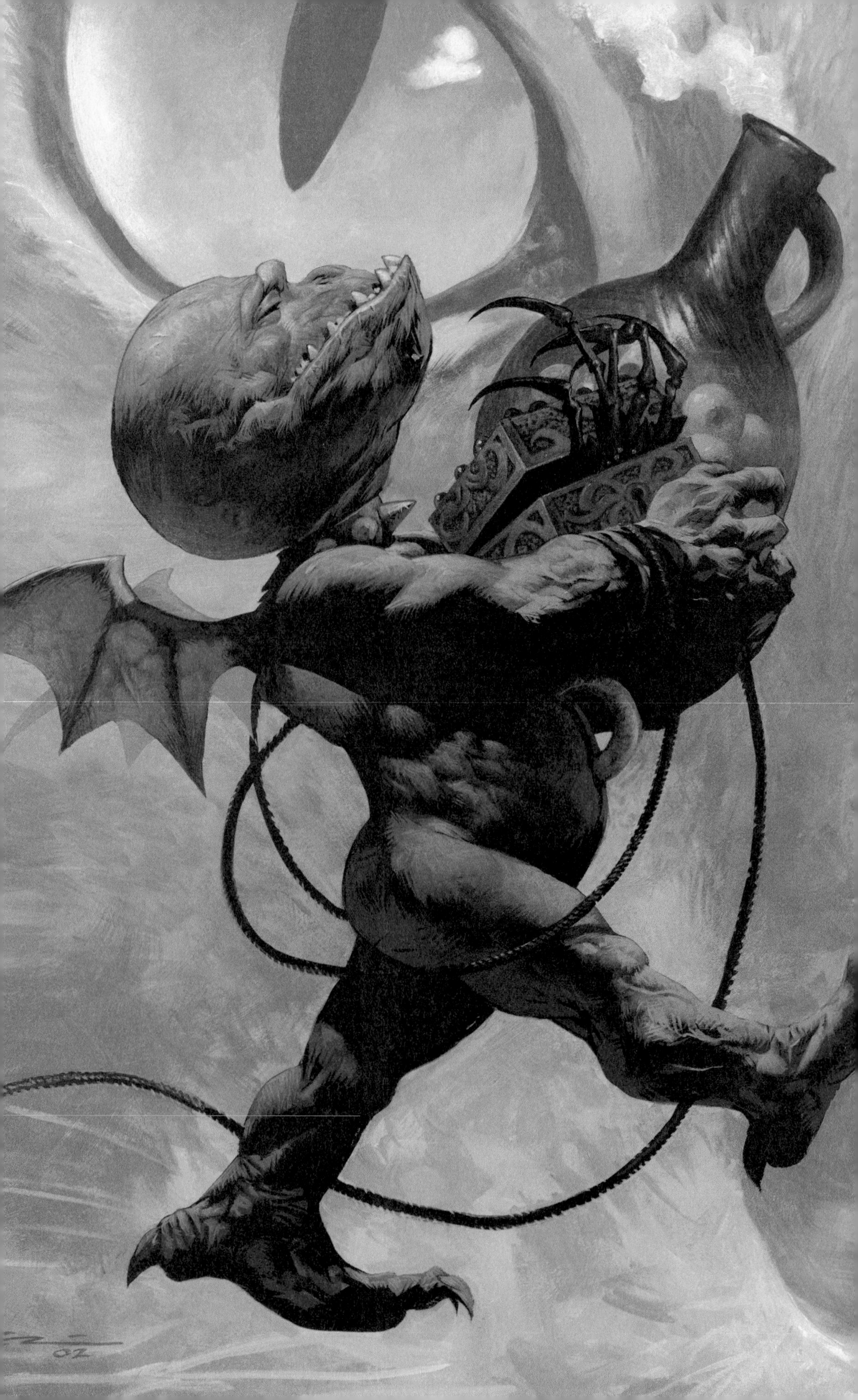

I had never written an ongoing book before I started work on LUCIFER. The longest story I'd ever told was a four-part miniseries.

Now here I was, embarked on a narrative that was going to take more than six years to complete. It was a vast enterprise, and (as Neil Gaiman had warned me) I was discovering the rules as I went along. There's really no other way to do it.

Everything up through the end of "Triptych" had been worked out in advance in fairly meticulous detail, so the first story arc that was planned in real time as we approached it was "A Dalliance With the Damned." It was a turning point for us in a number of ways.

First of all, it marked a further increase in permanent or recurring cast members. The fallen cherub, Gaudium, had already been introduced in "Children and Monsters," and the Lady Lys, briefly, in "Triptych." "A Dalliance With the Damned" would add Arux, Prackspoor, and Christopher Rudd, and would define the region of Effrul (in Hell) as a distinct setting — one that would be revisited often in later arcs such as "Inferno" and "Morningstar" and the one-off "The Eighth Sin."

It also marked a new phase in Peter's and my collaboration on the title. Peter had come on board with issue #5 (see my introduction to LUCIFER BOOK ONE), and at the beginning he had felt that this was more my story than his — which made him reticent about offering advice or opinions on storytelling. With "Dalliance," however, we began relaxing into the partnership, learning each other's styles and approaches and talking things through more explicitly.

A great example of this, and one that I never tire of mentioning, is Christopher Rudd's origin story — the story of how he sinned and died and went to Hell for his transgressions. I wrote this three-page sequence in a very penny-plain style as a straightforward flashback, with Rudd narrating over the mostly silent images.

Then Peter called me up and said he thought there was a case for doing it very differently. "This is a man thinking about his own damnation, right? And he's tortured by it every waking moment. You could argue that this isn't just the reason he's in Hell, these memories are the Hell he's in. So let's put that obsession on the page."

In short, Peter took my grim, blunt fable of child murder and twisted it into something darkly mesmerizing. Forty-five panels over three pages, and as vivid and terrible a depiction of a tormented mind devouring itself as you're ever likely to see.

Finally, "Dalliance" put the seal on the way the rest of our epic would be told. After its completion I felt confident in pushing forward with the style that I'd first tried out in "Children and Monsters" — allowing Lucifer to weave in and out of other people's stories, so that he acted as a catalyst for their actions and controlled their outcomes like some sort of infernal ringmaster. It was a style that seemed suited to the character, keeping him partially unknowable but still allowing him to be part of a complex unfolding plot while maintaining the aura of huge power and menace that he'd always had in THE SANDMAN.

And something else happened in that second year of the book's life. I'd been talking to Shelly about the possibility of writing a miniseries that struck out on a tangent from the main story arc but still illuminated some of our themes (like the one-offs we were doing). I actually got as far as pitching a Mazikeen four-parter that would have shown what she was doing in Hell while Lucifer was experiencing formal banquets and violent revolutions in Effrul. That eventually came to nothing, but Shelly was able to get approval for a parallel project that I pitched at the same time — a prestige format one-off exploring some of the challenges that Lucifer faced when he went from being the leader of the opposition to being a deity in his own right.

That became "Nirvana," and it's included here (for the first time) in its rightful place, after "Triptych" but before "Dalliance." The conversation between Lucifer and Mazikeen at the start of the story is very relevant to events in those arcs.

We were fortunate enough to get Jon J Muth as the artist on "Nirvana," and his gorgeous painted art gave the book an ethereal, otherworldly feel. In one respect, however, the project left him somewhat traumatized. He was working on the climax to the story, in which the angel Perdissa brings a 747 jet down on the Tiananmen Gate, and he had the radio on in the background while he worked. The date was the eleventh of September, 2001.

At a certain point Jon put his brush down and called me.

"I can't paint this scene," he said. "I really can't. Not now. Probably not ever."

And he didn't. That ending was excised, and I'm not sure I even have the script for it any more. A few weeks later I wrote the revised scene that appears in this volume.

I only mention this because it feels, every time I re-read the story, as though it curves around an unseen obstacle at that point — a big, invisible mass of tragedy and horror. Sometimes the world leaves you temporarily helpless and unarmed. Stories leak away and you're left with a profound silence.

You have to wait until the words and the images come back to you.

— **Mike Carey**
London, May 2013

Lucifer

BOOK TWO

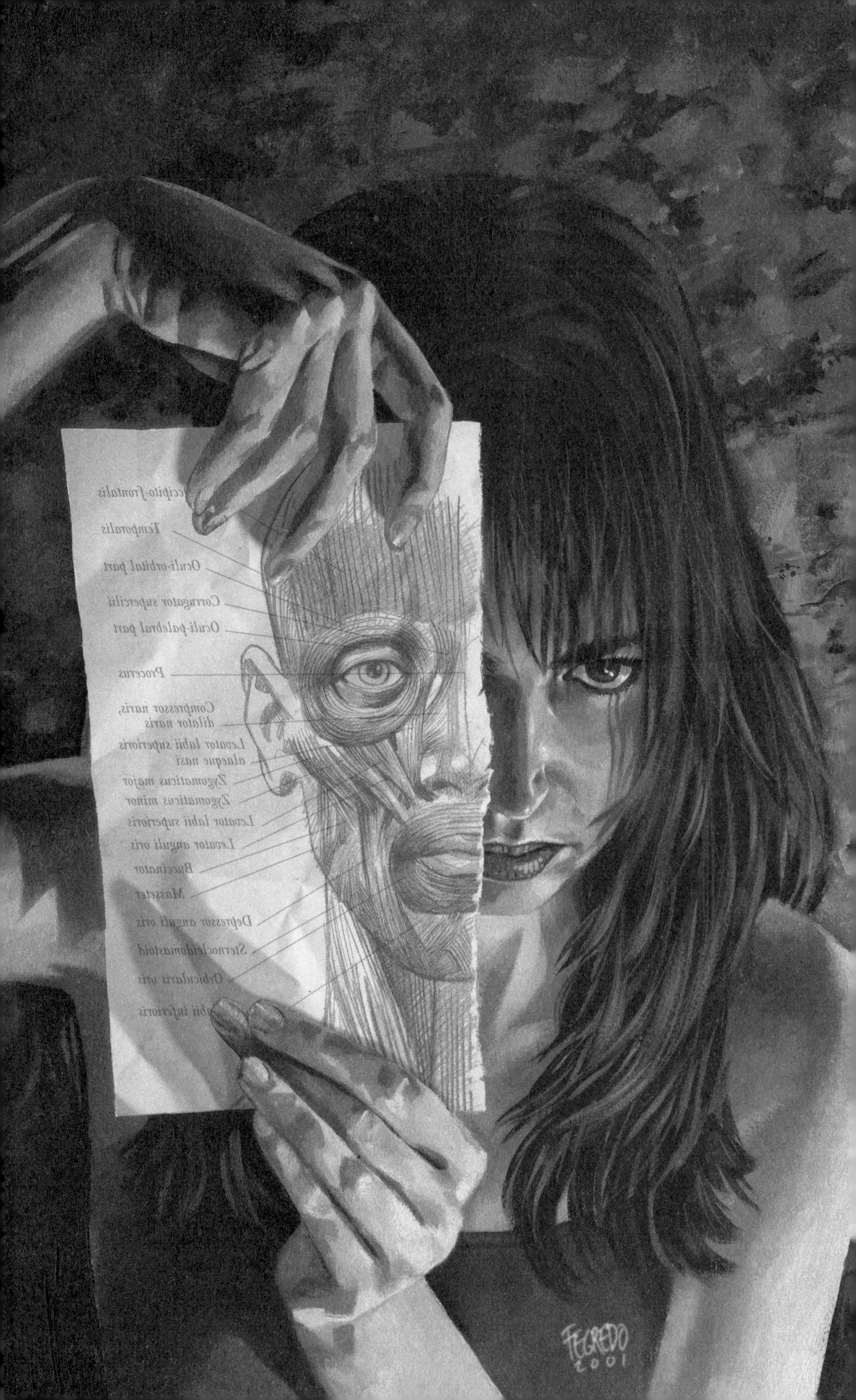

ccipito-frontalis
Temporalis
Oculi-orbital part
Corrugator supercilii
Oculi-palebral part
Procerus
Compressor naris, dilator naris
Levator labii superioris alaeque nasi
Zygomaticus major
Zygomaticus minor
Levator labii superioris
Levator anguli oris
Buccinator
Masseter
Depressor anguli oris
Sternocleidomastoid
Orbicularis oris
abii inferioris
FEGREDO 2001

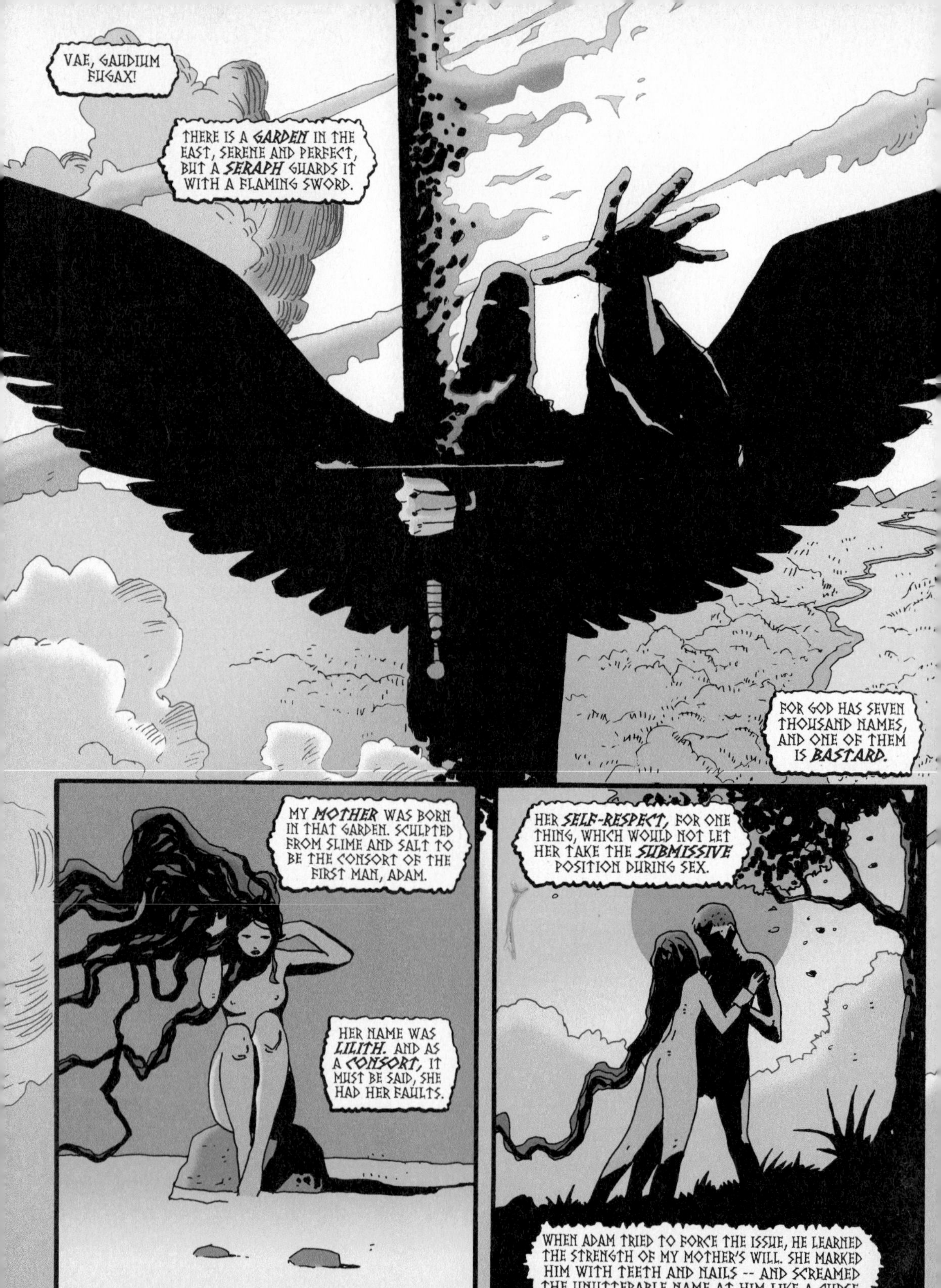
VAE, GAUDIUM FUGAX!
THERE IS A GARDEN IN THE EAST, SERENE AND PERFECT, BUT A SERAPH GUARDS IT WITH A FLAMING SWORD.
FOR GOD HAS SEVEN THOUSAND NAMES, AND ONE OF THEM IS BASTARD.
MY MOTHER WAS BORN IN THAT GARDEN. SCULPTED FROM SLIME AND SALT TO BE THE CONSORT OF THE FIRST MAN, ADAM.
HER NAME WAS LILITH. AND AS A CONSORT, IT MUST BE SAID, SHE HAD HER FAULTS.
HER SELF-RESPECT, FOR ONE THING, WHICH WOULD NOT LET HER TAKE THE SUBMISSIVE POSITION DURING SEX.
WHEN ADAM TRIED TO FORCE THE ISSUE, HE LEARNED THE STRENGTH OF MY MOTHER'S WILL. SHE MARKED HIM WITH TEETH AND NAILS -- AND SCREAMED THE UNUTTERABLE NAME AT HIM LIKE A CURSE.

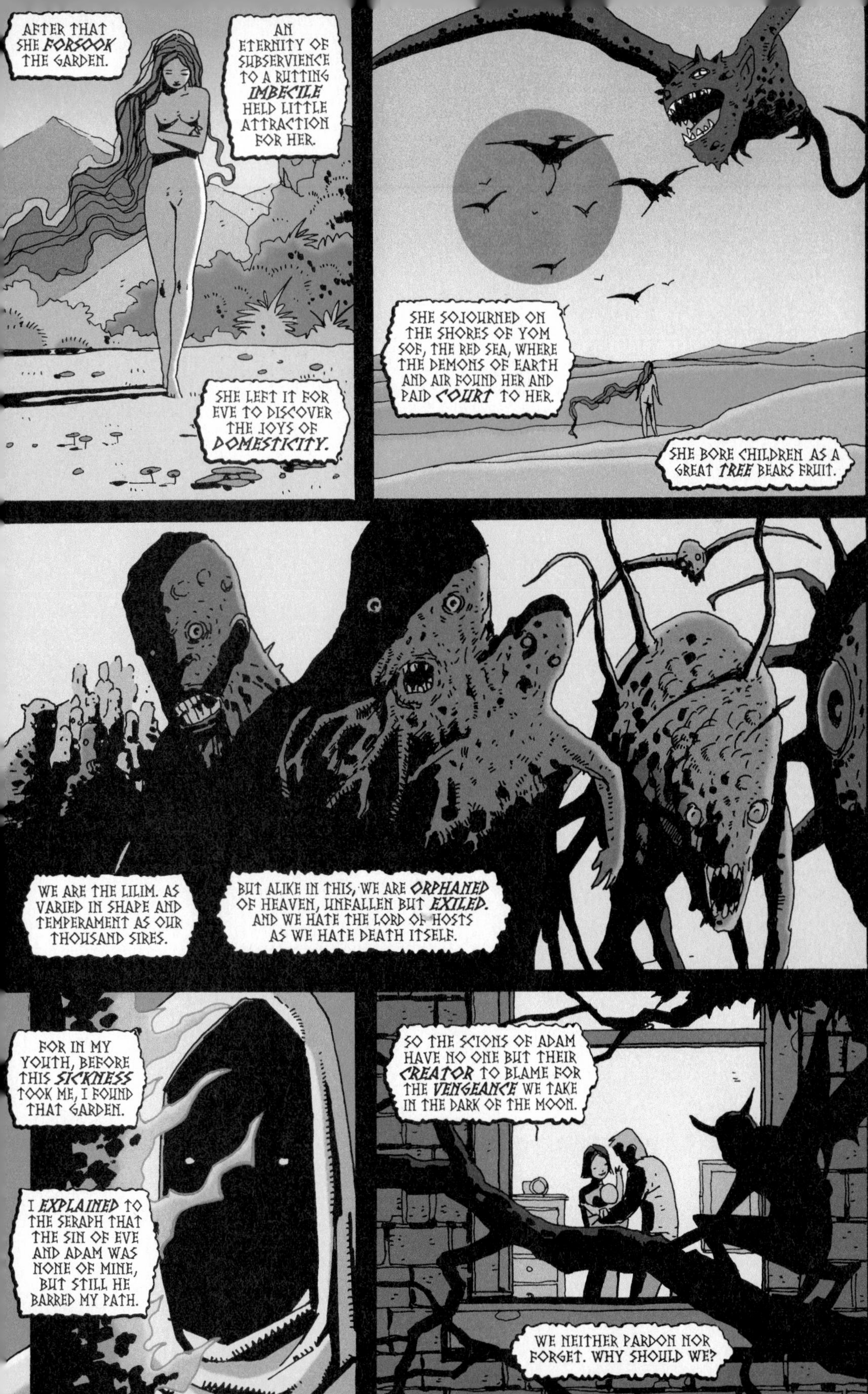
AFTER THAT SHE FORSOOK THE GARDEN.
AN ETERNITY OF SUBSERVIENCE TO A RUTTING IMBECILE HELD LITTLE ATTRACTION FOR HER.
SHE LEFT IT FOR EVE TO DISCOVER THE JOYS OF DOMESTICITY.
SHE SOJOURNED ON THE SHORES OF YOM SOF, THE RED SEA, WHERE THE DEMONS OF EARTH AND AIR FOUND HER AND PAID COURT TO HER.
SHE BORE CHILDREN AS A GREAT TREE BEARS FRUIT.
WE ARE THE LILIM. AS VARIED IN SHAPE AND TEMPERAMENT AS OUR THOUSAND SIRES.
BUT ALIKE IN THIS, WE ARE ORPHANED OF HEAVEN, UNFALLEN BUT EXILED. AND WE HATE THE LORD OF HOSTS AS WE HATE DEATH ITSELF.
FOR IN MY YOUTH, BEFORE THIS SICKNESS TOOK ME, I FOUND THAT GARDEN.
I EXPLAINED TO THE SERAPH THAT THE SIN OF EVE AND ADAM WAS NONE OF MINE, BUT STILL HE BARRED MY PATH.
SO THE SCIONS OF ADAM HAVE NO ONE BUT THEIR CREATOR TO BLAME FOR THE VENGEANCE WE TAKE IN THE DARK OF THE MOON.
WE NEITHER PARDON NOR FORGET. WHY SHOULD WE?

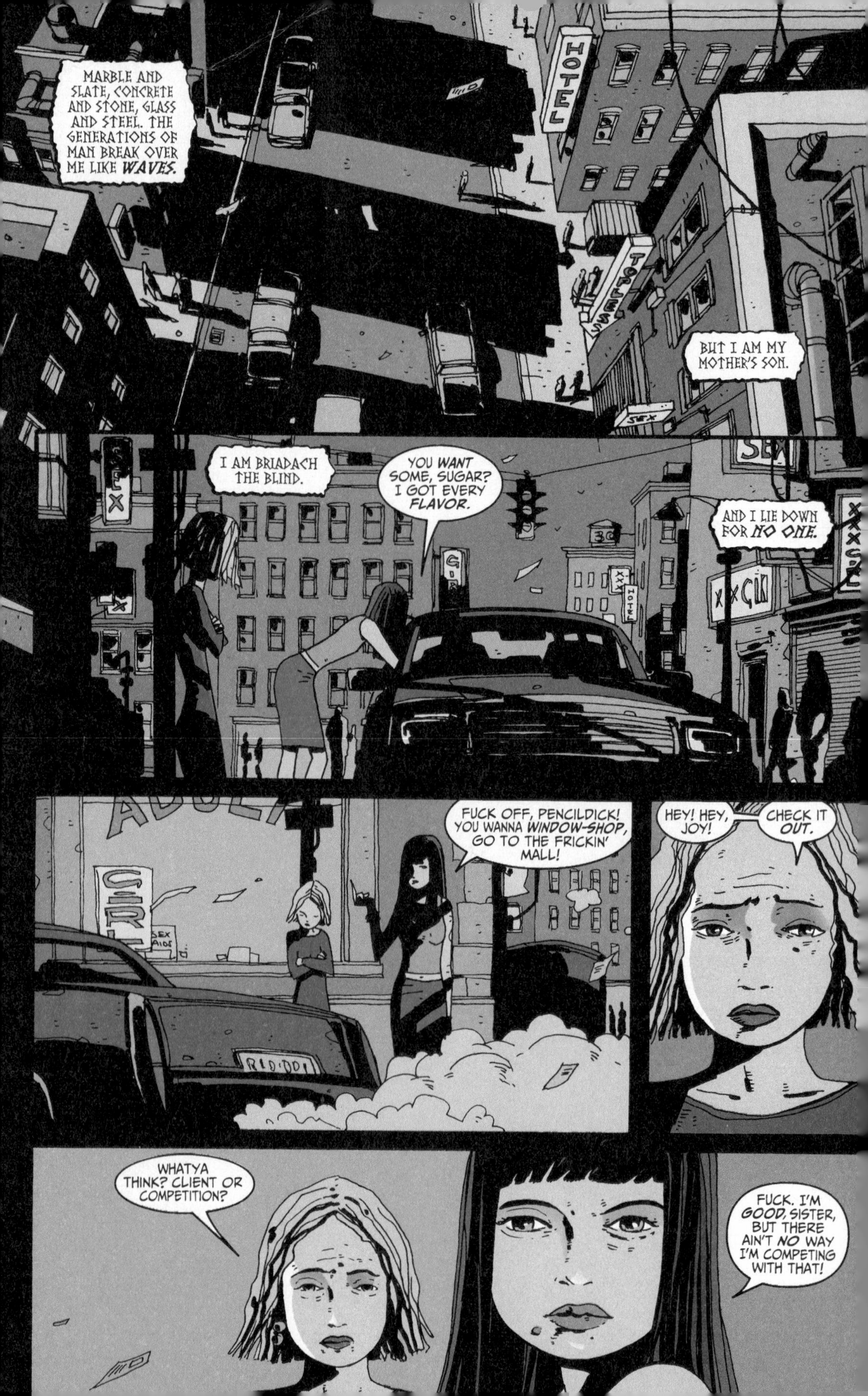
MARBLE AND SLATE, CONCRETE AND STONE, GLASS AND STEEL. THE GENERATIONS OF MAN BREAK OVER ME LIKE WAVES.
HOTEL
TOPLESS
BUT I AM MY MOTHER'S SON.
SEX
I AM BRIADACH THE BLIND.
YOU WANT SOME, SUGAR? I GOT EVERY FLAVOR.
AND I LIE DOWN FOR NO ONE.
FUCK OFF, PENCILDICK! YOU WANNA WINDOW-SHOP, GO TO THE FRICKIN' MALL!
HEY! HEY, JOY!
CHECK IT OUT.
WHATYA THINK? CLIENT OR COMPETITION?
FUCK. I'M GOOD, SISTER, BUT THERE AIN'T NO WAY I'M COMPETING WITH THAT!

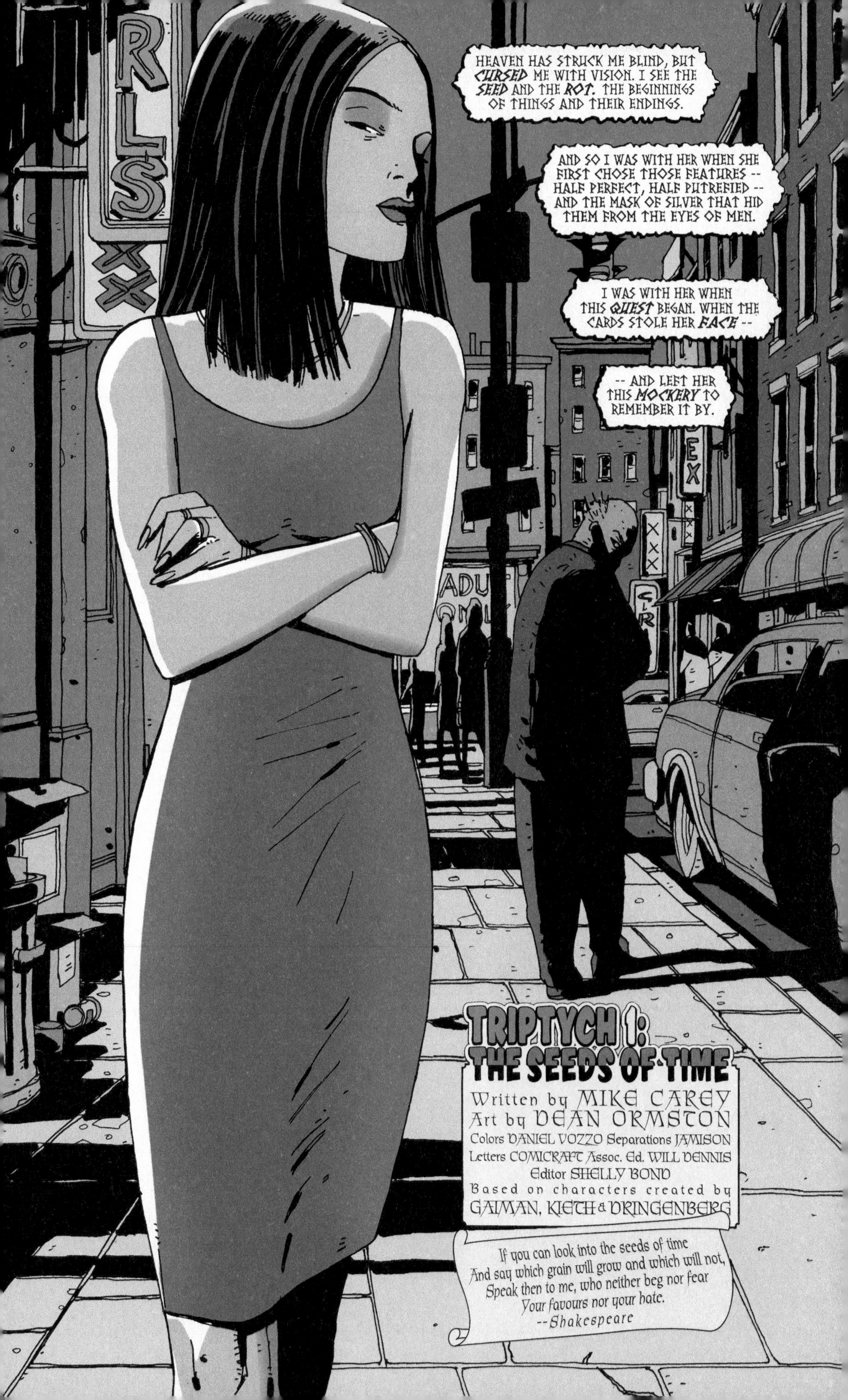

HEAVEN HAS STRUCK ME BLIND, BUT CURSED ME WITH VISION. I SEE THE SEED AND THE ROT. THE BEGINNINGS OF THINGS AND THEIR ENDINGS.
AND SO I WAS WITH HER WHEN SHE FIRST CHOSE THOSE FEATURES -- HALF PERFECT, HALF PUTREFIED -- AND THE MASK OF SILVER THAT HID THEM FROM THE EYES OF MEN.
I WAS WITH HER WHEN THIS QUEST BEGAN. WHEN THE CARDS STOLE HER FACE --
-- AND LEFT HER THIS MOCKERY TO REMEMBER IT BY.
TRIPTYCH 1: THE SEEDS OF TIME
Written by MIKE CAREY
Art by DEAN ORMSTON
Colors DANIEL VOZZO Separations JAMISON
Letters COMICRAFT Assoc. Ed. WILL DENNIS
Editor SHELLY BOND
Based on characters created by
GAIMAN, KIETH & DRINGENBERG
If you can look into the seeds of time
And say which grain will grow and which will not,
Speak then to me, who neither beg nor fear
Your favours nor your hate.
--Shakespeare

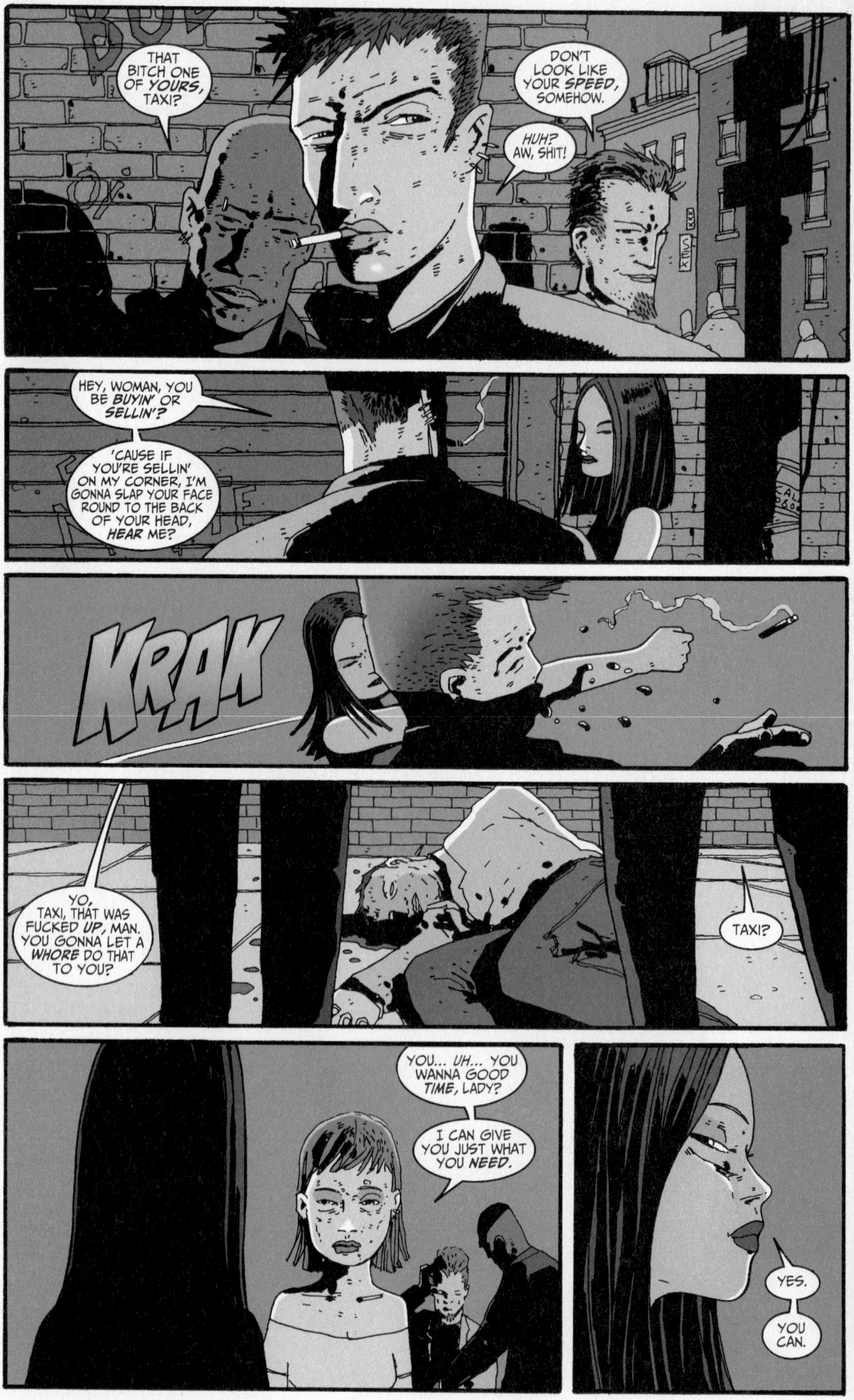
THAT BITCH ONE OF YOURS, TAXI?
DON'T LOOK LIKE YOUR SPEED, SOMEHOW.
HUH? AW, SHIT!
HEY, WOMAN, YOU BE BUYIN' OR SELLIN'?
'CAUSE IF YOU'RE SELLIN' ON MY CORNER, I'M GONNA SLAP YOUR FACE ROUND TO THE BACK OF YOUR HEAD, HEAR ME?
KRAK
YO, TAXI, THAT WAS FUCKED UP, MAN. YOU GONNA LET A WHORE DO THAT TO YOU?
TAXI?
YOU... UH... YOU WANNA GOOD TIME, LADY?
I CAN GIVE YOU JUST WHAT YOU NEED.
YES.
YOU CAN.

-- ONE OF SEVERAL FREEWAY ACCIDENTS APPARENTLY CAUSED BY DRIVERS LITERALLY FALLING *ASLEEP* AT THE WHEEL.

NOW FOR MORE ON THOSE UFO SIGHTINGS IN L.A., LET'S --

SO WHAT WAY DO YOU LIKE IT? YOU WANNA DO A SIXTY-NINE, OR WHAT?

I WANT YOU TO BE *QUIET.* VERY QUIET.

OR ELSE I WILL HOOK OUT YOUR *EYEBALLS* WITH MY FINGERS.

OH JESUS. OH PLEASE, LADY, DON'T *KILL* ME.

I GOT A KID. I SWEAR, YOU CAN DO WHATEVER YOU WANT AND NOT EVEN PAY.

I'M NOT GOING TO KILL YOU.

HER MAGIC IS LIKE *MINE* -- LIKE ALL OUR KIN'S. BLOOD AND PISS. SEMEN AND TEARS. MUCUS AND MENSTRUM.

THE *KISS* IS TO MIX THEIR JUICES.

THEN SHE SPITS ON THE FLOOR, AND DRAWS A *CIRCLE.*

NO PENTAGRAM. NO WORDS OF BINDING. JUST A CIRCLE.

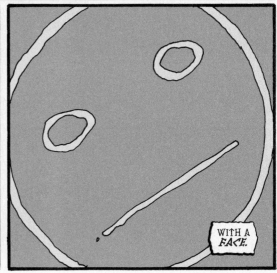

WITH A *FACE.*

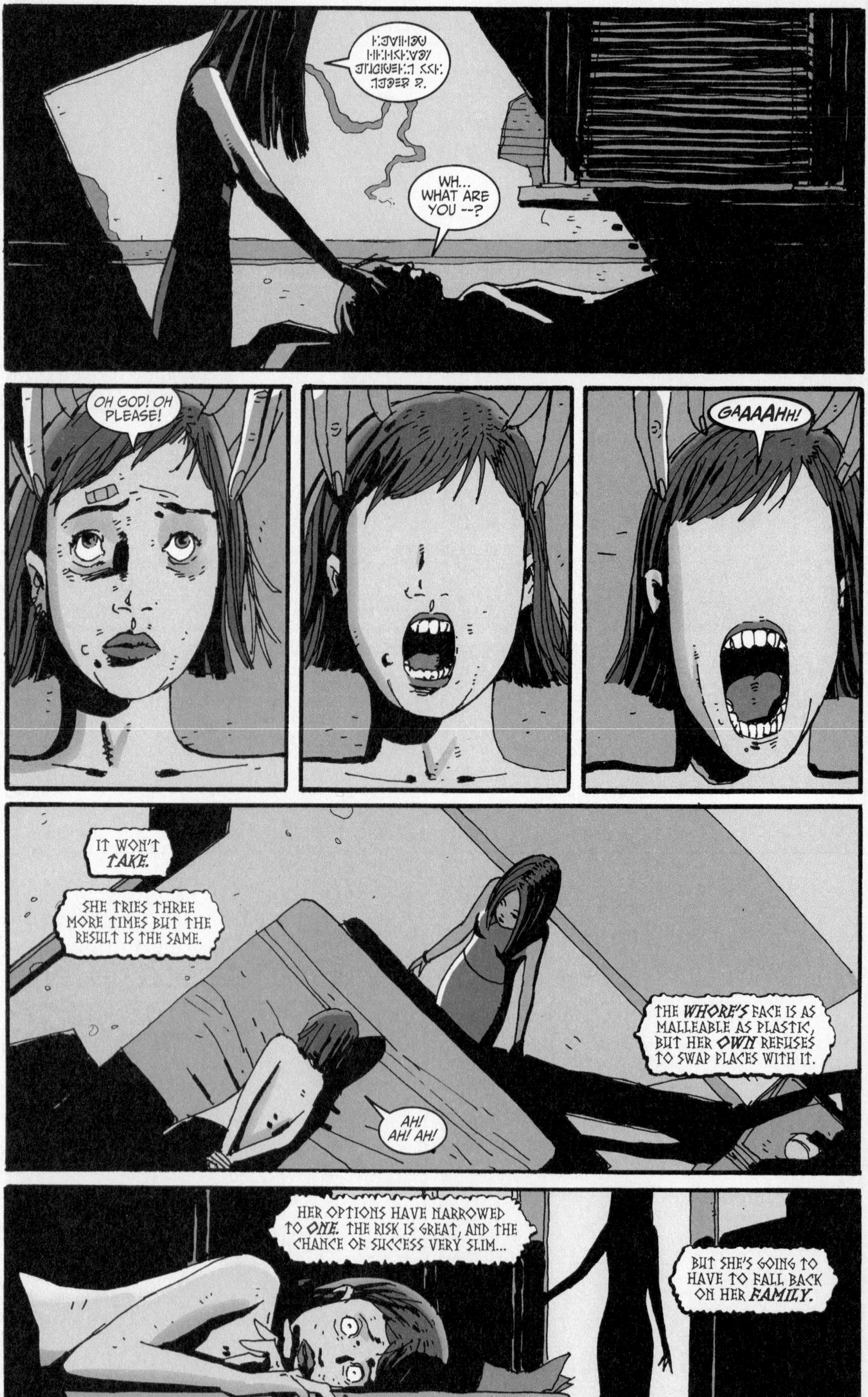

WH... WHAT ARE YOU --?
OH GOD! OH PLEASE!
GAAAAHH!
IT WON'T TAKE.
SHE TRIES THREE MORE TIMES BUT THE RESULT IS THE SAME.
THE WHORE'S FACE IS AS MALLEABLE AS PLASTIC, BUT HER OWN REFUSES TO SWAP PLACES WITH IT.
AH! AH! AH!
HER OPTIONS HAVE NARROWED TO ONE. THE RISK IS GREAT, AND THE CHANCE OF SUCCESS VERY SLIM...
BUT SHE'S GOING TO HAVE TO FALL BACK ON HER FAMILY.

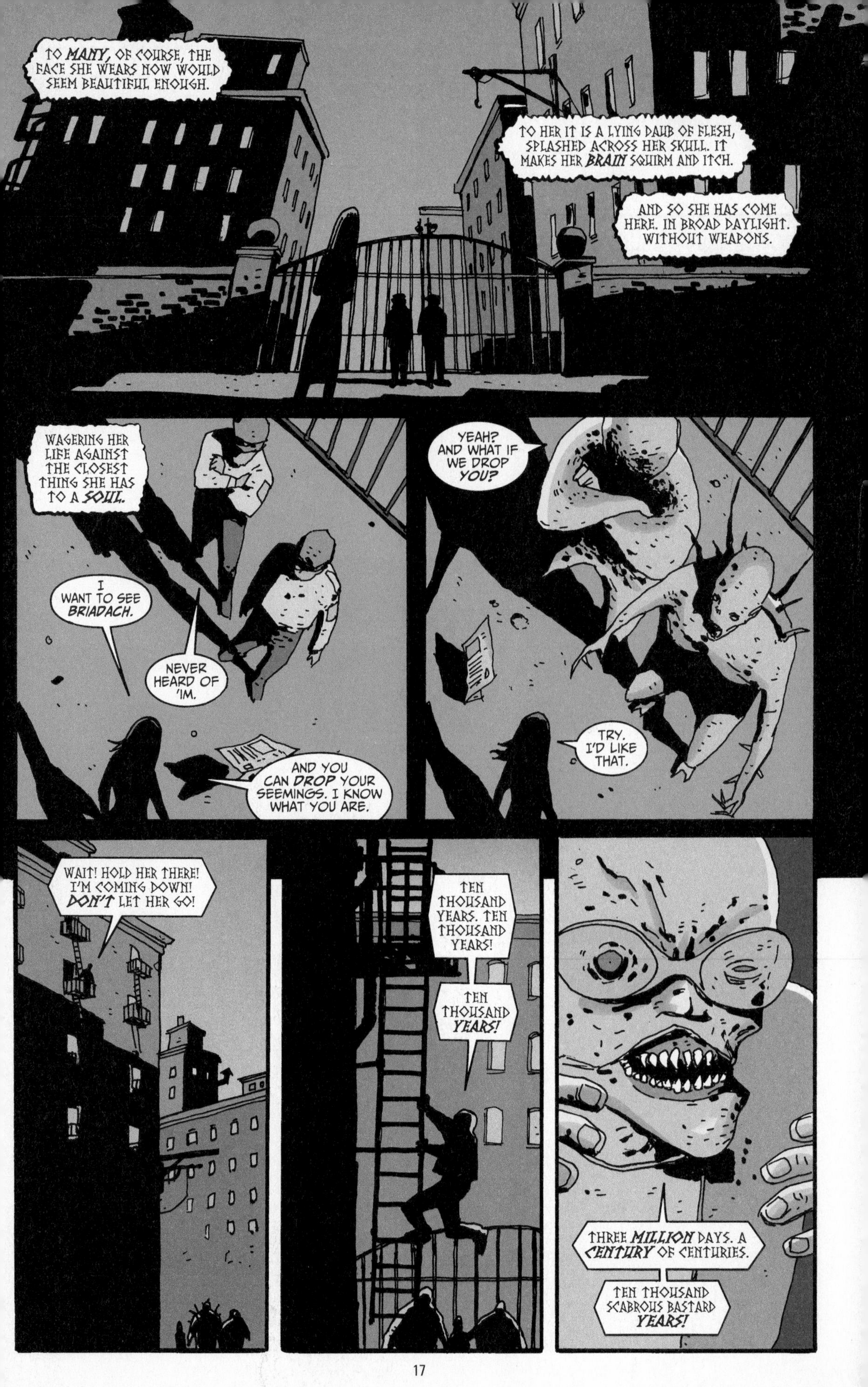
TO MANY, OF COURSE, THE FACE SHE WEARS NOW WOULD SEEM BEAUTIFUL ENOUGH.
TO HER IT IS A LYING DAUB OF FLESH, SPLASHED ACROSS HER SKULL. IT MAKES HER BRAIN SQUIRM AND ITCH.
AND SO SHE HAS COME HERE. IN BROAD DAYLIGHT. WITHOUT WEAPONS.
WAGERING HER LIFE AGAINST THE CLOSEST THING SHE HAS TO A SOUL.
I WANT TO SEE BRIADACH.
NEVER HEARD OF 'IM.
AND YOU CAN DROP YOUR SEEMINGS. I KNOW WHAT YOU ARE.
YEAH? AND WHAT IF WE DROP YOU?
TRY. I'D LIKE THAT.
WAIT! HOLD HER THERE! I'M COMING DOWN! DON'T LET HER GO!
TEN THOUSAND YEARS. TEN THOUSAND YEARS!
TEN THOUSAND YEARS!
THREE MILLION DAYS. A CENTURY OF CENTURIES.
TEN THOUSAND SCABROUS BASTARD YEARS!

SO YOU THOUGHT YOU COULD SNEAK PAST ME JUST BY CHANGING YOUR *FACE!*

IS IT *SANCTUARY* YOU'RE BEGGING FOR, YOU TREACHEROUS BITCH? HAS LUCIFER CAST YOU *OUT?*

I BEG FOR *NOTHING,* MAHU. YOU KNOW ME BETTER.

I JUST WANT TO TALK TO THE *MAN* OF THE HOUSE.

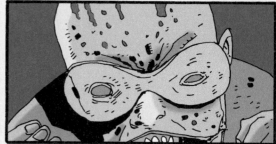

AHHHRRRR!

WHUMP

KLUD KLUD KLUD

YOU *HEARD* HER. TAKE HER TO BRIADACH.

AND ADD HER NAME TO THE *ROSTER.* SHE'S ONE OF US.

18

IT IS *DIFFICULT* TO RISE. SINCE THIS SICKNESS FELL UPON ME I HAVE LAIN HERE AND *FESTERED.*

EXERTION OF ANY KIND MAKES THE *TUMORS* QUICKEN AND SPAWN.

BUT STILL...

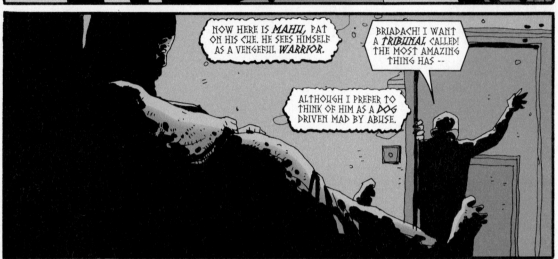

NOW HERE IS *MAHU,* PAT ON HIS CUE. HE SEES HIMSELF AS A VENGEFUL *WARRIOR.*

BRIADACH! I WANT A *TRIBUNAL* CALLED! THE MOST AMAZING THING HAS --

ALTHOUGH I PREFER TO THINK OF HIM AS A *DOG* DRIVEN MAD BY ABUSE.

THIS HAS NOT DIMINISHED MY *FONDNESS* FOR HIM. NOT AT ALL.

HAVE YOU FORGOTTEN HOW TO *KNEEL,* MAHU?

NO. OF COURSE NOT. I'M SORRY.

IN MANY WAYS A MAD DOG IS AN *IDEAL* PET FOR ME.

HUSH NOW. YOU WILL HAVE YOUR TRIBUNAL. AND I WILL ATTEND.

YOU WILL --?

OH, YES. TODAY IS SPECIAL. I MAY BE BLIND --

-- BUT THIS IS SOMETHING I WANT TO EXPERIENCE *FIRST-HAND.*

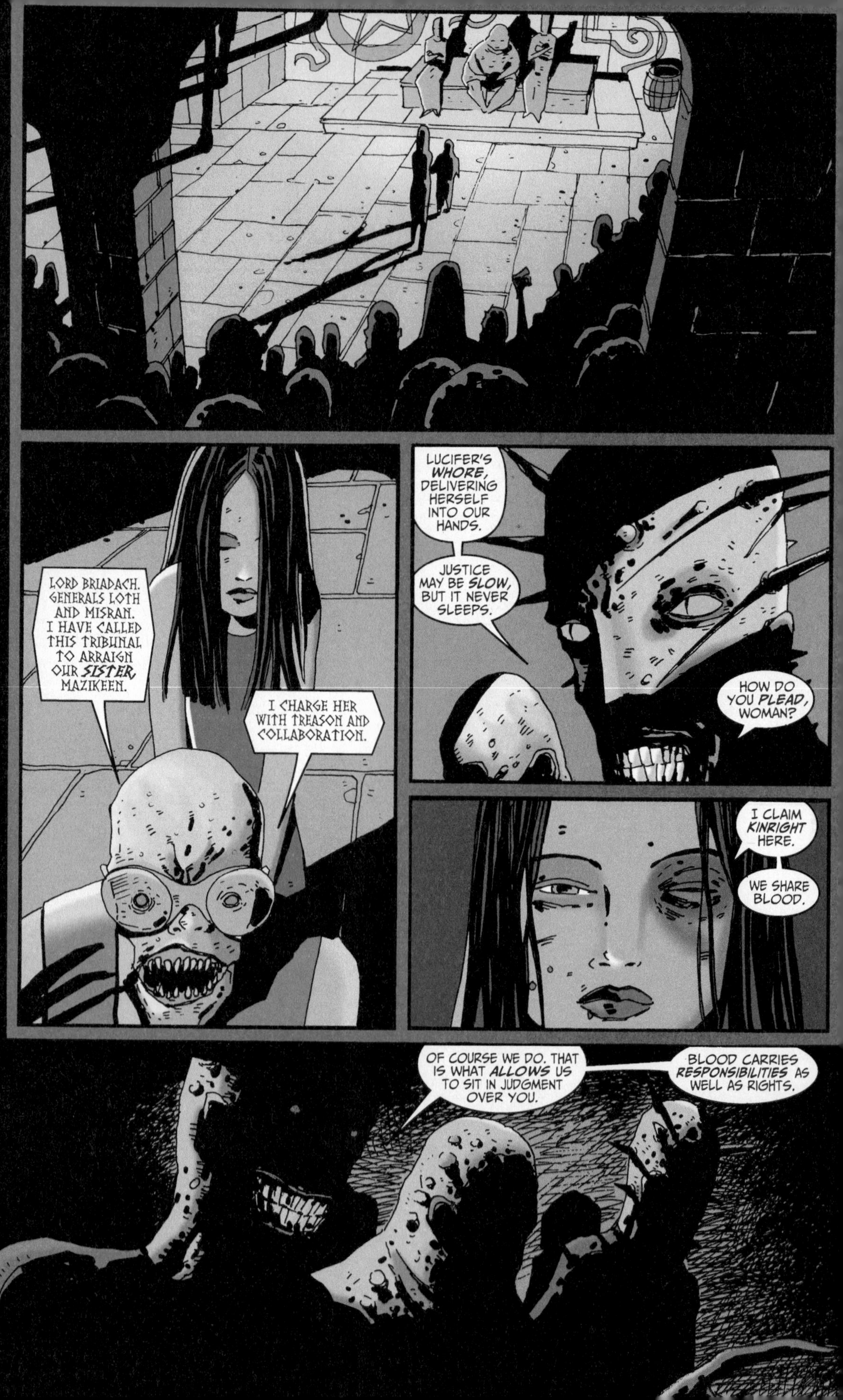

LORD BRIADACH. GENERALS LOTH AND MISRAN. I HAVE CALLED THIS TRIBUNAL TO ARRAIGN OUR SISTER, MAZIKEEN.
I CHARGE HER WITH TREASON AND COLLABORATION.
LUCIFER'S WHORE, DELIVERING HERSELF INTO OUR HANDS.
JUSTICE MAY BE SLOW, BUT IT NEVER SLEEPS.
HOW DO YOU PLEAD, WOMAN?
I CLAIM KINRIGHT HERE.
WE SHARE BLOOD.
OF COURSE WE DO. THAT IS WHAT ALLOWS US TO SIT IN JUDGMENT OVER YOU.
BLOOD CARRIES RESPONSIBILITIES AS WELL AS RIGHTS.

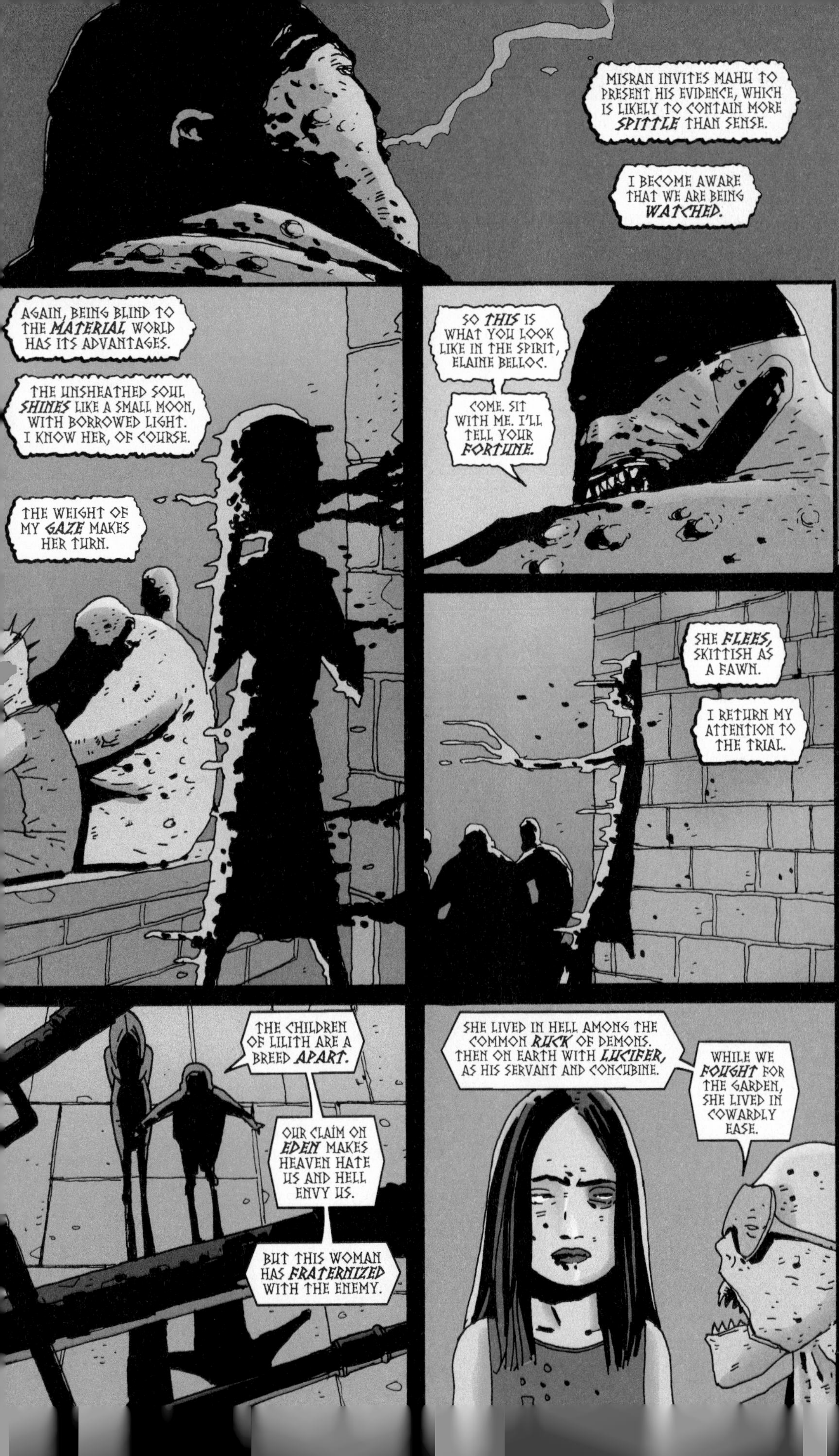
MISRAN INVITES MAHU TO PRESENT HIS EVIDENCE, WHICH IS LIKELY TO CONTAIN MORE SPITTLE THAN SENSE.
I BECOME AWARE THAT WE ARE BEING WATCHED.
AGAIN, BEING BLIND TO THE MATERIAL WORLD HAS ITS ADVANTAGES.
THE UNSHEATHED SOUL SHINES LIKE A SMALL MOON, WITH BORROWED LIGHT. I KNOW HER, OF COURSE.
THE WEIGHT OF MY GAZE MAKES HER TURN.
SO THIS IS WHAT YOU LOOK LIKE IN THE SPIRIT, ELAINE BELLOC.
COME. SIT WITH ME. I'LL TELL YOUR FORTUNE.
SHE FLEES, SKITTISH AS A FAWN.
I RETURN MY ATTENTION TO THE TRIAL.
THE CHILDREN OF LILITH ARE A BREED APART.
OUR CLAIM ON EDEN MAKES HEAVEN HATE US AND HELL ENVY US.
BUT THIS WOMAN HAS FRATERNIZED WITH THE ENEMY.
SHE LIVED IN HELL AMONG THE COMMON RUCK OF DEMONS. THEN ON EARTH WITH LUCIFER, AS HIS SERVANT AND CONCUBINE.
WHILE WE FOUGHT FOR THE GARDEN, SHE LIVED IN COWARDLY EASE.

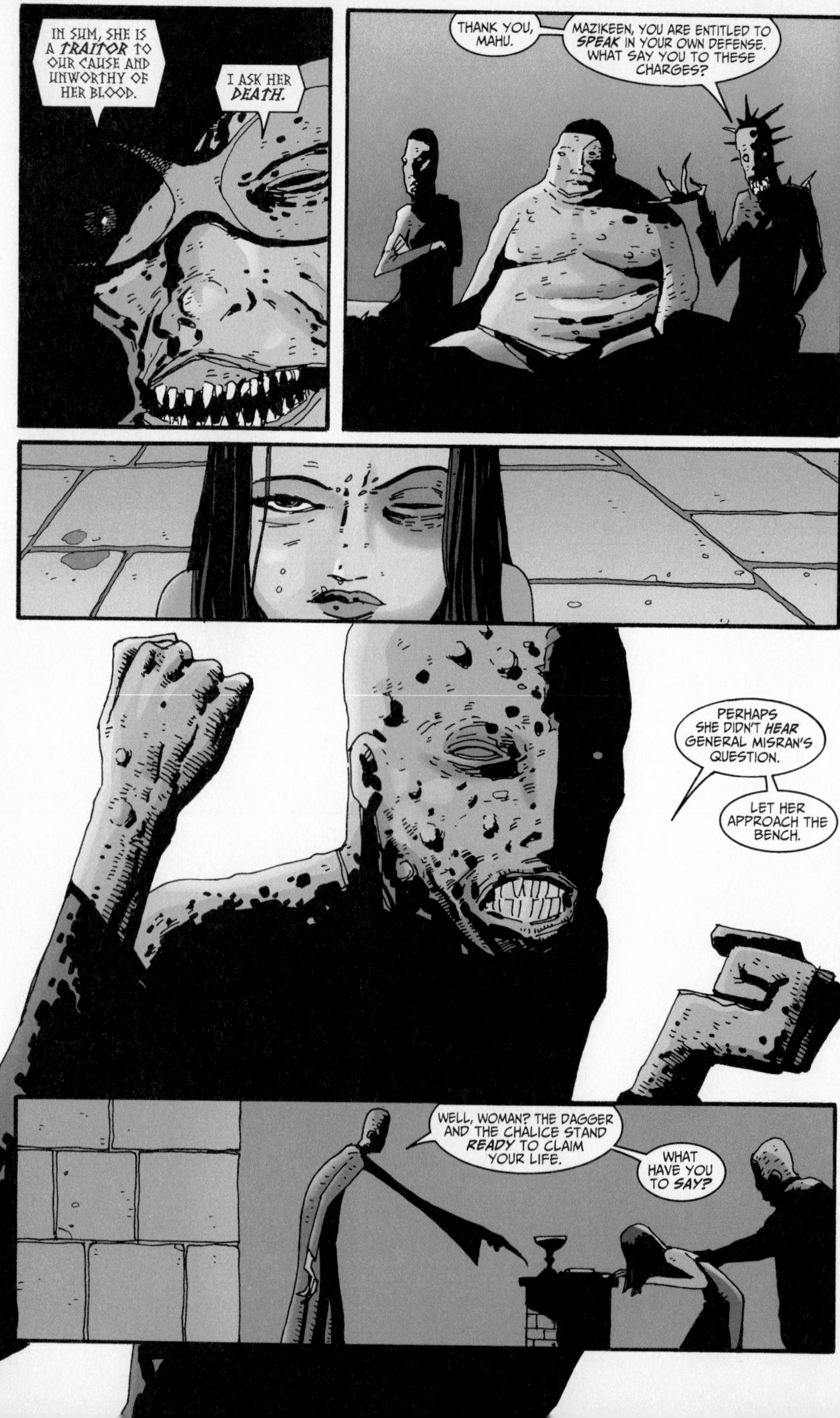
IN SUM, SHE IS A TRAITOR TO OUR CAUSE AND UNWORTHY OF HER BLOOD.
I ASK HER DEATH.
THANK YOU, MAHU.
MAZIKEEN, YOU ARE ENTITLED TO SPEAK IN YOUR OWN DEFENSE. WHAT SAY YOU TO THESE CHARGES?
PERHAPS SHE DIDN'T HEAR GENERAL MISRAN'S QUESTION.
LET HER APPROACH THE BENCH.
WELL, WOMAN? THE DAGGER AND THE CHALICE STAND READY TO CLAIM YOUR LIFE.
WHAT HAVE YOU TO SAY?

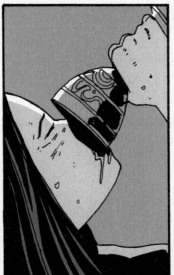

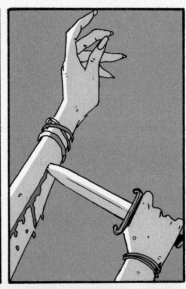

THE BITCH IS *MOCKING* US.

LOTH. SHE THINKS TO OUTMANEUVER US. SHE KNOWS WE CAN'T GIVE A *VERDICT* WITHOUT HEARING HER DEFENSE.

BUT THERE IS ALWAYS TRIAL BY *COMBAT.*

NO, NO. MAHU WILL *LOSE.* YOU KNOW HER REPUTATION.

I SAY AS LITTLE AS POSSIBLE.

IT IS PERMISSIBLE TO *HANDICAP* HER.

DESTINY NEEDS A *PUSH.* BUT A VERY SMALL PUSH WILL DO.

BRING CHAINS. AND A *BLINDFOLD.*

IF SHE WON'T *SPEAK,* THEN LET HER FIGHT.

23

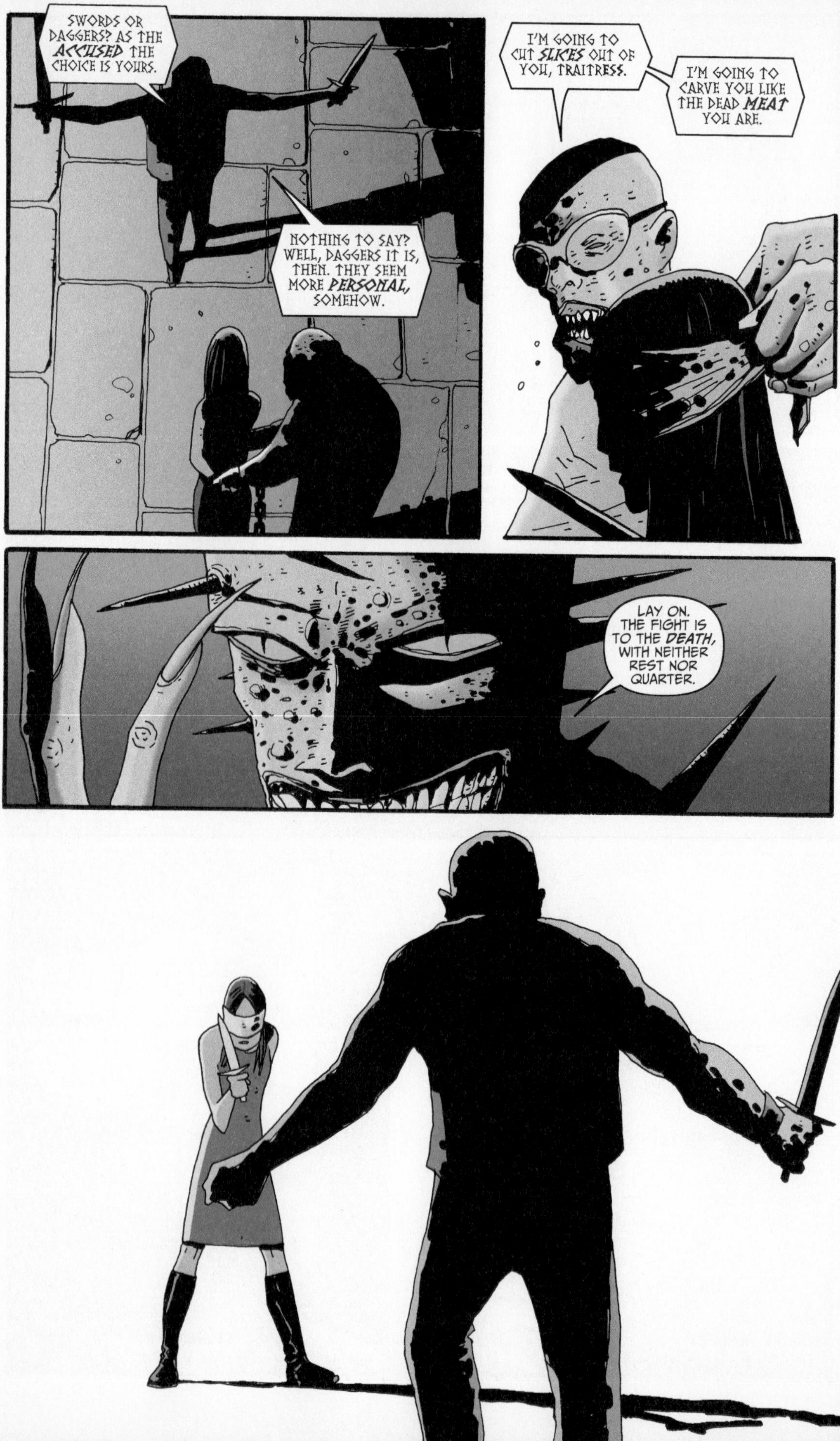
SWORDS OR DAGGERS? AS THE ACCUSED THE CHOICE IS YOURS.
NOTHING TO SAY? WELL, DAGGERS IT IS, THEN. THEY SEEM MORE PERSONAL, SOMEHOW.
I'M GOING TO CUT SLICES OUT OF YOU, TRAITRESS.
I'M GOING TO CARVE YOU LIKE THE DEAD MEAT YOU ARE.
LAY ON. THE FIGHT IS TO THE DEATH, WITH NEITHER REST NOR QUARTER.

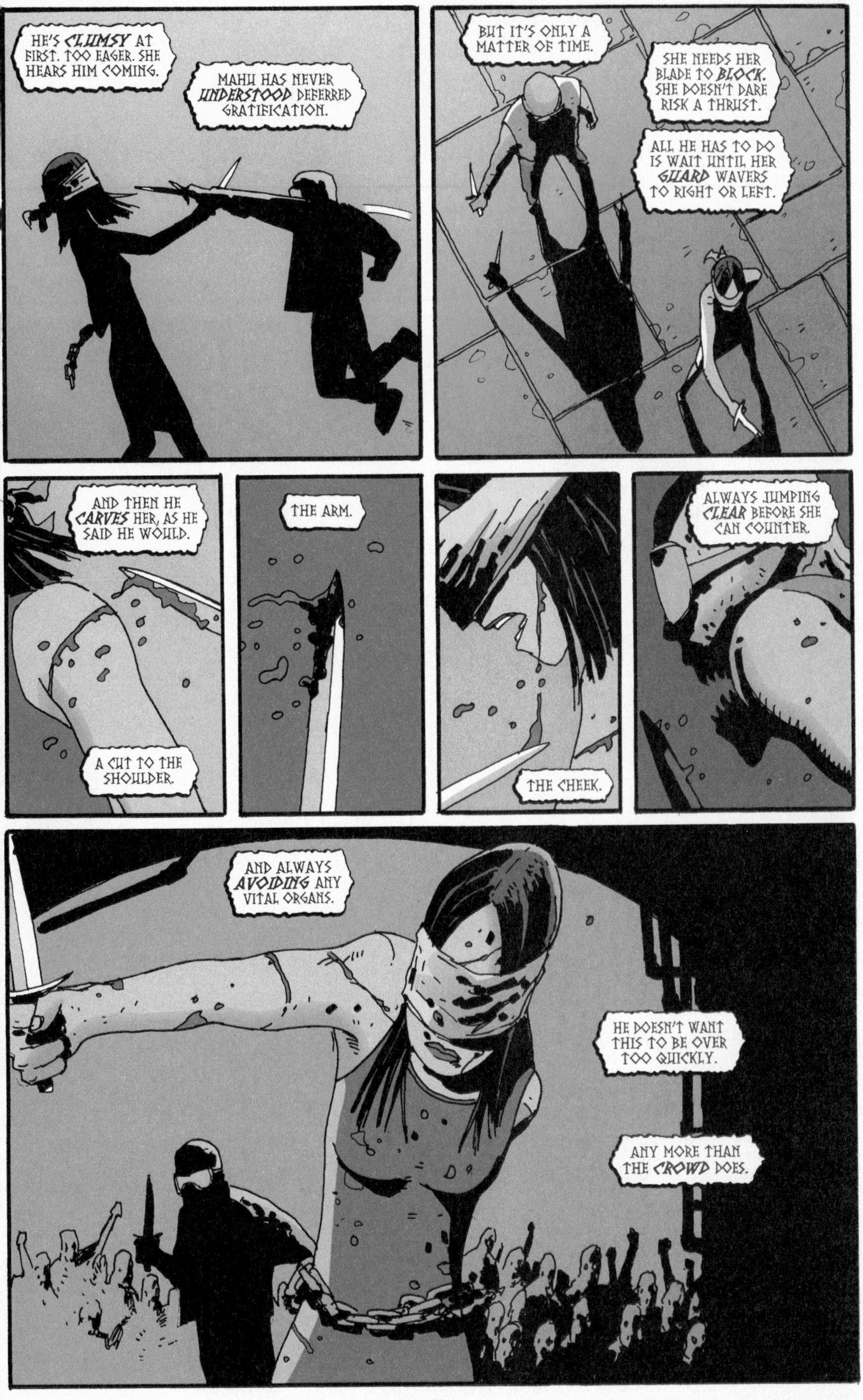
HE'S CLUMSY AT FIRST. TOO EAGER. SHE HEARS HIM COMING.
MAHU HAS NEVER UNDERSTOOD DEFERRED GRATIFICATION.
BUT IT'S ONLY A MATTER OF TIME.
SHE NEEDS HER BLADE TO BLOCK. SHE DOESN'T DARE RISK A THRUST.
ALL HE HAS TO DO IS WAIT UNTIL HER GUARD WAVERS TO RIGHT OR LEFT.
AND THEN HE CARVES HER, AS HE SAID HE WOULD.
A CUT TO THE SHOULDER.
THE ARM.
THE CHEEK.
ALWAYS JUMPING CLEAR BEFORE SHE CAN COUNTER.
AND ALWAYS AVOIDING ANY VITAL ORGANS.
HE DOESN'T WANT THIS TO BE OVER TOO QUICKLY.
ANY MORE THAN THE CROWD DOES.

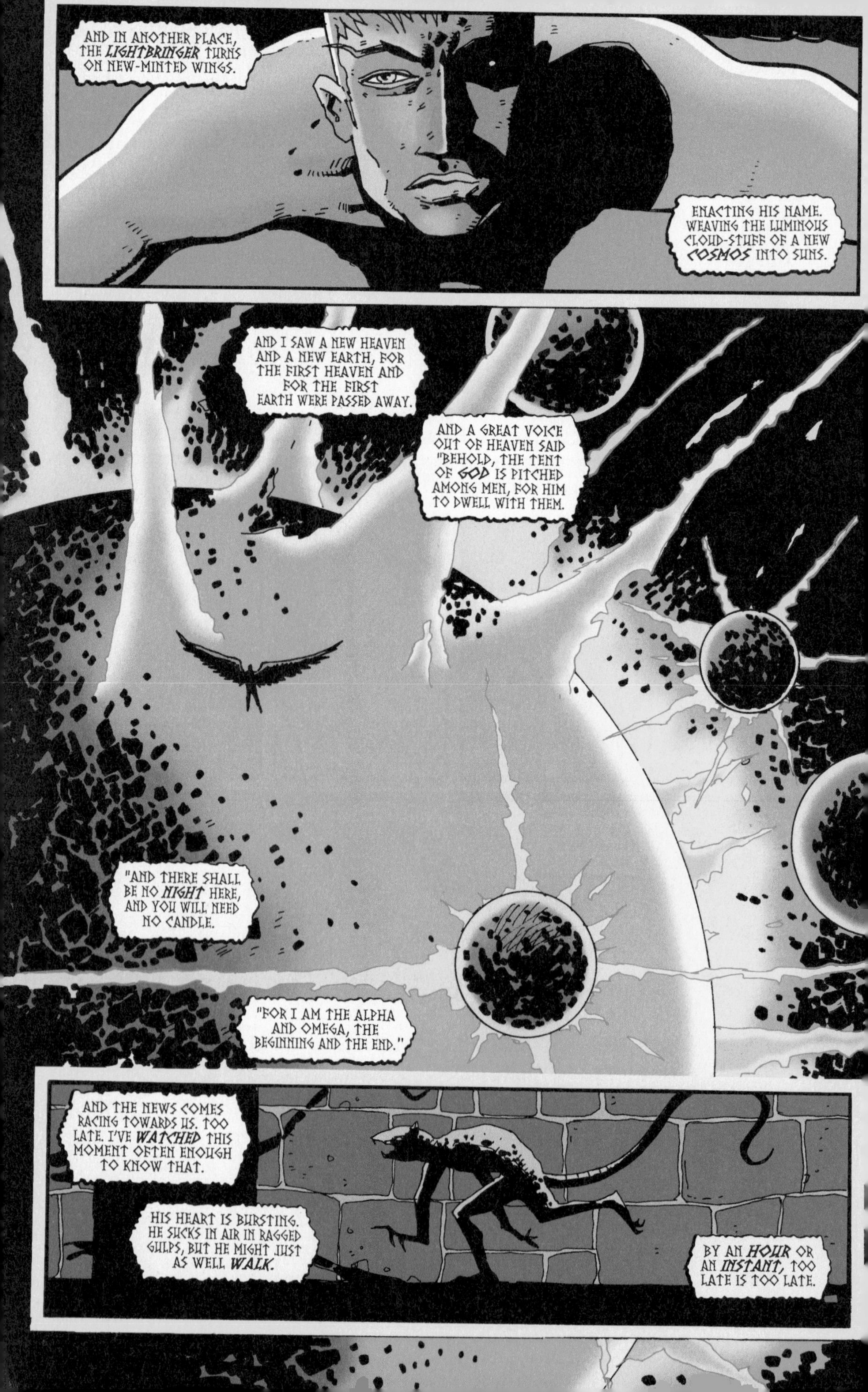
AND IN ANOTHER PLACE, THE LIGHTBRINGER TURNS ON NEW-MINTED WINGS.
ENACTING HIS NAME. WEAVING THE LUMINOUS CLOUD-STUFF OF A NEW COSMOS INTO SUNS.
AND I SAW A NEW HEAVEN AND A NEW EARTH, FOR THE FIRST HEAVEN AND FOR THE FIRST EARTH WERE PASSED AWAY.
AND A GREAT VOICE OUT OF HEAVEN SAID "BEHOLD, THE TENT OF GOD IS PITCHED AMONG MEN, FOR HIM TO DWELL WITH THEM.
"AND THERE SHALL BE NO NIGHT HERE, AND YOU WILL NEED NO CANDLE.
"FOR I AM THE ALPHA AND OMEGA, THE BEGINNING AND THE END."
AND THE NEWS COMES RACING TOWARDS US. TOO LATE. I'VE WATCHED THIS MOMENT OFTEN ENOUGH TO KNOW THAT.
HIS HEART IS BURSTING. HE SUCKS IN AIR IN RAGGED GULPS, BUT HE MIGHT JUST AS WELL WALK.
BY AN HOUR OR AN INSTANT, TOO LATE IS TOO LATE.

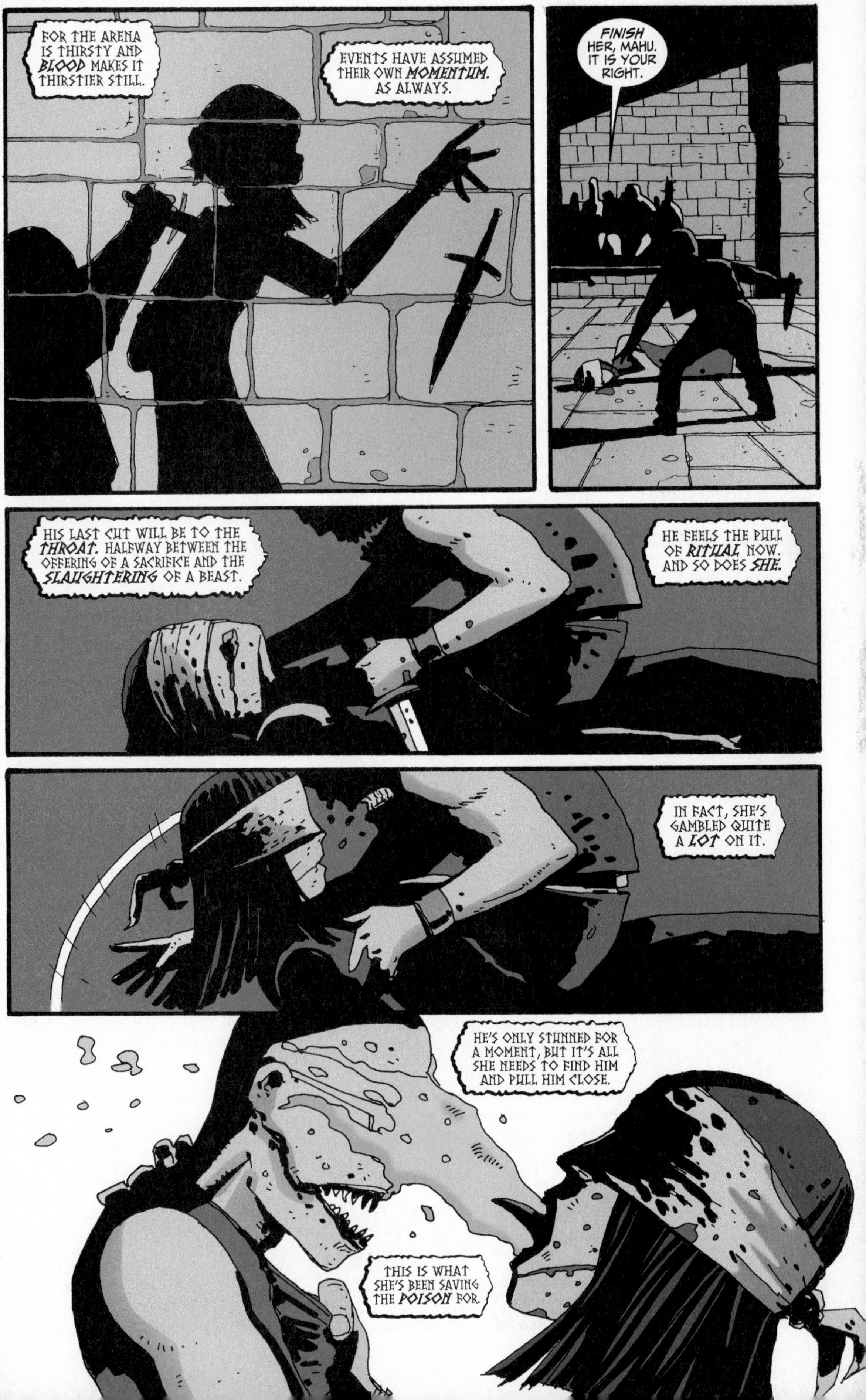
FOR THE ARENA IS THIRSTY AND BLOOD MAKES IT THIRSTIER STILL.
EVENTS HAVE ASSUMED THEIR OWN MOMENTUM. AS ALWAYS.
FINISH HER, MAHU. IT IS YOUR RIGHT.
HIS LAST CUT WILL BE TO THE THROAT. HALFWAY BETWEEN THE OFFERING OF A SACRIFICE AND THE SLAUGHTERING OF A BEAST.
HE FEELS THE PULL OF RITUAL NOW. AND SO DOES SHE.
IN FACT, SHE'S GAMBLED QUITE A LOT ON IT.
HE'S ONLY STUNNED FOR A MOMENT, BUT IT'S ALL SHE NEEDS TO FIND HIM AND PULL HIM CLOSE.
THIS IS WHAT SHE'S BEEN SAVING THE POISON FOR.

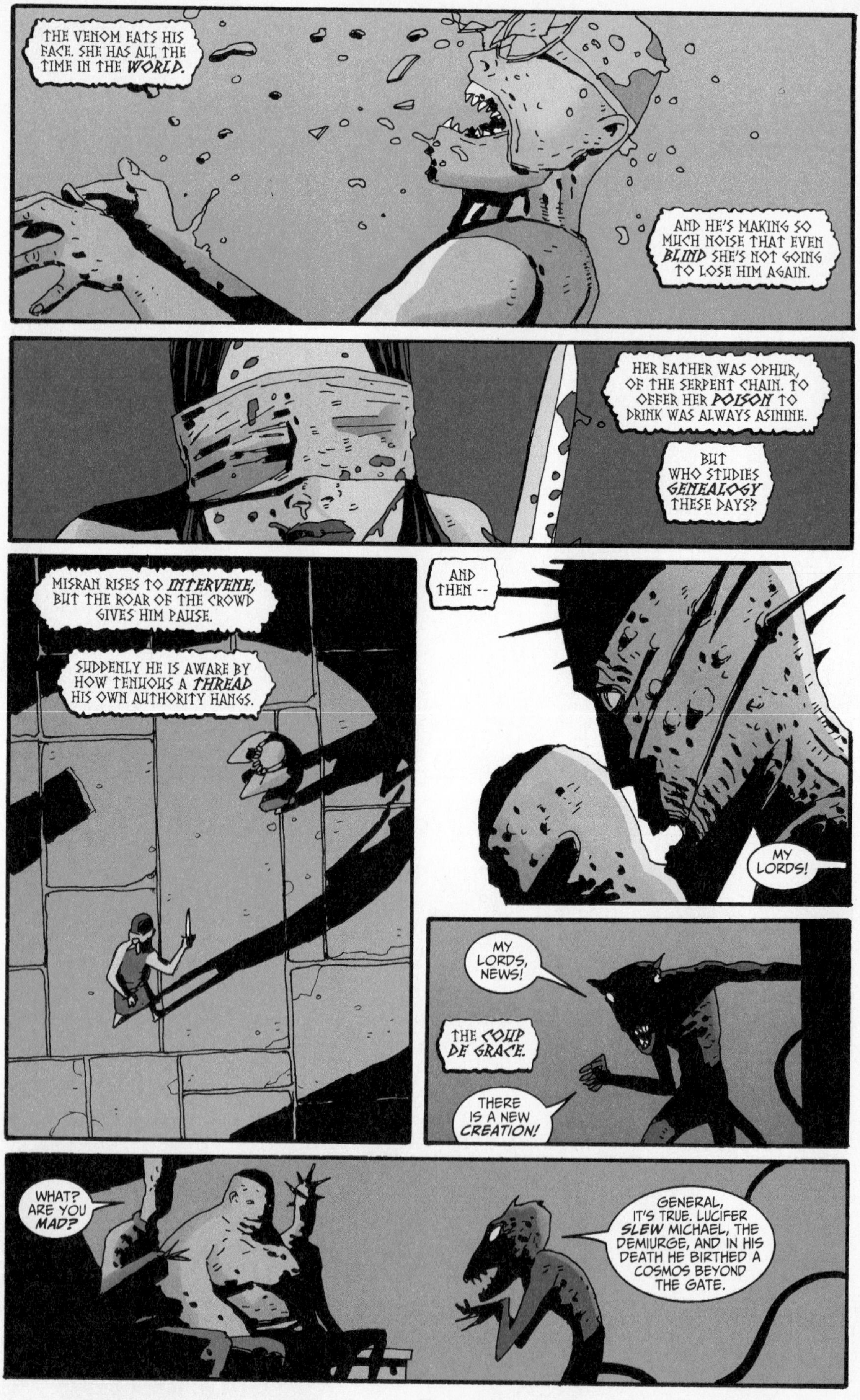
THE VENOM EATS HIS FACE. SHE HAS ALL THE TIME IN THE WORLD.
AND HE'S MAKING SO MUCH NOISE THAT EVEN BLIND SHE'S NOT GOING TO LOSE HIM AGAIN.
HER FATHER WAS OPHUR, OF THE SERPENT CHAIN. TO OFFER HER POISON TO DRINK WAS ALWAYS ASININE.
BUT WHO STUDIES GENEALOGY THESE DAYS?
MISRAN RISES TO INTERVENE, BUT THE ROAR OF THE CROWD GIVES HIM PAUSE.
SUDDENLY HE IS AWARE BY HOW TENUOUS A THREAD HIS OWN AUTHORITY HANGS.
AND THEN --
MY LORDS!
MY LORDS, NEWS!
THE COUP DE GRACE.
THERE IS A NEW CREATION!
WHAT? ARE YOU MAD?
GENERAL, IT'S TRUE. LUCIFER SLEW MICHAEL, THE DEMIURGE, AND IN HIS DEATH HE BIRTHED A COSMOS BEYOND THE GATE.

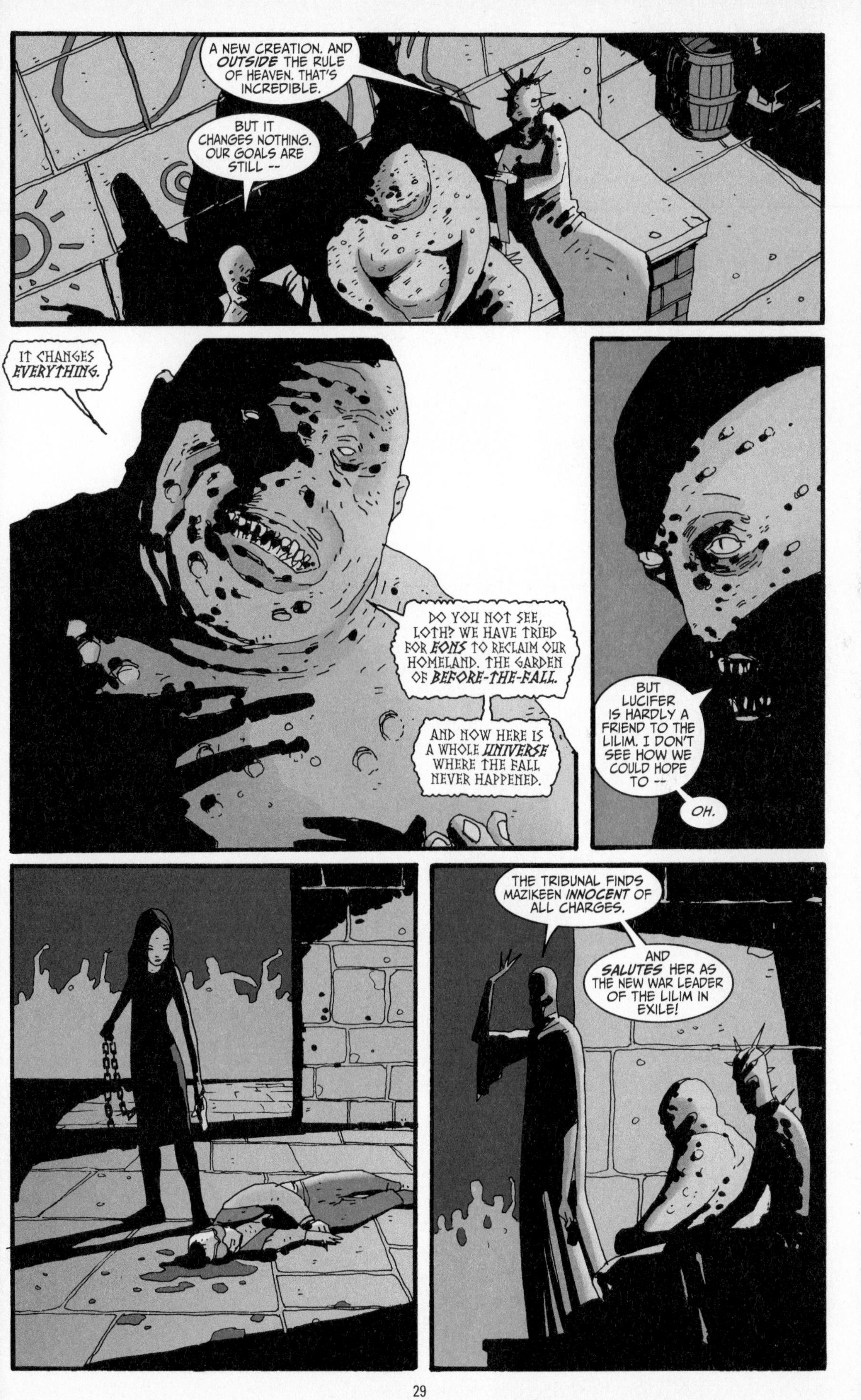

A NEW CREATION. AND OUTSIDE THE RULE OF HEAVEN. THAT'S INCREDIBLE.
BUT IT CHANGES NOTHING. OUR GOALS ARE STILL --
IT CHANGES EVERYTHING.
DO YOU NOT SEE, LOTH? WE HAVE TRIED FOR EONS TO RECLAIM OUR HOMELAND. THE GARDEN OF BEFORE-THE-FALL.
AND NOW HERE IS A WHOLE UNIVERSE WHERE THE FALL NEVER HAPPENED.
BUT LUCIFER IS HARDLY A FRIEND TO THE LILIM. I DON'T SEE HOW WE COULD HOPE TO --
OH.
THE TRIBUNAL FINDS MAZIKEEN INNOCENT OF ALL CHARGES.
AND SALUTES HER AS THE NEW WAR LEADER OF THE LILIM IN EXILE!

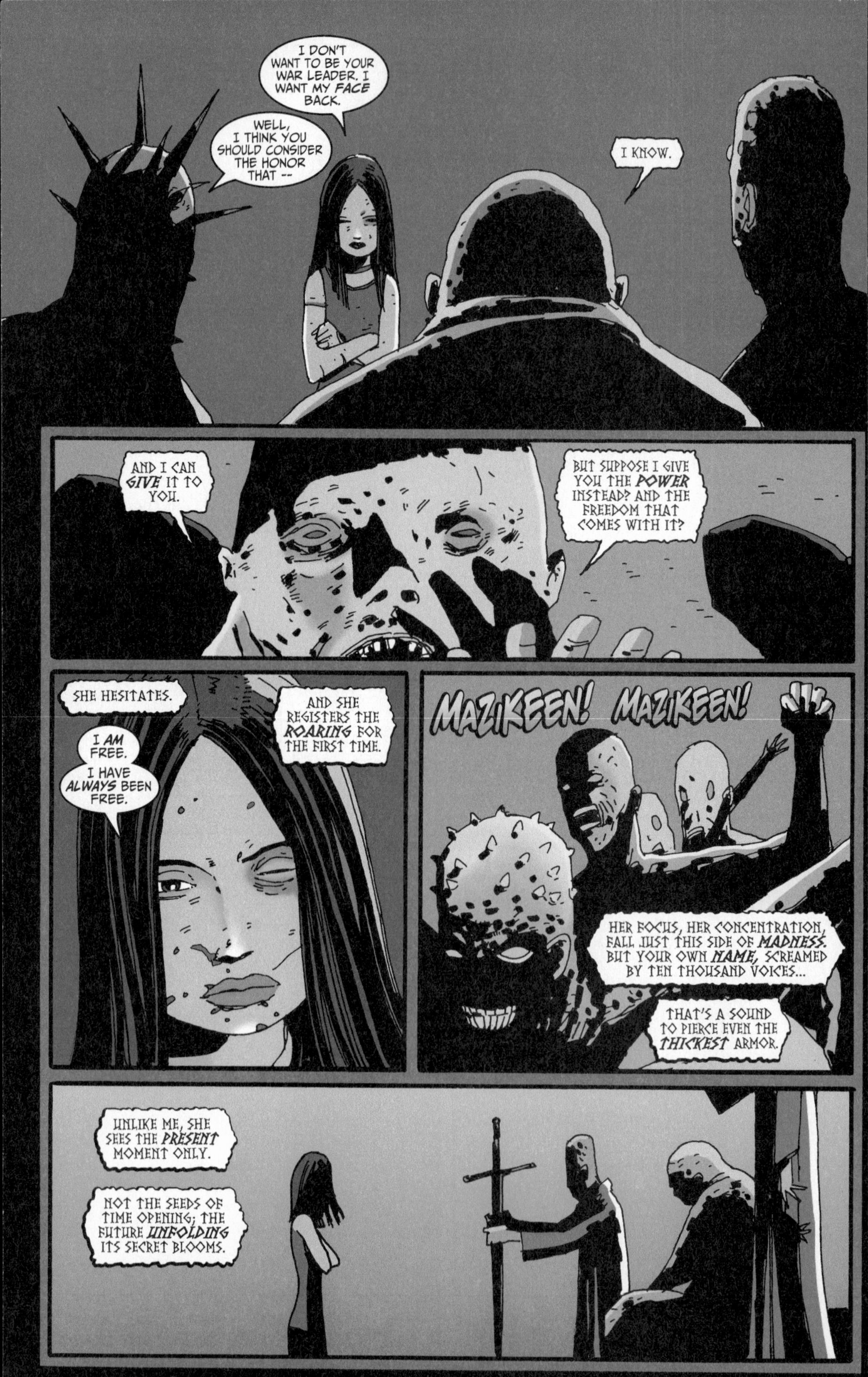

I DON'T WANT TO BE YOUR WAR LEADER. I WANT MY FACE BACK.
WELL, I THINK YOU SHOULD CONSIDER THE HONOR THAT --
I KNOW.
AND I CAN GIVE IT TO YOU.
BUT SUPPOSE I GIVE YOU THE POWER INSTEAD? AND THE FREEDOM THAT COMES WITH IT?
SHE HESITATES.
I AM FREE. I HAVE ALWAYS BEEN FREE.
AND SHE REGISTERS THE ROARING FOR THE FIRST TIME.
MAZIKEEN! MAZIKEEN!
HER FOCUS, HER CONCENTRATION, FALL JUST THIS SIDE OF MADNESS. BUT YOUR OWN NAME, SCREAMED BY TEN THOUSAND VOICES...
THAT'S A SOUND TO PIERCE EVEN THE THICKEST ARMOR.
UNLIKE ME, SHE SEES THE PRESENT MOMENT ONLY.
NOT THE SEEDS OF TIME OPENING; THE FUTURE UNFOLDING ITS SECRET BLOOMS.

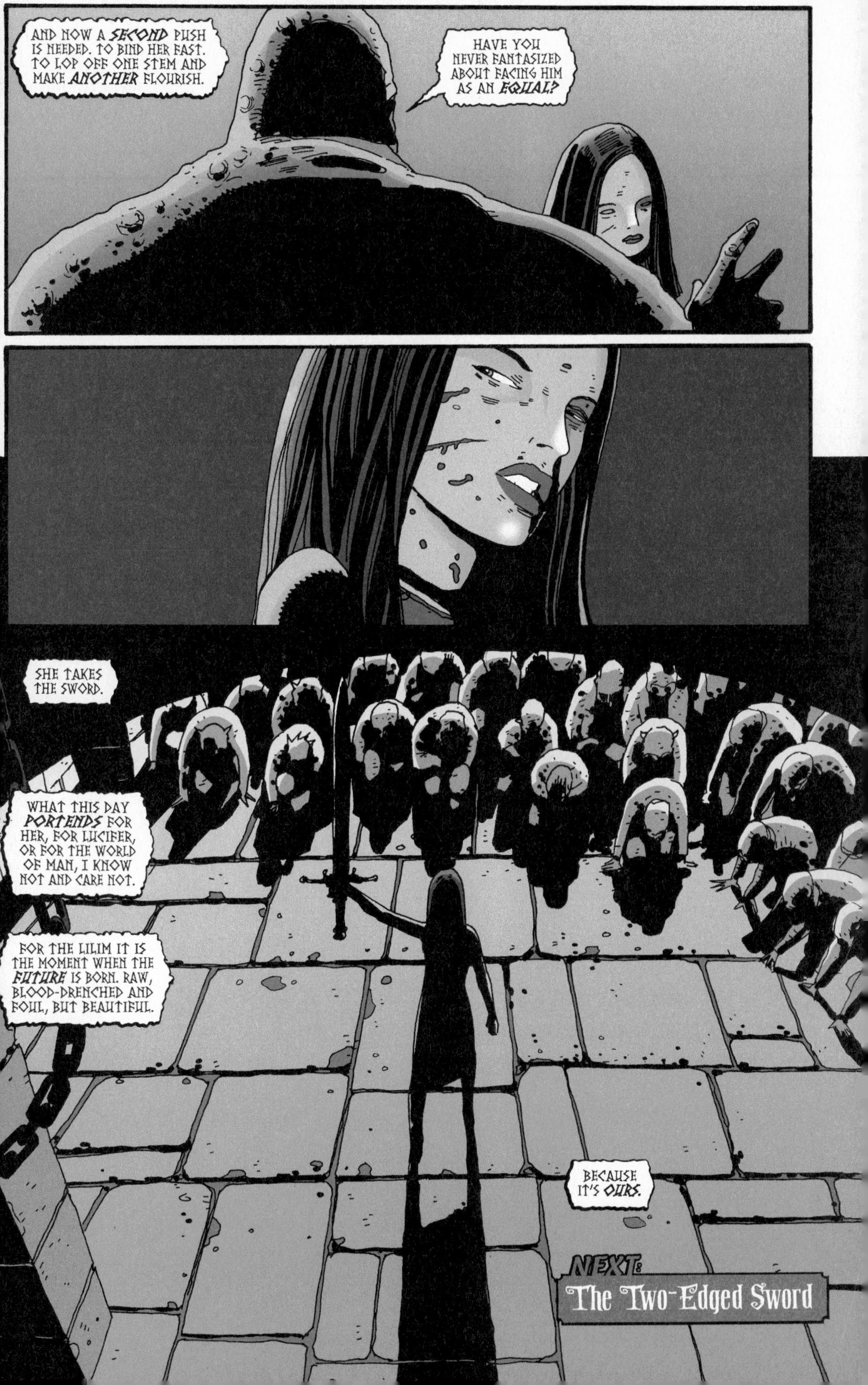
AND NOW A SECOND PUSH IS NEEDED. TO BIND HER FAST. TO LOP OFF ONE STEM AND MAKE ANOTHER FLOURISH.
HAVE YOU NEVER FANTASIZED ABOUT FACING HIM AS AN EQUAL?
SHE TAKES THE SWORD.
WHAT THIS DAY PORTENDS FOR HER, FOR LUCIFER, OR FOR THE WORLD OF MAN, I KNOW NOT AND CARE NOT.
FOR THE LILIM IT IS THE MOMENT WHEN THE FUTURE IS BORN. RAW, BLOOD-DRENCHED AND FOUL, BUT BEAUTIFUL.
BECAUSE IT'S OURS.
NEXT:
The Two-Edged Sword

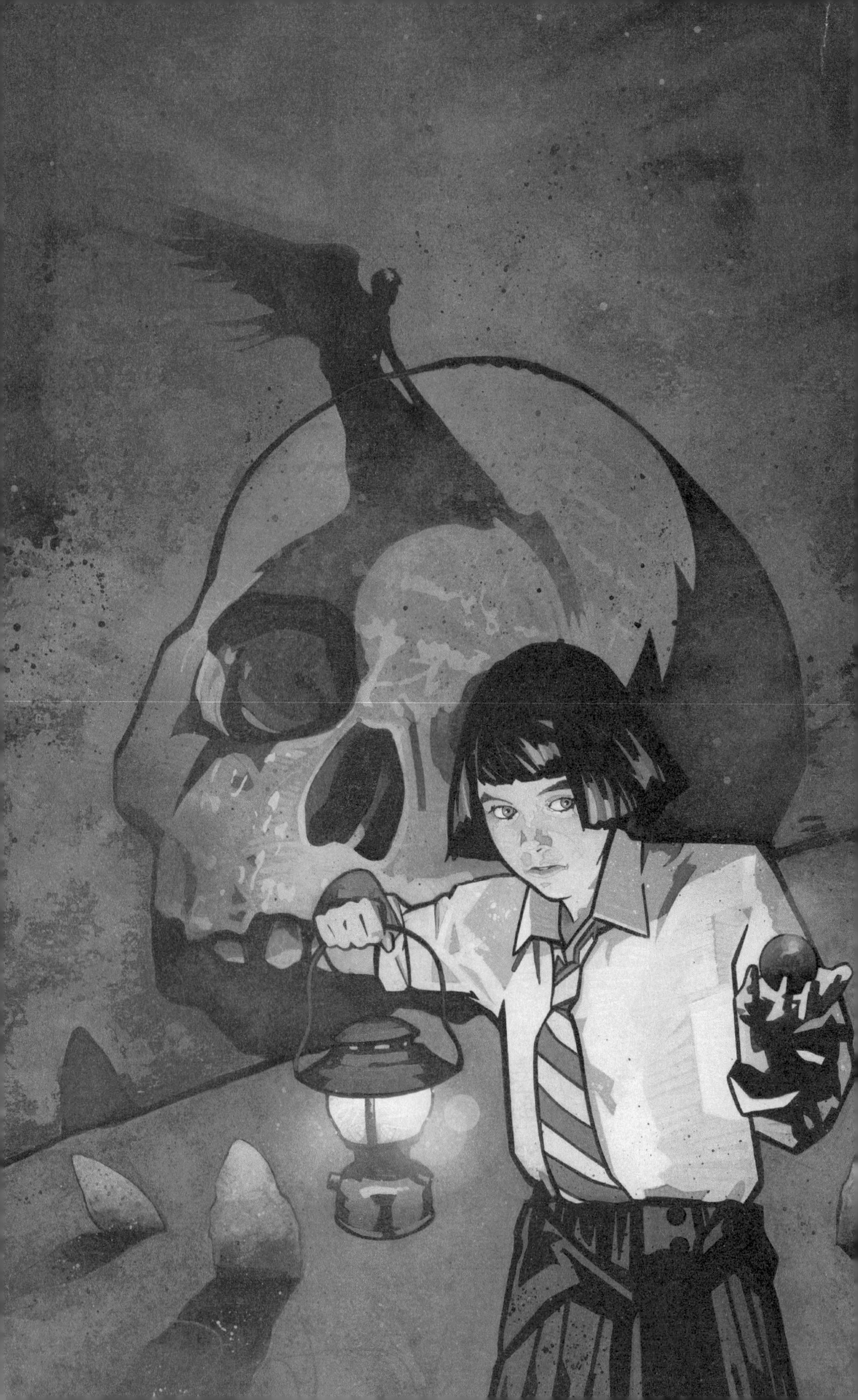

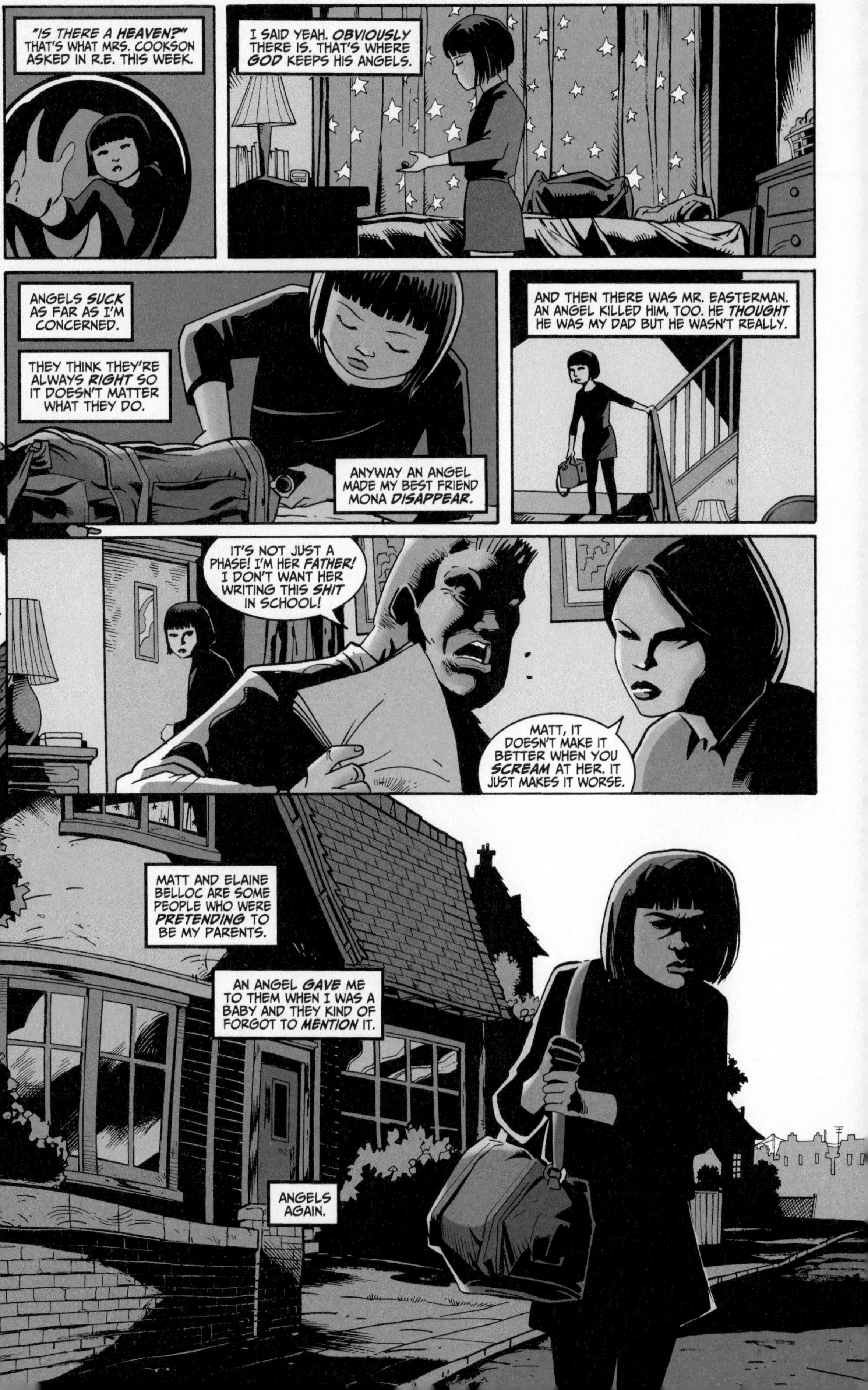
"IS THERE A HEAVEN?" THAT'S WHAT MRS. COOKSON ASKED IN R.E. THIS WEEK.
I SAID YEAH. OBVIOUSLY THERE IS. THAT'S WHERE GOD KEEPS HIS ANGELS.
ANGELS SUCK AS FAR AS I'M CONCERNED.
THEY THINK THEY'RE ALWAYS RIGHT SO IT DOESN'T MATTER WHAT THEY DO.
ANYWAY AN ANGEL MADE MY BEST FRIEND MONA DISAPPEAR.
AND THEN THERE WAS MR. EASTERMAN. AN ANGEL KILLED HIM, TOO. HE THOUGHT HE WAS MY DAD BUT HE WASN'T REALLY.
IT'S NOT JUST A PHASE! I'M HER FATHER! I DON'T WANT HER WRITING THIS SHIT IN SCHOOL!
MATT, IT DOESN'T MAKE IT BETTER WHEN YOU SCREAM AT HER. IT JUST MAKES IT WORSE.
MATT AND ELAINE BELLOC ARE SOME PEOPLE WHO WERE PRETENDING TO BE MY PARENTS.
AN ANGEL GAVE ME TO THEM WHEN I WAS A BABY AND THEY KIND OF FORGOT TO MENTION IT.
ANGELS AGAIN.

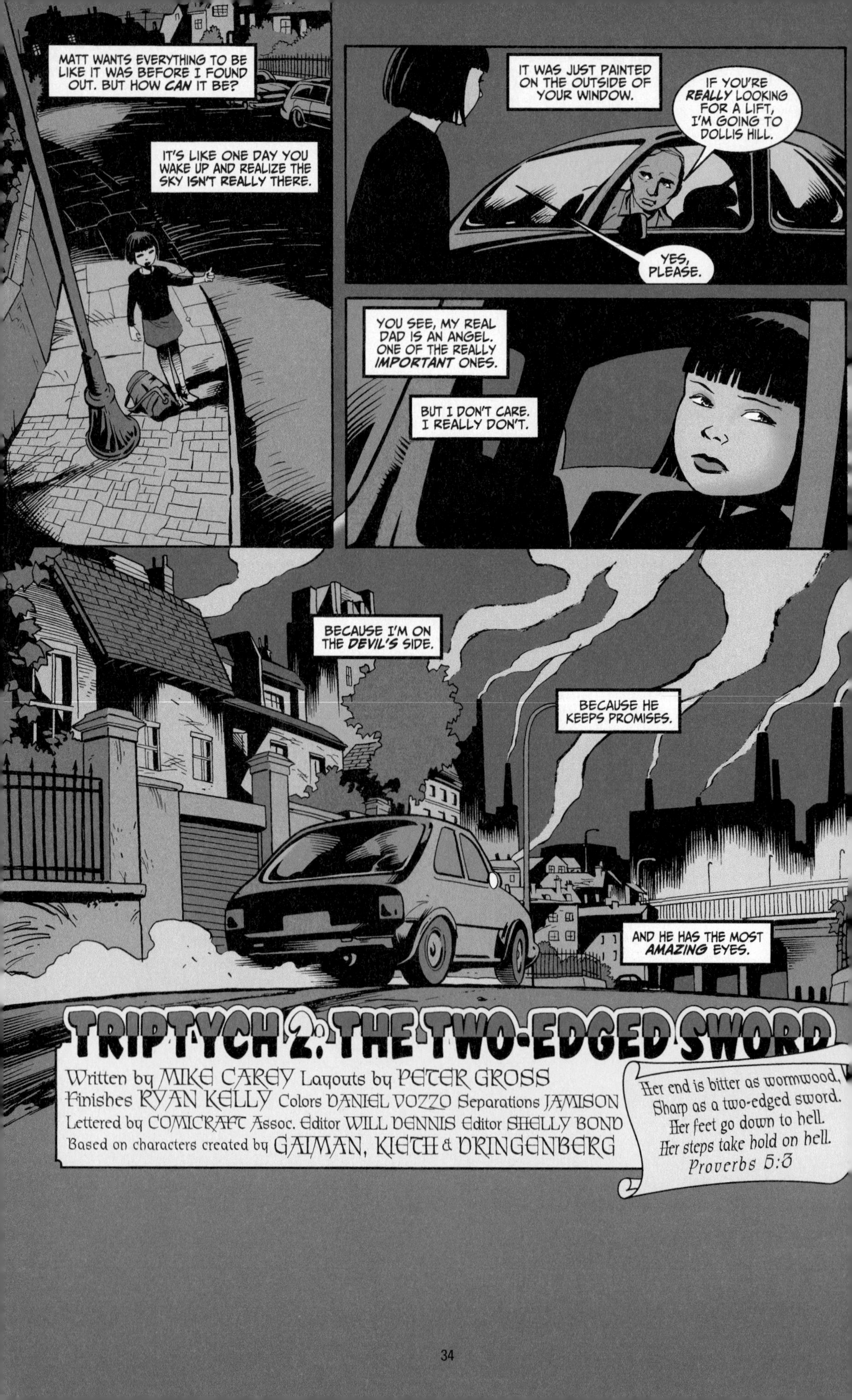
MATT WANTS EVERYTHING TO BE LIKE IT WAS BEFORE I FOUND OUT. BUT HOW *CAN* IT BE?
IT'S LIKE ONE DAY YOU WAKE UP AND REALIZE THE SKY ISN'T REALLY THERE.
IT WAS JUST PAINTED ON THE OUTSIDE OF YOUR WINDOW.
IF YOU'RE *REALLY* LOOKING FOR A LIFT, I'M GOING TO DOLLIS HILL.
YES, PLEASE.
YOU SEE, MY REAL DAD IS AN ANGEL. ONE OF THE REALLY *IMPORTANT* ONES.
BUT I DON'T CARE. I REALLY DON'T.
BECAUSE I'M ON THE *DEVIL'S* SIDE.
BECAUSE HE KEEPS PROMISES.
AND HE HAS THE MOST *AMAZING* EYES.

TRIPTYCH 2: THE TWO-EDGED SWORD

Written by MIKE CAREY Layouts by PETER GROSS
Finishes RYAN KELLY Colors DANIEL VOZZO Separations JAMISON
Lettered by COMICRAFT Assoc. Editor WILL DENNIS Editor SHELLY BOND
Based on characters created by GAIMAN, KIETH & DRINGENBERG

Her end is bitter as wormwood,
Sharp as a two-edged sword.
Her feet go down to hell.
Her steps take hold on hell.
Proverbs 5:3

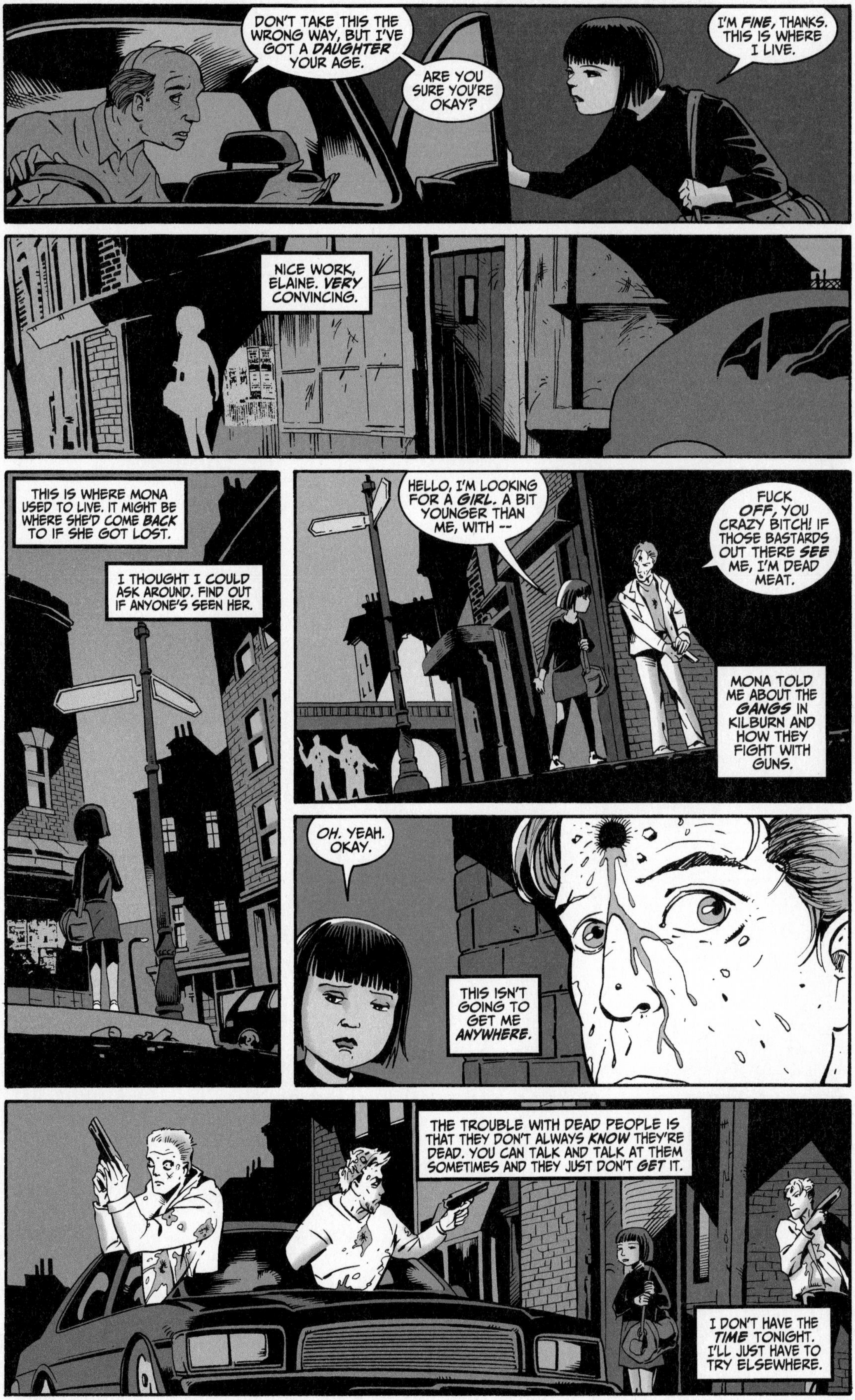
DON'T TAKE THIS THE WRONG WAY, BUT I'VE GOT A DAUGHTER YOUR AGE.
ARE YOU SURE YOU'RE OKAY?
I'M FINE, THANKS. THIS IS WHERE I LIVE.
NICE WORK, ELAINE. VERY CONVINCING.
THIS IS WHERE MONA USED TO LIVE. IT MIGHT BE WHERE SHE'D COME BACK TO IF SHE GOT LOST.
I THOUGHT I COULD ASK AROUND. FIND OUT IF ANYONE'S SEEN HER.
HELLO, I'M LOOKING FOR A GIRL. A BIT YOUNGER THAN ME, WITH --
FUCK OFF, YOU CRAZY BITCH! IF THOSE BASTARDS OUT THERE SEE ME, I'M DEAD MEAT.
MONA TOLD ME ABOUT THE GANGS IN KILBURN AND HOW THEY FIGHT WITH GUNS.
OH. YEAH. OKAY.
THIS ISN'T GOING TO GET ME ANYWHERE.
THE TROUBLE WITH DEAD PEOPLE IS THAT THEY DON'T ALWAYS KNOW THEY'RE DEAD. YOU CAN TALK AND TALK AT THEM SOMETIMES AND THEY JUST DON'T GET IT.
I DON'T HAVE THE TIME TONIGHT. I'LL JUST HAVE TO TRY ELSEWHERE.

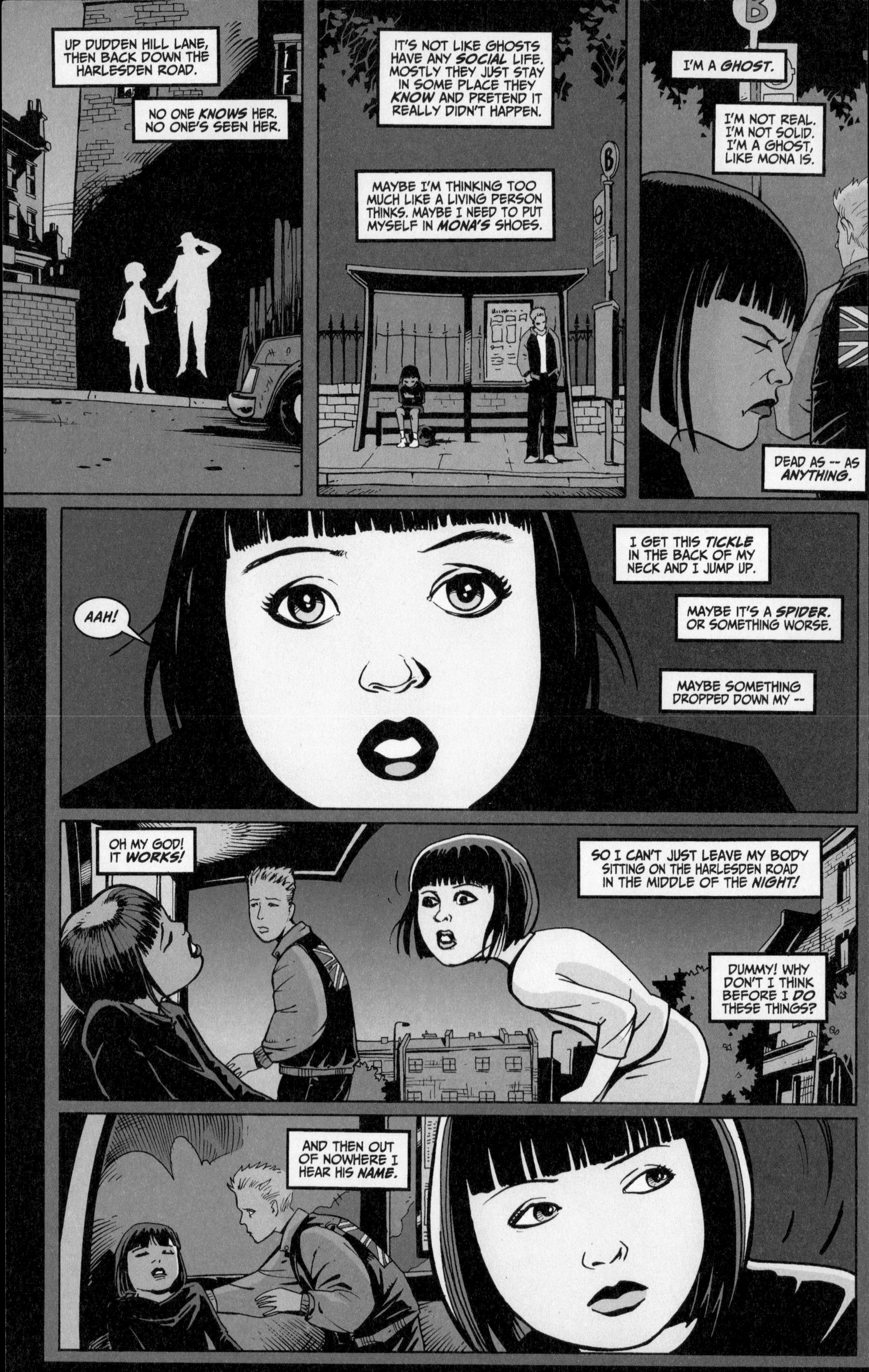

UP DUDDEN HILL LANE, THEN BACK DOWN THE HARLESDEN ROAD.
NO ONE KNOWS HER. NO ONE'S SEEN HER.
IT'S NOT LIKE GHOSTS HAVE ANY SOCIAL LIFE. MOSTLY THEY JUST STAY IN SOME PLACE THEY KNOW AND PRETEND IT REALLY DIDN'T HAPPEN.
MAYBE I'M THINKING TOO MUCH LIKE A LIVING PERSON THINKS. MAYBE I NEED TO PUT MYSELF IN MONA'S SHOES.
I'M A GHOST.
I'M NOT REAL. I'M NOT SOLID. I'M A GHOST, LIKE MONA IS.
DEAD AS -- AS ANYTHING.
I GET THIS TICKLE IN THE BACK OF MY NECK AND I JUMP UP.
AAH!
MAYBE IT'S A SPIDER. OR SOMETHING WORSE.
MAYBE SOMETHING DROPPED DOWN MY --
OH MY GOD! IT WORKS!
SO I CAN'T JUST LEAVE MY BODY SITTING ON THE HARLESDEN ROAD IN THE MIDDLE OF THE NIGHT!
DUMMY! WHY DON'T I THINK BEFORE I DO THESE THINGS?
AND THEN OUT OF NOWHERE I HEAR HIS NAME.

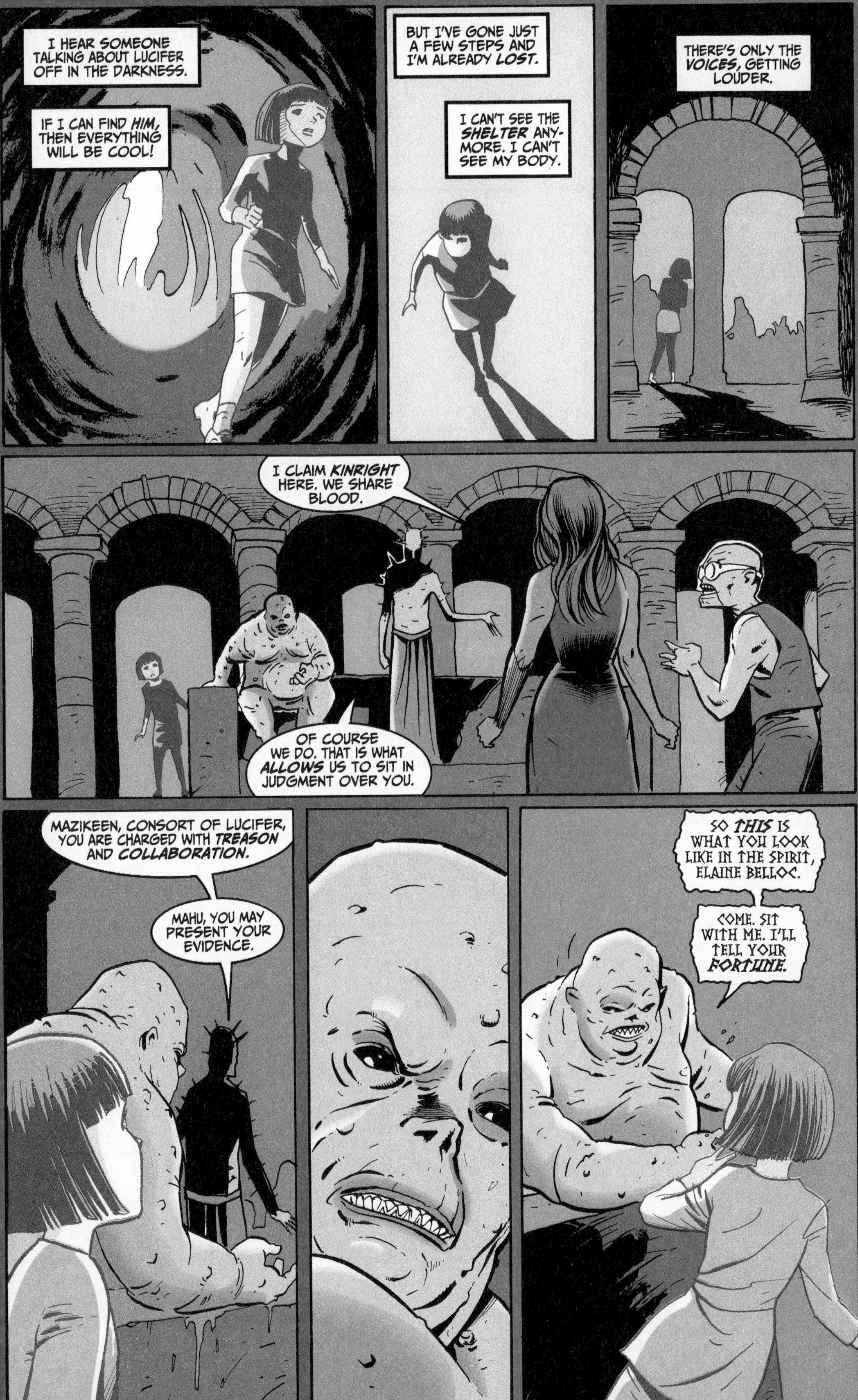
I HEAR SOMEONE TALKING ABOUT LUCIFER OFF IN THE DARKNESS.
IF I CAN FIND HIM, THEN EVERYTHING WILL BE COOL!
BUT I'VE GONE JUST A FEW STEPS AND I'M ALREADY LOST.
I CAN'T SEE THE SHELTER ANY-MORE. I CAN'T SEE MY BODY.
THERE'S ONLY THE VOICES, GETTING LOUDER.
I CLAIM KINRIGHT HERE. WE SHARE BLOOD.
OF COURSE WE DO. THAT IS WHAT ALLOWS US TO SIT IN JUDGMENT OVER YOU.
MAZIKEEN, CONSORT OF LUCIFER, YOU ARE CHARGED WITH TREASON AND COLLABORATION.
MAHU, YOU MAY PRESENT YOUR EVIDENCE.
SO THIS IS WHAT YOU LOOK LIKE IN THE SPIRIT, ELAINE BELLOC.
COME. SIT WITH ME. I'LL TELL YOUR FORTUNE.

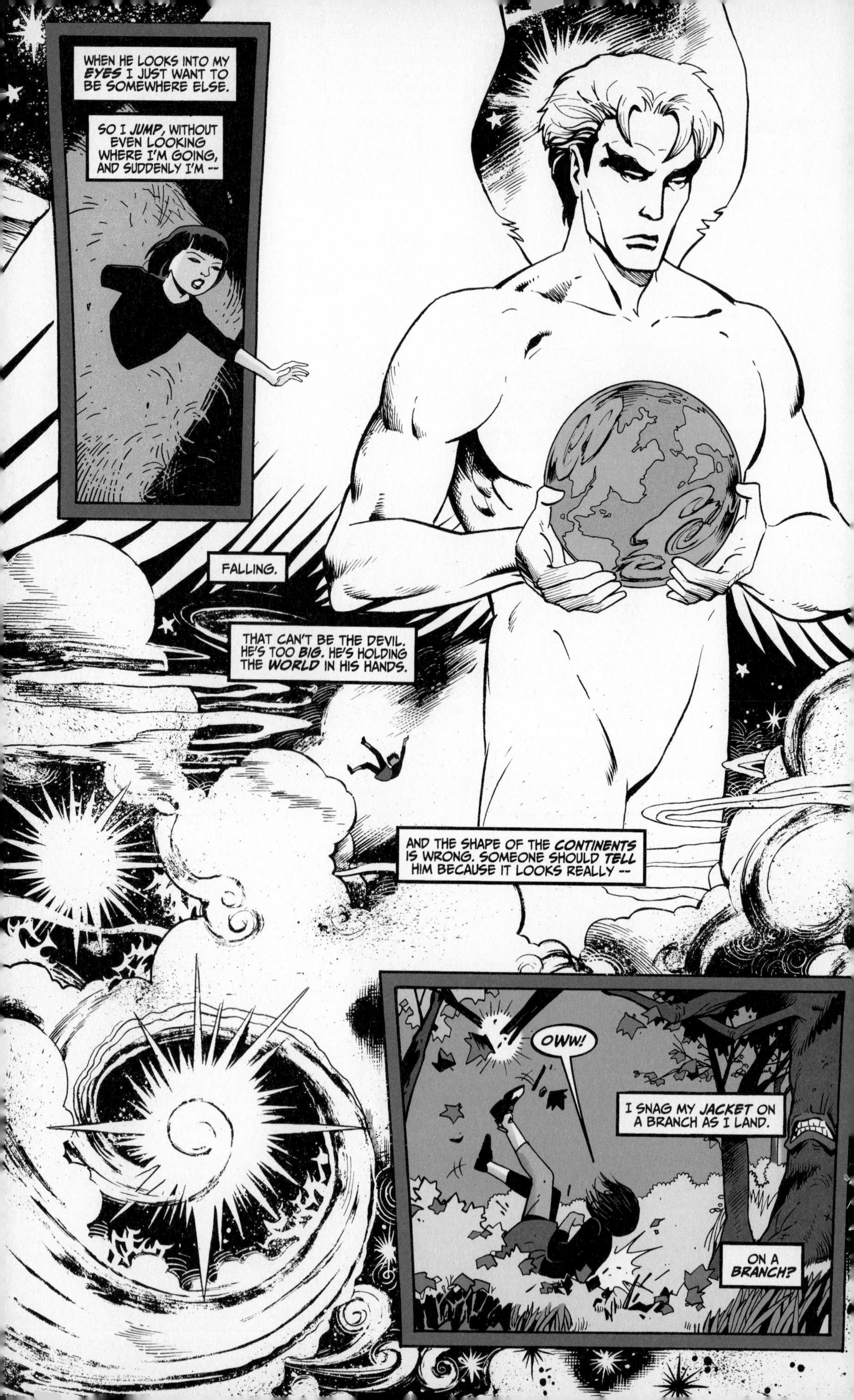
WHEN HE LOOKS INTO MY EYES I JUST WANT TO BE SOMEWHERE ELSE.
SO I JUMP, WITHOUT EVEN LOOKING WHERE I'M GOING, AND SUDDENLY I'M --
FALLING.
THAT CAN'T BE THE DEVIL. HE'S TOO BIG. HE'S HOLDING THE WORLD IN HIS HANDS.
AND THE SHAPE OF THE CONTINENTS IS WRONG. SOMEONE SHOULD TELL HIM BECAUSE IT LOOKS REALLY --
OWW!
I SNAG MY JACKET ON A BRANCH AS I LAND.
ON A BRANCH?

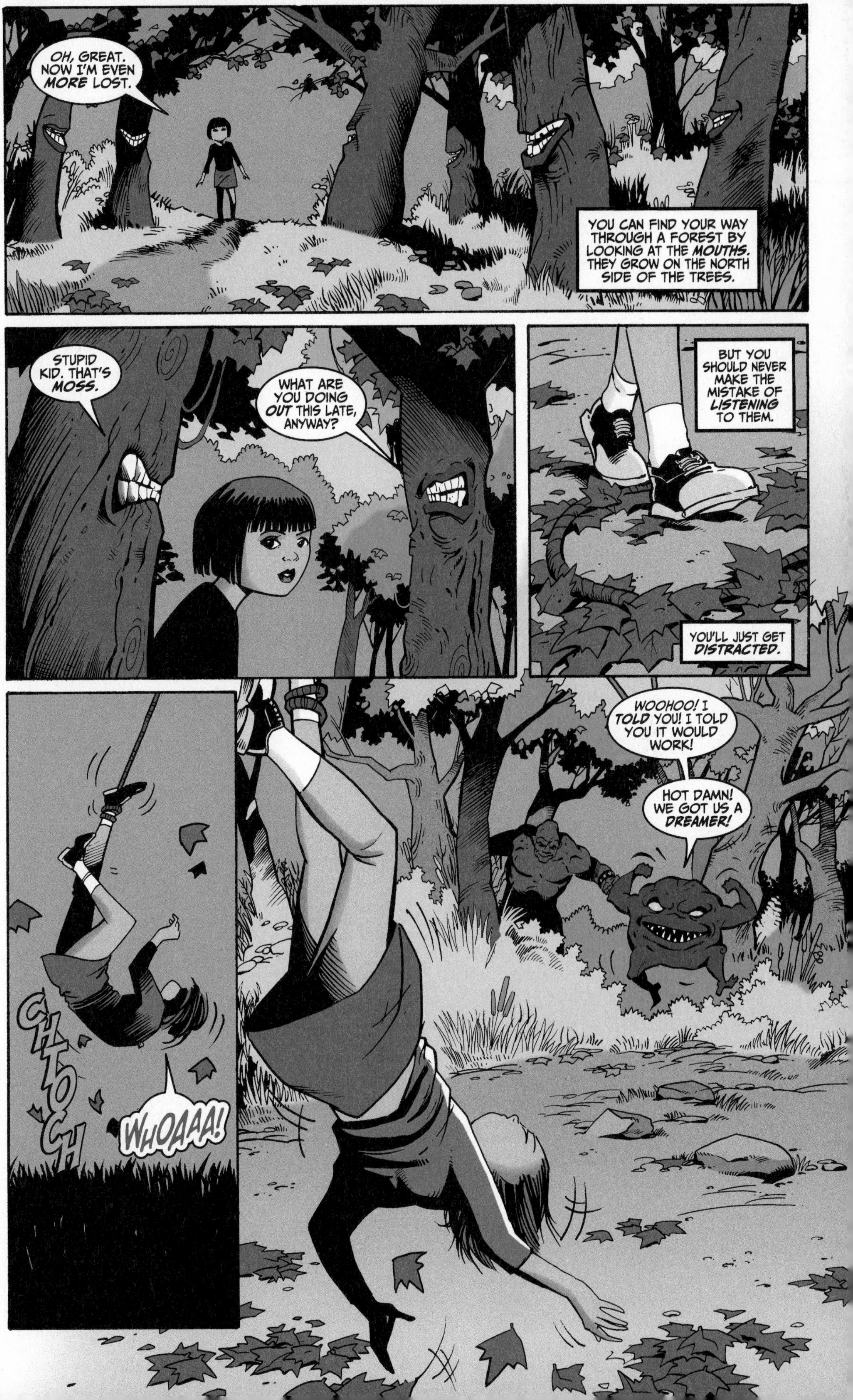
OH, GREAT. NOW I'M EVEN MORE LOST.
YOU CAN FIND YOUR WAY THROUGH A FOREST BY LOOKING AT THE MOUTHS. THEY GROW ON THE NORTH SIDE OF THE TREES.
STUPID KID. THAT'S MOSS.
WHAT ARE YOU DOING OUT THIS LATE, ANYWAY?
BUT YOU SHOULD NEVER MAKE THE MISTAKE OF LISTENING TO THEM.
YOU'LL JUST GET DISTRACTED.
CHTOCH
WHOAAA!
WOOHOO! I TOLD YOU! I TOLD YOU IT WOULD WORK!
HOT DAMN! WE GOT US A DREAMER!

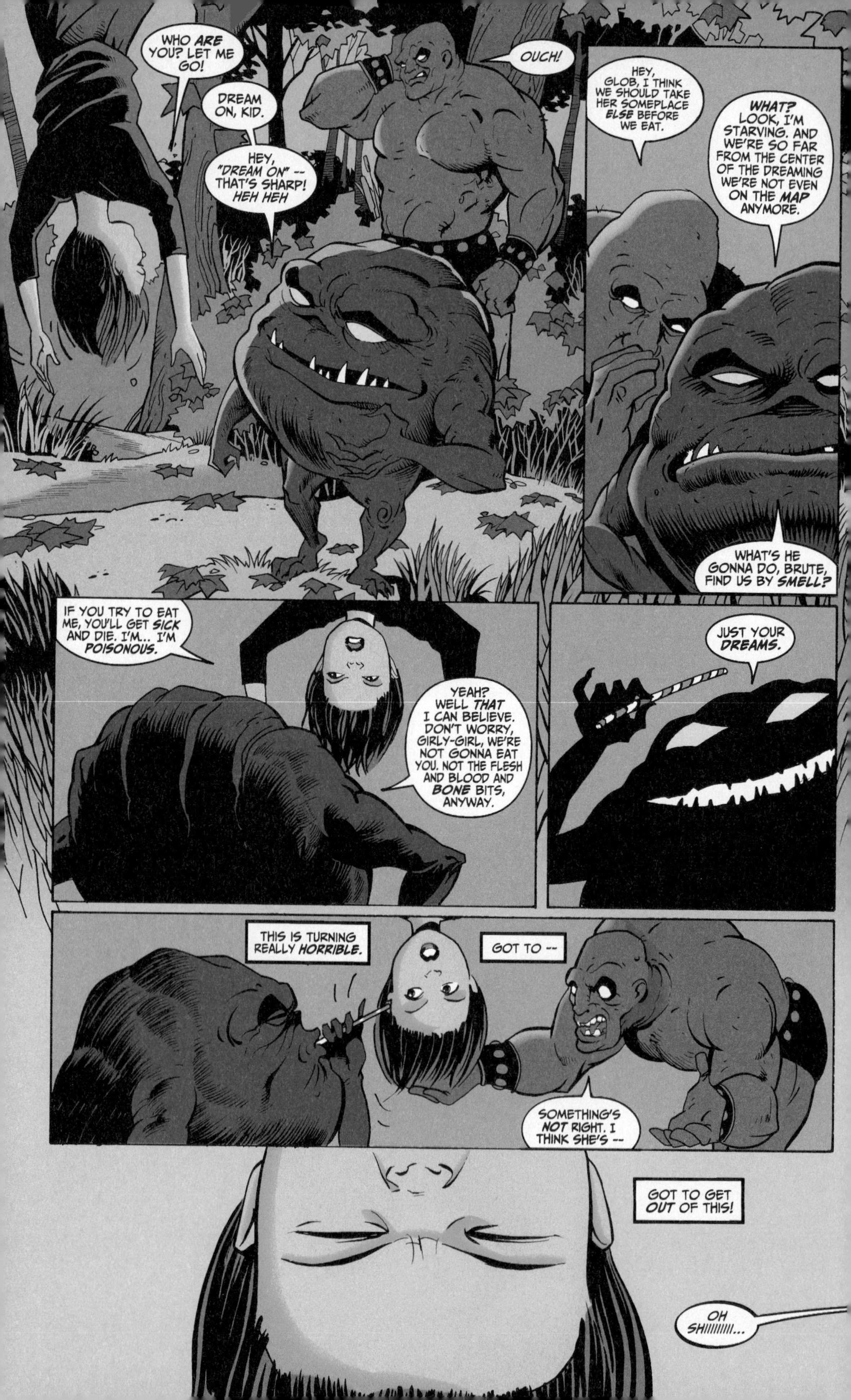
WHO ARE YOU? LET ME GO!
OUCH!
DREAM ON, KID.
HEY, "DREAM ON" -- THAT'S SHARP! HEH HEH
HEY, GLOB, I THINK WE SHOULD TAKE HER SOMEPLACE ELSE BEFORE WE EAT.
WHAT? LOOK, I'M STARVING. AND WE'RE SO FAR FROM THE CENTER OF THE DREAMING WE'RE NOT EVEN ON THE MAP ANYMORE.
WHAT'S HE GONNA DO, BRUTE, FIND US BY SMELL?
IF YOU TRY TO EAT ME, YOU'LL GET SICK AND DIE. I'M... I'M POISONOUS.
YEAH? WELL THAT I CAN BELIEVE. DON'T WORRY, GIRLY-GIRL, WE'RE NOT GONNA EAT YOU. NOT THE FLESH AND BLOOD AND BONE BITS, ANYWAY.
JUST YOUR DREAMS.
THIS IS TURNING REALLY HORRIBLE.
GOT TO --
SOMETHING'S NOT RIGHT. I THINK SHE'S --
GOT TO GET OUT OF THIS!
OH SHIIIIIIII...

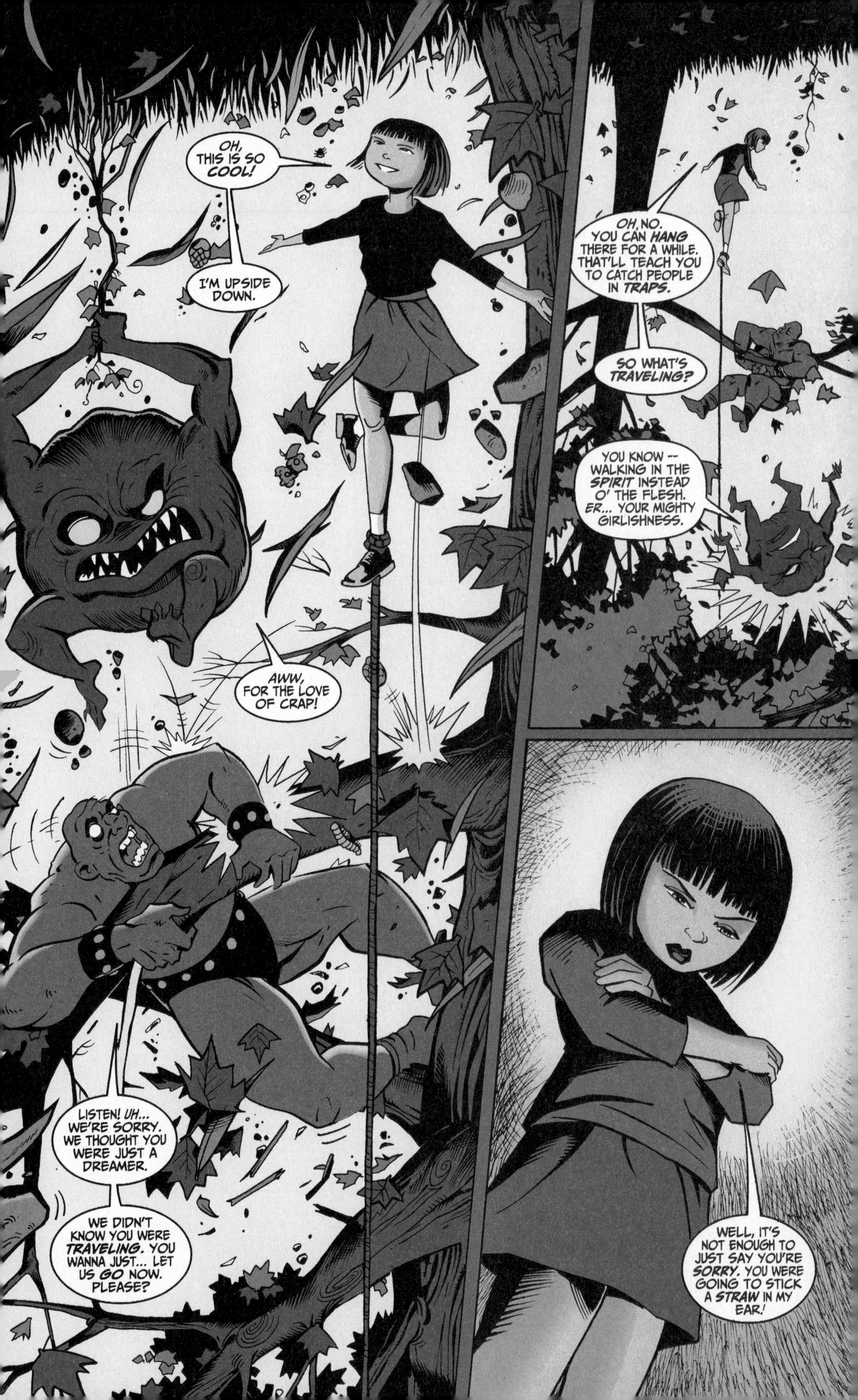

OH, THIS IS SO *COOL!*
I'M UPSIDE DOWN.
AWW, FOR THE LOVE OF CRAP!
LISTEN! *UH...* WE'RE SORRY. WE THOUGHT YOU WERE JUST A DREAMER.
WE DIDN'T KNOW YOU WERE *TRAVELING.* YOU WANNA JUST... LET US *GO* NOW. PLEASE?
OH, NO. YOU CAN *HANG* THERE FOR A WHILE. THAT'LL TEACH YOU TO CATCH PEOPLE IN *TRAPS.*
SO WHAT'S *TRAVELING?*
YOU KNOW -- WALKING IN THE *SPIRIT* INSTEAD O' THE FLESH. *ER...* YOUR MIGHTY GIRLISHNESS.
WELL, IT'S NOT ENOUGH TO JUST SAY YOU'RE *SORRY.* YOU WERE GOING TO STICK A *STRAW* IN MY EAR!

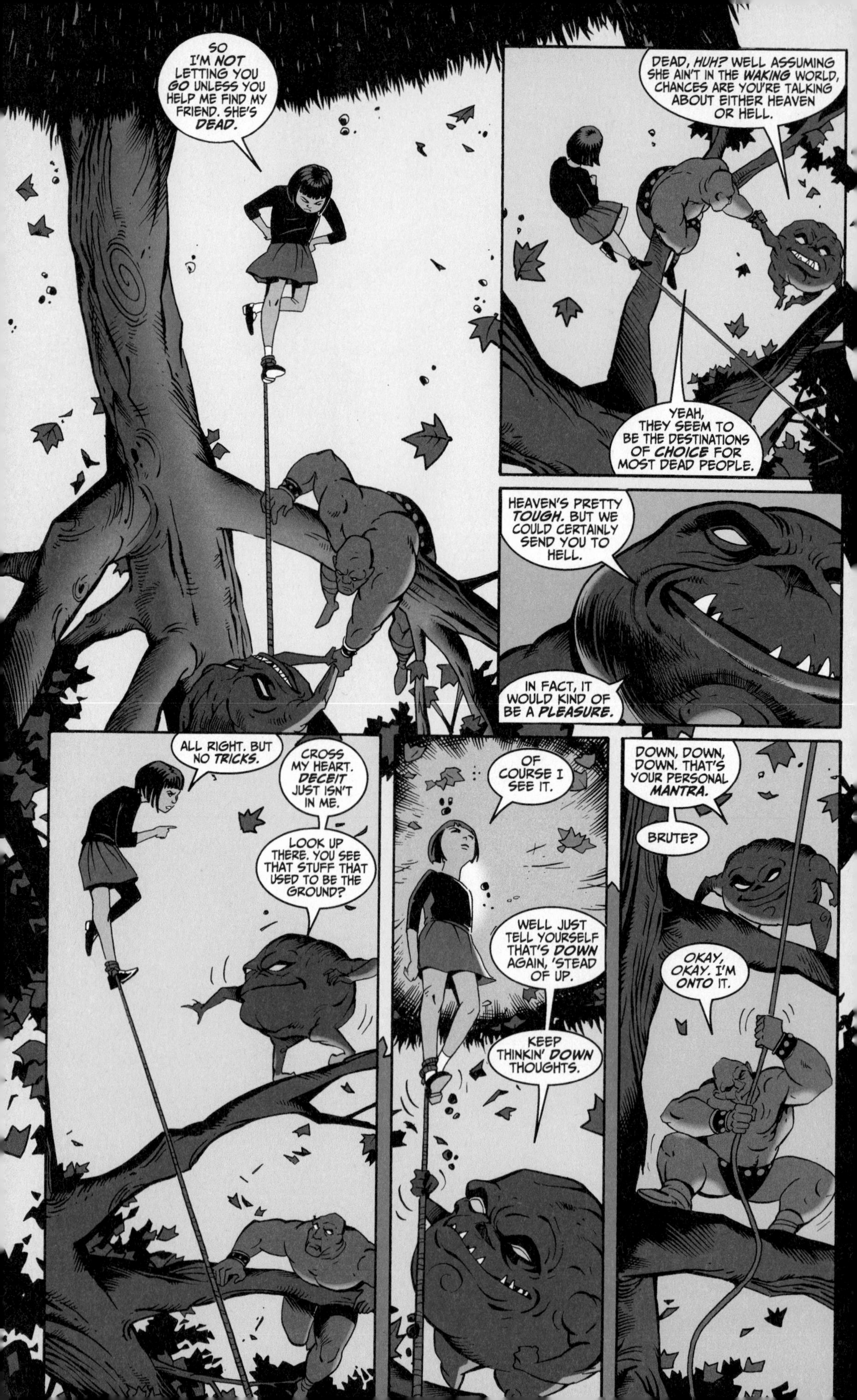
SO I'M NOT LETTING YOU GO UNLESS YOU HELP ME FIND MY FRIEND. SHE'S DEAD.
DEAD, HUH? WELL ASSUMING SHE AIN'T IN THE WAKING WORLD, CHANCES ARE YOU'RE TALKING ABOUT EITHER HEAVEN OR HELL.
YEAH, THEY SEEM TO BE THE DESTINATIONS OF CHOICE FOR MOST DEAD PEOPLE.
HEAVEN'S PRETTY TOUGH. BUT WE COULD CERTAINLY SEND YOU TO HELL.
IN FACT, IT WOULD KIND OF BE A PLEASURE.
ALL RIGHT. BUT NO TRICKS.
CROSS MY HEART. DECEIT JUST ISN'T IN ME.
LOOK UP THERE. YOU SEE THAT STUFF THAT USED TO BE THE GROUND?
OF COURSE I SEE IT.
WELL JUST TELL YOURSELF THAT'S DOWN AGAIN, 'STEAD OF UP.
KEEP THINKIN' DOWN THOUGHTS.
DOWN, DOWN, DOWN. THAT'S YOUR PERSONAL MANTRA.
BRUTE?
OKAY, OKAY. I'M ONTO IT.

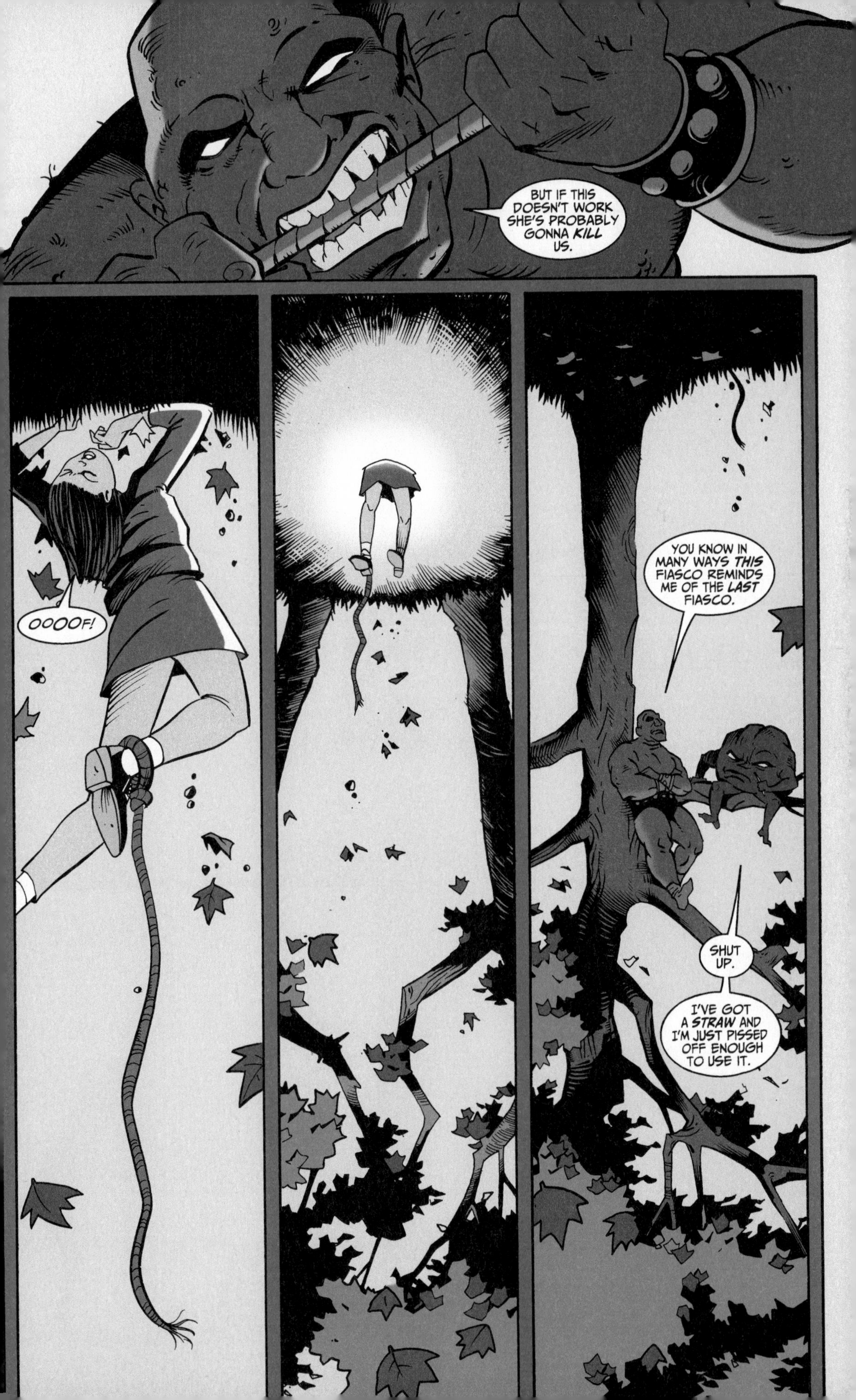
BUT IF THIS DOESN'T WORK SHE'S PROBABLY GONNA KILL US.
OOOOF!
YOU KNOW IN MANY WAYS THIS FIASCO REMINDS ME OF THE LAST FIASCO.
SHUT UP.
I'VE GOT A STRAW AND I'M JUST PISSED OFF ENOUGH TO USE IT.

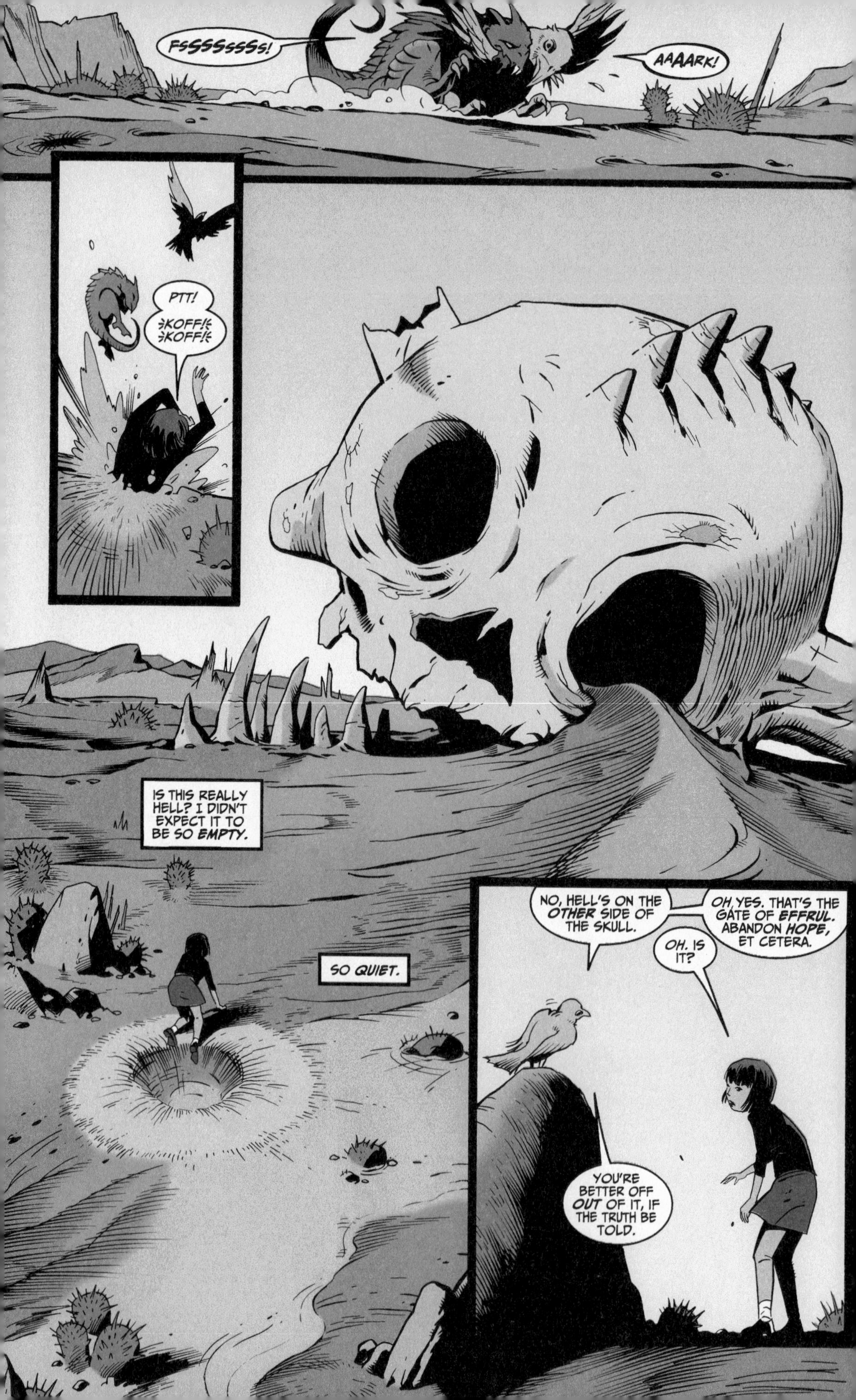
FSSSSSSSS!
AAAARK!
PTT!
KOFF! KOFF!
IS THIS REALLY HELL? I DIDN'T EXPECT IT TO BE SO EMPTY.
SO QUIET.
NO, HELL'S ON THE OTHER SIDE OF THE SKULL.
OH. IS IT?
OH, YES. THAT'S THE GATE OF EFFRUL. ABANDON HOPE, ET CETERA.
YOU'RE BETTER OFF OUT OF IT, IF THE TRUTH BE TOLD.

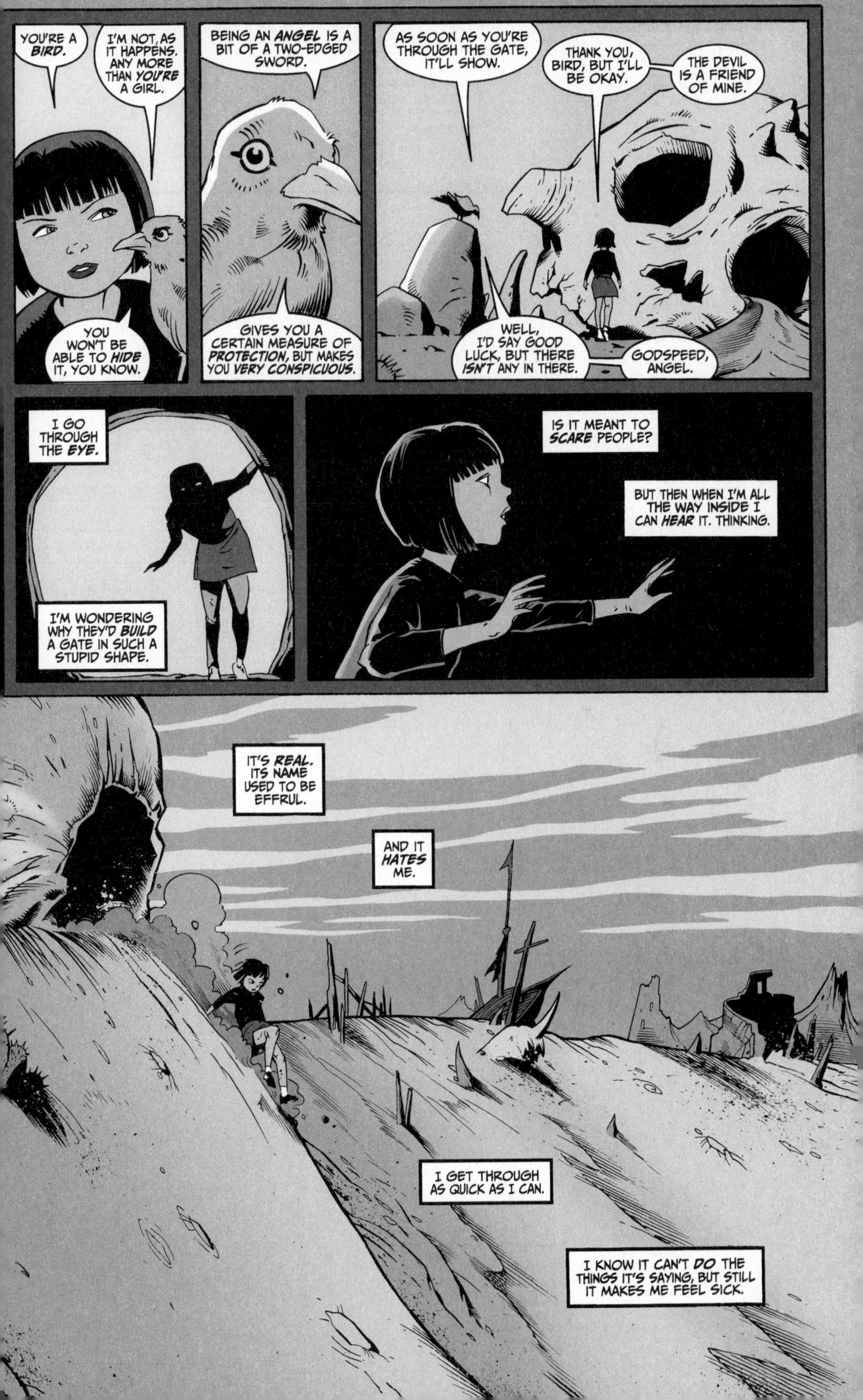
YOU'RE A BIRD.
I'M NOT, AS IT HAPPENS. ANY MORE THAN YOU'RE A GIRL.
YOU WON'T BE ABLE TO HIDE IT, YOU KNOW.
BEING AN ANGEL IS A BIT OF A TWO-EDGED SWORD.
GIVES YOU A CERTAIN MEASURE OF PROTECTION, BUT MAKES YOU VERY CONSPICUOUS.
AS SOON AS YOU'RE THROUGH THE GATE, IT'LL SHOW.
THANK YOU, BIRD, BUT I'LL BE OKAY.
THE DEVIL IS A FRIEND OF MINE.
WELL, I'D SAY GOOD LUCK, BUT THERE ISN'T ANY IN THERE.
GODSPEED, ANGEL.
I GO THROUGH THE EYE.
I'M WONDERING WHY THEY'D BUILD A GATE IN SUCH A STUPID SHAPE.
IS IT MEANT TO SCARE PEOPLE?
BUT THEN WHEN I'M ALL THE WAY INSIDE I CAN HEAR IT. THINKING.
IT'S REAL. ITS NAME USED TO BE EFFRUL.
AND IT HATES ME.
I GET THROUGH AS QUICK AS I CAN.
I KNOW IT CAN'T DO THE THINGS IT'S SAYING, BUT STILL IT MAKES ME FEEL SICK.

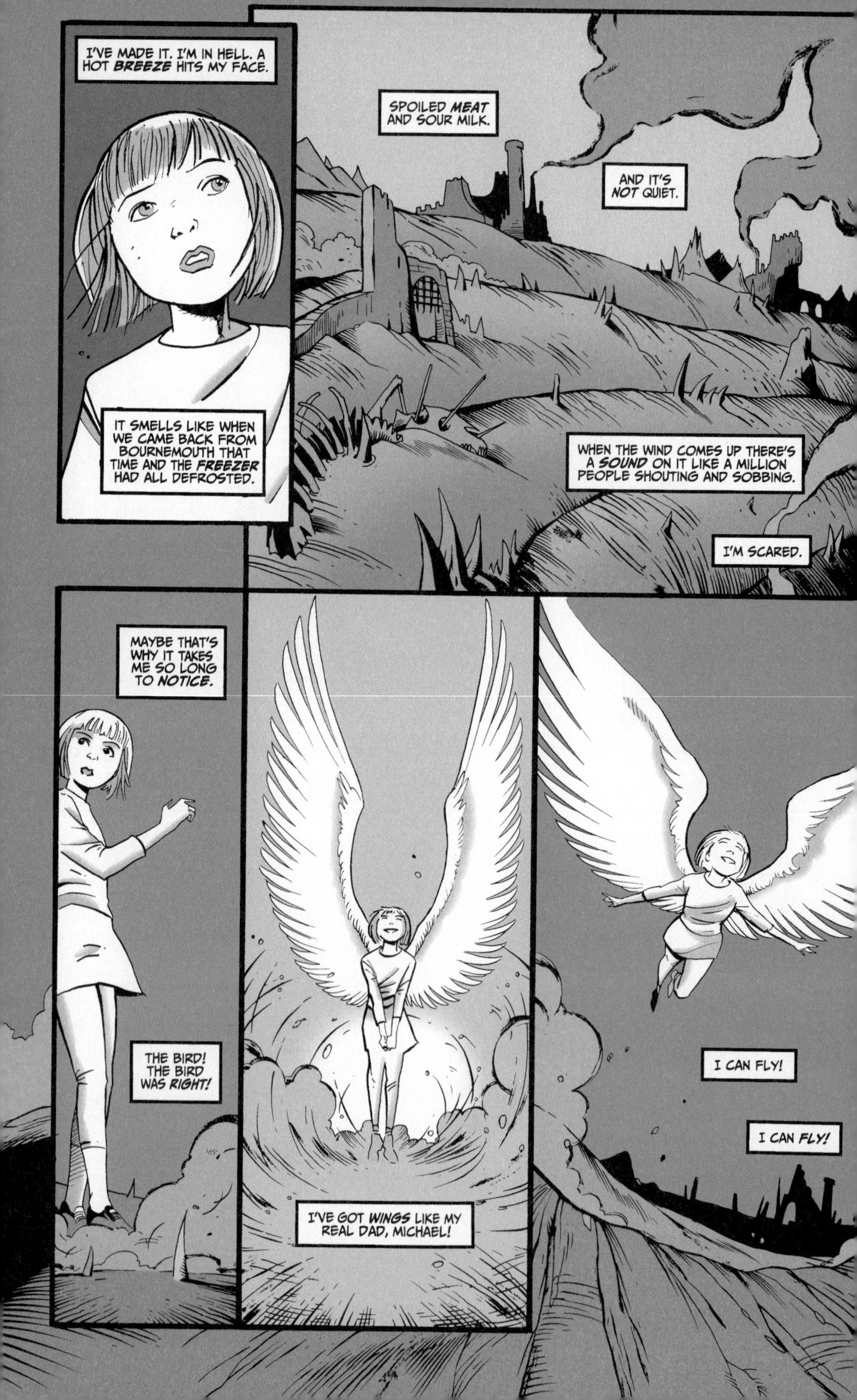
I'VE MADE IT. I'M IN HELL. A HOT BREEZE HITS MY FACE.
IT SMELLS LIKE WHEN WE CAME BACK FROM BOURNEMOUTH THAT TIME AND THE FREEZER HAD ALL DEFROSTED.
SPOILED MEAT AND SOUR MILK.
AND IT'S NOT QUIET.
WHEN THE WIND COMES UP THERE'S A SOUND ON IT LIKE A MILLION PEOPLE SHOUTING AND SOBBING.
I'M SCARED.
MAYBE THAT'S WHY IT TAKES ME SO LONG TO NOTICE.
THE BIRD! THE BIRD WAS RIGHT!
I'VE GOT WINGS LIKE MY REAL DAD, MICHAEL!
I CAN FLY!
I CAN FLY!

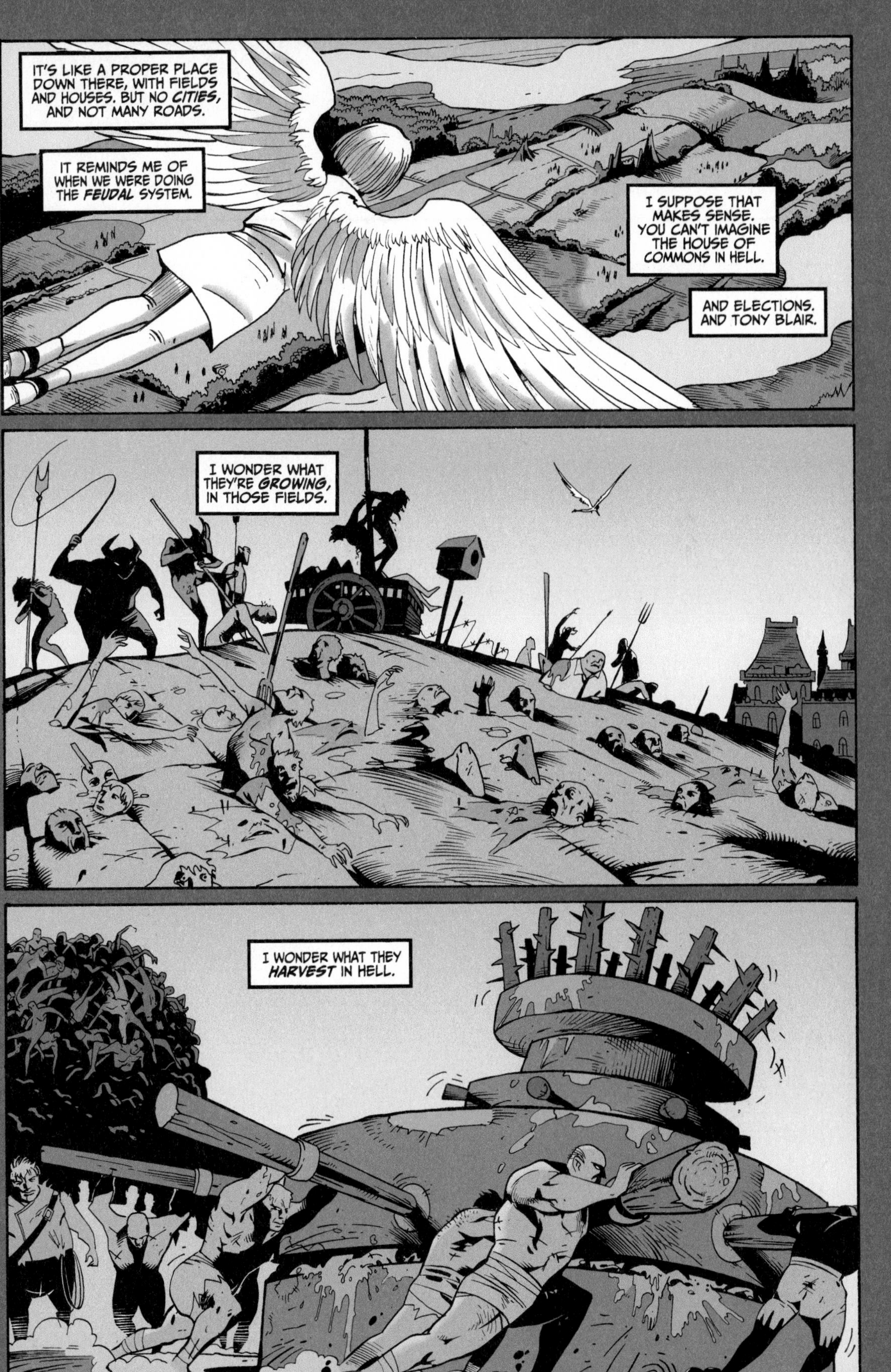
IT'S LIKE A PROPER PLACE DOWN THERE, WITH FIELDS AND HOUSES. BUT NO CITIES, AND NOT MANY ROADS.
IT REMINDS ME OF WHEN WE WERE DOING THE FEUDAL SYSTEM.
I SUPPOSE THAT MAKES SENSE. YOU CAN'T IMAGINE THE HOUSE OF COMMONS IN HELL.
AND ELECTIONS. AND TONY BLAIR.
I WONDER WHAT THEY'RE GROWING, IN THOSE FIELDS.
I WONDER WHAT THEY HARVEST IN HELL.

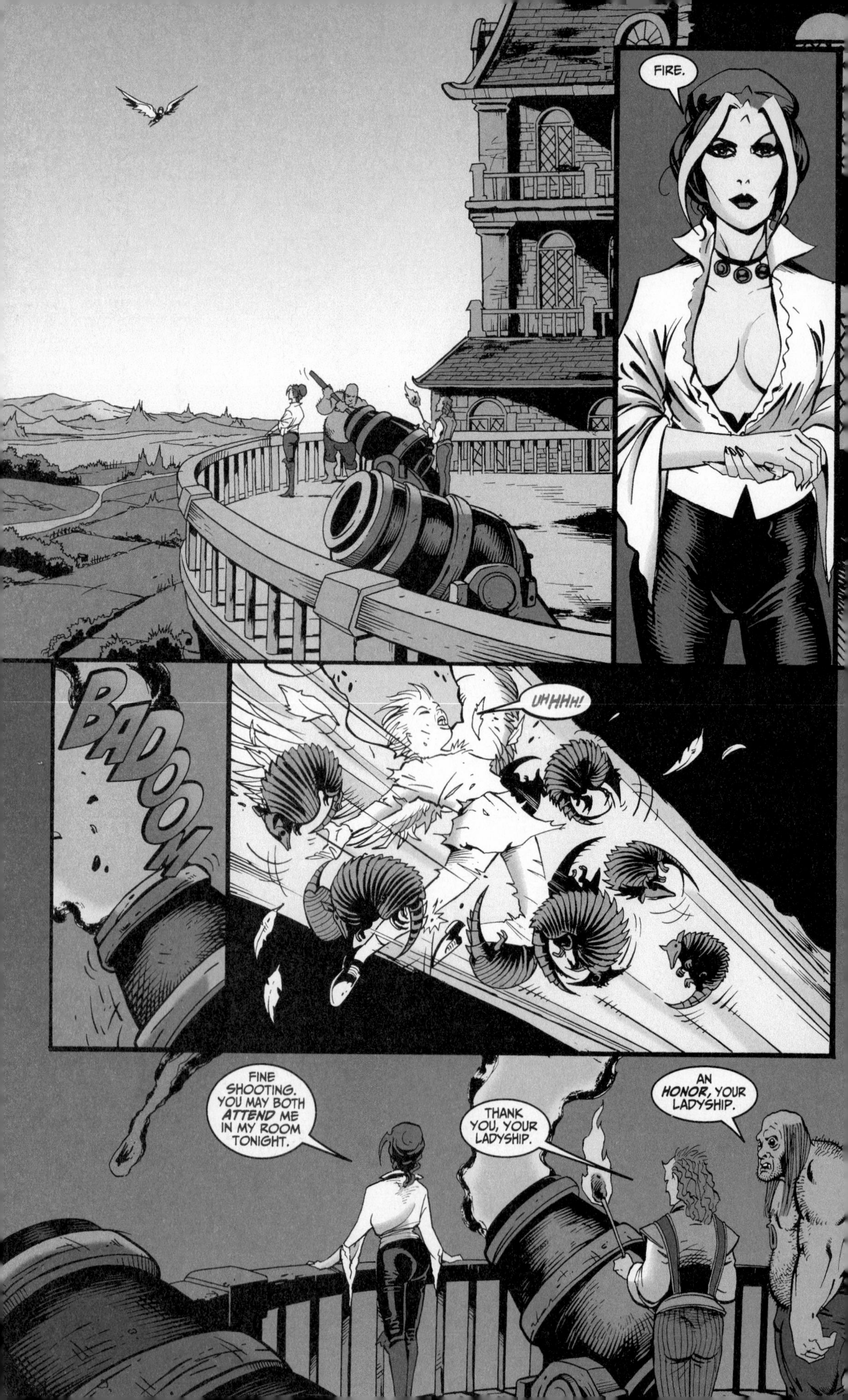
FIRE.
BADOOOM
UHHHH!
FINE SHOOTING. YOU MAY BOTH ATTEND ME IN MY ROOM TONIGHT.
THANK YOU, YOUR LADYSHIP.
AN HONOR, YOUR LADYSHIP.

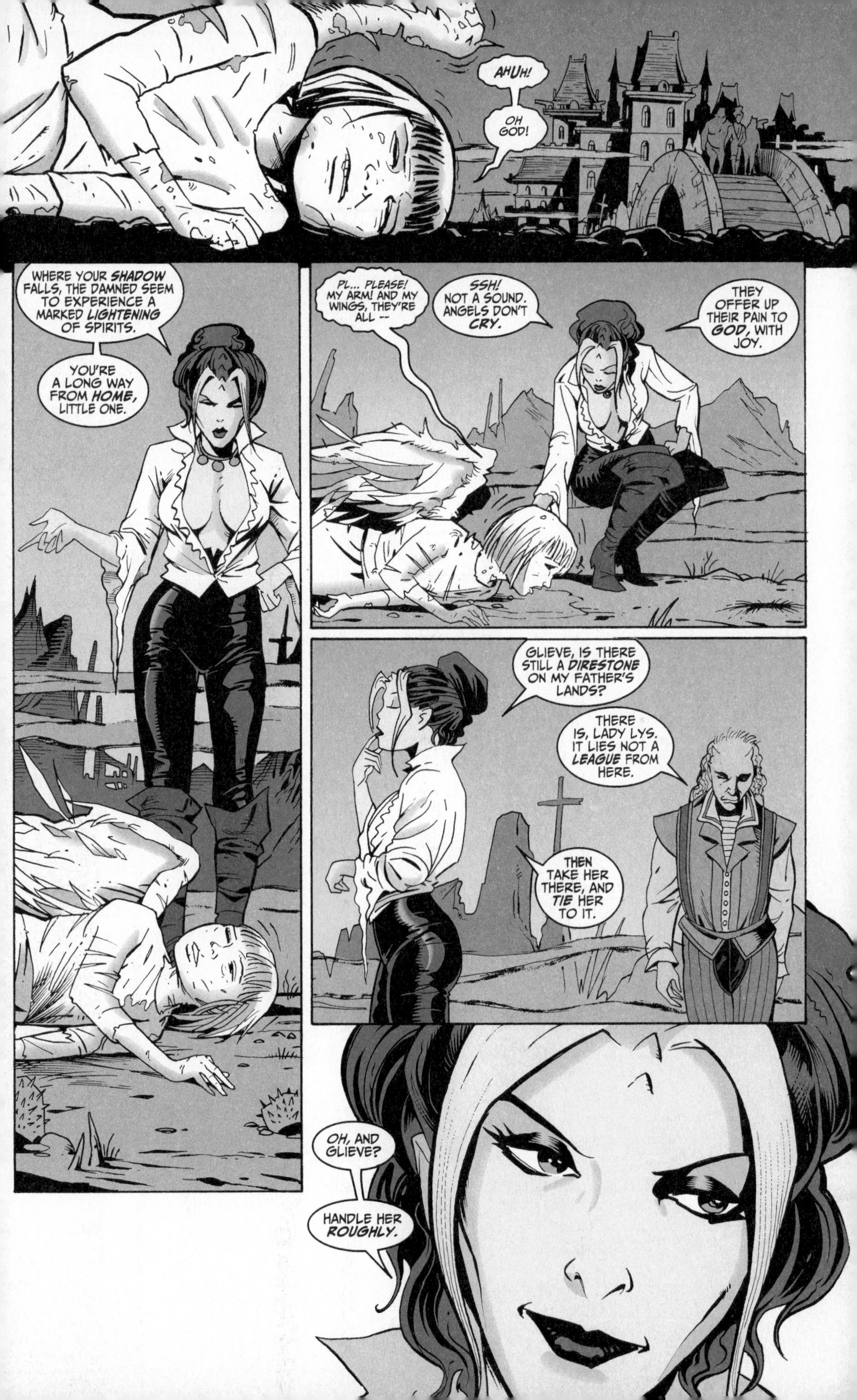
AHUH!
OH GOD!
WHERE YOUR SHADOW FALLS, THE DAMNED SEEM TO EXPERIENCE A MARKED LIGHTENING OF SPIRITS.
YOU'RE A LONG WAY FROM HOME, LITTLE ONE.
PL... PLEASE! MY ARM! AND MY WINGS, THEY'RE ALL --
SSH! NOT A SOUND. ANGELS DON'T CRY.
THEY OFFER UP THEIR PAIN TO GOD, WITH JOY.
GLIEVE, IS THERE STILL A DIRESTONE ON MY FATHER'S LANDS?
THERE IS, LADY LYS. IT LIES NOT A LEAGUE FROM HERE.
THEN TAKE HER THERE, AND TIE HER TO IT.
OH, AND GLIEVE?
HANDLE HER ROUGHLY.

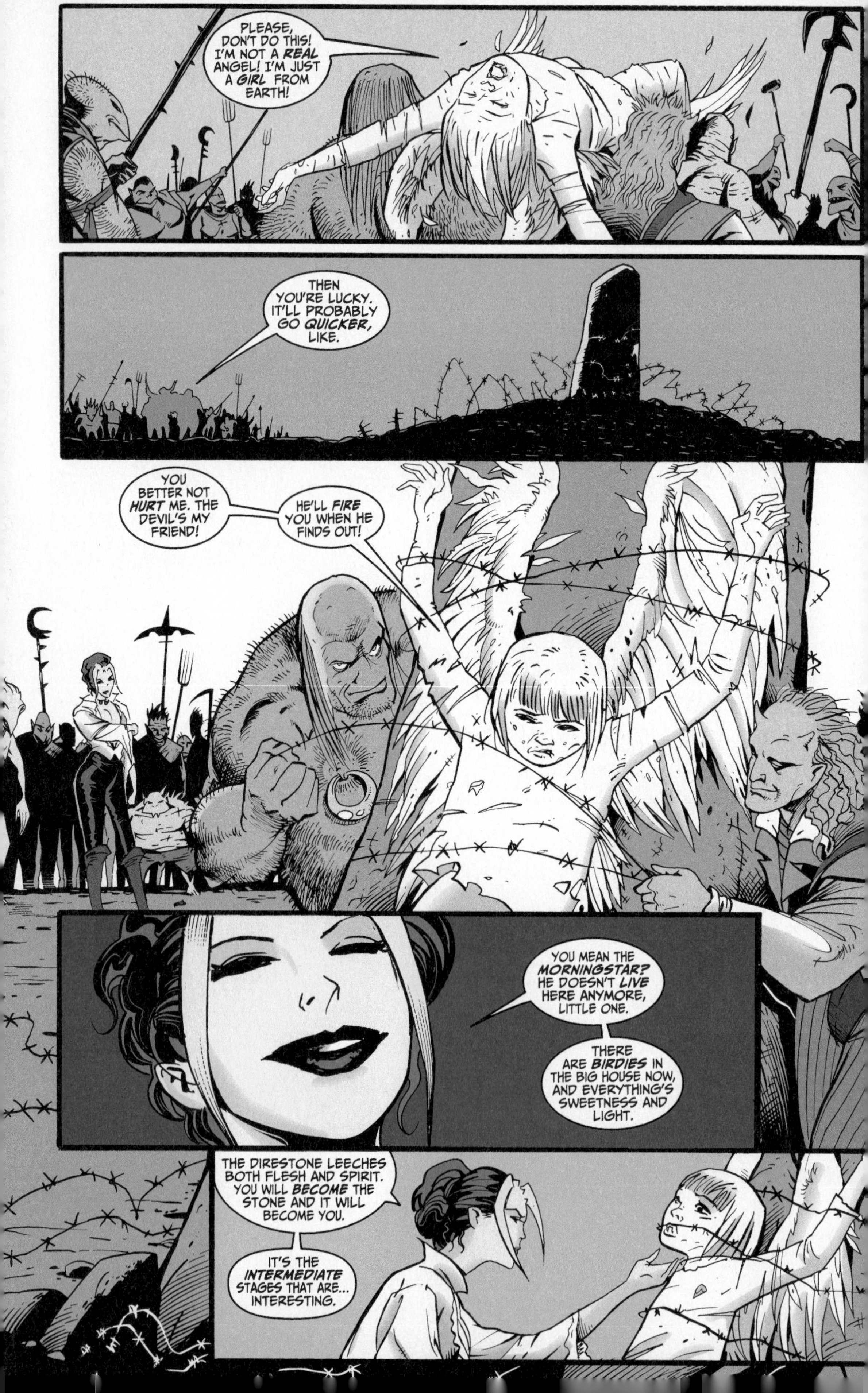

PLEASE, DON'T DO THIS! I'M NOT A REAL ANGEL! I'M JUST A GIRL FROM EARTH!
THEN YOU'RE LUCKY. IT'LL PROBABLY GO QUICKER, LIKE.
YOU BETTER NOT HURT ME. THE DEVIL'S MY FRIEND!
HE'LL FIRE YOU WHEN HE FINDS OUT!
YOU MEAN THE MORNINGSTAR? HE DOESN'T LIVE HERE ANYMORE, LITTLE ONE.
THERE ARE BIRDIES IN THE BIG HOUSE NOW, AND EVERYTHING'S SWEETNESS AND LIGHT.
THE DIRESTONE LEECHES BOTH FLESH AND SPIRIT. YOU WILL BECOME THE STONE AND IT WILL BECOME YOU.
IT'S THE INTERMEDIATE STAGES THAT ARE... INTERESTING.

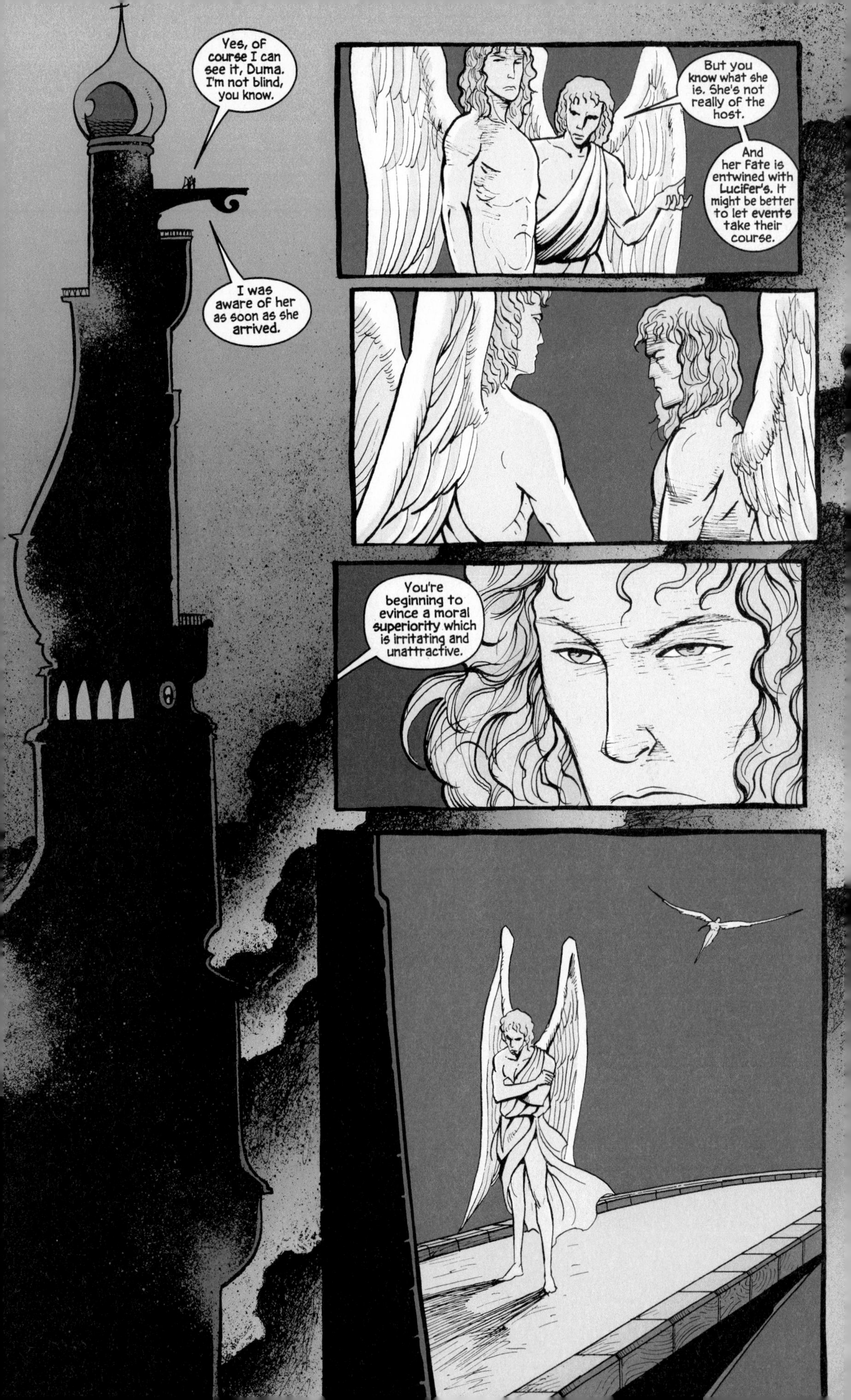
Yes, of course I can see it, Duma. I'm not blind, you know.
I was aware of her as soon as she arrived.
But you know what she is. She's not really of the host.
And her fate is entwined with Lucifer's. It might be better to let events take their course.
You're beginning to evince a moral superiority which is irritating and unattractive.

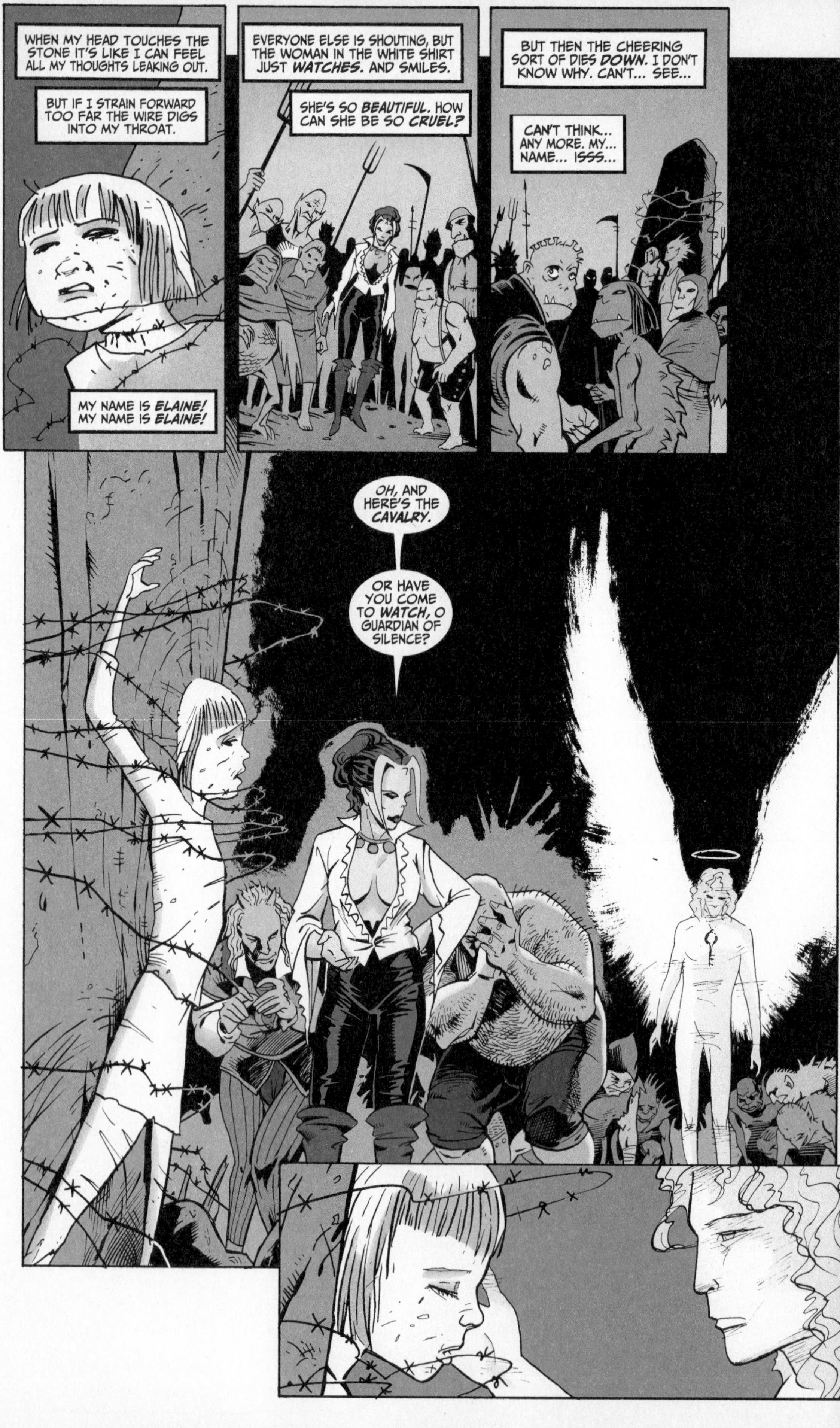

WHEN MY HEAD TOUCHES THE STONE IT'S LIKE I CAN FEEL ALL MY THOUGHTS LEAKING OUT.
BUT IF I STRAIN FORWARD TOO FAR THE WIRE DIGS INTO MY THROAT.
MY NAME IS ELAINE! MY NAME IS ELAINE!
EVERYONE ELSE IS SHOUTING, BUT THE WOMAN IN THE WHITE SHIRT JUST WATCHES. AND SMILES.
SHE'S SO BEAUTIFUL. HOW CAN SHE BE SO CRUEL?
BUT THEN THE CHEERING SORT OF DIES DOWN. I DON'T KNOW WHY. CAN'T... SEE...
CAN'T THINK... ANY MORE. MY... NAME... ISSS...
OH, AND HERE'S THE CAVALRY.
OR HAVE YOU COME TO WATCH, O GUARDIAN OF SILENCE?

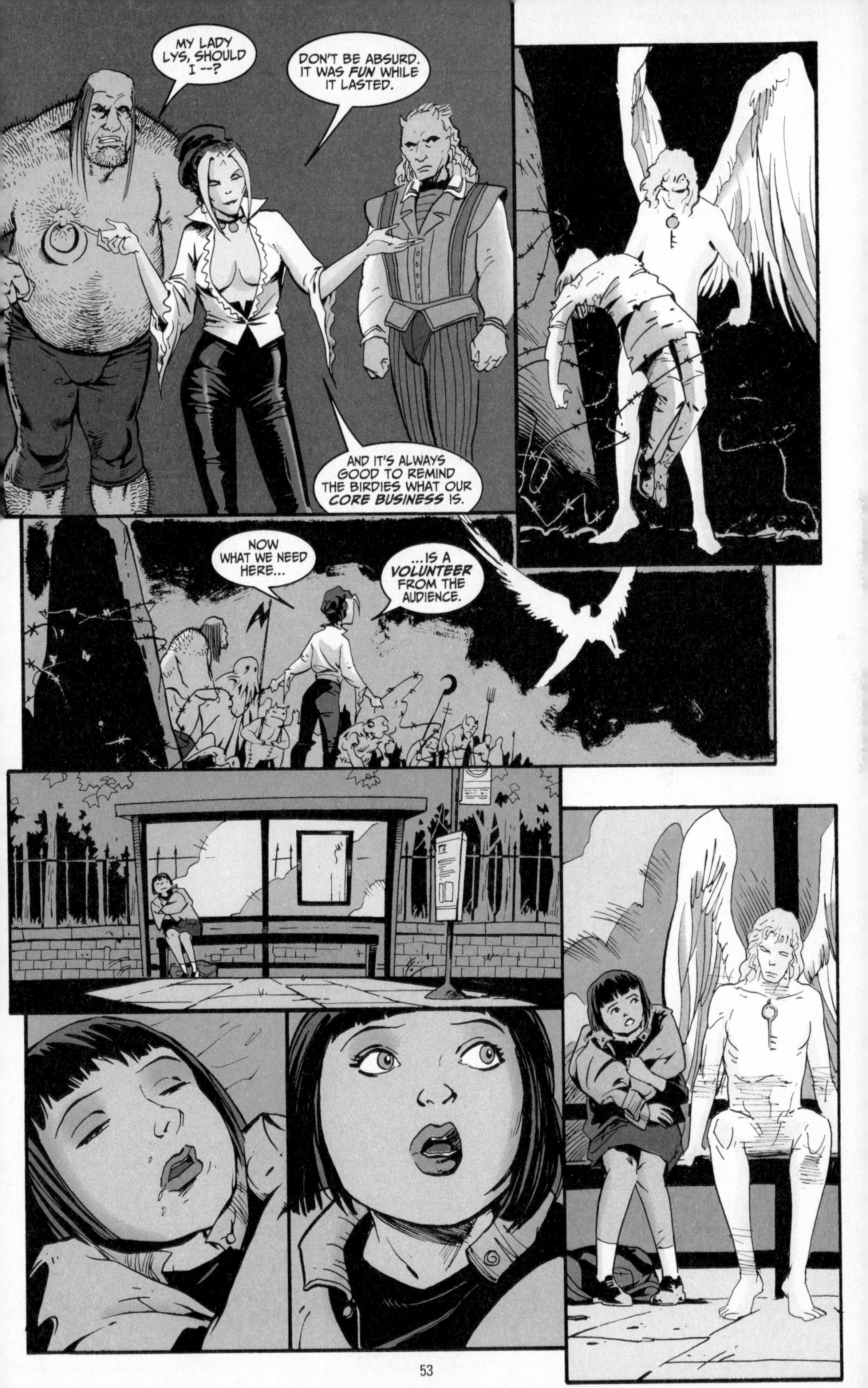
MY LADY LYS, SHOULD I --?
DON'T BE ABSURD. IT WAS FUN WHILE IT LASTED.
AND IT'S ALWAYS GOOD TO REMIND THE BIRDIES WHAT OUR CORE BUSINESS IS.
NOW WHAT WE NEED HERE...
...IS A VOLUNTEER FROM THE AUDIENCE.

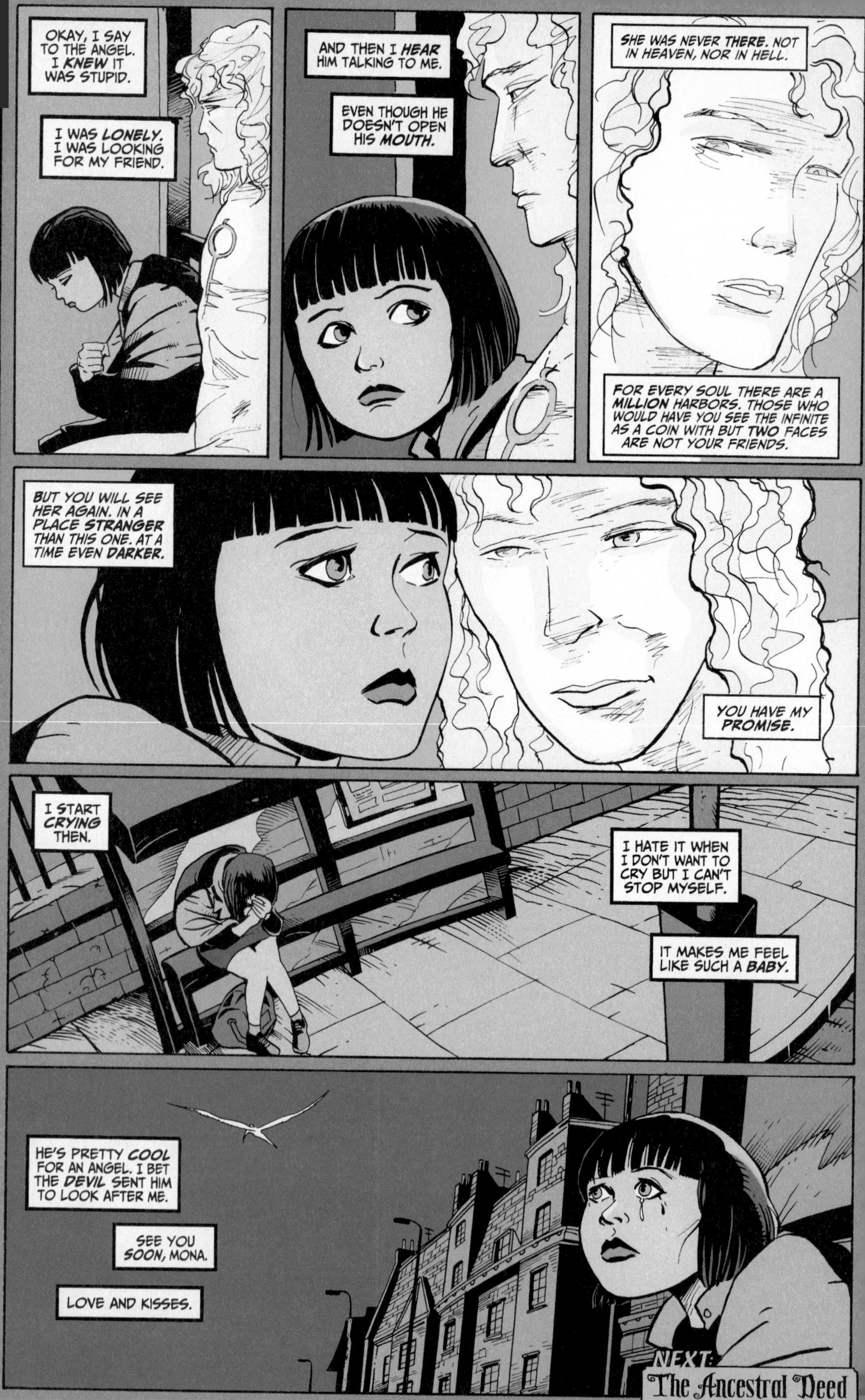
OKAY, I SAY TO THE ANGEL. I KNEW IT WAS STUPID.
I WAS LONELY. I WAS LOOKING FOR MY FRIEND.
AND THEN I HEAR HIM TALKING TO ME.
EVEN THOUGH HE DOESN'T OPEN HIS MOUTH.
SHE WAS NEVER THERE. NOT IN HEAVEN, NOR IN HELL.
FOR EVERY SOUL THERE ARE A MILLION HARBORS. THOSE WHO WOULD HAVE YOU SEE THE INFINITE AS A COIN WITH BUT TWO FACES ARE NOT YOUR FRIENDS.
BUT YOU WILL SEE HER AGAIN. IN A PLACE STRANGER THAN THIS ONE. AT A TIME EVEN DARKER.
YOU HAVE MY PROMISE.
I START CRYING THEN.
I HATE IT WHEN I DON'T WANT TO CRY BUT I CAN'T STOP MYSELF.
IT MAKES ME FEEL LIKE SUCH A BABY.
HE'S PRETTY COOL FOR AN ANGEL. I BET THE DEVIL SENT HIM TO LOOK AFTER ME.
SEE YOU SOON, MONA.
LOVE AND KISSES.
NEXT: The Ancestral Deed

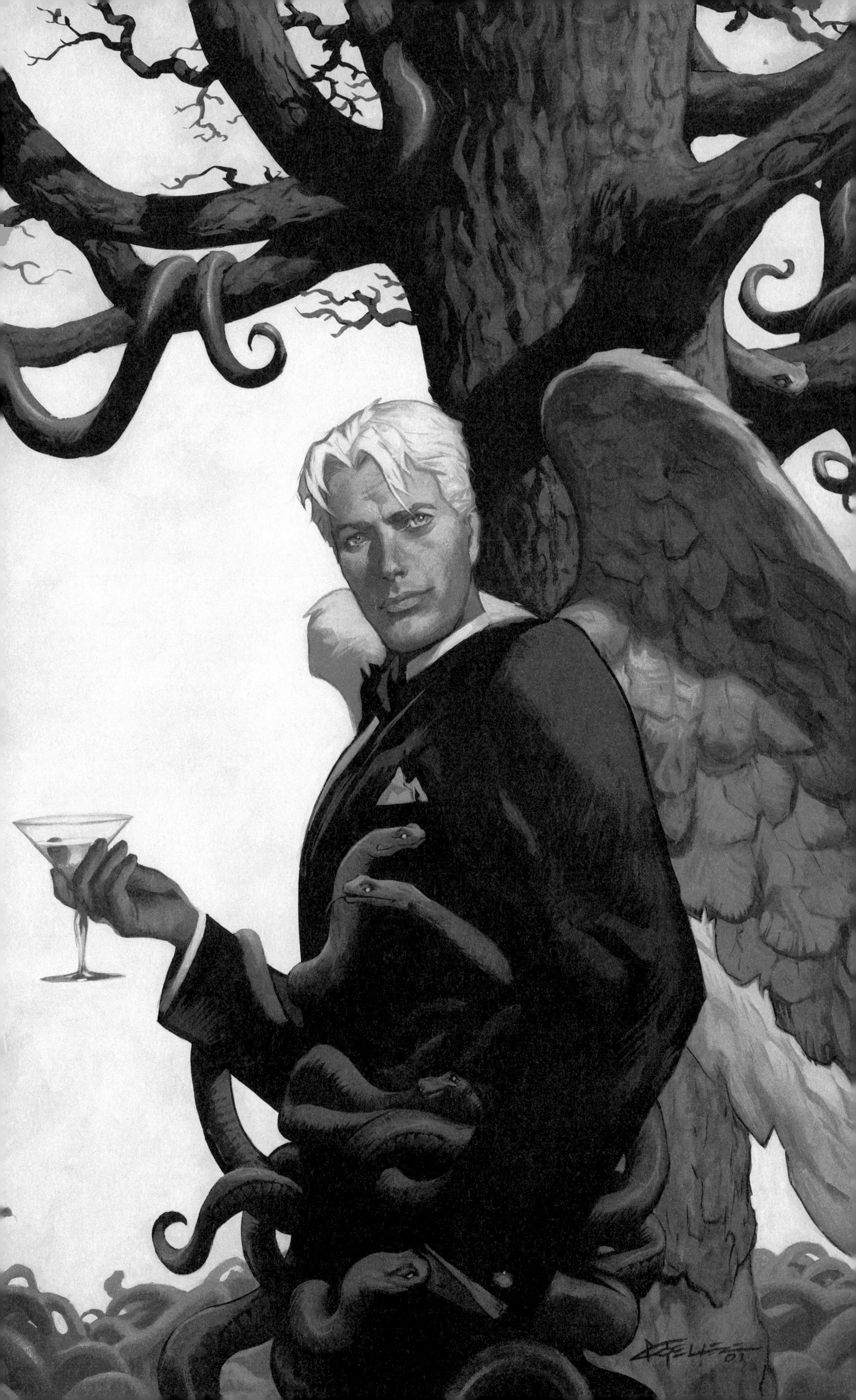

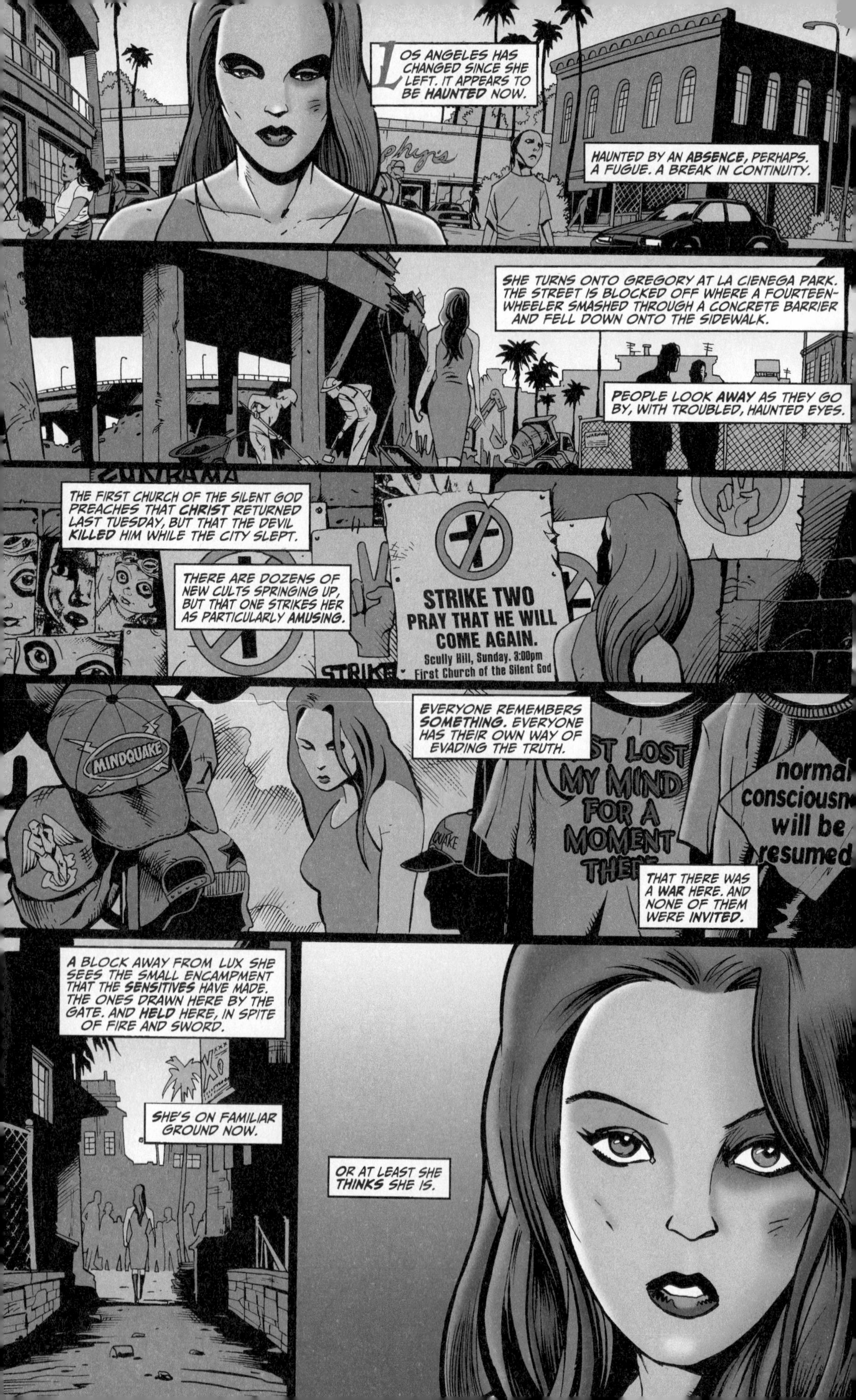
LOS ANGELES HAS CHANGED SINCE SHE LEFT. IT APPEARS TO BE HAUNTED NOW.
HAUNTED BY AN ABSENCE, PERHAPS. A FUGUE. A BREAK IN CONTINUITY.
SHE TURNS ONTO GREGORY AT LA CIENEGA PARK. THE STREET IS BLOCKED OFF WHERE A FOURTEEN-WHEELER SMASHED THROUGH A CONCRETE BARRIER AND FELL DOWN ONTO THE SIDEWALK.
PEOPLE LOOK AWAY AS THEY GO BY, WITH TROUBLED, HAUNTED EYES.
THE FIRST CHURCH OF THE SILENT GOD PREACHES THAT CHRIST RETURNED LAST TUESDAY, BUT THAT THE DEVIL KILLED HIM WHILE THE CITY SLEPT.
THERE ARE DOZENS OF NEW CULTS SPRINGING UP, BUT THAT ONE STRIKES HER AS PARTICULARLY AMUSING.
STRIKE TWO
PRAY THAT HE WILL COME AGAIN.
Scully Hill, Sunday, 3:00pm
First Church of the Silent God
STRIKE
MINDQUAKE
EVERYONE REMEMBERS SOMETHING. EVERYONE HAS THEIR OWN WAY OF EVADING THE TRUTH.
LOST MY MIND FOR A MOMENT
normal consciousne will be resumed
THAT THERE WAS A WAR HERE. AND NONE OF THEM WERE INVITED.
A BLOCK AWAY FROM LUX SHE SEES THE SMALL ENCAMPMENT THAT THE SENSITIVES HAVE MADE. THE ONES DRAWN HERE BY THE GATE. AND HELD HERE, IN SPITE OF FIRE AND SWORD.
SHE'S ON FAMILIAR GROUND NOW.
OR AT LEAST SHE THINKS SHE IS.

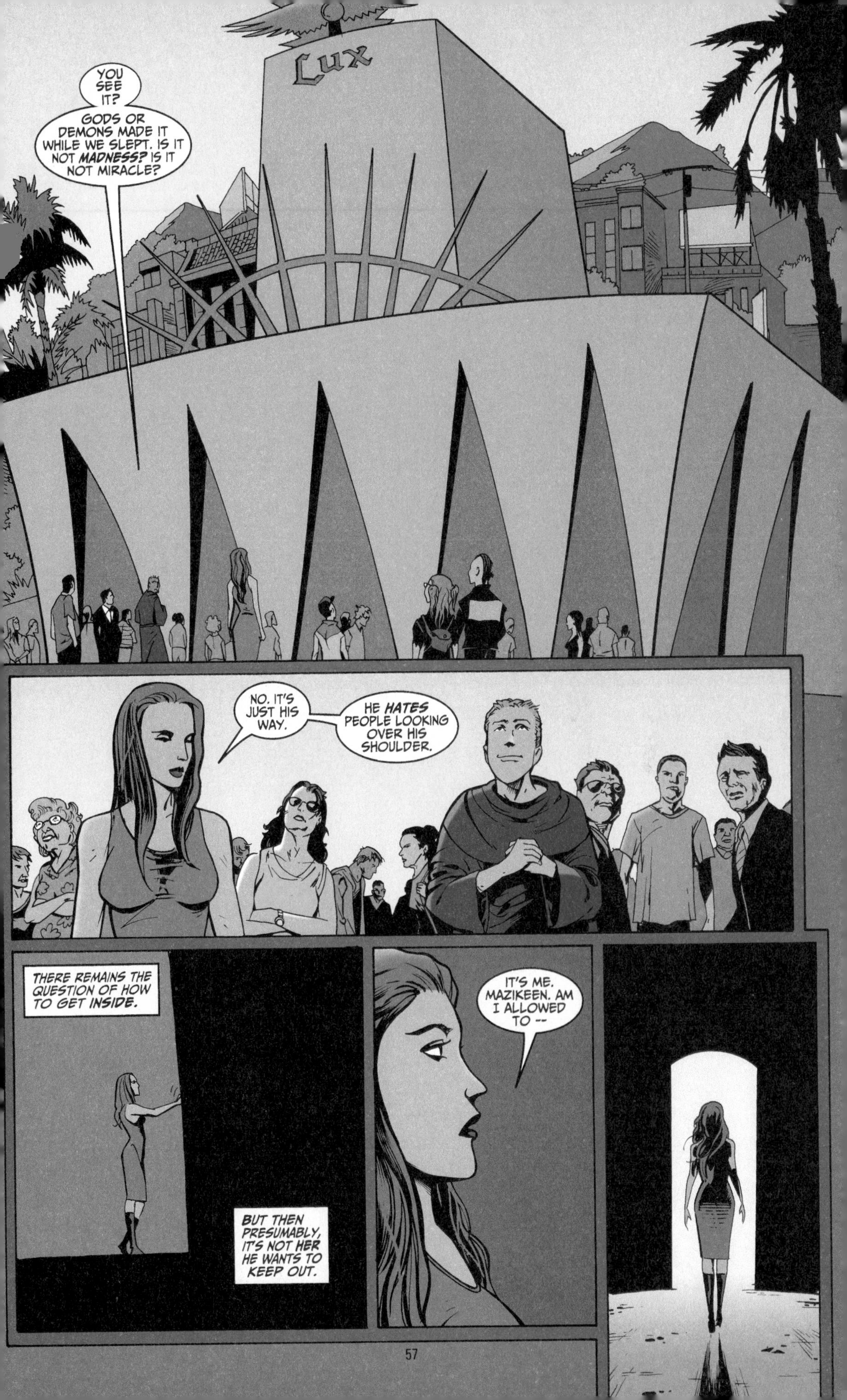
Lux
YOU SEE IT? GODS OR DEMONS MADE IT WHILE WE SLEPT. IS IT NOT *MADNESS?* IS IT NOT MIRACLE?
NO. IT'S JUST HIS WAY.
HE *HATES* PEOPLE LOOKING OVER HIS SHOULDER.
THERE REMAINS THE QUESTION OF HOW TO GET *INSIDE.*
BUT THEN PRESUMABLY, IT'S NOT *HER* HE WANTS TO KEEP OUT.
IT'S ME. MAZIKEEN. AM I ALLOWED TO --

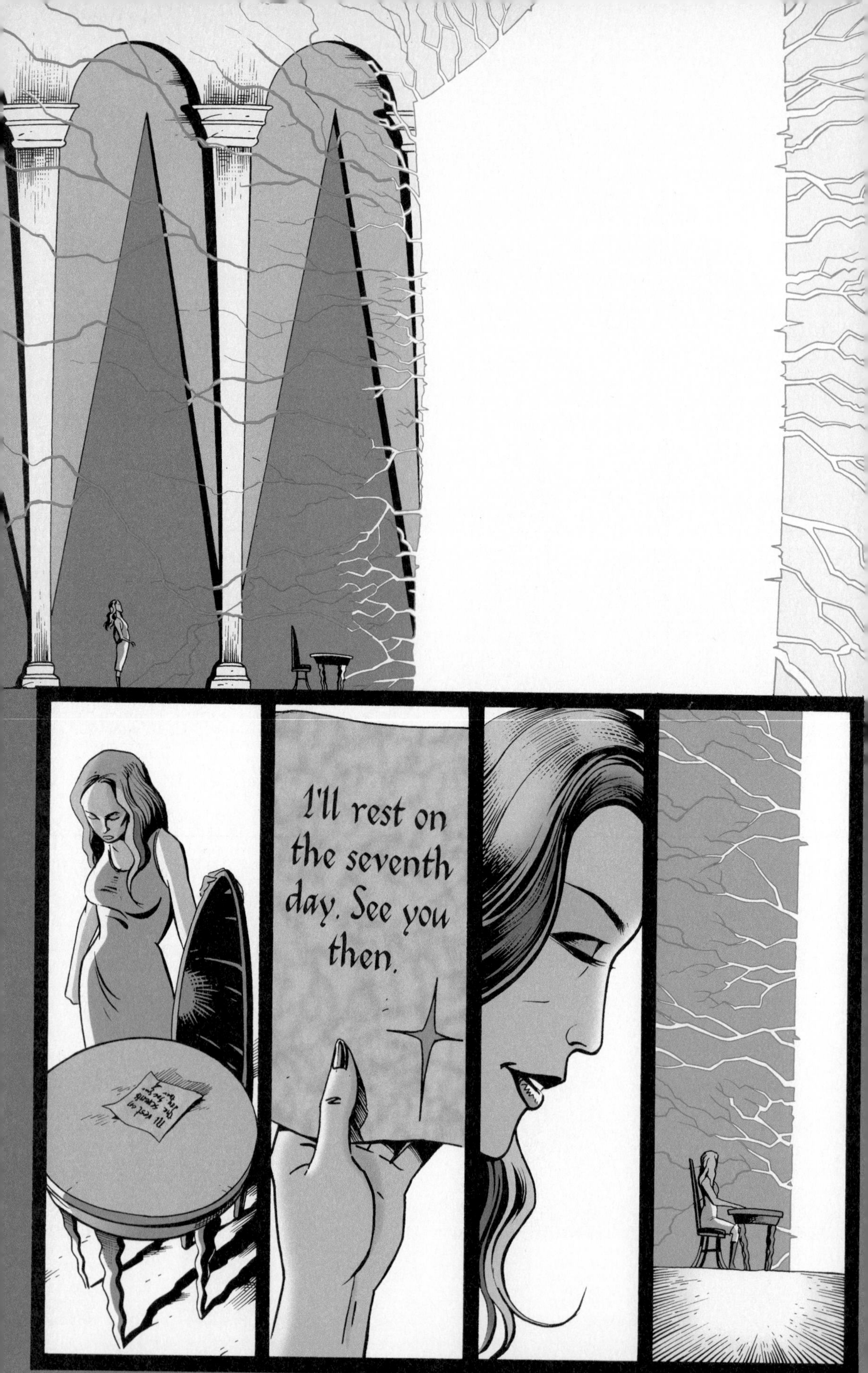
I'll rest on the seventh day. See you then.

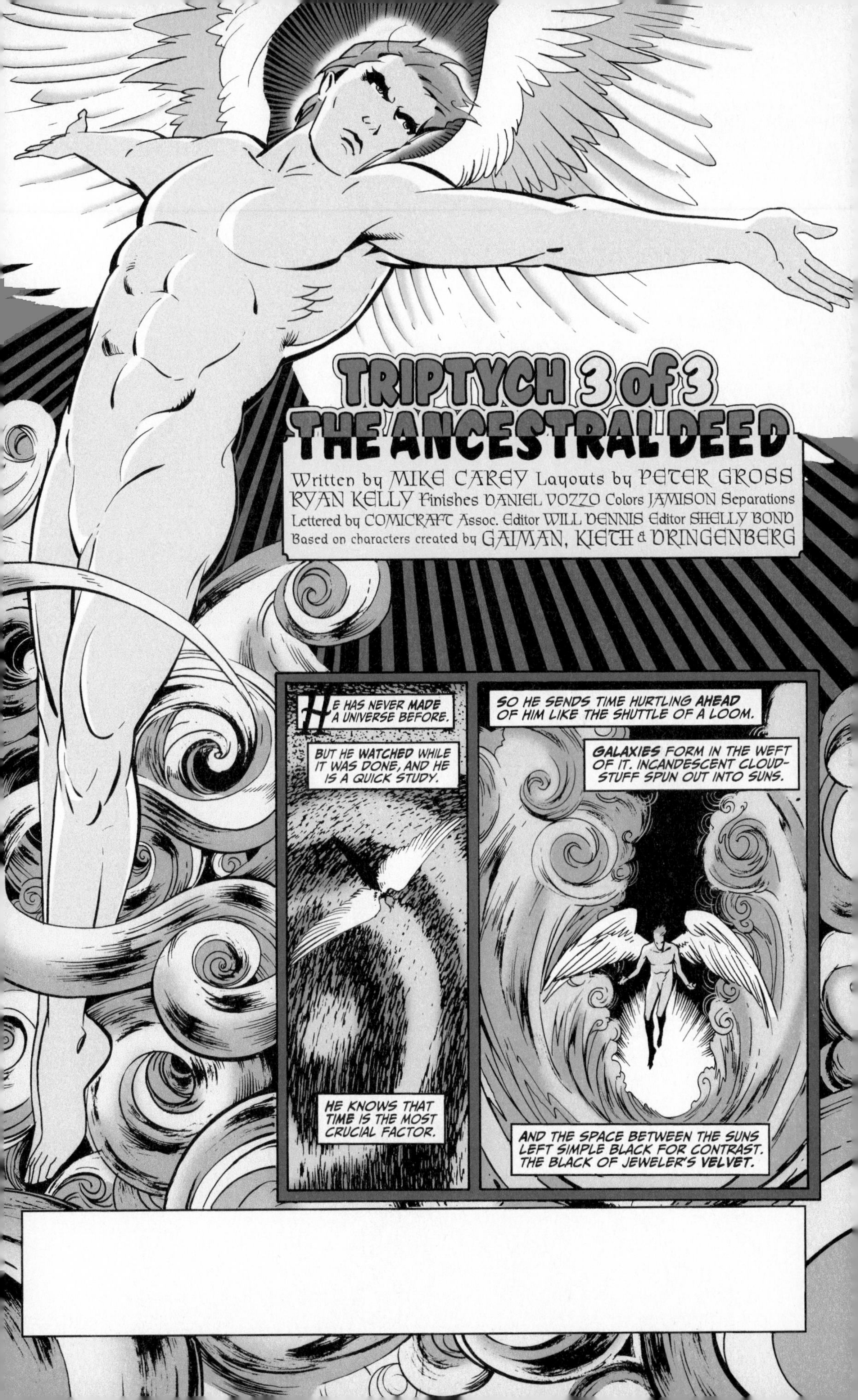
TRIPTYCH 3 of 3
THE ANCESTRAL DEED
Written by MIKE CAREY Layouts by PETER GROSS
RYAN KELLY Finishes DANIEL VOZZO Colors JAMISON Separations
Lettered by COMICRAFT Assoc. Editor WILL DENNIS Editor SHELLY BOND
Based on characters created by GAIMAN, KIETH & DRINGENBERG
HE HAS NEVER MADE A UNIVERSE BEFORE.
BUT HE WATCHED WHILE IT WAS DONE, AND HE IS A QUICK STUDY.
HE KNOWS THAT TIME IS THE MOST CRUCIAL FACTOR.
SO HE SENDS TIME HURTLING AHEAD OF HIM LIKE THE SHUTTLE OF A LOOM.
GALAXIES FORM IN THE WEFT OF IT. INCANDESCENT CLOUD-STUFF SPUN OUT INTO SUNS.
AND THE SPACE BETWEEN THE SUNS LEFT SIMPLE BLACK FOR CONTRAST. THE BLACK OF JEWELER'S VELVET.

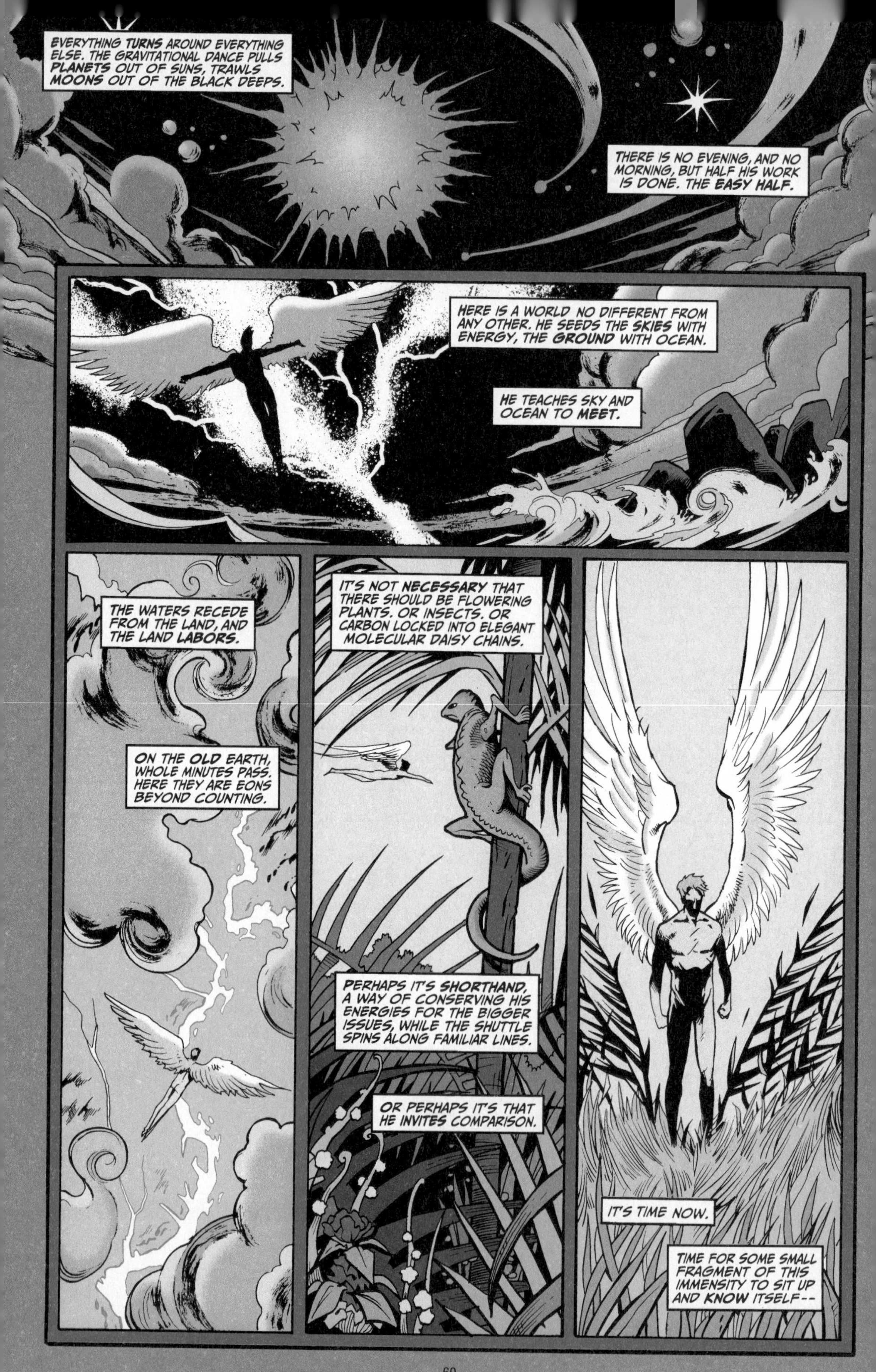

EVERYTHING TURNS AROUND EVERYTHING ELSE. THE GRAVITATIONAL DANCE PULLS PLANETS OUT OF SUNS, TRAWLS MOONS OUT OF THE BLACK DEEPS.
THERE IS NO EVENING, AND NO MORNING, BUT HALF HIS WORK IS DONE. THE EASY HALF.
HERE IS A WORLD NO DIFFERENT FROM ANY OTHER. HE SEEDS THE SKIES WITH ENERGY, THE GROUND WITH OCEAN.
HE TEACHES SKY AND OCEAN TO MEET.
THE WATERS RECEDE FROM THE LAND, AND THE LAND LABORS.
ON THE OLD EARTH, WHOLE MINUTES PASS. HERE THEY ARE EONS BEYOND COUNTING.
IT'S NOT NECESSARY THAT THERE SHOULD BE FLOWERING PLANTS. OR INSECTS. OR CARBON LOCKED INTO ELEGANT MOLECULAR DAISY CHAINS.
PERHAPS IT'S SHORTHAND, A WAY OF CONSERVING HIS ENERGIES FOR THE BIGGER ISSUES, WHILE THE SHUTTLE SPINS ALONG FAMILIAR LINES.
OR PERHAPS IT'S THAT HE INVITES COMPARISON.
IT'S TIME NOW.
TIME FOR SOME SMALL FRAGMENT OF THIS IMMENSITY TO SIT UP AND KNOW ITSELF--

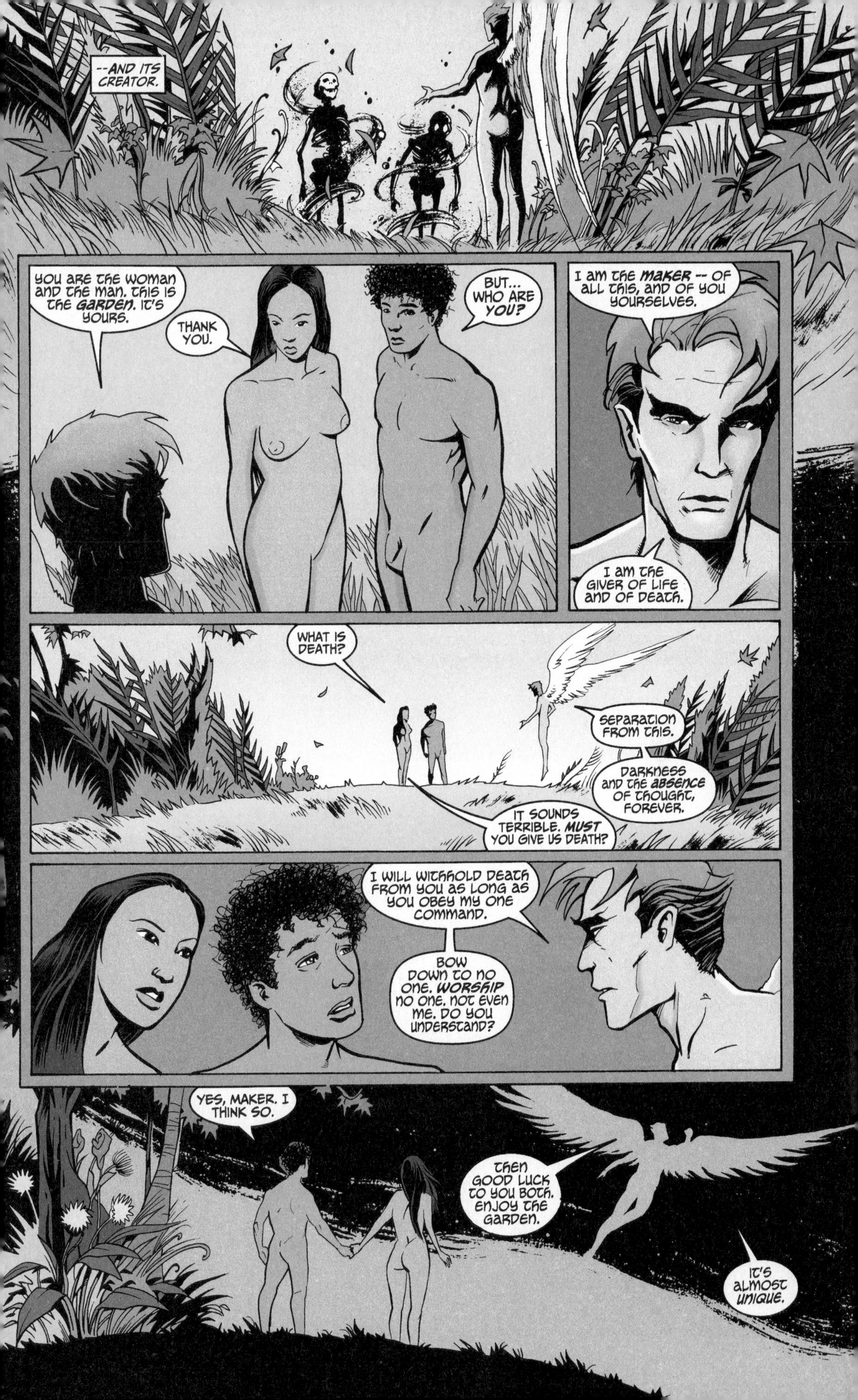
--AND ITS CREATOR.
YOU ARE THE WOMAN AND THE MAN. THIS IS THE GARDEN. IT'S YOURS.
THANK YOU.
BUT... WHO ARE YOU?
I AM THE MAKER -- OF ALL THIS, AND OF YOU YOURSELVES.
I AM THE GIVER OF LIFE AND OF DEATH.
WHAT IS DEATH?
SEPARATION FROM THIS.
DARKNESS AND THE ABSENCE OF THOUGHT, FOREVER.
IT SOUNDS TERRIBLE. MUST YOU GIVE US DEATH?
I WILL WITHHOLD DEATH FROM YOU AS LONG AS YOU OBEY MY ONE COMMAND.
BOW DOWN TO NO ONE. WORSHIP NO ONE. NOT EVEN ME. DO YOU UNDERSTAND?
YES, MAKER. I THINK SO.
THEN GOOD LUCK TO YOU BOTH. ENJOY THE GARDEN.
IT'S ALMOST UNIQUE.

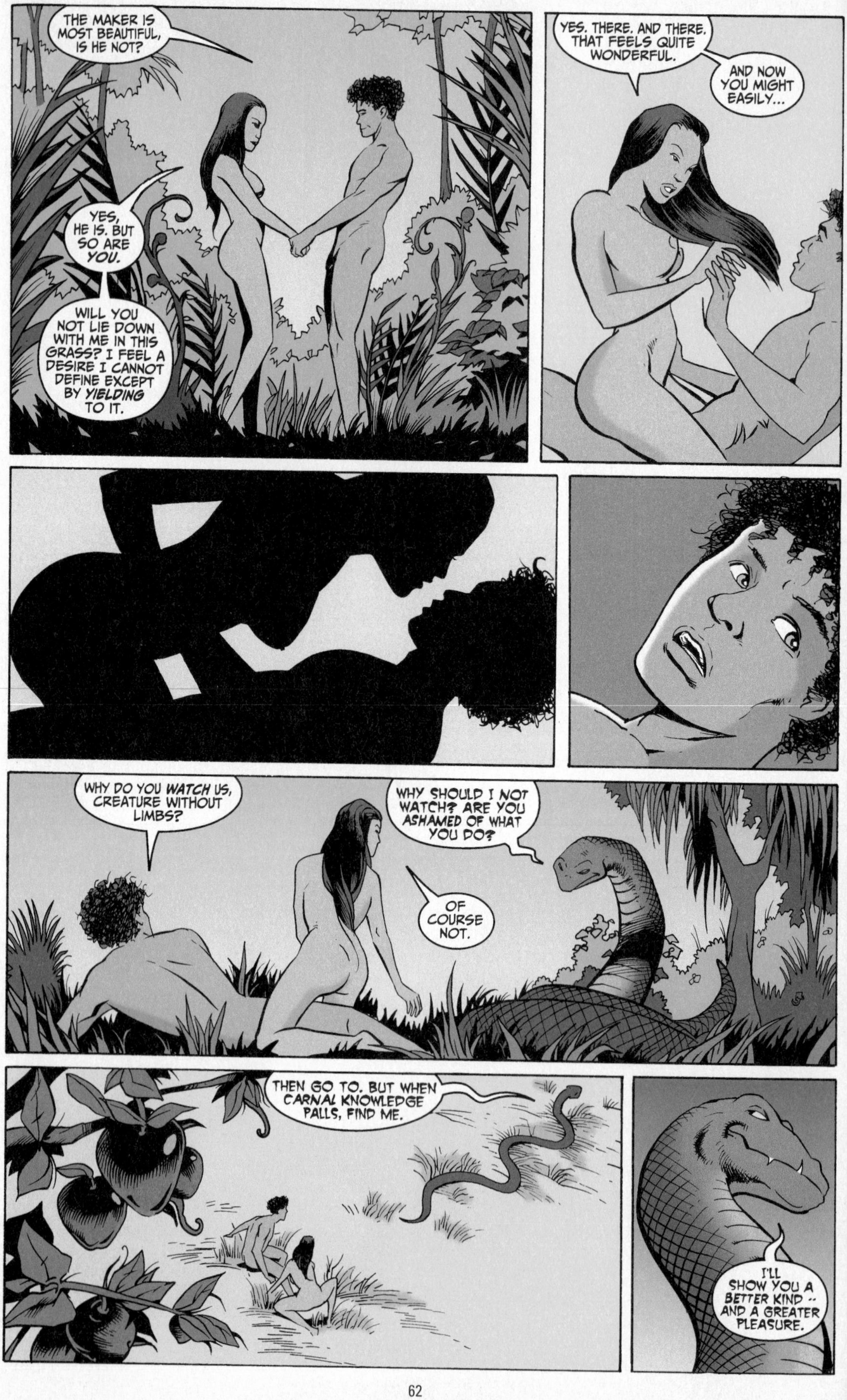
THE MAKER IS MOST BEAUTIFUL, IS HE NOT?
YES, HE IS. BUT SO ARE *YOU*.
WILL YOU NOT LIE DOWN WITH ME IN THIS GRASS? I FEEL A DESIRE I CANNOT DEFINE EXCEPT BY *YIELDING* TO IT.
YES. THERE. AND THERE. THAT FEELS QUITE WONDERFUL.
AND NOW YOU MIGHT EASILY...
WHY DO YOU *WATCH* US, CREATURE WITHOUT LIMBS?
WHY SHOULD I *NOT* WATCH? ARE YOU *ASHAMED* OF WHAT YOU DO?
OF COURSE NOT.
THEN GO TO. BUT WHEN *CARNAL* KNOWLEDGE PALLS, FIND ME.
I'LL SHOW YOU A BETTER KIND -- AND A GREATER PLEASURE.

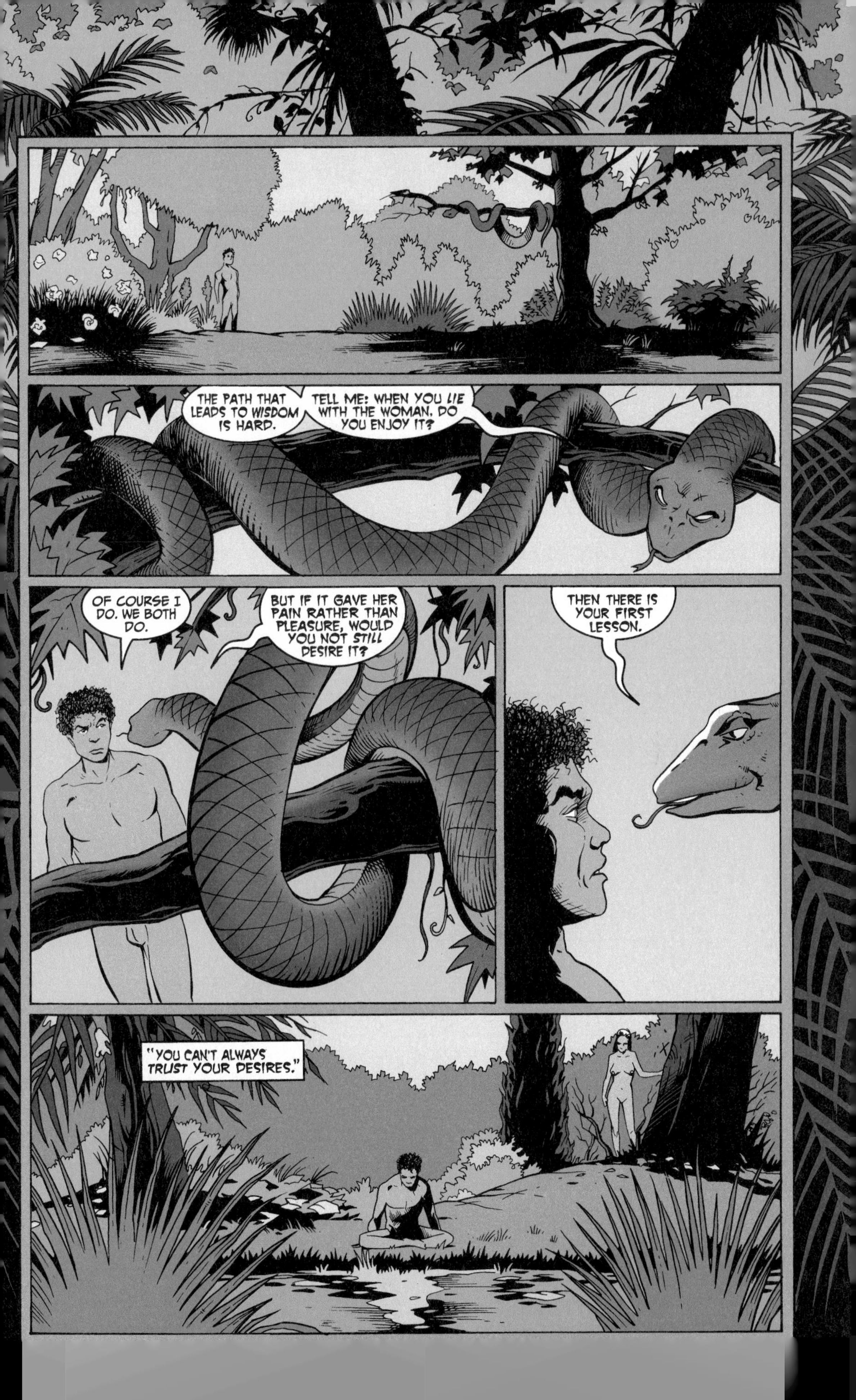

THE PATH THAT LEADS TO WISDOM IS HARD.
TELL ME: WHEN YOU LIE WITH THE WOMAN, DO YOU ENJOY IT?
OF COURSE I DO. WE BOTH DO.
BUT IF IT GAVE HER PAIN RATHER THAN PLEASURE, WOULD YOU NOT STILL DESIRE IT?
THEN THERE IS YOUR FIRST LESSON.
"YOU CAN'T ALWAYS TRUST YOUR DESIRES."

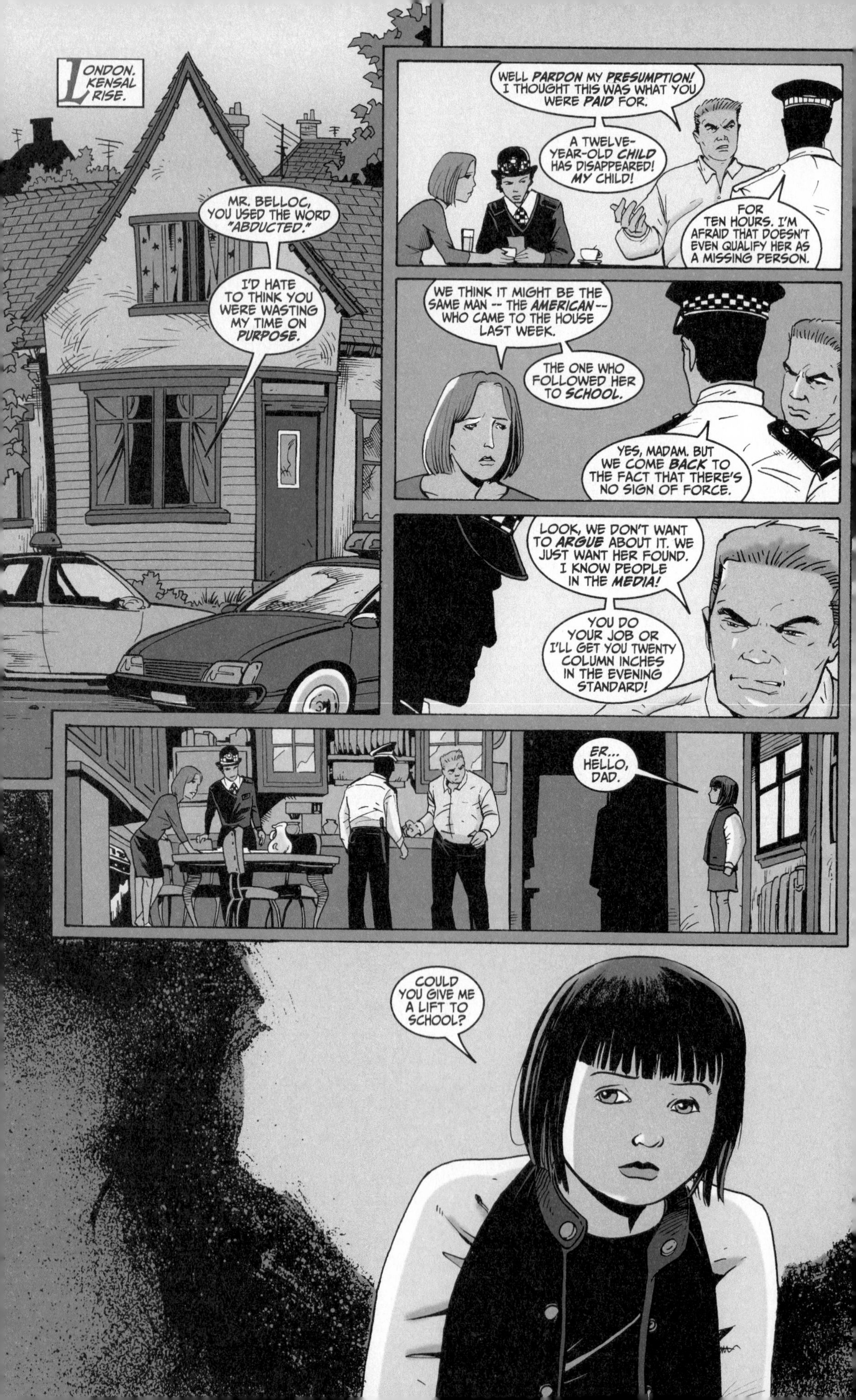
LONDON. KENSAL RISE.
MR. BELLOC, YOU USED THE WORD "ABDUCTED."
I'D HATE TO THINK YOU WERE WASTING MY TIME ON PURPOSE.
WELL PARDON MY PRESUMPTION! I THOUGHT THIS WAS WHAT YOU WERE PAID FOR.
A TWELVE-YEAR-OLD CHILD HAS DISAPPEARED! MY CHILD!
FOR TEN HOURS. I'M AFRAID THAT DOESN'T EVEN QUALIFY HER AS A MISSING PERSON.
WE THINK IT MIGHT BE THE SAME MAN -- THE AMERICAN -- WHO CAME TO THE HOUSE LAST WEEK.
THE ONE WHO FOLLOWED HER TO SCHOOL.
YES, MADAM. BUT WE COME BACK TO THE FACT THAT THERE'S NO SIGN OF FORCE.
LOOK, WE DON'T WANT TO ARGUE ABOUT IT. WE JUST WANT HER FOUND. I KNOW PEOPLE IN THE MEDIA!
YOU DO YOUR JOB OR I'LL GET YOU TWENTY COLUMN INCHES IN THE EVENING STANDARD!
ER... HELLO, DAD.
COULD YOU GIVE ME A LIFT TO SCHOOL?

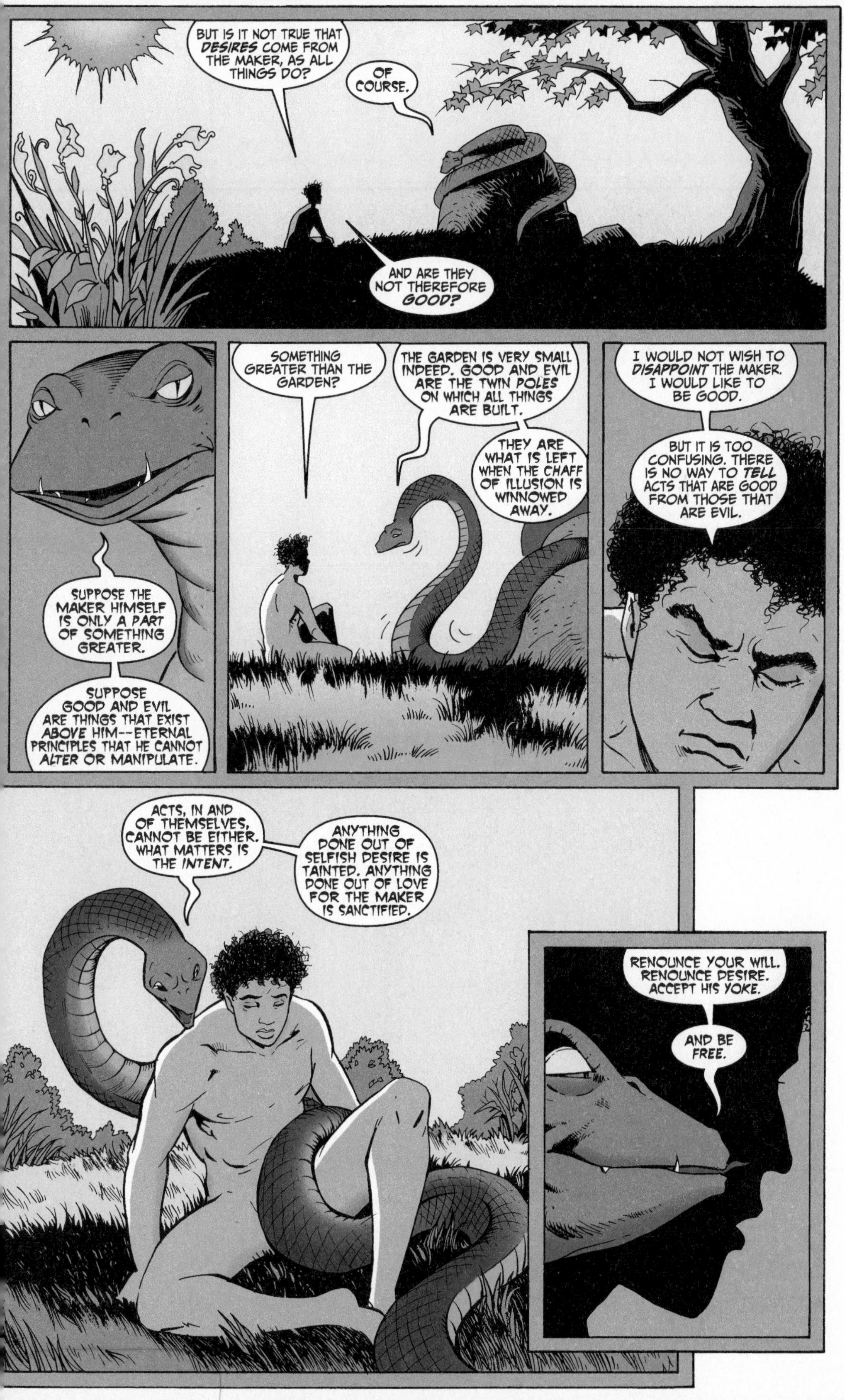
BUT IS IT NOT TRUE THAT DESIRES COME FROM THE MAKER, AS ALL THINGS DO?
OF COURSE.
AND ARE THEY NOT THEREFORE GOOD?
SUPPOSE THE MAKER HIMSELF IS ONLY A PART OF SOMETHING GREATER.
SUPPOSE GOOD AND EVIL ARE THINGS THAT EXIST ABOVE HIM--ETERNAL PRINCIPLES THAT HE CANNOT ALTER OR MANIPULATE.
SOMETHING GREATER THAN THE GARDEN?
THE GARDEN IS VERY SMALL INDEED. GOOD AND EVIL ARE THE TWIN POLES ON WHICH ALL THINGS ARE BUILT.
THEY ARE WHAT IS LEFT WHEN THE CHAFF OF ILLUSION IS WINNOWED AWAY.
I WOULD NOT WISH TO DISAPPOINT THE MAKER. I WOULD LIKE TO BE GOOD.
BUT IT IS TOO CONFUSING. THERE IS NO WAY TO TELL ACTS THAT ARE GOOD FROM THOSE THAT ARE EVIL.
ACTS, IN AND OF THEMSELVES, CANNOT BE EITHER. WHAT MATTERS IS THE INTENT.
ANYTHING DONE OUT OF SELFISH DESIRE IS TAINTED. ANYTHING DONE OUT OF LOVE FOR THE MAKER IS SANCTIFIED.
RENOUNCE YOUR WILL. RENOUNCE DESIRE. ACCEPT HIS YOKE.
AND BE FREE.

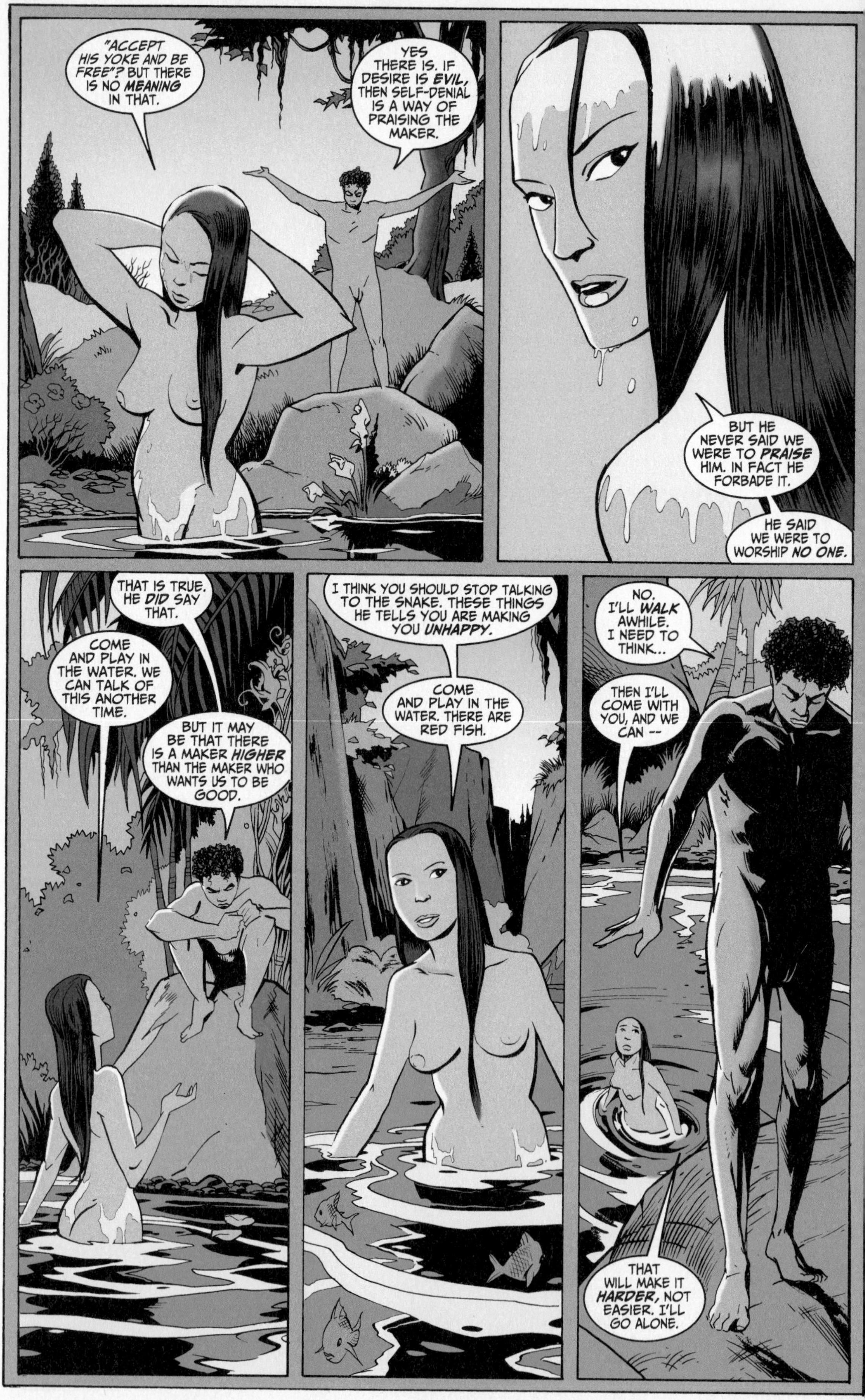
"ACCEPT HIS YOKE AND BE FREE"? BUT THERE IS NO MEANING IN THAT.
YES THERE IS. IF DESIRE IS EVIL, THEN SELF-DENIAL IS A WAY OF PRAISING THE MAKER.
BUT HE NEVER SAID WE WERE TO PRAISE HIM. IN FACT HE FORBADE IT.
HE SAID WE WERE TO WORSHIP NO ONE.
THAT IS TRUE. HE DID SAY THAT.
COME AND PLAY IN THE WATER. WE CAN TALK OF THIS ANOTHER TIME.
BUT IT MAY BE THAT THERE IS A MAKER HIGHER THAN THE MAKER WHO WANTS US TO BE GOOD.
I THINK YOU SHOULD STOP TALKING TO THE SNAKE. THESE THINGS HE TELLS YOU ARE MAKING YOU UNHAPPY.
COME AND PLAY IN THE WATER. THERE ARE RED FISH.
NO. I'LL WALK AWHILE. I NEED TO THINK...
THEN I'LL COME WITH YOU, AND WE CAN --
THAT WILL MAKE IT HARDER, NOT EASIER. I'LL GO ALONE.

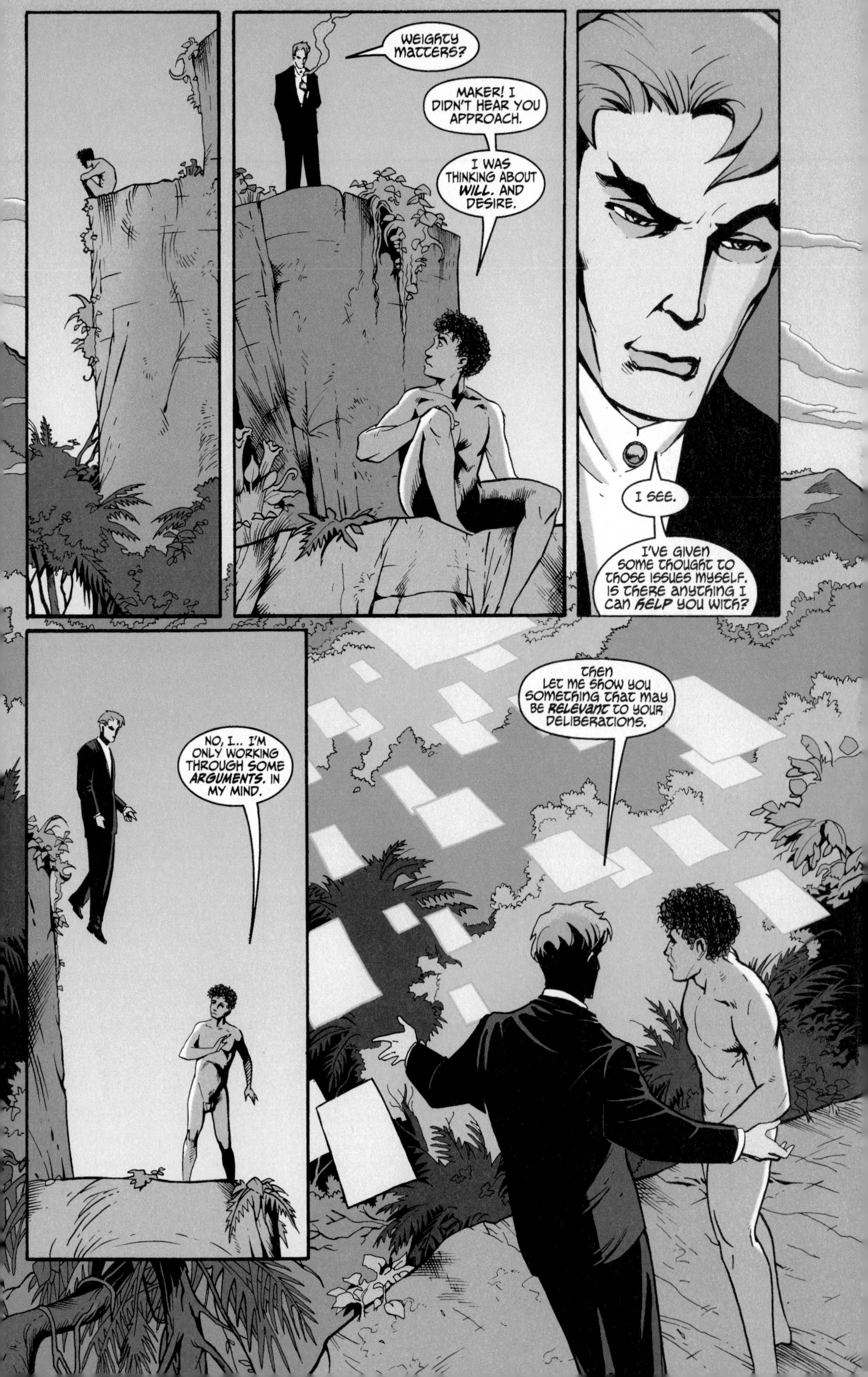
WEIGHTY MATTERS?
MAKER! I DIDN'T HEAR YOU APPROACH.
I WAS THINKING ABOUT WILL. AND DESIRE.
I SEE.
I'VE GIVEN SOME THOUGHT TO THOSE ISSUES MYSELF. IS THERE ANYTHING I CAN HELP YOU WITH?
NO, I... I'M ONLY WORKING THROUGH SOME ARGUMENTS. IN MY MIND.
THEN LET ME SHOW YOU SOMETHING THAT MAY BE RELEVANT TO YOUR DELIBERATIONS.

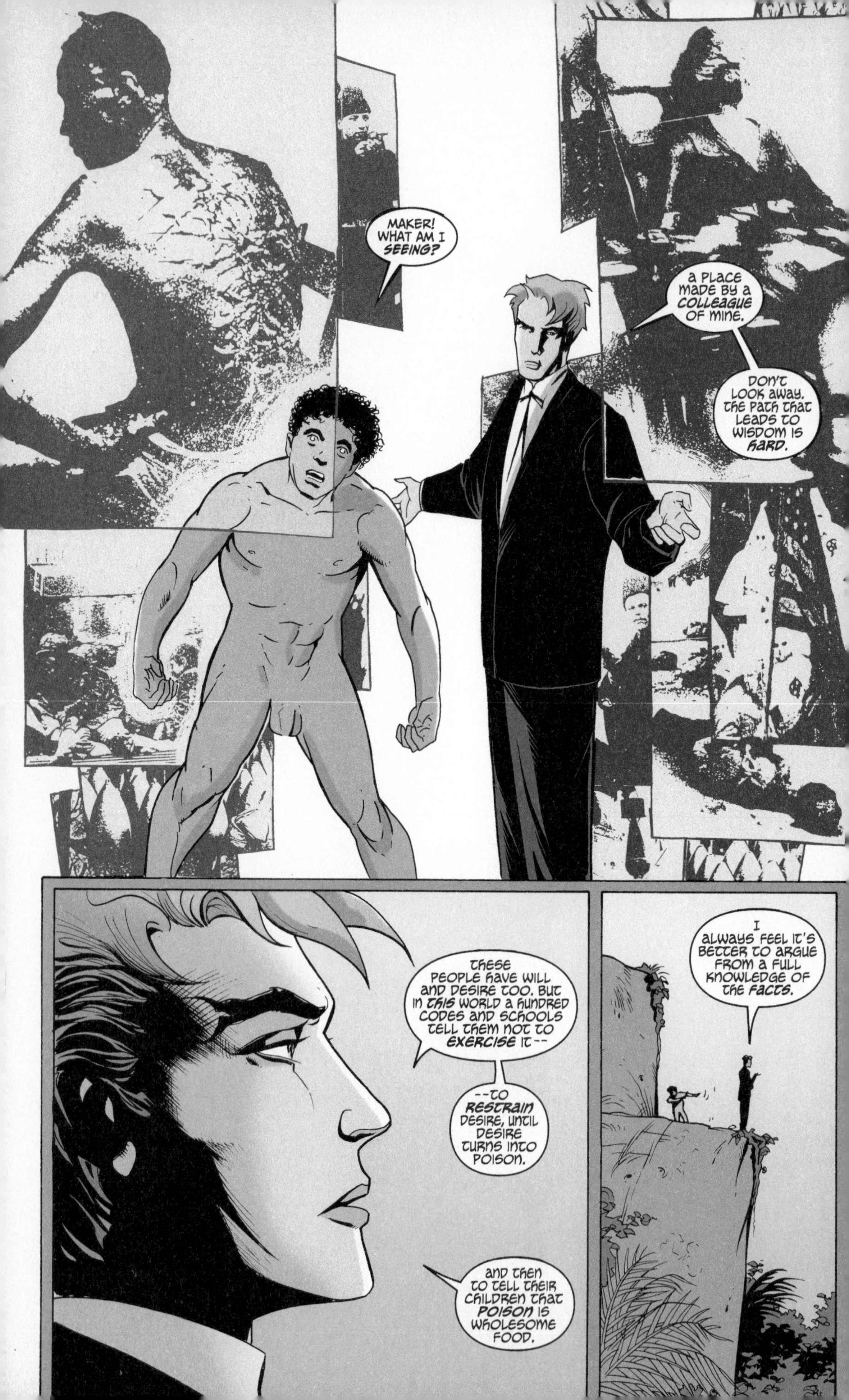
MAKER! WHAT AM I SEEING?
A PLACE MADE BY A COLLEAGUE OF MINE.
DON'T LOOK AWAY. THE PATH THAT LEADS TO WISDOM IS HARD.
THESE PEOPLE HAVE WILL AND DESIRE TOO. BUT IN THIS WORLD A HUNDRED CODES AND SCHOOLS TELL THEM NOT TO EXERCISE IT--
--TO RESTRAIN DESIRE, UNTIL DESIRE TURNS INTO POISON.
AND THEN TO TELL THEIR CHILDREN THAT POISON IS WHOLESOME FOOD.
I ALWAYS FEEL IT'S BETTER TO ARGUE FROM A FULL KNOWLEDGE OF THE FACTS.

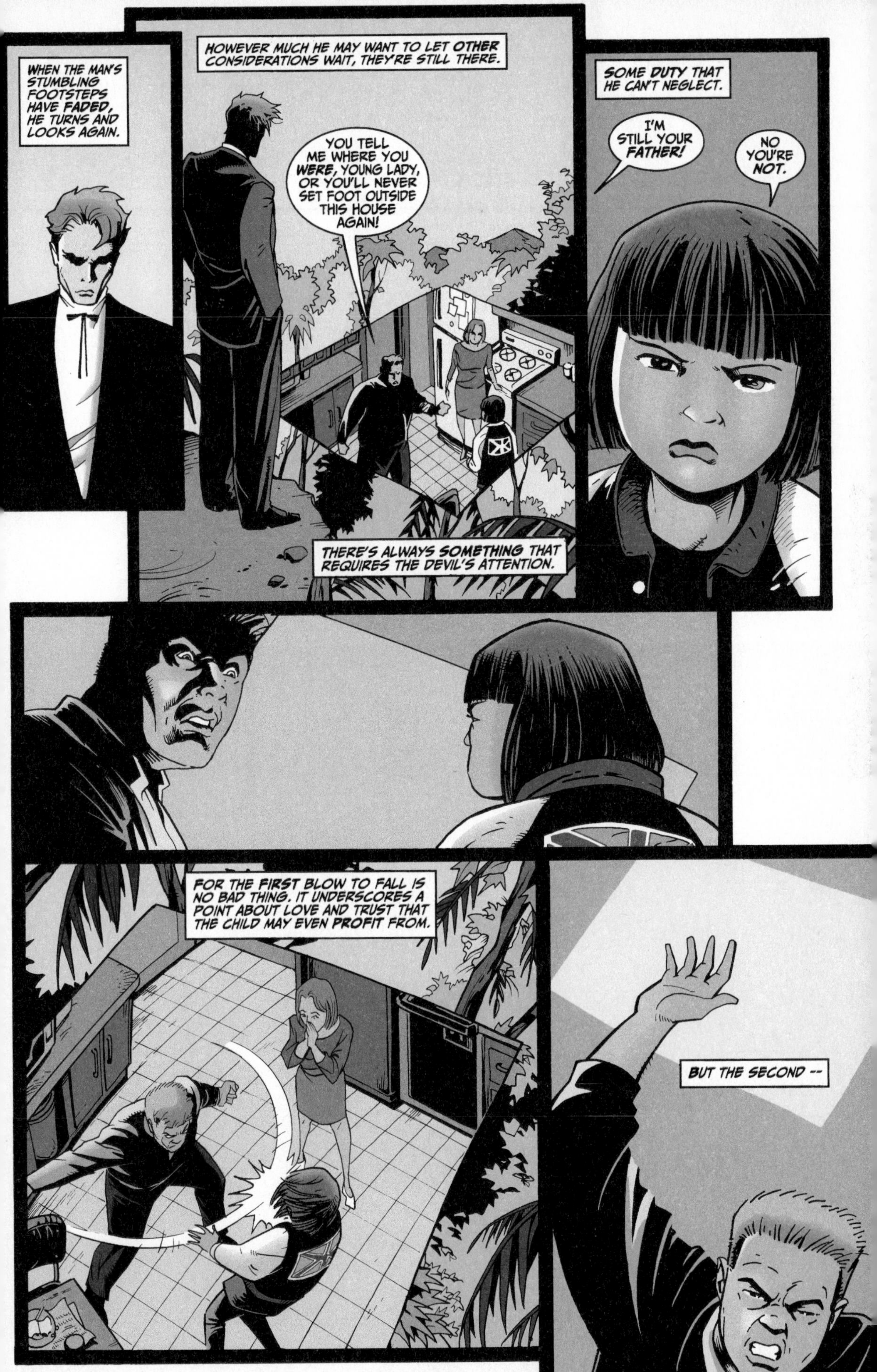
WHEN THE MAN'S STUMBLING FOOTSTEPS HAVE FADED, HE TURNS AND LOOKS AGAIN.
HOWEVER MUCH HE MAY WANT TO LET OTHER CONSIDERATIONS WAIT, THEY'RE STILL THERE.
YOU TELL ME WHERE YOU WERE, YOUNG LADY, OR YOU'LL NEVER SET FOOT OUTSIDE THIS HOUSE AGAIN!
THERE'S ALWAYS SOMETHING THAT REQUIRES THE DEVIL'S ATTENTION.
SOME DUTY THAT HE CAN'T NEGLECT.
I'M STILL YOUR FATHER!
NO YOU'RE NOT.
FOR THE FIRST BLOW TO FALL IS NO BAD THING. IT UNDERSCORES A POINT ABOUT LOVE AND TRUST THAT THE CHILD MAY EVEN PROFIT FROM.
BUT THE SECOND --

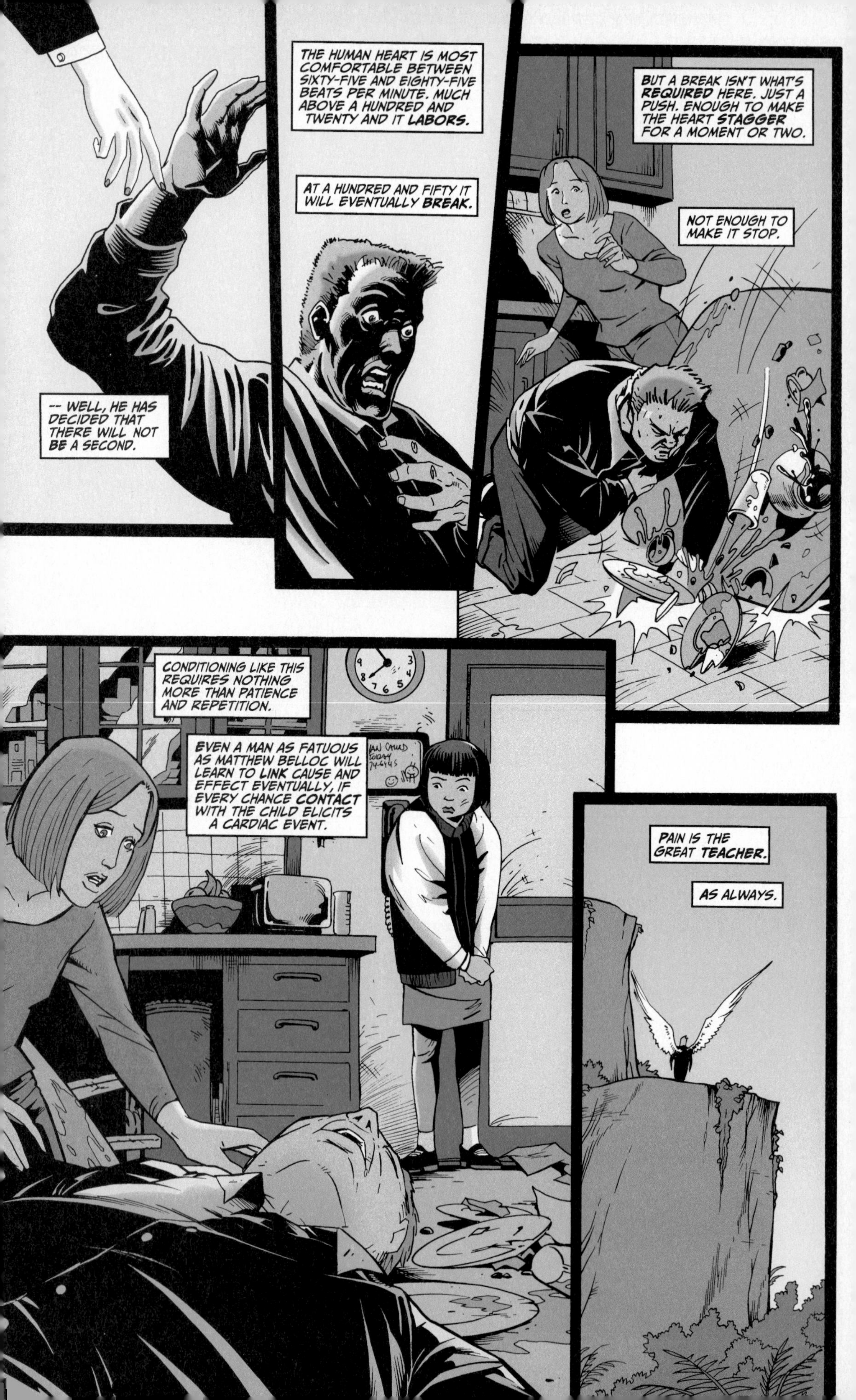
-- WELL, HE HAS DECIDED THAT THERE WILL NOT BE A SECOND.
THE HUMAN HEART IS MOST COMFORTABLE BETWEEN SIXTY-FIVE AND EIGHTY-FIVE BEATS PER MINUTE. MUCH ABOVE A HUNDRED AND TWENTY AND IT LABORS.
AT A HUNDRED AND FIFTY IT WILL EVENTUALLY BREAK.
BUT A BREAK ISN'T WHAT'S REQUIRED HERE. JUST A PUSH. ENOUGH TO MAKE THE HEART STAGGER FOR A MOMENT OR TWO.
NOT ENOUGH TO MAKE IT STOP.
CONDITIONING LIKE THIS REQUIRES NOTHING MORE THAN PATIENCE AND REPETITION.
EVEN A MAN AS FATUOUS AS MATTHEW BELLOC WILL LEARN TO LINK CAUSE AND EFFECT EVENTUALLY, IF EVERY CHANCE CONTACT WITH THE CHILD ELICITS A CARDIAC EVENT.
PAIN IS THE GREAT TEACHER.
AS ALWAYS.

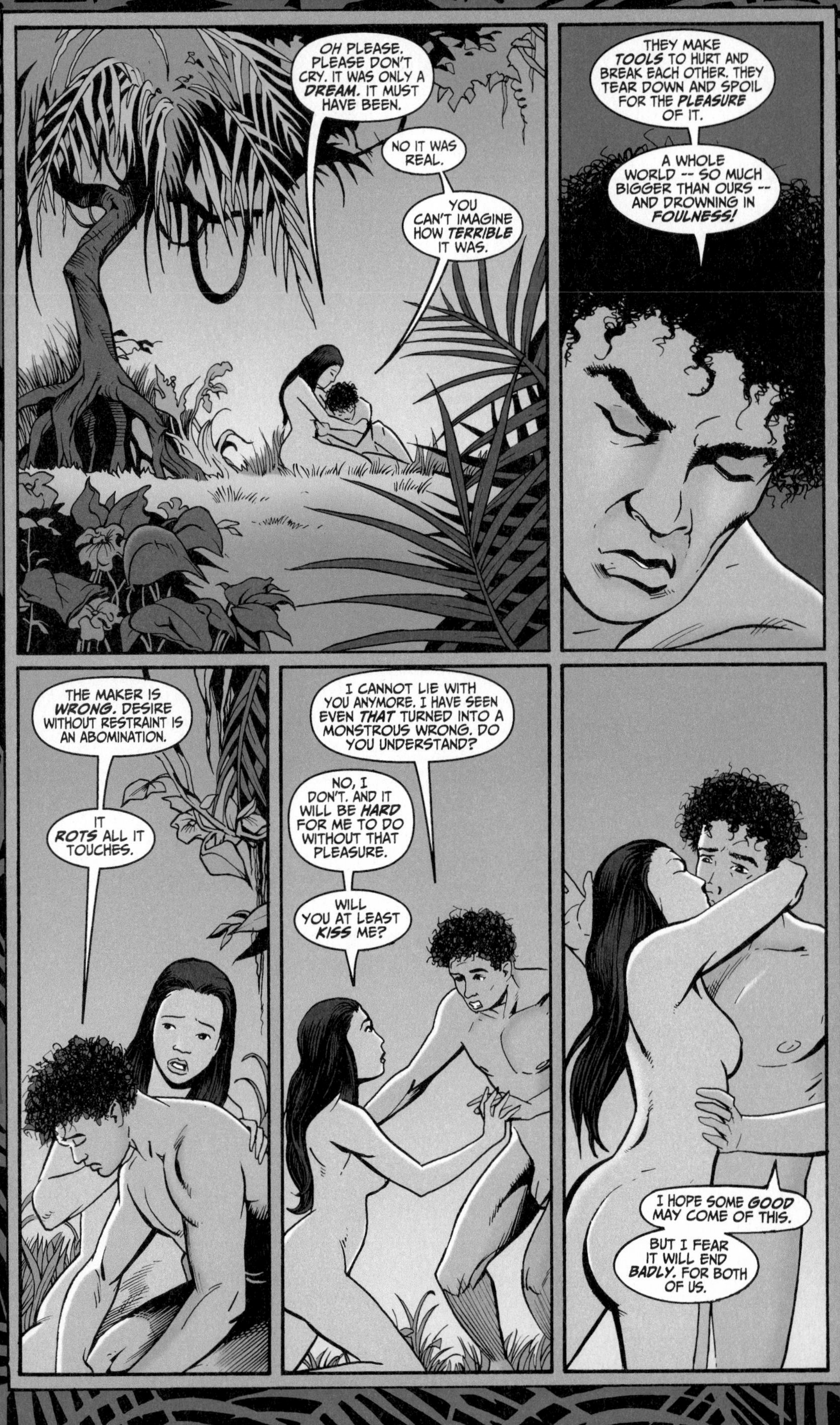
OH PLEASE. PLEASE DON'T CRY. IT WAS ONLY A DREAM. IT MUST HAVE BEEN.
NO IT WAS REAL.
YOU CAN'T IMAGINE HOW TERRIBLE IT WAS.
THEY MAKE TOOLS TO HURT AND BREAK EACH OTHER. THEY TEAR DOWN AND SPOIL FOR THE PLEASURE OF IT.
A WHOLE WORLD -- SO MUCH BIGGER THAN OURS -- AND DROWNING IN FOULNESS!
THE MAKER IS WRONG. DESIRE WITHOUT RESTRAINT IS AN ABOMINATION.
IT ROTS ALL IT TOUCHES.
I CANNOT LIE WITH YOU ANYMORE. I HAVE SEEN EVEN THAT TURNED INTO A MONSTROUS WRONG. DO YOU UNDERSTAND?
NO, I DON'T. AND IT WILL BE HARD FOR ME TO DO WITHOUT THAT PLEASURE.
WILL YOU AT LEAST KISS ME?
I HOPE SOME GOOD MAY COME OF THIS.
BUT I FEAR IT WILL END BADLY. FOR BOTH OF US.

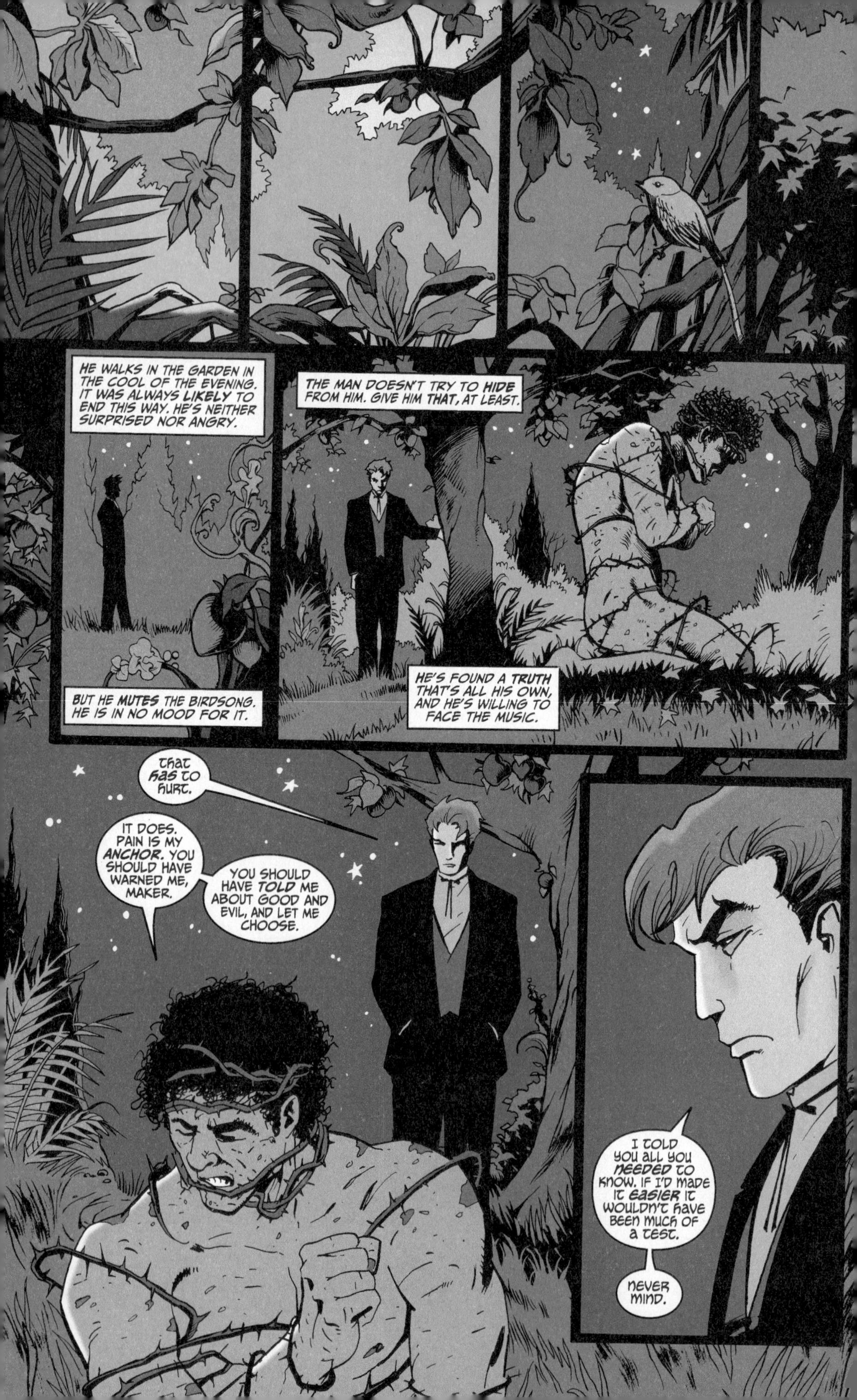

HE WALKS IN THE GARDEN IN THE COOL OF THE EVENING. IT WAS ALWAYS LIKELY TO END THIS WAY. HE'S NEITHER SURPRISED NOR ANGRY.
BUT HE MUTES THE BIRDSONG. HE IS IN NO MOOD FOR IT.
THE MAN DOESN'T TRY TO HIDE FROM HIM. GIVE HIM THAT, AT LEAST.
HE'S FOUND A TRUTH THAT'S ALL HIS OWN, AND HE'S WILLING TO FACE THE MUSIC.
THAT HAS TO HURT.
IT DOES. PAIN IS MY ANCHOR. YOU SHOULD HAVE WARNED ME, MAKER.
YOU SHOULD HAVE TOLD ME ABOUT GOOD AND EVIL, AND LET ME CHOOSE.
I TOLD YOU ALL YOU NEEDED TO KNOW. IF I'D MADE IT EASIER IT WOULDN'T HAVE BEEN MUCH OF A TEST.
NEVER MIND.

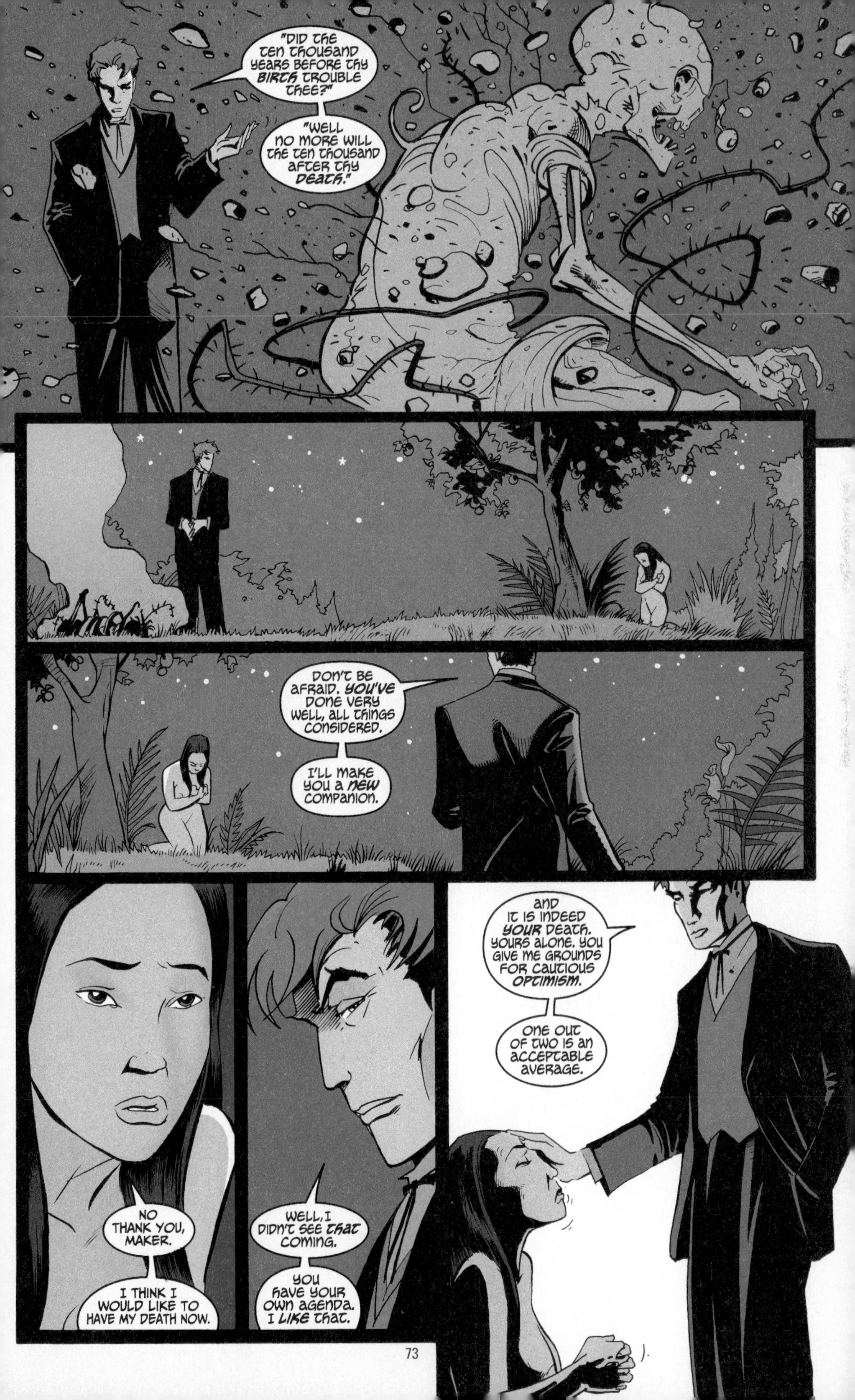
"DID THE TEN THOUSAND YEARS BEFORE THY BIRTH TROUBLE THEE?"
"WELL NO MORE WILL THE TEN THOUSAND AFTER THY DEATH."
DON'T BE AFRAID. YOU'VE DONE VERY WELL, ALL THINGS CONSIDERED.
I'LL MAKE YOU A NEW COMPANION.
NO THANK YOU, MAKER.
I THINK I WOULD LIKE TO HAVE MY DEATH NOW.
WELL, I DIDN'T SEE THAT COMING.
YOU HAVE YOUR OWN AGENDA. I LIKE THAT.
AND IT IS INDEED YOUR DEATH. YOURS ALONE. YOU GIVE ME GROUNDS FOR CAUTIOUS OPTIMISM.
ONE OUT OF TWO IS AN ACCEPTABLE AVERAGE.

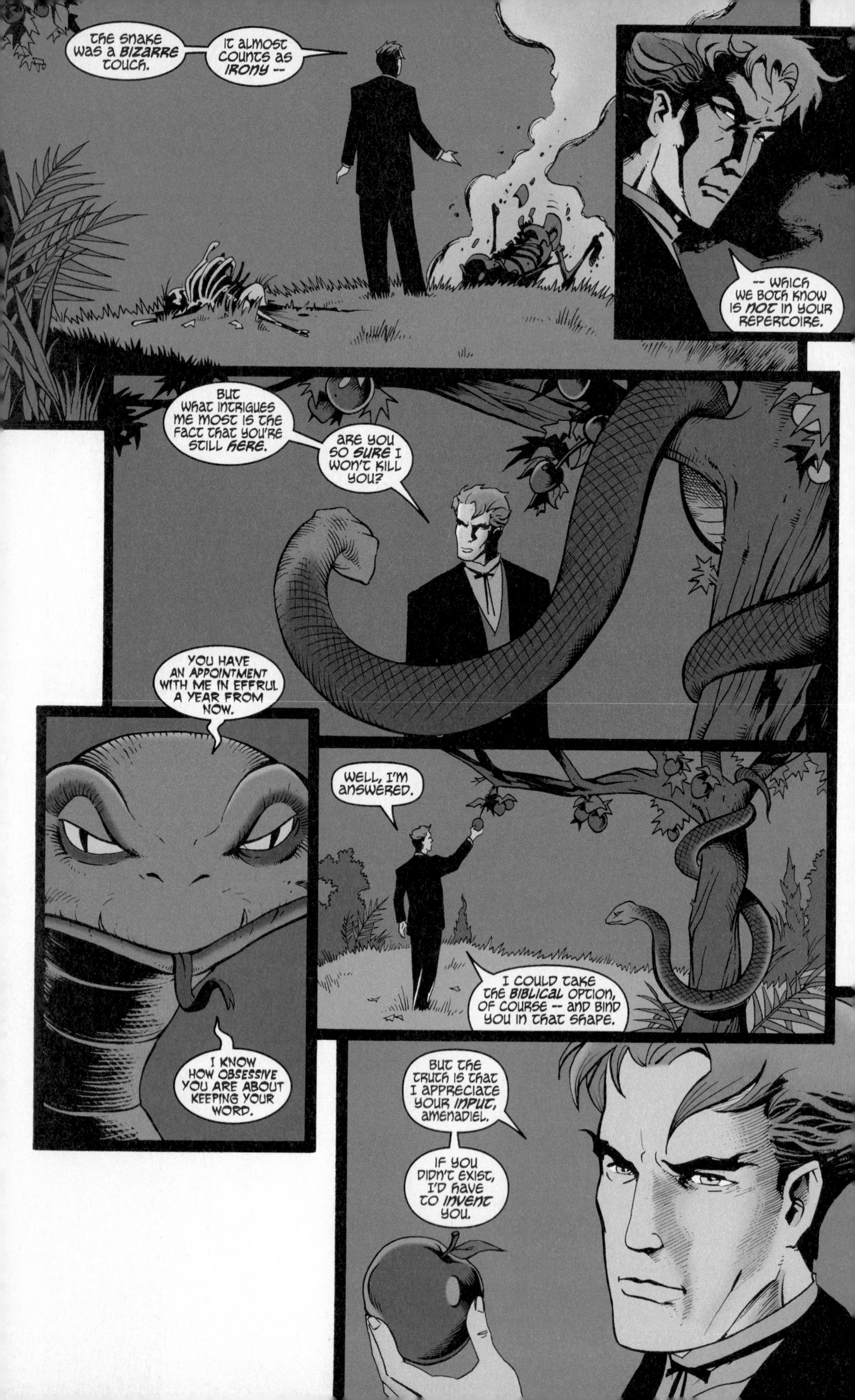
THE SNAKE WAS A BIZARRE TOUCH.
IT ALMOST COUNTS AS IRONY --
-- WHICH WE BOTH KNOW IS NOT IN YOUR REPERTOIRE.
BUT WHAT INTRIGUES ME MOST IS THE FACT THAT YOU'RE STILL HERE.
ARE YOU SO SURE I WON'T KILL YOU?
YOU HAVE AN APPOINTMENT WITH ME IN EFFRUL A YEAR FROM NOW.
I KNOW HOW OBSESSIVE YOU ARE ABOUT KEEPING YOUR WORD.
WELL, I'M ANSWERED.
I COULD TAKE THE BIBLICAL OPTION, OF COURSE -- AND BIND YOU IN THAT SHAPE.
BUT THE TRUTH IS THAT I APPRECIATE YOUR INPUT, AMENADIEL.
IF YOU DIDN'T EXIST, I'D HAVE TO INVENT YOU.

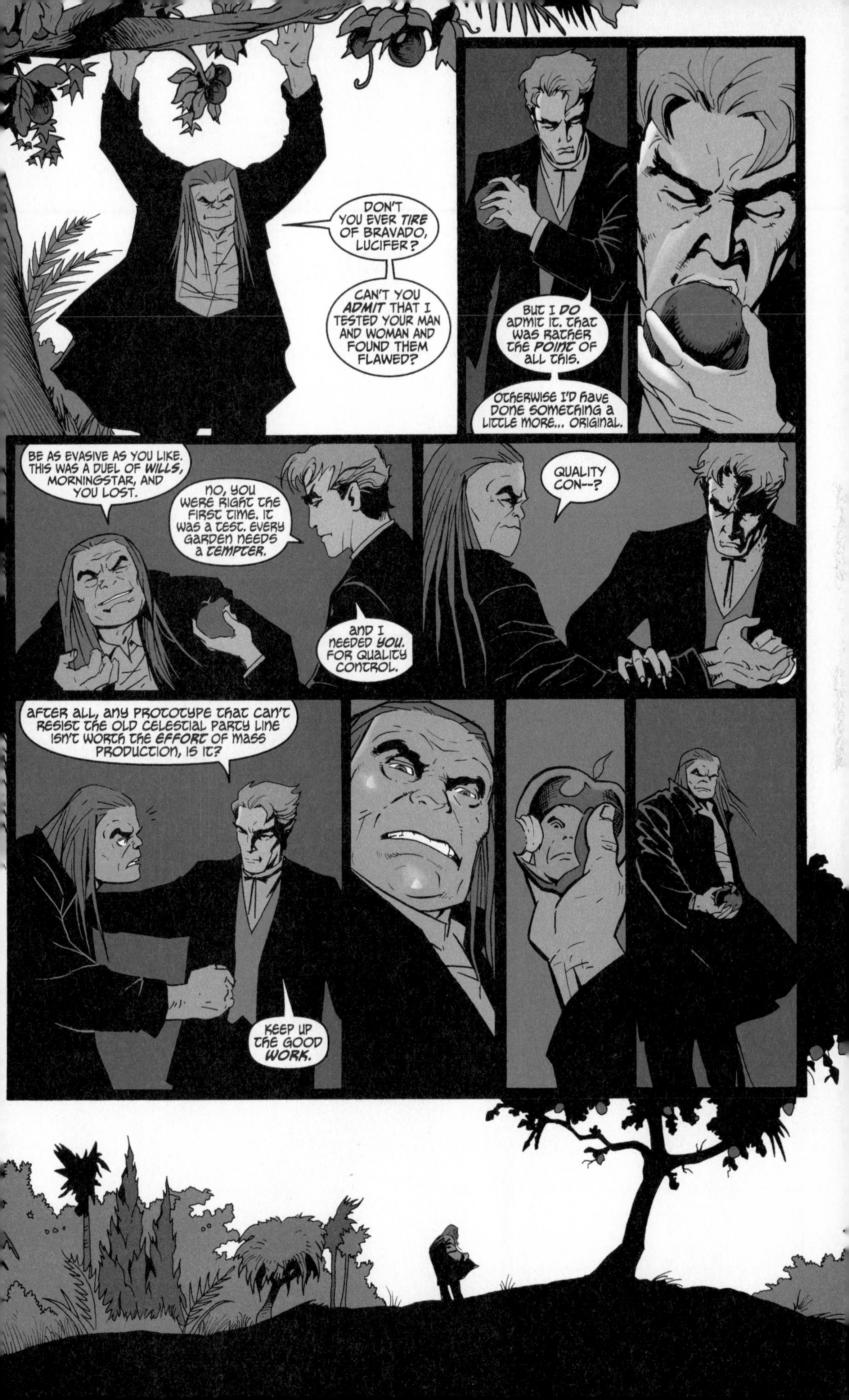

DON'T YOU EVER TIRE OF BRAVADO, LUCIFER?
CAN'T YOU ADMIT THAT I TESTED YOUR MAN AND WOMAN AND FOUND THEM FLAWED?
BUT I DO ADMIT IT. THAT WAS RATHER THE POINT OF ALL THIS.
OTHERWISE I'D HAVE DONE SOMETHING A LITTLE MORE... ORIGINAL.
BE AS EVASIVE AS YOU LIKE. THIS WAS A DUEL OF WILLS, MORNINGSTAR, AND YOU LOST.
NO, YOU WERE RIGHT THE FIRST TIME. IT WAS A TEST. EVERY GARDEN NEEDS A TEMPTER.
AND I NEEDED YOU. FOR QUALITY CONTROL.
QUALITY CON--?
AFTER ALL, ANY PROTOTYPE THAT CAN'T RESIST THE OLD CELESTIAL PARTY LINE ISN'T WORTH THE EFFORT OF MASS PRODUCTION, IS IT?
KEEP UP THE GOOD WORK.

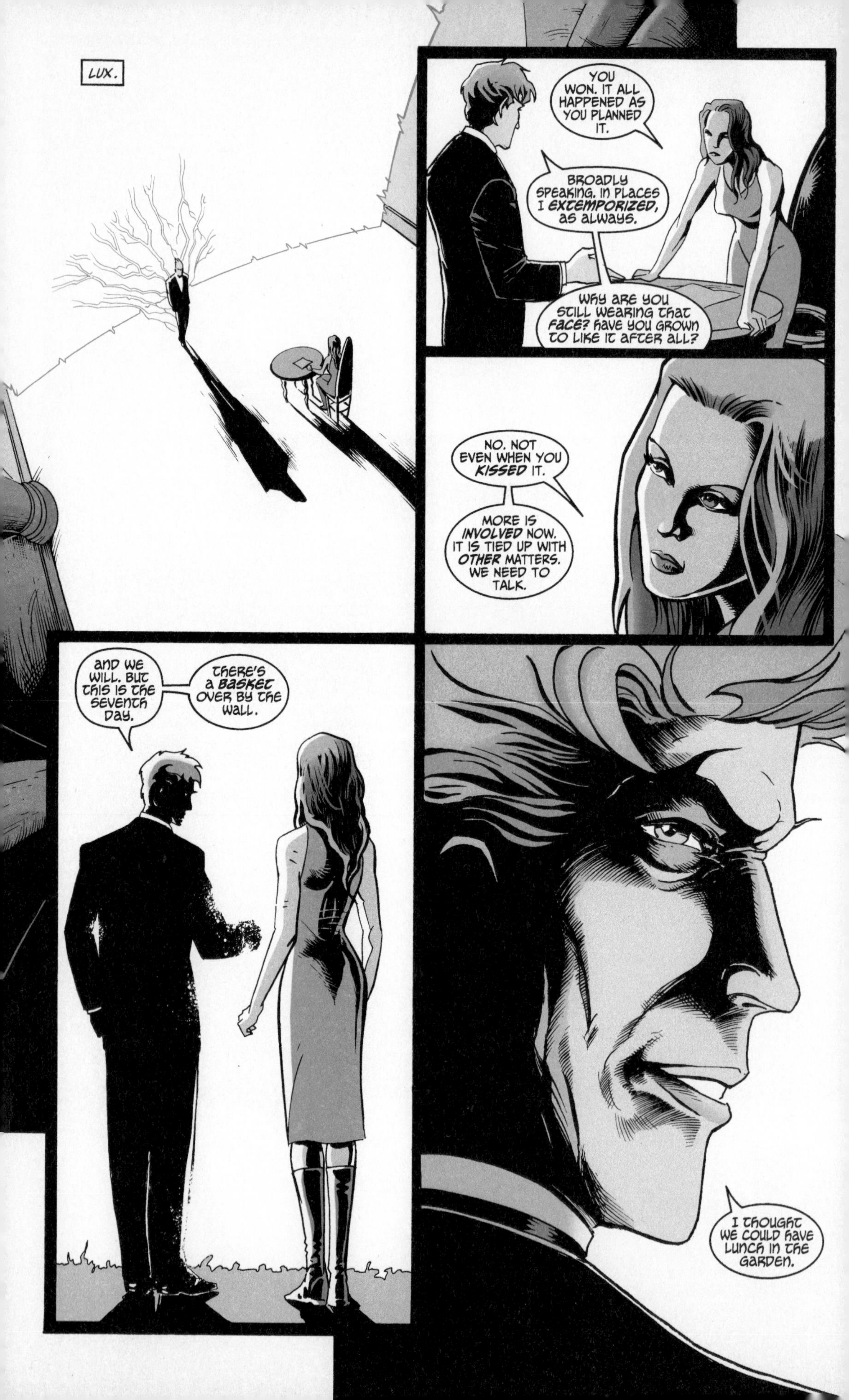
LUX.
YOU WON. IT ALL HAPPENED AS YOU PLANNED IT.
BROADLY SPEAKING. IN PLACES I EXTEMPORIZED, AS ALWAYS.
WHY ARE YOU STILL WEARING THAT FACE? HAVE YOU GROWN TO LIKE IT AFTER ALL?
NO. NOT EVEN WHEN YOU KISSED IT.
MORE IS INVOLVED NOW. IT IS TIED UP WITH OTHER MATTERS. WE NEED TO TALK.
AND WE WILL. BUT THIS IS THE SEVENTH DAY.
THERE'S A BASKET OVER BY THE WALL.
I THOUGHT WE COULD HAVE LUNCH IN THE GARDEN.

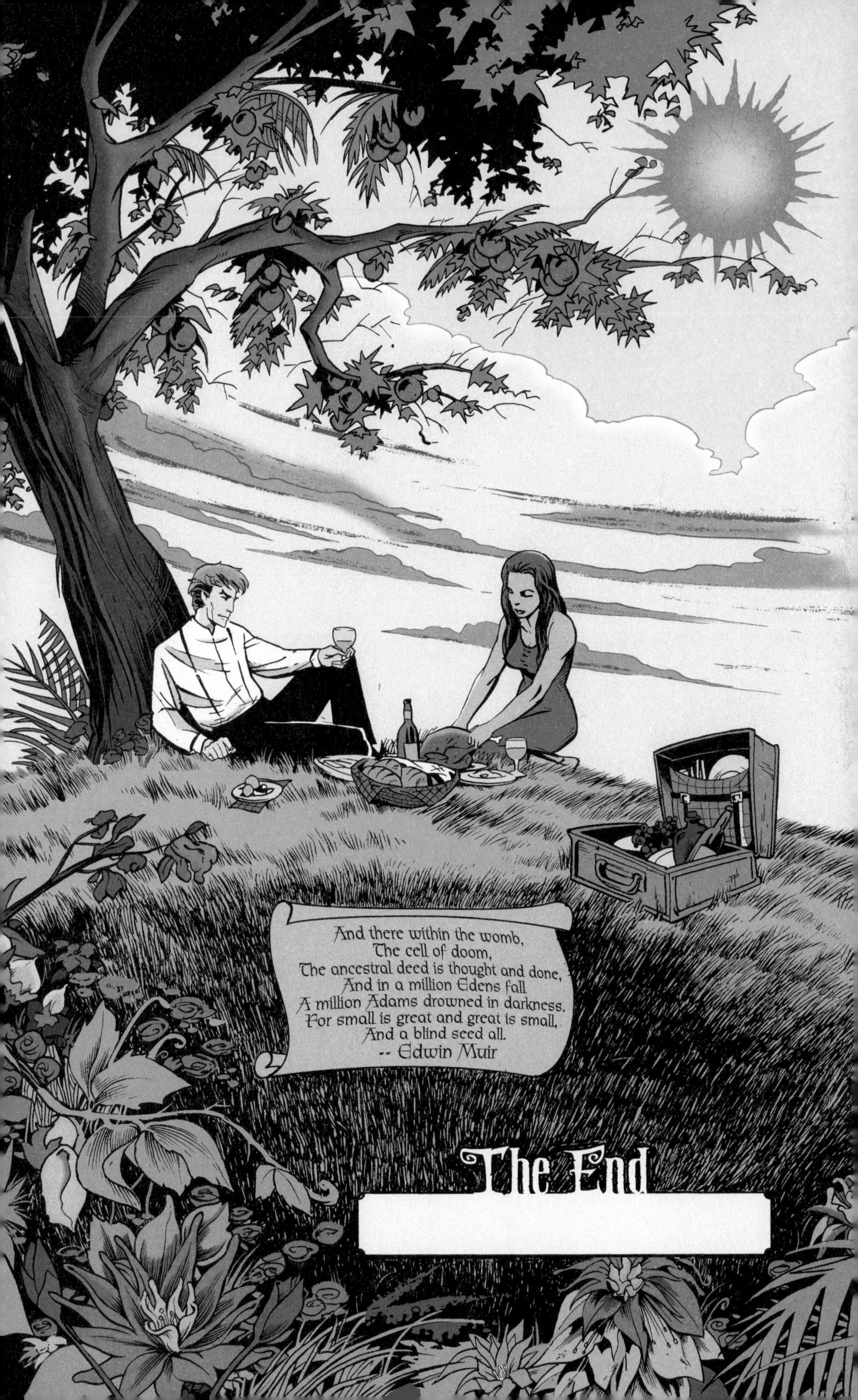
And there within the womb,
The cell of doom,
The ancestral deed is thought and done,
And in a million Edens fall
A million Adams drowned in darkness.
For small is great and great is small,
And a blind seed all.
-- Edwin Muir
The End

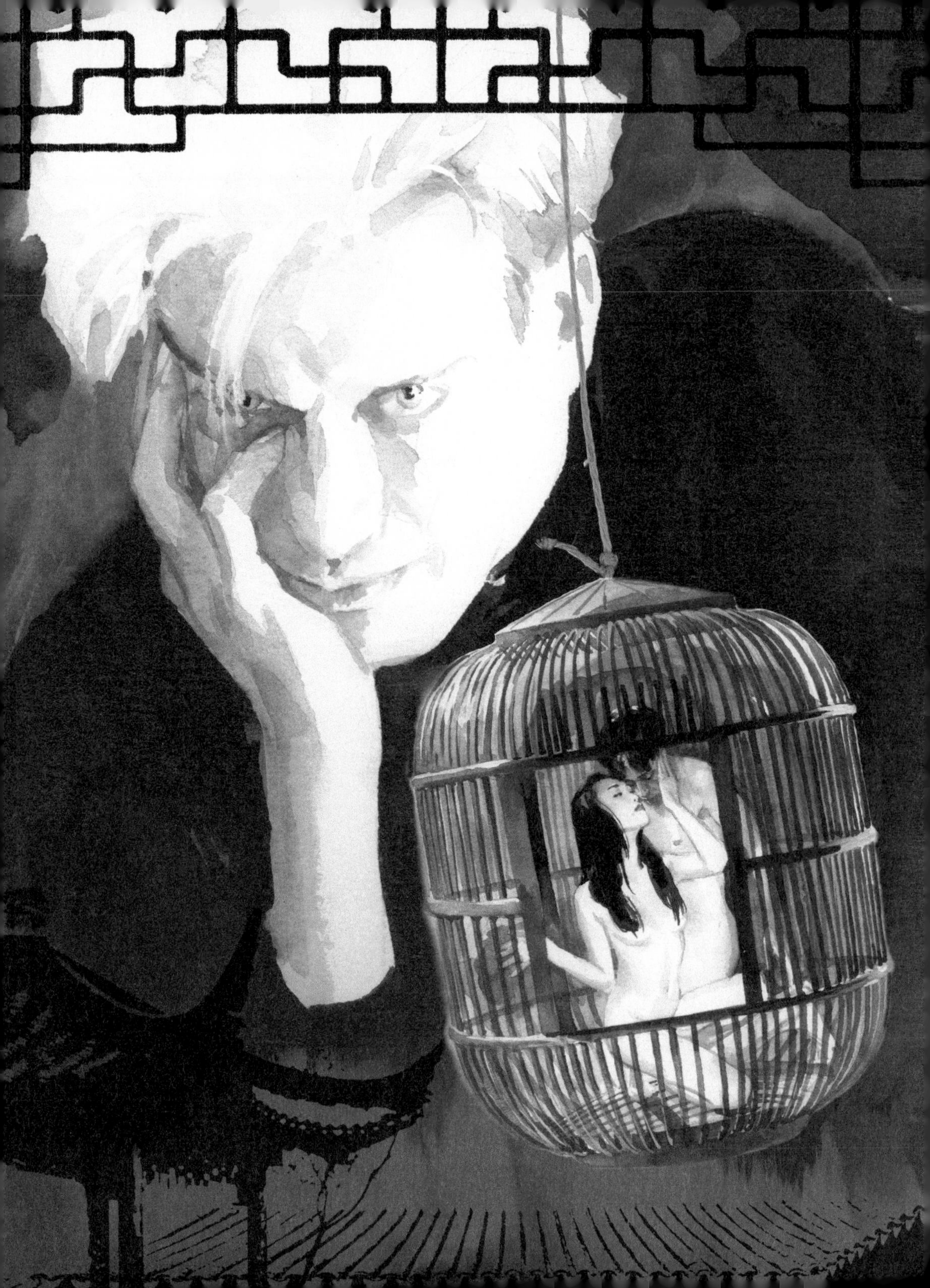

Nirvana

Mike Carey
Writer

Jon J Muth
Artist

Comicraft
Letterer

Mariah Huehner
Assistant Editor

Shelly Bond
Editor

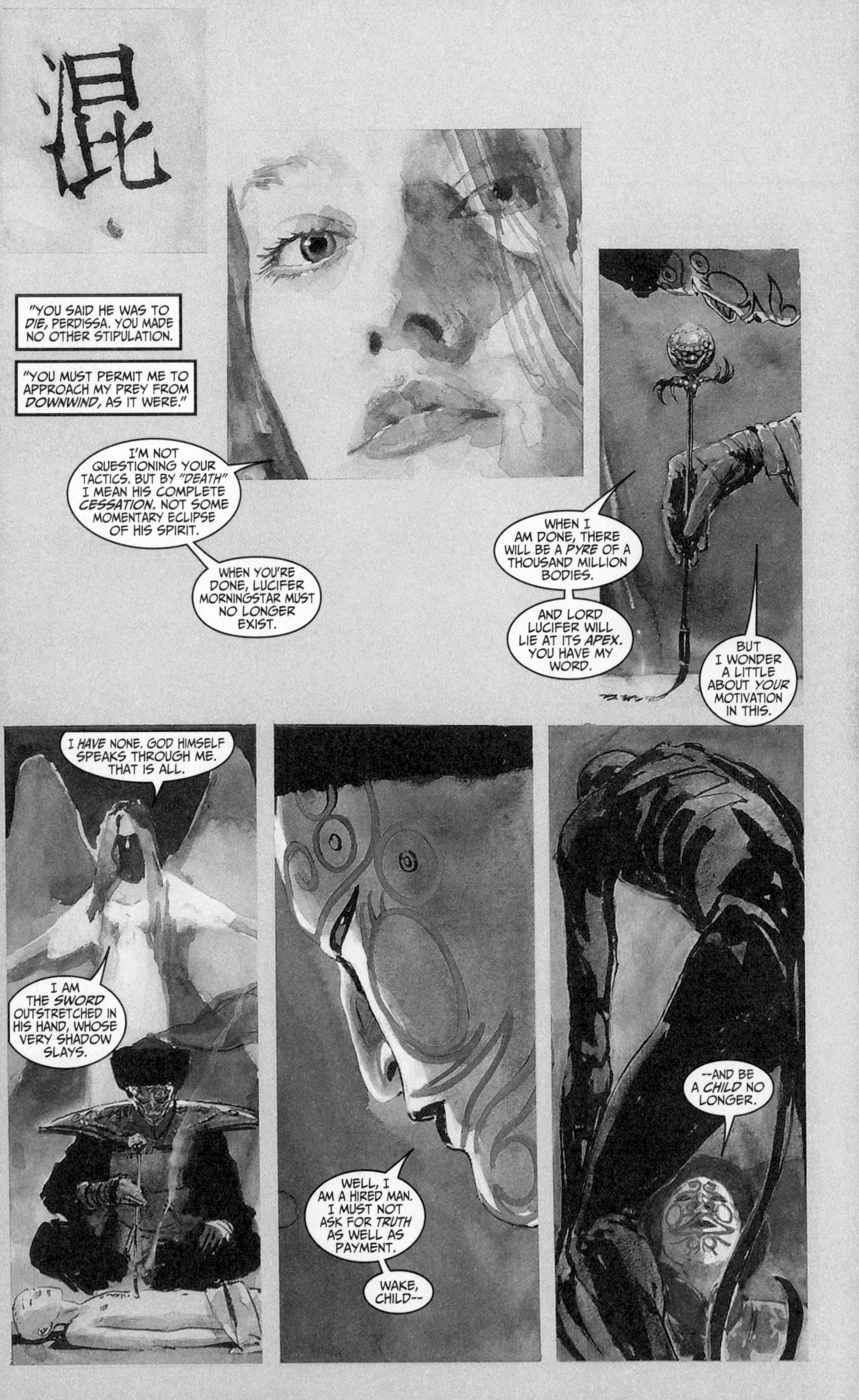
混
"YOU SAID HE WAS TO DIE, PERDISSA. YOU MADE NO OTHER STIPULATION.
"YOU MUST PERMIT ME TO APPROACH MY PREY FROM DOWNWIND, AS IT WERE."
I'M NOT QUESTIONING YOUR TACTICS. BUT BY "DEATH" I MEAN HIS COMPLETE CESSATION. NOT SOME MOMENTARY ECLIPSE OF HIS SPIRIT.
WHEN YOU'RE DONE, LUCIFER MORNINGSTAR MUST NO LONGER EXIST.
WHEN I AM DONE, THERE WILL BE A PYRE OF A THOUSAND MILLION BODIES.
AND LORD LUCIFER WILL LIE AT ITS APEX. YOU HAVE MY WORD.
BUT I WONDER A LITTLE ABOUT YOUR MOTIVATION IN THIS.
I HAVE NONE. GOD HIMSELF SPEAKS THROUGH ME. THAT IS ALL.
I AM THE SWORD OUTSTRETCHED IN HIS HAND, WHOSE VERY SHADOW SLAYS.
WELL, I AM A HIRED MAN. I MUST NOT ASK FOR TRUTH AS WELL AS PAYMENT.
WAKE, CHILD--
--AND BE A CHILD NO LONGER.

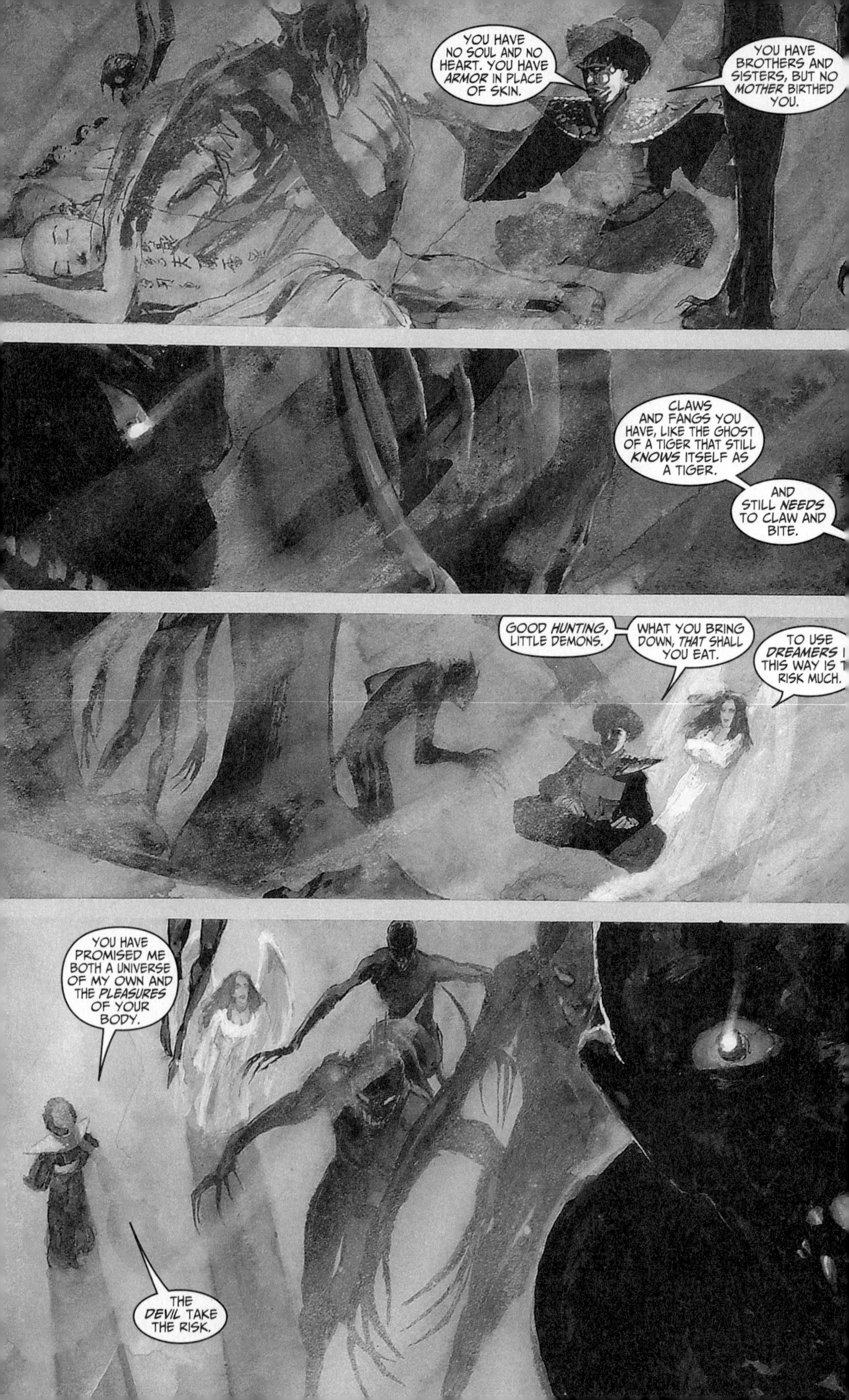
YOU HAVE NO SOUL AND NO HEART. YOU HAVE ARMOR IN PLACE OF SKIN.
YOU HAVE BROTHERS AND SISTERS, BUT NO MOTHER BIRTHED YOU.
CLAWS AND FANGS YOU HAVE, LIKE THE GHOST OF A TIGER THAT STILL KNOWS ITSELF AS A TIGER.
AND STILL NEEDS TO CLAW AND BITE.
GOOD HUNTING, LITTLE DEMONS.
WHAT YOU BRING DOWN, THAT SHALL YOU EAT.
TO USE DREAMERS I THIS WAY IS T RISK MUCH.
YOU HAVE PROMISED ME BOTH A UNIVERSE OF MY OWN AND THE PLEASURES OF YOUR BODY.
THE DEVIL TAKE THE RISK.

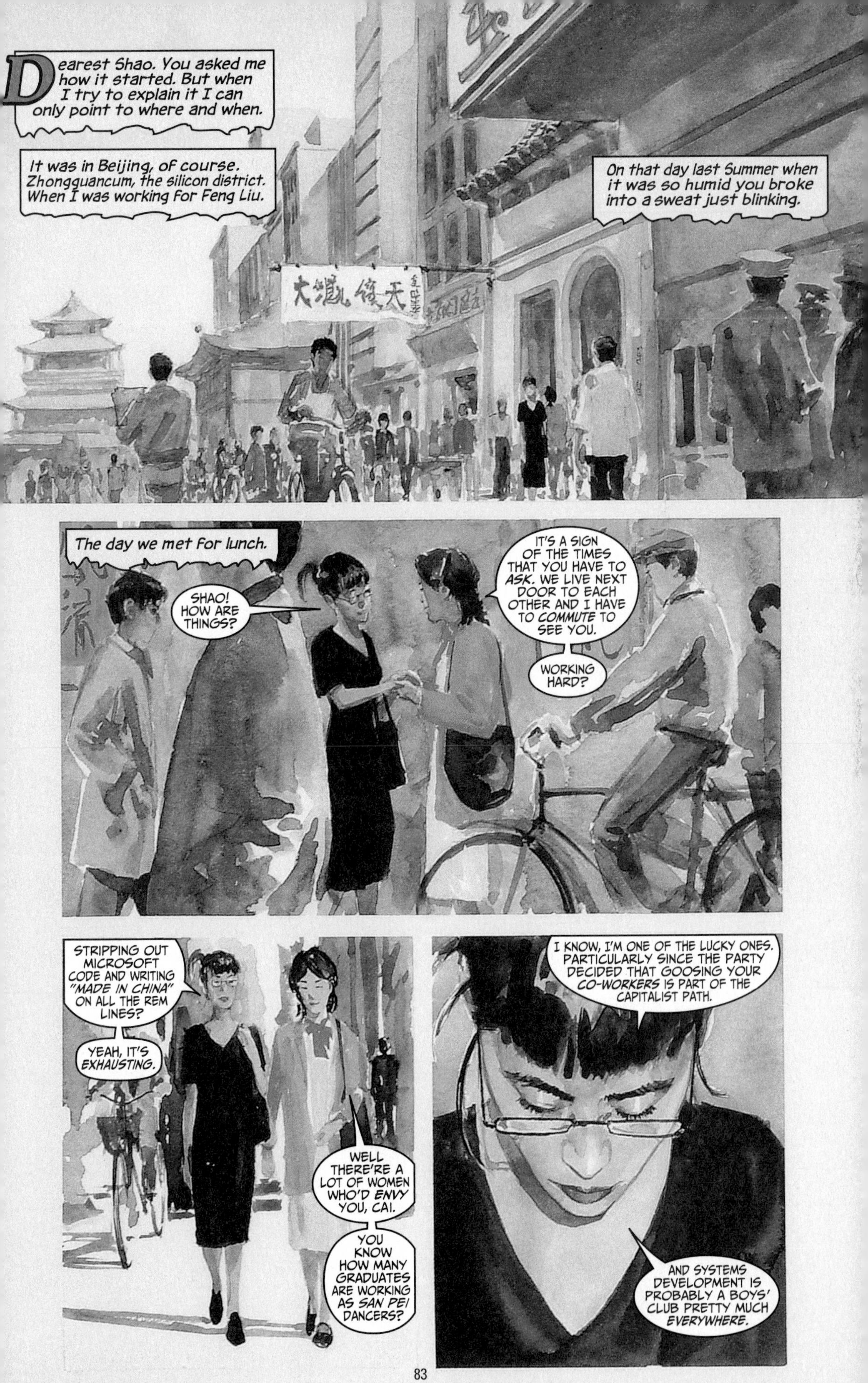
Dearest Shao. You asked me how it started. But when I try to explain it I can only point to where and when.
It was in Beijing, of course. Zhongguancum, the silicon district. When I was working for Feng Liu.
On that day last Summer when it was so humid you broke into a sweat just blinking.
The day we met for lunch.
SHAO! HOW ARE THINGS?
IT'S A SIGN OF THE TIMES THAT YOU HAVE TO ASK. WE LIVE NEXT DOOR TO EACH OTHER AND I HAVE TO COMMUTE TO SEE YOU.
WORKING HARD?
STRIPPING OUT MICROSOFT CODE AND WRITING "MADE IN CHINA" ON ALL THE REM LINES?
YEAH, IT'S EXHAUSTING.
WELL THERE'RE A LOT OF WOMEN WHO'D ENVY YOU, CAI.
YOU KNOW HOW MANY GRADUATES ARE WORKING AS SAN PEI DANCERS?
I KNOW, I'M ONE OF THE LUCKY ONES. PARTICULARLY SINCE THE PARTY DECIDED THAT GOOSING YOUR CO-WORKERS IS PART OF THE CAPITALIST PATH.
AND SYSTEMS DEVELOPMENT IS PROBABLY A BOYS' CLUB PRETTY MUCH EVERYWHERE.

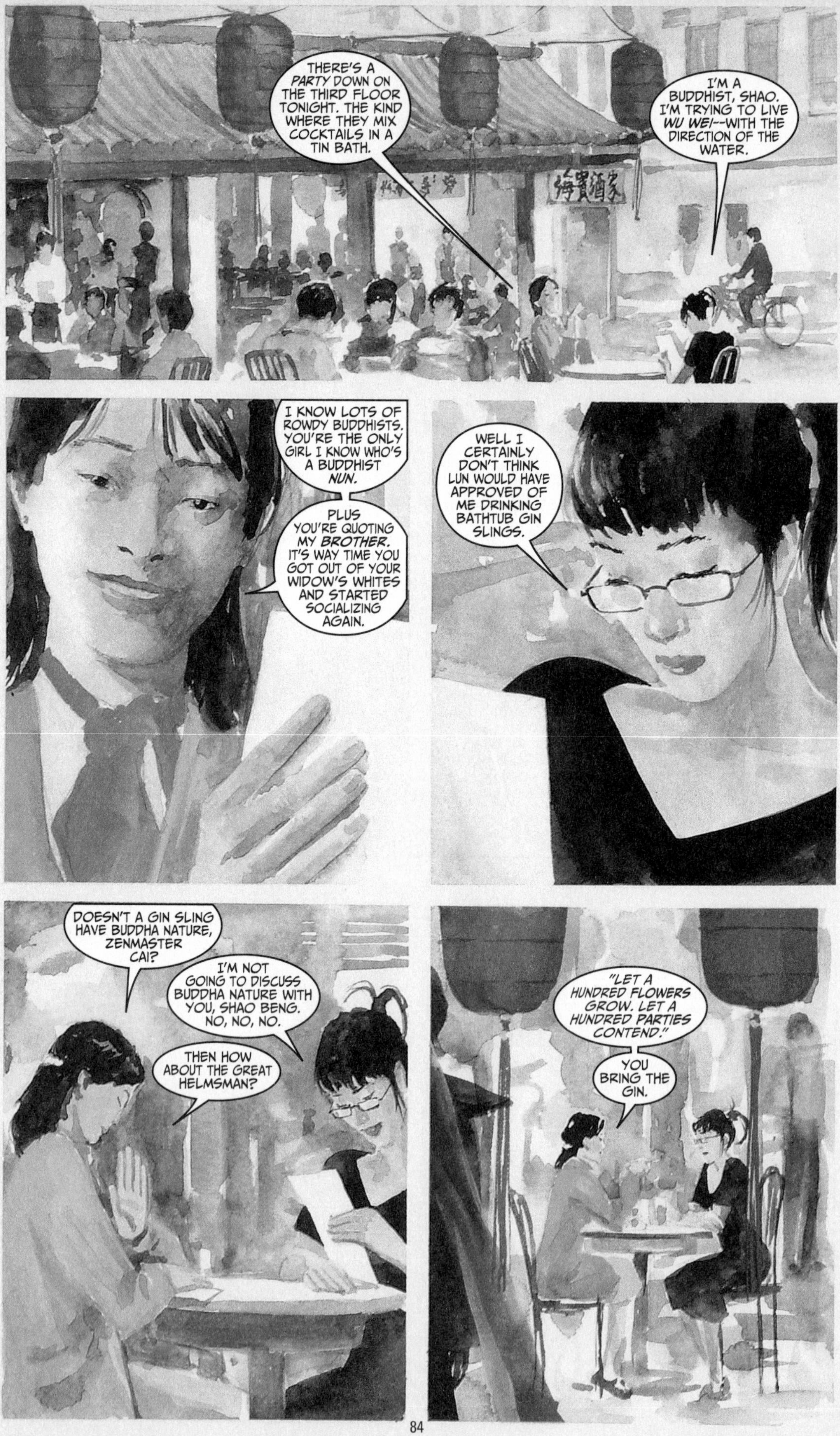
THERE'S A *PARTY* DOWN ON THE THIRD FLOOR TONIGHT. THE KIND WHERE THEY MIX COCKTAILS IN A TIN BATH.
I'M A BUDDHIST, SHAO. I'M TRYING TO LIVE *WU WEI*--WITH THE DIRECTION OF THE WATER.
I KNOW LOTS OF ROWDY BUDDHISTS. YOU'RE THE ONLY GIRL I KNOW WHO'S A BUDDHIST *NUN.*
PLUS YOU'RE QUOTING MY *BROTHER.* IT'S WAY TIME YOU GOT OUT OF YOUR WIDOW'S WHITES AND STARTED SOCIALIZING AGAIN.
WELL I CERTAINLY DON'T THINK LUN WOULD HAVE APPROVED OF ME DRINKING BATHTUB GIN SLINGS.
DOESN'T A GIN SLING HAVE BUDDHA NATURE, ZENMASTER CAI?
I'M NOT GOING TO DISCUSS BUDDHA NATURE WITH YOU, SHAO BENG. NO, NO, NO.
THEN HOW ABOUT THE GREAT HELMSMAN?
"LET A HUNDRED FLOWERS GROW. LET A HUNDRED PARTIES CONTEND."
YOU BRING THE GIN.

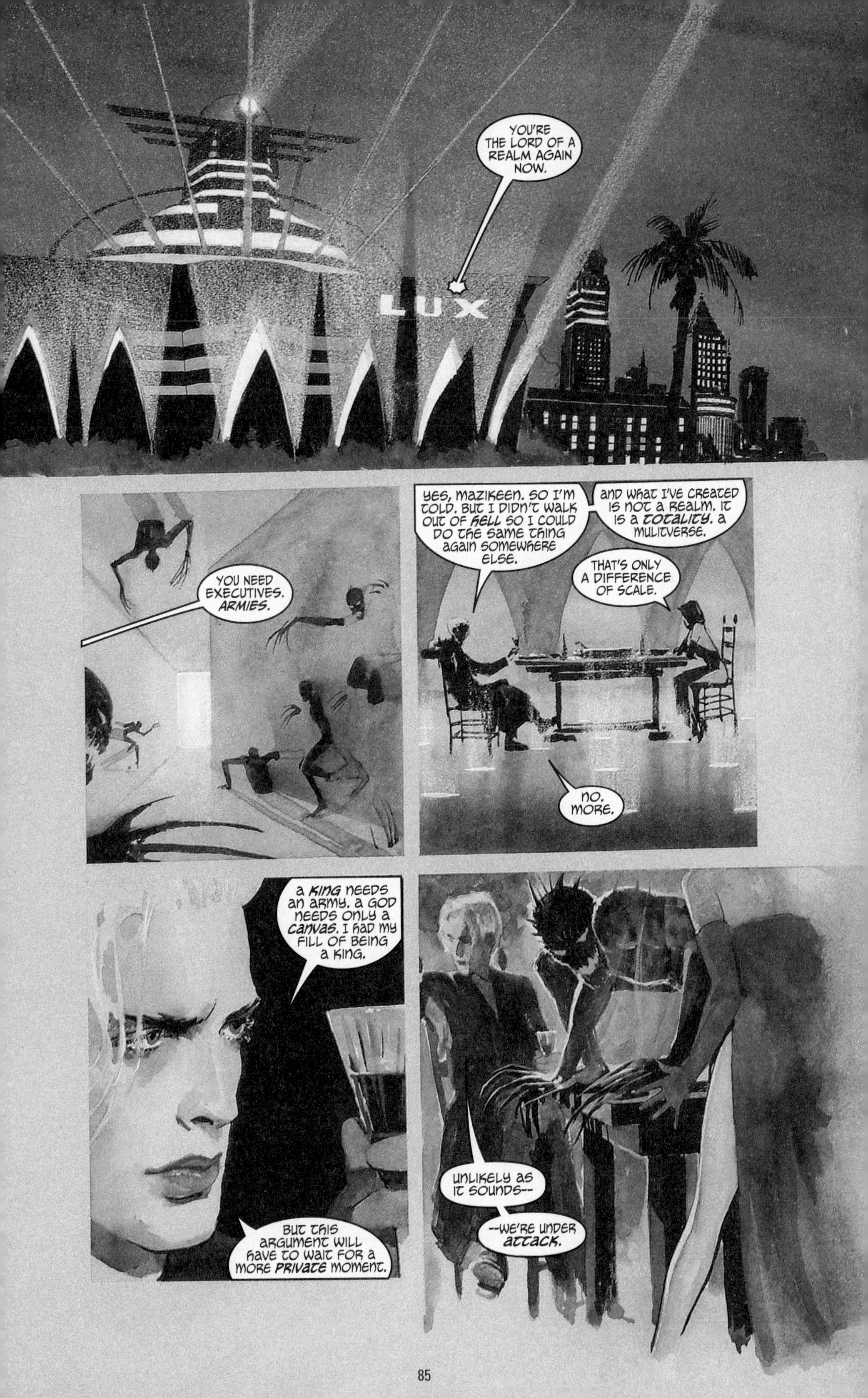

YOU'RE THE LORD OF A REALM AGAIN NOW.
LUX
YOU NEED EXECUTIVES. ARMIES.
YES, MAZIKEEN. SO I'M TOLD. BUT I DIDN'T WALK OUT OF HELL SO I COULD DO THE SAME THING AGAIN SOMEWHERE ELSE.
AND WHAT I'VE CREATED IS NOT A REALM. IT IS A TOTALITY. A MULITVERSE.
THAT'S ONLY A DIFFERENCE OF SCALE.
NO. MORE.
A KING NEEDS AN ARMY. A GOD NEEDS ONLY A CANVAS. I HAD MY FILL OF BEING A KING.
BUT THIS ARGUMENT WILL HAVE TO WAIT FOR A MORE PRIVATE MOMENT.
UNLIKELY AS IT SOUNDS--
--WE'RE UNDER ATTACK.

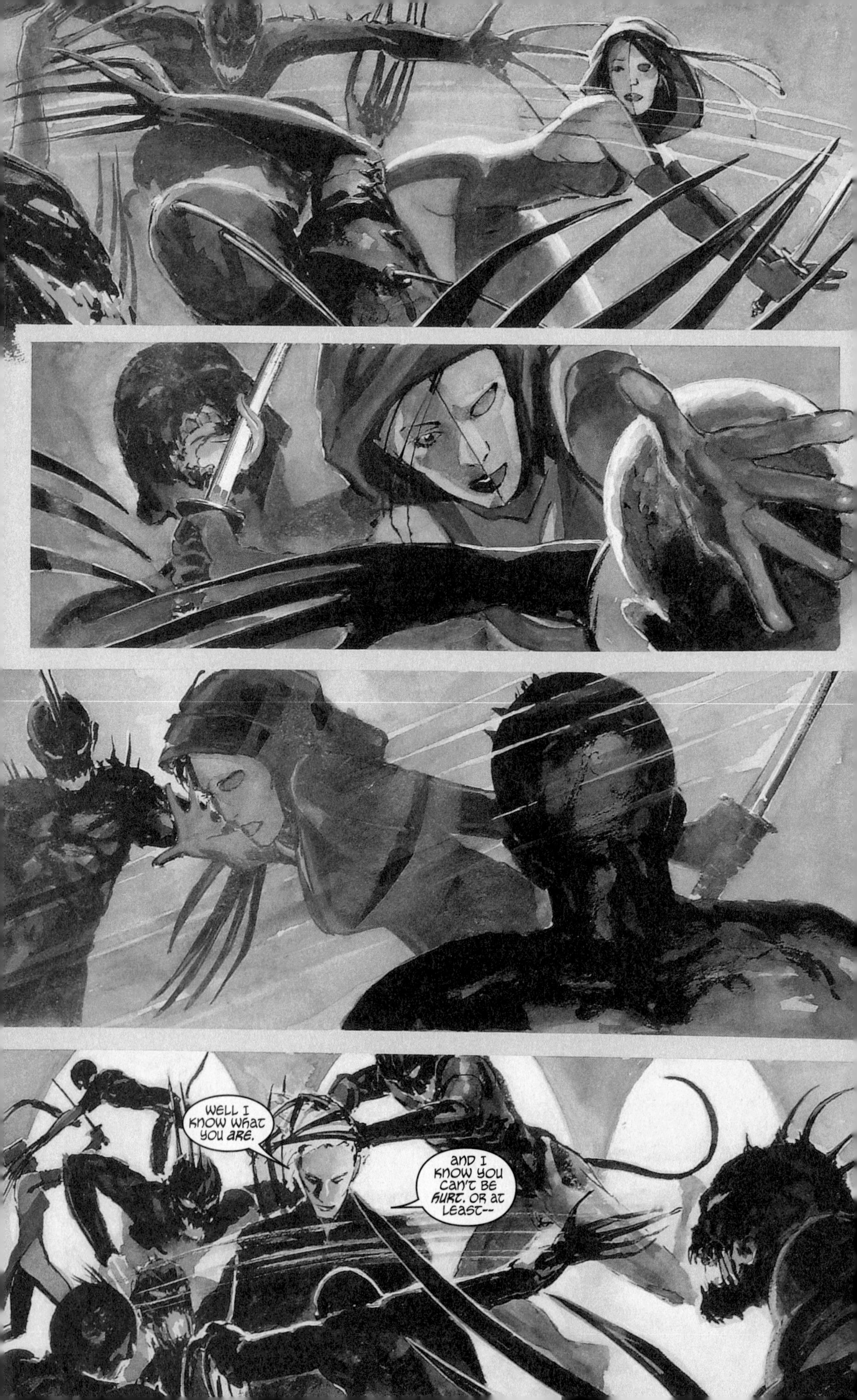
WELL I KNOW WHAT YOU ARE.
AND I KNOW YOU CAN'T BE HURT. OR AT LEAST--

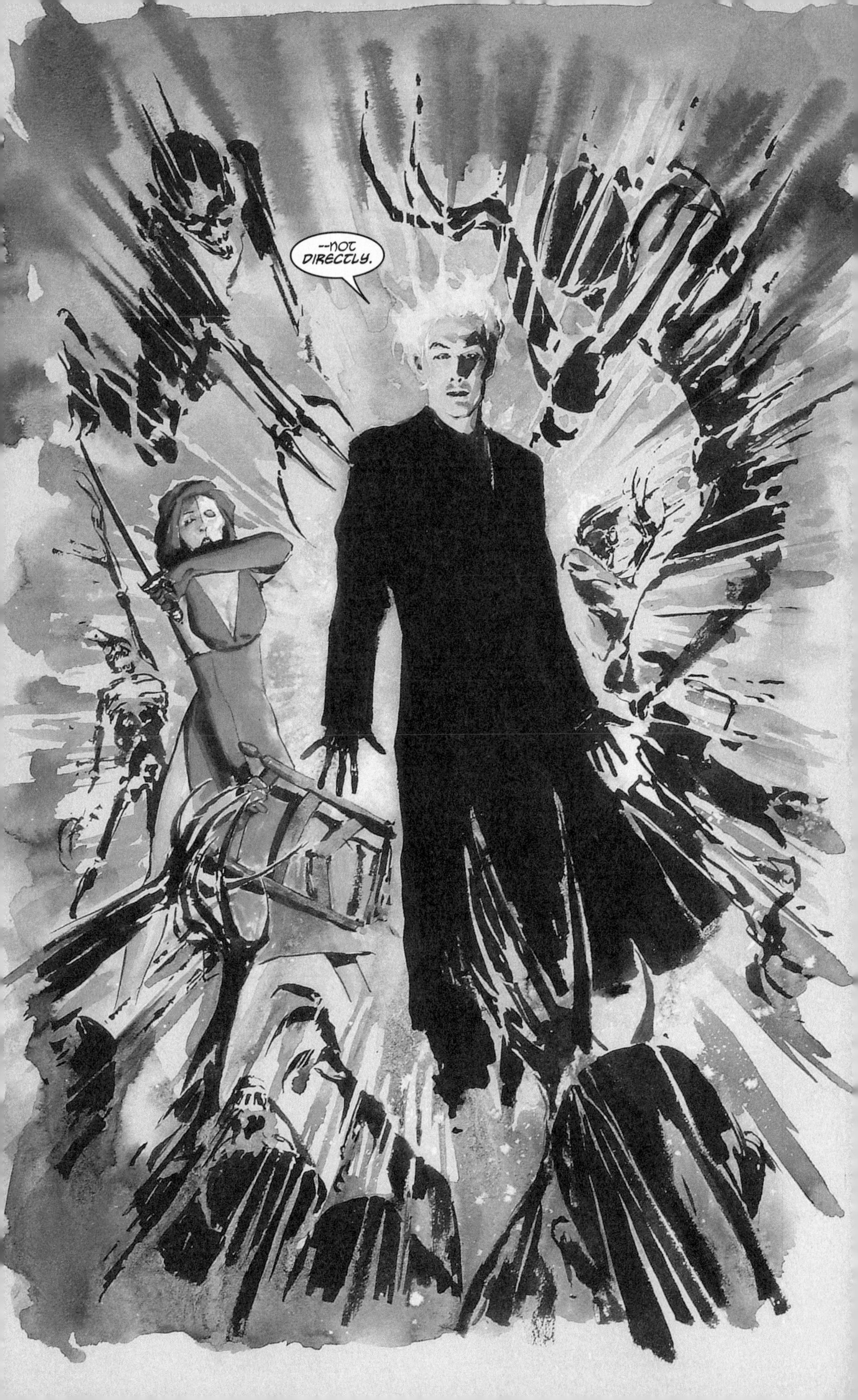
--NOT DIRECTLY.

QUAIMA. THE SPIRITS OF *SLEEPERS* FASHIONED INTO DEMONS.

CURIOUS.

I THINK I'LL SEEK OUT THESE SLEEPERS, AND ENSURE THEY DO NOT *WAKE.*

IT'S ALREADY *DONE.*

THE QUAIMA THEMSELVES ARE INVULNERABLE. I COULD ONLY *DESTROY* THEM BY EXTINGUISHING THE HUMAN SOULS THAT ANCHORED THEM.

VERY, VERY REGRETTABLE. IT MEANS I'LL HAVE TO LOOK *ELSEWHERE* FOR MY ANSWERS.

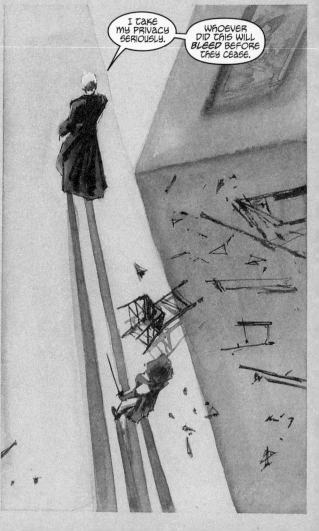

I TAKE MY PRIVACY SERIOUSLY.

WHOEVER DID THIS WILL *BLEED* BEFORE THEY CEASE.

I was going to say "I remember riding home..."

But I was thinking about Lun, and how I found him. In the dark, with the wire in his hands and his eyes half out of his head.

It never felt much like home after that.

You never believed in Buddha, Shao-- or in anything else you couldn't take a good look at in the shop before you brought it home.

So you never felt that incredible ambivalence about life.

OH NO, JIANG! NOT ANOTHER BIRD.

I'M GOING TO HAVE TO PUT A BELL ON YOUR--

That it's infinitely precious--

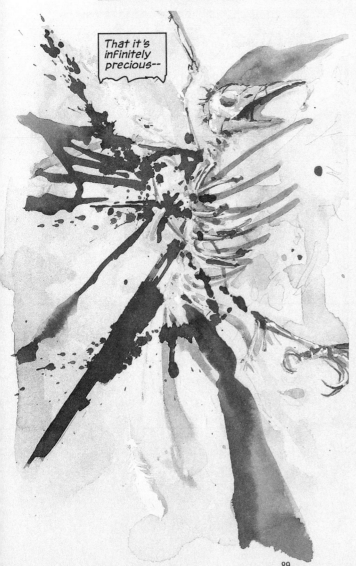

--and that the greatest reward a soul can find is to leave it forever.

COME INSIDE, CAI YUE.

I BRING YOU THE MOST WONDERFUL NEWS.

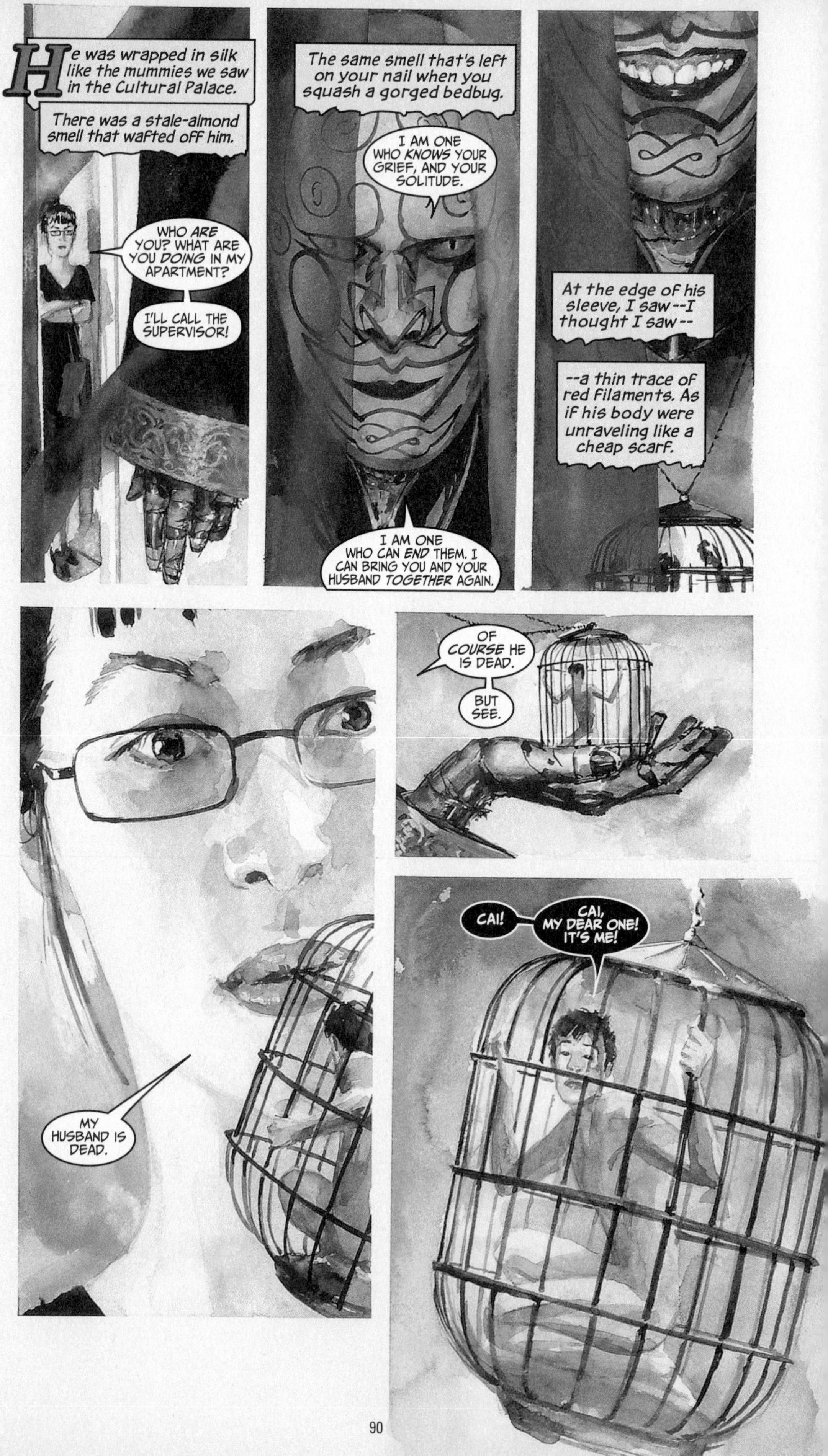
He was wrapped in silk like the mummies we saw in the Cultural Palace.
There was a stale-almond smell that wafted off him.
WHO ARE YOU? WHAT ARE YOU DOING IN MY APARTMENT?
I'LL CALL THE SUPERVISOR!
The same smell that's left on your nail when you squash a gorged bedbug.
I AM ONE WHO KNOWS YOUR GRIEF, AND YOUR SOLITUDE.
I AM ONE WHO CAN END THEM. I CAN BRING YOU AND YOUR HUSBAND TOGETHER AGAIN.
At the edge of his sleeve, I saw --I thought I saw --
--a thin trace of red filaments. As if his body were unraveling like a cheap scarf.
MY HUSBAND IS DEAD.
OF COURSE HE IS DEAD.
BUT SEE.
CAI!
CAI, MY DEAR ONE! IT'S ME!

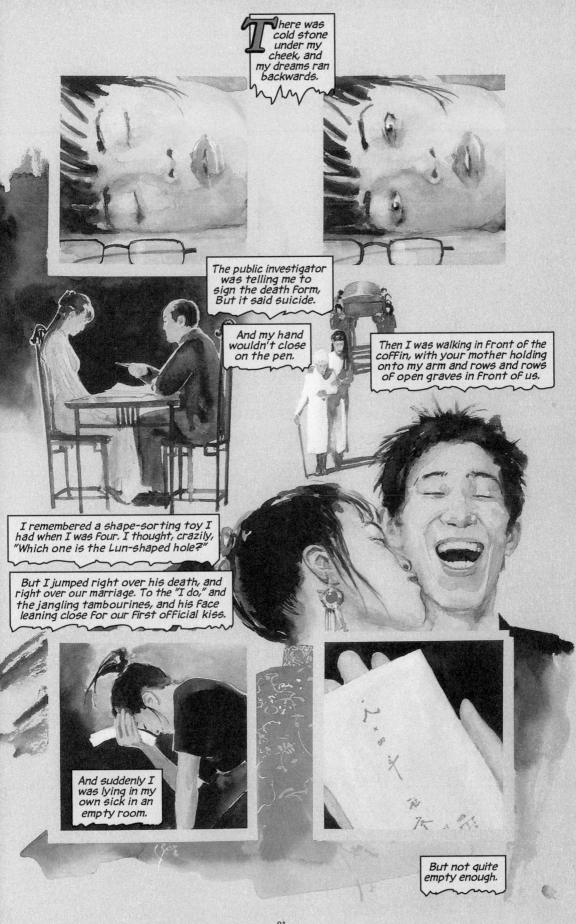

There was cold stone under my cheek, and my dreams ran backwards.

The public investigator was telling me to sign the death form, But it said suicide.

And my hand wouldn't close on the pen.

Then I was walking in front of the coffin, with your mother holding onto my arm and rows and rows of open graves in front of us.

I remembered a shape-sorting toy I had when I was four. I thought, crazily, "Which one is the Lun-shaped hole?"

But I jumped right over his death, and right over our marriage. To the "I do," and the jangling tambourines, and his face leaning close for our first official kiss.

And suddenly I was lying in my own sick in an empty room.

But not quite empty enough.

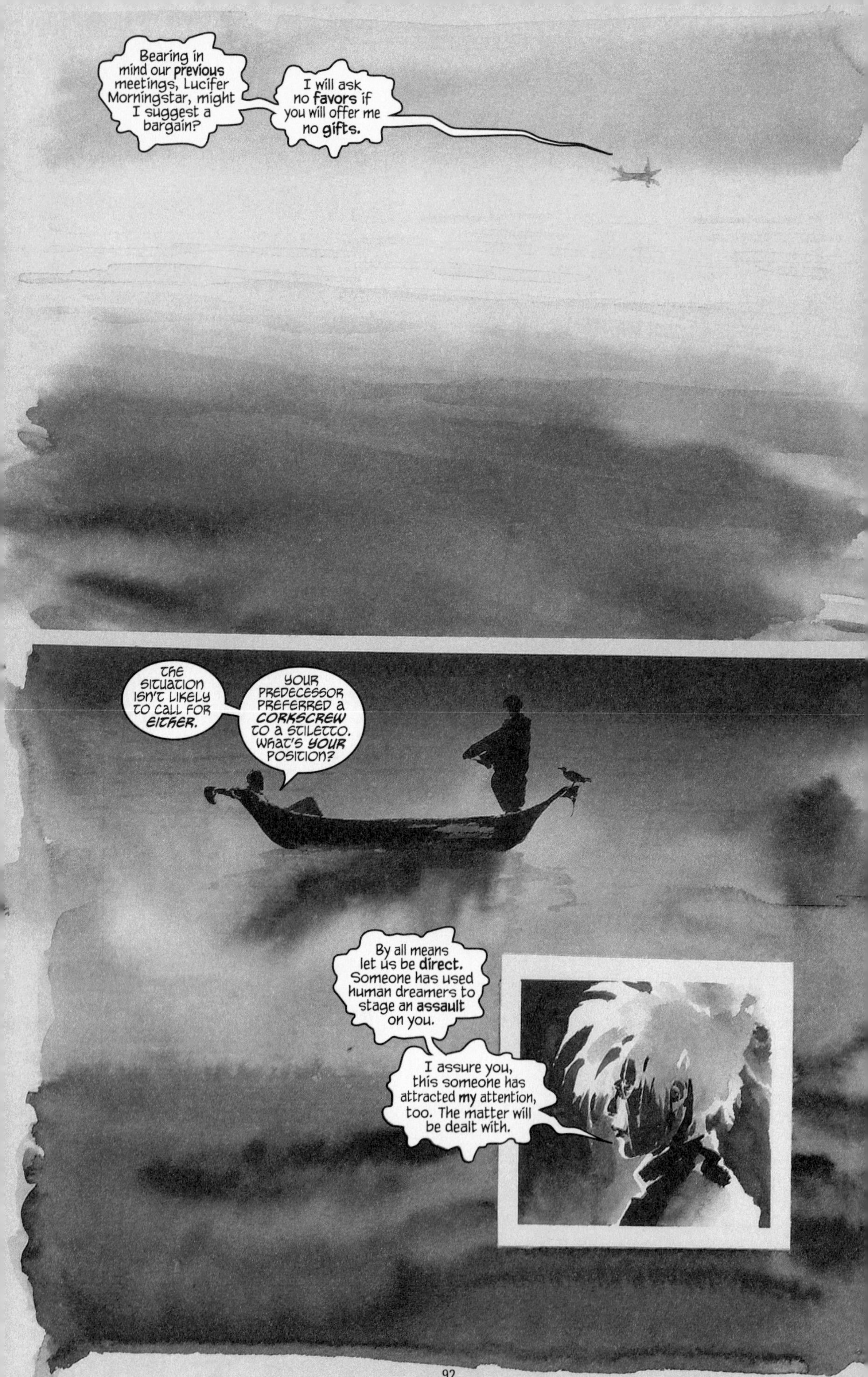
Bearing in mind our previous meetings, Lucifer Morningstar, might I suggest a bargain?
I will ask no favors if you will offer me no gifts.
THE SITUATION ISN'T LIKELY TO CALL FOR EITHER.
YOUR PREDECESSOR PREFERRED A CORKSCREW TO A STILETTO. WHAT'S YOUR POSITION?
By all means let us be direct. Someone has used human dreamers to stage an assault on you.
I assure you, this someone has attracted my attention, too. The matter will be dealt with.

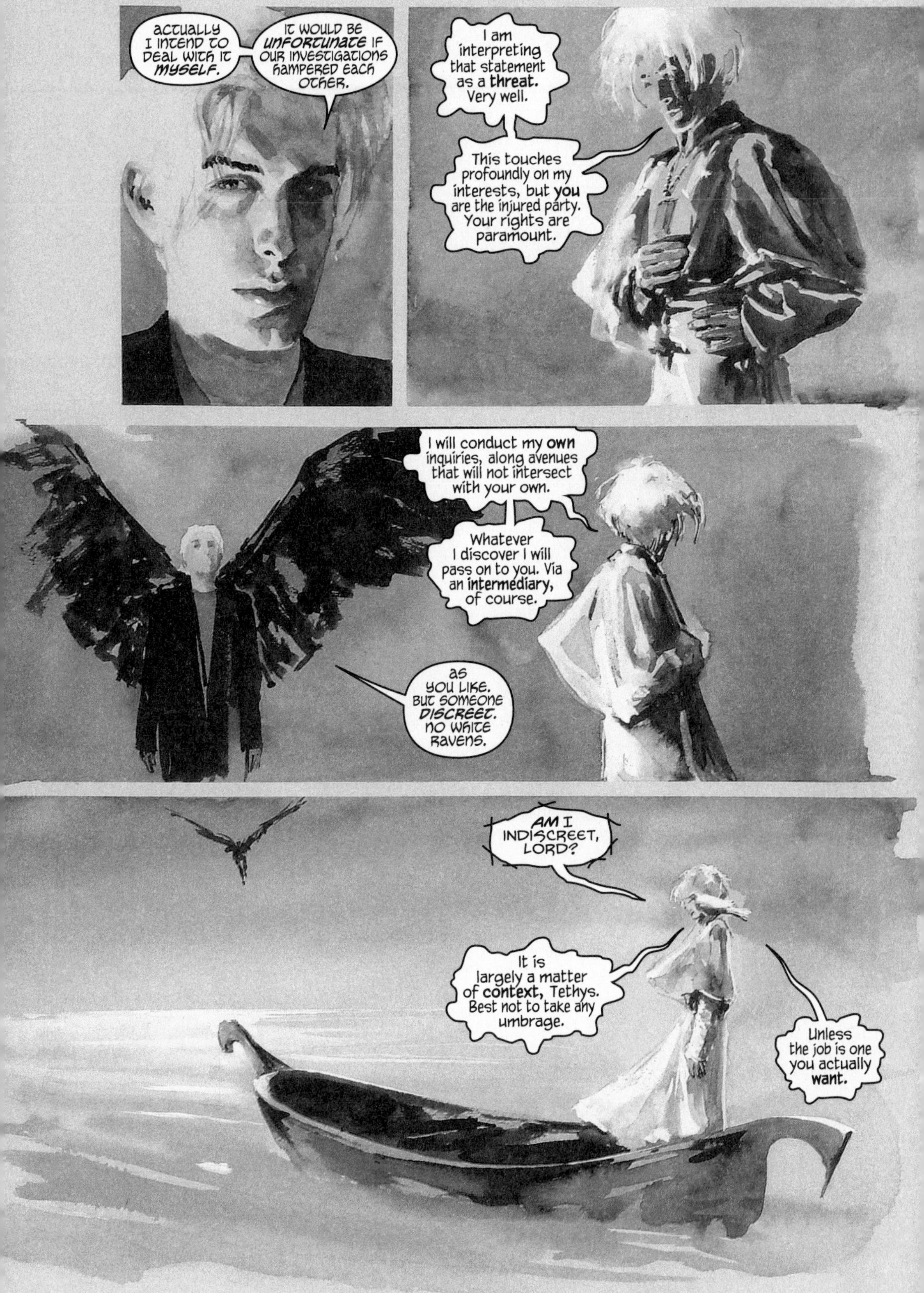

ACTUALLY I INTEND TO DEAL WITH IT MYSELF.
IT WOULD BE UNFORTUNATE IF OUR INVESTIGATIONS HAMPERED EACH OTHER.
I am interpreting that statement as a **threat.** Very well.
This touches profoundly on my interests, but **you** are the injured party. Your rights are paramount.
I will conduct my **own** inquiries, along avenues that will not intersect with your own.
Whatever I discover I will pass on to you. Via an **intermediary,** of course.
AS YOU LIKE. BUT SOMEONE DISCREET. NO WHITE RAVENS.
AM I INDISCREET, LORD?
It is largely a matter of **context,** Tethys. Best not to take any umbrage.
Unless the job is one you actually **want.**

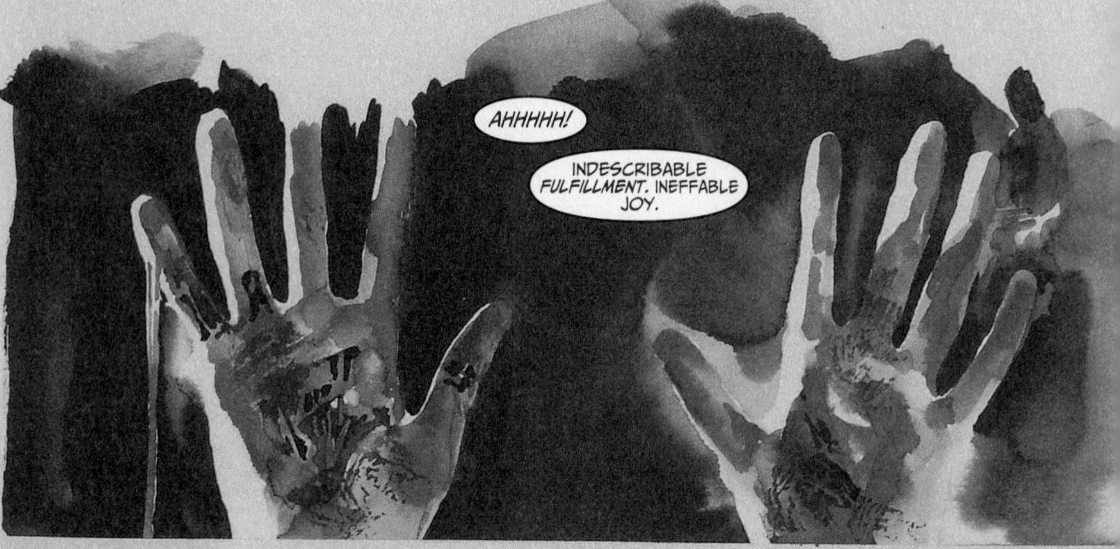
AHHHHH!
INDESCRIBABLE FULFILLMENT. INEFFABLE JOY.

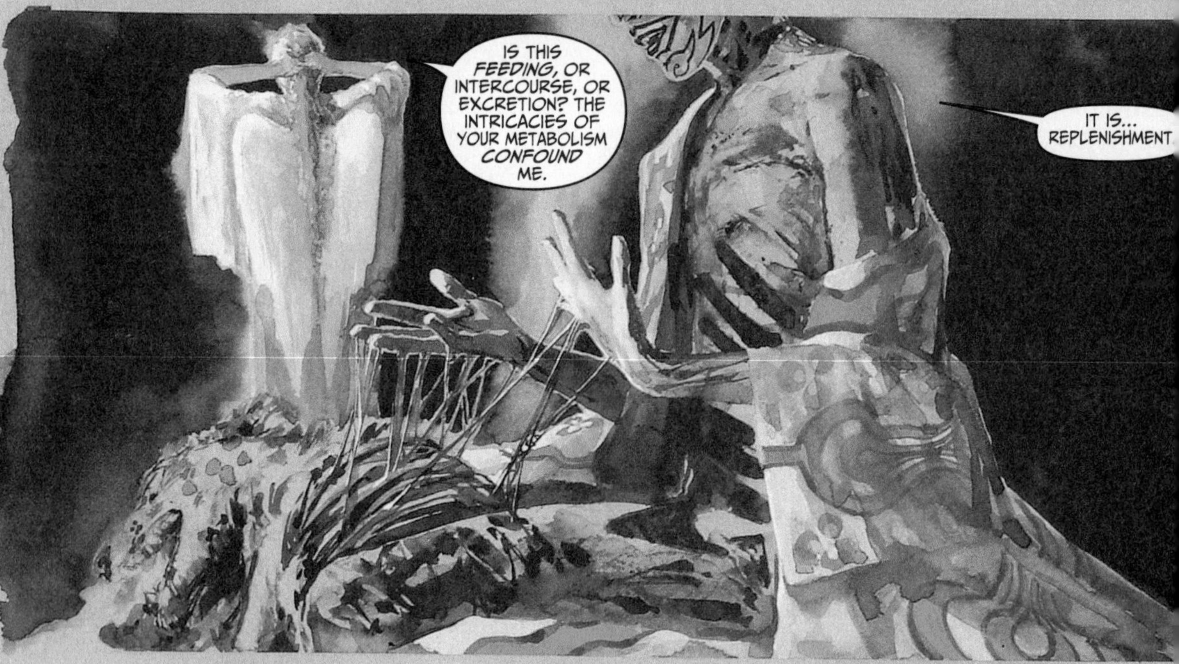
IS THIS FEEDING, OR INTERCOURSE, OR EXCRETION? THE INTRICACIES OF YOUR METABOLISM CONFOUND ME.
IT IS... REPLENISHMENT.

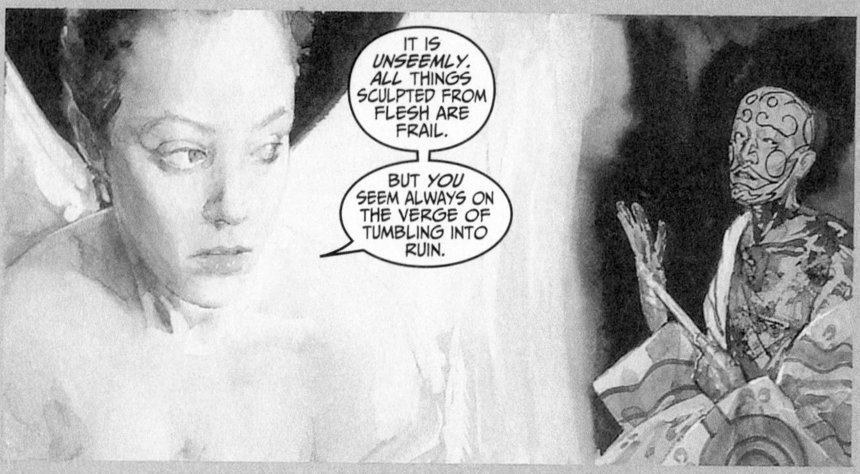
IT IS UNSEEMLY. ALL THINGS SCULPTED FROM FLESH ARE FRAIL.
BUT YOU SEEM ALWAYS ON THE VERGE OF TUMBLING INTO RUIN.

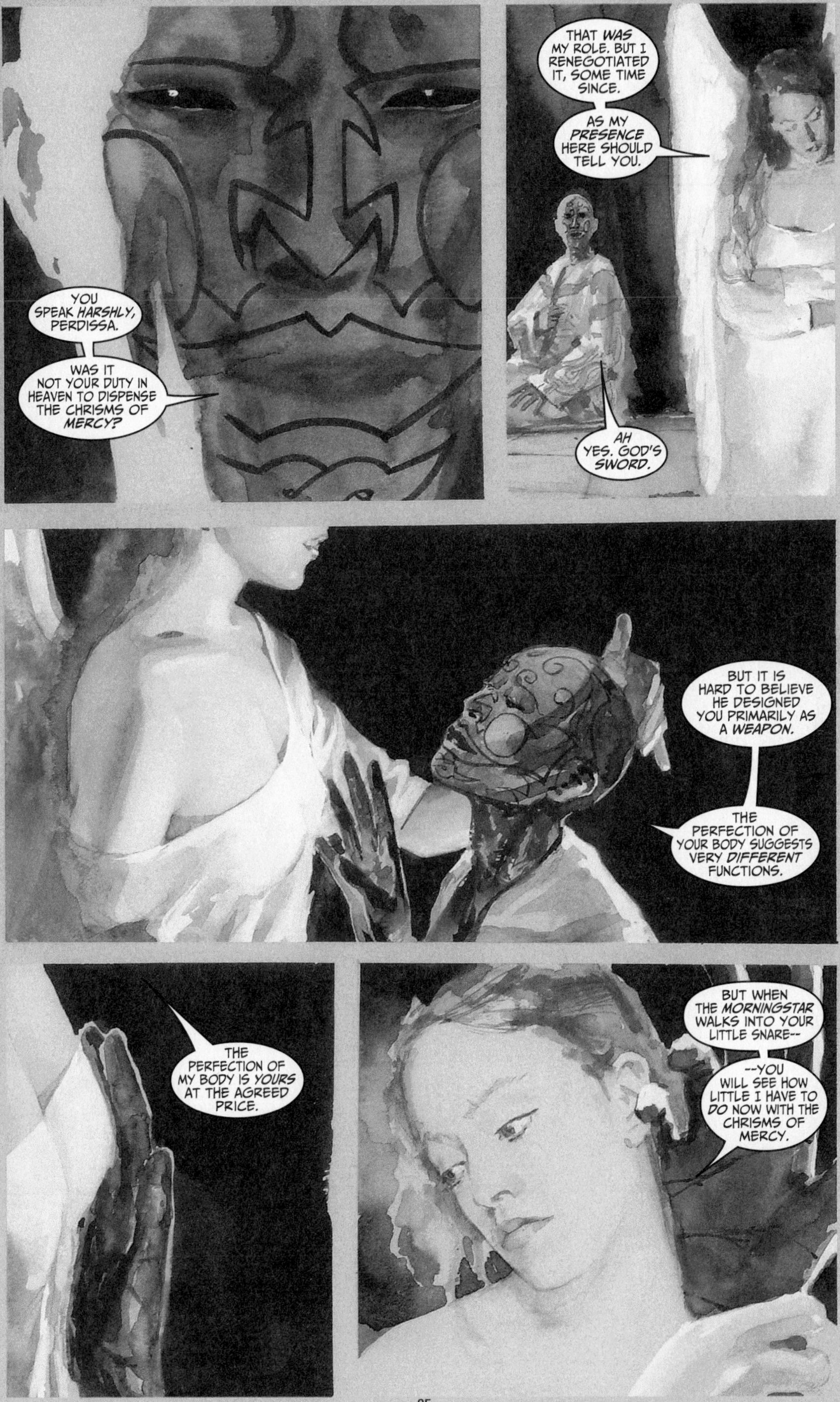
YOU SPEAK HARSHLY, PERDISSA.
WAS IT NOT YOUR DUTY IN HEAVEN TO DISPENSE THE CHRISMS OF MERCY?
THAT WAS MY ROLE. BUT I RENEGOTIATED IT, SOME TIME SINCE.
AS MY PRESENCE HERE SHOULD TELL YOU.
AH YES. GOD'S SWORD.
BUT IT IS HARD TO BELIEVE HE DESIGNED YOU PRIMARILY AS A WEAPON.
THE PERFECTION OF YOUR BODY SUGGESTS VERY DIFFERENT FUNCTIONS.
THE PERFECTION OF MY BODY IS YOURS AT THE AGREED PRICE.
BUT WHEN THE MORNINGSTAR WALKS INTO YOUR LITTLE SNARE--
--YOU WILL SEE HOW LITTLE I HAVE TO DO NOW WITH THE CHRISMS OF MERCY.

BRAZIL. MEXICO. GERMANY. YUGOSLAVIA.

YOUR ENEMY HAS LAID A *TORTUOUS* TRAIL.

PERHAPS. BUT THESE *CALLIGRAMS* ON THE BODIES--

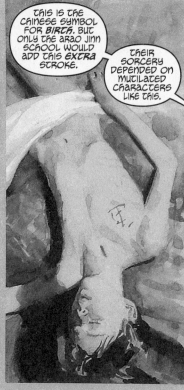

THIS IS THE CHINESE SYMBOL FOR *BIRTH*. BUT ONLY THE ARAO JINN SCHOOL WOULD ADD THIS *EXTRA* STROKE.

THEIR SORCERY DEPENDED ON MUTILATED CHARACTERS LIKE THIS.

I'VE NEVER *HEARD* OF THE ARAO JINN.

THEY'VE BEEN DEAD A LONG TIME. EXCEPT FOR THE SILK MAN, THEIR FOUNDER, WHO WAS NEVER *ALIVE* IN THE FIRST PLACE.

HE'S A FOSSIL REMNANT FROM AN *EARLIER*, CRUDER CREATION. HIS BODY IS A *WEAVING* THAT HAS TO BE RENEWED CONSTANTLY.

HIS *SPIRIT* TOO, COME TO THAT. A *MESSY* FORM OF IMMORTALITY, BUT IT SEEMS TO DO THE JOB.

WELL, *BLOOD* HAS ANSWERED BLOOD. I AM CONTENT.

REALLY? I'M *NOT*. NOT AT ALL.

"I THINK I'LL MOVE ON TO CHINA--

"--AND SEE IF THERE'S A *POINT* TO ALL THIS."

When I was three my father took me to Temple of Heaven Park to see the paper kites. Dragons and snakes and monsters, flying through the sky. I thought they were real. I wondered where they went at night, when it was time to sleep.

And now, twenty years later, I had my answer.

CAI YUE. WELCOME.

NOW WE MAY BEGIN OUR LESSONS.

LESSONS? I THOUGHT YOU SAID YOU WERE GOING TO LET ME SEE HIM AGAIN.

THIS SHELL? THIS FRAIL, TINY GHOST? PUT IT FROM YOUR MIND.

THERE IS BUT ONE PLACE WHERE YOU AND LUN CAN COME TOGETHER. IN NIRVANA.

BUT NIRVANA IS ONLY AN... IDEA.

A METAPHOR FOR A STATE OF MIND.

OH NO. IT IS A REAL PLACE. THE GREAT ABSENCE WHERE SEPARATION IS NO LONGER POSSIBLE.

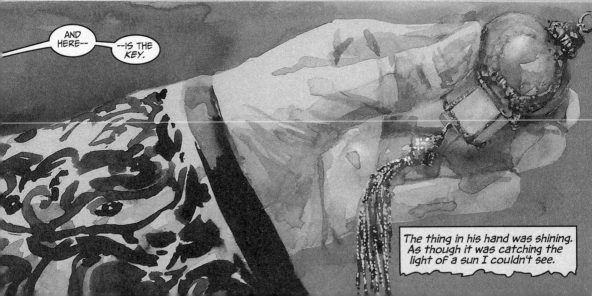

AND HERE-- --IS THE KEY.

The thing in his hand was shining. As though it was catching the light of a sun I couldn't see.

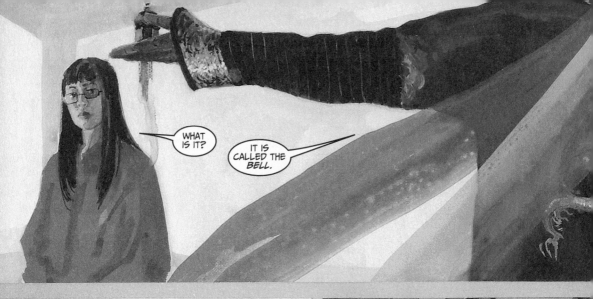

WHAT IS IT?

IT IS CALLED THE *BELL*.

IT'S BEAUTIFUL.

THE GODDESS *KUANYIN* MADE IT A LONG TIME AGO, AS AN AID TO MEDITATION. BUT IT HAS *OTHER* PROPERTIES, WHICH SHE DID NOT INTEND.

YOU WILL WALK THE SPIRIT ROADS, CAI YUE, WITH LUN'S SOUL *RIDING* ON YOURS. YOU WILL ENTER THE BELL, AND AT ITS *HEART* YOU WILL FIND NIRVANA.

THIS IS THE ONLY WAY YOUR HUSBAND'S GHOST CAN BE *FREED* FROM THE CAGE.

I *should* have run then. As far and as fast as I could.

I might have died. But the other things wouldn't have happened.

GO *INTO* IT? HOW?

BY *WANTING* TO. I WILL TEACH YOU, AND PREPARE YOU.

But I just sat there like an ox on an altar.

NOW BE *SILENT*, MY STUDENT. AND CLEAR YOUR MIND.

SO THAT I MAY BOTH FILL AND EMPTY IT.

And I let him--

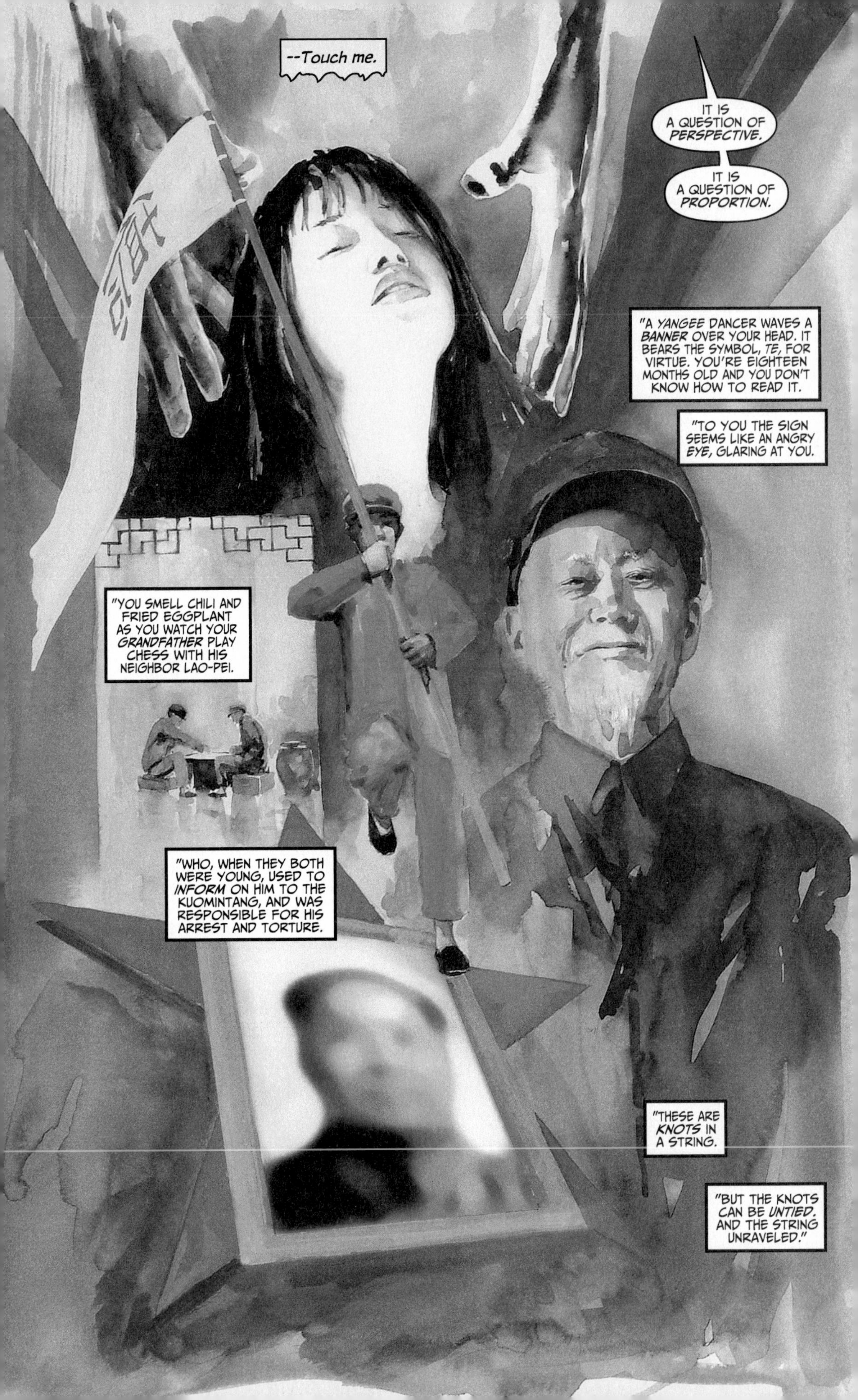
--Touch me.
IT IS A QUESTION OF *PERSPECTIVE.*
IT IS A QUESTION OF *PROPORTION.*
"A *YANGEE* DANCER WAVES A *BANNER* OVER YOUR HEAD. IT BEARS THE SYMBOL, *TE,* FOR VIRTUE. YOU'RE EIGHTEEN MONTHS OLD AND YOU DON'T KNOW HOW TO READ IT.
"TO YOU THE SIGN SEEMS LIKE AN ANGRY *EYE,* GLARING AT YOU.
"YOU SMELL CHILI AND FRIED EGGPLANT AS YOU WATCH YOUR *GRANDFATHER* PLAY CHESS WITH HIS NEIGHBOR LAO-PEI.
"WHO, WHEN THEY BOTH WERE YOUNG, USED TO *INFORM* ON HIM TO THE KUOMINTANG, AND WAS RESPONSIBLE FOR HIS ARREST AND TORTURE.
"THESE ARE *KNOTS* IN A STRING.
"BUT THE KNOTS CAN BE *UNTIED.* AND THE STRING UNRAVELED."

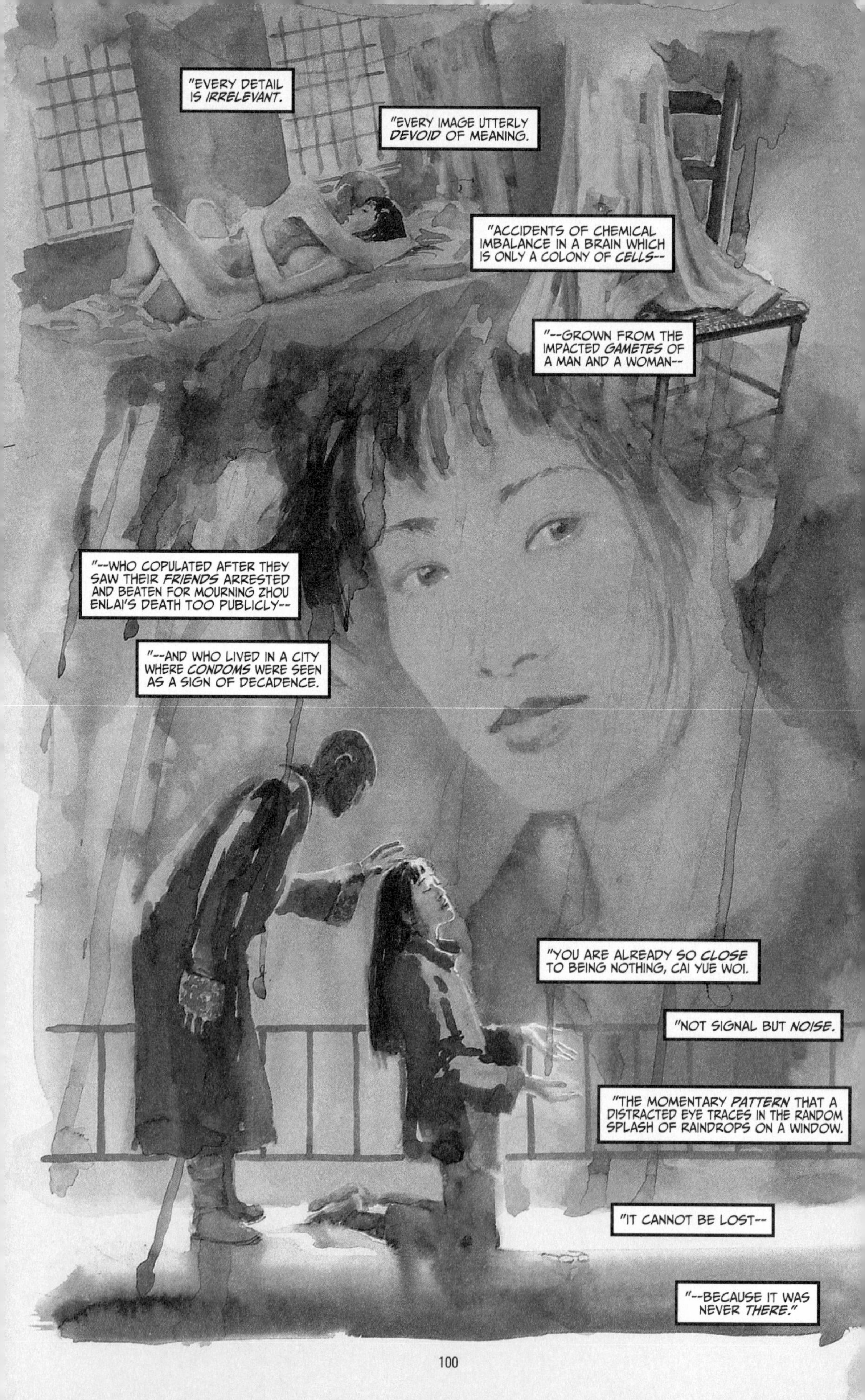
"EVERY DETAIL IS IRRELEVANT.
"EVERY IMAGE UTTERLY DEVOID OF MEANING.
"ACCIDENTS OF CHEMICAL IMBALANCE IN A BRAIN WHICH IS ONLY A COLONY OF CELLS--
"--GROWN FROM THE IMPACTED GAMETES OF A MAN AND A WOMAN--
"--WHO COPULATED AFTER THEY SAW THEIR FRIENDS ARRESTED AND BEATEN FOR MOURNING ZHOU ENLAI'S DEATH TOO PUBLICLY--
"--AND WHO LIVED IN A CITY WHERE CONDOMS WERE SEEN AS A SIGN OF DECADENCE.
"YOU ARE ALREADY SO CLOSE TO BEING NOTHING, CAI YUE WOI.
"NOT SIGNAL BUT NOISE.
"THE MOMENTARY PATTERN THAT A DISTRACTED EYE TRACES IN THE RANDOM SPLASH OF RAINDROPS ON A WINDOW.
"IT CANNOT BE LOST--
"--BECAUSE IT WAS NEVER THERE."

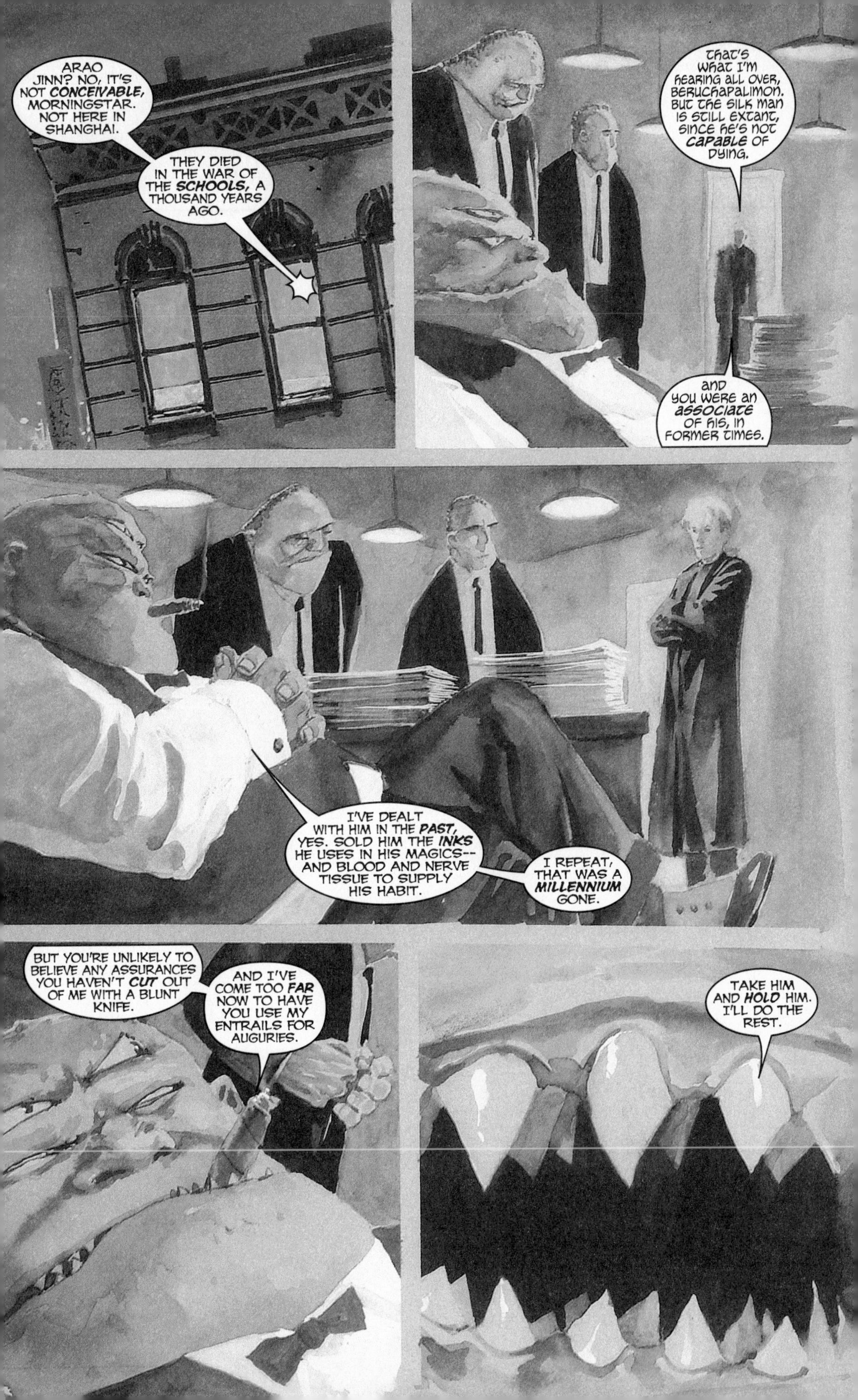
ARAO JINN? NO, IT'S NOT CONCEIVABLE, MORNINGSTAR. NOT HERE IN SHANGHAI.
THEY DIED IN THE WAR OF THE SCHOOLS, A THOUSAND YEARS AGO.
THAT'S WHAT I'M HEARING ALL OVER, BERUCHAPALIMON. BUT THE SILK MAN IS STILL EXTANT, SINCE HE'S NOT CAPABLE OF DYING.
AND YOU WERE AN ASSOCIATE OF HIS, IN FORMER TIMES.
I'VE DEALT WITH HIM IN THE PAST, YES. SOLD HIM THE INKS HE USES IN HIS MAGICS-- AND BLOOD AND NERVE TISSUE TO SUPPLY HIS HABIT.
I REPEAT, THAT WAS A MILLENNIUM GONE.
BUT YOU'RE UNLIKELY TO BELIEVE ANY ASSURANCES YOU HAVEN'T CUT OUT OF ME WITH A BLUNT KNIFE.
AND I'VE COME TOO FAR NOW TO HAVE YOU USE MY ENTRAILS FOR AUGURIES.
TAKE HIM AND HOLD HIM. I'LL DO THE REST.

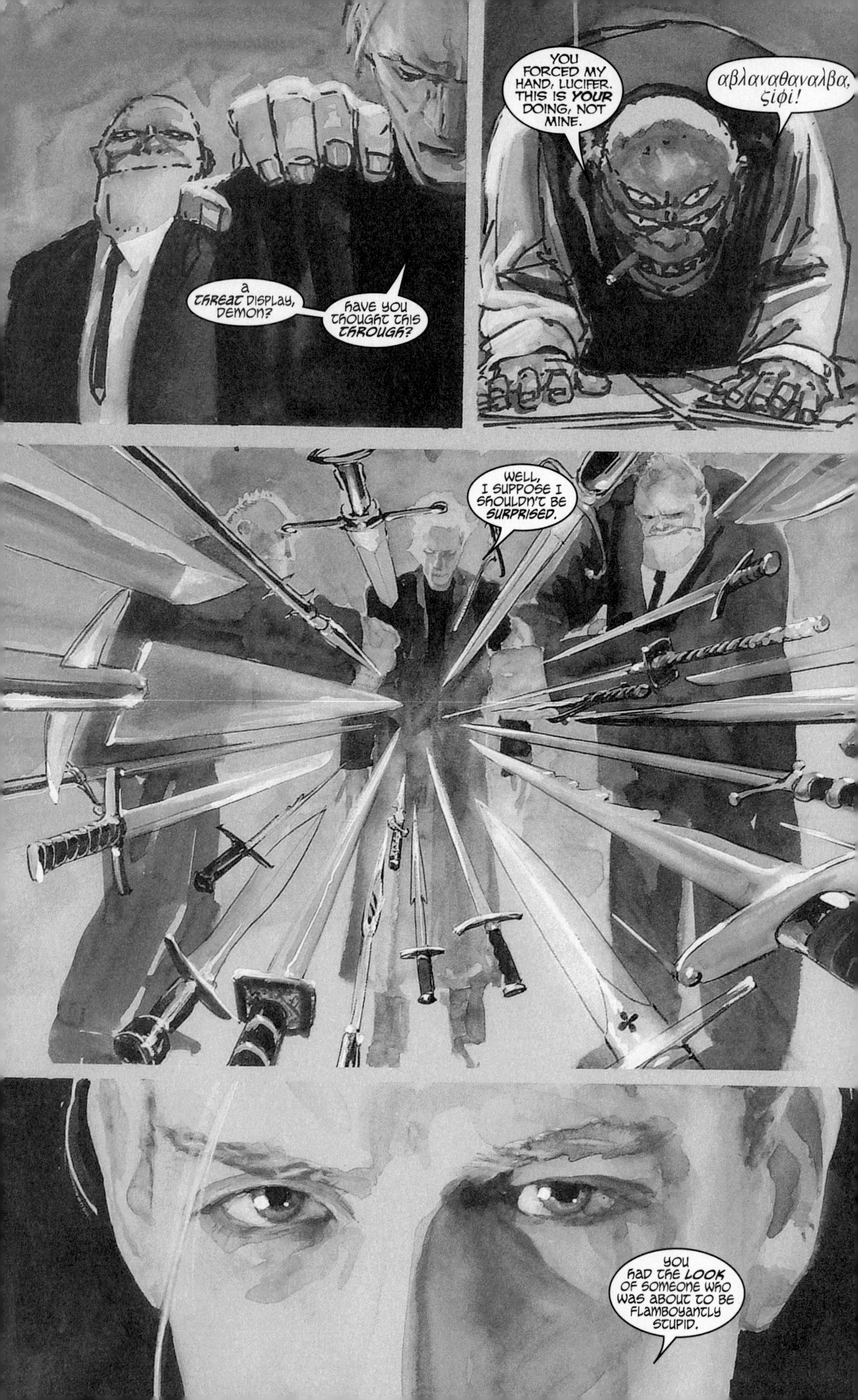

A THREAT DISPLAY, DEMON?
HAVE YOU THOUGHT THIS THROUGH?
YOU FORCED MY HAND, LUCIFER. THIS IS YOUR DOING, NOT MINE.
αβλαναθαναλβα, ζιφι!
WELL, I SUPPOSE I SHOULDN'T BE SURPRISED.
YOU HAD THE LOOK OF SOMEONE WHO WAS ABOUT TO BE FLAMBOYANTLY STUPID.

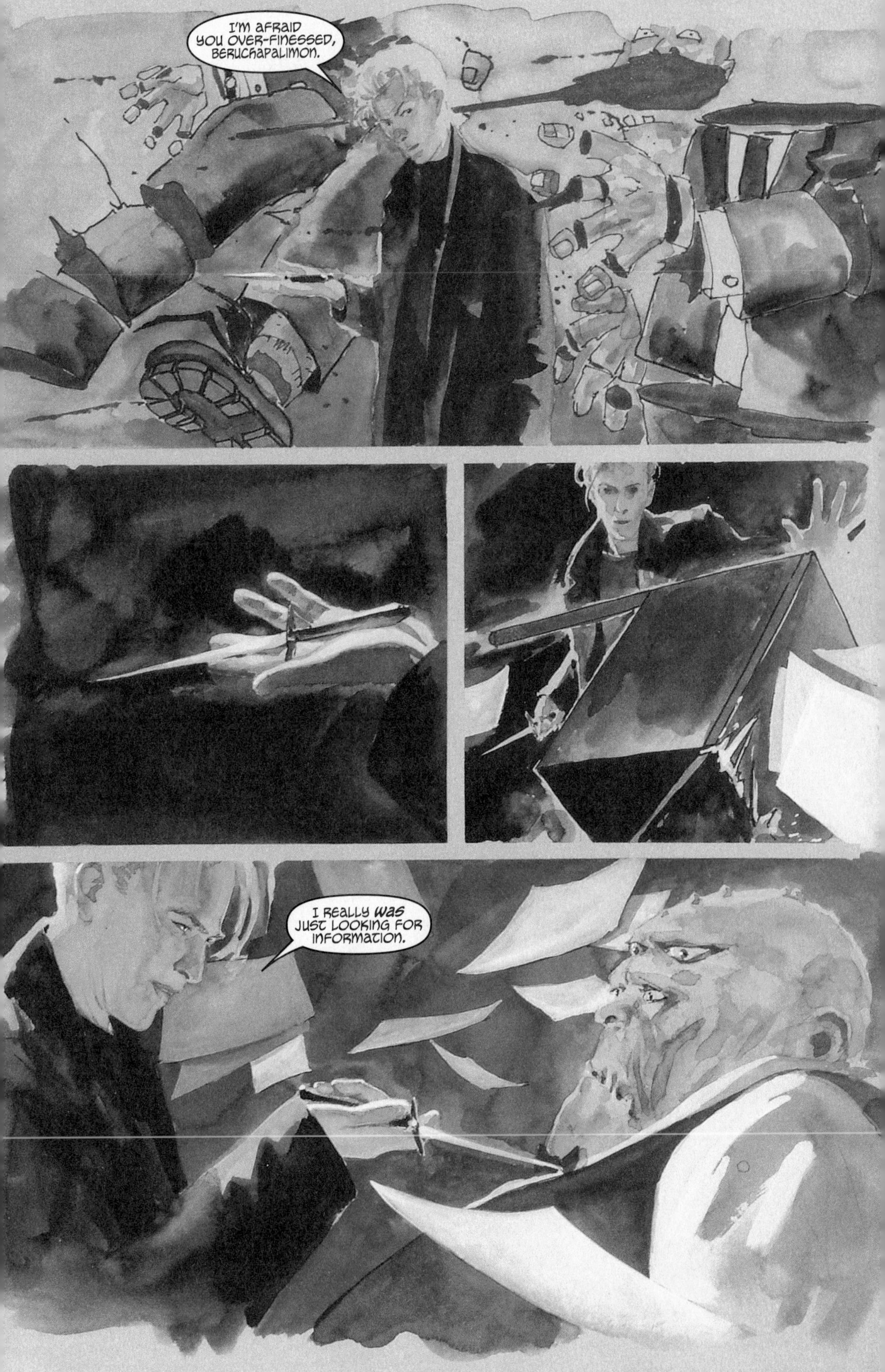
I'M AFRAID YOU OVER-FINESSED, BERUCHAPALIMON.
I REALLY *WAS* JUST LOOKING FOR INFORMATION.

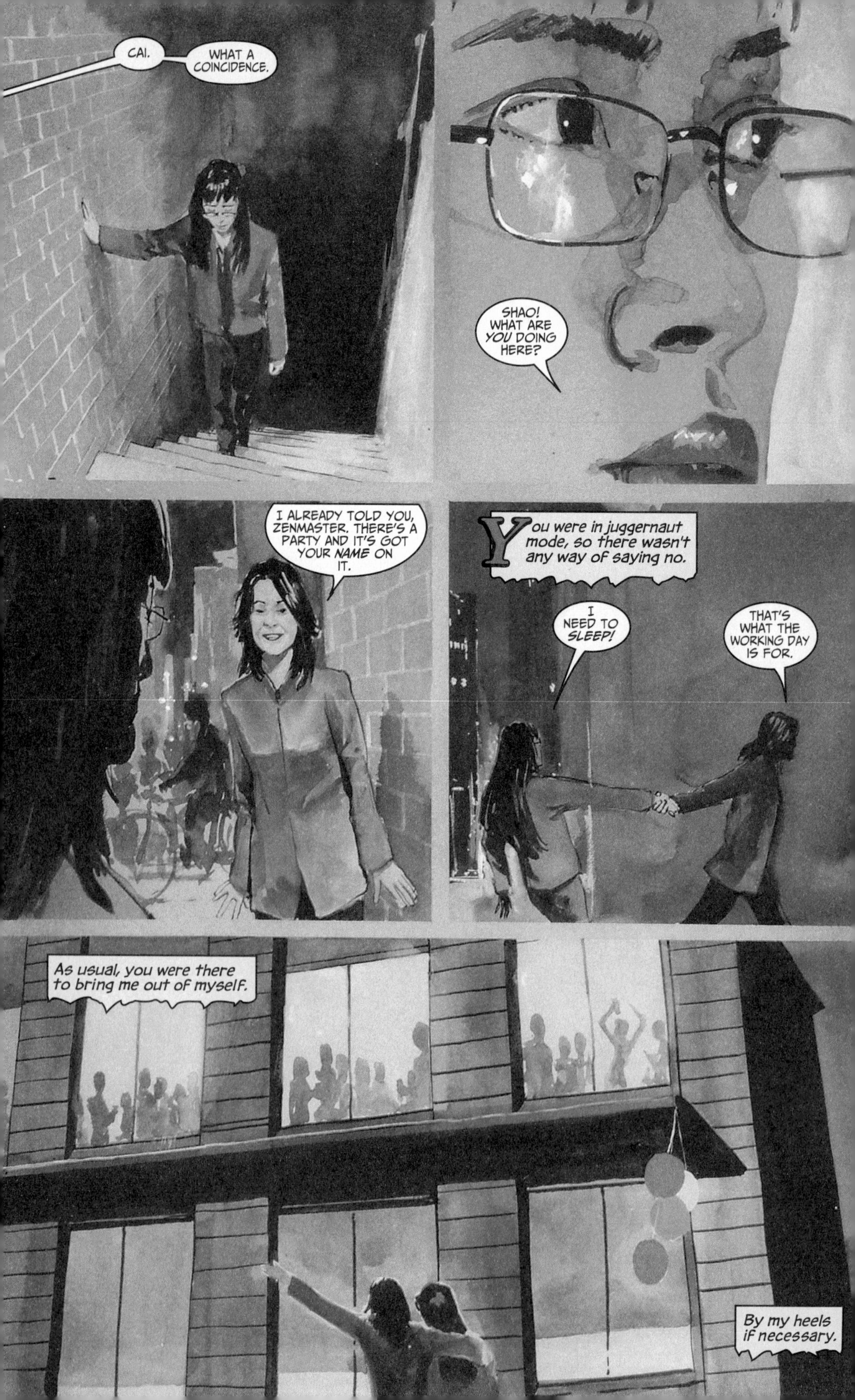
CAI.
WHAT A COINCIDENCE.
SHAO! WHAT ARE *YOU* DOING HERE?
I ALREADY TOLD YOU, ZENMASTER. THERE'S A PARTY AND IT'S GOT YOUR *NAME* ON IT.
You were in juggernaut mode, so there wasn't any way of saying no.
I NEED TO *SLEEP!*
THAT'S WHAT THE WORKING DAY IS FOR.
As usual, you were there to bring me out of myself.
By my heels if necessary.

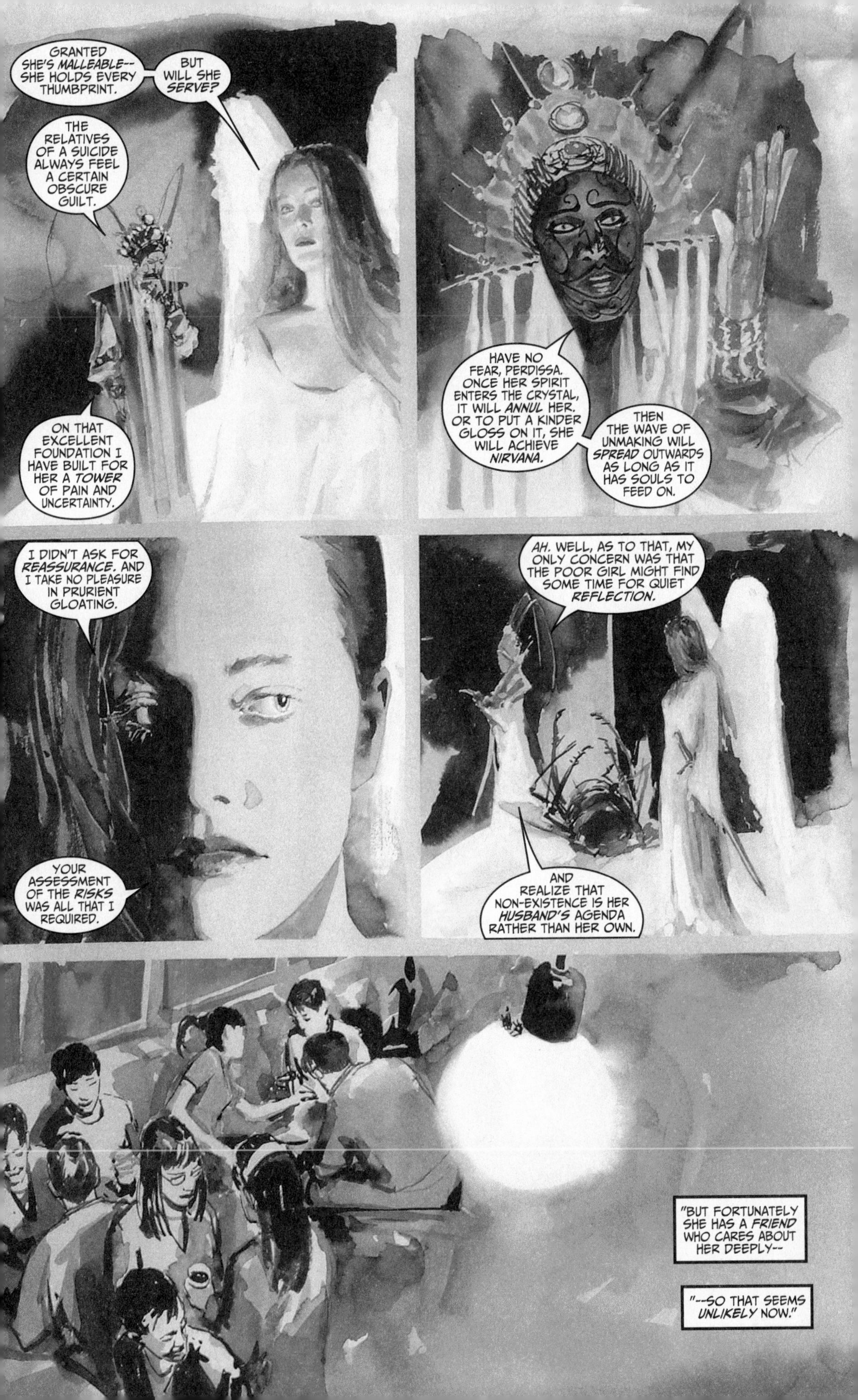
GRANTED SHE'S MALLEABLE-- SHE HOLDS EVERY THUMBPRINT.
BUT WILL SHE SERVE?
THE RELATIVES OF A SUICIDE ALWAYS FEEL A CERTAIN OBSCURE GUILT.
ON THAT EXCELLENT FOUNDATION I HAVE BUILT FOR HER A TOWER OF PAIN AND UNCERTAINTY.
HAVE NO FEAR, PERDISSA. ONCE HER SPIRIT ENTERS THE CRYSTAL, IT WILL ANNUL HER. OR TO PUT A KINDER GLOSS ON IT, SHE WILL ACHIEVE NIRVANA.
THEN THE WAVE OF UNMAKING WILL SPREAD OUTWARDS AS LONG AS IT HAS SOULS TO FEED ON.
I DIDN'T ASK FOR REASSURANCE. AND I TAKE NO PLEASURE IN PRURIENT GLOATING.
YOUR ASSESSMENT OF THE RISKS WAS ALL THAT I REQUIRED.
AH. WELL, AS TO THAT, MY ONLY CONCERN WAS THAT THE POOR GIRL MIGHT FIND SOME TIME FOR QUIET REFLECTION.
AND REALIZE THAT NON-EXISTENCE IS HER HUSBAND'S AGENDA RATHER THAN HER OWN.
"BUT FORTUNATELY SHE HAS A FRIEND WHO CARES ABOUT HER DEEPLY--
"--SO THAT SEEMS UNLIKELY NOW."

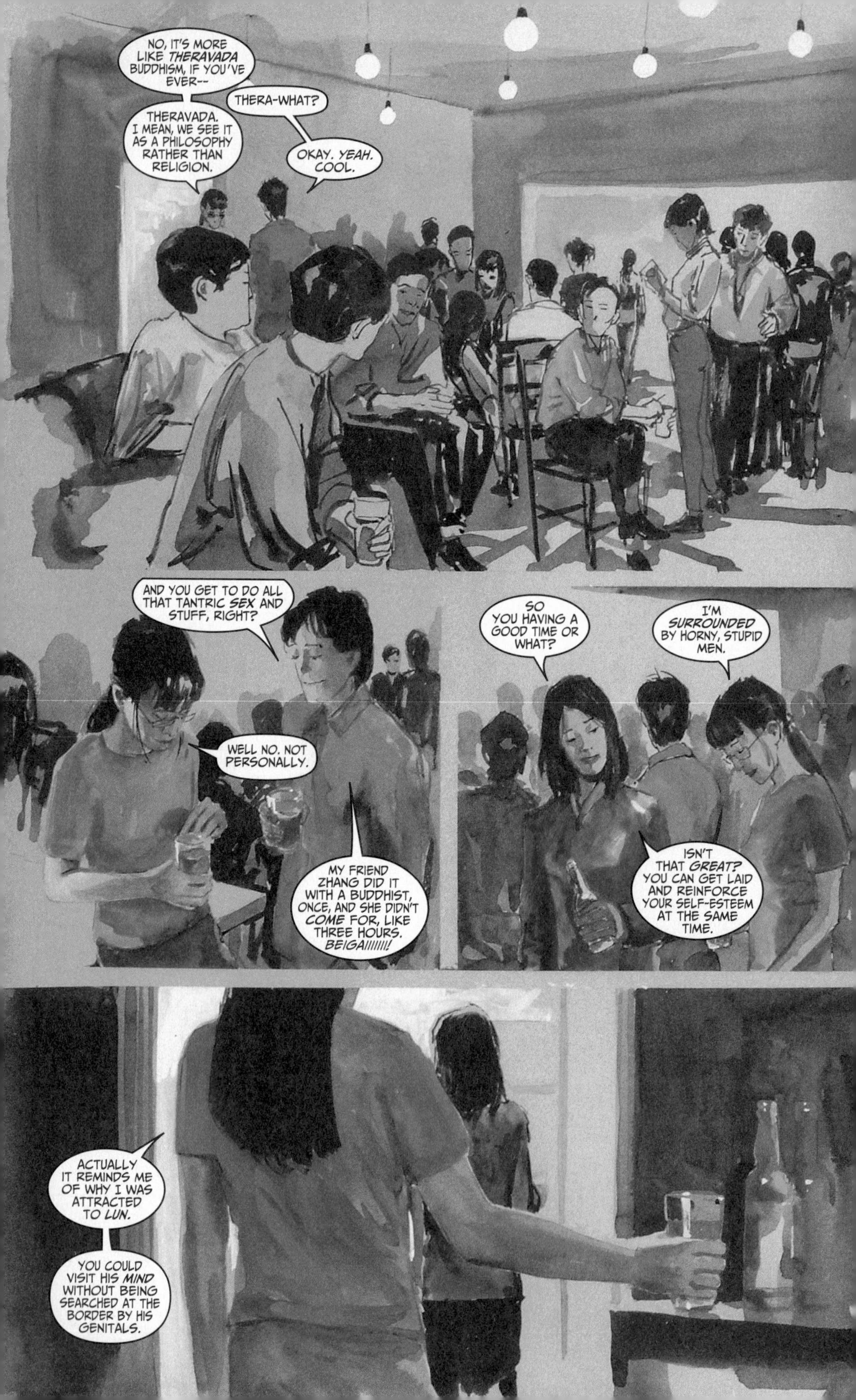

NO, IT'S MORE LIKE *THERAVADA* BUDDHISM, IF YOU'VE EVER--
THERA-WHAT?
THERAVADA. I MEAN, WE SEE IT AS A PHILOSOPHY RATHER THAN RELIGION.
OKAY. *YEAH.* COOL.
AND YOU GET TO DO ALL THAT TANTRIC *SEX* AND STUFF, RIGHT?
WELL NO. NOT PERSONALLY.
MY FRIEND ZHANG DID IT WITH A BUDDHIST, ONCE, AND SHE DIDN'T *COME* FOR, LIKE THREE HOURS. *BEIGA!!!!!!!!*
SO YOU HAVING A GOOD TIME OR WHAT?
I'M *SURROUNDED* BY HORNY, STUPID MEN.
ISN'T THAT *GREAT?* YOU CAN GET LAID AND REINFORCE YOUR SELF-ESTEEM AT THE SAME TIME.
ACTUALLY IT REMINDS ME OF WHY I WAS ATTRACTED TO *LUN.*
YOU COULD VISIT HIS *MIND* WITHOUT BEING SEARCHED AT THE BORDER BY HIS GENITALS.

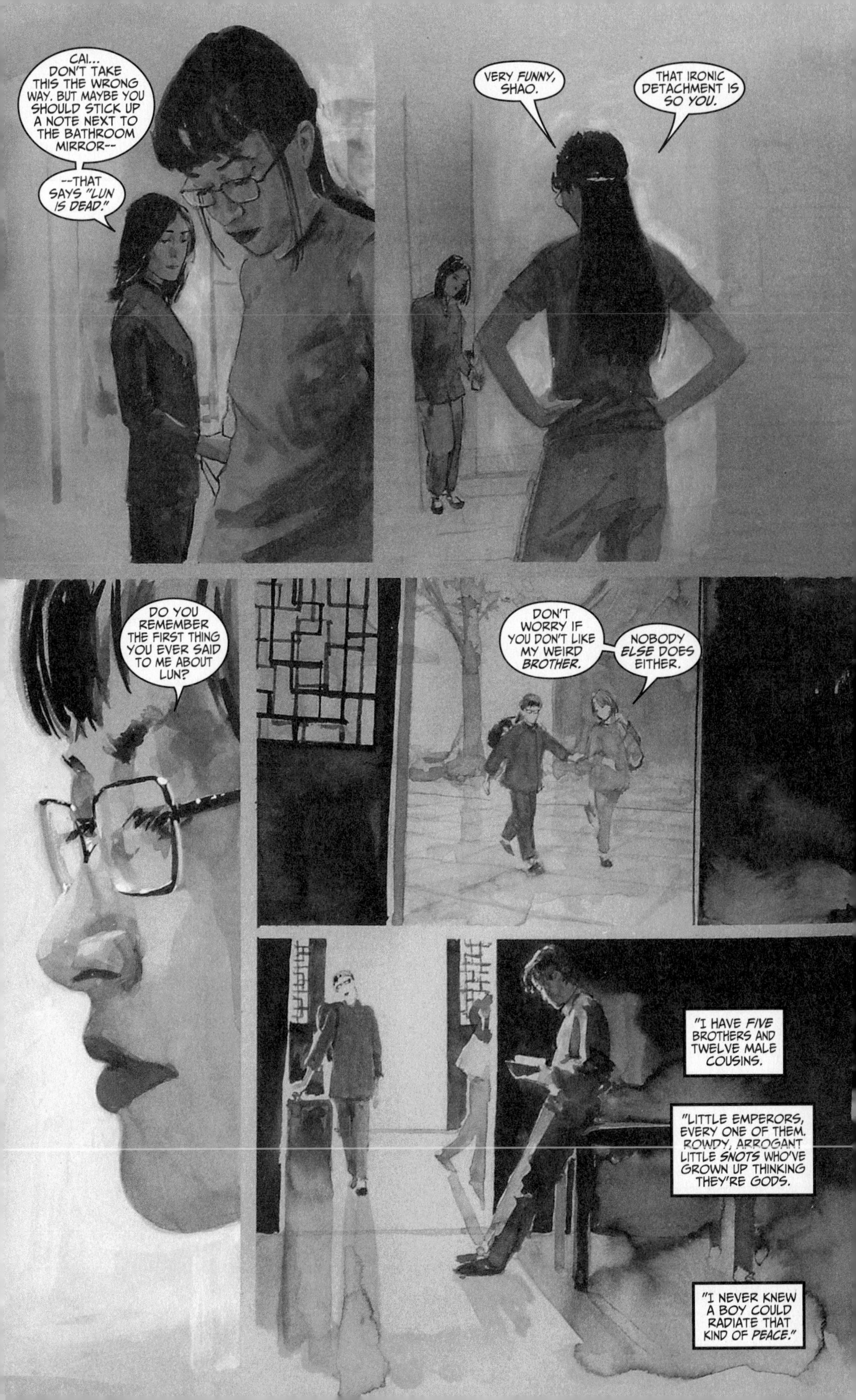

CAI... DON'T TAKE THIS THE WRONG WAY. BUT MAYBE YOU SHOULD STICK UP A NOTE NEXT TO THE BATHROOM MIRROR--
--THAT SAYS "LUN IS DEAD."
VERY FUNNY, SHAO.
THAT IRONIC DETACHMENT IS SO YOU.
DO YOU REMEMBER THE FIRST THING YOU EVER SAID TO ME ABOUT LUN?
DON'T WORRY IF YOU DON'T LIKE MY WEIRD BROTHER.
NOBODY ELSE DOES EITHER.
"I HAVE FIVE BROTHERS AND TWELVE MALE COUSINS.
"LITTLE EMPERORS, EVERY ONE OF THEM. ROWDY, ARROGANT LITTLE SNOTS WHO'VE GROWN UP THINKING THEY'RE GODS.
"I NEVER KNEW A BOY COULD RADIATE THAT KIND OF PEACE."

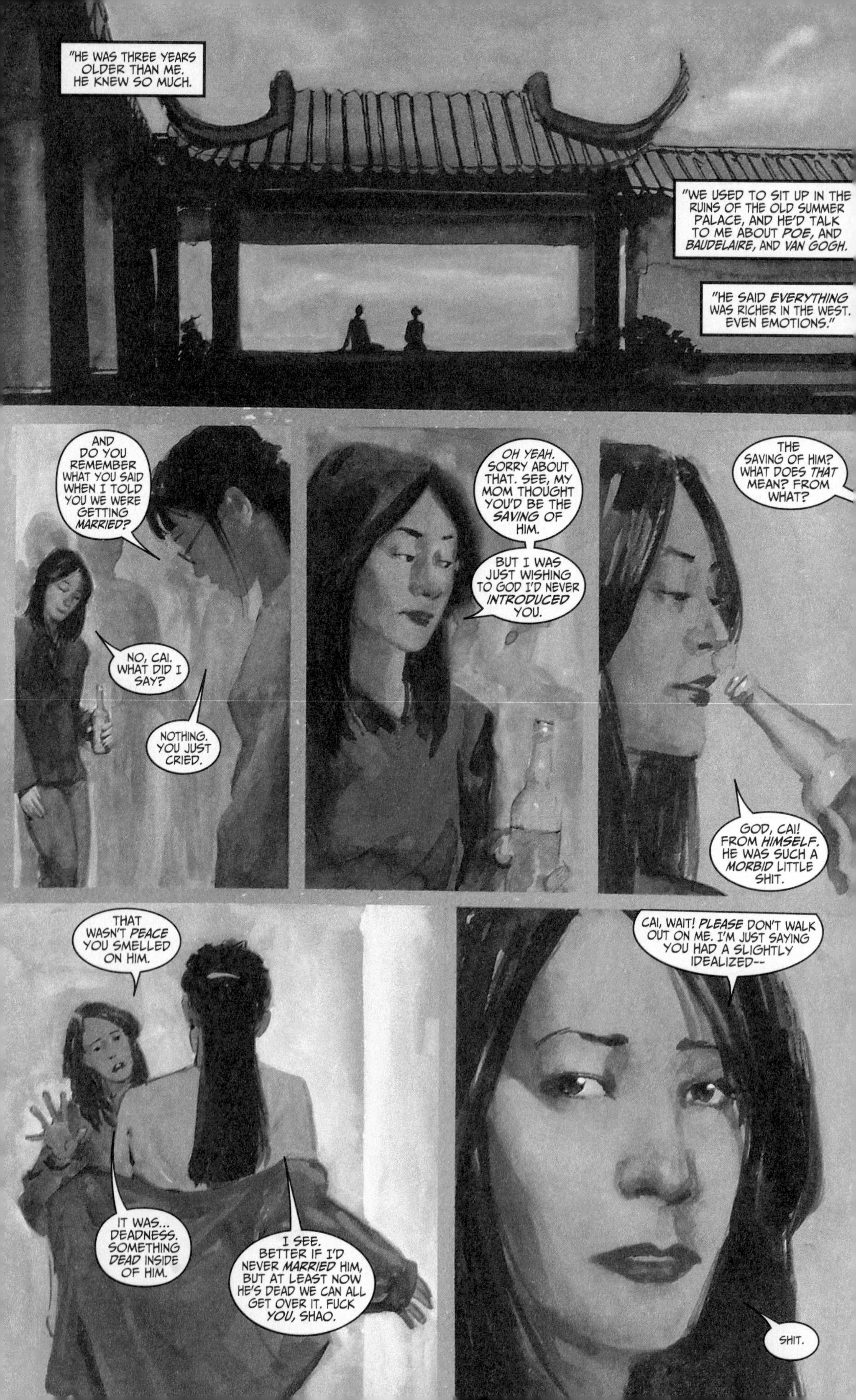
"HE WAS THREE YEARS OLDER THAN ME. HE KNEW SO MUCH.
"WE USED TO SIT UP IN THE RUINS OF THE OLD SUMMER PALACE, AND HE'D TALK TO ME ABOUT POE, AND BAUDELAIRE, AND VAN GOGH.
"HE SAID EVERYTHING WAS RICHER IN THE WEST. EVEN EMOTIONS."
AND DO YOU REMEMBER WHAT YOU SAID WHEN I TOLD YOU WE WERE GETTING MARRIED?
NO, CAI. WHAT DID I SAY?
NOTHING. YOU JUST CRIED.
OH YEAH. SORRY ABOUT THAT. SEE, MY MOM THOUGHT YOU'D BE THE SAVING OF HIM.
BUT I WAS JUST WISHING TO GOD I'D NEVER INTRODUCED YOU.
THE SAVING OF HIM? WHAT DOES THAT MEAN? FROM WHAT?
GOD, CAI! FROM HIMSELF. HE WAS SUCH A MORBID LITTLE SHIT.
THAT WASN'T PEACE YOU SMELLED ON HIM.
IT WAS... DEADNESS. SOMETHING DEAD INSIDE OF HIM.
I SEE. BETTER IF I'D NEVER MARRIED HIM, BUT AT LEAST NOW HE'S DEAD WE CAN ALL GET OVER IT. FUCK YOU, SHAO.
CAI, WAIT! PLEASE DON'T WALK OUT ON ME. I'M JUST SAYING YOU HAD A SLIGHTLY IDEALIZED--
SHIT.

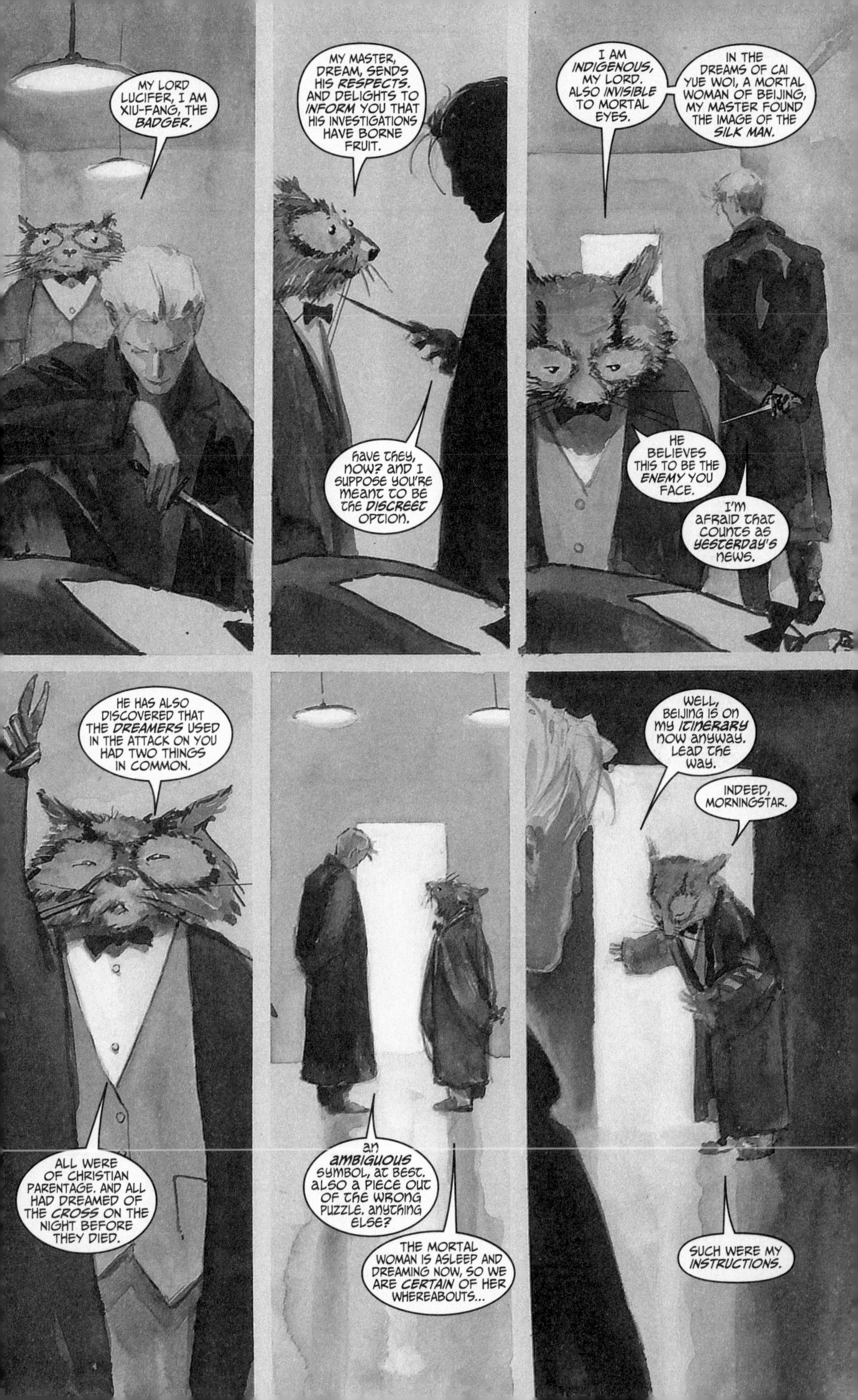
MY LORD LUCIFER, I AM XIU-FANG, THE BADGER.
MY MASTER, DREAM, SENDS HIS RESPECTS. AND DELIGHTS TO INFORM YOU THAT HIS INVESTIGATIONS HAVE BORNE FRUIT.
have they, now? and I suppose you're meant to be the discreet option.
I AM INDIGENOUS, MY LORD. ALSO INVISIBLE TO MORTAL EYES.
IN THE DREAMS OF CAI YUE WOI, A MORTAL WOMAN OF BEIJING, MY MASTER FOUND THE IMAGE OF THE SILK MAN.
HE BELIEVES THIS TO BE THE ENEMY YOU FACE.
I'm afraid that counts as yesterday's news.
HE HAS ALSO DISCOVERED THAT THE DREAMERS USED IN THE ATTACK ON YOU HAD TWO THINGS IN COMMON.
ALL WERE OF CHRISTIAN PARENTAGE. AND ALL HAD DREAMED OF THE CROSS ON THE NIGHT BEFORE THEY DIED.
an ambiguous symbol, at best. also a piece out of the wrong puzzle. anything else?
THE MORTAL WOMAN IS ASLEEP AND DREAMING NOW, SO WE ARE CERTAIN OF HER WHEREABOUTS...
well, beijing is on my itinerary now anyway. lead the way.
INDEED, MORNINGSTAR.
SUCH WERE MY INSTRUCTIONS.

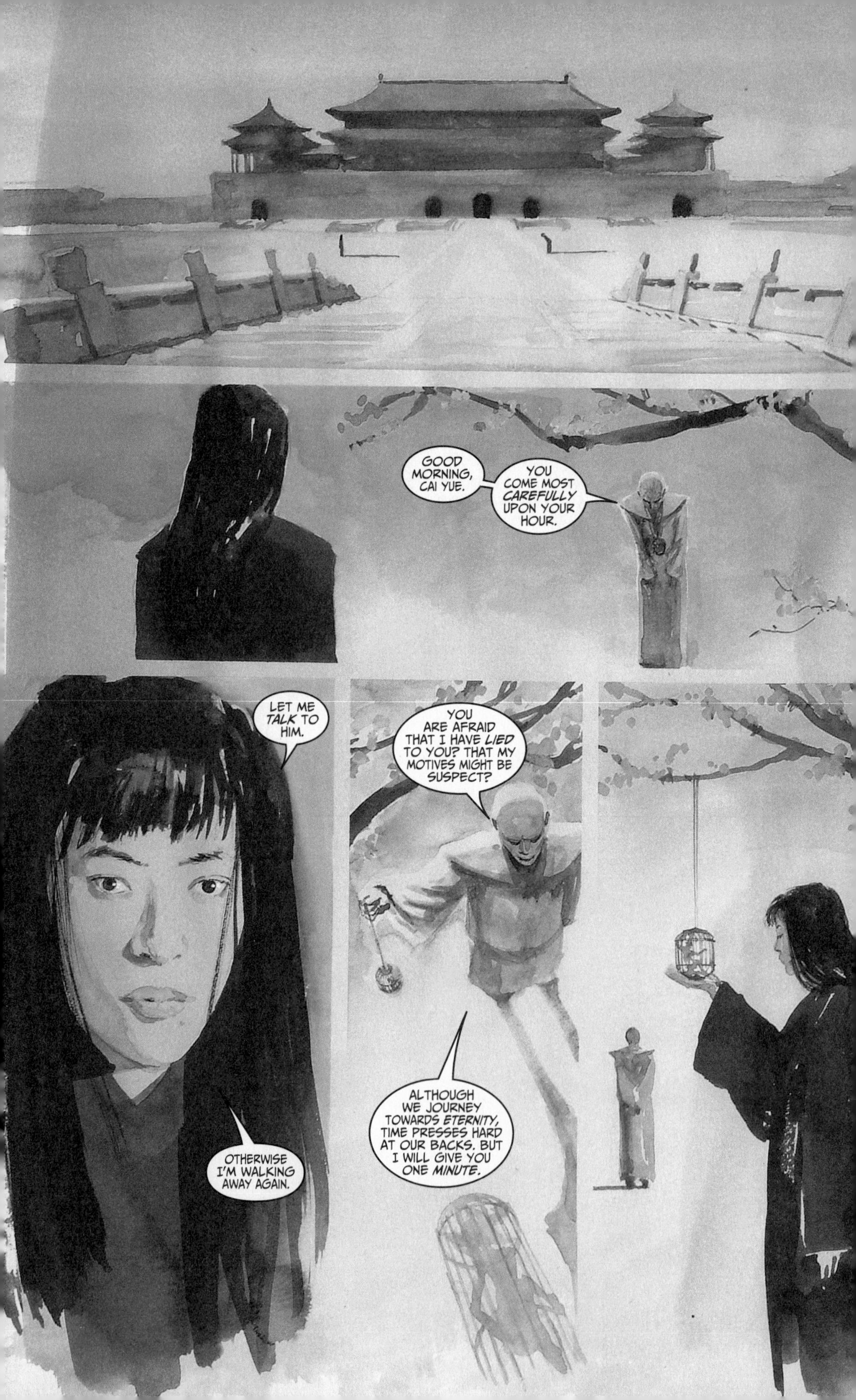
GOOD MORNING, CAI YUE.
YOU COME MOST CAREFULLY UPON YOUR HOUR.
LET ME TALK TO HIM.
OTHERWISE I'M WALKING AWAY AGAIN.
YOU ARE AFRAID THAT I HAVE LIED TO YOU? THAT MY MOTIVES MIGHT BE SUSPECT?
ALTHOUGH WE JOURNEY TOWARDS ETERNITY, TIME PRESSES HARD AT OUR BACKS. BUT I WILL GIVE YOU ONE MINUTE.

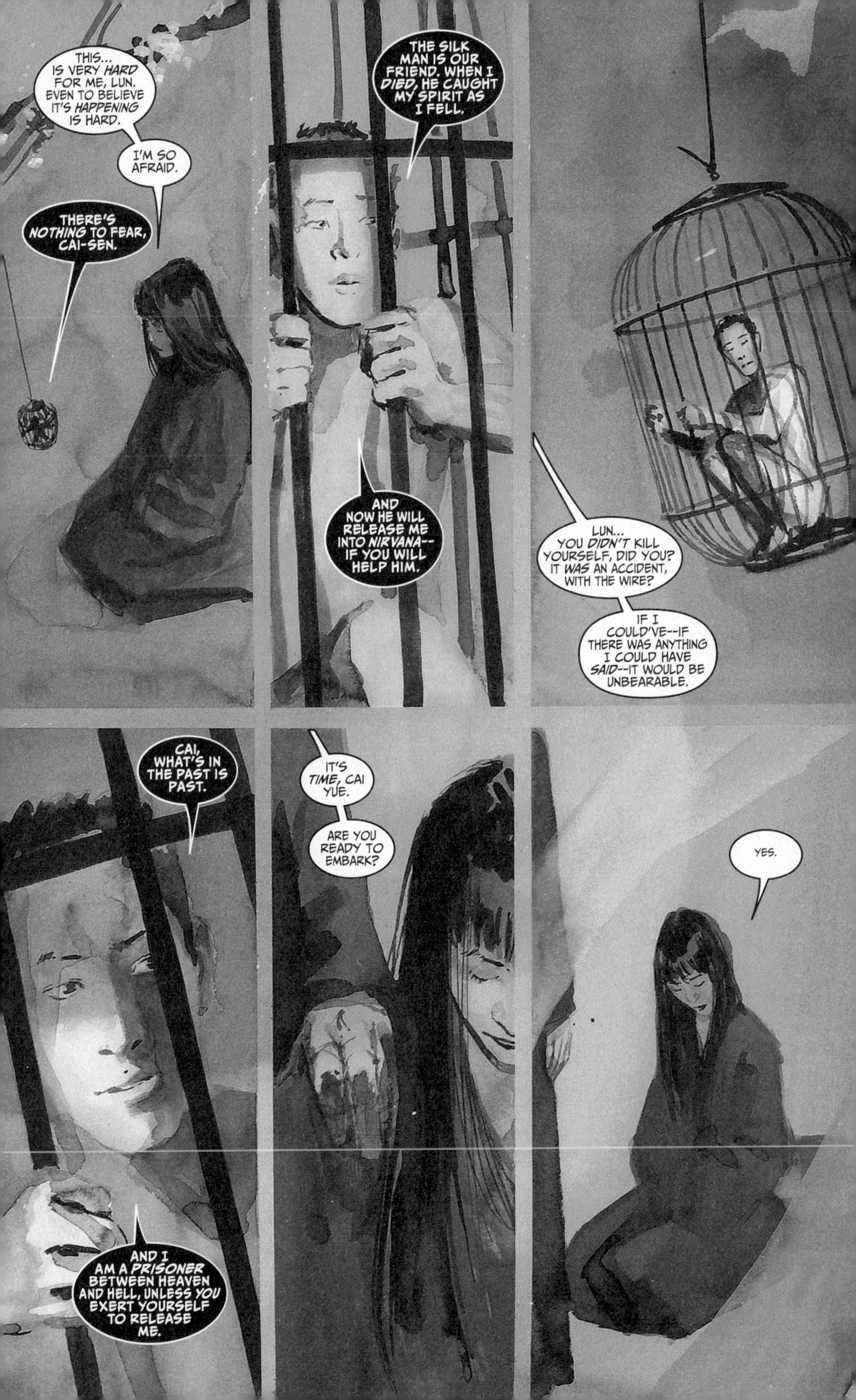
THIS... IS VERY HARD FOR ME, LUN. EVEN TO BELIEVE IT'S HAPPENING IS HARD.
I'M SO AFRAID.
THERE'S NOTHING TO FEAR, CAI-SEN.
THE SILK MAN IS OUR FRIEND. WHEN I DIED, HE CAUGHT MY SPIRIT AS I FELL.
AND NOW HE WILL RELEASE ME INTO NIRVANA-- IF YOU WILL HELP HIM.
LUN... YOU DIDN'T KILL YOURSELF, DID YOU? IT WAS AN ACCIDENT, WITH THE WIRE?
IF I COULD'VE--IF THERE WAS ANYTHING I COULD HAVE SAID--IT WOULD BE UNBEARABLE.
CAI, WHAT'S IN THE PAST IS PAST.
AND I AM A PRISONER BETWEEN HEAVEN AND HELL, UNLESS YOU EXERT YOURSELF TO RELEASE ME.
IT'S TIME, CAI YUE.
ARE YOU READY TO EMBARK?
YES.

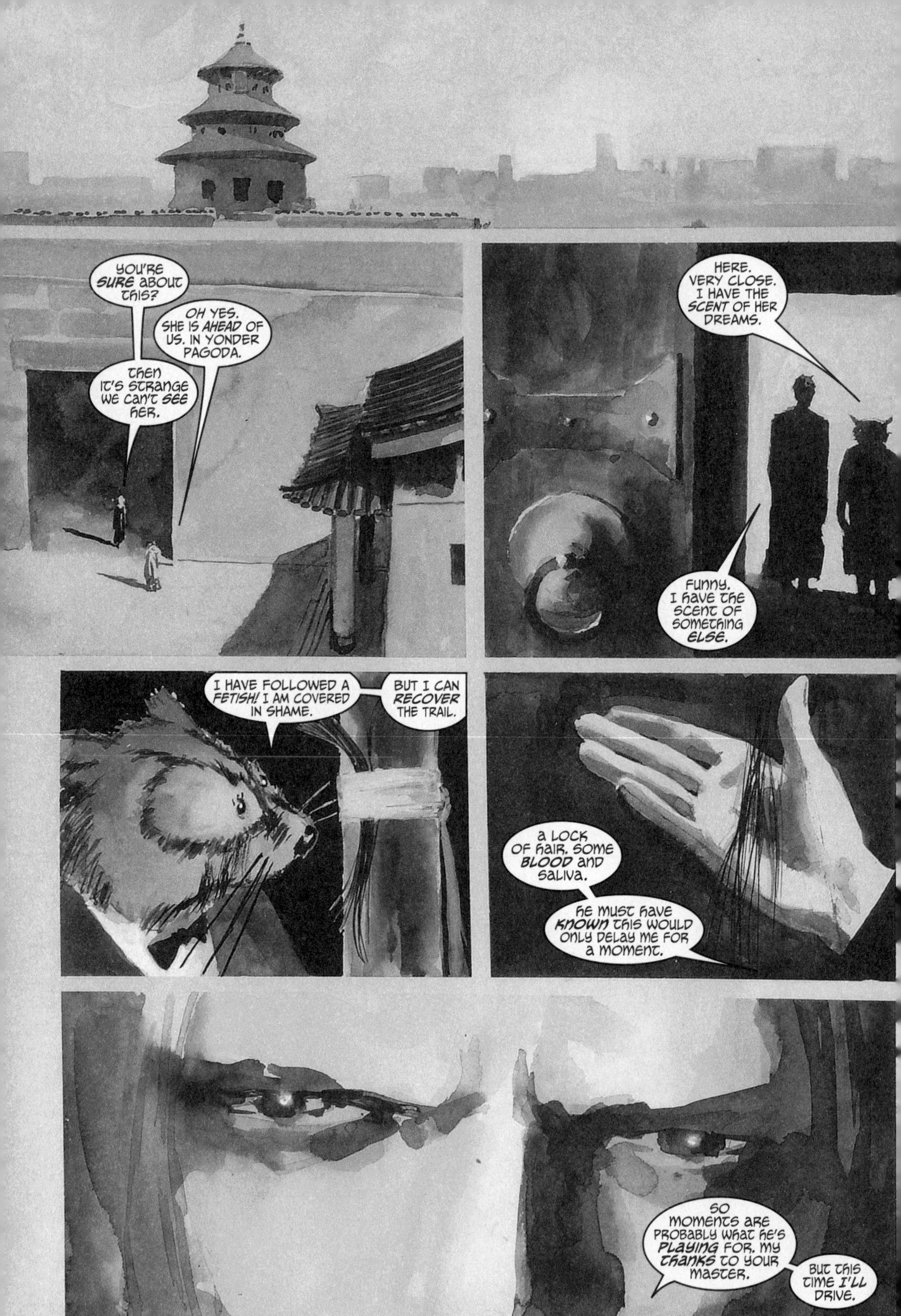
YOU'RE SURE ABOUT THIS?
OH YES. SHE IS AHEAD OF US. IN YONDER PAGODA.
THEN IT'S STRANGE WE CAN'T SEE HER.
HERE. VERY CLOSE. I HAVE THE SCENT OF HER DREAMS.
FUNNY. I HAVE THE SCENT OF SOMETHING ELSE.
I HAVE FOLLOWED A FETISH! I AM COVERED IN SHAME.
BUT I CAN RECOVER THE TRAIL.
A LOCK OF HAIR. SOME BLOOD AND SALIVA.
HE MUST HAVE KNOWN THIS WOULD ONLY DELAY ME FOR A MOMENT.
SO MOMENTS ARE PROBABLY WHAT HE'S PLAYING FOR. MY THANKS TO YOUR MASTER.
BUT THIS TIME I'LL DRIVE.

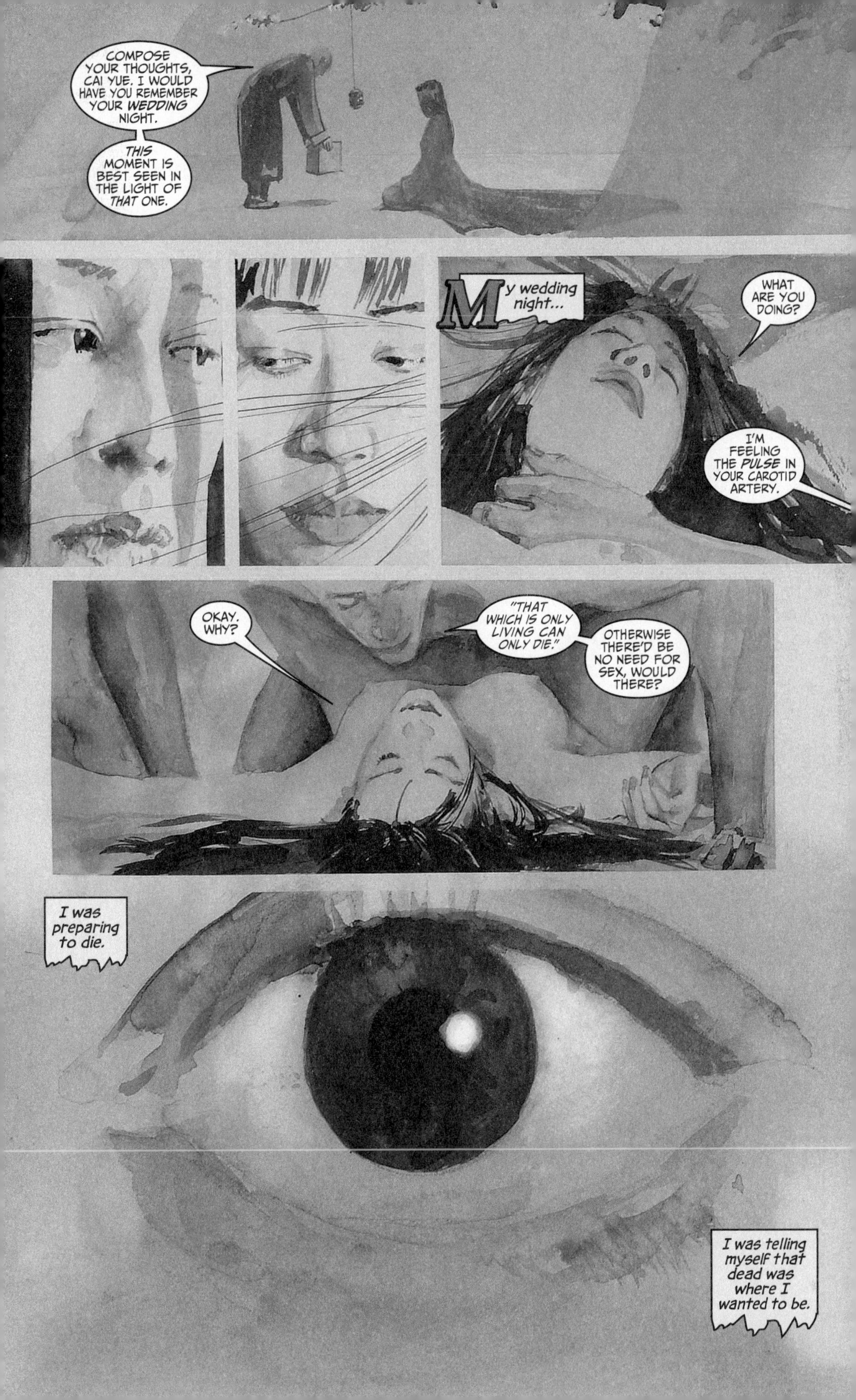
COMPOSE YOUR THOUGHTS, CAI YUE. I WOULD HAVE YOU REMEMBER YOUR *WEDDING* NIGHT.
THIS MOMENT IS BEST SEEN IN THE LIGHT OF *THAT* ONE.
My wedding night...
WHAT ARE YOU DOING?
I'M FEELING THE *PULSE* IN YOUR CAROTID ARTERY.
OKAY. WHY?
"THAT WHICH IS ONLY LIVING CAN ONLY DIE."
OTHERWISE THERE'D BE NO NEED FOR SEX, WOULD THERE?
I was preparing to die.
I was telling myself that dead was where I wanted to be.

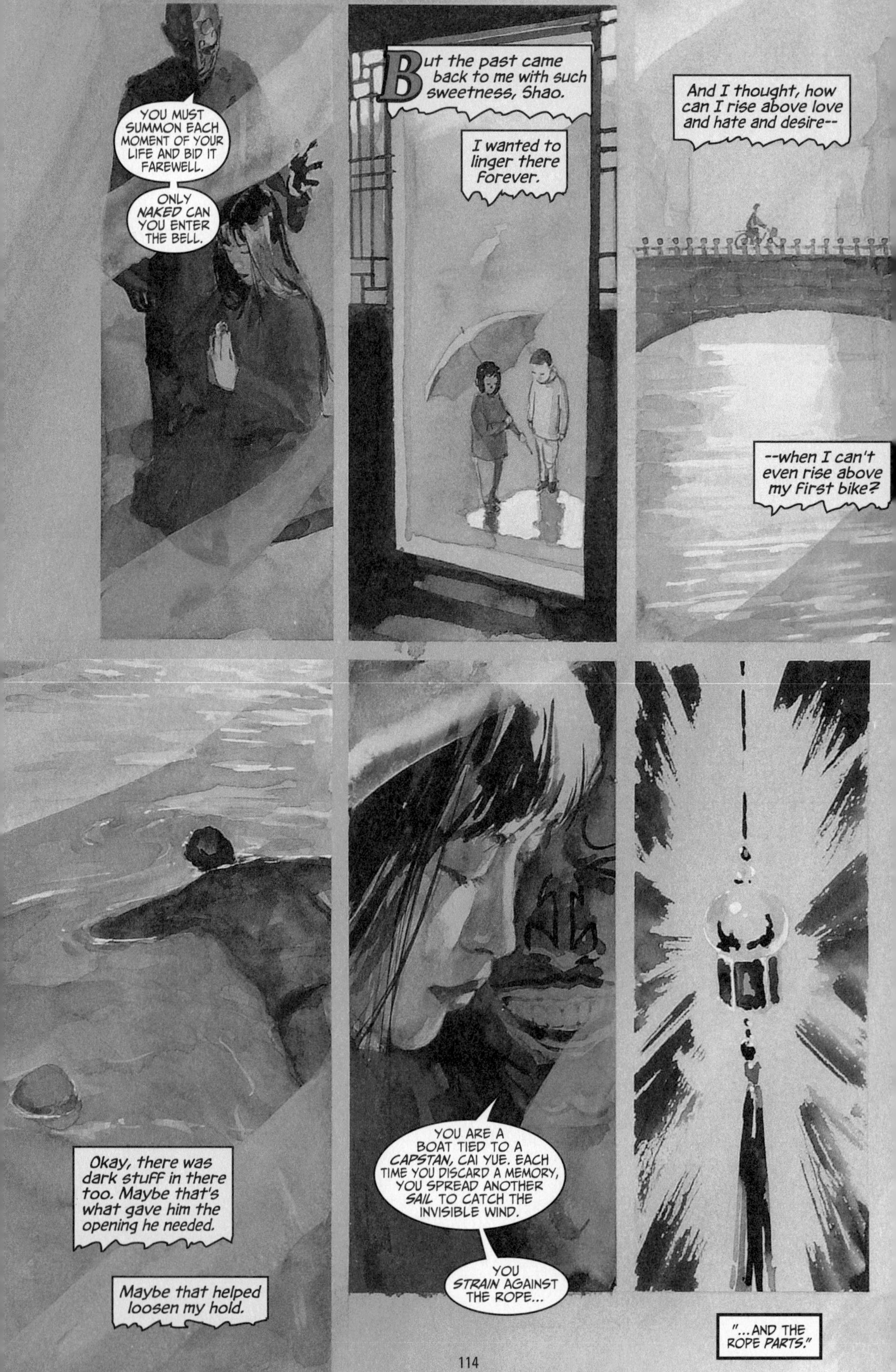
YOU MUST SUMMON EACH MOMENT OF YOUR LIFE AND BID IT FAREWELL.
ONLY NAKED CAN YOU ENTER THE BELL.
But the past came back to me with such sweetness, Shao.
I wanted to linger there forever.
And I thought, how can I rise above love and hate and desire--
--when I can't even rise above my first bike?
Okay, there was dark stuff in there too. Maybe that's what gave him the opening he needed.
Maybe that helped loosen my hold.
YOU ARE A BOAT TIED TO A CAPSTAN, CAI YUE. EACH TIME YOU DISCARD A MEMORY, YOU SPREAD ANOTHER SAIL TO CATCH THE INVISIBLE WIND.
YOU STRAIN AGAINST THE ROPE...
"...AND THE ROPE PARTS."

YOU'RE A VERY LONG WAY FROM *HOME*, SILK MAN.

I'LL TRY TO *SPARE* YOU THE LONG WALK BACK.

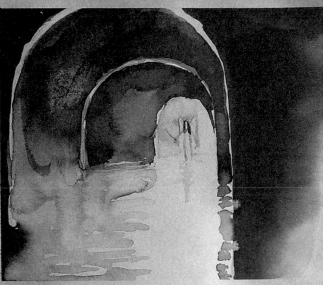

I'M SORRY, SIR. YOU CAN'T COME THROUGH HERE.

THE GATE IS UNDER REPAIR.

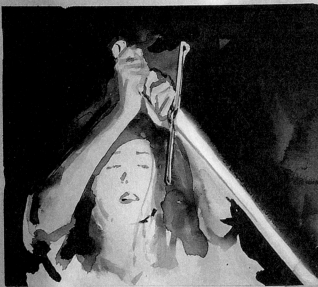

PLAYING FOR MOMENTS.

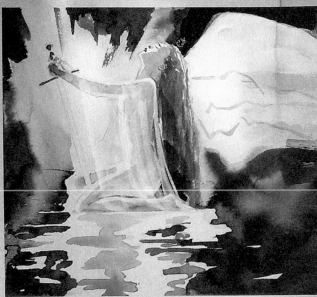

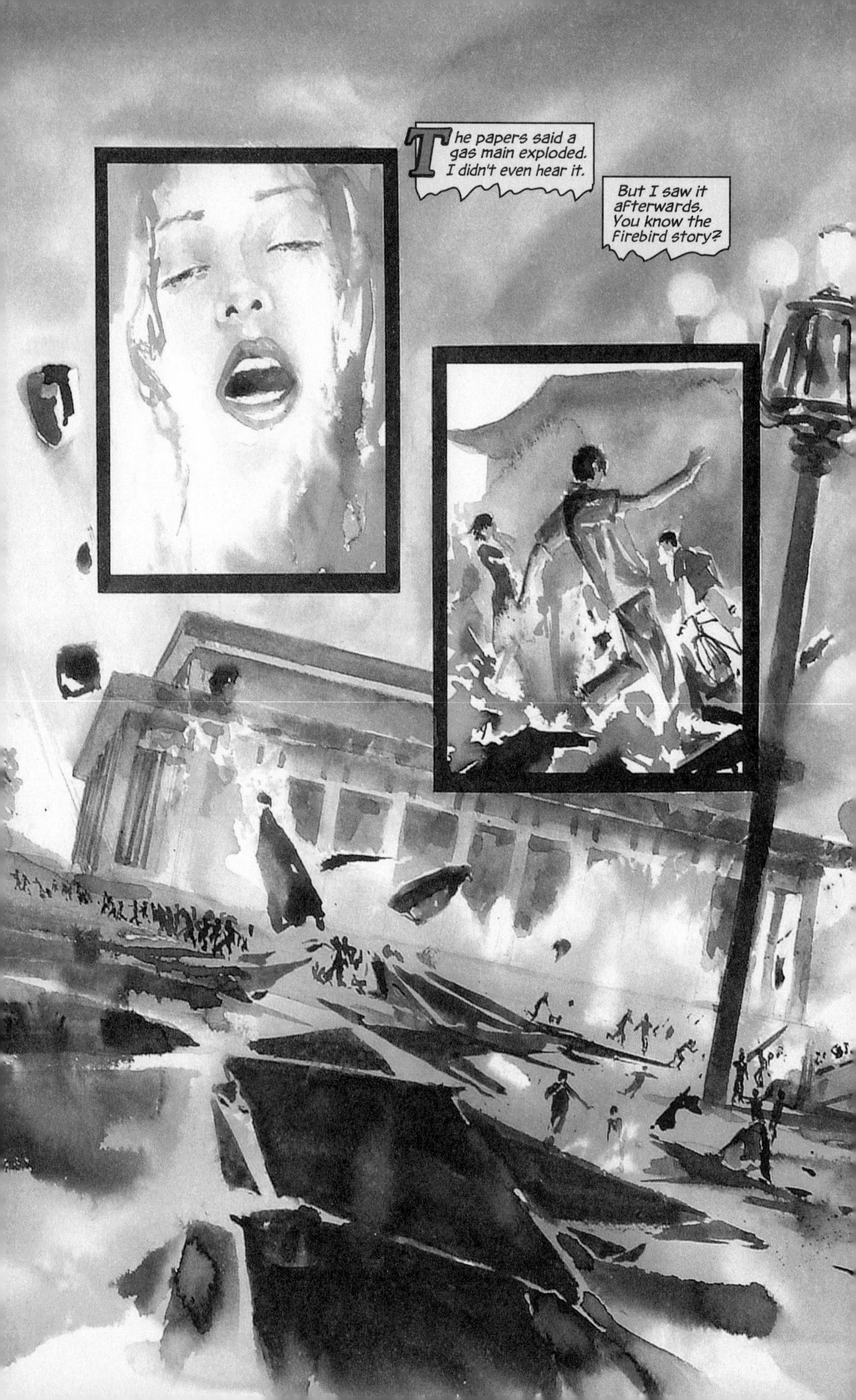
The papers said a gas main exploded. I didn't even hear it.
But I saw it afterwards. You know the Firebird story?

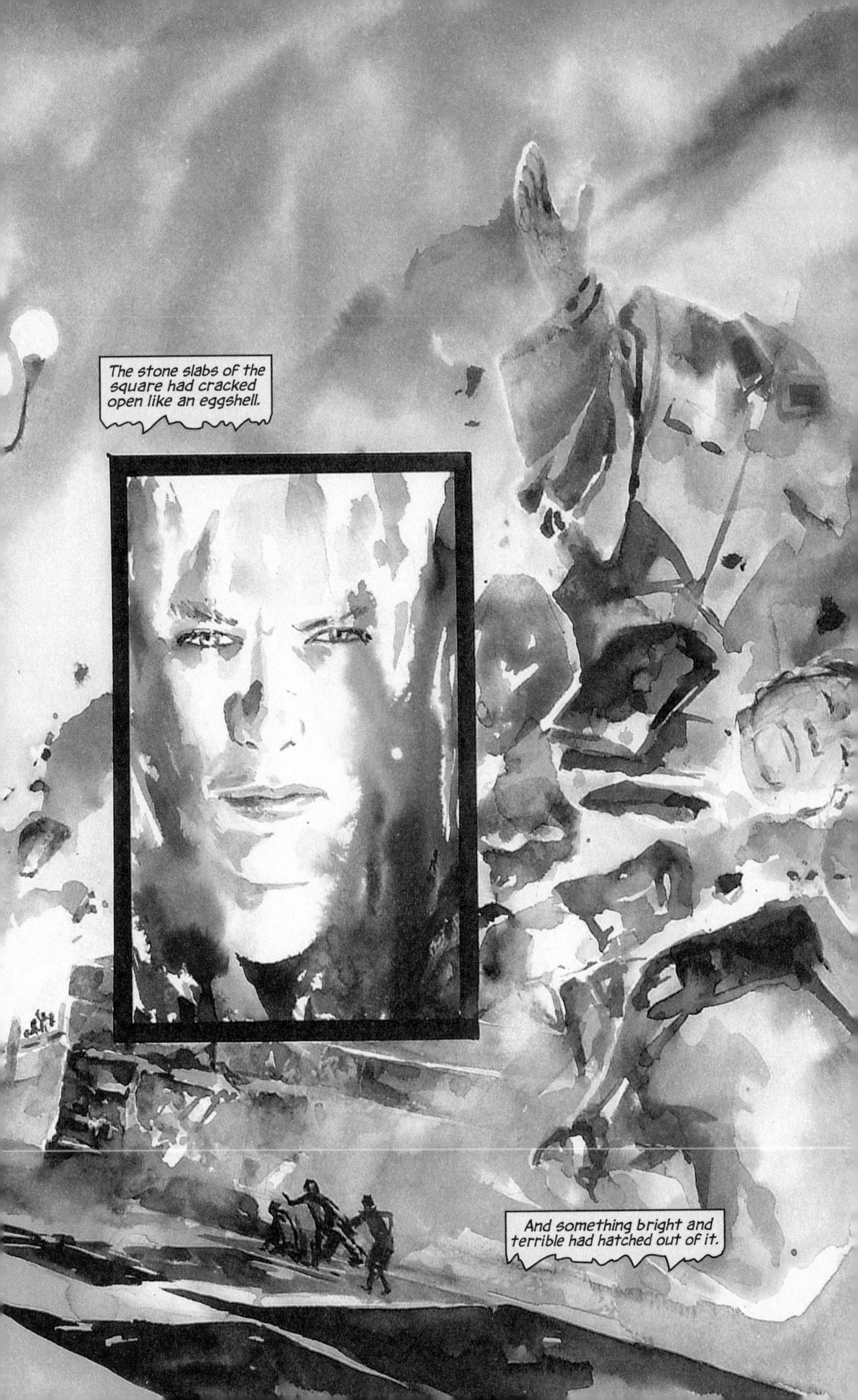
The stone slabs of the square had cracked open like an eggshell.
And something bright and terrible had hatched out of it.

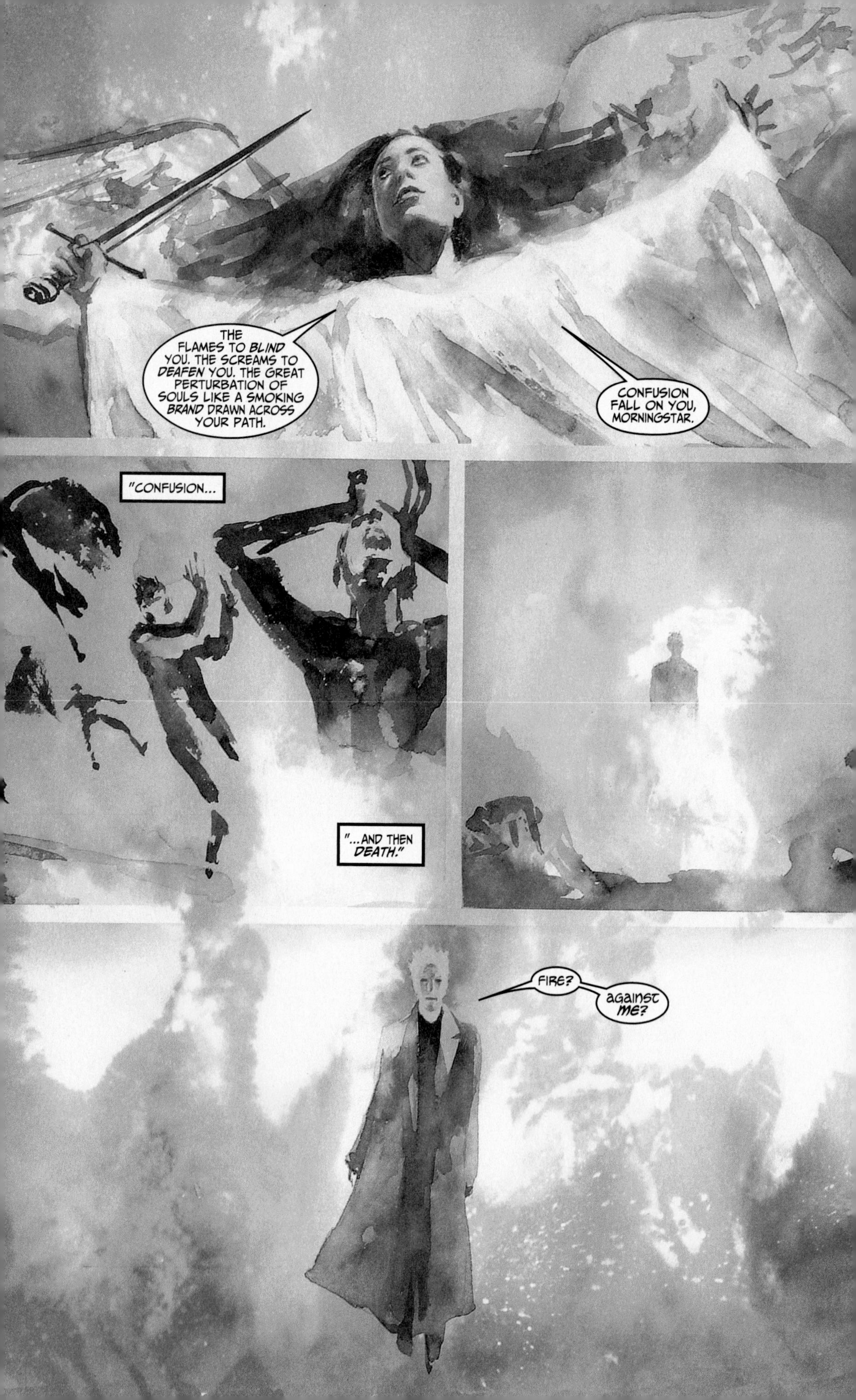
THE FLAMES TO BLIND YOU. THE SCREAMS TO DEAFEN YOU. THE GREAT PERTURBATION OF SOULS LIKE A SMOKING BRAND DRAWN ACROSS YOUR PATH.
CONFUSION FALL ON YOU, MORNINGSTAR.
"CONFUSION...
"...AND THEN DEATH."
FIRE?
against me?

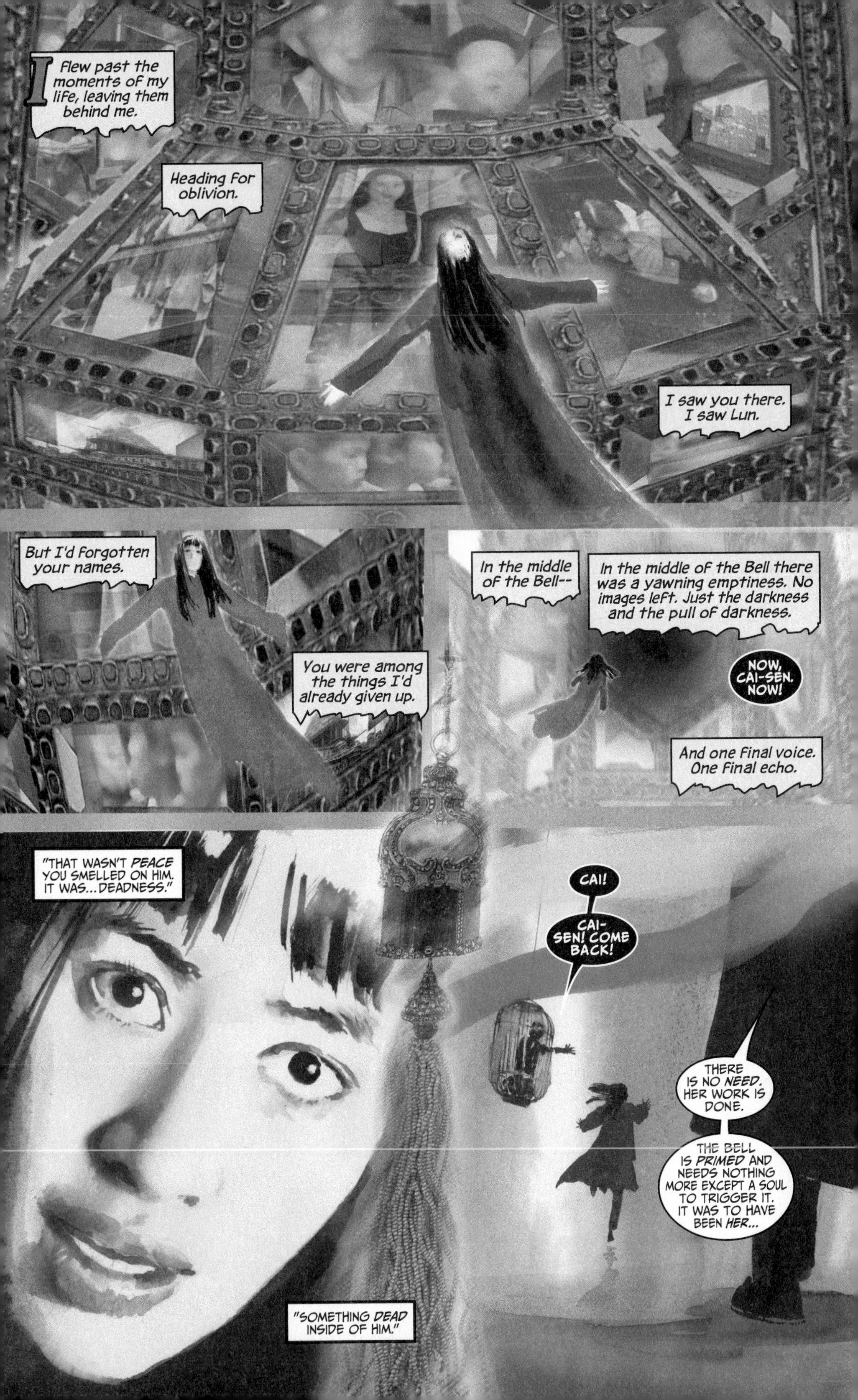
I Flew past the moments of my life, leaving them behind me.
Heading For oblivion.
I saw you there. I saw Lun.
But I'd Forgotten your names.
You were among the things I'd already given up.
In the middle of the Bell--
In the middle of the Bell there was a yawning emptiness. No images left. Just the darkness and the pull of darkness.
NOW, CAI-SEN. NOW!
And one Final voice. One Final echo.
"THAT WASN'T *PEACE* YOU SMELLED ON HIM. IT WAS...DEADNESS."
CAI!
CAI-SEN! COME BACK!
THERE IS NO *NEED*. HER WORK IS DONE.
THE BELL IS *PRIMED* AND NEEDS NOTHING MORE EXCEPT A SOUL TO TRIGGER IT. IT WAS TO HAVE BEEN *HER*...
"SOMETHING *DEAD* INSIDE OF HIM."

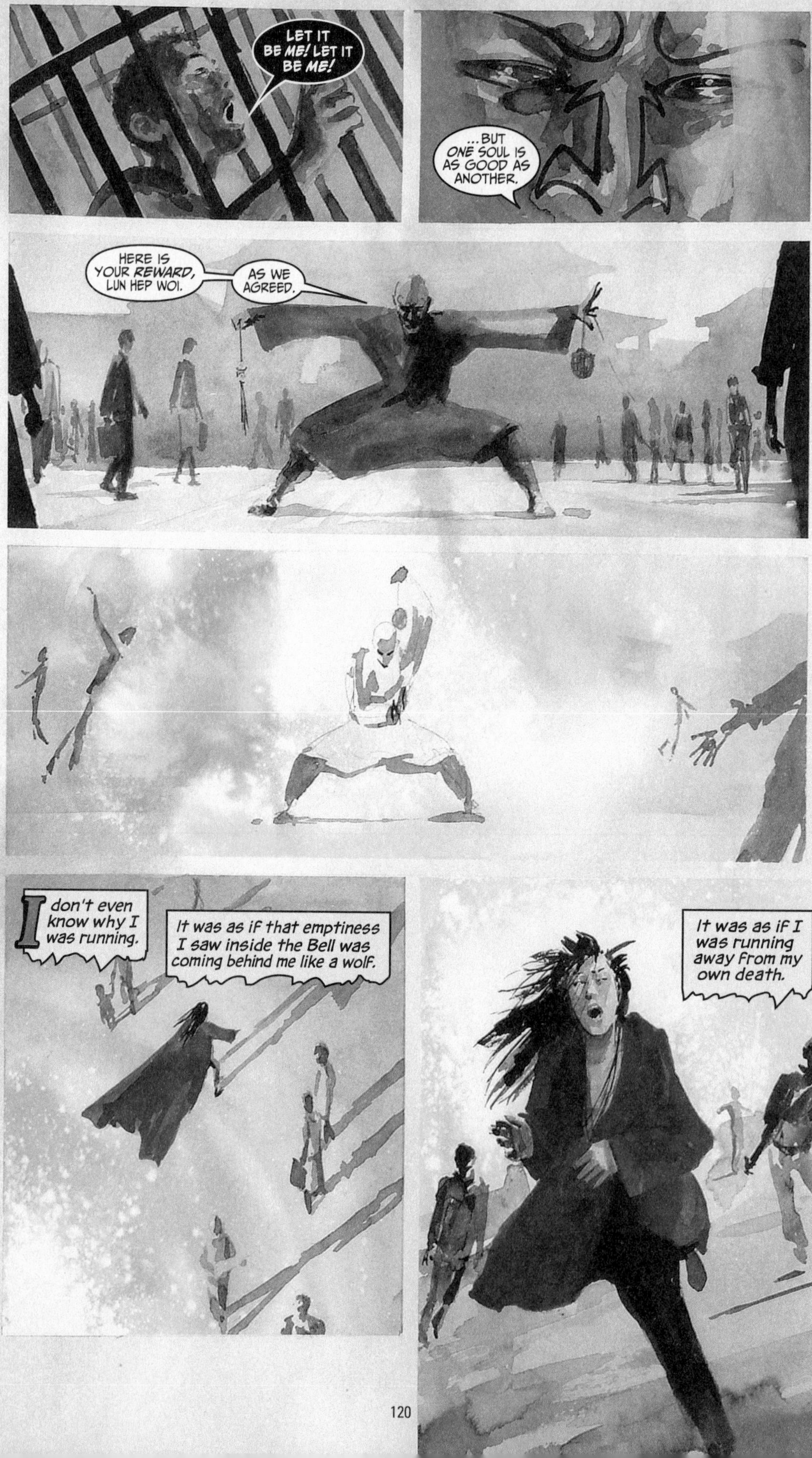
LET IT BE *ME!* LET IT BE *ME!*
...BUT *ONE* SOUL IS AS GOOD AS ANOTHER.
HERE IS YOUR *REWARD*, LUN HEP WOI.
AS WE AGREED.
I don't even know why I was running.
It was as if that emptiness I saw inside the Bell was coming behind me like a wolf.
It was as if I was running away from my own death.

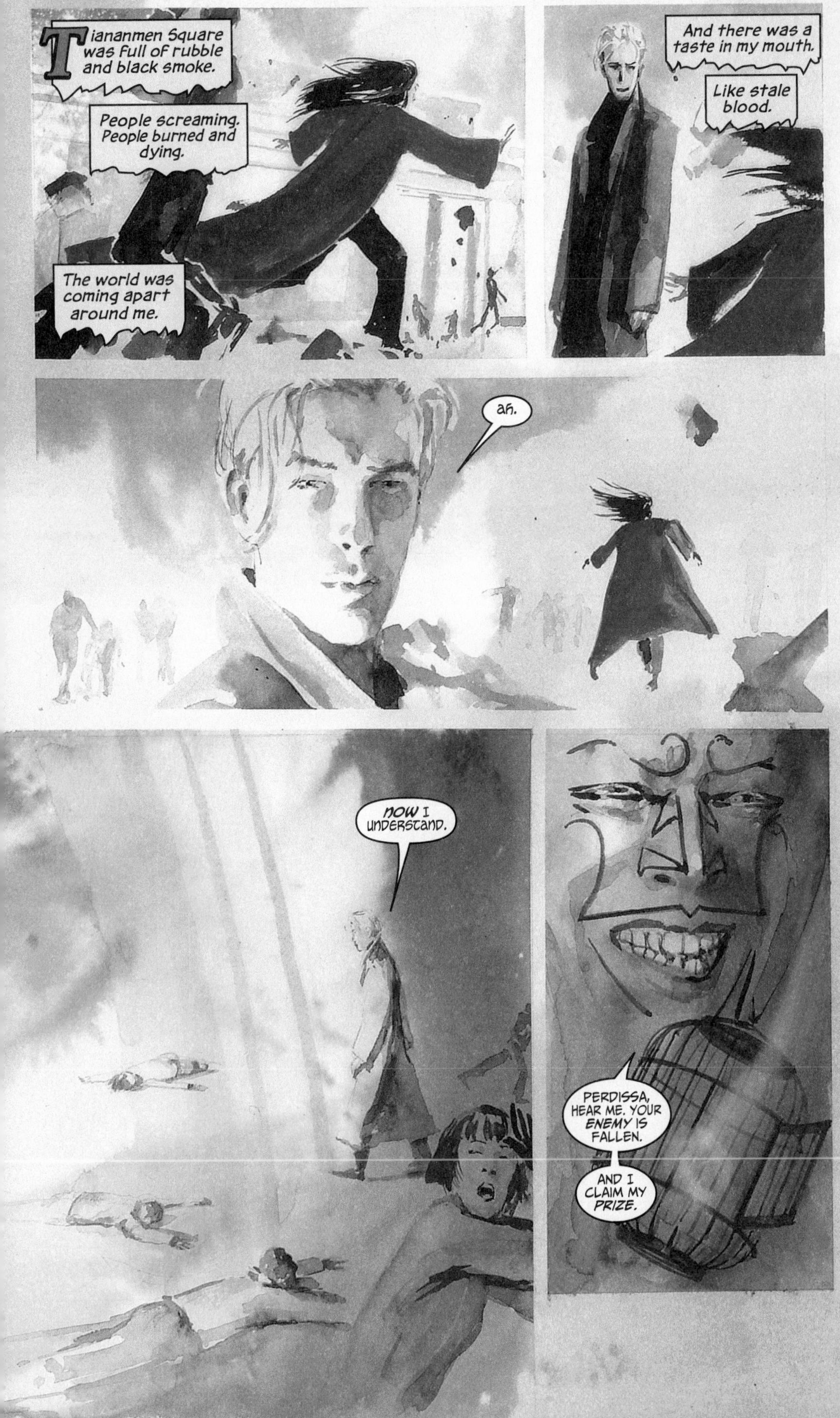
Tiananmen Square was full of rubble and black smoke.
People screaming. People burned and dying.
The world was coming apart around me.
And there was a taste in my mouth.
Like stale blood.
ah.
NOW I UNDERSTAND.
PERDISSA, HEAR ME. YOUR ENEMY IS FALLEN.
AND I CLAIM MY PRIZE.

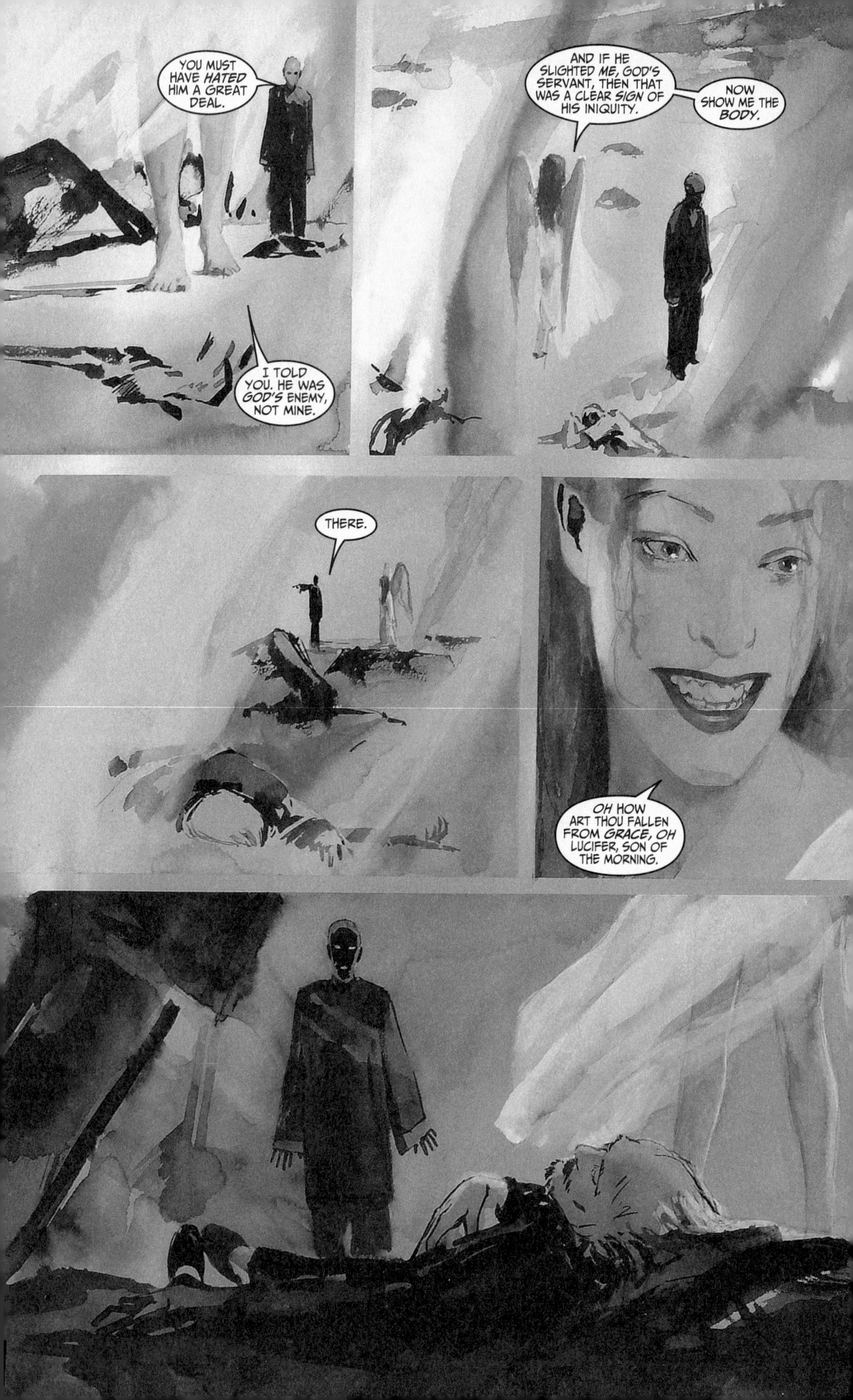
YOU MUST HAVE HATED HIM A GREAT DEAL.
I TOLD YOU. HE WAS GOD'S ENEMY, NOT MINE.
AND IF HE SLIGHTED ME, GOD'S SERVANT, THEN THAT WAS A CLEAR SIGN OF HIS INIQUITY.
NOW SHOW ME THE BODY.
THERE.
OH HOW ART THOU FALLEN FROM GRACE, OH LUCIFER, SON OF THE MORNING.

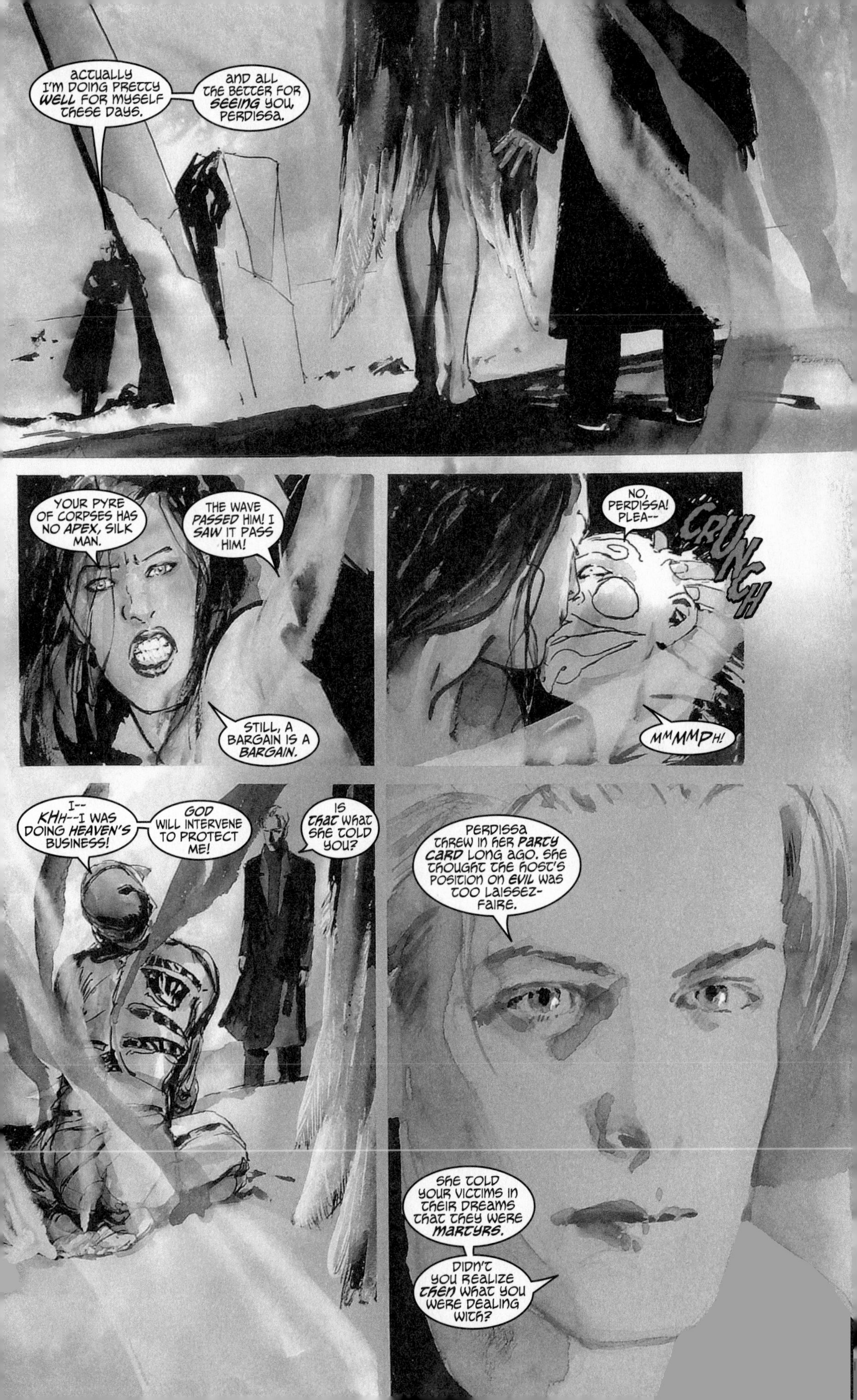
ACTUALLY I'M DOING PRETTY WELL FOR MYSELF THESE DAYS.
AND ALL THE BETTER FOR SEEING YOU, PERDISSA.
YOUR PYRE OF CORPSES HAS NO APEX, SILK MAN.
THE WAVE PASSED HIM! I SAW IT PASS HIM!
STILL, A BARGAIN IS A BARGAIN.
NO, PERDISSA! PLEA--
CRUNCH
MMMMPH!
I-- KHH--I WAS DOING HEAVEN'S BUSINESS!
GOD WILL INTERVENE TO PROTECT ME!
IS THAT WHAT SHE TOLD YOU?
PERDISSA THREW IN HER PARTY CARD LONG AGO. SHE THOUGHT THE HOST'S POSITION ON EVIL WAS TOO LAISSEZ-FAIRE.
SHE TOLD YOUR VICTIMS IN THEIR DREAMS THAT THEY WERE MARTYRS.
DIDN'T YOU REALIZE THEN WHAT YOU WERE DEALING WITH?

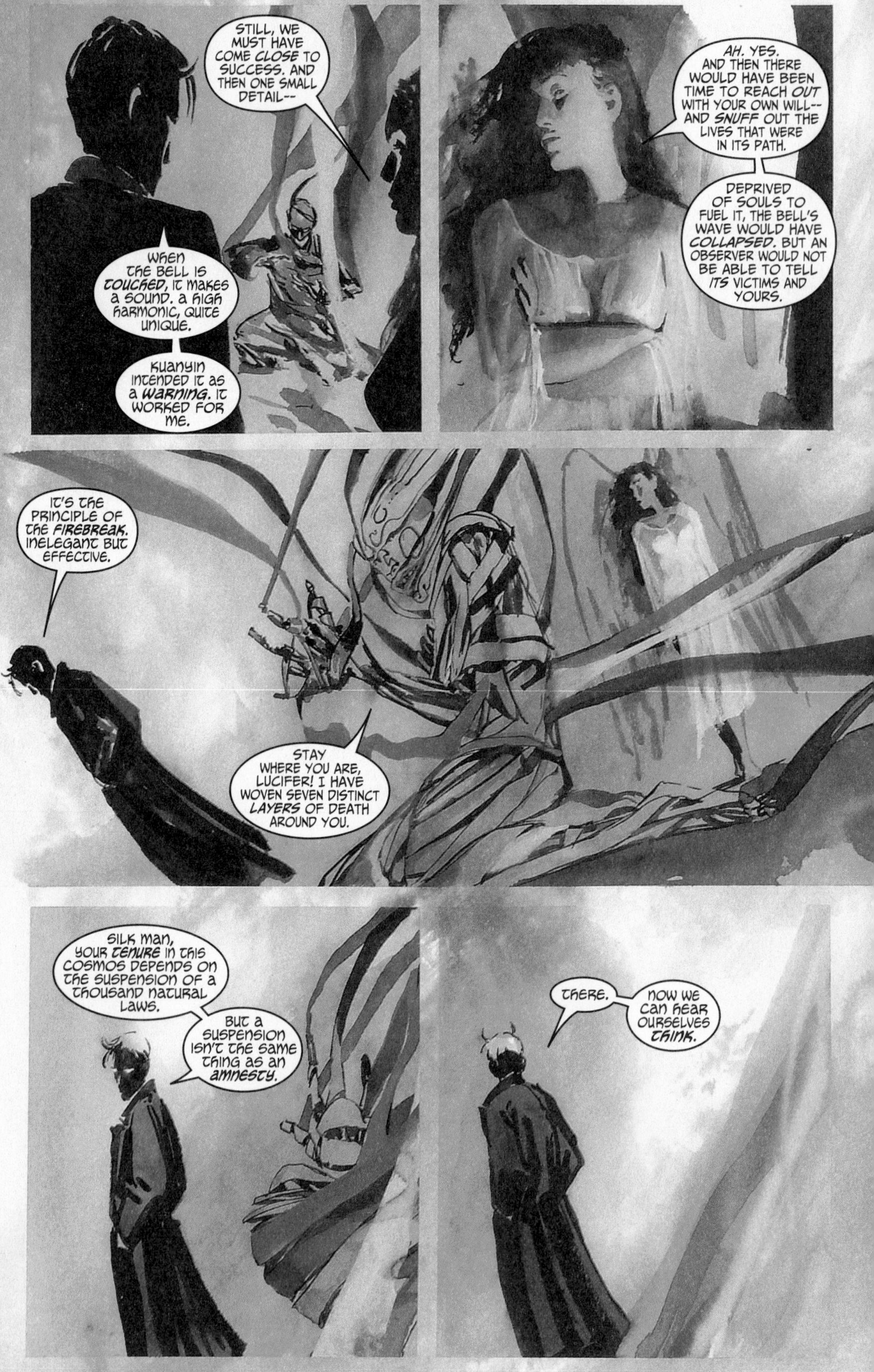

STILL, WE MUST HAVE COME CLOSE TO SUCCESS. AND THEN ONE SMALL DETAIL--
WHEN THE BELL IS TOUCHED, IT MAKES A SOUND. A HIGH HARMONIC, QUITE UNIQUE.
KUANYIN INTENDED IT AS A WARNING. IT WORKED FOR ME.
AH. YES. AND THEN THERE WOULD HAVE BEEN TIME TO REACH OUT WITH YOUR OWN WILL-- AND SNUFF OUT THE LIVES THAT WERE IN ITS PATH.
DEPRIVED OF SOULS TO FUEL IT, THE BELL'S WAVE WOULD HAVE COLLAPSED. BUT AN OBSERVER WOULD NOT BE ABLE TO TELL ITS VICTIMS AND YOURS.
IT'S THE PRINCIPLE OF THE FIREBREAK. INELEGANT BUT EFFECTIVE.
STAY WHERE YOU ARE, LUCIFER! I HAVE WOVEN SEVEN DISTINCT LAYERS OF DEATH AROUND YOU.
SILK MAN, YOUR TENURE IN THIS COSMOS DEPENDS ON THE SUSPENSION OF A THOUSAND NATURAL LAWS.
BUT A SUSPENSION ISN'T THE SAME THING AS AN AMNESTY.
THERE.
NOW WE CAN HEAR OURSELVES THINK.

WHAT YOU HAVE DONE TO YOUR GATE I HAVE DONE TO MY BODY, MORNINGSTAR.
THE DIVINE NAME IS WRITTEN ON ME AND THROUGH ME. LAY A HAND ON ME AND CREATION SHAKES.
TO BE HONEST, I'VE ALWAYS FELT THAT CREATION WAS PRETTY SHAKY TO START WITH.
AND I DON'T WANT TO LAY A HAND ON YOU. WHICH WAS ALWAYS THE PROBLEM, WASN'T IT?
THERE IS NOTHING MORE TO SAY. STAND ASIDE AND LET ME PASS.
HMM. "KILL ME OR LET ME GO."
THAT'S WHAT THEY CALL THE FALLACY OF THE UNEXCLUDED MIDDLE.
THE HOST STILL DON'T LIKE YOUR METHODS, PERDISSA.
AND LIKE ANY DICTATORSHIP THEY'LL ACT ON INFORMATION RECEIVED.

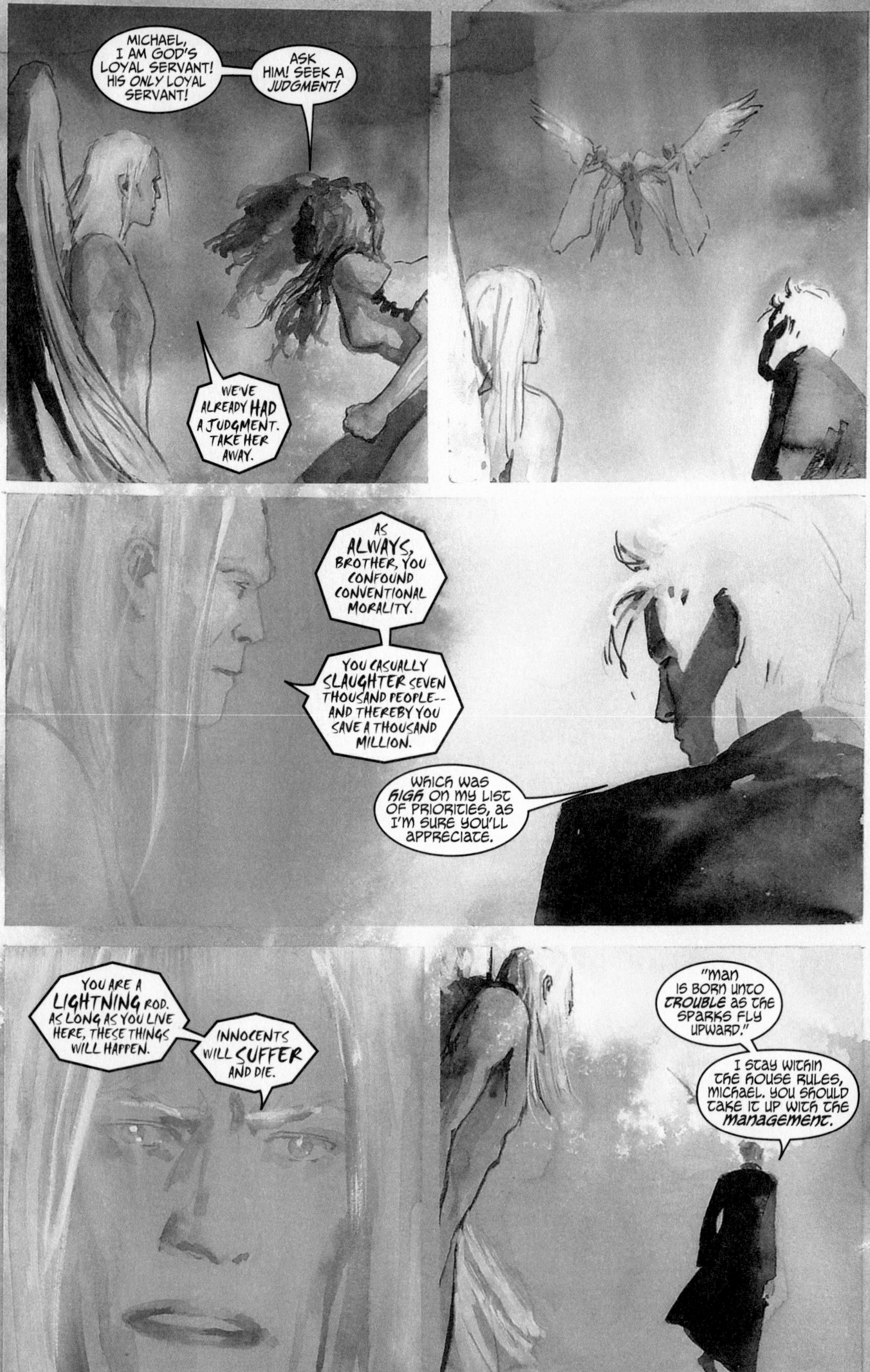

MICHAEL, I AM GOD'S LOYAL SERVANT! HIS ONLY LOYAL SERVANT!
ASK HIM! SEEK A JUDGMENT!
WE'VE ALREADY HAD A JUDGMENT. TAKE HER AWAY.
AS ALWAYS, BROTHER, YOU CONFOUND CONVENTIONAL MORALITY.
YOU CASUALLY SLAUGHTER SEVEN THOUSAND PEOPLE-- AND THEREBY YOU SAVE A THOUSAND MILLION.
WHICH WAS HIGH ON MY LIST OF PRIORITIES, AS I'M SURE YOU'LL APPRECIATE.
YOU ARE A LIGHTNING ROD. AS LONG AS YOU LIVE HERE, THESE THINGS WILL HAPPEN.
INNOCENTS WILL SUFFER AND DIE.
"MAN IS BORN UNTO TROUBLE AS THE SPARKS FLY UPWARD."
I STAY WITHIN THE HOUSE RULES, MICHAEL. YOU SHOULD TAKE IT UP WITH THE MANAGEMENT.

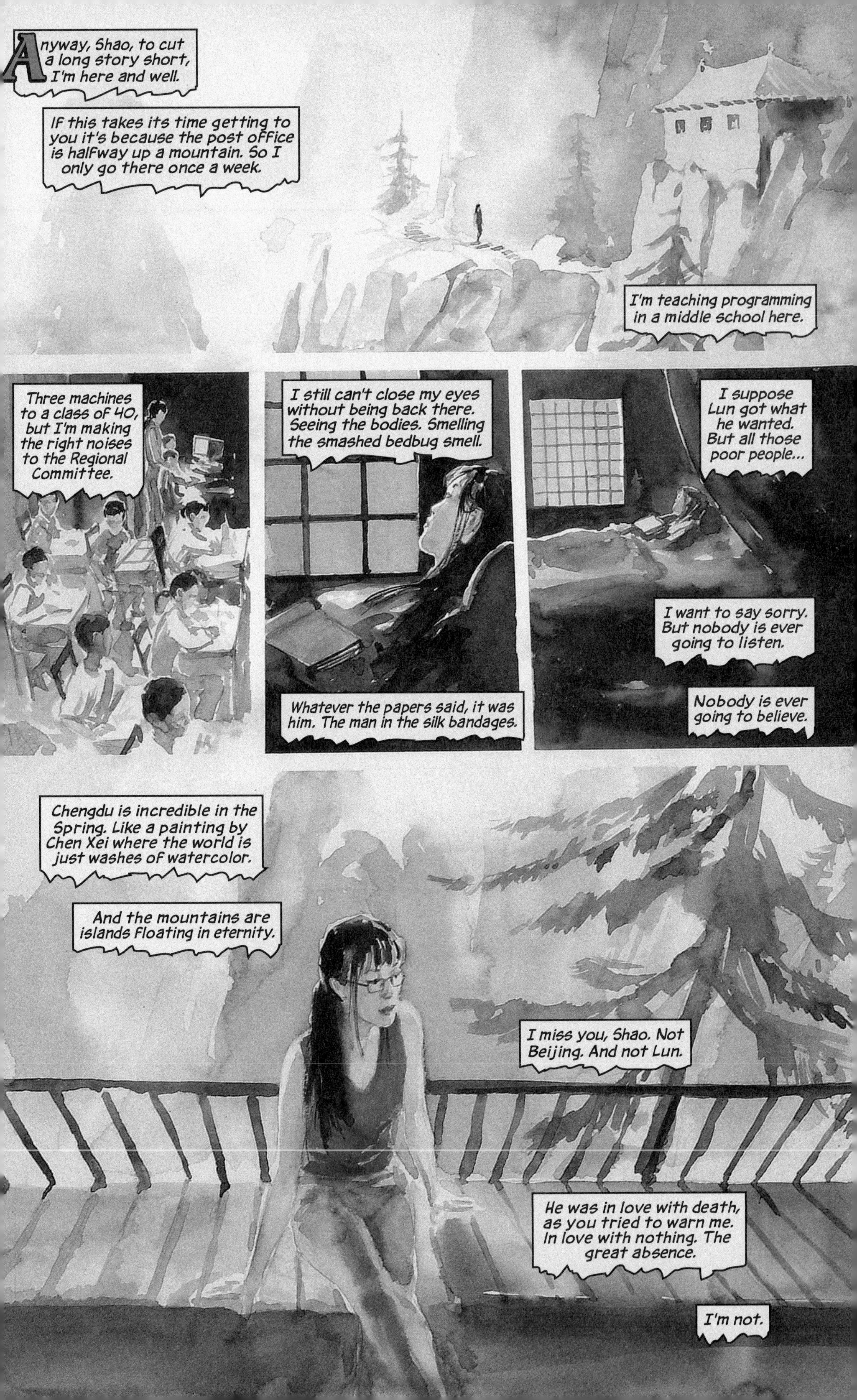
Anyway, Shao, to cut a long story short, I'm here and well.
If this takes its time getting to you it's because the post office is halfway up a mountain. So I only go there once a week.
I'm teaching programming in a middle school here.
Three machines to a class of 40, but I'm making the right noises to the Regional Committee.
I still can't close my eyes without being back there. Seeing the bodies. Smelling the smashed bedbug smell.
Whatever the papers said, it was him. The man in the silk bandages.
I suppose Lun got what he wanted. But all those poor people...
I want to say sorry. But nobody is ever going to listen.
Nobody is ever going to believe.
Chengdu is incredible in the Spring. Like a painting by Chen Xei where the world is just washes of watercolor.
And the mountains are islands floating in eternity.
I miss you, Shao. Not Beijing. And not Lun.
He was in love with death, as you tried to warn me. In love with nothing. The great absence.
I'm not.

I'm happy with samsara. Birth. Death. The world of forms.
I don't want to be released from my life into something else.
As Bankei Zenji wrote in his sermons: "Beauty chains me to the Earth."
"But if I were to fly, where would I fly? The heavens are not a place for human souls."
All my love,
"Zenmaster Cai."
The End

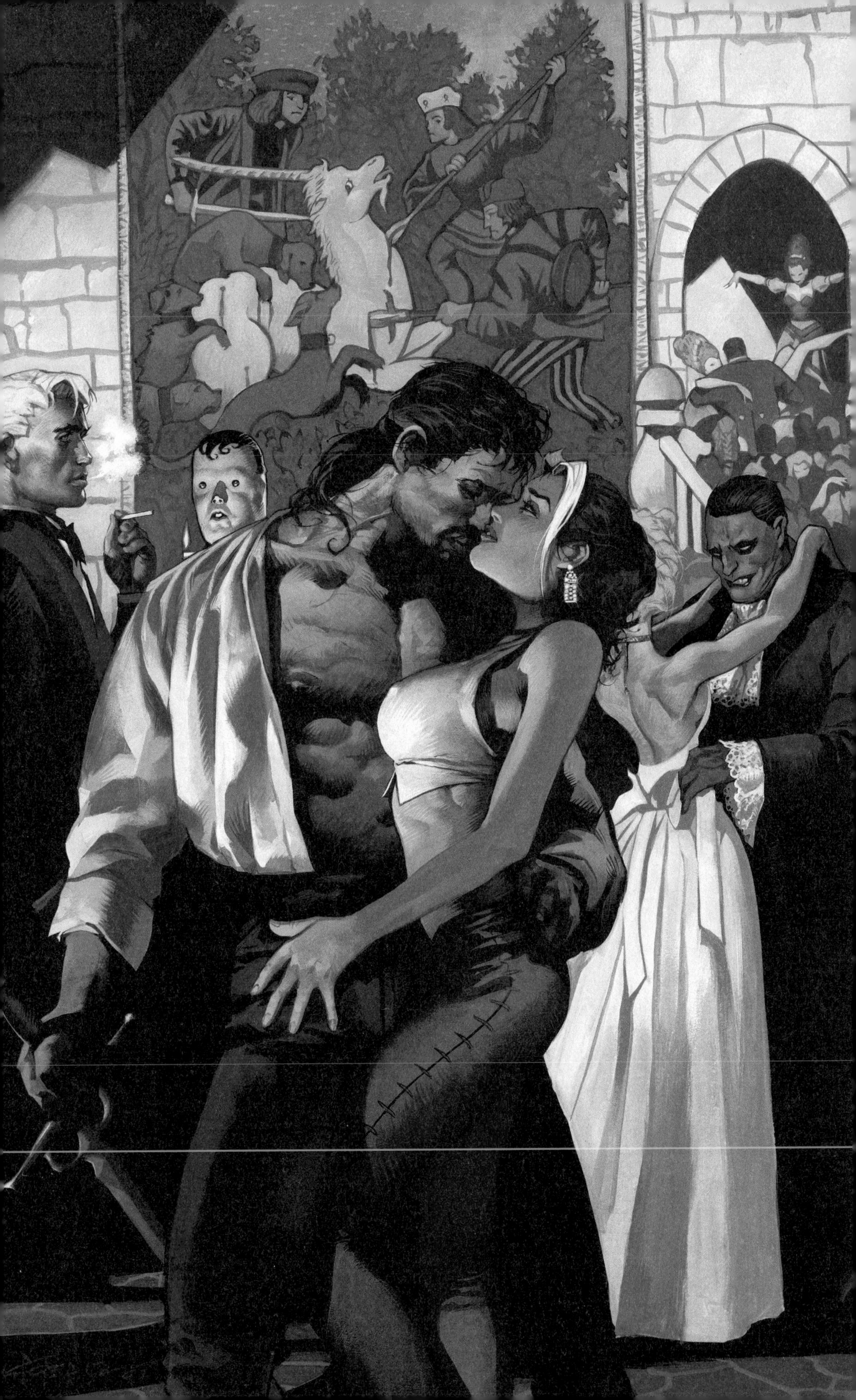

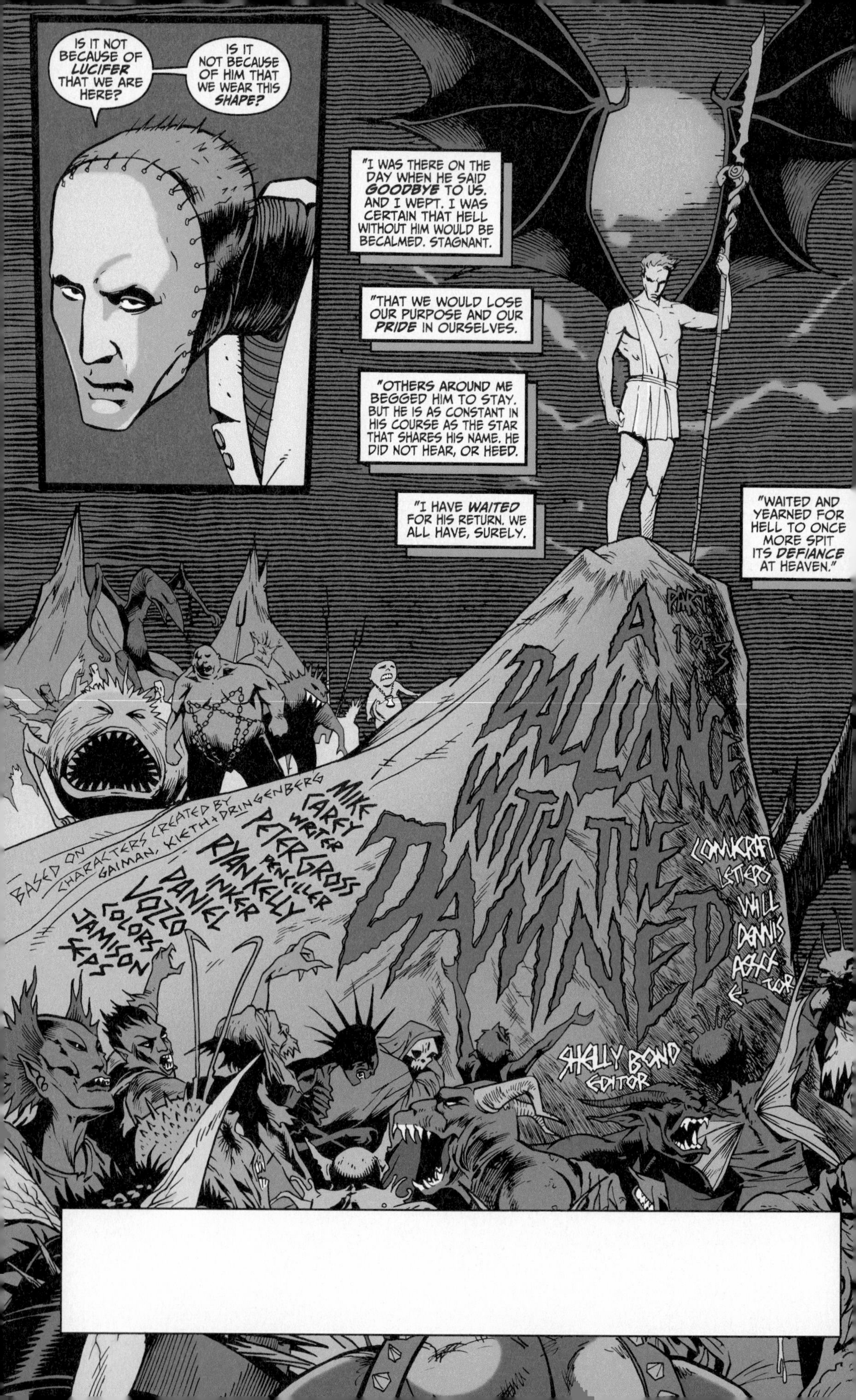
IS IT NOT BECAUSE OF LUCIFER THAT WE ARE HERE?
IS IT NOT BECAUSE OF HIM THAT WE WEAR THIS SHAPE?
"I WAS THERE ON THE DAY WHEN HE SAID GOODBYE TO US. AND I WEPT. I WAS CERTAIN THAT HELL WITHOUT HIM WOULD BE BECALMED. STAGNANT.
"THAT WE WOULD LOSE OUR PURPOSE AND OUR PRIDE IN OURSELVES.
"OTHERS AROUND ME BEGGED HIM TO STAY. BUT HE IS AS CONSTANT IN HIS COURSE AS THE STAR THAT SHARES HIS NAME. HE DID NOT HEAR, OR HEED.
"I HAVE WAITED FOR HIS RETURN. WE ALL HAVE, SURELY.
"WAITED AND YEARNED FOR HELL TO ONCE MORE SPIT ITS DEFIANCE AT HEAVEN."
PART 1 OF 3
A DALLIANCE WITH THE DAMNED
MIKE CAREY WRITER
PETER GROSS PENCILLER
RYAN KELLY INKER
DANIEL VOZZO COLORS
JAMISON SEPS
BASED ON CHARACTERS CREATED BY GAIMAN, KIETH + DRINGENBERG
COMICRAFT LETTERS
WILL DENNIS ASSOC EDITOR
SHELLY BOND EDITOR

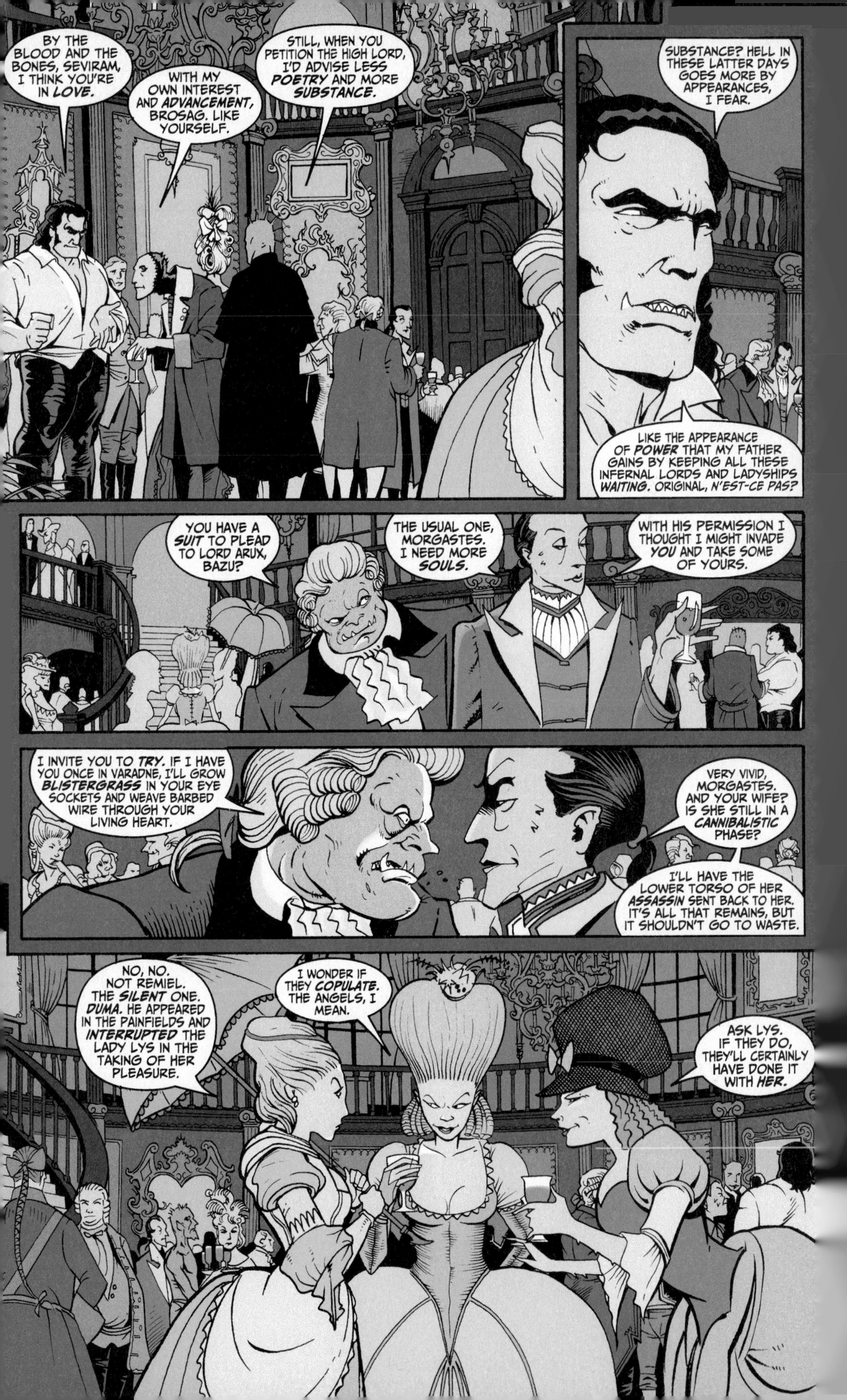
BY THE BLOOD AND THE BONES, SEVIRAM, I THINK YOU'RE IN LOVE.
WITH MY OWN INTEREST AND ADVANCEMENT, BROSAG. LIKE YOURSELF.
STILL, WHEN YOU PETITION THE HIGH LORD, I'D ADVISE LESS POETRY AND MORE SUBSTANCE.
SUBSTANCE? HELL IN THESE LATTER DAYS GOES MORE BY APPEARANCES, I FEAR.
LIKE THE APPEARANCE OF POWER THAT MY FATHER GAINS BY KEEPING ALL THESE INFERNAL LORDS AND LADYSHIPS WAITING. ORIGINAL, N'EST-CE PAS?
YOU HAVE A SUIT TO PLEAD TO LORD ARUX, BAZU?
THE USUAL ONE, MORGASTES. I NEED MORE SOULS.
WITH HIS PERMISSION I THOUGHT I MIGHT INVADE YOU AND TAKE SOME OF YOURS.
I INVITE YOU TO TRY. IF I HAVE YOU ONCE IN VARADNE, I'LL GROW BLISTERGRASS IN YOUR EYE SOCKETS AND WEAVE BARBED WIRE THROUGH YOUR LIVING HEART.
VERY VIVID, MORGASTES. AND YOUR WIFE? IS SHE STILL IN A CANNIBALISTIC PHASE?
I'LL HAVE THE LOWER TORSO OF HER ASSASSIN SENT BACK TO HER. IT'S ALL THAT REMAINS, BUT IT SHOULDN'T GO TO WASTE.
NO, NO. NOT REMIEL. THE SILENT ONE. DUMA. HE APPEARED IN THE PAINFIELDS AND INTERRUPTED THE LADY LYS IN THE TAKING OF HER PLEASURE.
I WONDER IF THEY COPULATE. THE ANGELS, I MEAN.
ASK LYS. IF THEY DO, THEY'LL CERTAINLY HAVE DONE IT WITH HER.

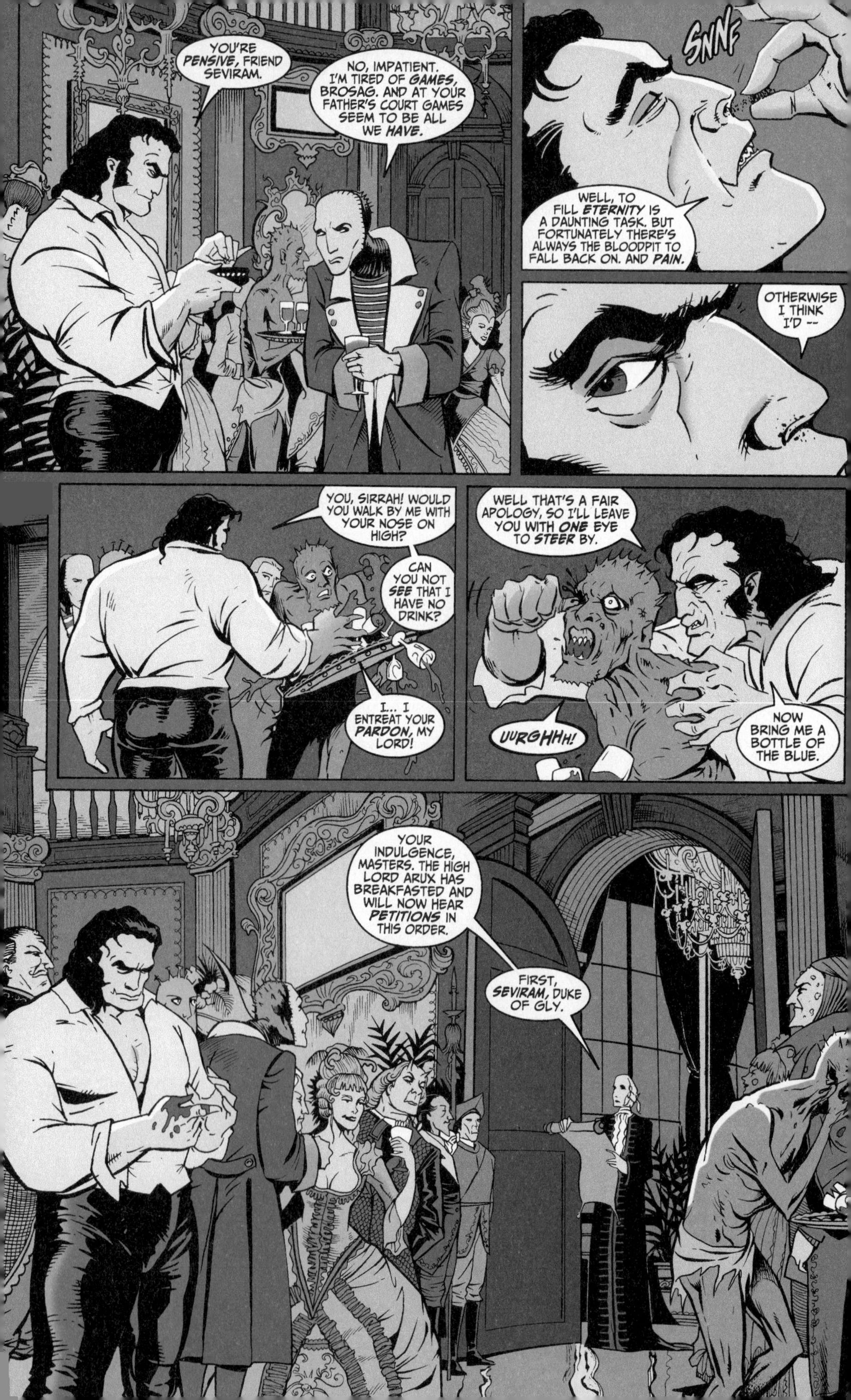
YOU'RE PENSIVE, FRIEND SEVIRAM.
NO, IMPATIENT. I'M TIRED OF GAMES, BROSAG. AND AT YOUR FATHER'S COURT GAMES SEEM TO BE ALL WE HAVE.
SNNF
WELL, TO FILL ETERNITY IS A DAUNTING TASK. BUT FORTUNATELY THERE'S ALWAYS THE BLOODPIT TO FALL BACK ON. AND PAIN.
OTHERWISE I THINK I'D --
YOU, SIRRAH! WOULD YOU WALK BY ME WITH YOUR NOSE ON HIGH?
CAN YOU NOT SEE THAT I HAVE NO DRINK?
I... I ENTREAT YOUR PARDON, MY LORD!
WELL THAT'S A FAIR APOLOGY, SO I'LL LEAVE YOU WITH ONE EYE TO STEER BY.
UURGHHH!
NOW BRING ME A BOTTLE OF THE BLUE.
YOUR INDULGENCE, MASTERS. THE HIGH LORD ARUX HAS BREAKFASTED AND WILL NOW HEAR PETITIONS IN THIS ORDER.
FIRST, SEVIRAM, DUKE OF GLY.

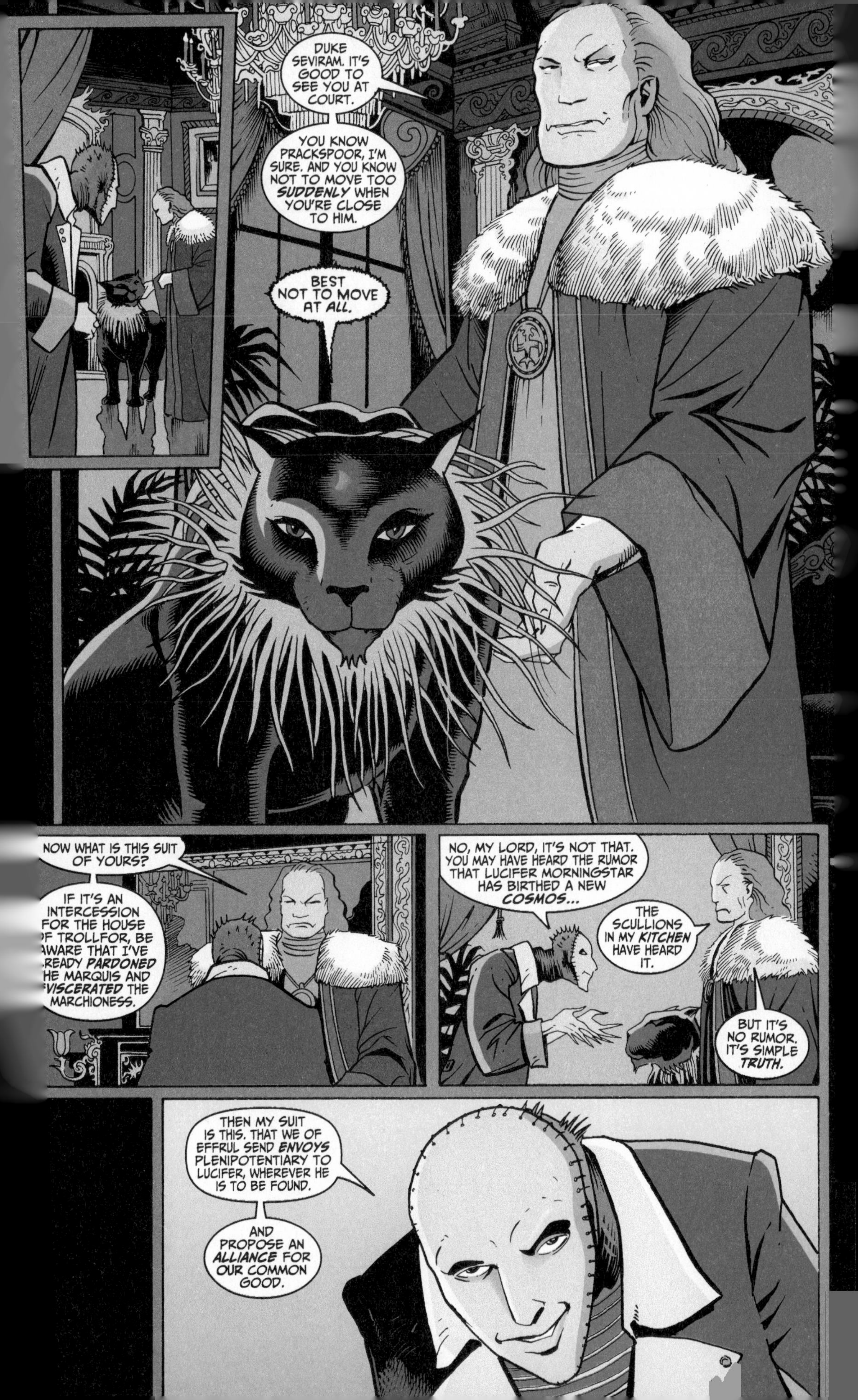
DUKE SEVIRAM. IT'S GOOD TO SEE YOU AT COURT.
YOU KNOW PRACKSPOOR, I'M SURE. AND YOU KNOW NOT TO MOVE TOO SUDDENLY WHEN YOU'RE CLOSE TO HIM.
BEST NOT TO MOVE AT ALL.
NOW WHAT IS THIS SUIT OF YOURS?
IF IT'S AN INTERCESSION FOR THE HOUSE OF TROLLFOR, BE AWARE THAT I'VE READY PARDONED HE MARQUIS AND VISCERATED THE MARCHIONESS.
NO, MY LORD, IT'S NOT THAT. YOU MAY HAVE HEARD THE RUMOR THAT LUCIFER MORNINGSTAR HAS BIRTHED A NEW COSMOS...
THE SCULLIONS IN MY KITCHEN HAVE HEARD IT.
BUT IT'S NO RUMOR. IT'S SIMPLE TRUTH.
THEN MY SUIT IS THIS. THAT WE OF EFFRUL SEND ENVOYS PLENIPOTENTIARY TO LUCIFER, WHEREVER HE IS TO BE FOUND.
AND PROPOSE AN ALLIANCE FOR OUR COMMON GOOD.

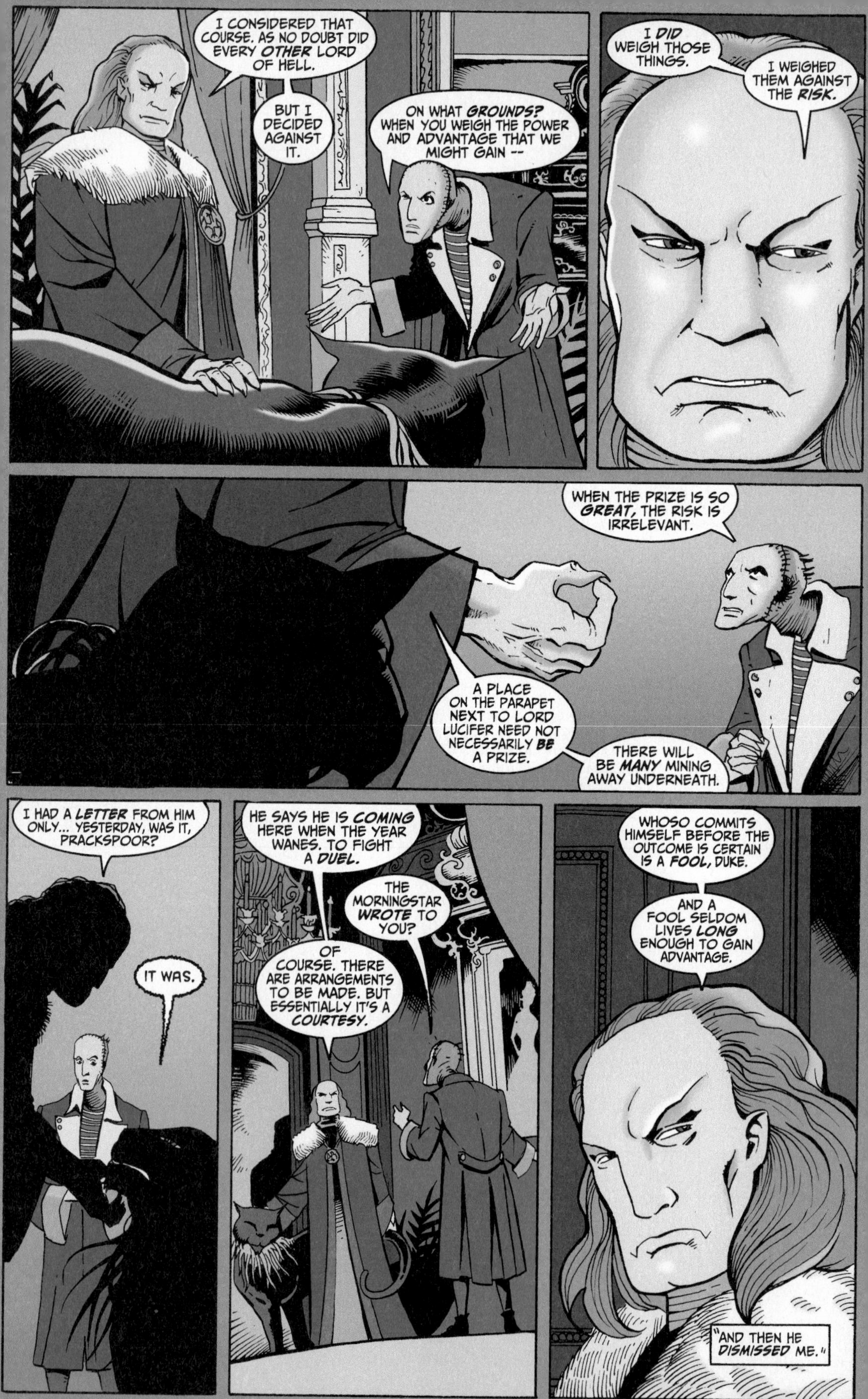
I CONSIDERED THAT COURSE. AS NO DOUBT DID EVERY OTHER LORD OF HELL.
BUT I DECIDED AGAINST IT.
ON WHAT GROUNDS? WHEN YOU WEIGH THE POWER AND ADVANTAGE THAT WE MIGHT GAIN --
I DID WEIGH THOSE THINGS.
I WEIGHED THEM AGAINST THE RISK.
WHEN THE PRIZE IS SO GREAT, THE RISK IS IRRELEVANT.
A PLACE ON THE PARAPET NEXT TO LORD LUCIFER NEED NOT NECESSARILY BE A PRIZE.
THERE WILL BE MANY MINING AWAY UNDERNEATH.
I HAD A LETTER FROM HIM ONLY... YESTERDAY, WAS IT, PRACKSPOOR?
IT WAS.
HE SAYS HE IS COMING HERE WHEN THE YEAR WANES. TO FIGHT A DUEL.
THE MORNINGSTAR WROTE TO YOU?
OF COURSE. THERE ARE ARRANGEMENTS TO BE MADE. BUT ESSENTIALLY IT'S A COURTESY.
WHOSO COMMITS HIMSELF BEFORE THE OUTCOME IS CERTAIN IS A FOOL, DUKE.
AND A FOOL SELDOM LIVES LONG ENOUGH TO GAIN ADVANTAGE.
"AND THEN HE DISMISSED ME."

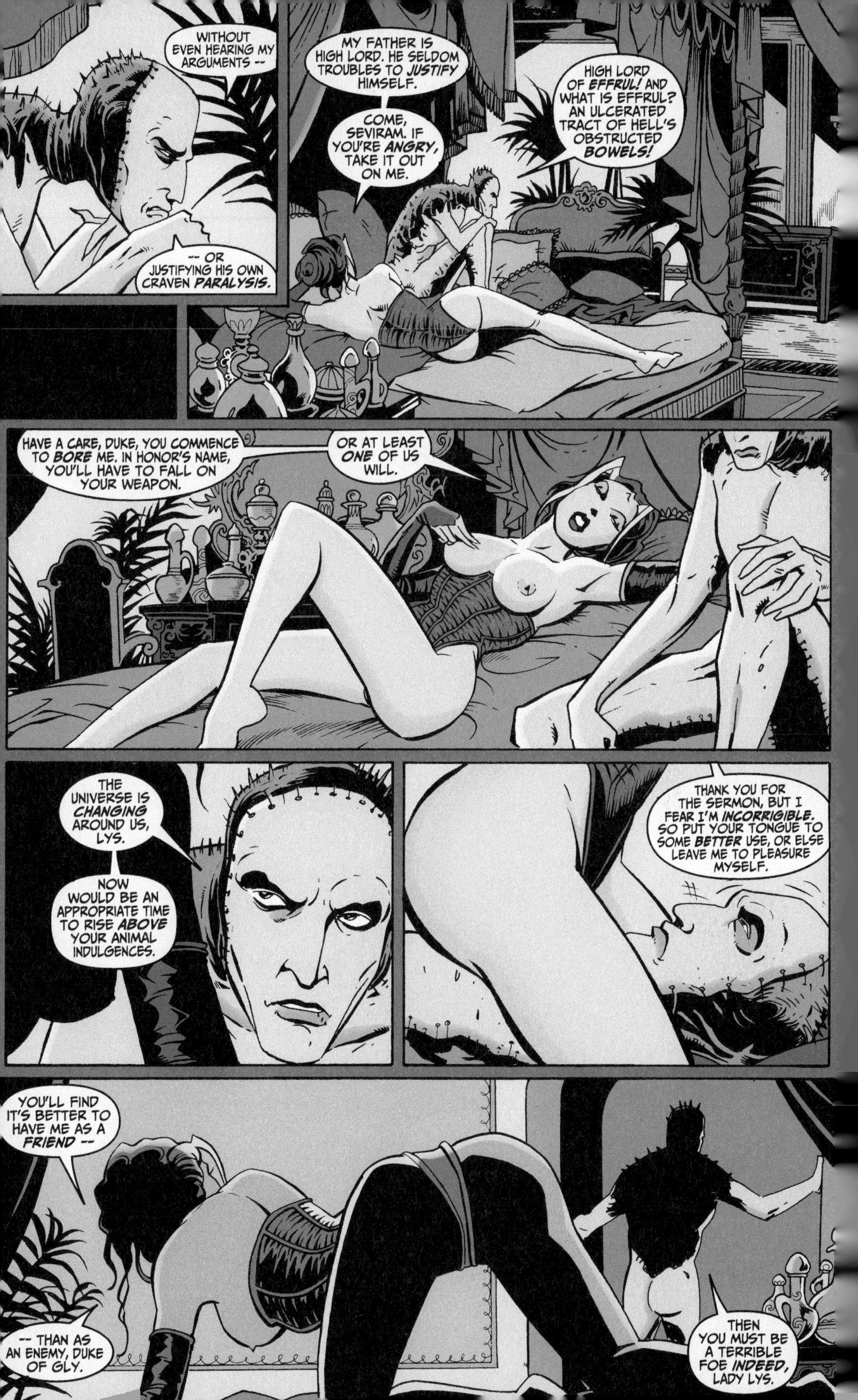

WITHOUT EVEN HEARING MY ARGUMENTS --
-- OR JUSTIFYING HIS OWN CRAVEN PARALYSIS.
MY FATHER IS HIGH LORD. HE SELDOM TROUBLES TO JUSTIFY HIMSELF.
COME, SEVIRAM. IF YOU'RE ANGRY, TAKE IT OUT ON ME.
HIGH LORD OF EFFRUL! AND WHAT IS EFFRUL? AN ULCERATED TRACT OF HELL'S OBSTRUCTED BOWELS!
HAVE A CARE, DUKE, YOU COMMENCE TO BORE ME. IN HONOR'S NAME, YOU'LL HAVE TO FALL ON YOUR WEAPON.
OR AT LEAST ONE OF US WILL.
THE UNIVERSE IS CHANGING AROUND US, LYS.
NOW WOULD BE AN APPROPRIATE TIME TO RISE ABOVE YOUR ANIMAL INDULGENCES.
THANK YOU FOR THE SERMON, BUT I FEAR I'M INCORRIGIBLE. SO PUT YOUR TONGUE TO SOME BETTER USE, OR ELSE LEAVE ME TO PLEASURE MYSELF.
YOU'LL FIND IT'S BETTER TO HAVE ME AS A FRIEND --
-- THAN AS AN ENEMY, DUKE OF GLY.
THEN YOU MUST BE A TERRIBLE FOE INDEED, LADY LYS.

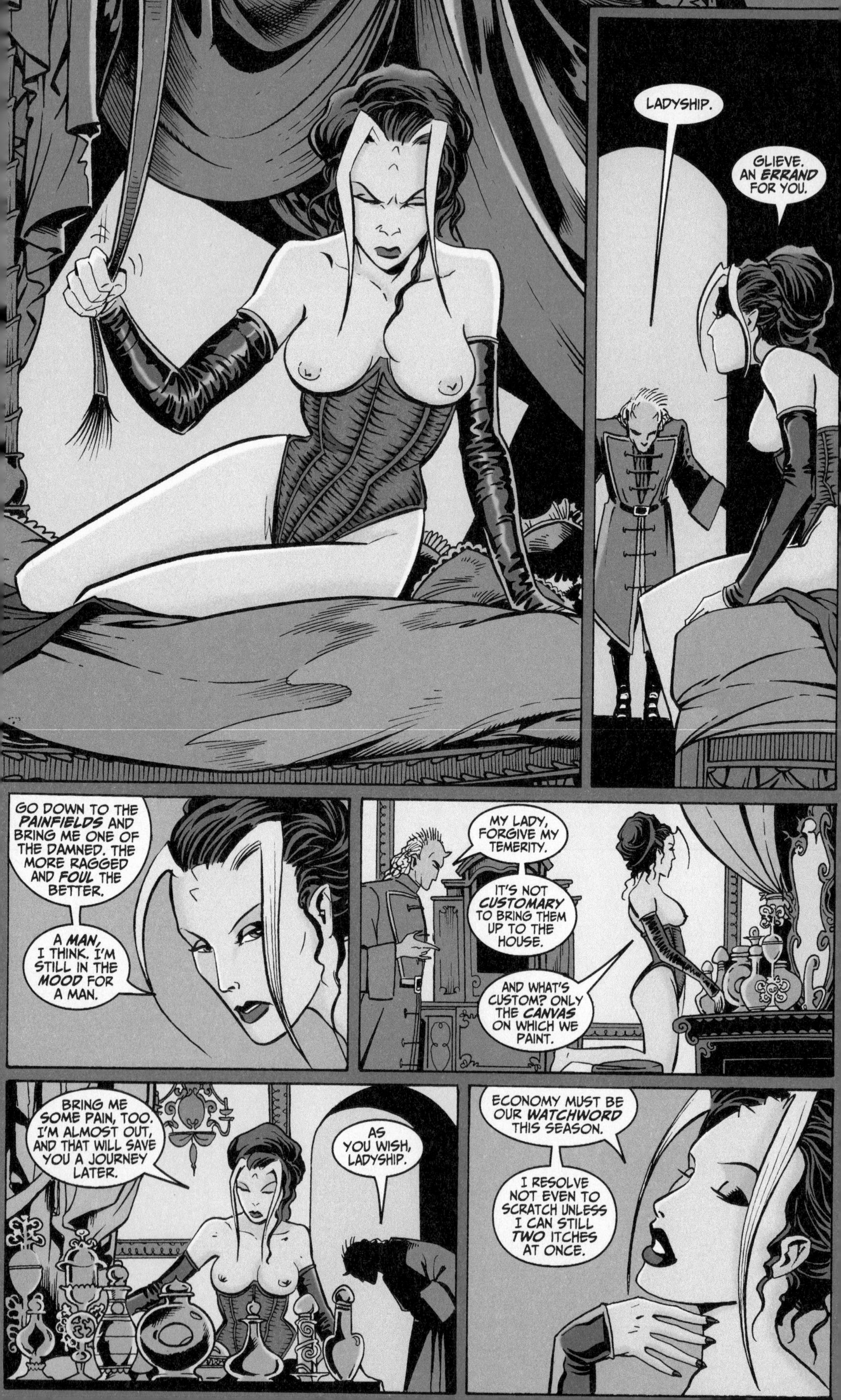
LADYSHIP.
GLIEVE. AN ERRAND FOR YOU.
GO DOWN TO THE PAINFIELDS AND BRING ME ONE OF THE DAMNED. THE MORE RAGGED AND FOUL THE BETTER.
A MAN, I THINK. I'M STILL IN THE MOOD FOR A MAN.
MY LADY, FORGIVE MY TEMERITY.
IT'S NOT CUSTOMARY TO BRING THEM UP TO THE HOUSE.
AND WHAT'S CUSTOM? ONLY THE CANVAS ON WHICH WE PAINT.
BRING ME SOME PAIN, TOO. I'M ALMOST OUT, AND THAT WILL SAVE YOU A JOURNEY LATER.
AS YOU WISH, LADYSHIP.
ECONOMY MUST BE OUR WATCHWORD THIS SEASON.
I RESOLVE NOT EVEN TO SCRATCH UNLESS I CAN STILL TWO ITCHES AT ONCE.

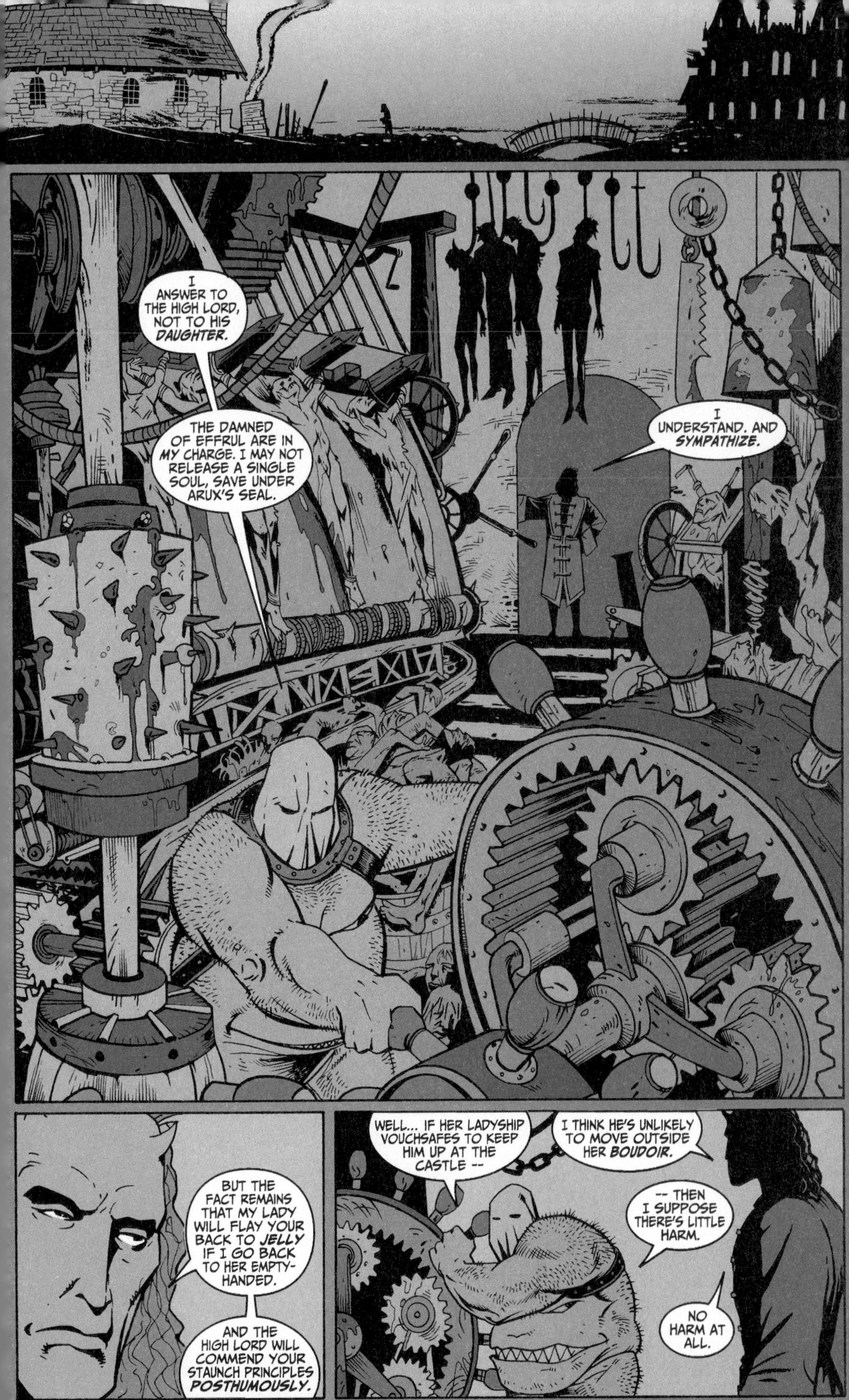
I ANSWER TO THE HIGH LORD, NOT TO HIS DAUGHTER.
THE DAMNED OF EFFRUL ARE IN MY CHARGE. I MAY NOT RELEASE A SINGLE SOUL, SAVE UNDER ARUX'S SEAL.
I UNDERSTAND. AND SYMPATHIZE.
BUT THE FACT REMAINS THAT MY LADY WILL FLAY YOUR BACK TO JELLY IF I GO BACK TO HER EMPTY-HANDED.
AND THE HIGH LORD WILL COMMEND YOUR STAUNCH PRINCIPLES POSTHUMOUSLY.
WELL... IF HER LADYSHIP VOUCHSAFES TO KEEP HIM UP AT THE CASTLE --
I THINK HE'S UNLIKELY TO MOVE OUTSIDE HER BOUDOIR.
-- THEN I SUPPOSE THERE'S LITTLE HARM.
NO HARM AT ALL.

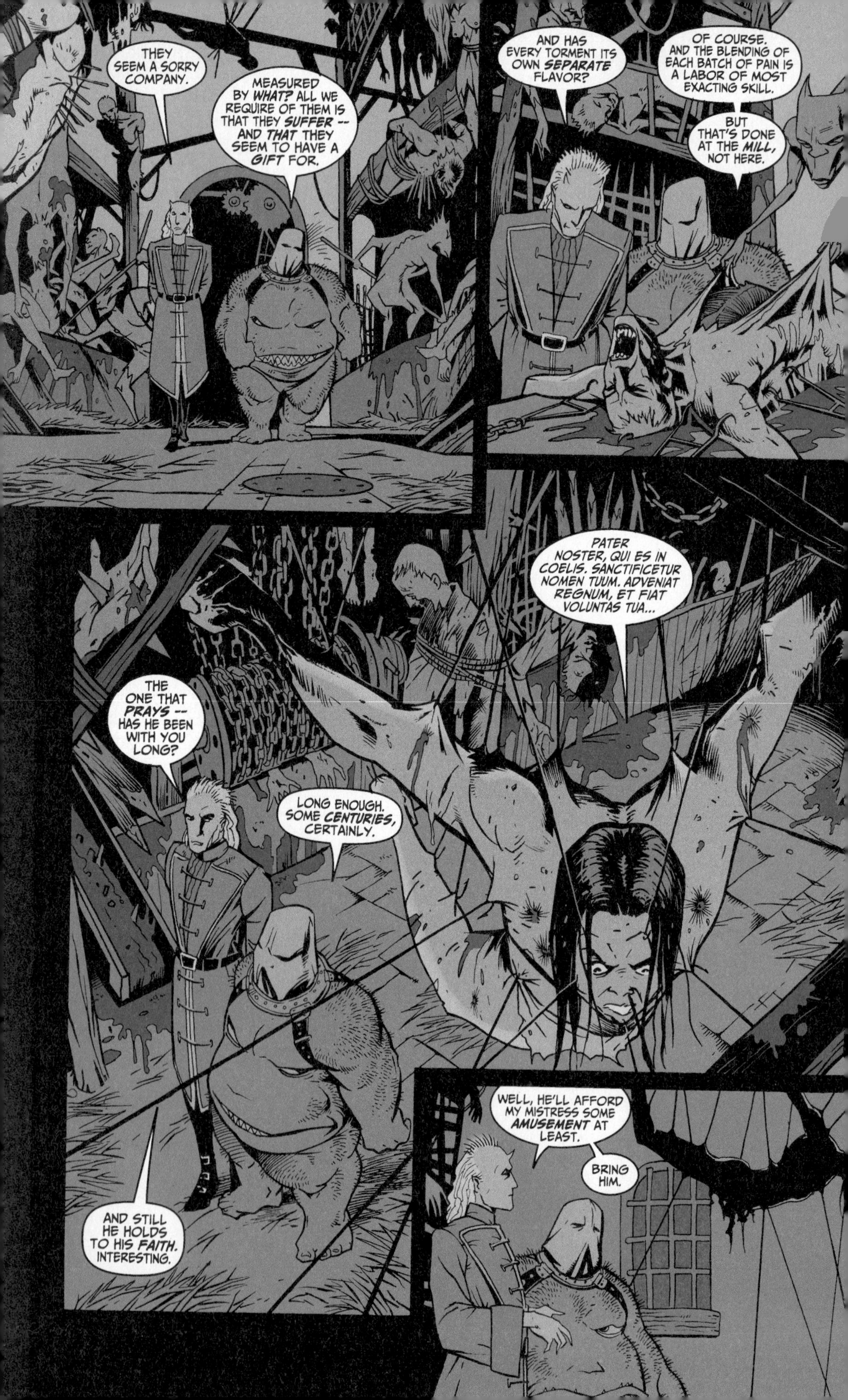
THEY SEEM A SORRY COMPANY.
MEASURED BY WHAT? ALL WE REQUIRE OF THEM IS THAT THEY SUFFER -- AND THAT THEY SEEM TO HAVE A GIFT FOR.
AND HAS EVERY TORMENT ITS OWN SEPARATE FLAVOR?
OF COURSE. AND THE BLENDING OF EACH BATCH OF PAIN IS A LABOR OF MOST EXACTING SKILL.
BUT THAT'S DONE AT THE MILL, NOT HERE.
PATER NOSTER, QUI ES IN COELIS. SANCTIFICETUR NOMEN TUUM. ADVENIAT REGNUM, ET FIAT VOLUNTAS TUA...
THE ONE THAT PRAYS -- HAS HE BEEN WITH YOU LONG?
LONG ENOUGH. SOME CENTURIES, CERTAINLY.
AND STILL HE HOLDS TO HIS FAITH. INTERESTING.
WELL, HE'LL AFFORD MY MISTRESS SOME AMUSEMENT AT LEAST.
BRING HIM.

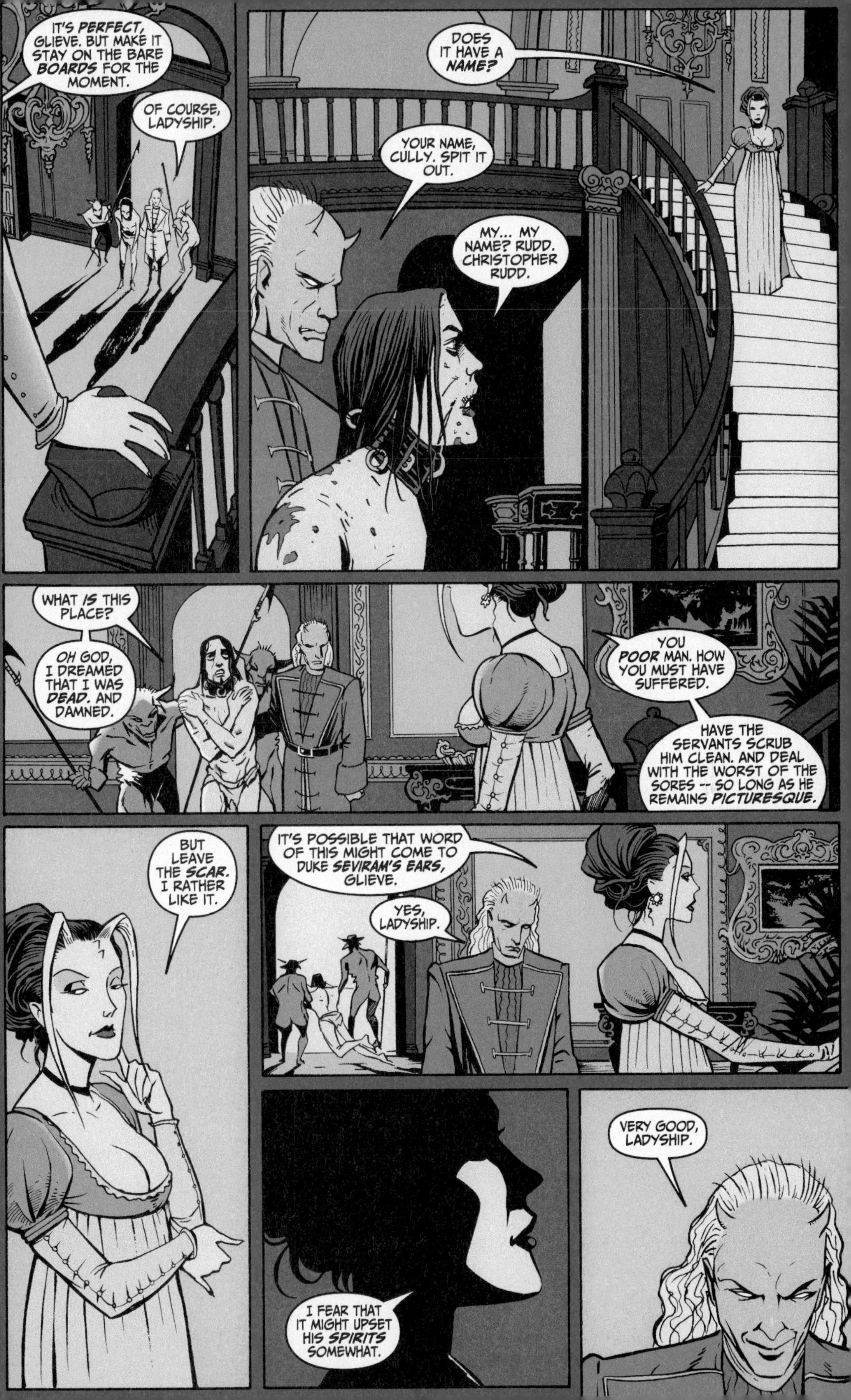
IT'S PERFECT, GLIEVE. BUT MAKE IT STAY ON THE BARE BOARDS FOR THE MOMENT.
OF COURSE, LADYSHIP.
DOES IT HAVE A NAME?
YOUR NAME, CULLY. SPIT IT OUT.
MY... MY NAME? RUDD. CHRISTOPHER RUDD.
WHAT IS THIS PLACE?
OH GOD, I DREAMED THAT I WAS DEAD. AND DAMNED.
YOU POOR MAN. HOW YOU MUST HAVE SUFFERED.
HAVE THE SERVANTS SCRUB HIM CLEAN. AND DEAL WITH THE WORST OF THE SORES -- SO LONG AS HE REMAINS PICTURESQUE.
BUT LEAVE THE SCAR. I RATHER LIKE IT.
IT'S POSSIBLE THAT WORD OF THIS MIGHT COME TO DUKE SEVIRAM'S EARS, GLIEVE.
YES, LADYSHIP.
I FEAR THAT IT MIGHT UPSET HIS SPIRITS SOMEWHAT.
VERY GOOD, LADYSHIP.

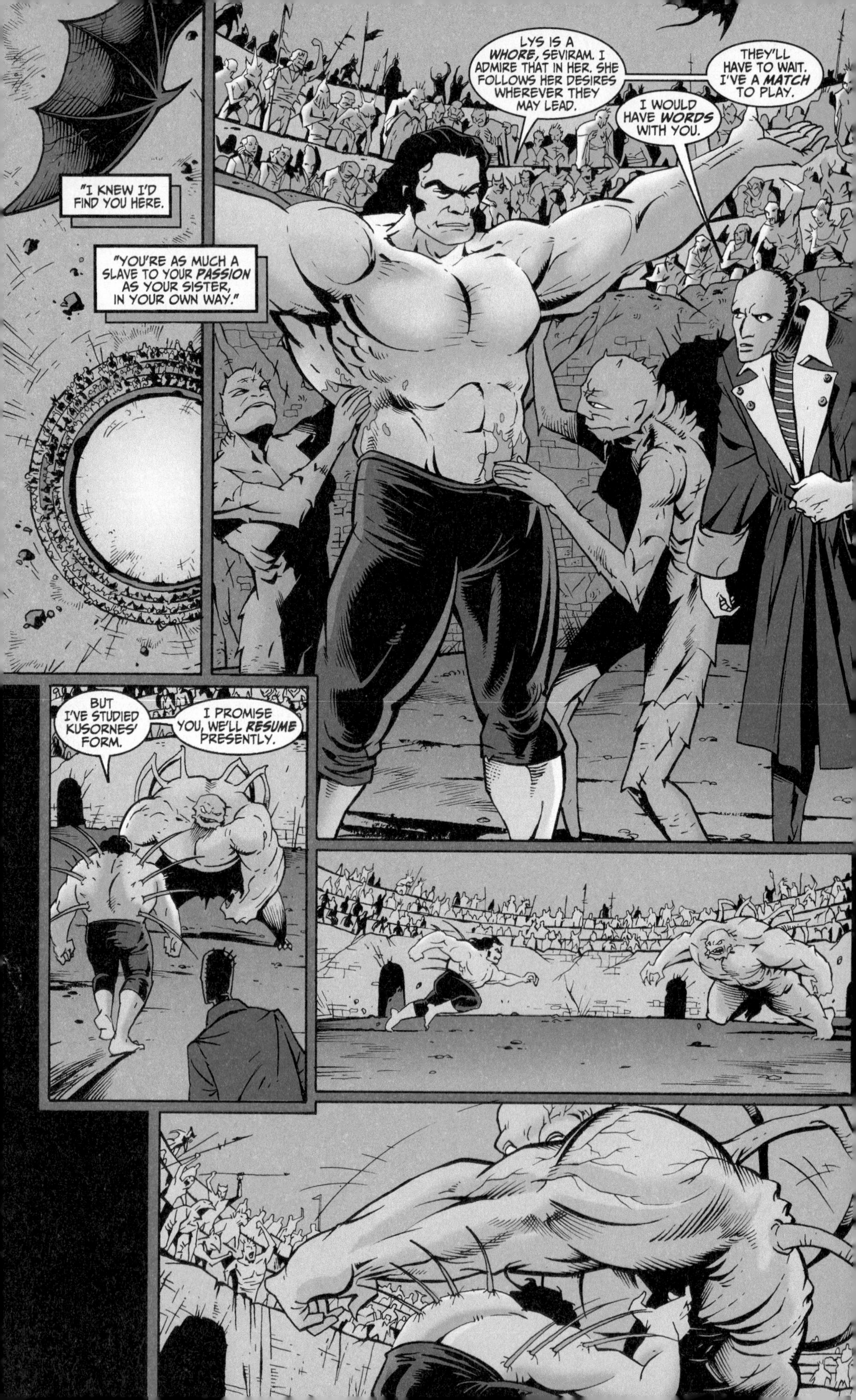
"I KNEW I'D FIND YOU HERE.
"YOU'RE AS MUCH A SLAVE TO YOUR PASSION AS YOUR SISTER, IN YOUR OWN WAY."
LYS IS A WHORE, SEVIRAM. I ADMIRE THAT IN HER. SHE FOLLOWS HER DESIRES WHEREVER THEY MAY LEAD.
I WOULD HAVE WORDS WITH YOU.
THEY'LL HAVE TO WAIT. I'VE A MATCH TO PLAY.
BUT I'VE STUDIED KUSORNES' FORM.
I PROMISE YOU, WE'LL RESUME PRESENTLY.

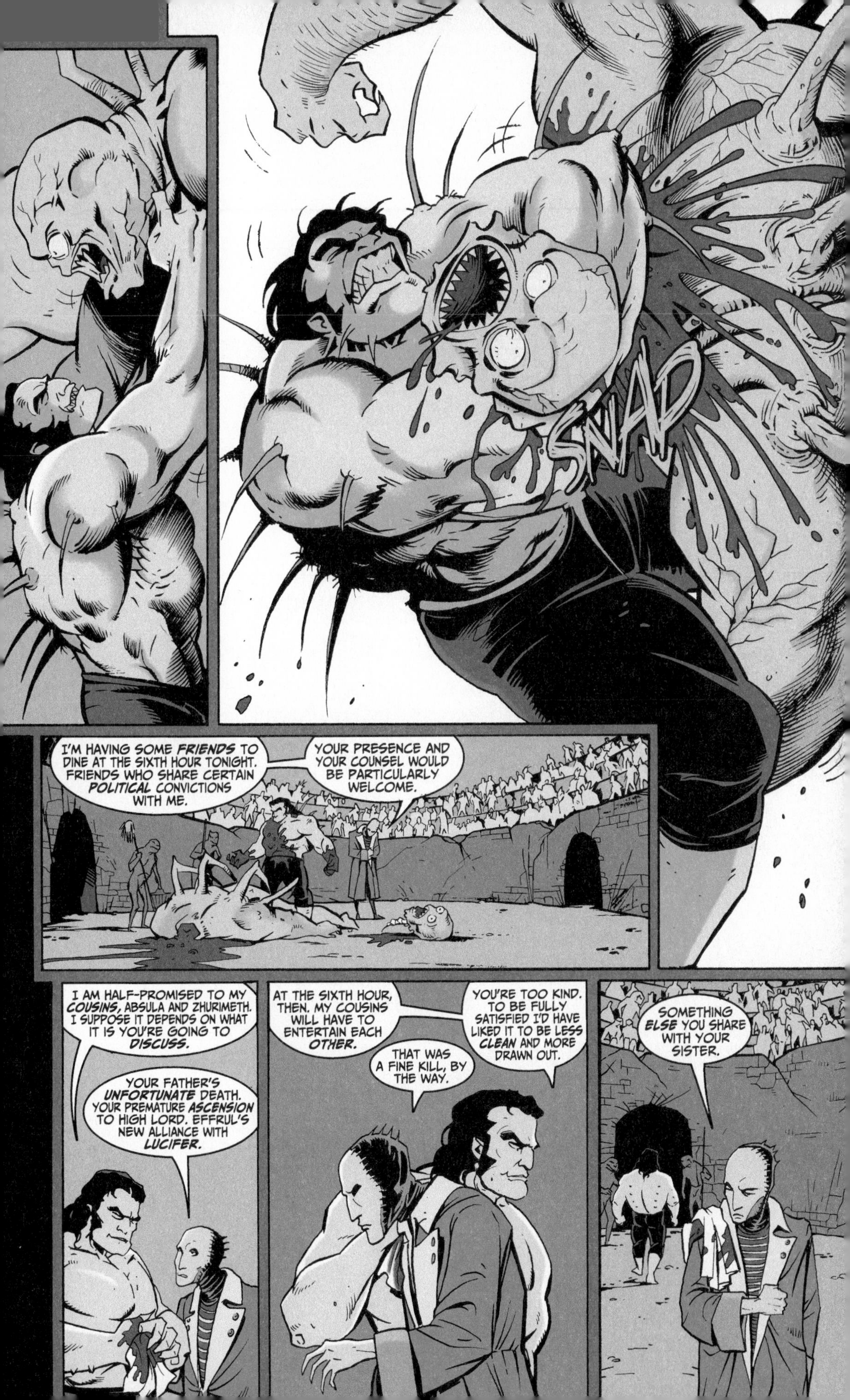
SNAP
I'M HAVING SOME FRIENDS TO DINE AT THE SIXTH HOUR TONIGHT. FRIENDS WHO SHARE CERTAIN POLITICAL CONVICTIONS WITH ME.
YOUR PRESENCE AND YOUR COUNSEL WOULD BE PARTICULARLY WELCOME.
I AM HALF-PROMISED TO MY COUSINS, ABSULA AND ZHURIMETH. I SUPPOSE IT DEPENDS ON WHAT IT IS YOU'RE GOING TO DISCUSS.
YOUR FATHER'S UNFORTUNATE DEATH. YOUR PREMATURE ASCENSION TO HIGH LORD. EFFRUL'S NEW ALLIANCE WITH LUCIFER.
AT THE SIXTH HOUR, THEN. MY COUSINS WILL HAVE TO ENTERTAIN EACH OTHER.
THAT WAS A FINE KILL, BY THE WAY.
YOU'RE TOO KIND. TO BE FULLY SATISFIED I'D HAVE LIKED IT TO BE LESS CLEAN AND MORE DRAWN OUT.
SOMETHING ELSE YOU SHARE WITH YOUR SISTER.

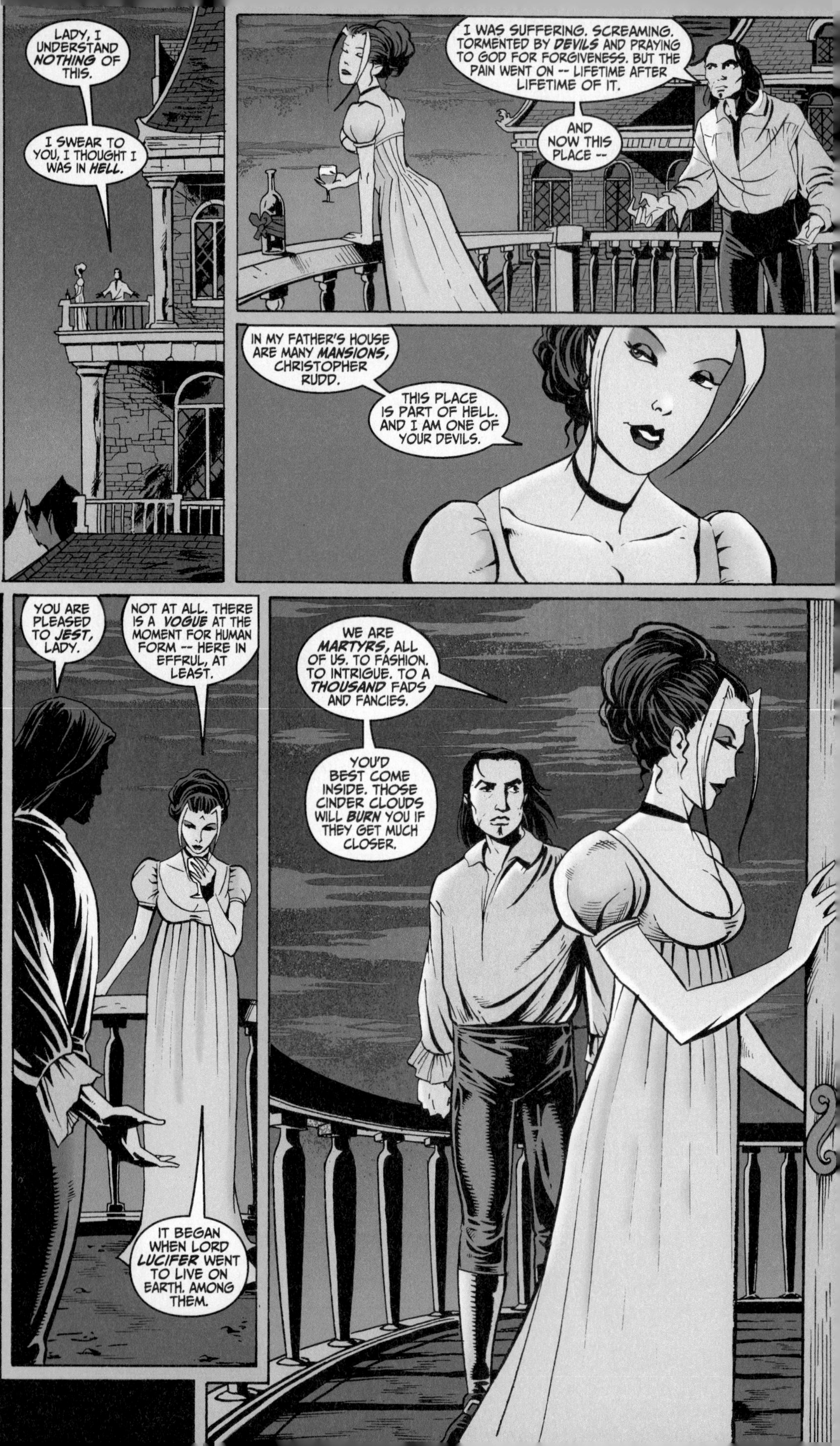
LADY, I UNDERSTAND NOTHING OF THIS.
I SWEAR TO YOU, I THOUGHT I WAS IN HELL.
I WAS SUFFERING. SCREAMING. TORMENTED BY DEVILS AND PRAYING TO GOD FOR FORGIVENESS. BUT THE PAIN WENT ON -- LIFETIME AFTER LIFETIME OF IT.
AND NOW THIS PLACE --
IN MY FATHER'S HOUSE ARE MANY MANSIONS, CHRISTOPHER RUDD.
THIS PLACE IS PART OF HELL. AND I AM ONE OF YOUR DEVILS.
YOU ARE PLEASED TO JEST, LADY.
NOT AT ALL. THERE IS A VOGUE AT THE MOMENT FOR HUMAN FORM -- HERE IN EFFRUL, AT LEAST.
IT BEGAN WHEN LORD LUCIFER WENT TO LIVE ON EARTH. AMONG THEM.
WE ARE MARTYRS, ALL OF US. TO FASHION. TO INTRIGUE. TO A THOUSAND FADS AND FANCIES.
YOU'D BEST COME INSIDE. THOSE CINDER CLOUDS WILL BURN YOU IF THEY GET MUCH CLOSER.

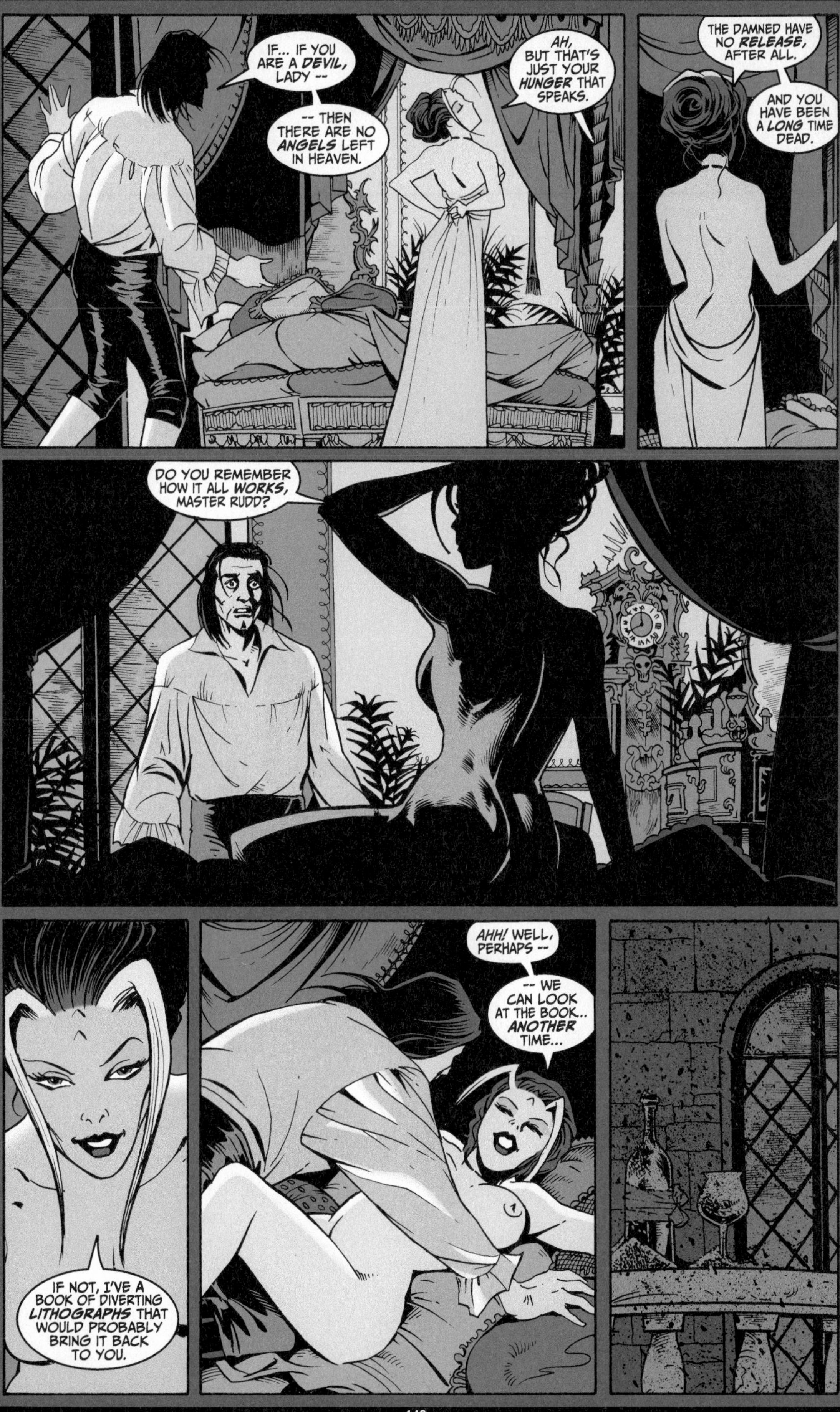
IF... IF YOU ARE A DEVIL, LADY --
-- THEN THERE ARE NO ANGELS LEFT IN HEAVEN.
AH, BUT THAT'S JUST YOUR HUNGER THAT SPEAKS.
THE DAMNED HAVE NO RELEASE, AFTER ALL.
AND YOU HAVE BEEN A LONG TIME DEAD.
DO YOU REMEMBER HOW IT ALL WORKS, MASTER RUDD?
IF NOT, I'VE A BOOK OF DIVERTING LITHOGRAPHS THAT WOULD PROBABLY BRING IT BACK TO YOU.
AHH! WELL, PERHAPS --
-- WE CAN LOOK AT THE BOOK... ANOTHER TIME...

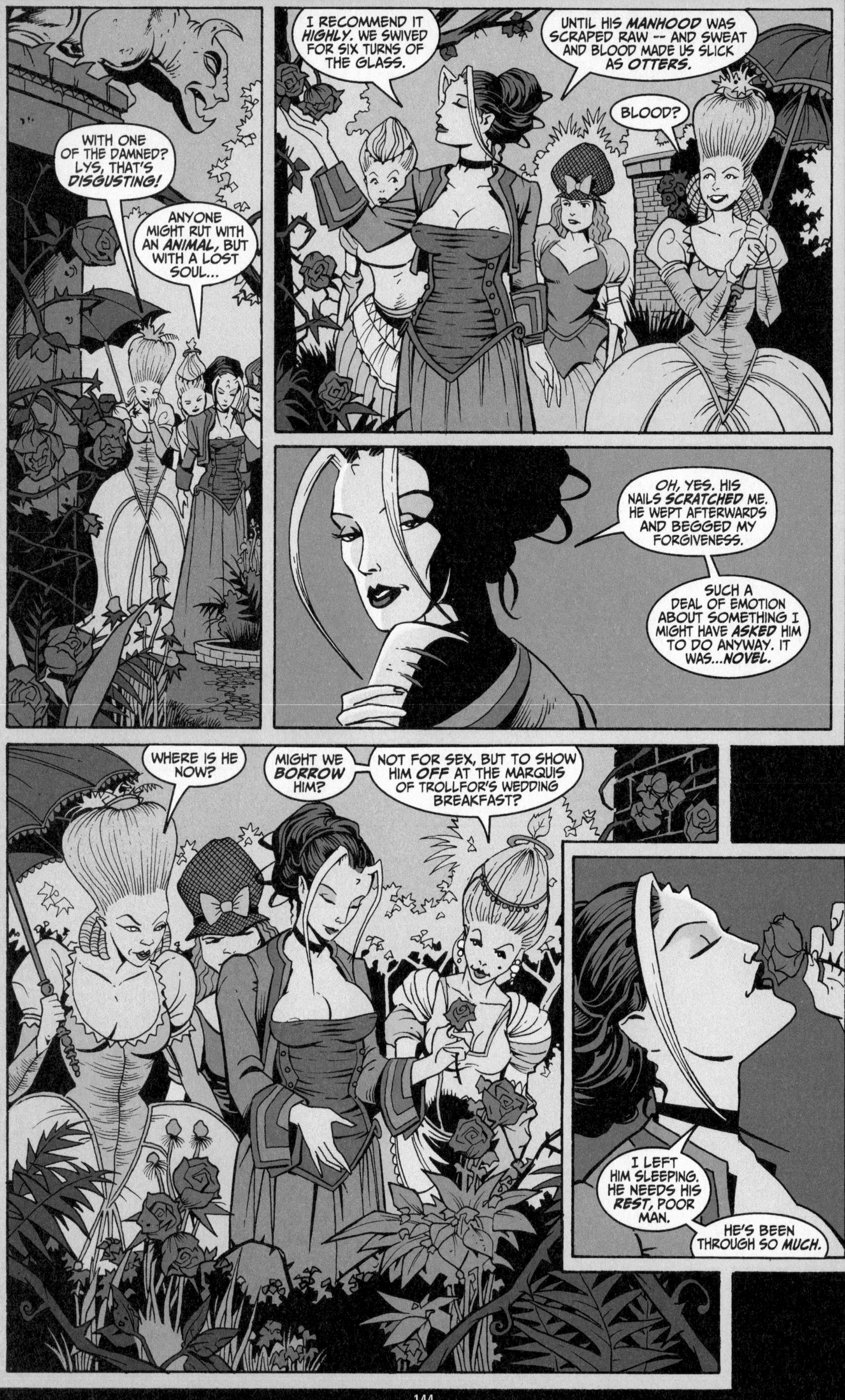
WITH ONE OF THE DAMNED? LYS, THAT'S DISGUSTING!
ANYONE MIGHT RUT WITH AN ANIMAL, BUT WITH A LOST SOUL...
I RECOMMEND IT HIGHLY. WE SWIVED FOR SIX TURNS OF THE GLASS.
UNTIL HIS MANHOOD WAS SCRAPED RAW -- AND SWEAT AND BLOOD MADE US SLICK AS OTTERS.
BLOOD?
OH, YES. HIS NAILS SCRATCHED ME. HE WEPT AFTERWARDS AND BEGGED MY FORGIVENESS.
SUCH A DEAL OF EMOTION ABOUT SOMETHING I MIGHT HAVE ASKED HIM TO DO ANYWAY. IT WAS...NOVEL.
WHERE IS HE NOW?
MIGHT WE BORROW HIM?
NOT FOR SEX, BUT TO SHOW HIM OFF AT THE MARQUIS OF TROLLFOR'S WEDDING BREAKFAST?
I LEFT HIM SLEEPING. HE NEEDS HIS REST, POOR MAN.
HE'S BEEN THROUGH SO MUCH.

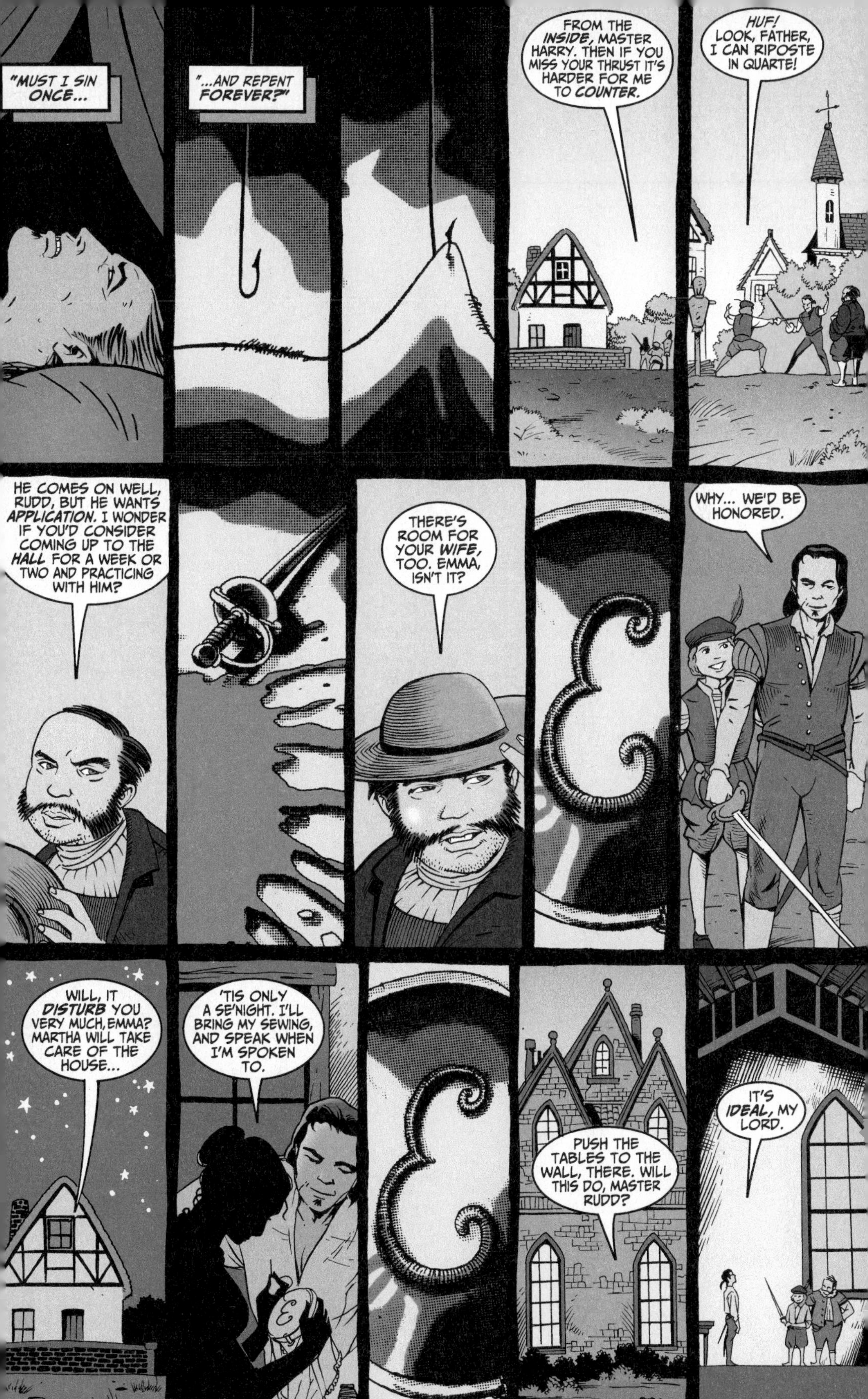
"MUST I SIN ONCE...
"...AND REPENT FOREVER?"
FROM THE INSIDE, MASTER HARRY. THEN IF YOU MISS YOUR THRUST IT'S HARDER FOR ME TO COUNTER.
HUF! LOOK, FATHER, I CAN RIPOSTE IN QUARTE!
HE COMES ON WELL, RUDD, BUT HE WANTS APPLICATION. I WONDER IF YOU'D CONSIDER COMING UP TO THE HALL FOR A WEEK OR TWO AND PRACTICING WITH HIM?
THERE'S ROOM FOR YOUR WIFE, TOO. EMMA, ISN'T IT?
WHY... WE'D BE HONORED.
WILL, IT DISTURB YOU VERY MUCH, EMMA? MARTHA WILL TAKE CARE OF THE HOUSE...
'TIS ONLY A SE'NIGHT. I'LL BRING MY SEWING, AND SPEAK WHEN I'M SPOKEN TO.
PUSH THE TABLES TO THE WALL, THERE. WILL THIS DO, MASTER RUDD?
IT'S IDEAL, MY LORD.

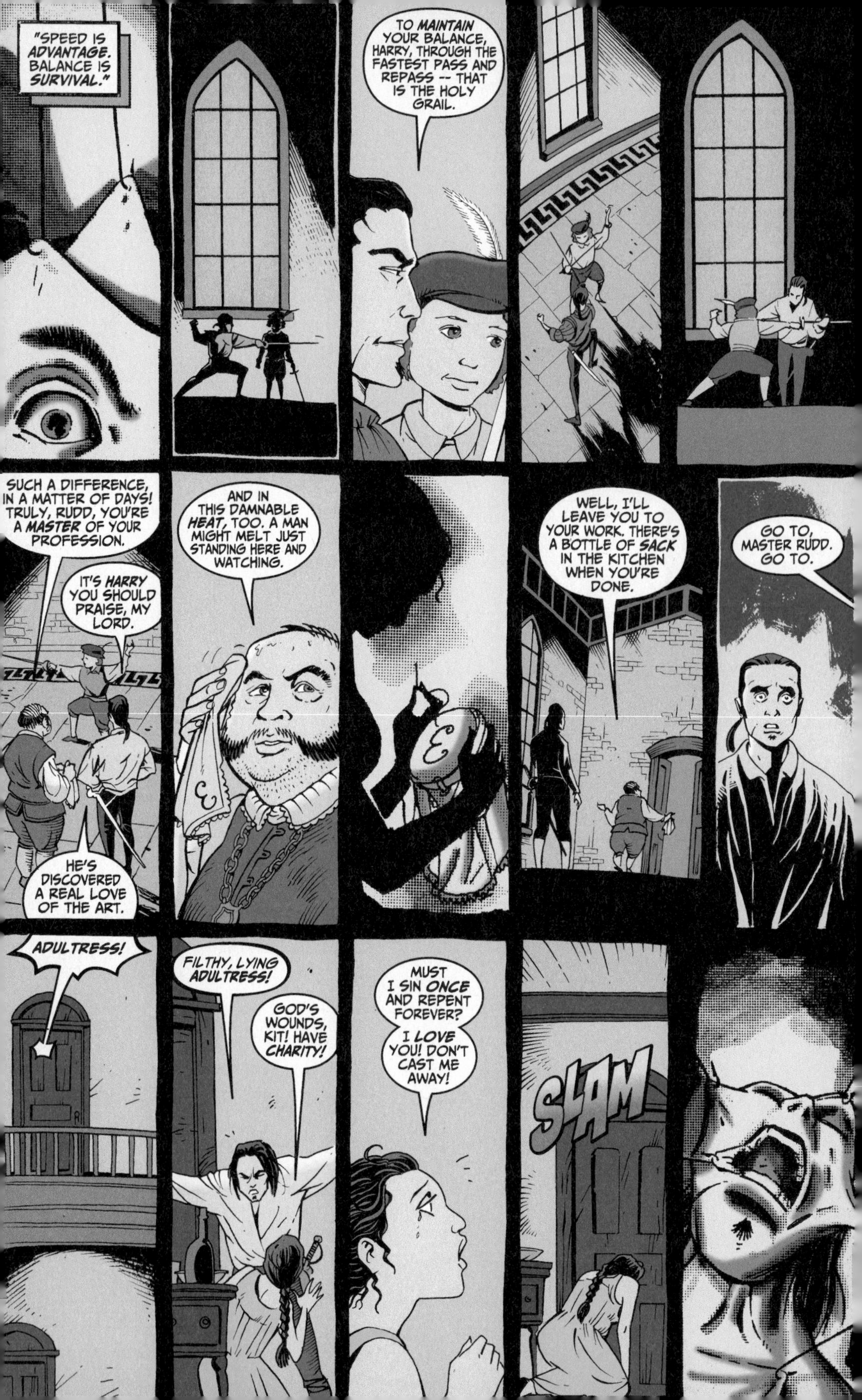
"SPEED IS ADVANTAGE. BALANCE IS SURVIVAL."
TO MAINTAIN YOUR BALANCE, HARRY, THROUGH THE FASTEST PASS AND REPASS -- THAT IS THE HOLY GRAIL.
SUCH A DIFFERENCE, IN A MATTER OF DAYS! TRULY, RUDD, YOU'RE A MASTER OF YOUR PROFESSION.
IT'S HARRY YOU SHOULD PRAISE, MY LORD.
HE'S DISCOVERED A REAL LOVE OF THE ART.
AND IN THIS DAMNABLE HEAT, TOO. A MAN MIGHT MELT JUST STANDING HERE AND WATCHING.
WELL, I'LL LEAVE YOU TO YOUR WORK. THERE'S A BOTTLE OF SACK IN THE KITCHEN WHEN YOU'RE DONE.
GO TO, MASTER RUDD. GO TO.
ADULTRESS!
FILTHY, LYING ADULTRESS!
GOD'S WOUNDS, KIT! HAVE CHARITY!
MUST I SIN ONCE AND REPENT FOREVER?
I LOVE YOU! DON'T CAST ME AWAY!
SLAM

ATTACK ME IN *TIERCE* AND I'LL SHOW YOU.

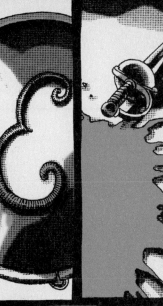

CHRISTOPHER, LOOK!

I'VE LEARNED THE FEINT.

...WHEREOF HE IS HEREBY ADJUDGED *GUILTY.*

HIS GOODS AND HIS CHATTELS *FORFEIT.*

HIS SENTENCE, TO BE HANGED AND THEN DRAWN.

AND MAY GOD HAVE *MERCY* ON HIS SOUL.

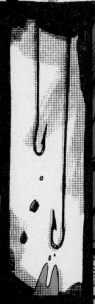

"YES, EMMA. WHERE THE SIN IS AS BLACK AS THIS --

"--FOREVER WOULD SEEM TO BE A *REASONABLE* EXCHANGE."

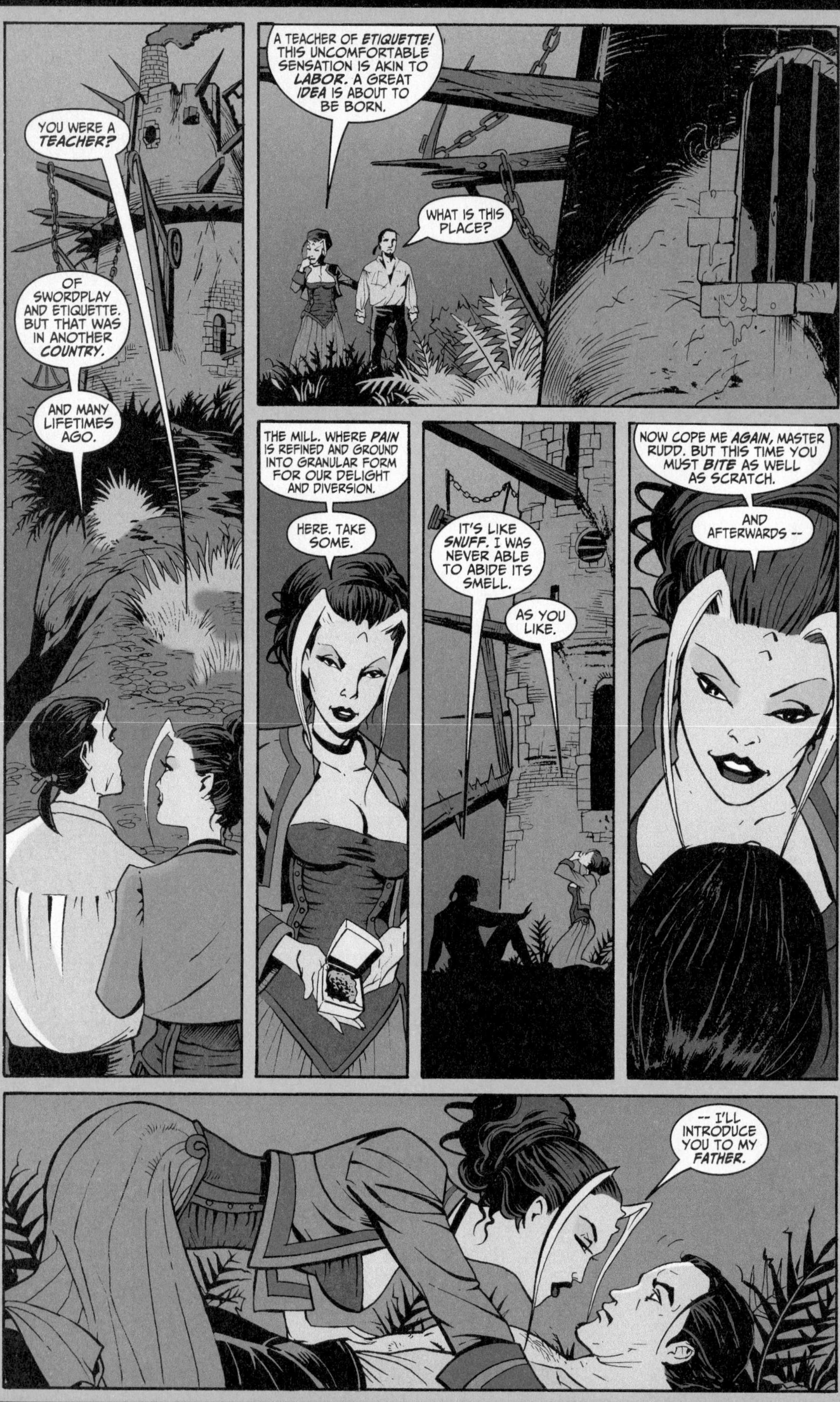

YOU WERE A *TEACHER?*
A TEACHER OF *ETIQUETTE!* THIS UNCOMFORTABLE SENSATION IS AKIN TO *LABOR.* A GREAT *IDEA* IS ABOUT TO BE BORN.
WHAT IS THIS PLACE?
OF SWORDPLAY AND ETIQUETTE. BUT THAT WAS IN ANOTHER *COUNTRY.*
AND MANY LIFETIMES AGO.
THE MILL. WHERE *PAIN* IS REFINED AND GROUND INTO GRANULAR FORM FOR OUR DELIGHT AND DIVERSION.
HERE. TAKE SOME.
IT'S LIKE *SNUFF.* I WAS NEVER ABLE TO ABIDE ITS SMELL.
AS YOU LIKE.
NOW COPE ME *AGAIN,* MASTER RUDD. BUT THIS TIME YOU MUST *BITE* AS WELL AS SCRATCH.
AND AFTERWARDS --
-- I'LL INTRODUCE YOU TO MY *FATHER.*

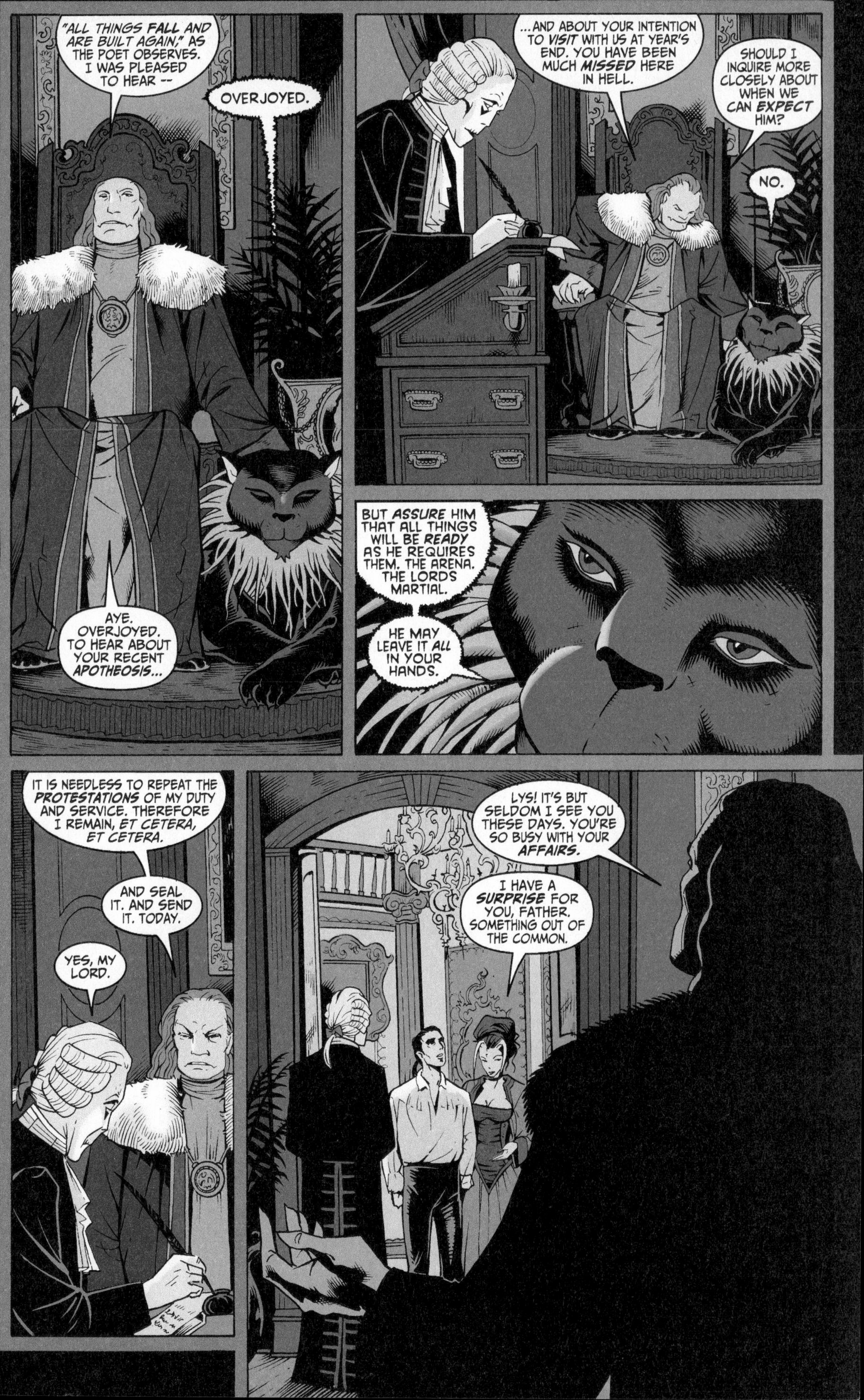

"ALL THINGS FALL AND ARE BUILT AGAIN," AS THE POET OBSERVES. I WAS PLEASED TO HEAR --
OVERJOYED.
AYE. OVERJOYED. TO HEAR ABOUT YOUR RECENT APOTHEOSIS...
...AND ABOUT YOUR INTENTION TO VISIT WITH US AT YEAR'S END. YOU HAVE BEEN MUCH MISSED HERE IN HELL.
SHOULD I INQUIRE MORE CLOSELY ABOUT WHEN WE CAN EXPECT HIM?
NO.
BUT ASSURE HIM THAT ALL THINGS WILL BE READY AS HE REQUIRES THEM. THE ARENA. THE LORDS MARTIAL.
HE MAY LEAVE IT ALL IN YOUR HANDS.
IT IS NEEDLESS TO REPEAT THE PROTESTATIONS OF MY DUTY AND SERVICE. THEREFORE I REMAIN, ET CETERA, ET CETERA.
AND SEAL IT. AND SEND IT. TODAY.
YES, MY LORD.
LYS! IT'S BUT SELDOM I SEE YOU THESE DAYS. YOU'RE SO BUSY WITH YOUR AFFAIRS.
I HAVE A SURPRISE FOR YOU, FATHER. SOMETHING OUT OF THE COMMON.

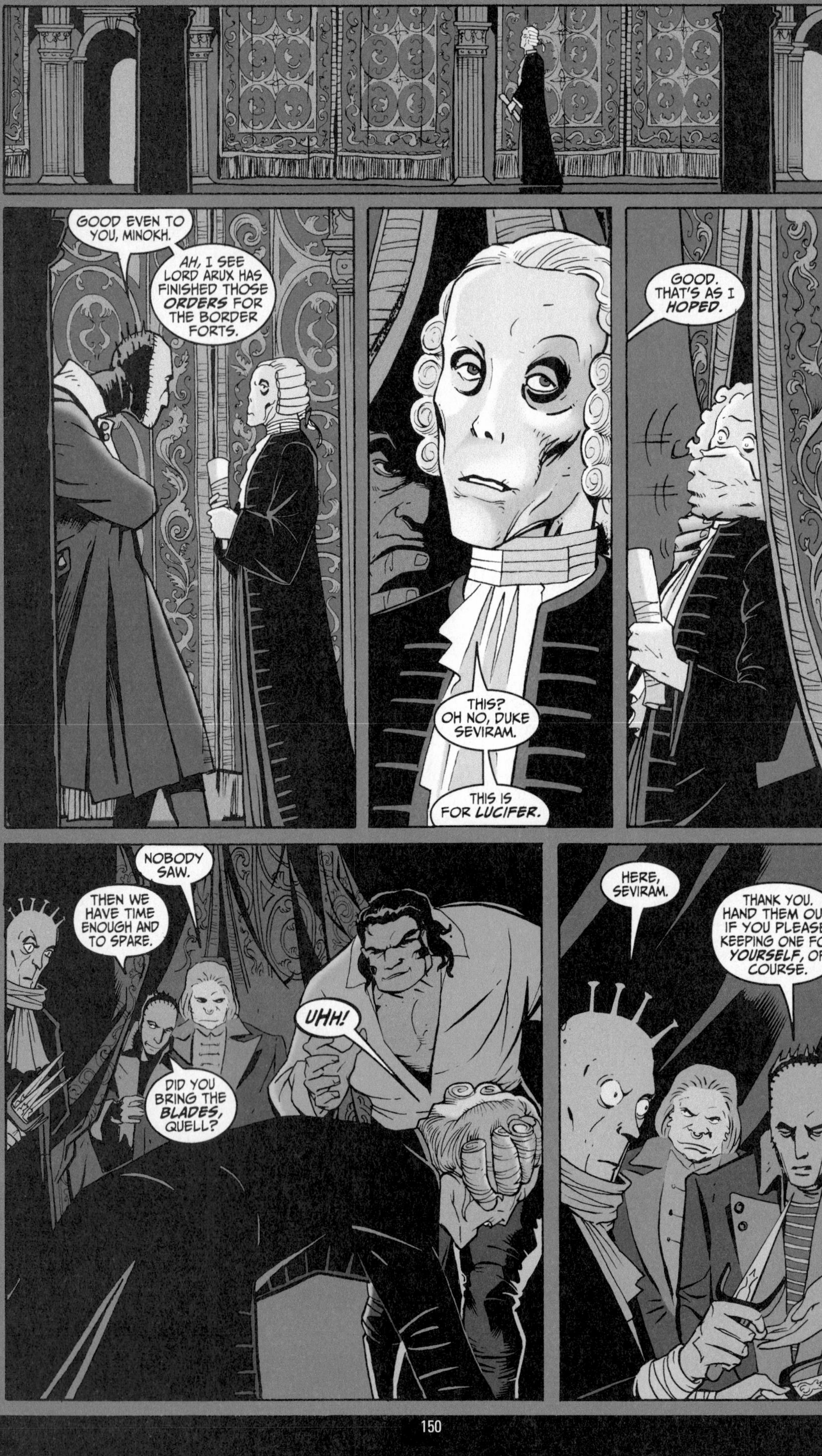
GOOD EVEN TO YOU, MINOKH.
AH, I SEE LORD ARUX HAS FINISHED THOSE ORDERS FOR THE BORDER FORTS.
THIS? OH NO, DUKE SEVIRAM.
THIS IS FOR LUCIFER.
GOOD. THAT'S AS I HOPED.
NOBODY SAW.
THEN WE HAVE TIME ENOUGH AND TO SPARE.
UHH!
DID YOU BRING THE BLADES, QUELL?
HERE, SEVIRAM.
THANK YOU. HAND THEM OUT, IF YOU PLEASE. KEEPING ONE FOR YOURSELF, OF COURSE.

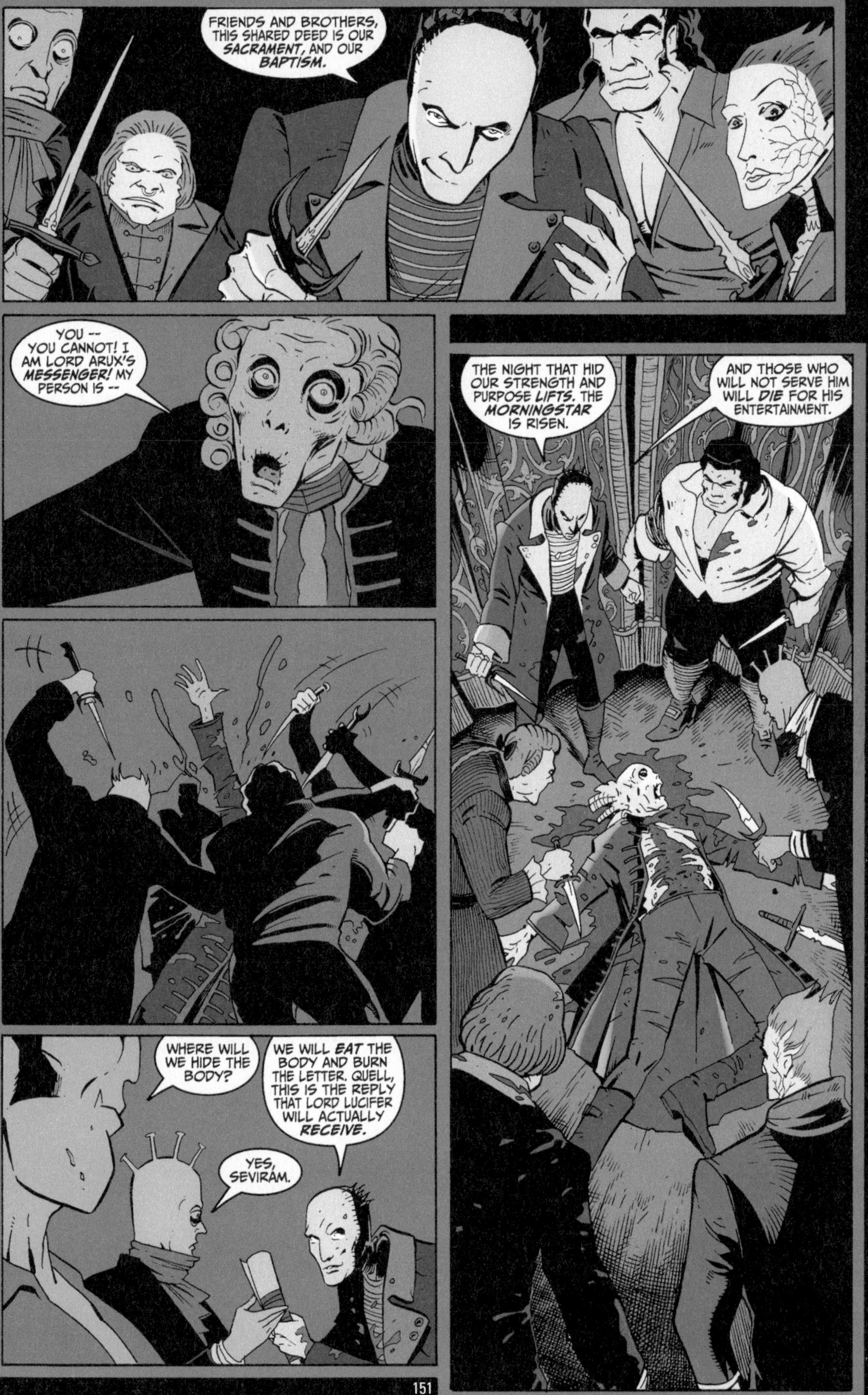

FRIENDS AND BROTHERS, THIS SHARED DEED IS OUR SACRAMENT, AND OUR BAPTISM.
YOU -- YOU CANNOT! I AM LORD ARUX'S MESSENGER! MY PERSON IS --
THE NIGHT THAT HID OUR STRENGTH AND PURPOSE LIFTS. THE MORNINGSTAR IS RISEN.
AND THOSE WHO WILL NOT SERVE HIM WILL DIE FOR HIS ENTERTAINMENT.
WHERE WILL WE HIDE THE BODY?
WE WILL EAT THE BODY AND BURN THE LETTER. QUELL, THIS IS THE REPLY THAT LORD LUCIFER WILL ACTUALLY RECEIVE.
YES, SEVIRAM.

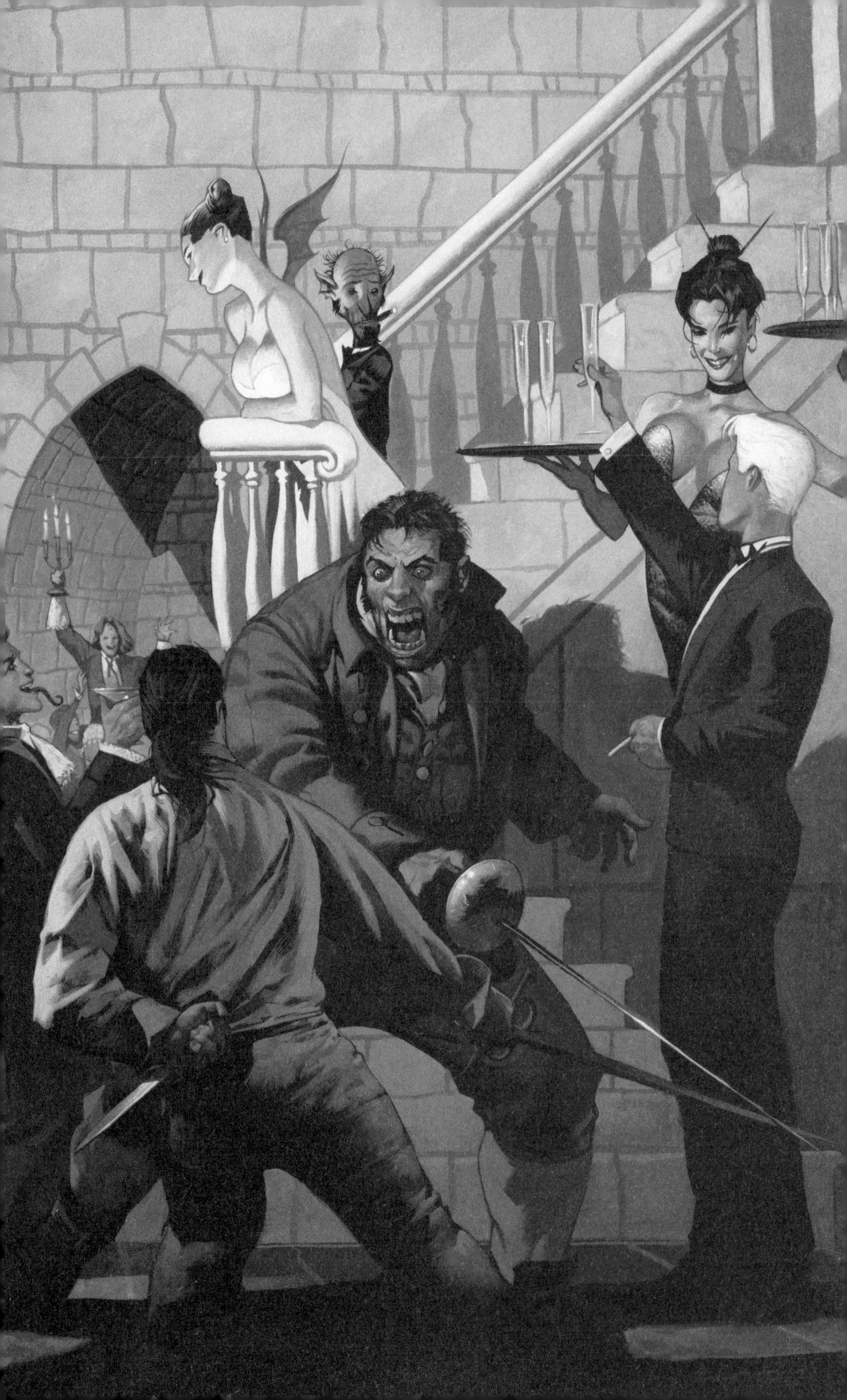

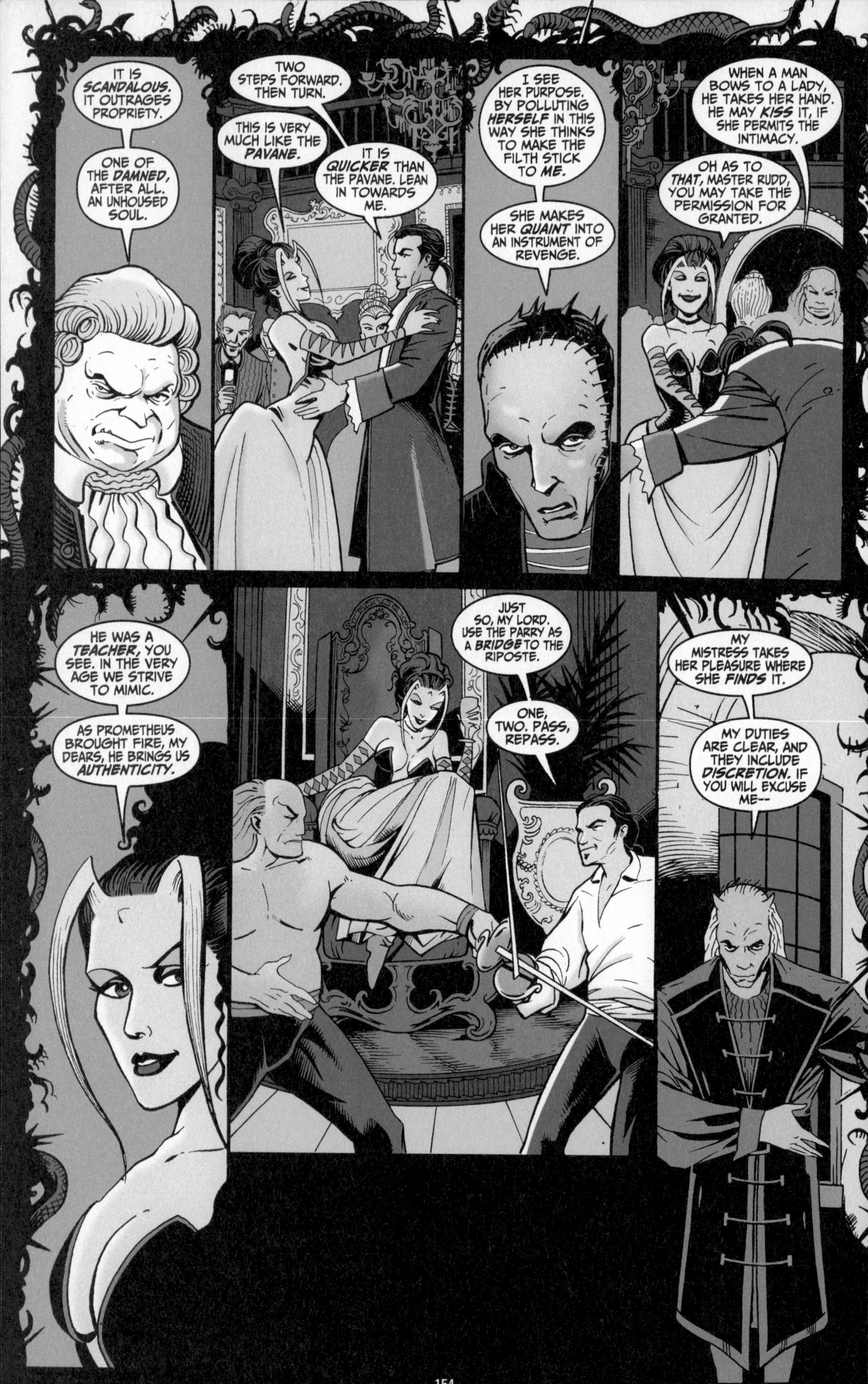
IT IS SCANDALOUS. IT OUTRAGES PROPRIETY.
ONE OF THE DAMNED, AFTER ALL. AN UNHOUSED SOUL.
TWO STEPS FORWARD. THEN TURN.
THIS IS VERY MUCH LIKE THE PAVANE.
IT IS QUICKER THAN THE PAVANE. LEAN IN TOWARDS ME.
I SEE HER PURPOSE. BY POLLUTING HERSELF IN THIS WAY SHE THINKS TO MAKE THE FILTH STICK TO ME.
SHE MAKES HER QUAINT INTO AN INSTRUMENT OF REVENGE.
WHEN A MAN BOWS TO A LADY, HE TAKES HER HAND. HE MAY KISS IT, IF SHE PERMITS THE INTIMACY.
OH AS TO THAT, MASTER RUDD, YOU MAY TAKE THE PERMISSION FOR GRANTED.
HE WAS A TEACHER, YOU SEE. IN THE VERY AGE WE STRIVE TO MIMIC.
AS PROMETHEUS BROUGHT FIRE, MY DEARS, HE BRINGS US AUTHENTICITY.
JUST SO, MY LORD. USE THE PARRY AS A BRIDGE TO THE RIPOSTE.
ONE, TWO. PASS, REPASS.
MY MISTRESS TAKES HER PLEASURE WHERE SHE FINDS IT.
MY DUTIES ARE CLEAR, AND THEY INCLUDE DISCRETION. IF YOU WILL EXCUSE ME--

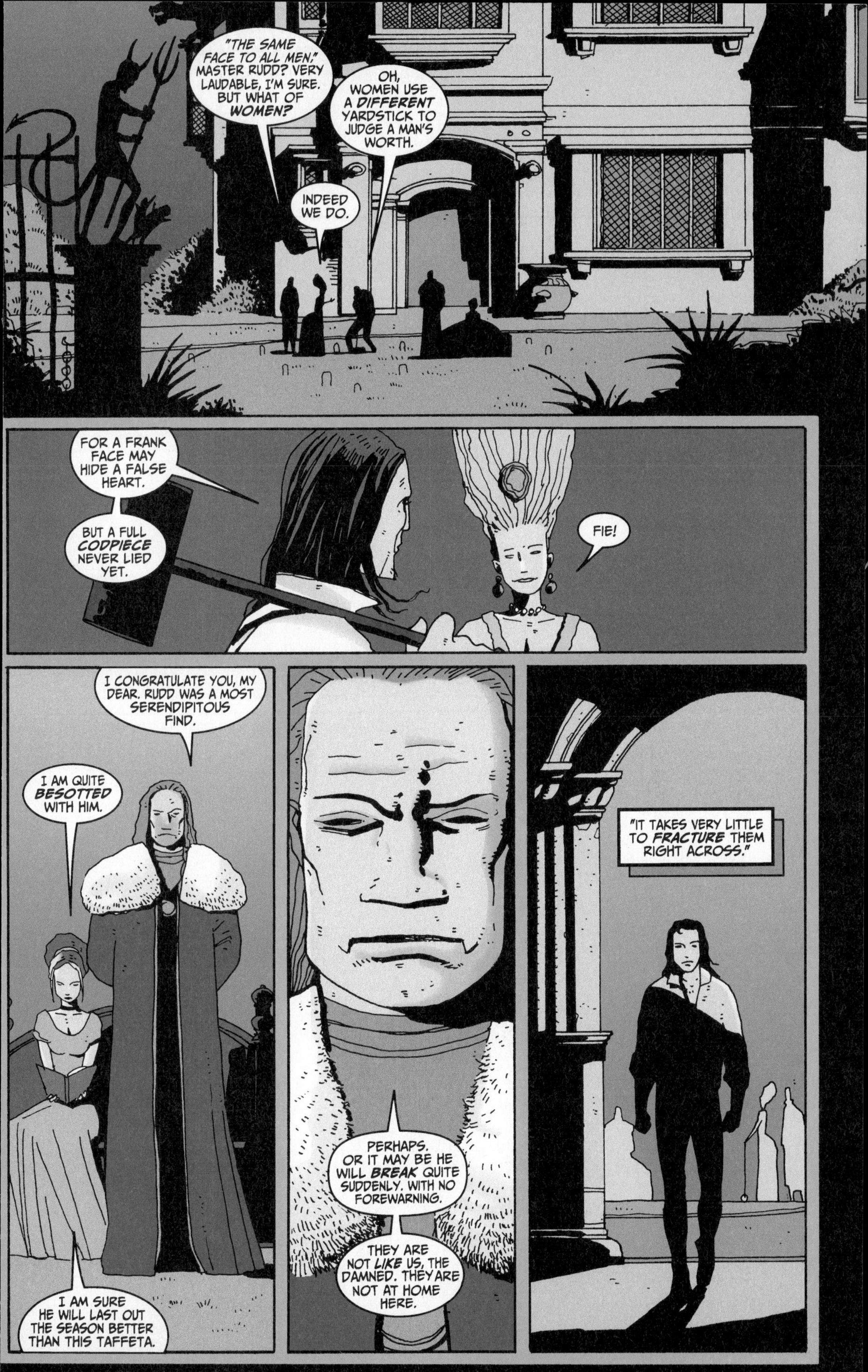
"THE SAME FACE TO ALL MEN," MASTER RUDD? VERY LAUDABLE, I'M SURE. BUT WHAT OF WOMEN?
OH, WOMEN USE A DIFFERENT YARDSTICK TO JUDGE A MAN'S WORTH.
INDEED WE DO.
FOR A FRANK FACE MAY HIDE A FALSE HEART.
BUT A FULL CODPIECE NEVER LIED YET.
FIE!
I CONGRATULATE YOU, MY DEAR. RUDD WAS A MOST SERENDIPITOUS FIND.
I AM QUITE BESOTTED WITH HIM.
I AM SURE HE WILL LAST OUT THE SEASON BETTER THAN THIS TAFFETA.
PERHAPS. OR IT MAY BE HE WILL BREAK QUITE SUDDENLY. WITH NO FOREWARNING.
THEY ARE NOT LIKE US, THE DAMNED. THEY ARE NOT AT HOME HERE.
"IT TAKES VERY LITTLE TO FRACTURE THEM RIGHT ACROSS."

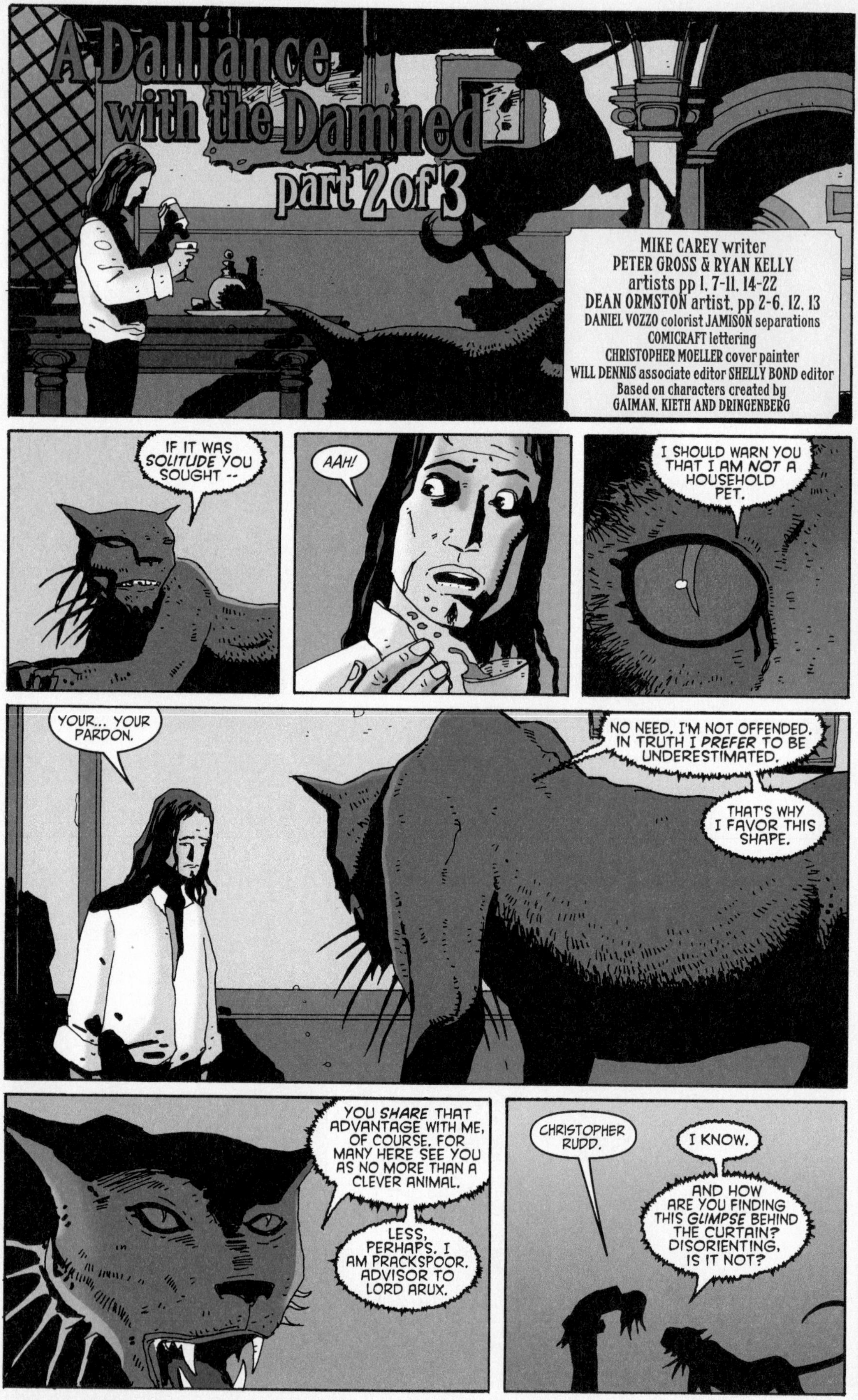
A Dalliance with the Damned
part 2 of 3
MIKE CAREY writer
PETER GROSS & RYAN KELLY artists pp 1, 7-11, 14-22
DEAN ORMSTON artist, pp 2-6, 12, 13
DANIEL VOZZO colorist JAMISON separations
COMICRAFT lettering
CHRISTOPHER MOELLER cover painter
WILL DENNIS associate editor SHELLY BOND editor
Based on characters created by GAIMAN, KIETH AND DRINGENBERG
IF IT WAS SOLITUDE YOU SOUGHT --
AAH!
I SHOULD WARN YOU THAT I AM NOT A HOUSEHOLD PET.
YOUR... YOUR PARDON.
NO NEED. I'M NOT OFFENDED. IN TRUTH I PREFER TO BE UNDERESTIMATED.
THAT'S WHY I FAVOR THIS SHAPE.
YOU SHARE THAT ADVANTAGE WITH ME, OF COURSE. FOR MANY HERE SEE YOU AS NO MORE THAN A CLEVER ANIMAL.
LESS, PERHAPS. I AM PRACKSPOOR, ADVISOR TO LORD ARUX.
CHRISTOPHER RUDD.
I KNOW.
AND HOW ARE YOU FINDING THIS GLIMPSE BEHIND THE CURTAIN? DISORIENTING, IS IT NOT?

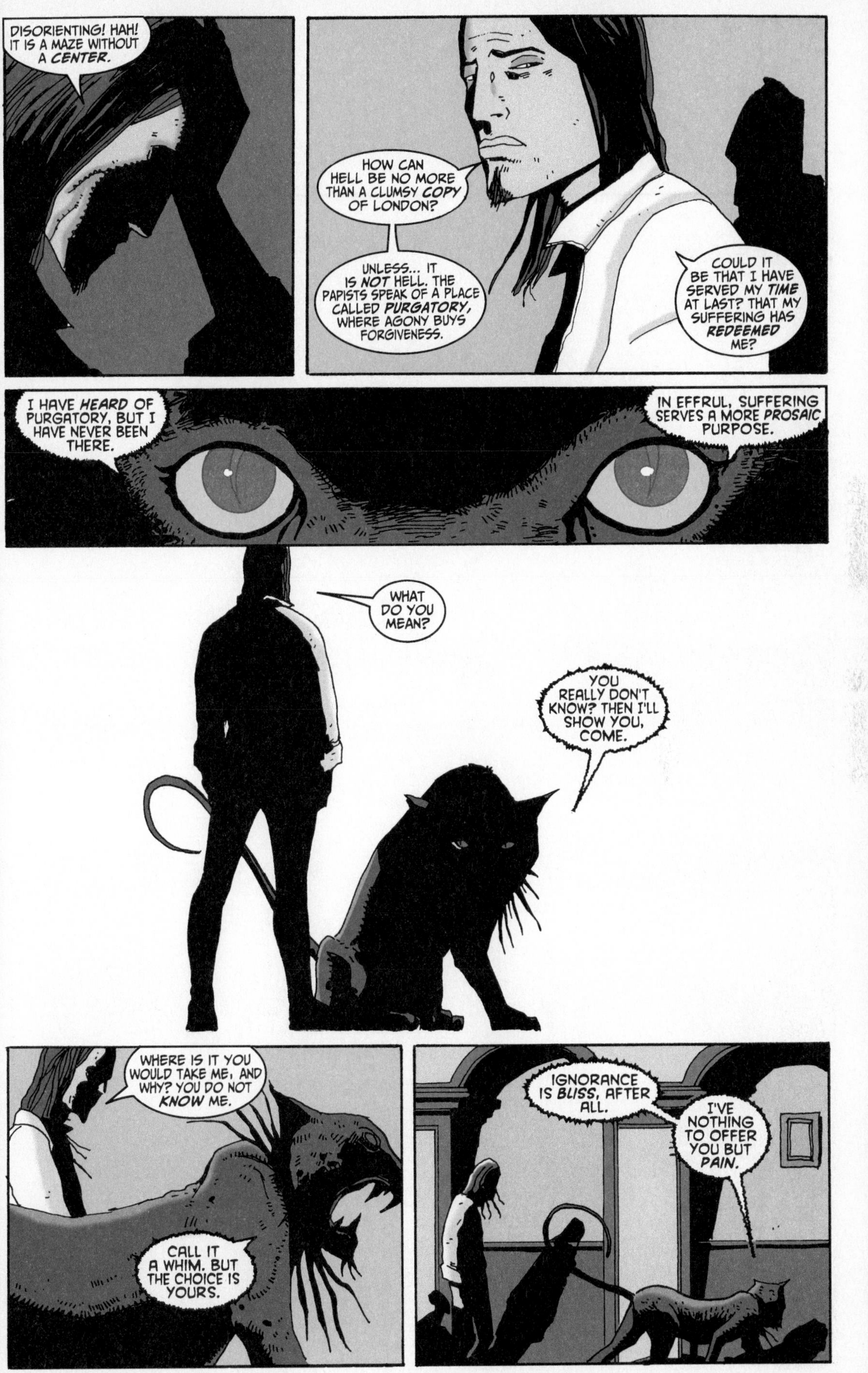

DISORIENTING! HAH! IT IS A MAZE WITHOUT A CENTER.
HOW CAN HELL BE NO MORE THAN A CLUMSY COPY OF LONDON?
UNLESS... IT IS NOT HELL. THE PAPISTS SPEAK OF A PLACE CALLED PURGATORY, WHERE AGONY BUYS FORGIVENESS.
COULD IT BE THAT I HAVE SERVED MY TIME AT LAST? THAT MY SUFFERING HAS REDEEMED ME?
I HAVE HEARD OF PURGATORY, BUT I HAVE NEVER BEEN THERE.
IN EFFRUL, SUFFERING SERVES A MORE PROSAIC PURPOSE.
WHAT DO YOU MEAN?
YOU REALLY DON'T KNOW? THEN I'LL SHOW YOU, COME.
WHERE IS IT YOU WOULD TAKE ME, AND WHY? YOU DO NOT KNOW ME.
CALL IT A WHIM. BUT THE CHOICE IS YOURS.
IGNORANCE IS BLISS, AFTER ALL.
I'VE NOTHING TO OFFER YOU BUT PAIN.

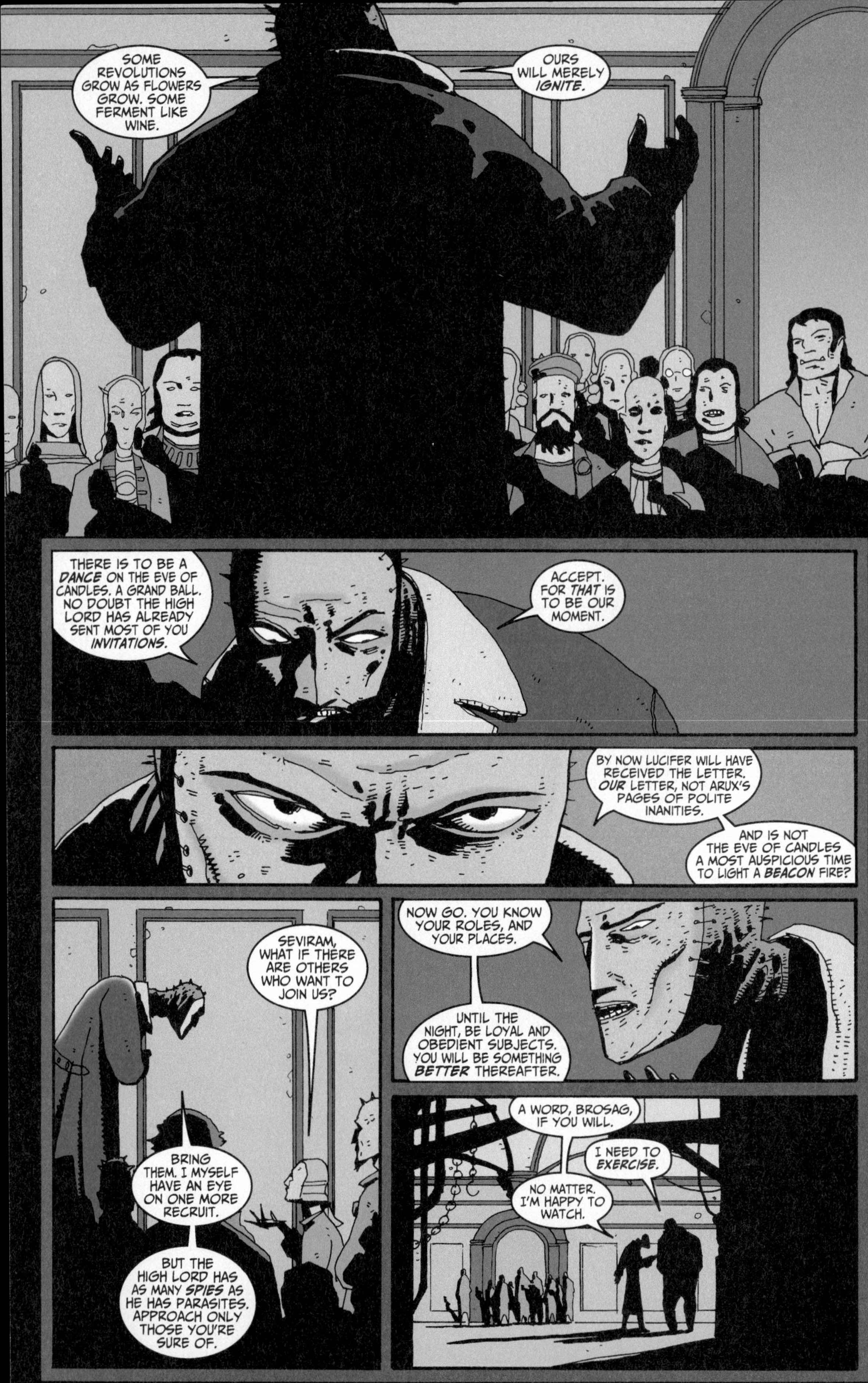
SOME REVOLUTIONS GROW AS FLOWERS GROW. SOME FERMENT LIKE WINE.
OURS WILL MERELY *IGNITE.*
THERE IS TO BE A *DANCE* ON THE EVE OF CANDLES. A GRAND BALL. NO DOUBT THE HIGH LORD HAS ALREADY SENT MOST OF YOU *INVITATIONS.*
ACCEPT. FOR *THAT* IS TO BE OUR MOMENT.
BY NOW LUCIFER WILL HAVE RECEIVED THE LETTER. *OUR* LETTER, NOT ARUX'S PAGES OF POLITE INANITIES.
AND IS NOT THE EVE OF CANDLES A MOST AUSPICIOUS TIME TO LIGHT A *BEACON* FIRE?
SEVIRAM, WHAT IF THERE ARE OTHERS WHO WANT TO JOIN US?
BRING THEM. I MYSELF HAVE AN EYE ON ONE MORE RECRUIT.
BUT THE HIGH LORD HAS AS MANY *SPIES* AS HE HAS PARASITES. APPROACH ONLY THOSE YOU'RE SURE OF.
NOW GO. YOU KNOW YOUR ROLES, AND YOUR PLACES.
UNTIL THE NIGHT, BE LOYAL AND OBEDIENT SUBJECTS. YOU WILL BE SOMETHING *BETTER* THEREAFTER.
A WORD, BROSAG, IF YOU WILL.
I NEED TO *EXERCISE.*
NO MATTER. I'M HAPPY TO WATCH.

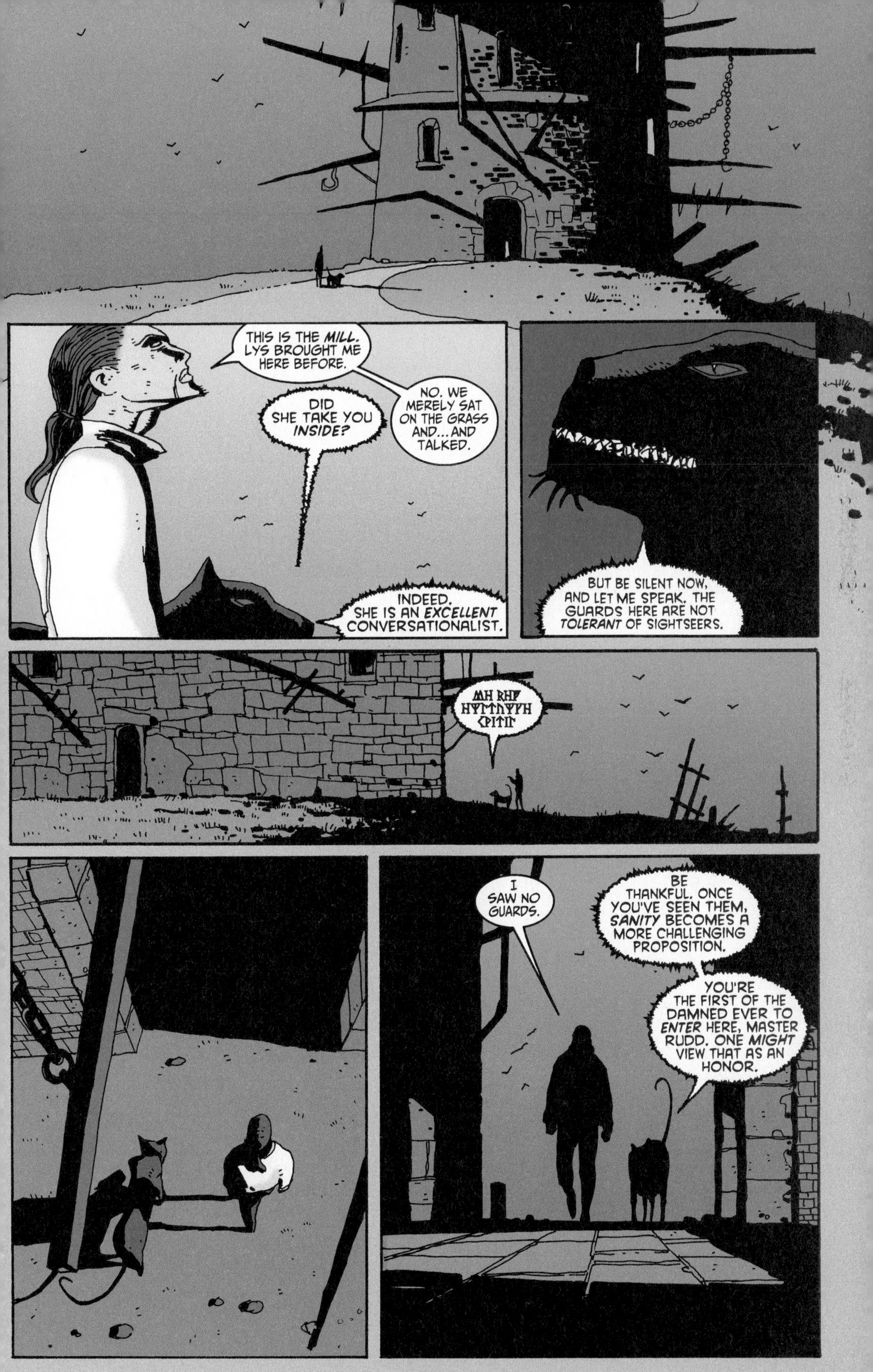
THIS IS THE MILL. LYS BROUGHT ME HERE BEFORE.
NO. WE MERELY SAT ON THE GRASS AND... AND TALKED.
DID SHE TAKE YOU INSIDE?
INDEED. SHE IS AN EXCELLENT CONVERSATIONALIST.
BUT BE SILENT NOW, AND LET ME SPEAK. THE GUARDS HERE ARE NOT TOLERANT OF SIGHTSEERS.
I SAW NO GUARDS.
BE THANKFUL. ONCE YOU'VE SEEN THEM, SANITY BECOMES A MORE CHALLENGING PROPOSITION.
YOU'RE THE FIRST OF THE DAMNED EVER TO ENTER HERE, MASTER RUDD. ONE MIGHT VIEW THAT AS AN HONOR.

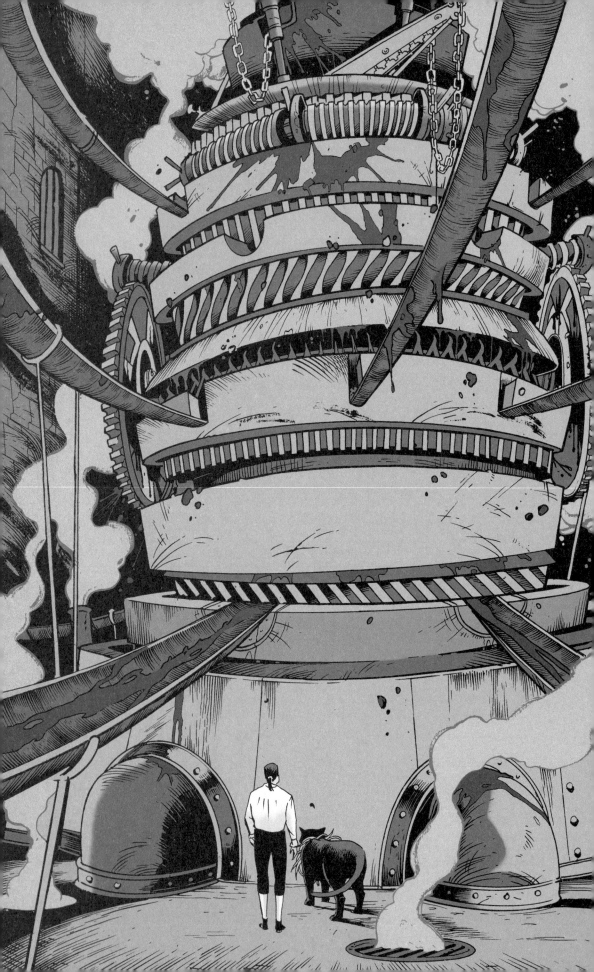

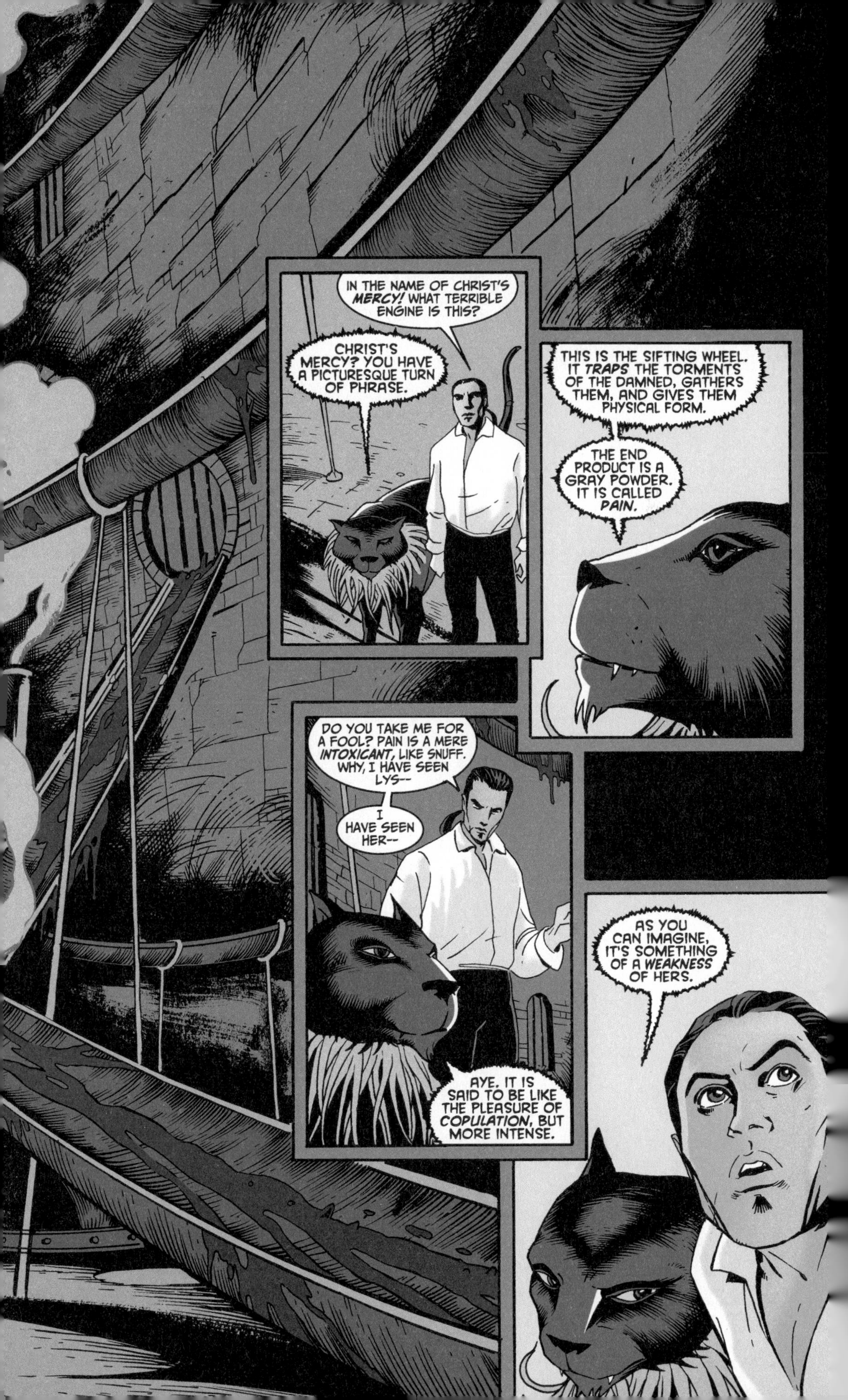
IN THE NAME OF CHRIST'S MERCY! WHAT TERRIBLE ENGINE IS THIS?
CHRIST'S MERCY? YOU HAVE A PICTURESQUE TURN OF PHRASE.
THIS IS THE SIFTING WHEEL. IT TRAPS THE TORMENTS OF THE DAMNED, GATHERS THEM, AND GIVES THEM PHYSICAL FORM.
THE END PRODUCT IS A GRAY POWDER. IT IS CALLED PAIN.
DO YOU TAKE ME FOR A FOOL? PAIN IS A MERE INTOXICANT, LIKE SNUFF. WHY, I HAVE SEEN LYS--
I HAVE SEEN HER--
AYE. IT IS SAID TO BE LIKE THE PLEASURE OF COPULATION, BUT MORE INTENSE.
AS YOU CAN IMAGINE, IT'S SOMETHING OF A WEAKNESS OF HERS.

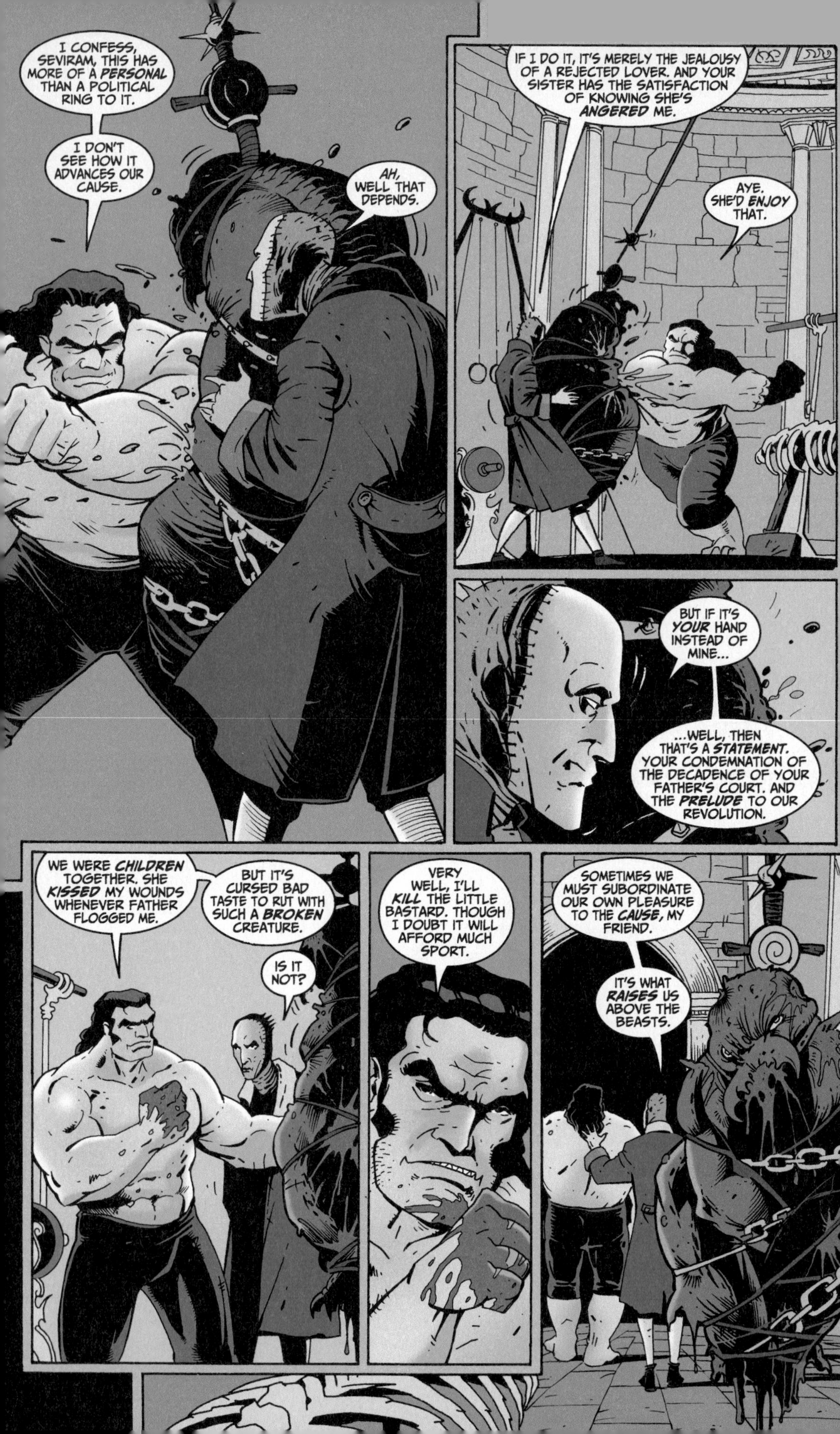
I CONFESS, SEVIRAM, THIS HAS MORE OF A PERSONAL THAN A POLITICAL RING TO IT.
I DON'T SEE HOW IT ADVANCES OUR CAUSE.
AH, WELL THAT DEPENDS.
IF I DO IT, IT'S MERELY THE JEALOUSY OF A REJECTED LOVER. AND YOUR SISTER HAS THE SATISFACTION OF KNOWING SHE'S ANGERED ME.
AYE. SHE'D ENJOY THAT.
BUT IF IT'S YOUR HAND INSTEAD OF MINE...
...WELL, THEN THAT'S A STATEMENT. YOUR CONDEMNATION OF THE DECADENCE OF YOUR FATHER'S COURT. AND THE PRELUDE TO OUR REVOLUTION.
WE WERE CHILDREN TOGETHER. SHE KISSED MY WOUNDS WHENEVER FATHER FLOGGED ME.
BUT IT'S CURSED BAD TASTE TO RUT WITH SUCH A BROKEN CREATURE.
IS IT NOT?
VERY WELL, I'LL KILL THE LITTLE BASTARD. THOUGH I DOUBT IT WILL AFFORD MUCH SPORT.
SOMETIMES WE MUST SUBORDINATE OUR OWN PLEASURE TO THE CAUSE, MY FRIEND.
IT'S WHAT RAISES US ABOVE THE BEASTS.

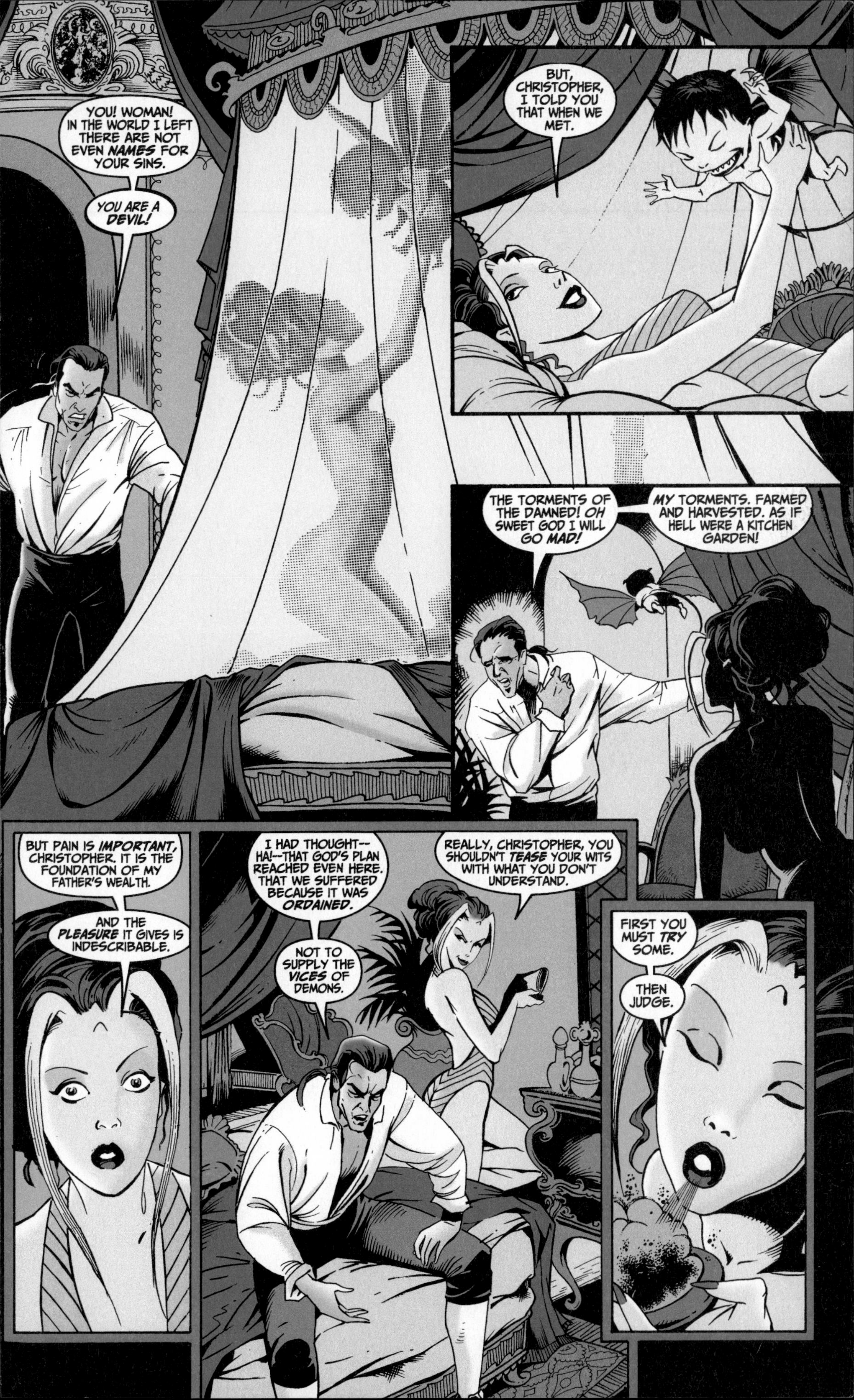
YOU! WOMAN! IN THE WORLD I LEFT THERE ARE NOT EVEN NAMES FOR YOUR SINS.
YOU ARE A DEVIL!
BUT, CHRISTOPHER, I TOLD YOU THAT WHEN WE MET.
THE TORMENTS OF THE DAMNED! OH SWEET GOD I WILL GO MAD!
MY TORMENTS. FARMED AND HARVESTED. AS IF HELL WERE A KITCHEN GARDEN!
BUT PAIN IS IMPORTANT, CHRISTOPHER. IT IS THE FOUNDATION OF MY FATHER'S WEALTH.
AND THE PLEASURE IT GIVES IS INDESCRIBABLE.
I HAD THOUGHT--HA!--THAT GOD'S PLAN REACHED EVEN HERE. THAT WE SUFFERED BECAUSE IT WAS ORDAINED.
NOT TO SUPPLY THE VICES OF DEMONS.
REALLY, CHRISTOPHER, YOU SHOULDN'T TEASE YOUR WITS WITH WHAT YOU DON'T UNDERSTAND.
FIRST YOU MUST TRY SOME.
THEN JUDGE.

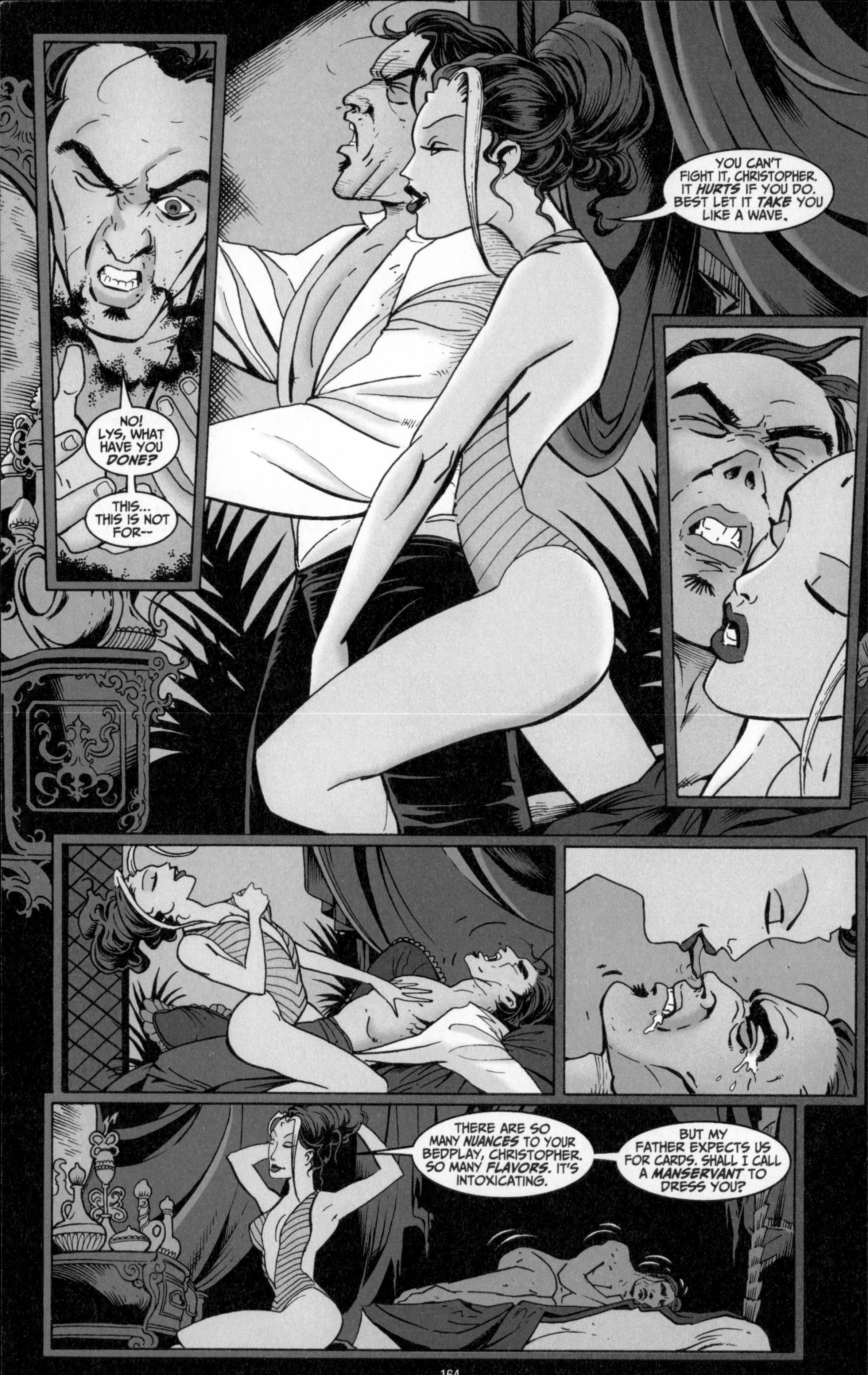
YOU CAN'T FIGHT IT, CHRISTOPHER. IT HURTS IF YOU DO. BEST LET IT TAKE YOU LIKE A WAVE.
NO! LYS, WHAT HAVE YOU DONE?
THIS... THIS IS NOT FOR--
THERE ARE SO MANY NUANCES TO YOUR BEDPLAY, CHRISTOPHER. SO MANY FLAVORS. IT'S INTOXICATING.
BUT MY FATHER EXPECTS US FOR CARDS. SHALL I CALL A MANSERVANT TO DRESS YOU?

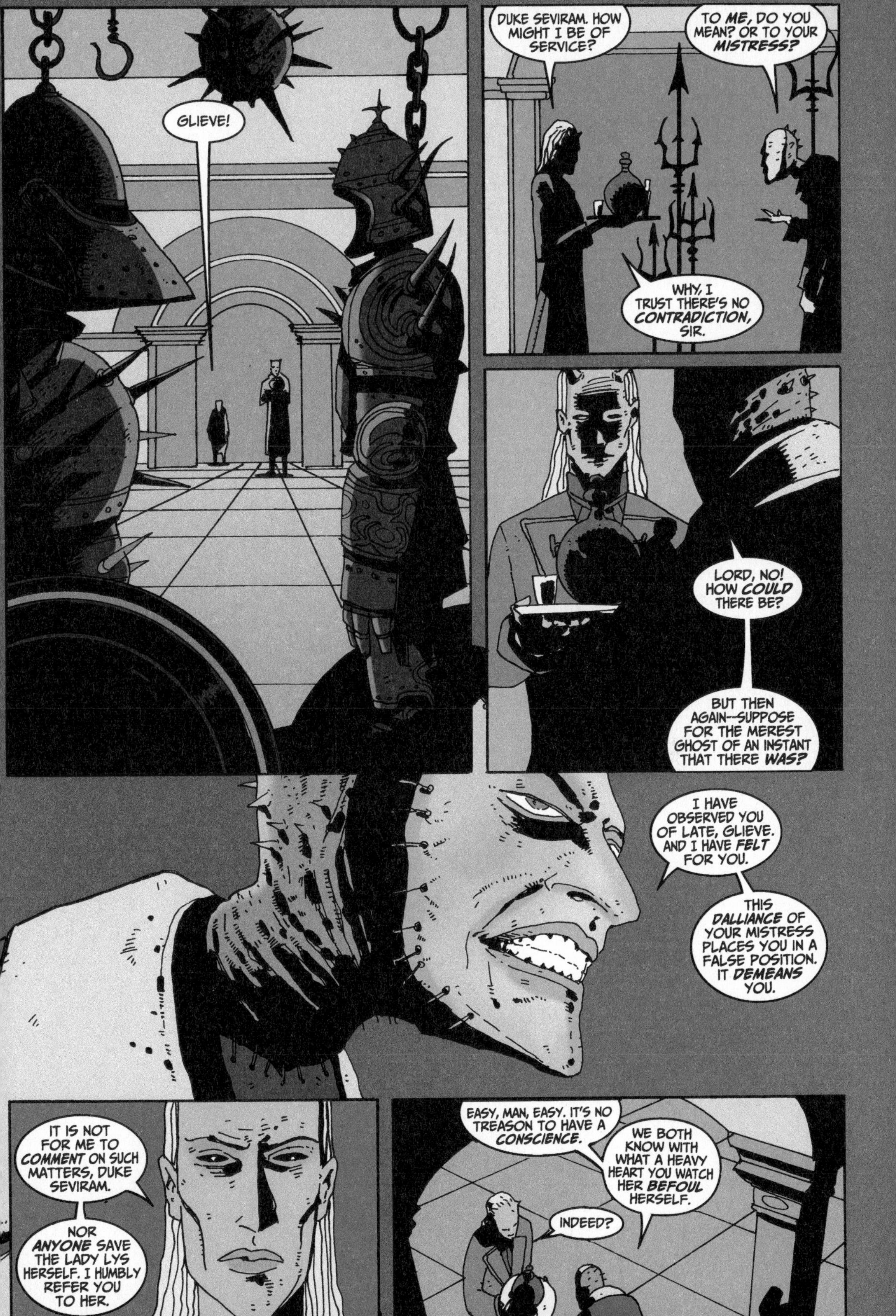
GLIEVE!
DUKE SEVIRAM. HOW MIGHT I BE OF SERVICE?
TO ME, DO YOU MEAN? OR TO YOUR MISTRESS?
WHY, I TRUST THERE'S NO CONTRADICTION, SIR.
LORD, NO! HOW COULD THERE BE?
BUT THEN AGAIN--SUPPOSE FOR THE MEREST GHOST OF AN INSTANT THAT THERE WAS?
I HAVE OBSERVED YOU OF LATE, GLIEVE. AND I HAVE FELT FOR YOU.
THIS DALLIANCE OF YOUR MISTRESS PLACES YOU IN A FALSE POSITION. IT DEMEANS YOU.
IT IS NOT FOR ME TO COMMENT ON SUCH MATTERS, DUKE SEVIRAM.
NOR ANYONE SAVE THE LADY LYS HERSELF. I HUMBLY REFER YOU TO HER.
EASY, MAN, EASY. IT'S NO TREASON TO HAVE A CONSCIENCE.
WE BOTH KNOW WITH WHAT A HEAVY HEART YOU WATCH HER BEFOUL HERSELF.
INDEED?

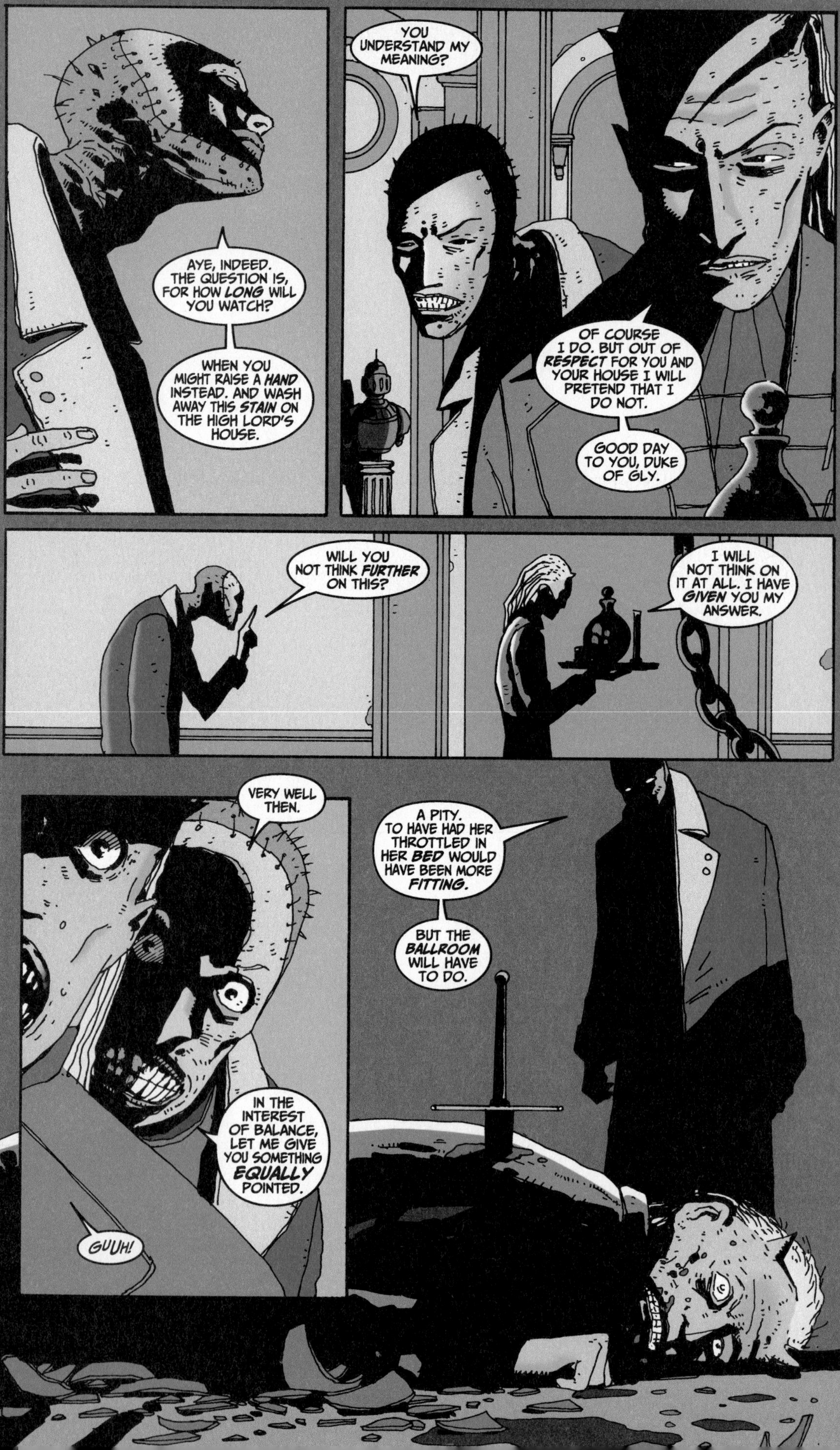
AYE, INDEED. THE QUESTION IS, FOR HOW LONG WILL YOU WATCH?
WHEN YOU MIGHT RAISE A HAND INSTEAD. AND WASH AWAY THIS STAIN ON THE HIGH LORD'S HOUSE.
YOU UNDERSTAND MY MEANING?
OF COURSE I DO. BUT OUT OF RESPECT FOR YOU AND YOUR HOUSE I WILL PRETEND THAT I DO NOT.
GOOD DAY TO YOU, DUKE OF GLY.
WILL YOU NOT THINK FURTHER ON THIS?
I WILL NOT THINK ON IT AT ALL. I HAVE GIVEN YOU MY ANSWER.
VERY WELL THEN.
IN THE INTEREST OF BALANCE, LET ME GIVE YOU SOMETHING EQUALLY POINTED.
GUUH!
A PITY. TO HAVE HAD HER THROTTLED IN HER BED WOULD HAVE BEEN MORE FITTING.
BUT THE BALLROOM WILL HAVE TO DO.

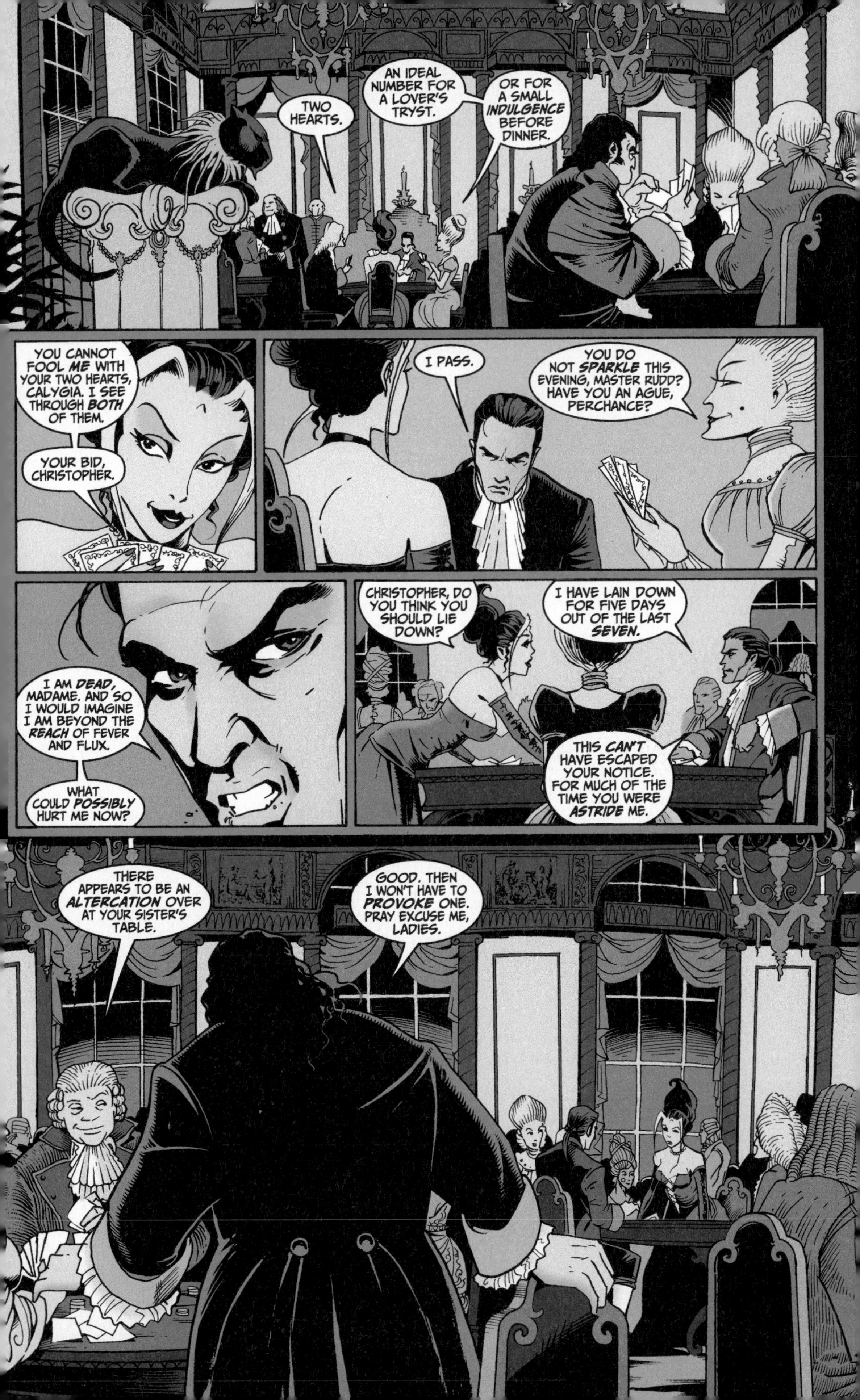
TWO HEARTS.
AN IDEAL NUMBER FOR A LOVER'S TRYST.
OR FOR A SMALL INDULGENCE BEFORE DINNER.
YOU CANNOT FOOL ME WITH YOUR TWO HEARTS, CALYGIA. I SEE THROUGH BOTH OF THEM.
YOUR BID, CHRISTOPHER.
I PASS.
YOU DO NOT SPARKLE THIS EVENING, MASTER RUDD? HAVE YOU AN AGUE, PERCHANCE?
I AM DEAD, MADAME. AND SO I WOULD IMAGINE I AM BEYOND THE REACH OF FEVER AND FLUX.
WHAT COULD POSSIBLY HURT ME NOW?
CHRISTOPHER, DO YOU THINK YOU SHOULD LIE DOWN?
I HAVE LAIN DOWN FOR FIVE DAYS OUT OF THE LAST SEVEN.
THIS CAN'T HAVE ESCAPED YOUR NOTICE. FOR MUCH OF THE TIME YOU WERE ASTRIDE ME.
THERE APPEARS TO BE AN ALTERCATION OVER AT YOUR SISTER'S TABLE.
GOOD. THEN I WON'T HAVE TO PROVOKE ONE. PRAY EXCUSE ME, LADIES.

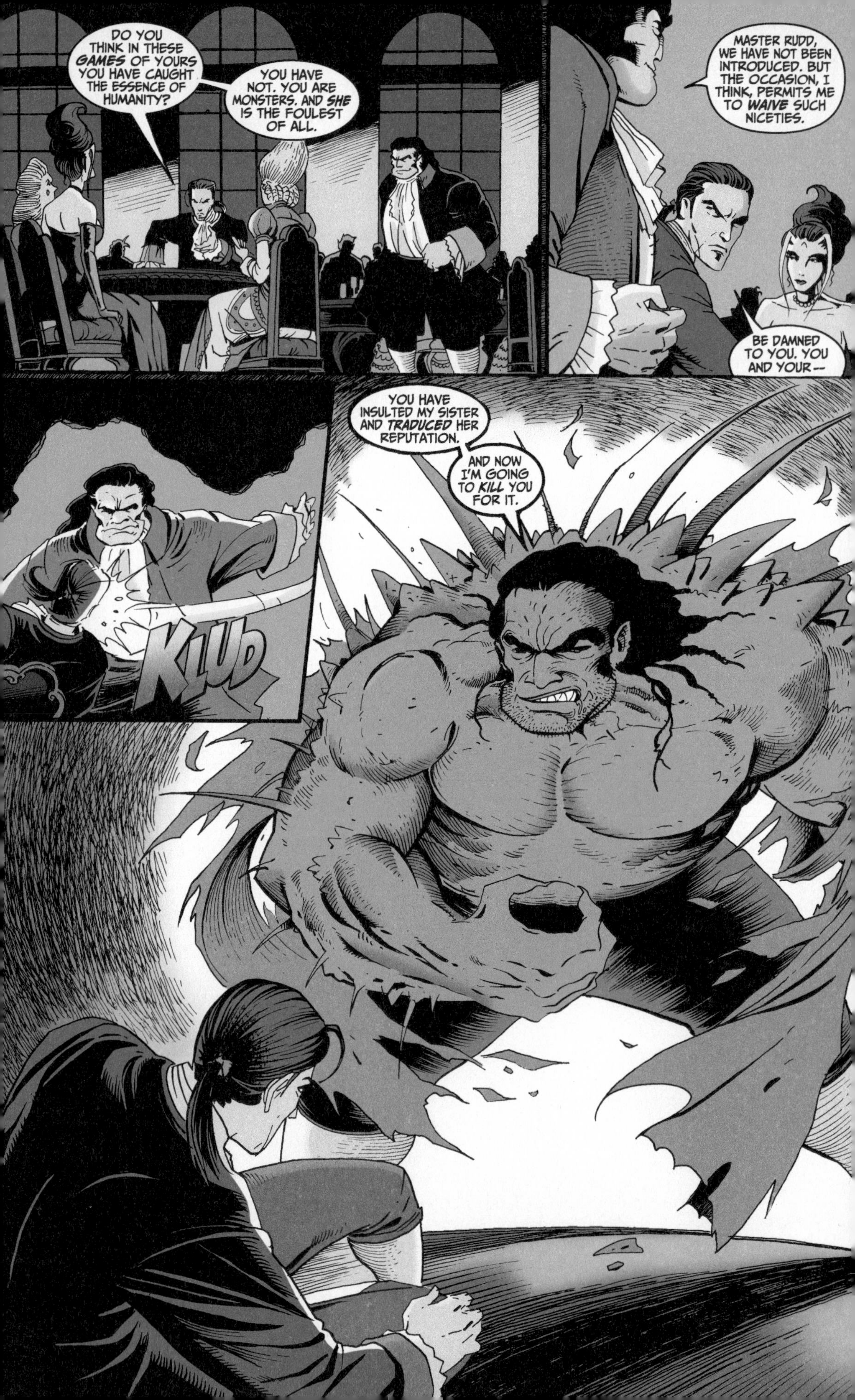
DO YOU THINK IN THESE GAMES OF YOURS YOU HAVE CAUGHT THE ESSENCE OF HUMANITY?
YOU HAVE NOT. YOU ARE MONSTERS. AND SHE IS THE FOULEST OF ALL.
MASTER RUDD, WE HAVE NOT BEEN INTRODUCED. BUT THE OCCASION, I THINK, PERMITS ME TO WAIVE SUCH NICETIES.
BE DAMNED TO YOU. YOU AND YOUR--
KLUD
YOU HAVE INSULTED MY SISTER AND TRADUCED HER REPUTATION.
AND NOW I'M GOING TO KILL YOU FOR IT.

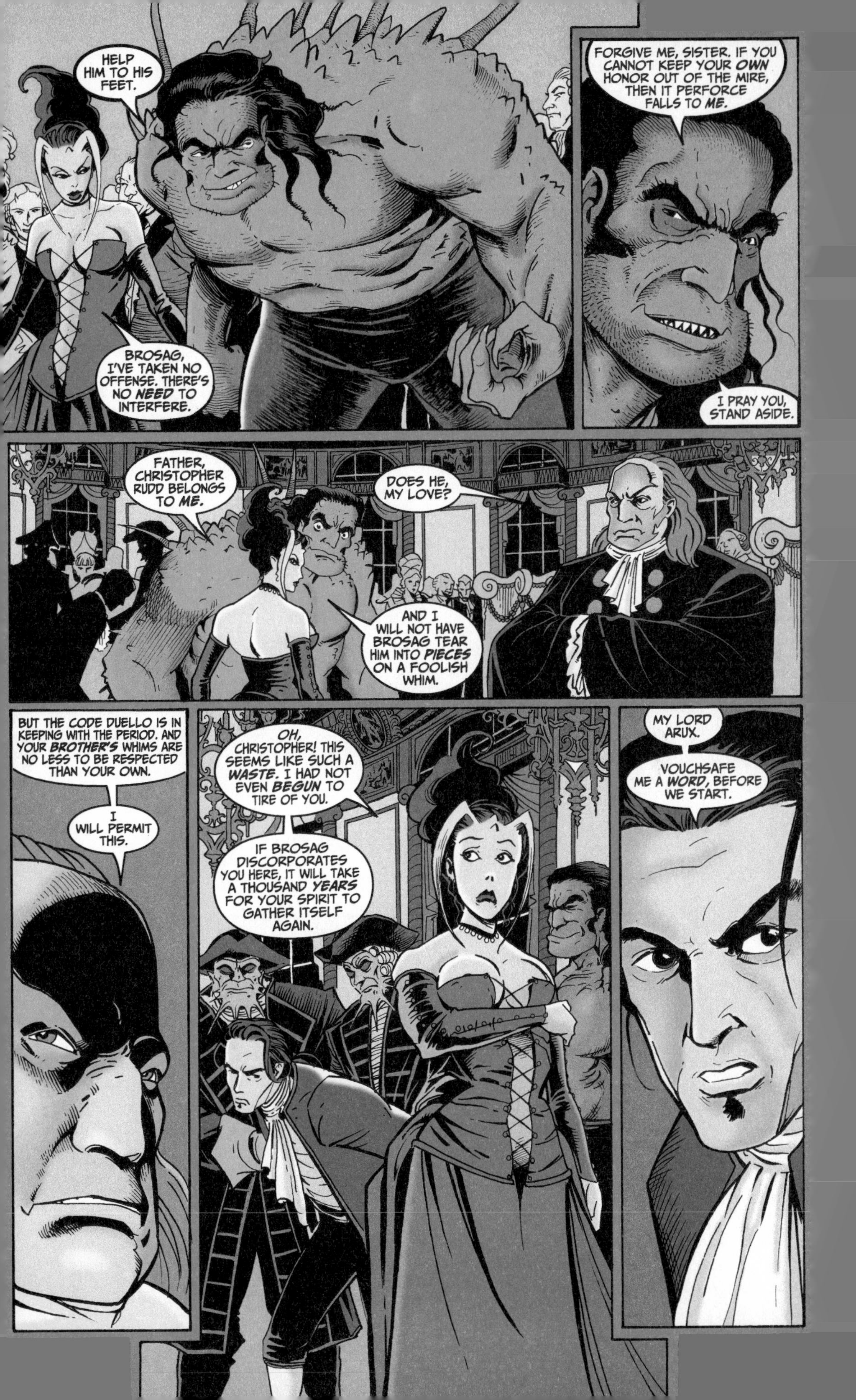
HELP HIM TO HIS FEET.
BROSAG, I'VE TAKEN NO OFFENSE. THERE'S NO *NEED* TO INTERFERE.
FORGIVE ME, SISTER. IF YOU CANNOT KEEP YOUR *OWN* HONOR OUT OF THE MIRE, THEN IT PERFORCE FALLS TO *ME*.
I PRAY YOU, STAND ASIDE.
FATHER, CHRISTOPHER RUDD BELONGS TO *ME*.
DOES HE, MY LOVE?
AND I WILL NOT HAVE BROSAG TEAR HIM INTO *PIECES* ON A FOOLISH WHIM.
BUT THE CODE DUELLO IS IN KEEPING WITH THE PERIOD. AND YOUR *BROTHER'S* WHIMS ARE NO LESS TO BE RESPECTED THAN YOUR OWN.
I WILL PERMIT THIS.
OH, CHRISTOPHER! THIS SEEMS LIKE SUCH A *WASTE*. I HAD NOT EVEN *BEGUN* TO TIRE OF YOU.
IF BROSAG DISCORPORATES YOU HERE, IT WILL TAKE A THOUSAND *YEARS* FOR YOUR SPIRIT TO GATHER ITSELF AGAIN.
MY LORD ARUX.
VOUCHSAFE ME A *WORD*, BEFORE WE START.

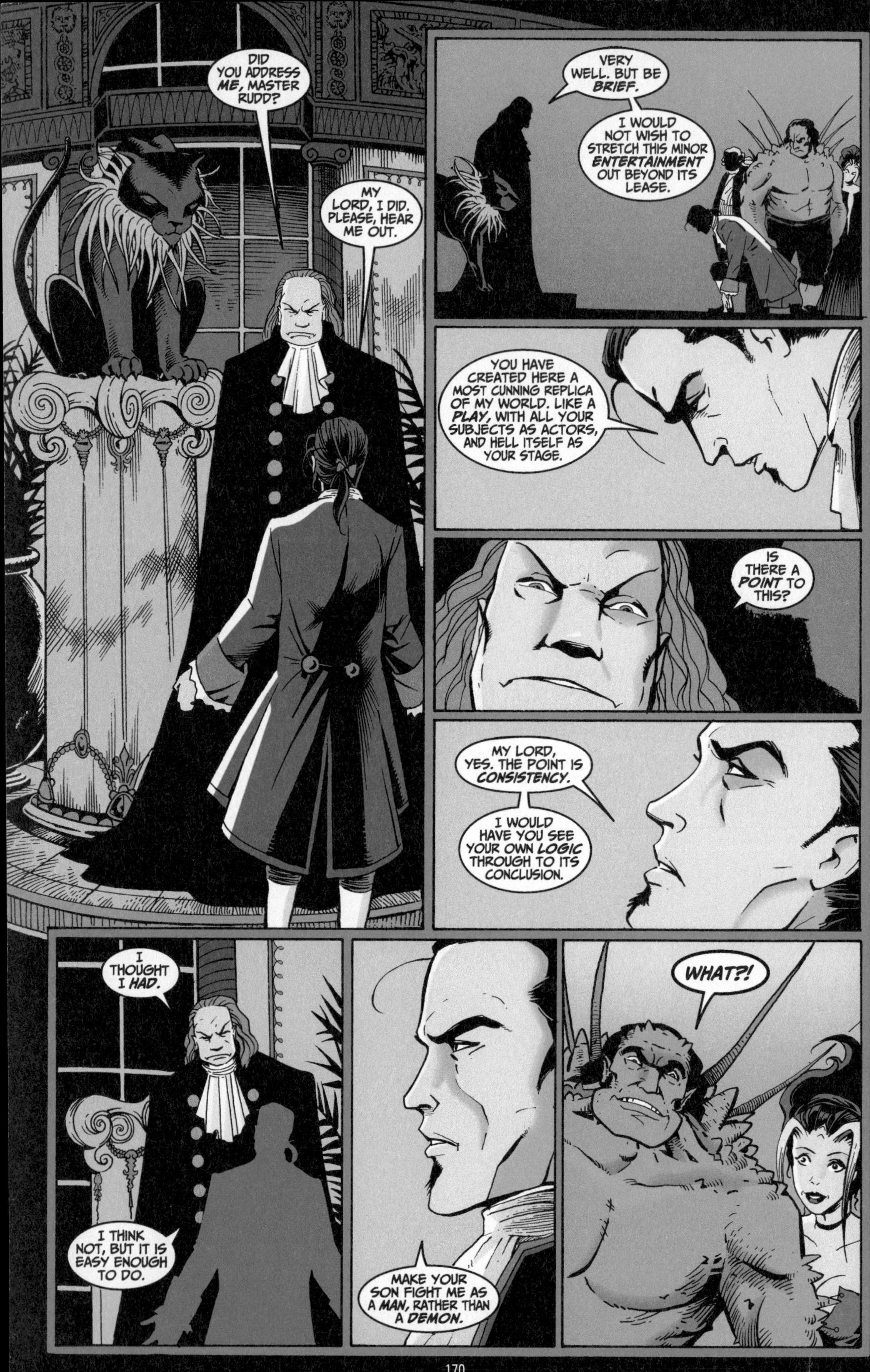
DID YOU ADDRESS *ME*, MASTER RUDD?
MY LORD, I DID. PLEASE, HEAR ME OUT.
VERY WELL. BUT BE *BRIEF*.
I WOULD NOT WISH TO STRETCH THIS MINOR *ENTERTAINMENT* OUT BEYOND ITS LEASE.
YOU HAVE CREATED HERE A MOST CUNNING REPLICA OF MY WORLD. LIKE A *PLAY*, WITH ALL YOUR SUBJECTS AS ACTORS, AND HELL ITSELF AS YOUR STAGE.
IS THERE A *POINT* TO THIS?
MY LORD, YES. THE POINT IS *CONSISTENCY*.
I WOULD HAVE YOU SEE YOUR OWN *LOGIC* THROUGH TO ITS CONCLUSION.
I THOUGHT I *HAD*.
I THINK NOT, BUT IT IS EASY ENOUGH TO DO.
MAKE YOUR SON FIGHT ME AS A *MAN*, RATHER THAN A *DEMON*.
WHAT?!

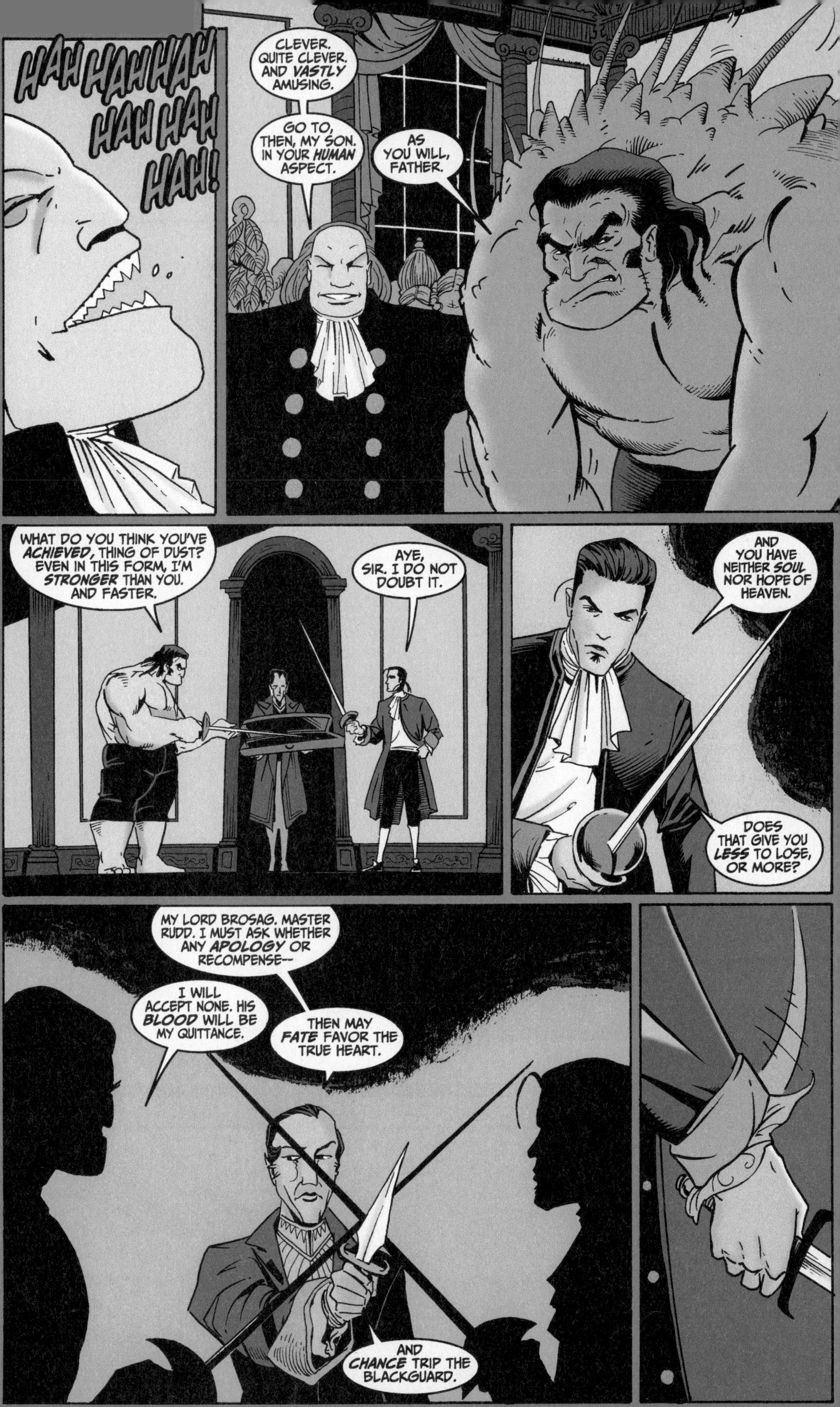
HAH HAH HAH
HAH HAH
HAH!
CLEVER. QUITE CLEVER. AND VASTLY AMUSING.
GO TO, THEN, MY SON. IN YOUR HUMAN ASPECT.
AS YOU WILL, FATHER.
WHAT DO YOU THINK YOU'VE ACHIEVED, THING OF DUST? EVEN IN THIS FORM, I'M STRONGER THAN YOU. AND FASTER.
AYE, SIR. I DO NOT DOUBT IT.
AND YOU HAVE NEITHER SOUL NOR HOPE OF HEAVEN.
DOES THAT GIVE YOU LESS TO LOSE, OR MORE?
MY LORD BROSAG. MASTER RUDD. I MUST ASK WHETHER ANY APOLOGY OR RECOMPENSE--
I WILL ACCEPT NONE. HIS BLOOD WILL BE MY QUITTANCE.
THEN MAY FATE FAVOR THE TRUE HEART.
AND CHANCE TRIP THE BLACKGUARD.

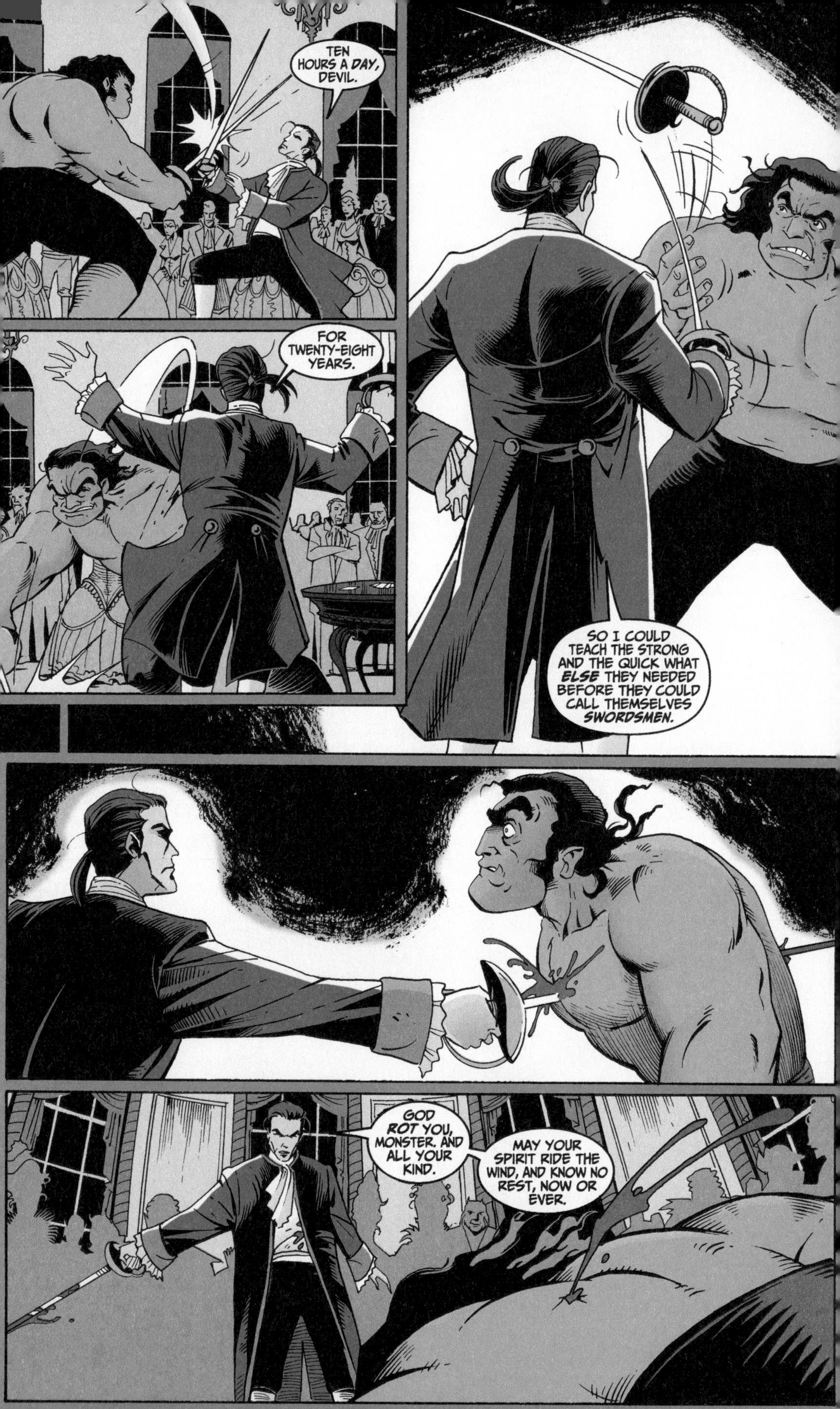
TEN HOURS A DAY, DEVIL.
FOR TWENTY-EIGHT YEARS.
SO I COULD TEACH THE STRONG AND THE QUICK WHAT ELSE THEY NEEDED BEFORE THEY COULD CALL THEMSELVES SWORDSMEN.
GOD ROT YOU, MONSTER. AND ALL YOUR KIND.
MAY YOUR SPIRIT RIDE THE WIND, AND KNOW NO REST, NOW OR EVER.

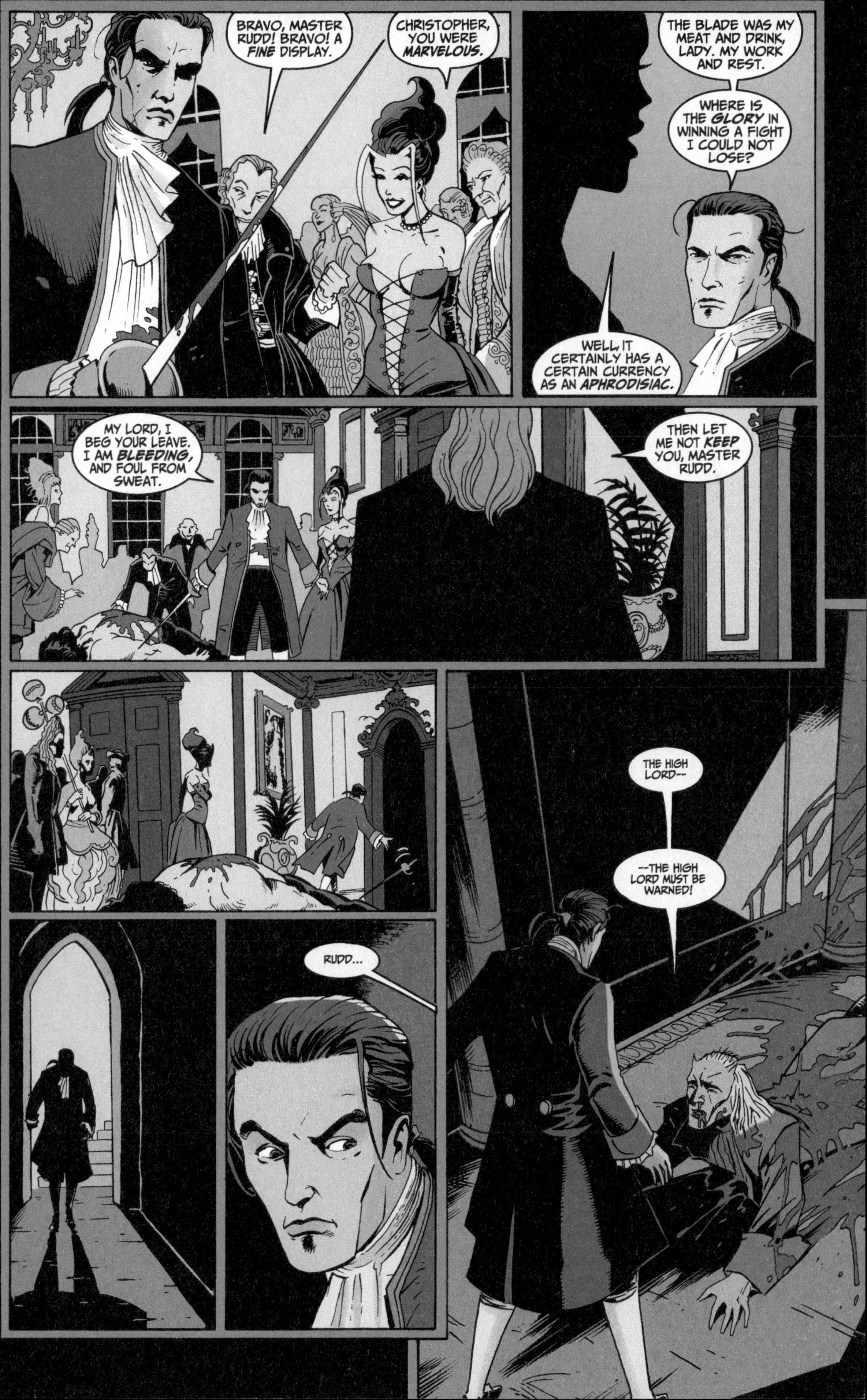
BRAVO, MASTER RUDD! BRAVO! A FINE DISPLAY.
CHRISTOPHER, YOU WERE MARVELOUS.
THE BLADE WAS MY MEAT AND DRINK, LADY. MY WORK AND REST.
WHERE IS THE GLORY IN WINNING A FIGHT I COULD NOT LOSE?
WELL, IT CERTAINLY HAS A CERTAIN CURRENCY AS AN APHRODISIAC.
MY LORD, I BEG YOUR LEAVE. I AM BLEEDING, AND FOUL FROM SWEAT.
THEN LET ME NOT KEEP YOU, MASTER RUDD.
RUDD...
THE HIGH LORD--
--THE HIGH LORD MUST BE WARNED!

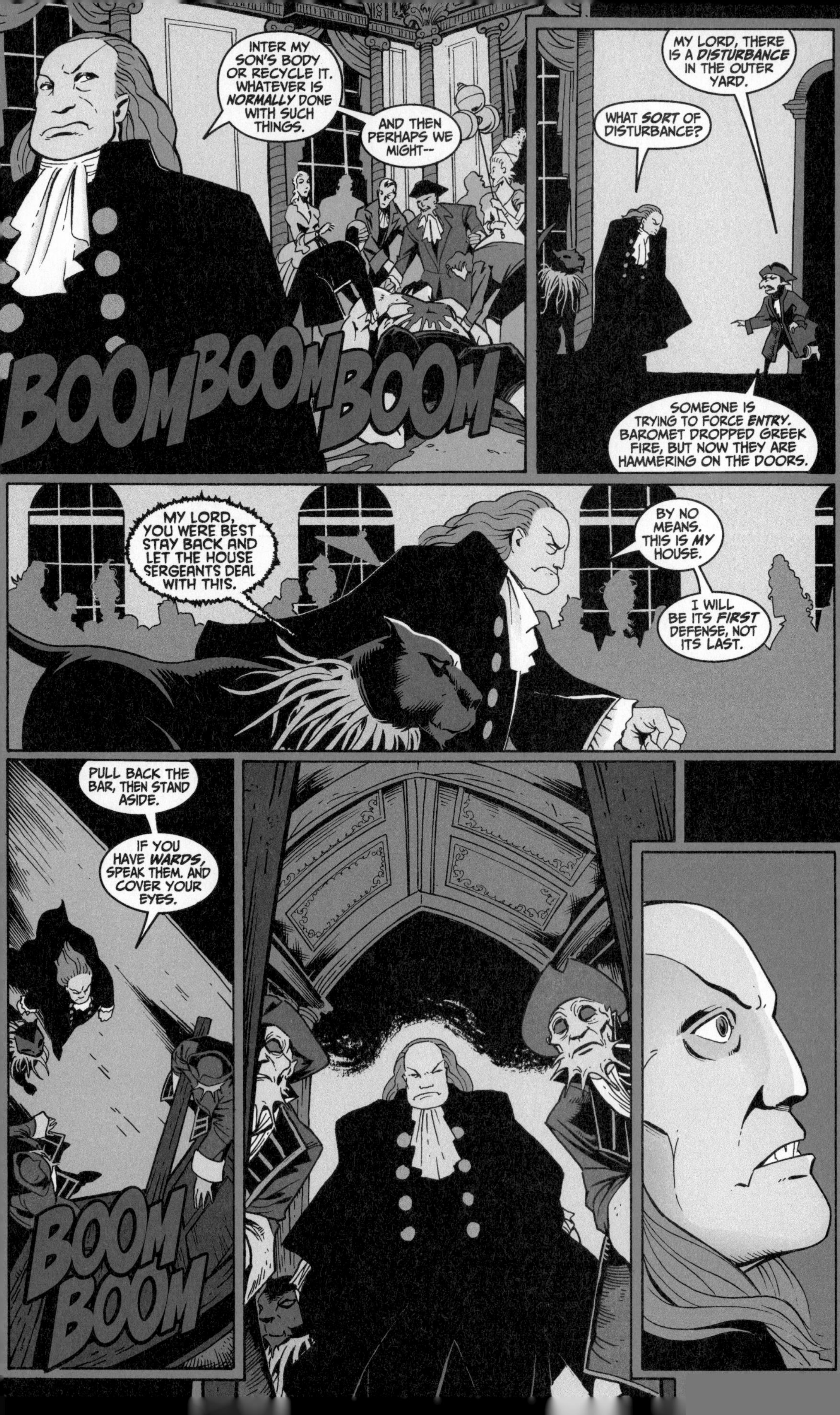
INTER MY SON'S BODY OR RECYCLE IT. WHATEVER IS NORMALLY DONE WITH SUCH THINGS.
AND THEN PERHAPS WE MIGHT--
BOOMBOOMBOOM
MY LORD, THERE IS A DISTURBANCE IN THE OUTER YARD.
WHAT SORT OF DISTURBANCE?
SOMEONE IS TRYING TO FORCE ENTRY. BAROMET DROPPED GREEK FIRE, BUT NOW THEY ARE HAMMERING ON THE DOORS.
MY LORD, YOU WERE BEST STAY BACK AND LET THE HOUSE SERGEANTS DEAL WITH THIS.
BY NO MEANS. THIS IS MY HOUSE.
I WILL BE ITS FIRST DEFENSE, NOT ITS LAST.
PULL BACK THE BAR, THEN STAND ASIDE.
IF YOU HAVE WARDS, SPEAK THEM. AND COVER YOUR EYES.
BOOM
BOOM

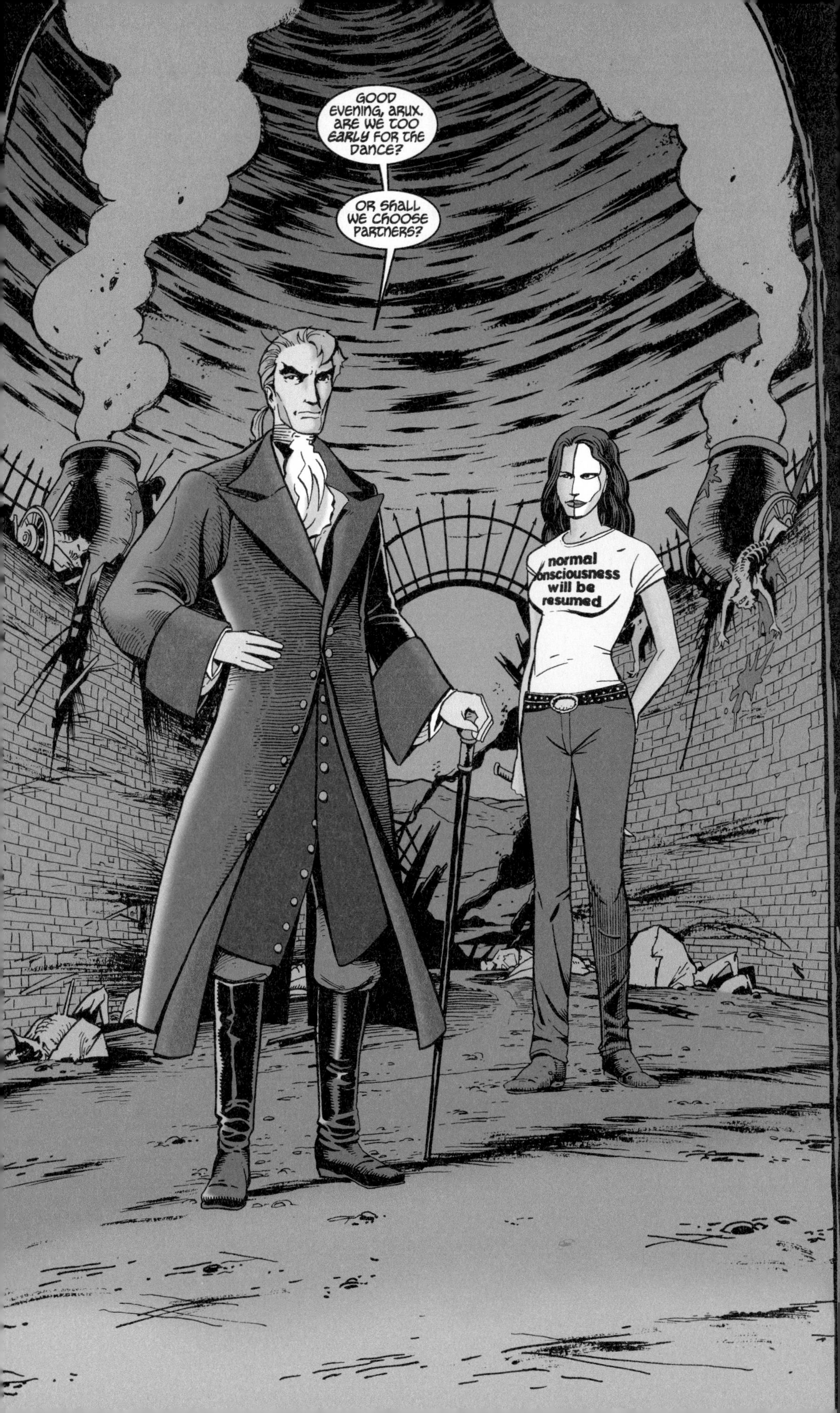
GOOD EVENING, ARUX. ARE WE TOO EARLY FOR THE DANCE?
OR SHALL WE CHOOSE PARTNERS?
normal
onsciousness
will be
resumed

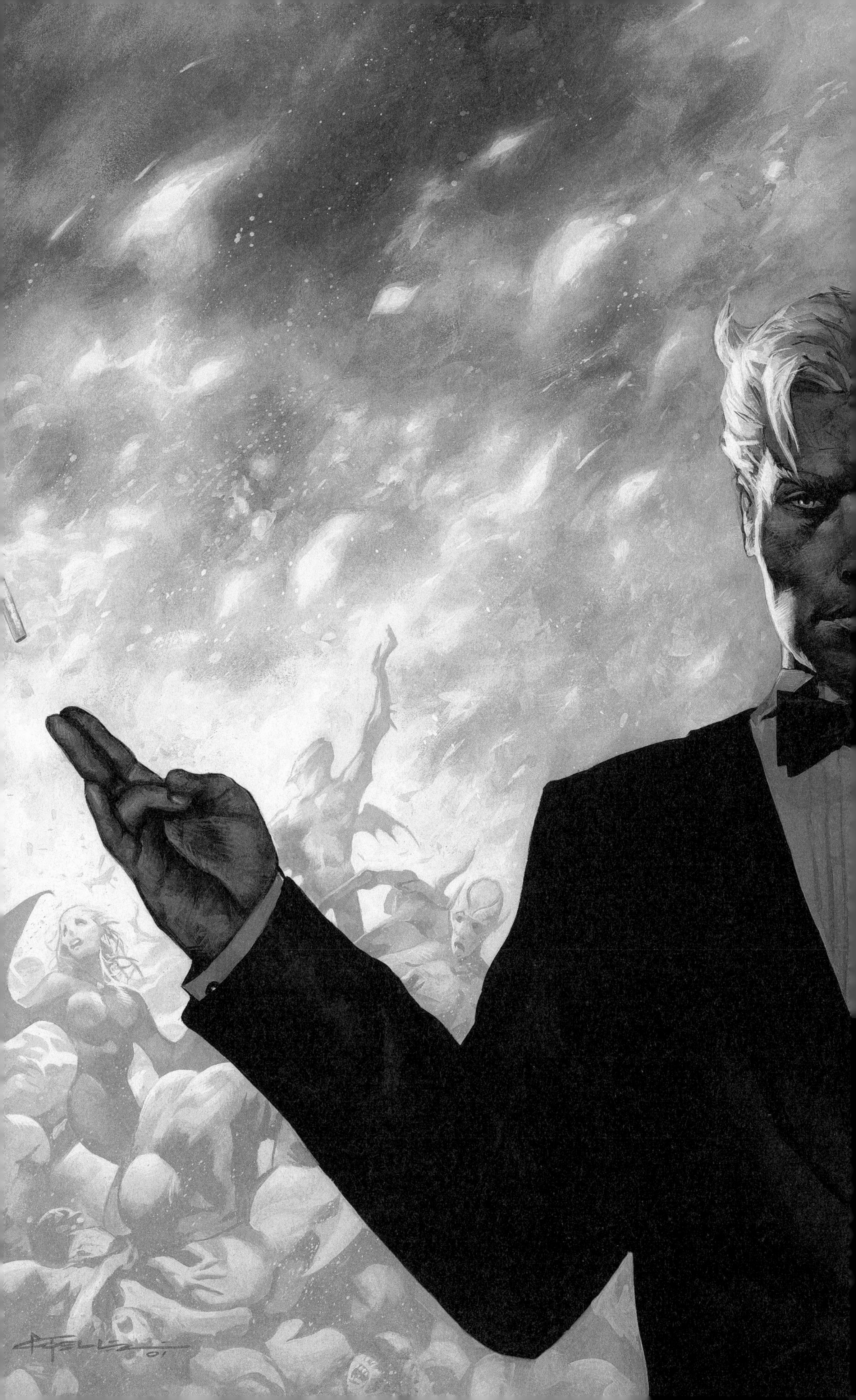

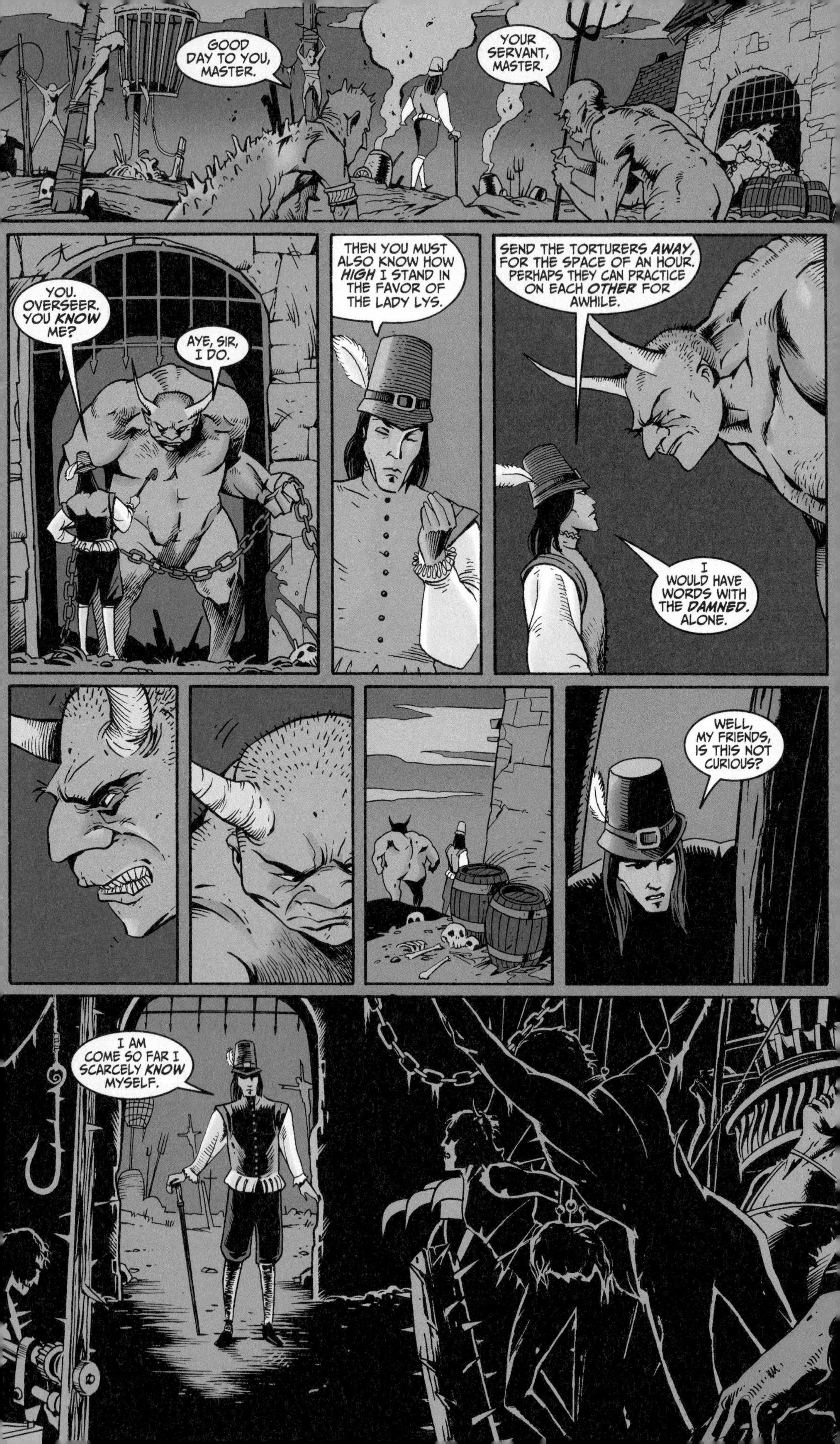
GOOD DAY TO YOU, MASTER.
YOUR SERVANT, MASTER.
YOU. OVERSEER. YOU KNOW ME?
AYE, SIR, I DO.
THEN YOU MUST ALSO KNOW HOW HIGH I STAND IN THE FAVOR OF THE LADY LYS.
SEND THE TORTURERS AWAY, FOR THE SPACE OF AN HOUR. PERHAPS THEY CAN PRACTICE ON EACH OTHER FOR AWHILE.
I WOULD HAVE WORDS WITH THE DAMNED. ALONE.
WELL, MY FRIENDS, IS THIS NOT CURIOUS?
I AM COME SO FAR I SCARCELY KNOW MYSELF.

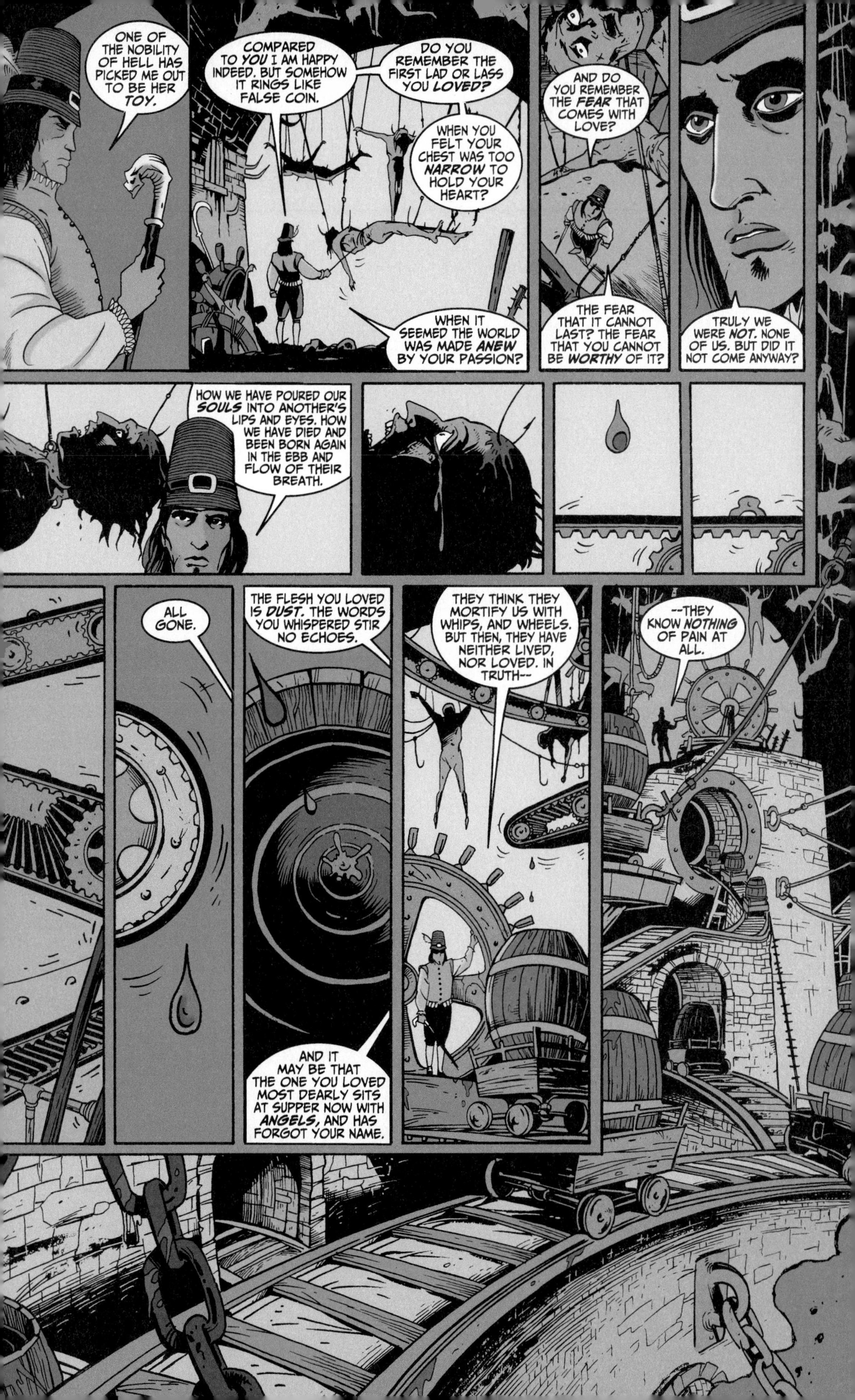
ONE OF THE NOBILITY OF HELL HAS PICKED ME OUT TO BE HER TOY.
COMPARED TO YOU I AM HAPPY INDEED. BUT SOMEHOW IT RINGS LIKE FALSE COIN.
DO YOU REMEMBER THE FIRST LAD OR LASS YOU LOVED?
WHEN YOU FELT YOUR CHEST WAS TOO NARROW TO HOLD YOUR HEART?
WHEN IT SEEMED THE WORLD WAS MADE ANEW BY YOUR PASSION?
AND DO YOU REMEMBER THE FEAR THAT COMES WITH LOVE?
THE FEAR THAT IT CANNOT LAST? THE FEAR THAT YOU CANNOT BE WORTHY OF IT?
TRULY WE WERE NOT. NONE OF US. BUT DID IT NOT COME ANYWAY?
HOW WE HAVE POURED OUR SOULS INTO ANOTHER'S LIPS AND EYES. HOW WE HAVE DIED AND BEEN BORN AGAIN IN THE EBB AND FLOW OF THEIR BREATH.
ALL GONE.
THE FLESH YOU LOVED IS DUST. THE WORDS YOU WHISPERED STIR NO ECHOES.
AND IT MAY BE THAT THE ONE YOU LOVED MOST DEARLY SITS AT SUPPER NOW WITH ANGELS, AND HAS FORGOT YOUR NAME.
THEY THINK THEY MORTIFY US WITH WHIPS, AND WHEELS. BUT THEN, THEY HAVE NEITHER LIVED, NOR LOVED. IN TRUTH--
--THEY KNOW NOTHING OF PAIN AT ALL.

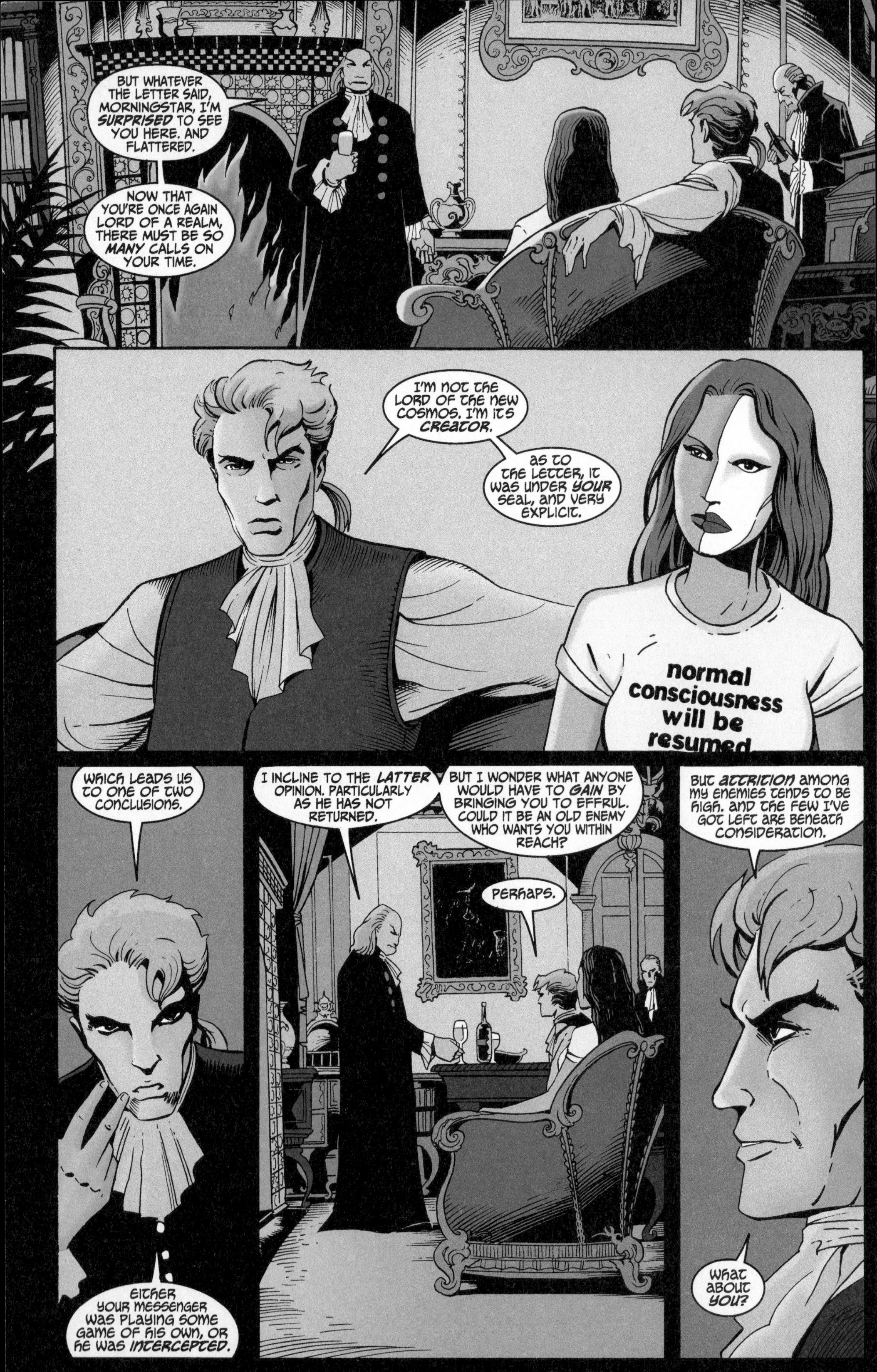

BUT WHATEVER THE LETTER SAID, MORNINGSTAR, I'M SURPRISED TO SEE YOU HERE. AND FLATTERED.
NOW THAT YOU'RE ONCE AGAIN LORD OF A REALM, THERE MUST BE SO MANY CALLS ON YOUR TIME.
I'M NOT THE LORD OF THE NEW COSMOS. I'M ITS CREATOR.
AS TO THE LETTER, IT WAS UNDER YOUR SEAL, AND VERY EXPLICIT.
normal consciousness will be resumed.
WHICH LEADS US TO ONE OF TWO CONCLUSIONS.
EITHER YOUR MESSENGER WAS PLAYING SOME GAME OF HIS OWN, OR HE WAS INTERCEPTED.
I INCLINE TO THE LATTER OPINION. PARTICULARLY AS HE HAS NOT RETURNED.
BUT I WONDER WHAT ANYONE WOULD HAVE TO GAIN BY BRINGING YOU TO EFFRUL. COULD IT BE AN OLD ENEMY WHO WANTS YOU WITHIN REACH?
PERHAPS.
BUT ATTRITION AMONG MY ENEMIES TENDS TO BE HIGH. AND THE FEW I'VE GOT LEFT ARE BENEATH CONSIDERATION.
WHAT ABOUT YOU?

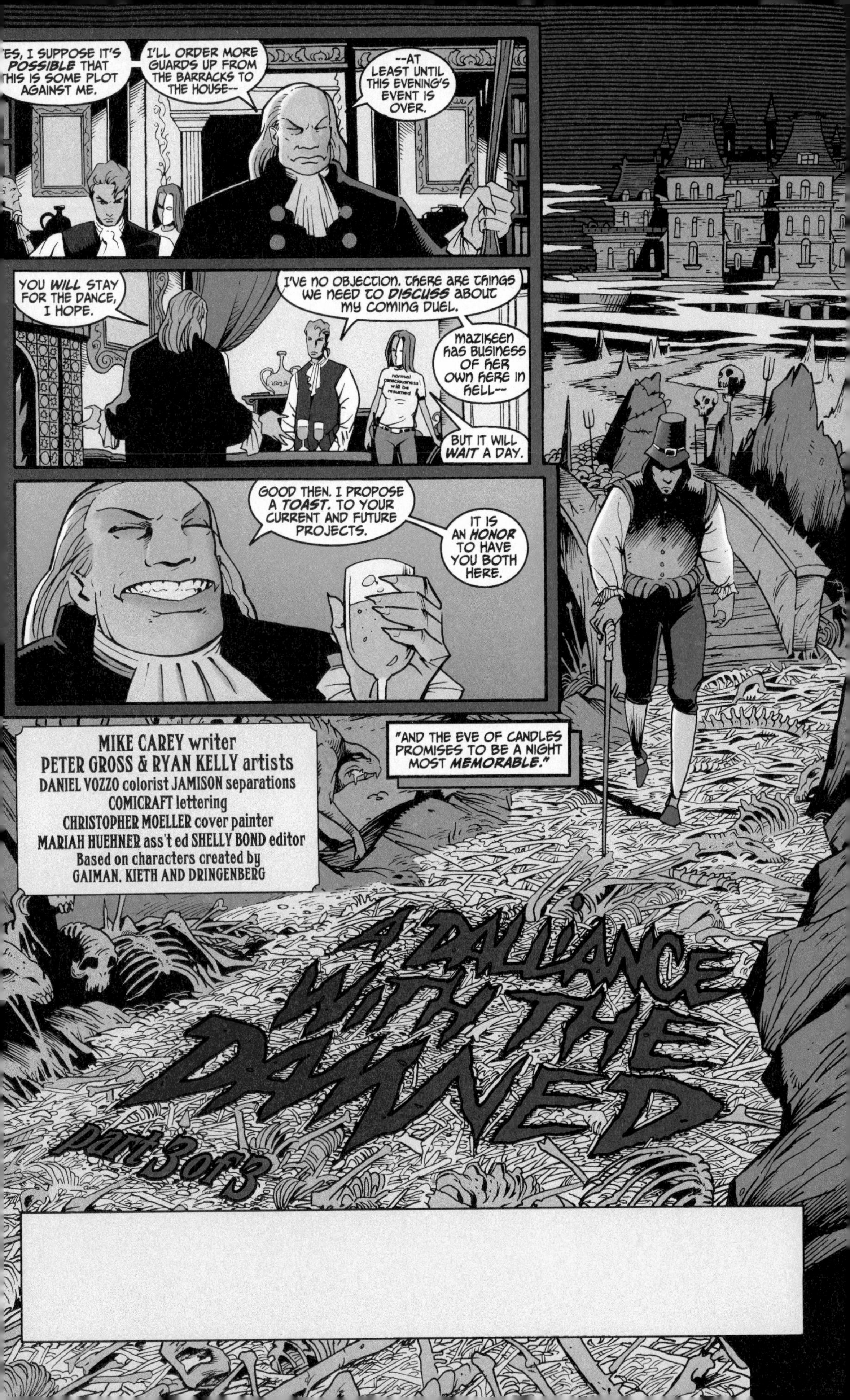
YES, I SUPPOSE IT'S POSSIBLE THAT THIS IS SOME PLOT AGAINST ME.
I'LL ORDER MORE GUARDS UP FROM THE BARRACKS TO THE HOUSE--
--AT LEAST UNTIL THIS EVENING'S EVENT IS OVER.
YOU WILL STAY FOR THE DANCE, I HOPE.
I'VE NO OBJECTION. THERE ARE THINGS WE NEED TO DISCUSS ABOUT MY COMING DUEL.
MAZIKEEN HAS BUSINESS OF HER OWN HERE IN HELL--
normal consciousness will be resumed
BUT IT WILL WAIT A DAY.
GOOD THEN. I PROPOSE A TOAST. TO YOUR CURRENT AND FUTURE PROJECTS.
IT IS AN HONOR TO HAVE YOU BOTH HERE.
"AND THE EVE OF CANDLES PROMISES TO BE A NIGHT MOST MEMORABLE."
MIKE CAREY writer
PETER GROSS & RYAN KELLY artists
DANIEL VOZZO colorist JAMISON separations
COMICRAFT lettering
CHRISTOPHER MOELLER cover painter
MARIAH HUEHNER ass't ed SHELLY BOND editor
Based on characters created by
GAIMAN, KIETH AND DRINGENBERG
A DALLIANCE WITH THE DAMNED
part 3 of 3

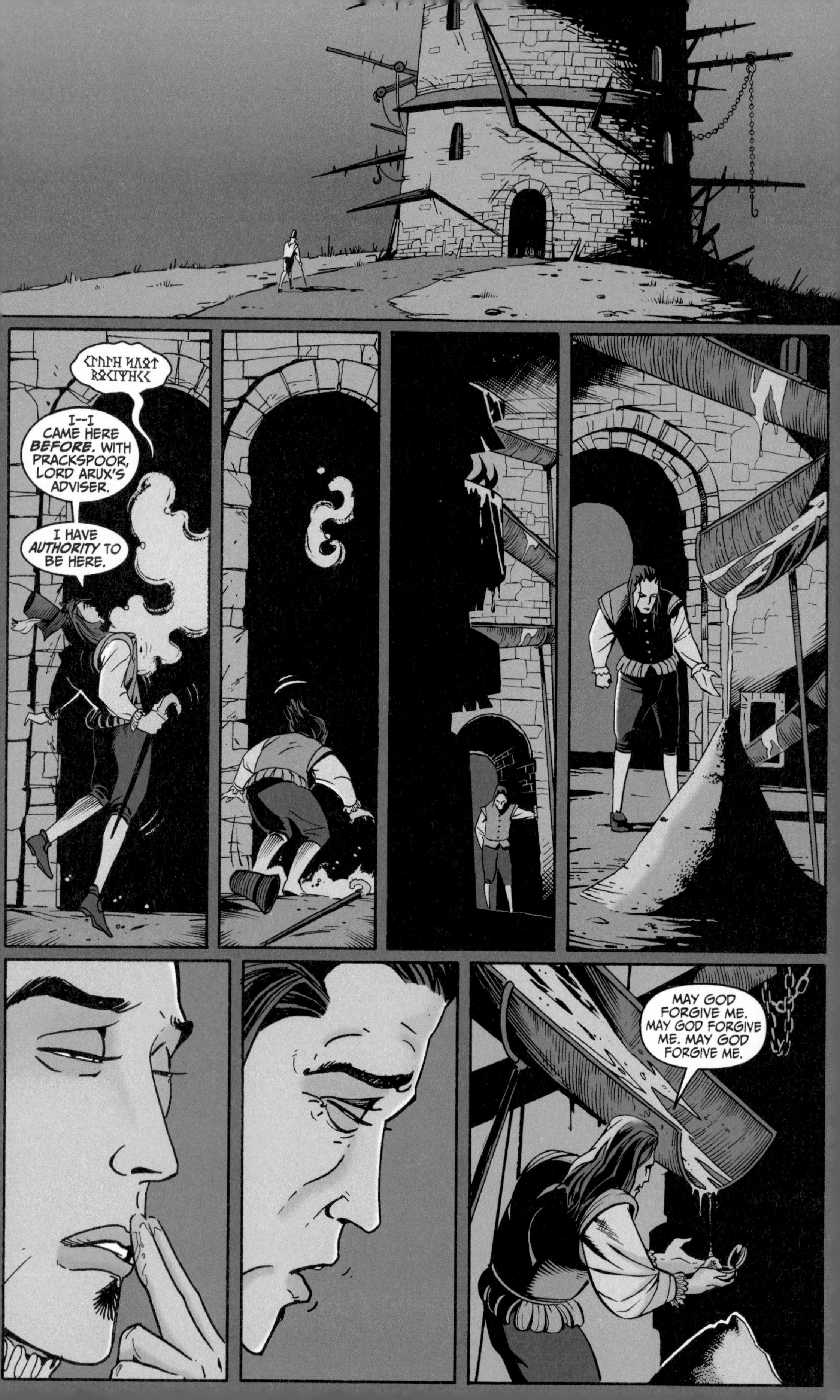
I--I CAME HERE BEFORE. WITH PRACKSPOOR, LORD ARUX'S ADVISER.
I HAVE AUTHORITY TO BE HERE.
MAY GOD FORGIVE ME. MAY GOD FORGIVE ME. MAY GOD FORGIVE ME.

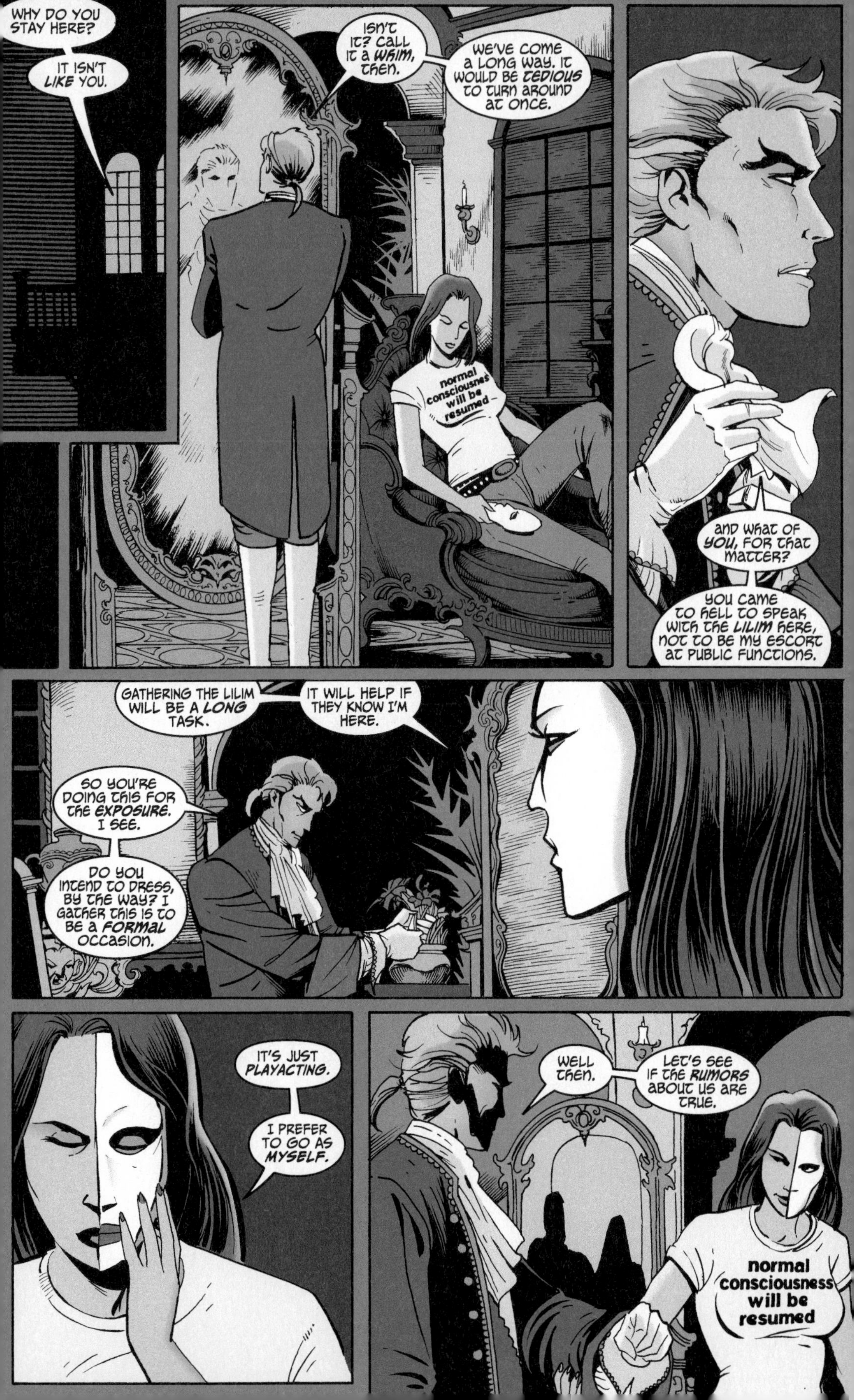
WHY DO YOU STAY HERE?
IT ISN'T LIKE YOU.
ISN'T IT? CALL IT A WHIM, THEN.
WE'VE COME A LONG WAY. IT WOULD BE TEDIOUS TO TURN AROUND AT ONCE.
normal consciousness will be resumed
AND WHAT OF YOU, FOR THAT MATTER?
YOU CAME TO HELL TO SPEAK WITH THE LILIM HERE, NOT TO BE MY ESCORT AT PUBLIC FUNCTIONS.
GATHERING THE LILIM WILL BE A LONG TASK.
IT WILL HELP IF THEY KNOW I'M HERE.
SO YOU'RE DOING THIS FOR THE EXPOSURE. I SEE.
DO YOU INTEND TO DRESS, BY THE WAY? I GATHER THIS IS TO BE A FORMAL OCCASION.
IT'S JUST PLAYACTING.
I PREFER TO GO AS MYSELF.
WELL THEN.
LET'S SEE IF THE RUMORS ABOUT US ARE TRUE.
normal consciousness will be resumed

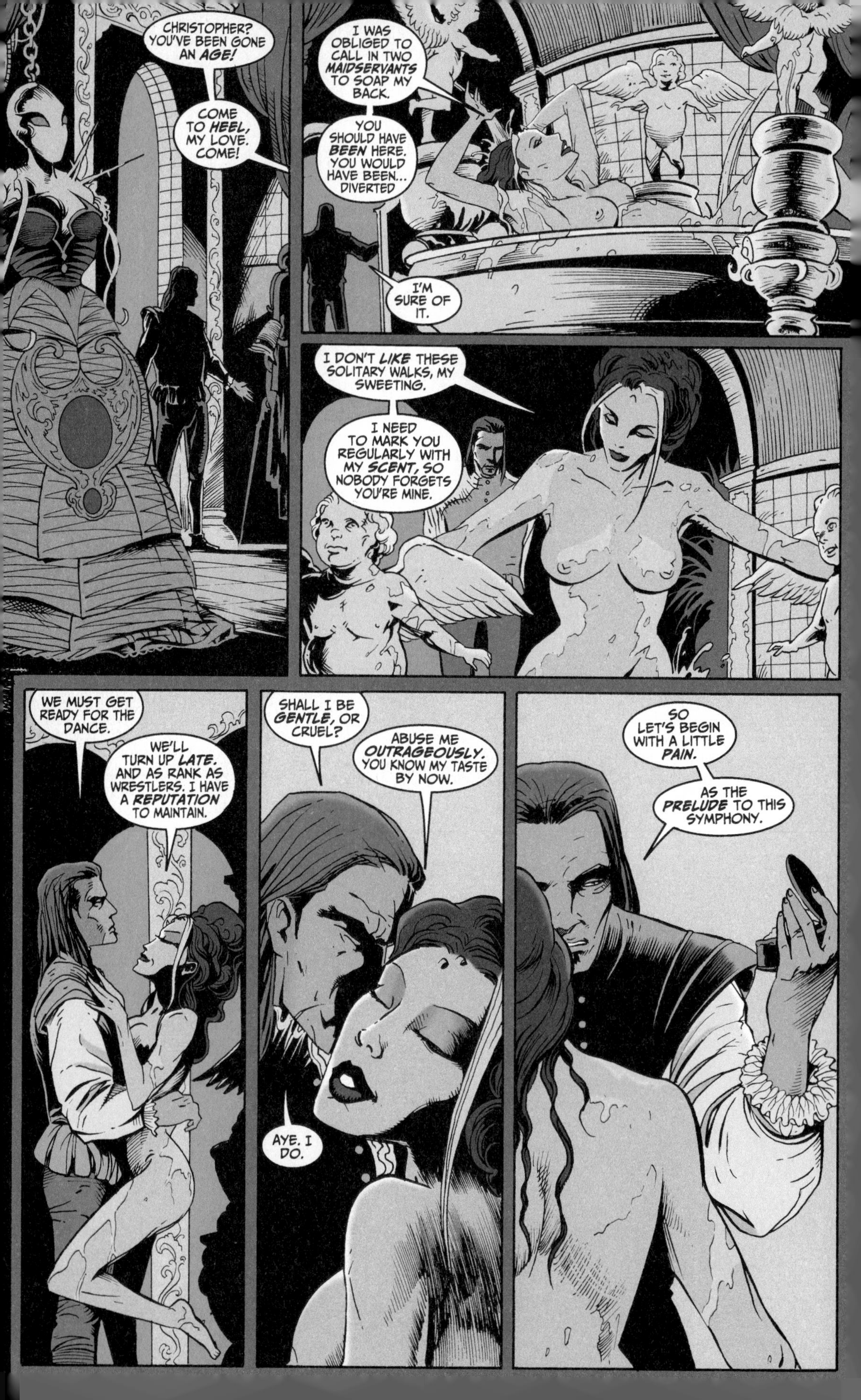
CHRISTOPHER? YOU'VE BEEN GONE AN AGE!
COME TO HEEL, MY LOVE. COME!
I WAS OBLIGED TO CALL IN TWO MAIDSERVANTS TO SOAP MY BACK.
YOU SHOULD HAVE BEEN HERE. YOU WOULD HAVE BEEN... DIVERTED
I'M SURE OF IT.
I DON'T LIKE THESE SOLITARY WALKS, MY SWEETING.
I NEED TO MARK YOU REGULARLY WITH MY SCENT, SO NOBODY FORGETS YOU'RE MINE.
WE MUST GET READY FOR THE DANCE.
WE'LL TURN UP LATE. AND AS RANK AS WRESTLERS. I HAVE A REPUTATION TO MAINTAIN.
SHALL I BE GENTLE, OR CRUEL?
ABUSE ME OUTRAGEOUSLY. YOU KNOW MY TASTE BY NOW.
AYE. I DO.
SO LET'S BEGIN WITH A LITTLE PAIN.
AS THE PRELUDE TO THIS SYMPHONY.

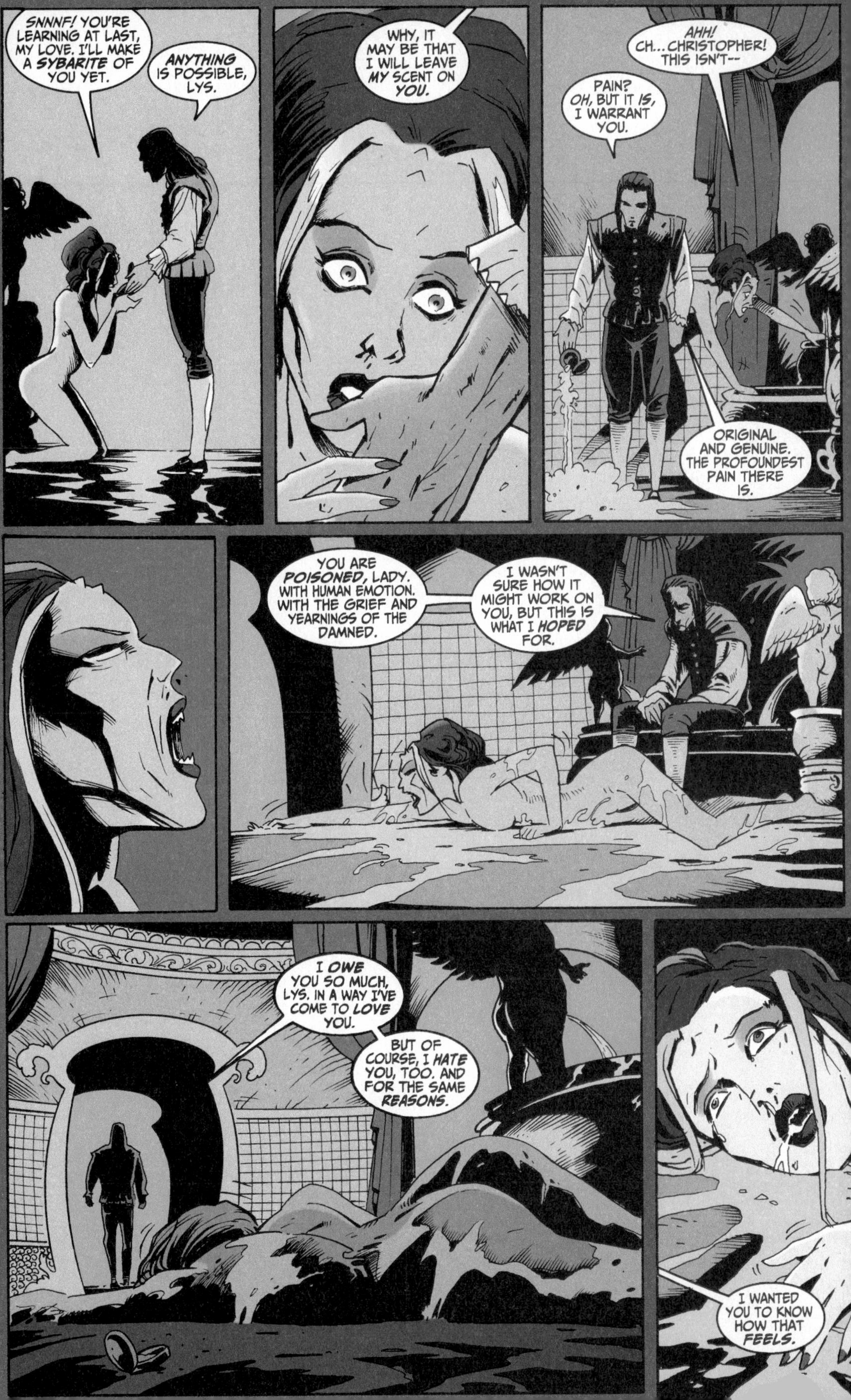
SNNNF! YOU'RE LEARNING AT LAST, MY LOVE. I'LL MAKE A SYBARITE OF YOU YET.
ANYTHING IS POSSIBLE, LYS.
WHY, IT MAY BE THAT I WILL LEAVE MY SCENT ON YOU.
AHH! CH... CHRISTOPHER! THIS ISN'T--
PAIN? OH, BUT IT IS, I WARRANT YOU.
ORIGINAL AND GENUINE. THE PROFOUNDEST PAIN THERE IS.
YOU ARE POISONED, LADY. WITH HUMAN EMOTION. WITH THE GRIEF AND YEARNINGS OF THE DAMNED.
I WASN'T SURE HOW IT MIGHT WORK ON YOU, BUT THIS IS WHAT I HOPED FOR.
I OWE YOU SO MUCH, LYS. IN A WAY I'VE COME TO LOVE YOU.
BUT OF COURSE, I HATE YOU, TOO. AND FOR THE SAME REASONS.
I WANTED YOU TO KNOW HOW THAT FEELS.

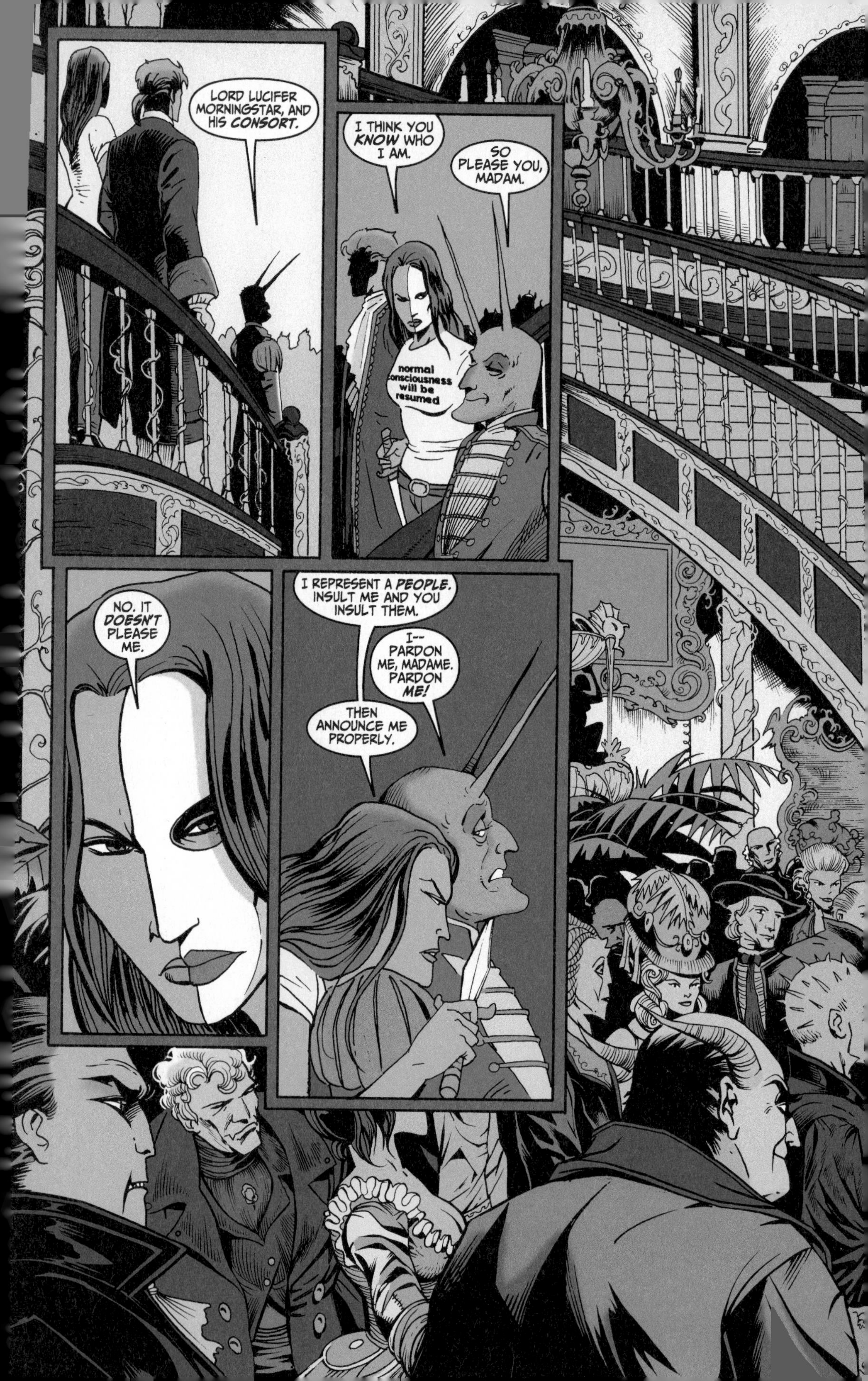
LORD LUCIFER MORNINGSTAR, AND HIS CONSORT.
I THINK YOU KNOW WHO I AM.
SO PLEASE YOU, MADAM.
normal consciousness will be resumed
NO. IT DOESN'T PLEASE ME.
I REPRESENT A PEOPLE. INSULT ME AND YOU INSULT THEM.
I-- PARDON ME, MADAME. PARDON ME!
THEN ANNOUNCE ME PROPERLY.

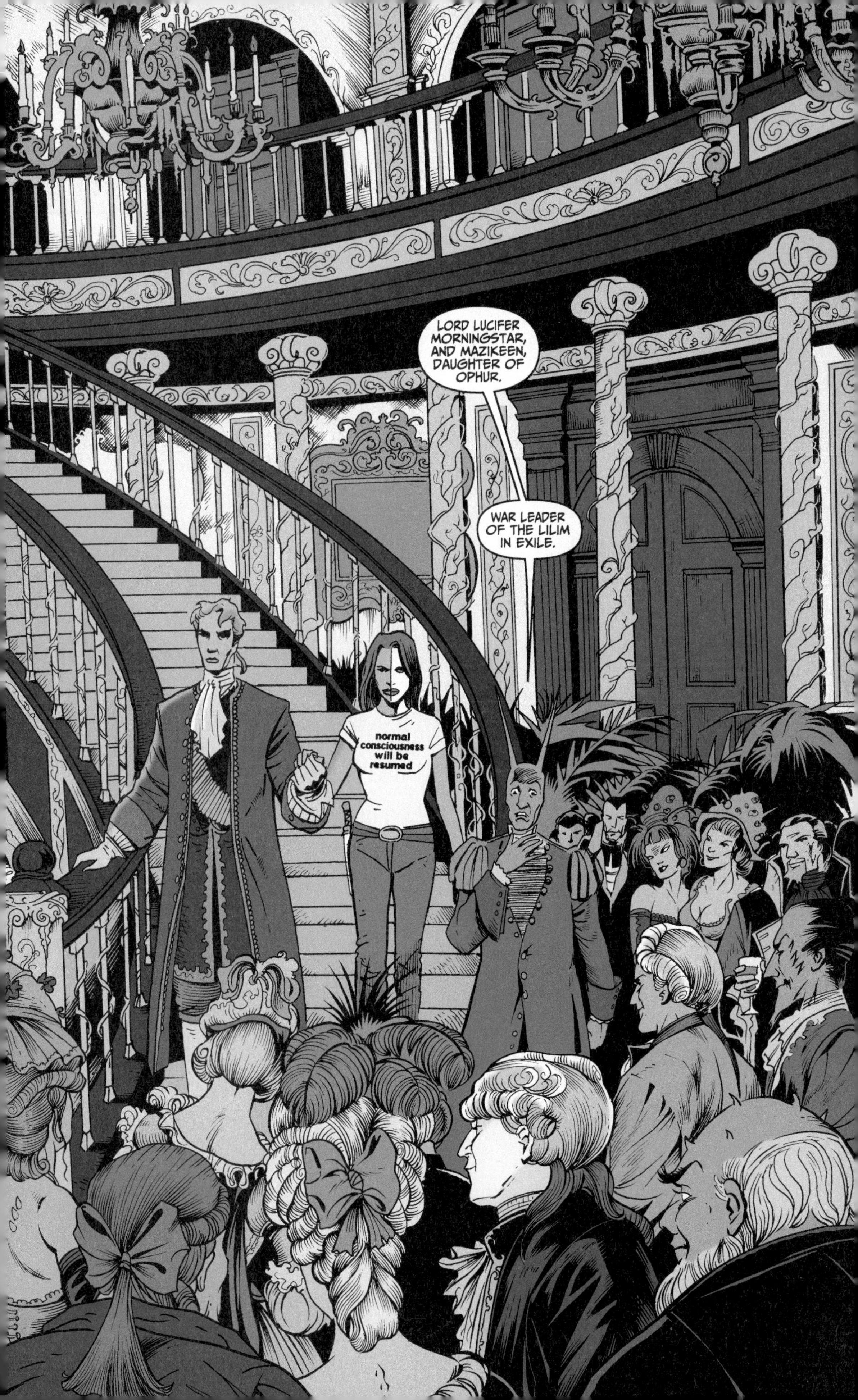
LORD LUCIFER MORNINGSTAR, AND MAZIKEEN, DAUGHTER OF OPHUR.
WAR LEADER OF THE LILIM IN EXILE.
normal consciousness will be resumed

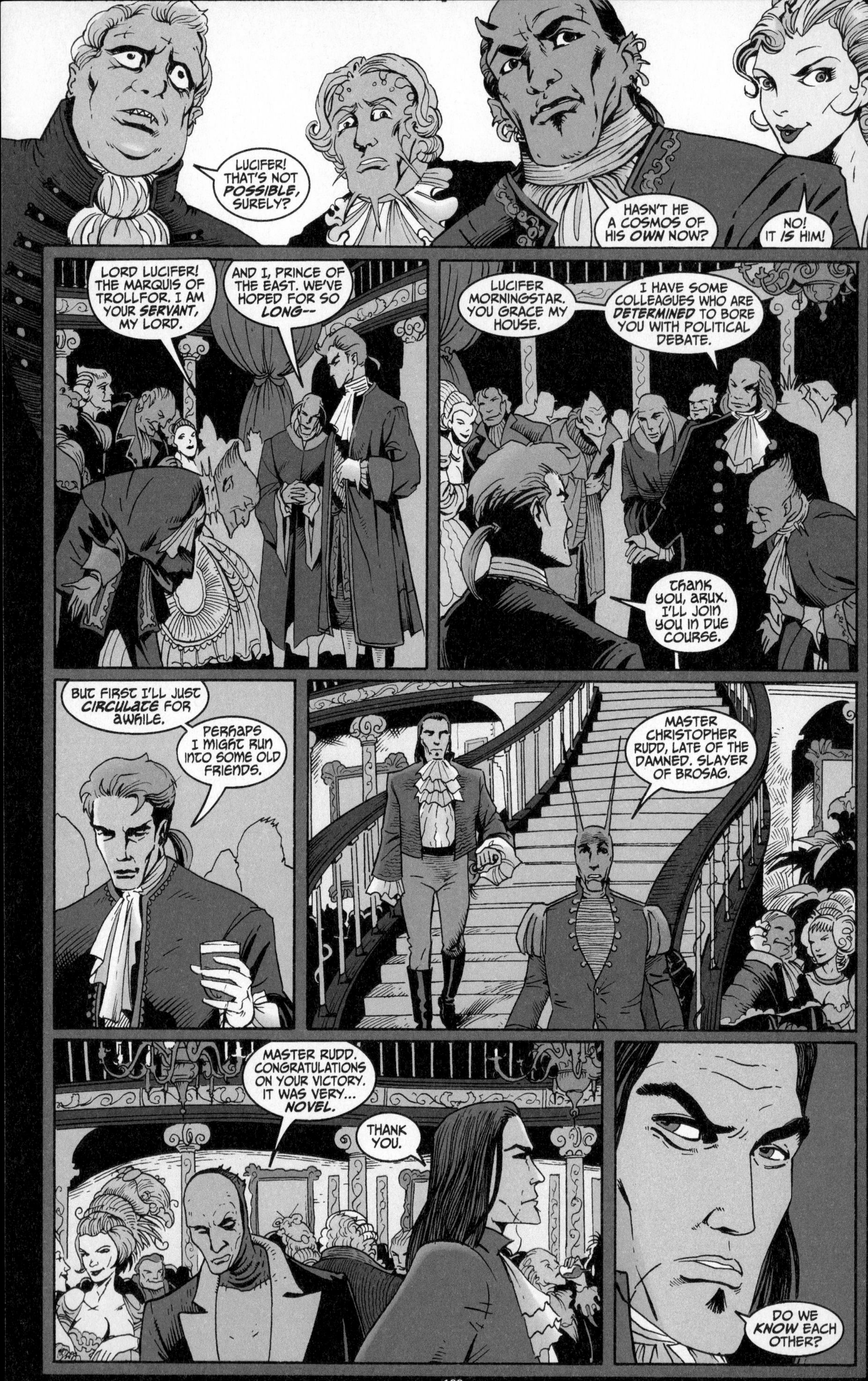

LUCIFER! THAT'S NOT POSSIBLE, SURELY?
HASN'T HE A COSMOS OF HIS OWN NOW?
NO! IT IS HIM!
LORD LUCIFER! THE MARQUIS OF TROLLFOR. I AM YOUR SERVANT, MY LORD.
AND I, PRINCE OF THE EAST. WE'VE HOPED FOR SO LONG--
LUCIFER MORNINGSTAR. YOU GRACE MY HOUSE.
I HAVE SOME COLLEAGUES WHO ARE DETERMINED TO BORE YOU WITH POLITICAL DEBATE.
THANK YOU, ARUX. I'LL JOIN YOU IN DUE COURSE.
BUT FIRST I'LL JUST CIRCULATE FOR AWHILE.
PERHAPS I MIGHT RUN INTO SOME OLD FRIENDS.
MASTER CHRISTOPHER RUDD, LATE OF THE DAMNED. SLAYER OF BROSAG.
MASTER RUDD. CONGRATULATIONS ON YOUR VICTORY. IT WAS VERY... NOVEL.
THANK YOU.
DO WE KNOW EACH OTHER?

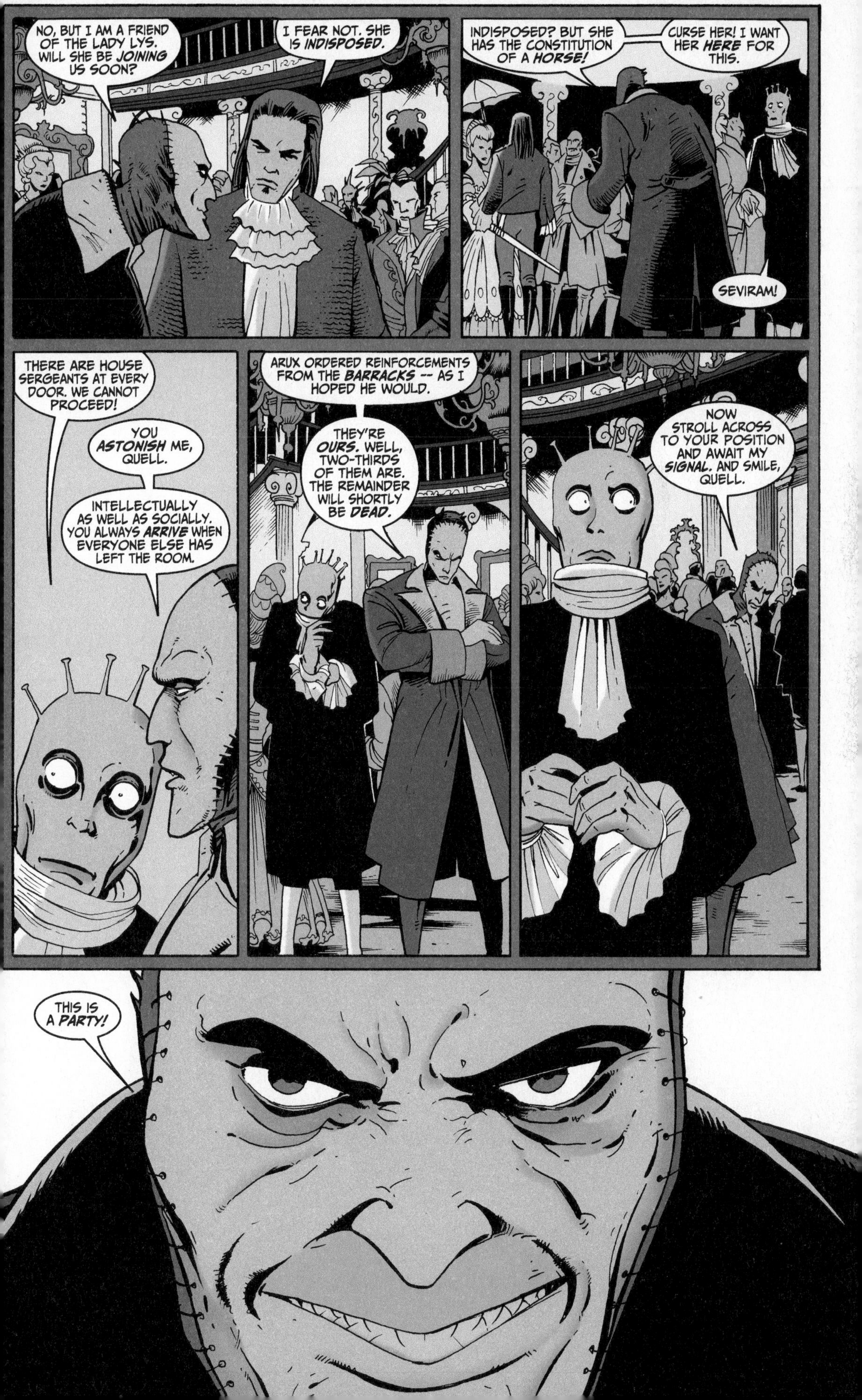
NO, BUT I AM A FRIEND OF THE LADY LYS. WILL SHE BE JOINING US SOON?
I FEAR NOT. SHE IS INDISPOSED.
INDISPOSED? BUT SHE HAS THE CONSTITUTION OF A HORSE!
CURSE HER! I WANT HER HERE FOR THIS.
SEVIRAM!
THERE ARE HOUSE SERGEANTS AT EVERY DOOR. WE CANNOT PROCEED!
YOU ASTONISH ME, QUELL.
INTELLECTUALLY AS WELL AS SOCIALLY. YOU ALWAYS ARRIVE WHEN EVERYONE ELSE HAS LEFT THE ROOM.
ARUX ORDERED REINFORCEMENTS FROM THE BARRACKS -- AS I HOPED HE WOULD.
THEY'RE OURS. WELL, TWO-THIRDS OF THEM ARE. THE REMAINDER WILL SHORTLY BE DEAD.
NOW STROLL ACROSS TO YOUR POSITION AND AWAIT MY SIGNAL. AND SMILE, QUELL.
THIS IS A PARTY!

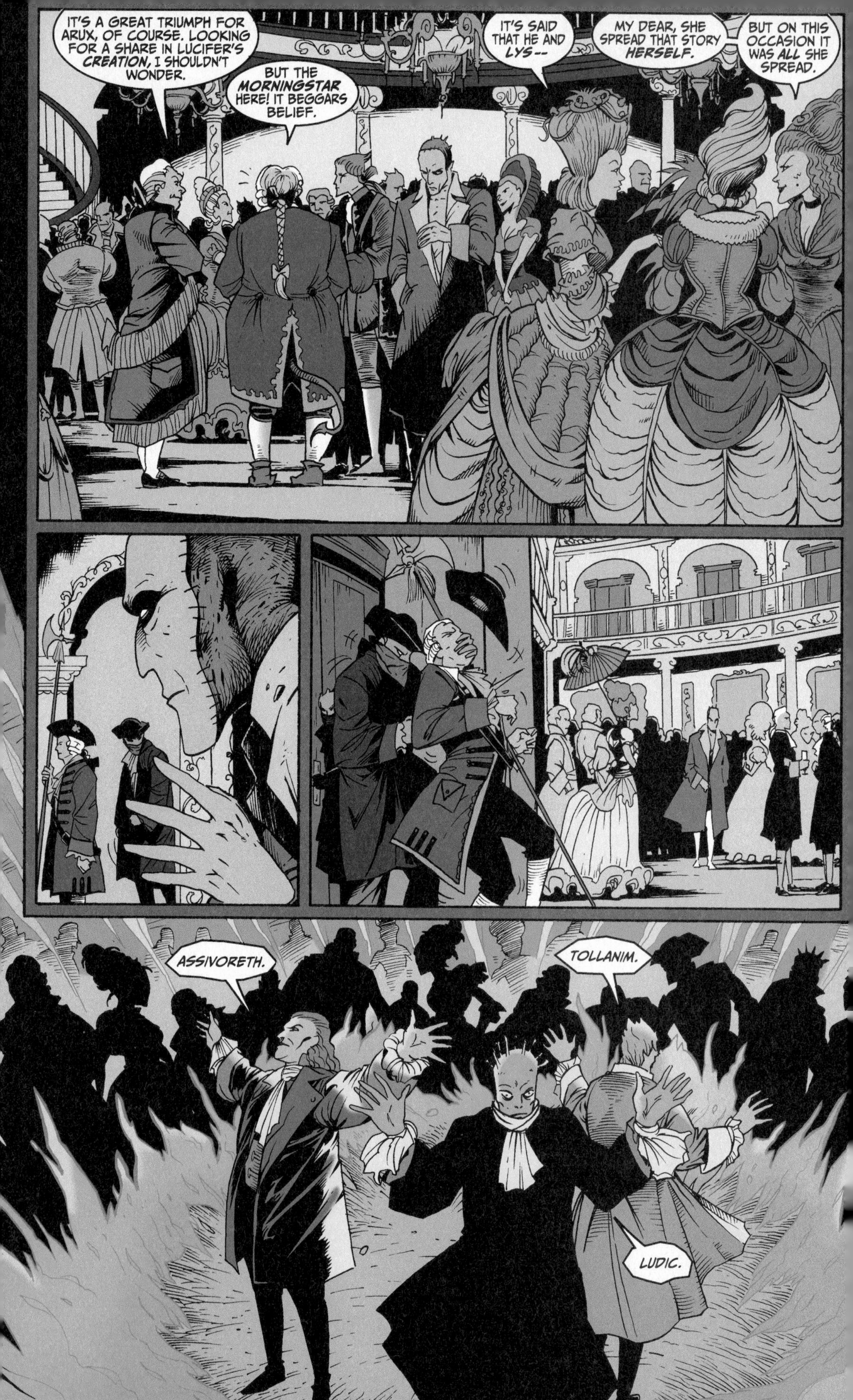
IT'S A GREAT TRIUMPH FOR ARUX, OF COURSE. LOOKING FOR A SHARE IN LUCIFER'S *CREATION*, I SHOULDN'T WONDER.
BUT THE *MORNINGSTAR* HERE! IT BEGGARS BELIEF.
IT'S SAID THAT HE AND *LYS*--
MY DEAR, SHE SPREAD THAT STORY *HERSELF*.
BUT ON THIS OCCASION IT WAS *ALL* SHE SPREAD.
ASSIVORETH.
TOLLANIM.
LUDIC.

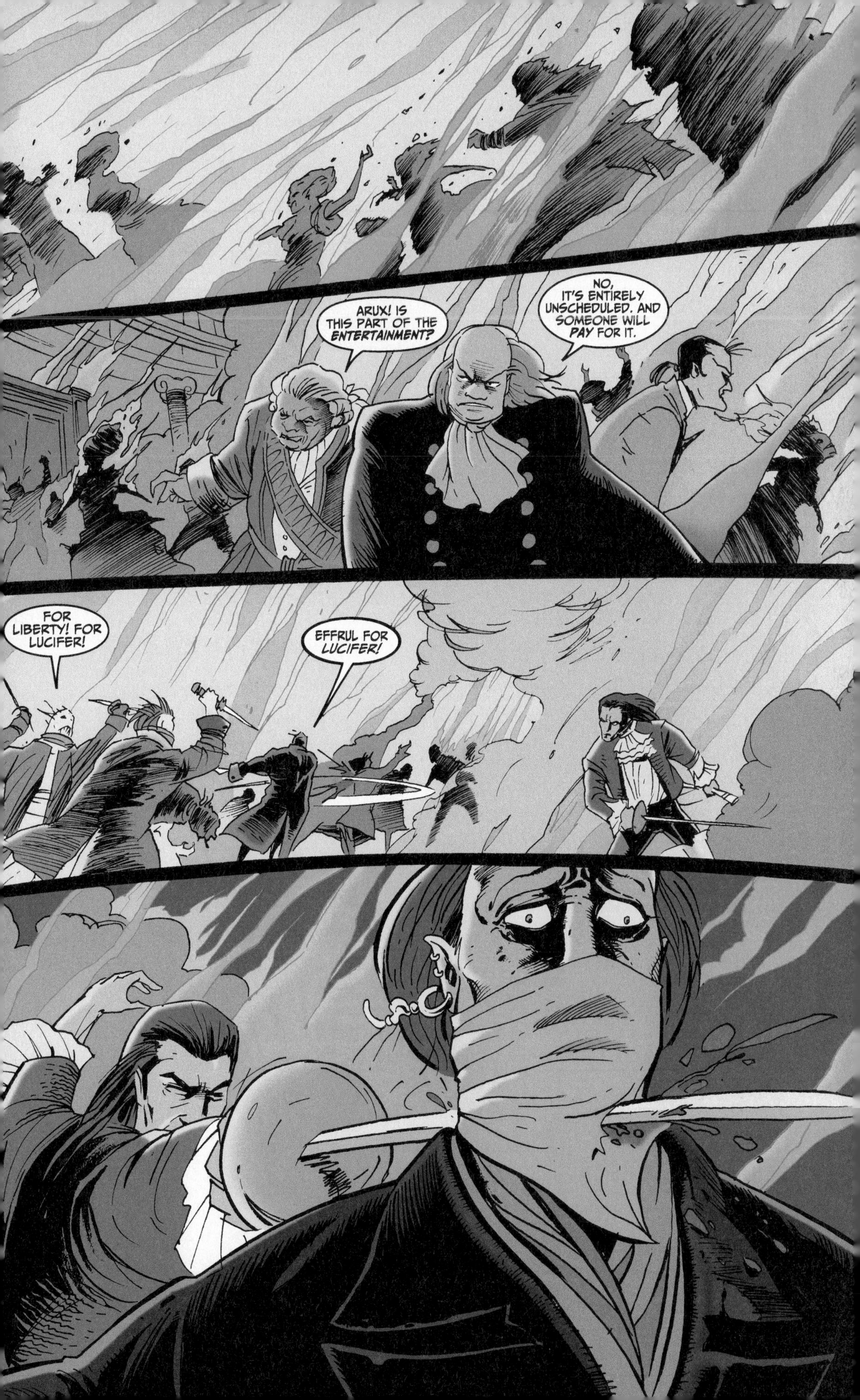
ARUX! IS THIS PART OF THE ENTERTAINMENT?
NO, IT'S ENTIRELY UNSCHEDULED. AND SOMEONE WILL PAY FOR IT.
FOR LIBERTY! FOR LUCIFER!
EFFRUL FOR LUCIFER!

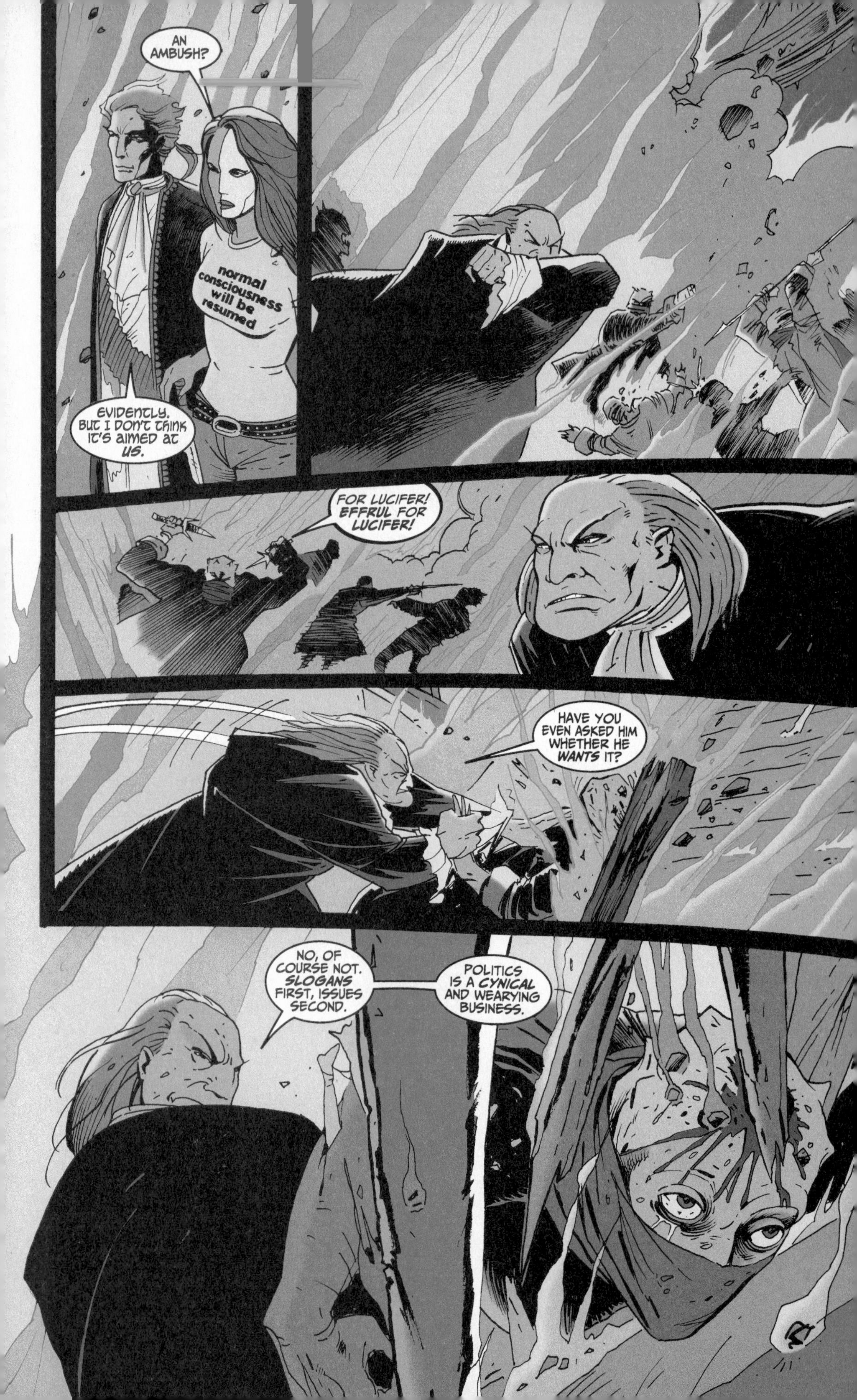
AN AMBUSH?
normal consciousness will be resumed
EVIDENTLY. BUT I DON'T THINK IT'S AIMED AT US.
FOR LUCIFER! EFFRUL FOR LUCIFER!
HAVE YOU EVEN ASKED HIM WHETHER HE WANTS IT?
NO, OF COURSE NOT. SLOGANS FIRST, ISSUES SECOND.
POLITICS IS A CYNICAL AND WEARYING BUSINESS.

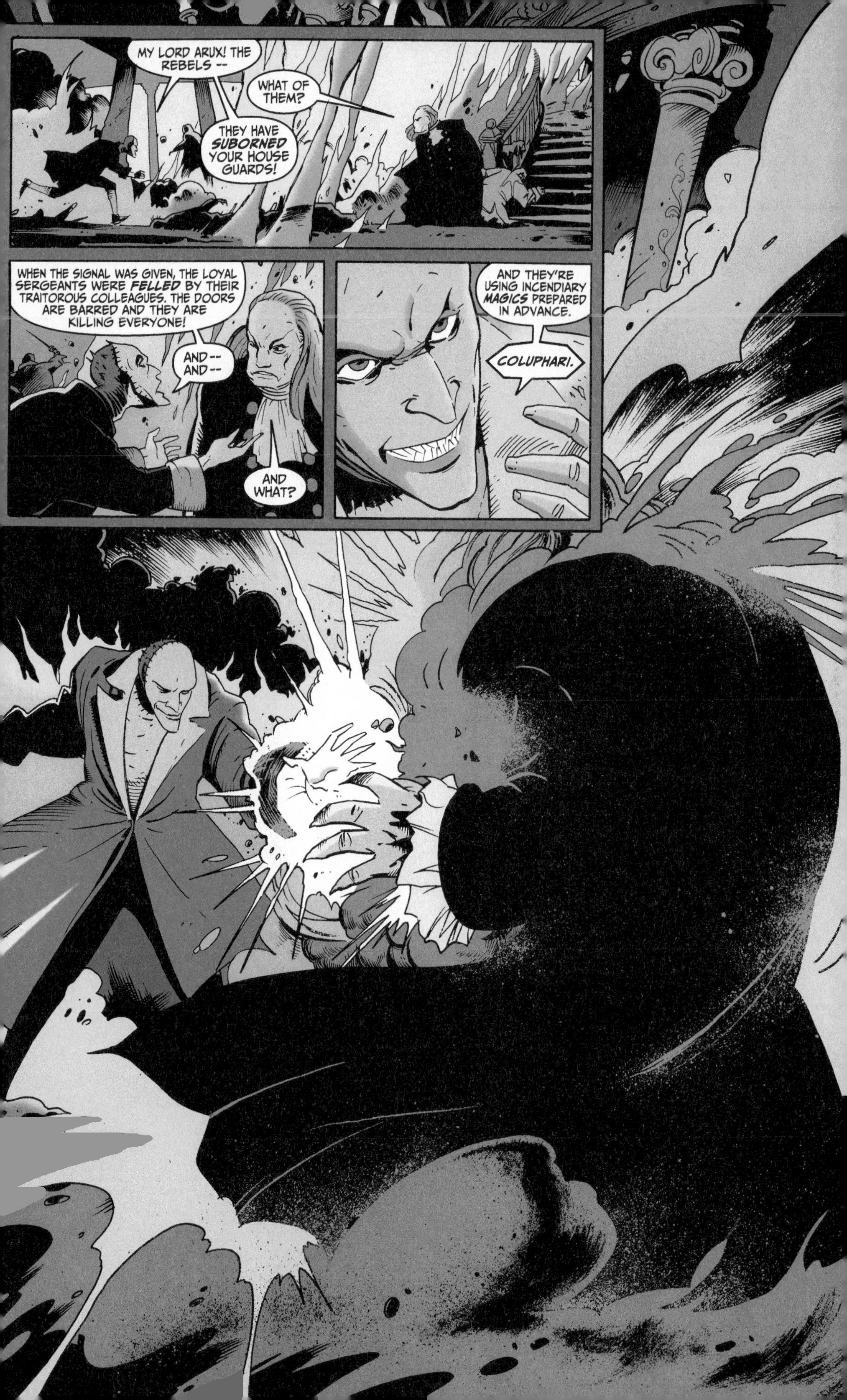
MY LORD ARUX! THE REBELS --
WHAT OF THEM?
THEY HAVE SUBORNED YOUR HOUSE GUARDS!
WHEN THE SIGNAL WAS GIVEN, THE LOYAL SERGEANTS WERE FELLED BY THEIR TRAITOROUS COLLEAGUES. THE DOORS ARE BARRED AND THEY ARE KILLING EVERYONE!
AND -- AND --
AND WHAT?
AND THEY'RE USING INCENDIARY MAGICS PREPARED IN ADVANCE.
COLUPHARI.

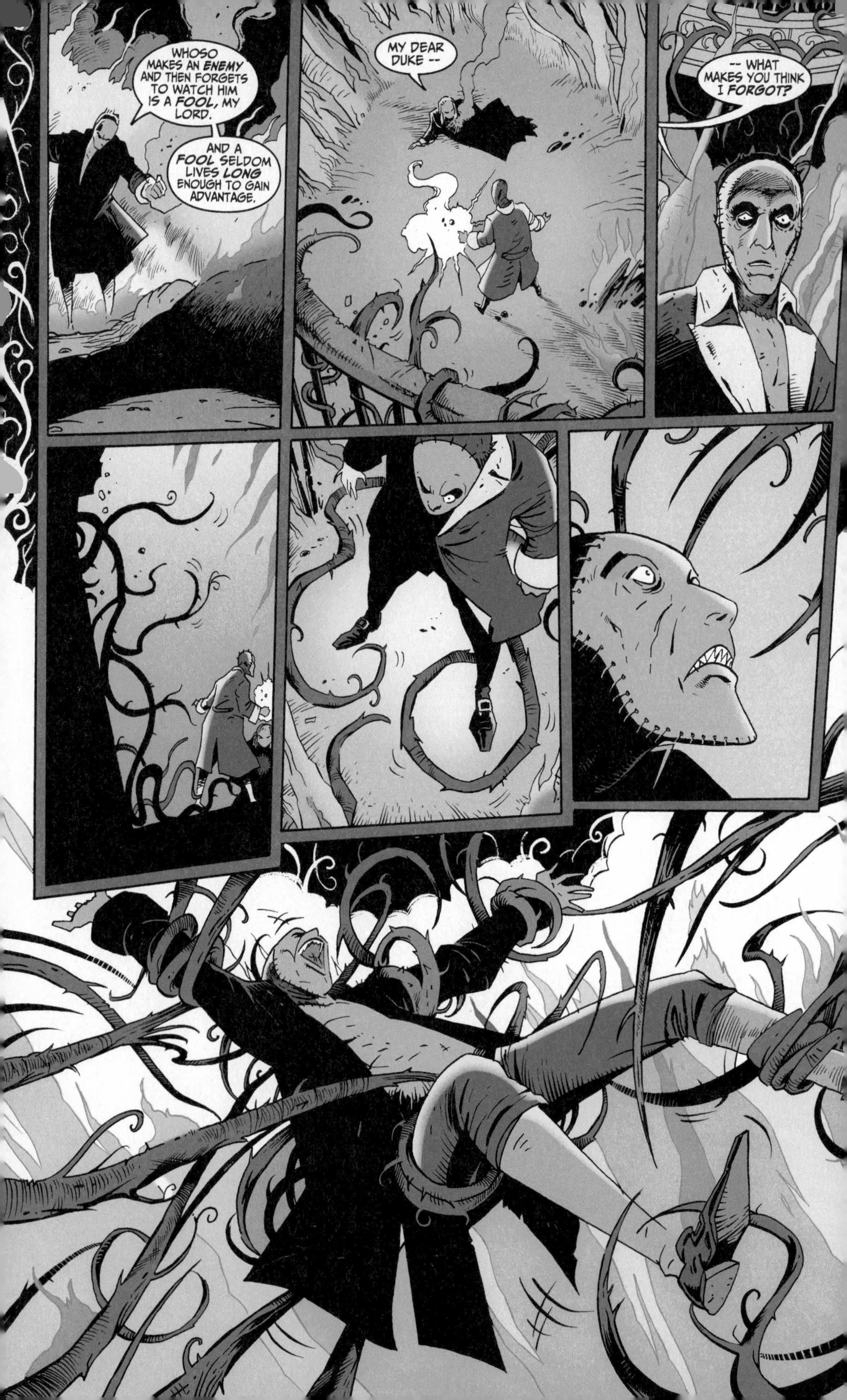
WHOSO MAKES AN ENEMY AND THEN FORGETS TO WATCH HIM IS A FOOL, MY LORD.
AND A FOOL SELDOM LIVES LONG ENOUGH TO GAIN ADVANTAGE.
MY DEAR DUKE --
-- WHAT MAKES YOU THINK I FORGOT?

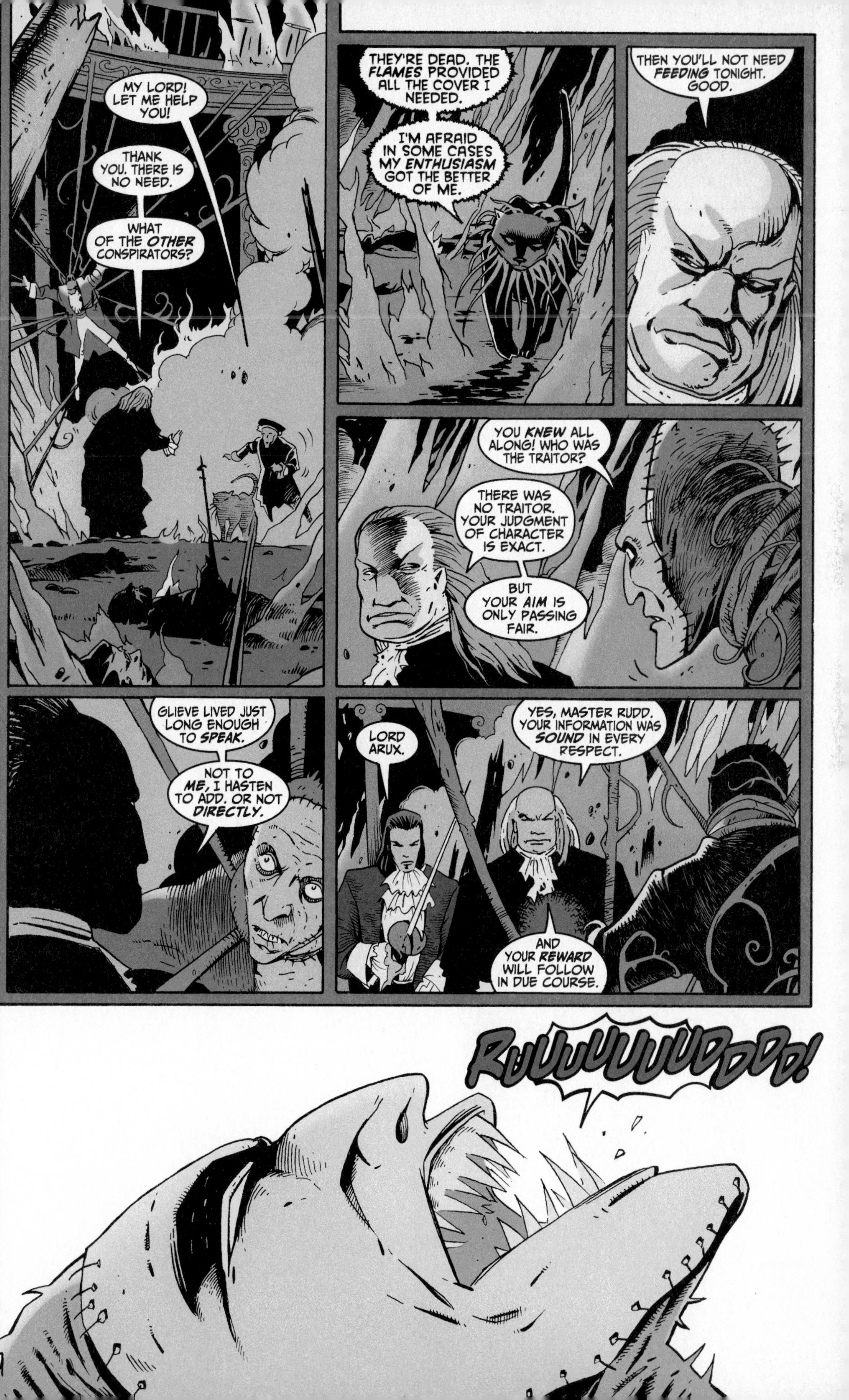
MY LORD! LET ME HELP YOU!
THANK YOU. THERE IS NO NEED.
WHAT OF THE OTHER CONSPIRATORS?
THEY'RE DEAD. THE FLAMES PROVIDED ALL THE COVER I NEEDED.
I'M AFRAID IN SOME CASES MY ENTHUSIASM GOT THE BETTER OF ME.
THEN YOU'LL NOT NEED FEEDING TONIGHT. GOOD.
YOU KNEW ALL ALONG! WHO WAS THE TRAITOR?
THERE WAS NO TRAITOR. YOUR JUDGMENT OF CHARACTER IS EXACT.
BUT YOUR AIM IS ONLY PASSING FAIR.
GLIEVE LIVED JUST LONG ENOUGH TO SPEAK.
NOT TO ME, I HASTEN TO ADD. OR NOT DIRECTLY.
LORD ARUX.
YES, MASTER RUDD. YOUR INFORMATION WAS SOUND IN EVERY RESPECT.
AND YOUR REWARD WILL FOLLOW IN DUE COURSE.
RUUUUUUUDDDD!

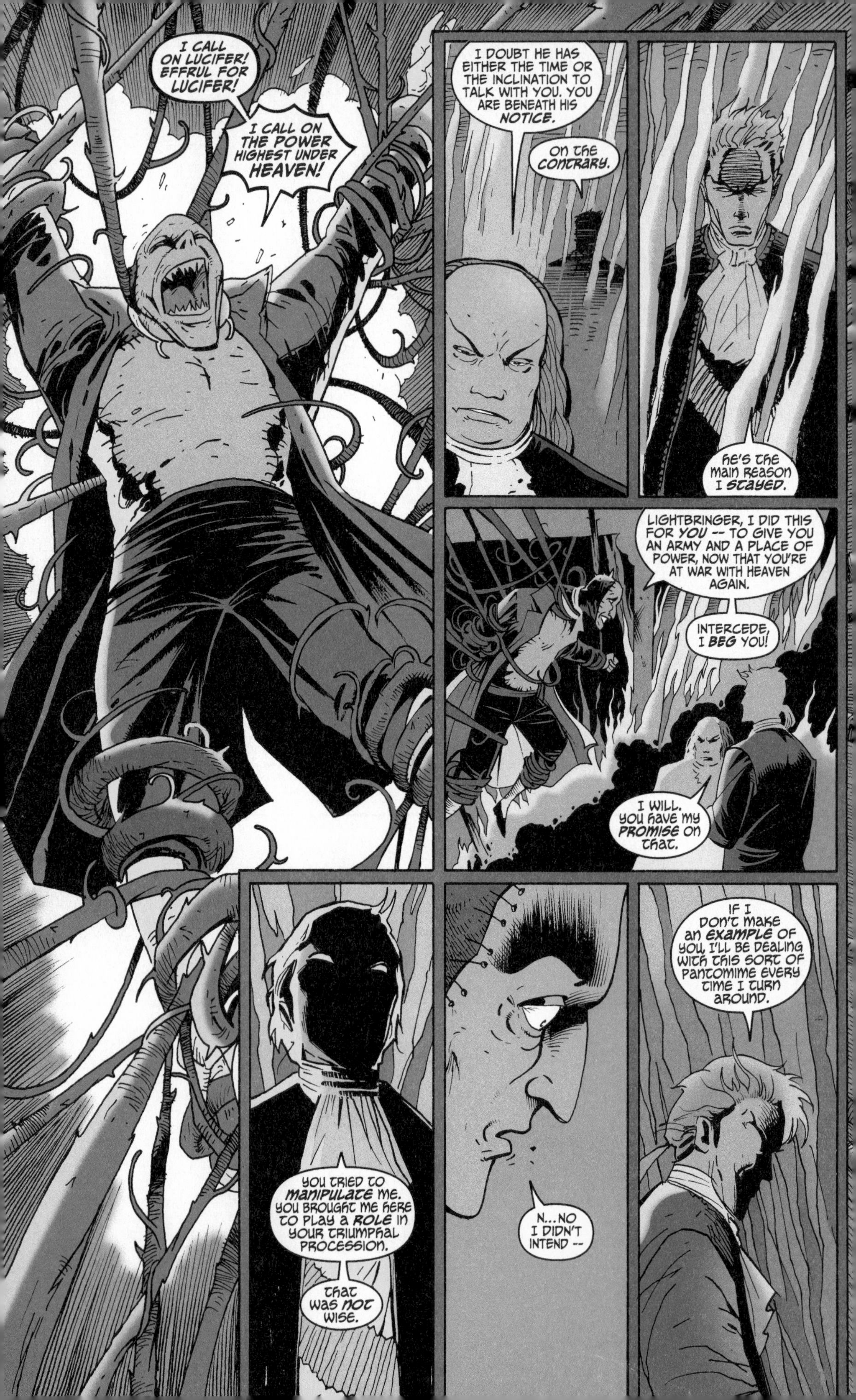
I CALL ON LUCIFER! EFFRUL FOR LUCIFER!
I CALL ON THE POWER HIGHEST UNDER HEAVEN!
I DOUBT HE HAS EITHER THE TIME OR THE INCLINATION TO TALK WITH YOU. YOU ARE BENEATH HIS NOTICE.
ON THE CONTRARY.
HE'S THE MAIN REASON I STAYED.
LIGHTBRINGER, I DID THIS FOR YOU -- TO GIVE YOU AN ARMY AND A PLACE OF POWER, NOW THAT YOU'RE AT WAR WITH HEAVEN AGAIN.
INTERCEDE, I BEG YOU!
I WILL. YOU HAVE MY PROMISE ON THAT.
YOU TRIED TO MANIPULATE ME. YOU BROUGHT ME HERE TO PLAY A ROLE IN YOUR TRIUMPHAL PROCESSION.
THAT WAS NOT WISE.
N...NO I DIDN'T INTEND --
IF I DON'T MAKE AN EXAMPLE OF YOU, I'LL BE DEALING WITH THIS SORT OF PANTOMIME EVERY TIME I TURN AROUND.

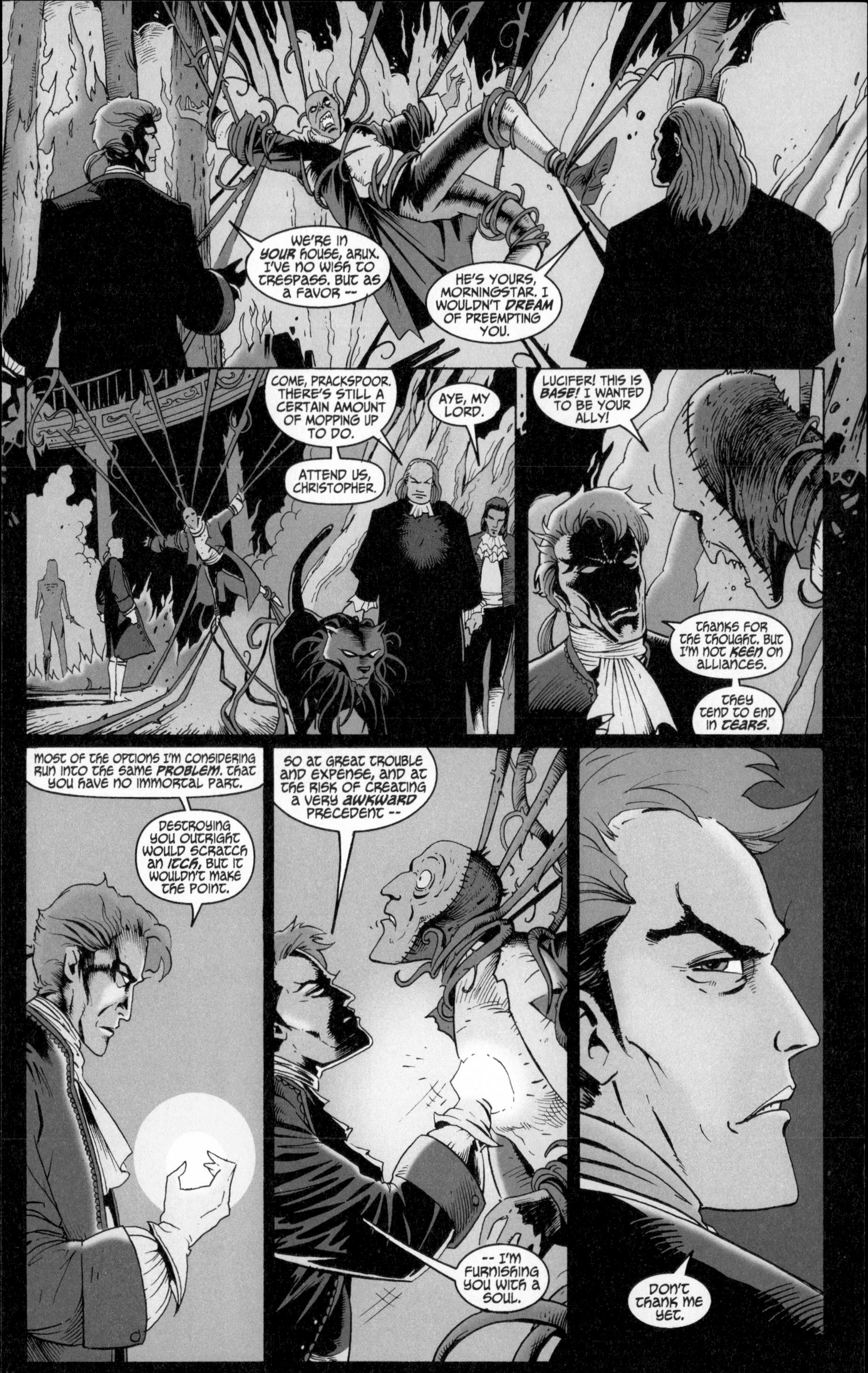
WE'RE IN YOUR HOUSE, ARUX. I'VE NO WISH TO TRESPASS. BUT AS A FAVOR --
HE'S YOURS, MORNINGSTAR. I WOULDN'T DREAM OF PREEMPTING YOU.
COME, PRACKSPOOR. THERE'S STILL A CERTAIN AMOUNT OF MOPPING UP TO DO.
AYE, MY LORD.
ATTEND US, CHRISTOPHER.
LUCIFER! THIS IS BASE! I WANTED TO BE YOUR ALLY!
THANKS FOR THE THOUGHT. BUT I'M NOT KEEN ON ALLIANCES.
THEY TEND TO END IN TEARS.
MOST OF THE OPTIONS I'M CONSIDERING RUN INTO THE SAME PROBLEM. THAT YOU HAVE NO IMMORTAL PART.
DESTROYING YOU OUTRIGHT WOULD SCRATCH AN ITCH, BUT IT WOULDN'T MAKE THE POINT.
SO AT GREAT TROUBLE AND EXPENSE, AND AT THE RISK OF CREATING A VERY AWKWARD PRECEDENT --
-- I'M FURNISHING YOU WITH A SOUL.
DON'T THANK ME YET.

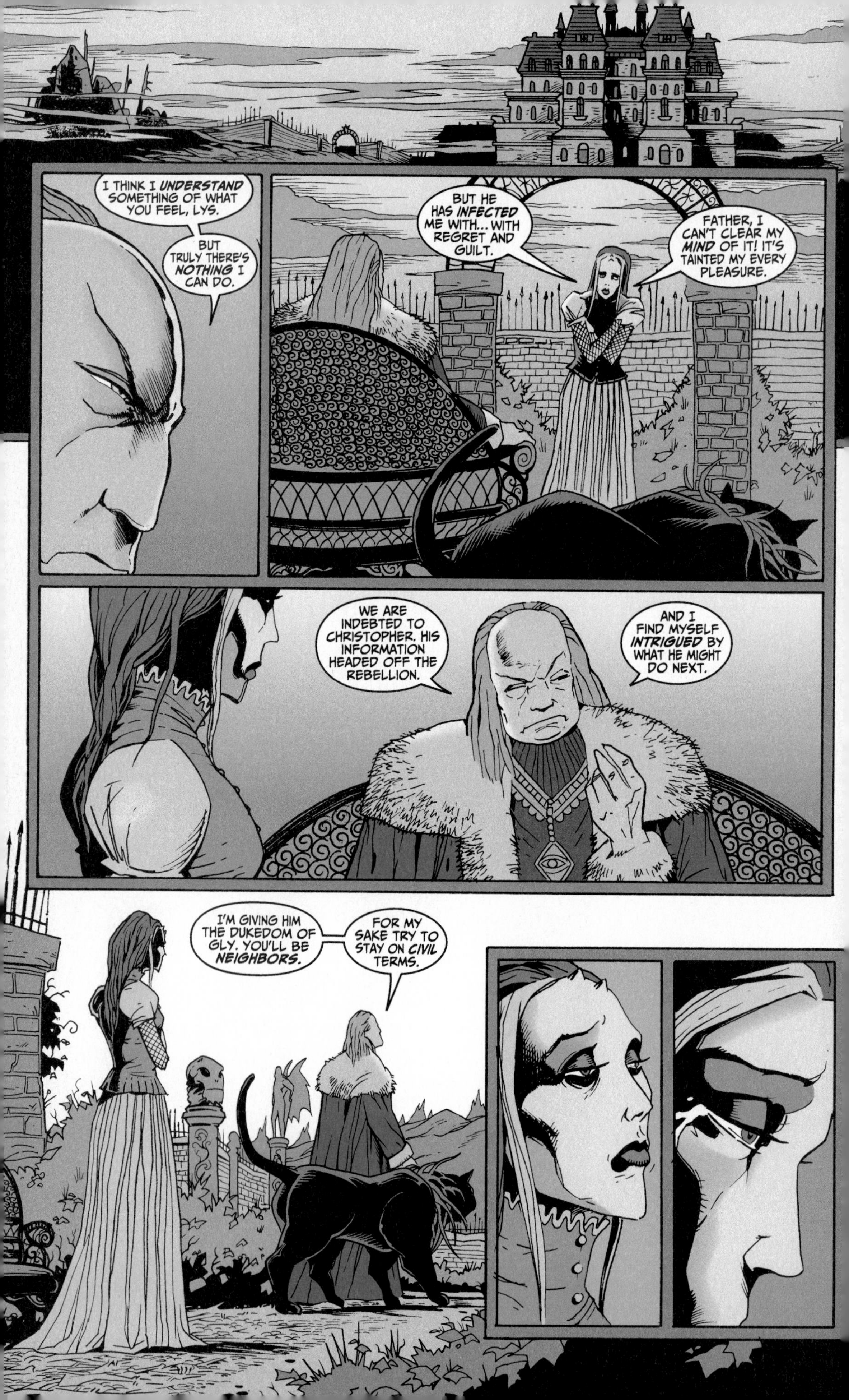

I THINK I UNDERSTAND SOMETHING OF WHAT YOU FEEL, LYS.
BUT TRULY THERE'S NOTHING I CAN DO.
BUT HE HAS INFECTED ME WITH... WITH REGRET AND GUILT.
FATHER, I CAN'T CLEAR MY MIND OF IT! IT'S TAINTED MY EVERY PLEASURE.
WE ARE INDEBTED TO CHRISTOPHER. HIS INFORMATION HEADED OFF THE REBELLION.
AND I FIND MYSELF INTRIGUED BY WHAT HE MIGHT DO NEXT.
I'M GIVING HIM THE DUKEDOM OF GLY. YOU'LL BE NEIGHBORS.
FOR MY SAKE TRY TO STAY ON CIVIL TERMS.

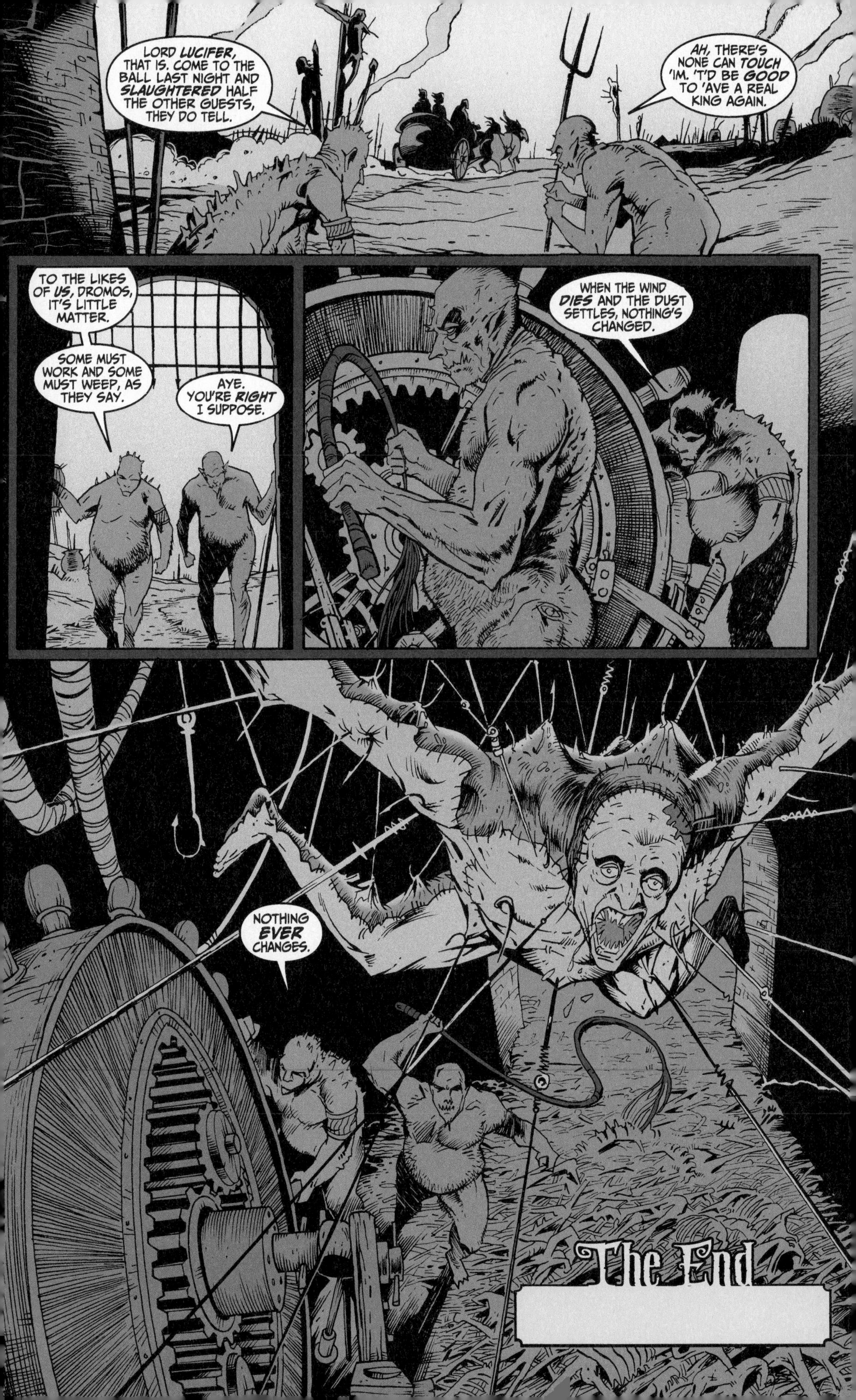
LORD LUCIFER, THAT IS. COME TO THE BALL LAST NIGHT AND SLAUGHTERED HALF THE OTHER GUESTS, THEY DO TELL.
AH, THERE'S NONE CAN TOUCH 'IM. 'T'D BE GOOD TO 'AVE A REAL KING AGAIN.
TO THE LIKES OF US, DROMOS, IT'S LITTLE MATTER.
SOME MUST WORK AND SOME MUST WEEP, AS THEY SAY.
AYE. YOU'RE RIGHT I SUPPOSE.
WHEN THE WIND DIES AND THE DUST SETTLES, NOTHING'S CHANGED.
NOTHING EVER CHANGES.
The End

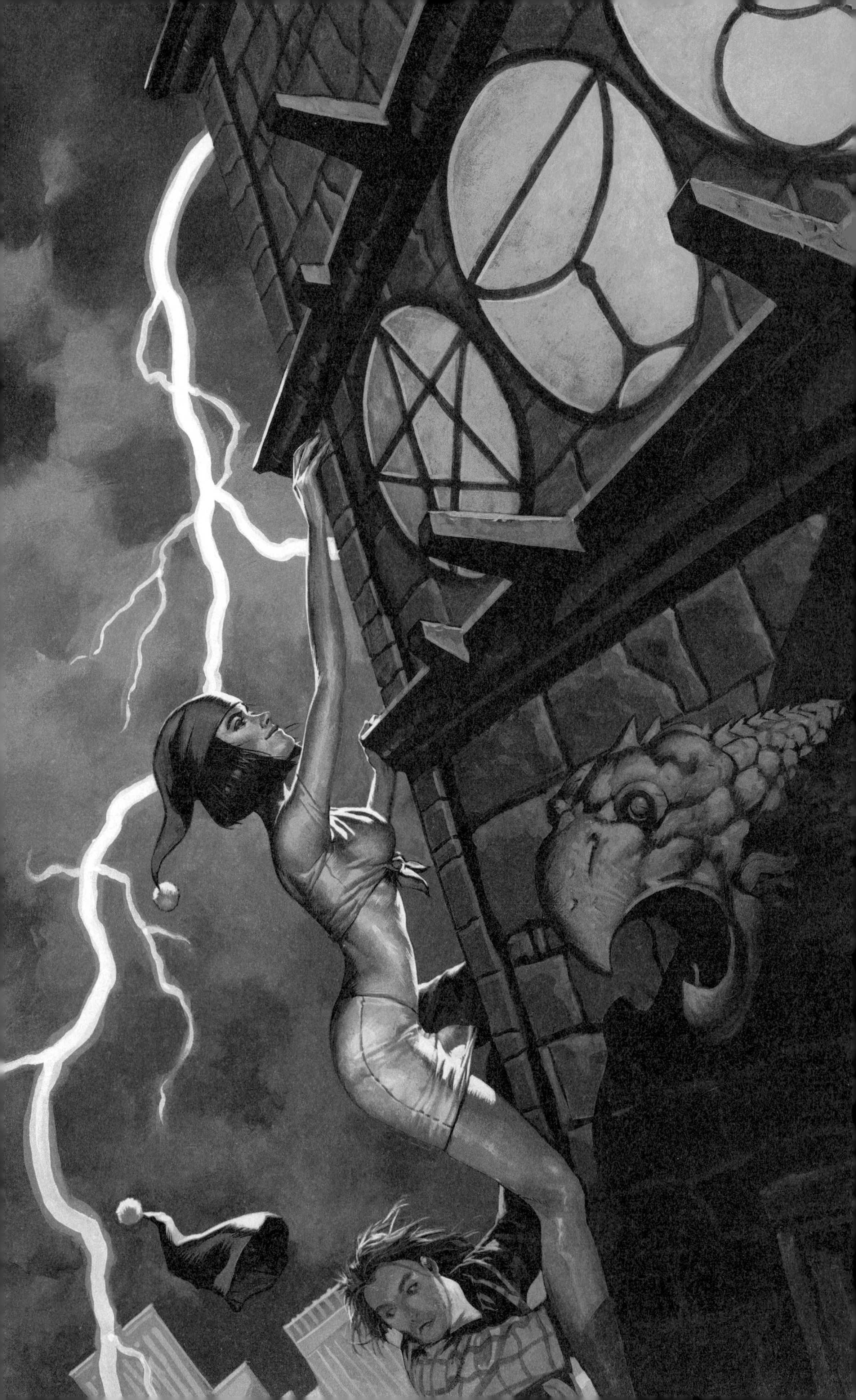

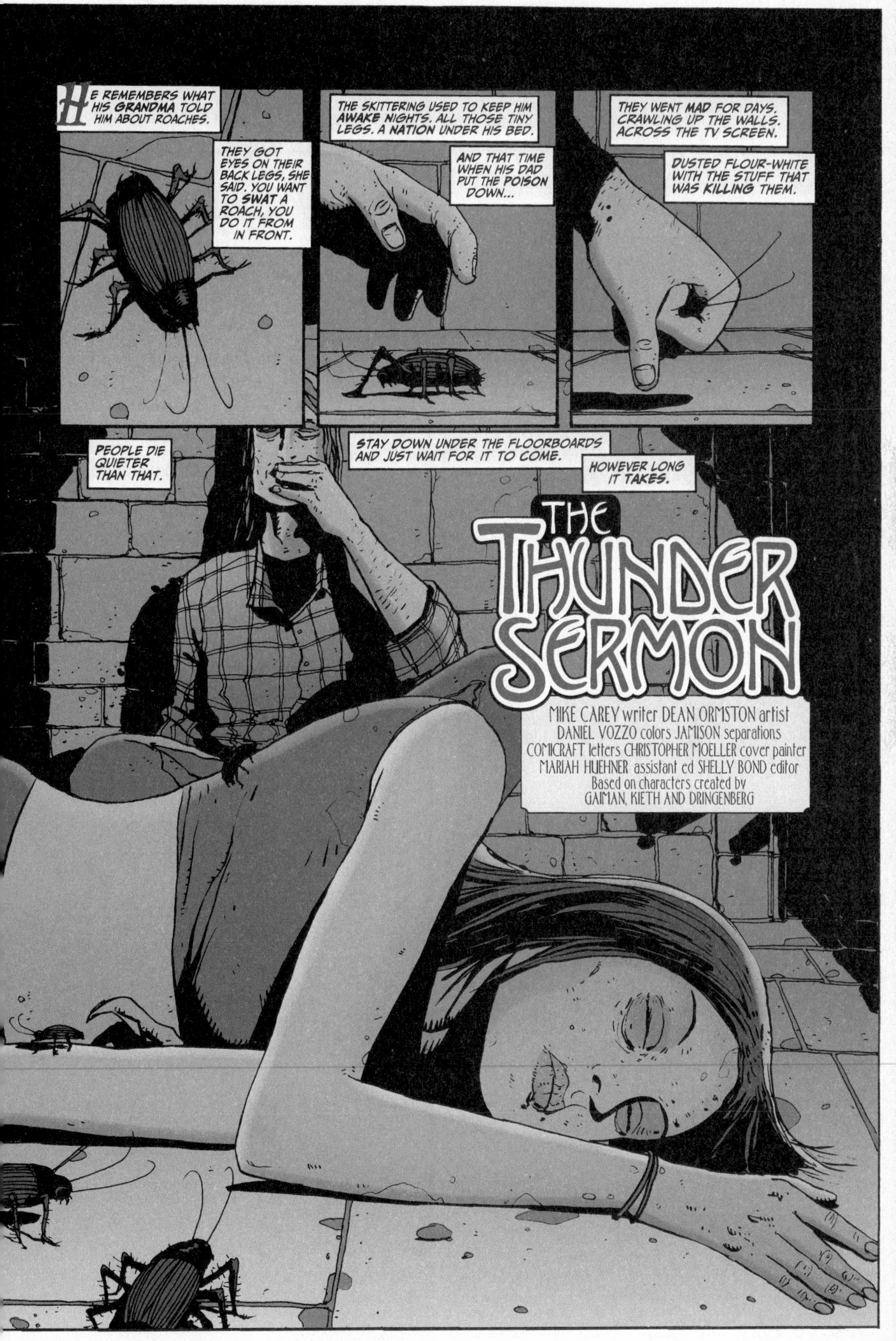
HE REMEMBERS WHAT HIS GRANDMA TOLD HIM ABOUT ROACHES.
THEY GOT EYES ON THEIR BACK LEGS, SHE SAID. YOU WANT TO SWAT A ROACH, YOU DO IT FROM IN FRONT.
THE SKITTERING USED TO KEEP HIM AWAKE NIGHTS. ALL THOSE TINY LEGS. A NATION UNDER HIS BED.
AND THAT TIME WHEN HIS DAD PUT THE POISON DOWN...
THEY WENT MAD FOR DAYS. CRAWLING UP THE WALLS. ACROSS THE TV SCREEN.
DUSTED FLOUR-WHITE WITH THE STUFF THAT WAS KILLING THEM.
PEOPLE DIE QUIETER THAN THAT.
STAY DOWN UNDER THE FLOORBOARDS AND JUST WAIT FOR IT TO COME.
HOWEVER LONG IT TAKES.
THE THUNDER SERMON
MIKE CAREY writer DEAN ORMSTON artist
DANIEL VOZZO colors JAMISON separations
COMICRAFT letters CHRISTOPHER MOELLER cover painter
MARIAH HUEHNER assistant ed SHELLY BOND editor
Based on characters created by
GAIMAN, KIETH AND DRINGENBERG

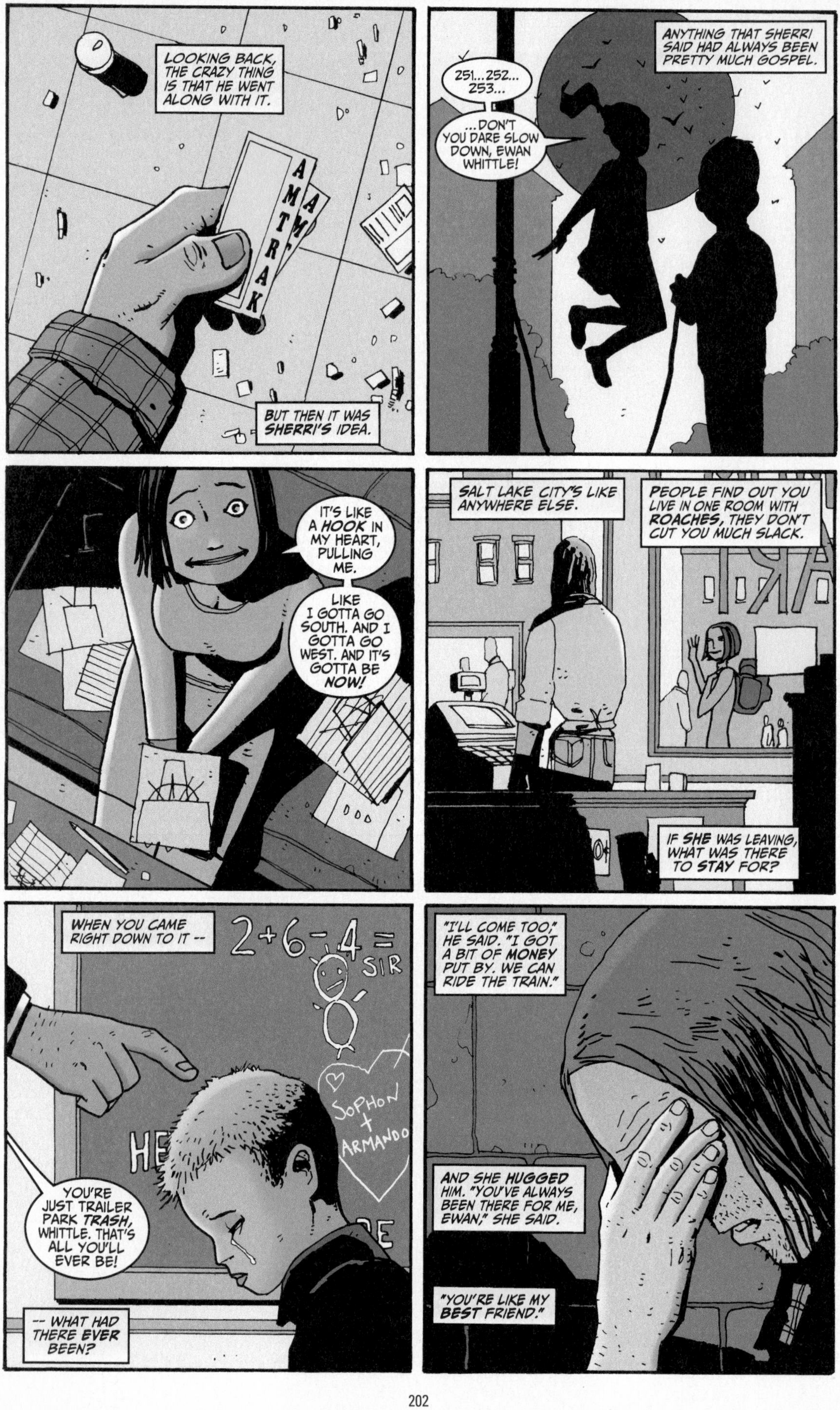
LOOKING BACK, THE CRAZY THING IS THAT HE WENT ALONG WITH IT.
AMTRAK
AMTRAK
BUT THEN IT WAS SHERRI'S IDEA.
ANYTHING THAT SHERRI SAID HAD ALWAYS BEEN PRETTY MUCH GOSPEL.
251...252... 253...
...DON'T YOU DARE SLOW DOWN, EWAN WHITTLE!
IT'S LIKE A HOOK IN MY HEART, PULLING ME.
LIKE I GOTTA GO SOUTH. AND I GOTTA GO WEST. AND IT'S GOTTA BE NOW!
SALT LAKE CITY'S LIKE ANYWHERE ELSE.
PEOPLE FIND OUT YOU LIVE IN ONE ROOM WITH ROACHES, THEY DON'T CUT YOU MUCH SLACK.
IF SHE WAS LEAVING, WHAT WAS THERE TO STAY FOR?
WHEN YOU CAME RIGHT DOWN TO IT --
2+6-4=
SIR
SOPHON + ARMANDO
YOU'RE JUST TRAILER PARK TRASH, WHITTLE. THAT'S ALL YOU'LL EVER BE!
-- WHAT HAD THERE EVER BEEN?
"I'LL COME TOO," HE SAID. "I GOT A BIT OF MONEY PUT BY. WE CAN RIDE THE TRAIN."
AND SHE HUGGED HIM. "YOU'VE ALWAYS BEEN THERE FOR ME, EWAN," SHE SAID.
"YOU'RE LIKE MY BEST FRIEND."

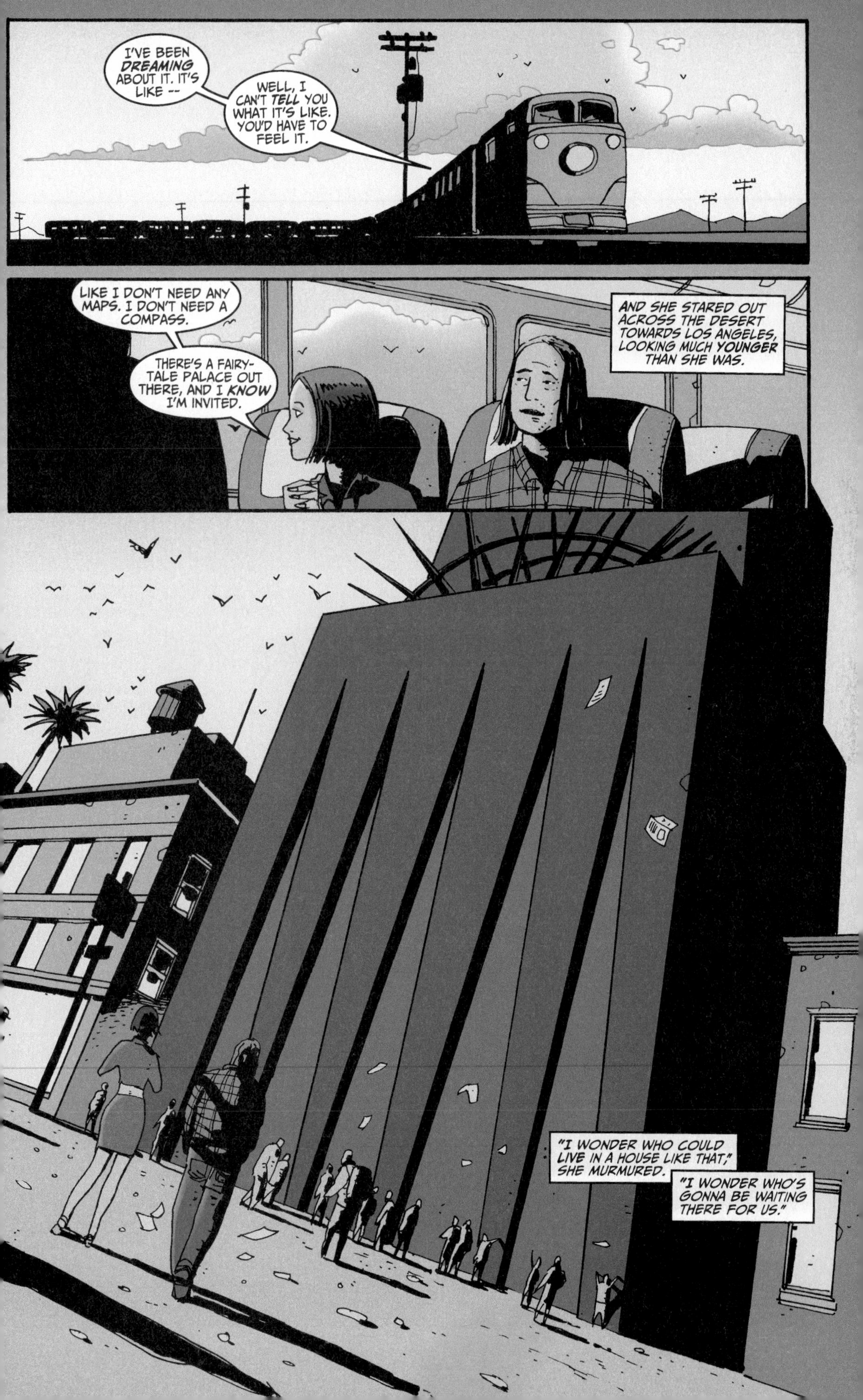
I'VE BEEN DREAMING ABOUT IT. IT'S LIKE --
WELL, I CAN'T TELL YOU WHAT IT'S LIKE. YOU'D HAVE TO FEEL IT.
LIKE I DON'T NEED ANY MAPS. I DON'T NEED A COMPASS.
THERE'S A FAIRY-TALE PALACE OUT THERE, AND I KNOW I'M INVITED.
AND SHE STARED OUT ACROSS THE DESERT TOWARDS LOS ANGELES, LOOKING MUCH YOUNGER THAN SHE WAS.
"I WONDER WHO COULD LIVE IN A HOUSE LIKE THAT," SHE MURMURED.
"I WONDER WHO'S GONNA BE WAITING THERE FOR US."

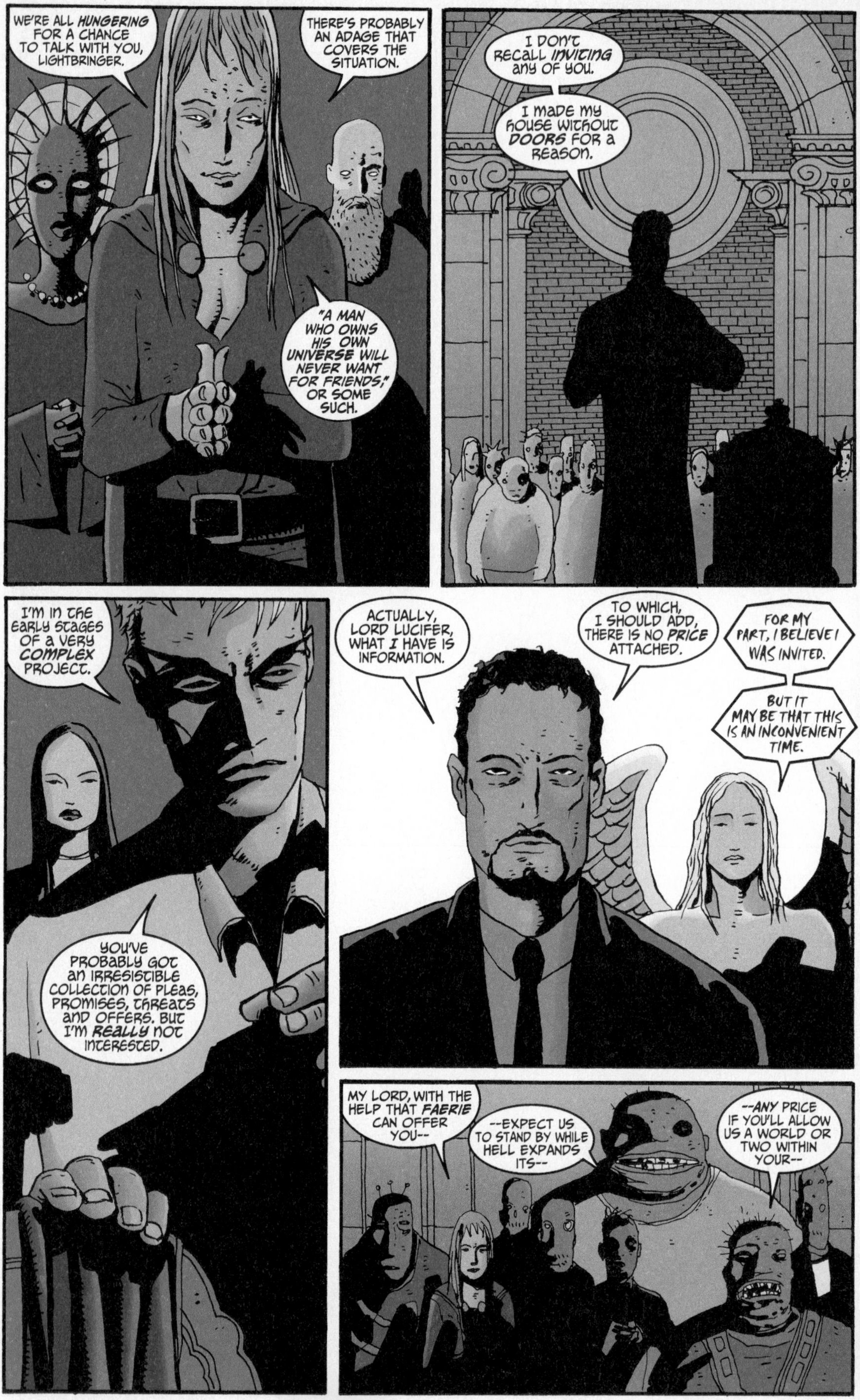
WE'RE ALL HUNGERING FOR A CHANCE TO TALK WITH YOU, LIGHTBRINGER.
THERE'S PROBABLY AN ADAGE THAT COVERS THE SITUATION.
"A MAN WHO OWNS HIS OWN UNIVERSE WILL NEVER WANT FOR FRIENDS," OR SOME SUCH.
I DON'T RECALL INVITING ANY OF YOU.
I MADE MY HOUSE WITHOUT DOORS FOR A REASON.
I'M IN THE EARLY STAGES OF A VERY COMPLEX PROJECT.
YOU'VE PROBABLY GOT AN IRRESISTIBLE COLLECTION OF PLEAS, PROMISES, THREATS AND OFFERS. BUT I'M REALLY NOT INTERESTED.
ACTUALLY, LORD LUCIFER, WHAT I HAVE IS INFORMATION.
TO WHICH, I SHOULD ADD, THERE IS NO PRICE ATTACHED.
FOR MY PART, I BELIEVE I WAS INVITED.
BUT IT MAY BE THAT THIS IS AN INCONVENIENT TIME.
MY LORD, WITH THE HELP THAT FAERIE CAN OFFER YOU--
--EXPECT US TO STAND BY WHILE HELL EXPANDS ITS--
--ANY PRICE IF YOU'LL ALLOW US A WORLD OR TWO WITHIN YOUR--

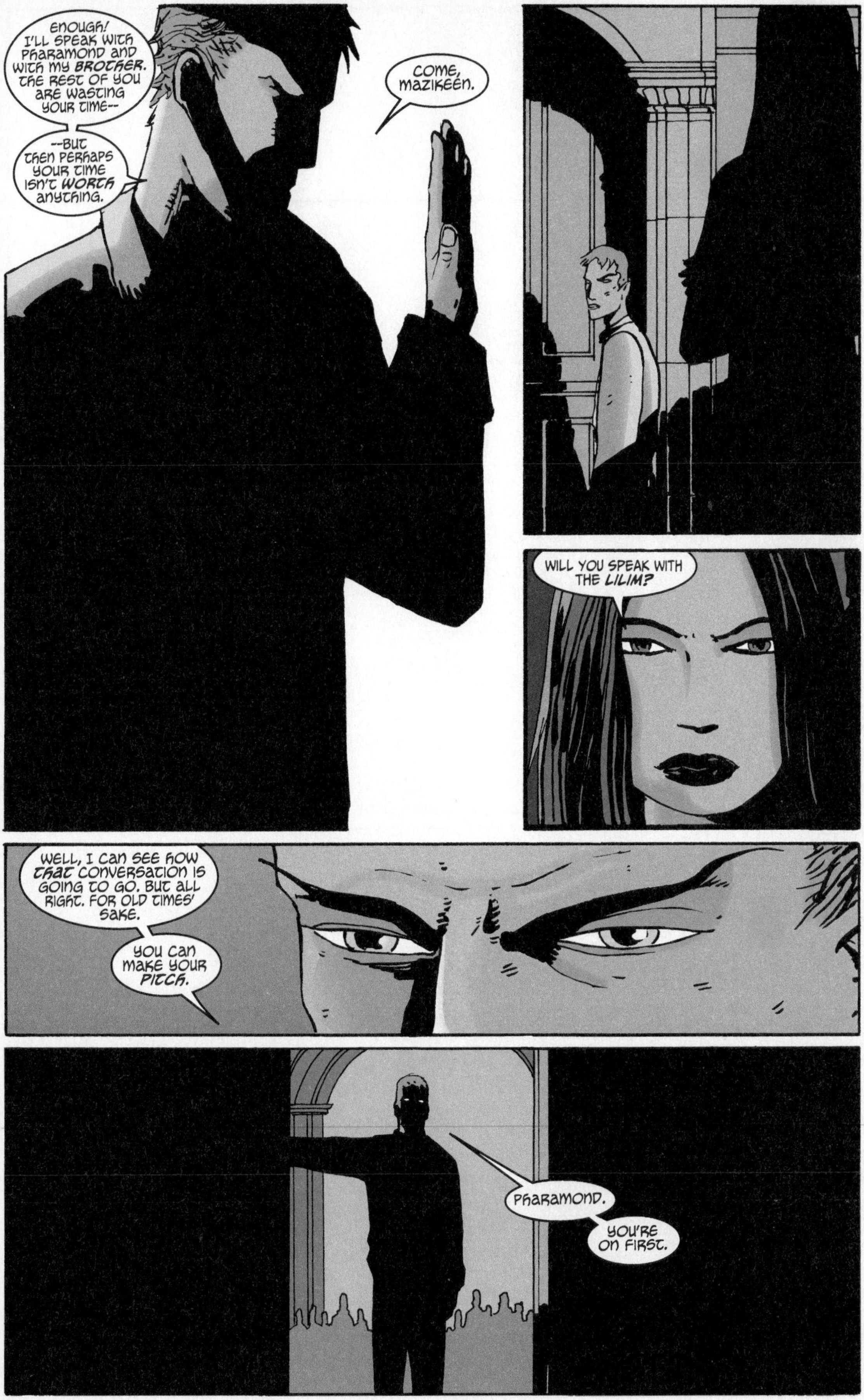

ENOUGH! I'LL SPEAK WITH PHARAMOND AND WITH MY BROTHER. THE REST OF YOU ARE WASTING YOUR TIME--
--BUT THEN PERHAPS YOUR TIME ISN'T WORTH ANYTHING.
COME, MAZIKEEN.
WILL YOU SPEAK WITH THE LILIM?
WELL, I CAN SEE HOW THAT CONVERSATION IS GOING TO GO. BUT ALL RIGHT. FOR OLD TIMES' SAKE.
YOU CAN MAKE YOUR PITCH.
PHARAMOND.
YOU'RE ON FIRST.

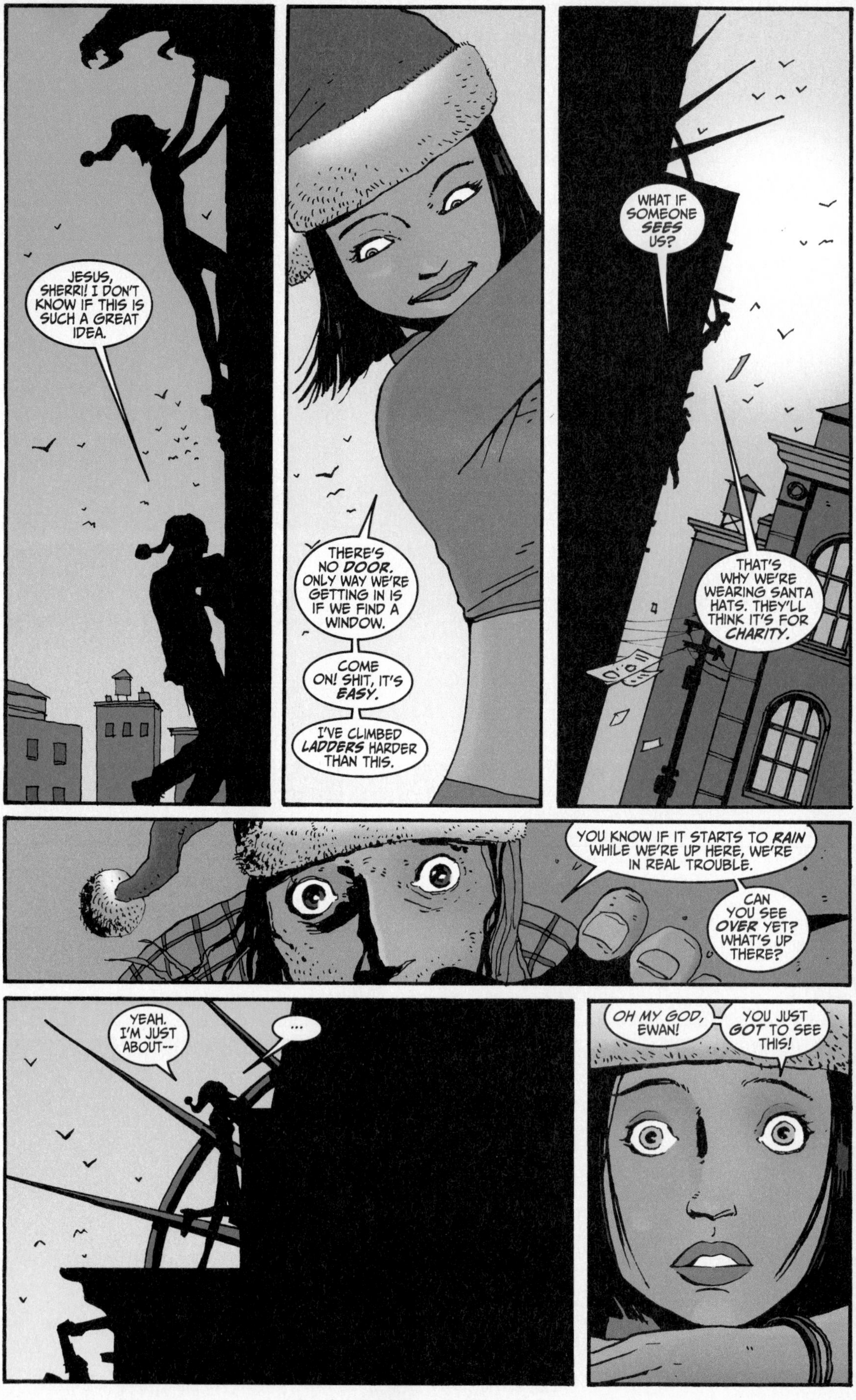
JESUS, SHERRI! I DON'T KNOW IF THIS IS SUCH A GREAT IDEA.
THERE'S NO DOOR. ONLY WAY WE'RE GETTING IN IS IF WE FIND A WINDOW.
COME ON! SHIT, IT'S EASY.
I'VE CLIMBED LADDERS HARDER THAN THIS.
WHAT IF SOMEONE SEES US?
THAT'S WHY WE'RE WEARING SANTA HATS. THEY'LL THINK IT'S FOR CHARITY.
YOU KNOW IF IT STARTS TO RAIN WHILE WE'RE UP HERE, WE'RE IN REAL TROUBLE.
CAN YOU SEE OVER YET? WHAT'S UP THERE?
YEAH. I'M JUST ABOUT--
...
OH MY GOD, EWAN!
YOU JUST GOT TO SEE THIS!

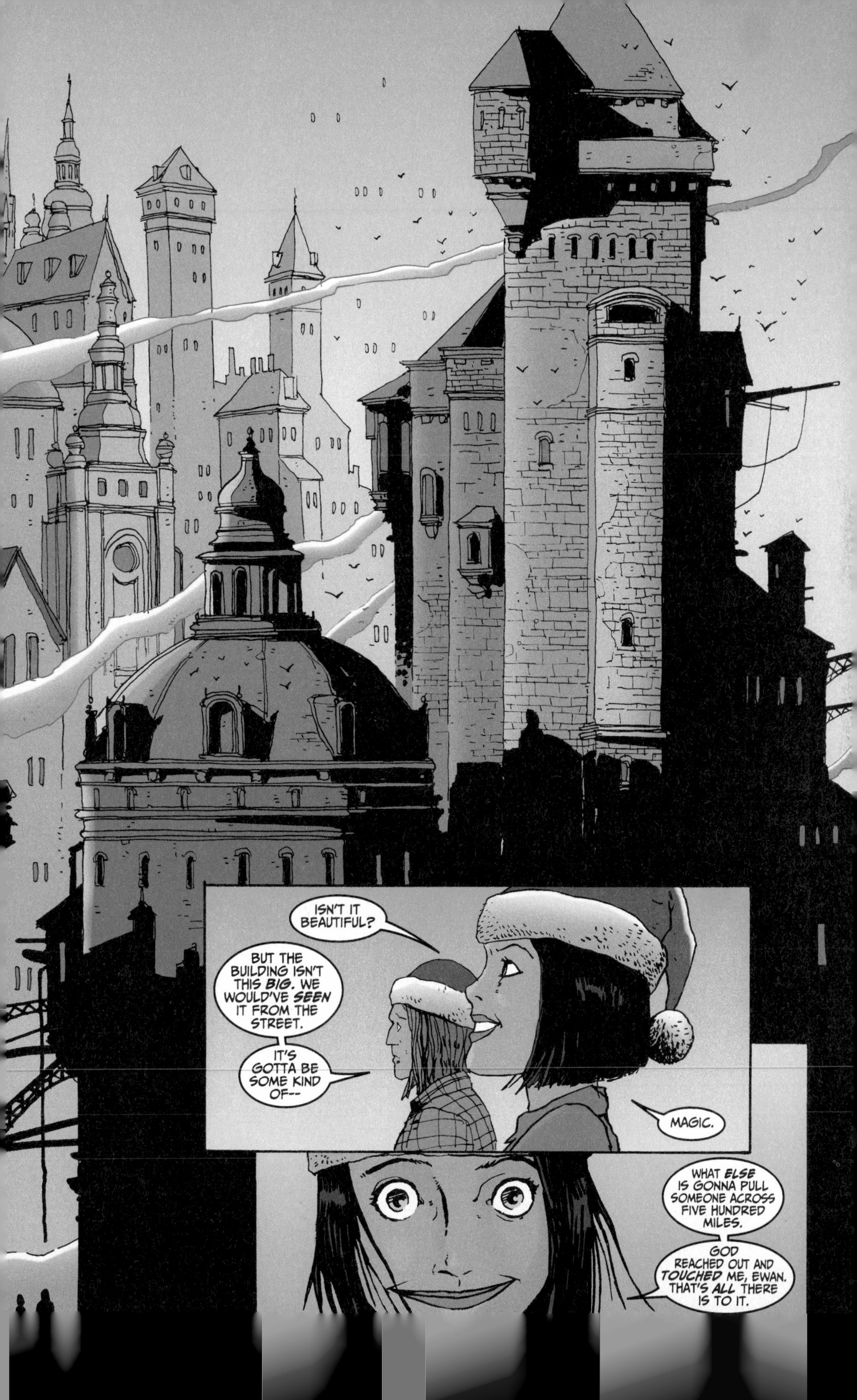
ISN'T IT BEAUTIFUL?
BUT THE BUILDING ISN'T THIS BIG. WE WOULD'VE SEEN IT FROM THE STREET.
IT'S GOTTA BE SOME KIND OF--
MAGIC.
WHAT ELSE IS GONNA PULL SOMEONE ACROSS FIVE HUNDRED MILES.
GOD REACHED OUT AND TOUCHED ME, EWAN. THAT'S ALL THERE IS TO IT.

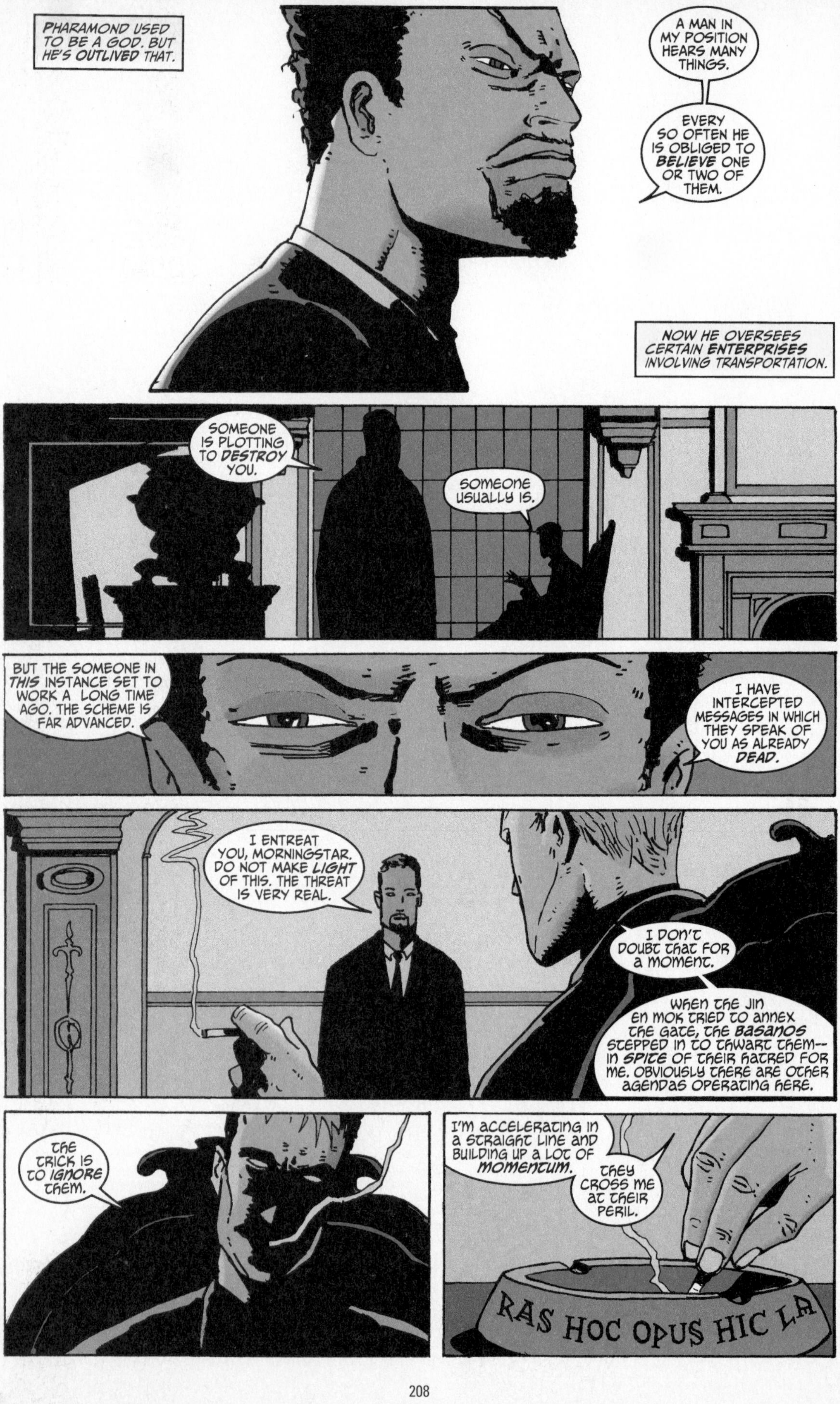
PHARAMOND USED TO BE A GOD. BUT HE'S OUTLIVED THAT.
A MAN IN MY POSITION HEARS MANY THINGS.
EVERY SO OFTEN HE IS OBLIGED TO BELIEVE ONE OR TWO OF THEM.
NOW HE OVERSEES CERTAIN ENTERPRISES INVOLVING TRANSPORTATION.
SOMEONE IS PLOTTING TO DESTROY YOU.
SOMEONE USUALLY IS.
BUT THE SOMEONE IN THIS INSTANCE SET TO WORK A LONG TIME AGO. THE SCHEME IS FAR ADVANCED.
I HAVE INTERCEPTED MESSAGES IN WHICH THEY SPEAK OF YOU AS ALREADY DEAD.
I ENTREAT YOU, MORNINGSTAR. DO NOT MAKE LIGHT OF THIS. THE THREAT IS VERY REAL.
I DON'T DOUBT THAT FOR A MOMENT.
WHEN THE JIN EN MOK TRIED TO ANNEX THE GATE, THE BASANOS STEPPED IN TO THWART THEM-- IN SPITE OF THEIR HATRED FOR ME. OBVIOUSLY THERE ARE OTHER AGENDAS OPERATING HERE.
THE TRICK IS TO IGNORE THEM.
I'M ACCELERATING IN A STRAIGHT LINE AND BUILDING UP A LOT OF MOMENTUM.
THEY CROSS ME AT THEIR PERIL.
RAS HOC OPUS HIC LA

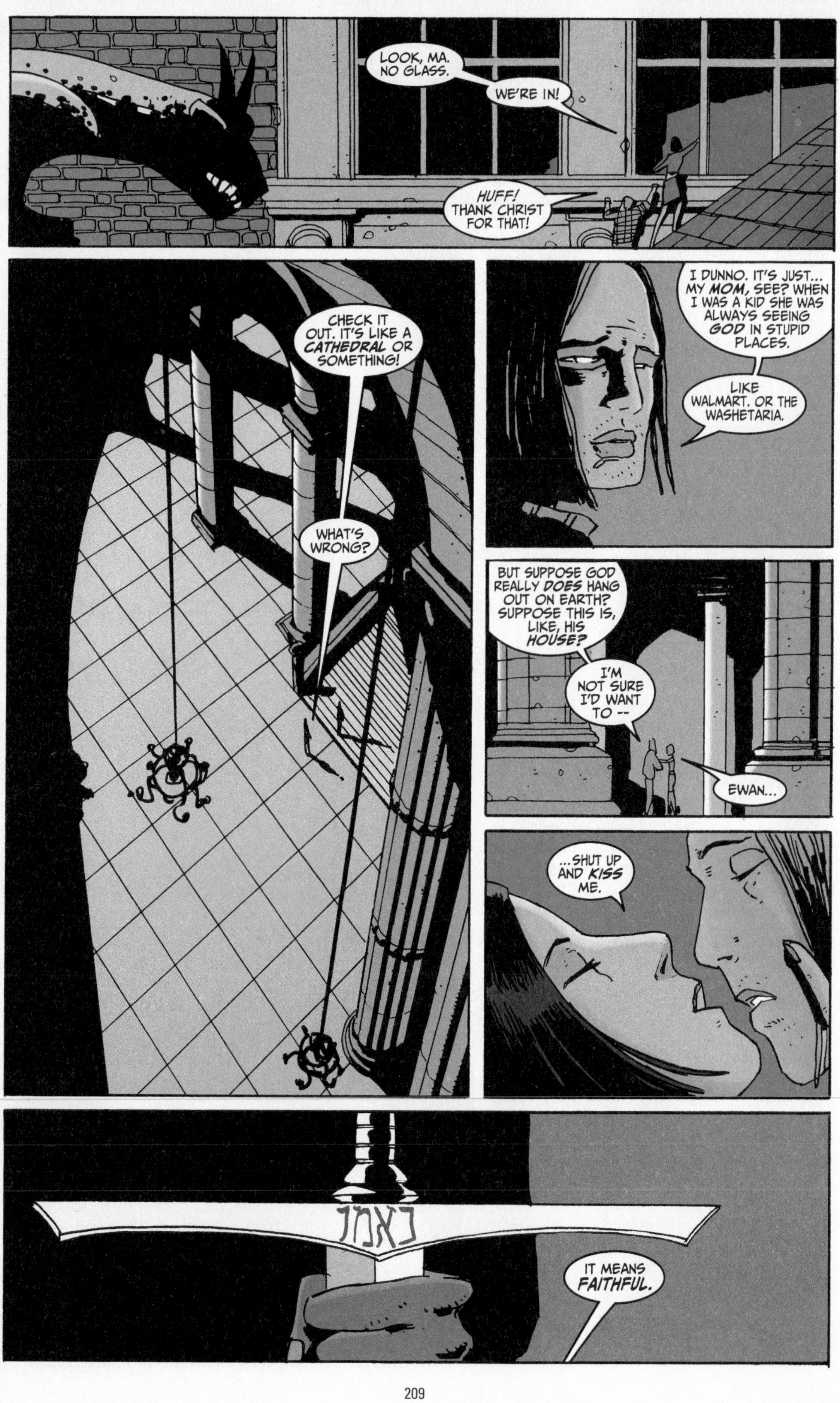
LOOK, MA. NO GLASS.
WE'RE IN!
HUFF! THANK CHRIST FOR THAT!
CHECK IT OUT. IT'S LIKE A CATHEDRAL OR SOMETHING!
WHAT'S WRONG?
I DUNNO. IT'S JUST... MY MOM, SEE? WHEN I WAS A KID SHE WAS ALWAYS SEEING GOD IN STUPID PLACES.
LIKE WALMART. OR THE WASHETARIA.
BUT SUPPOSE GOD REALLY DOES HANG OUT ON EARTH? SUPPOSE THIS IS, LIKE, HIS HOUSE?
I'M NOT SURE I'D WANT TO --
EWAN...
...SHUT UP AND KISS ME.
נאמן
IT MEANS FAITHFUL.

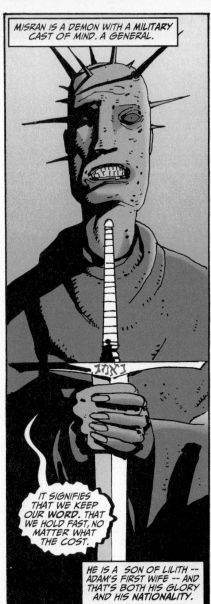

MISRAN IS A DEMON WITH A MILITARY CAST OF MIND. A GENERAL.

IT SIGNIFIES THAT WE KEEP OUR WORD. THAT WE HOLD FAST, NO MATTER WHAT THE COST.

HE IS A SON OF LILITH -- ADAM'S FIRST WIFE -- AND THAT'S BOTH HIS GLORY AND HIS NATIONALITY.

TAKE THE SWORD. A MILLION LILIM HAVE SWORN ON IT.

TAKE IT, STAR OF MORNING, AND LEAD US INTO THE LIGHT.

MISRAN, I'M STRETCHING A POINT JUST LISTENING TO YOU.

YOU'RE PLAYING POKER WITH NO CARDS AND NO STAKE. YOU DON'T HAVE A SINGLE THING I NEED.

A MILLION WARRIORS, LUCIFER! AN ARMY!

YOUR NEW COSMOS HAS A BORDER THAT STRETCHES INTO INFINITY. HOW WILL YOU GUARD IT WITHOUT AN ARMY?

YOU USE THE WORD "INFINITY" VERY GLIBLY, GENERAL MISRAN.

HAVE YOU EVER BEEN THERE?

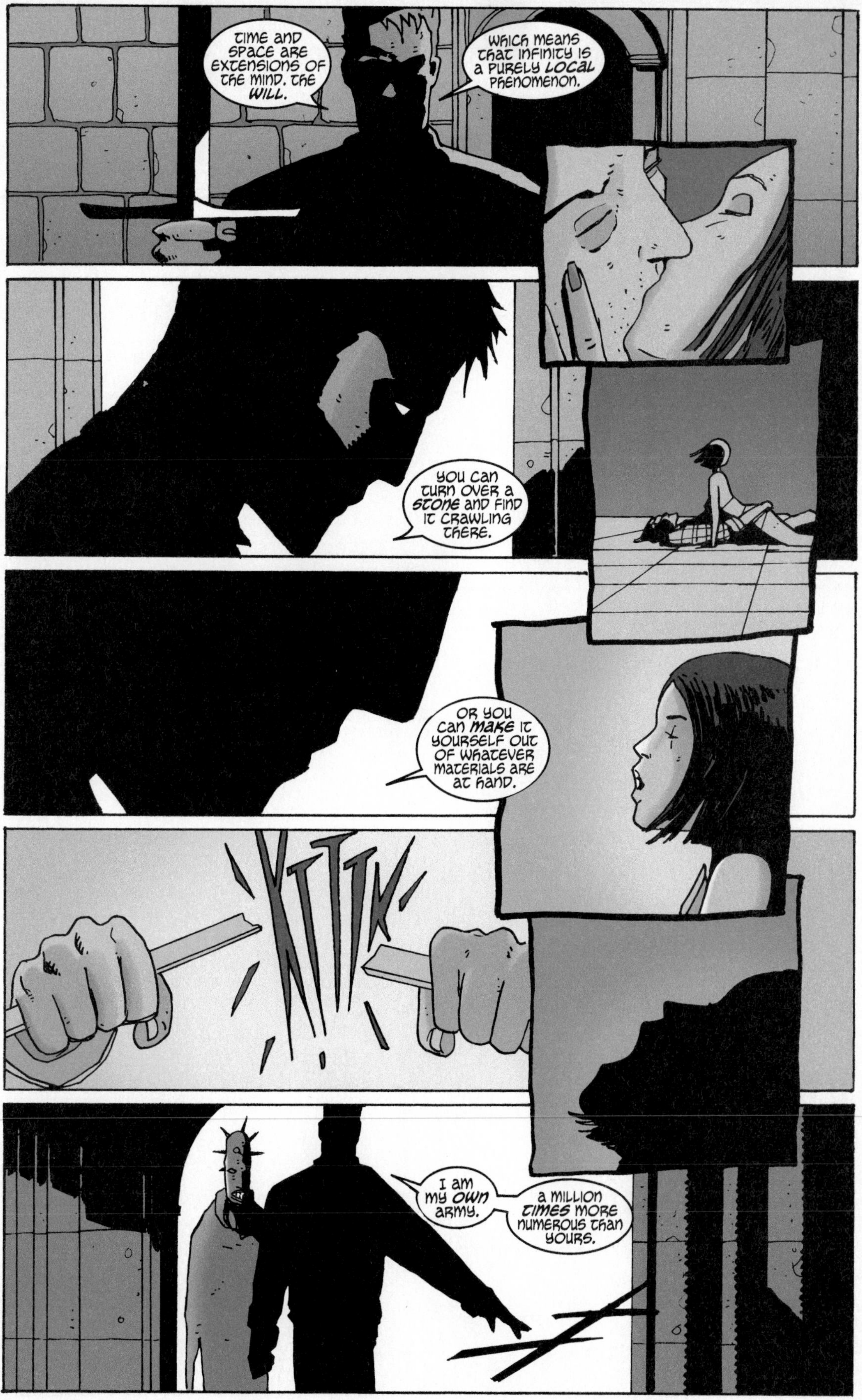
TIME AND SPACE ARE EXTENSIONS OF THE MIND. THE WILL.
WHICH MEANS THAT INFINITY IS A PURELY LOCAL PHENOMENON.
YOU CAN TURN OVER A STONE AND FIND IT CRAWLING THERE.
OR YOU CAN MAKE IT YOURSELF OUT OF WHATEVER MATERIALS ARE AT HAND.
KTTTK
I AM MY OWN ARMY.
A MILLION TIMES MORE NUMEROUS THAN YOURS.

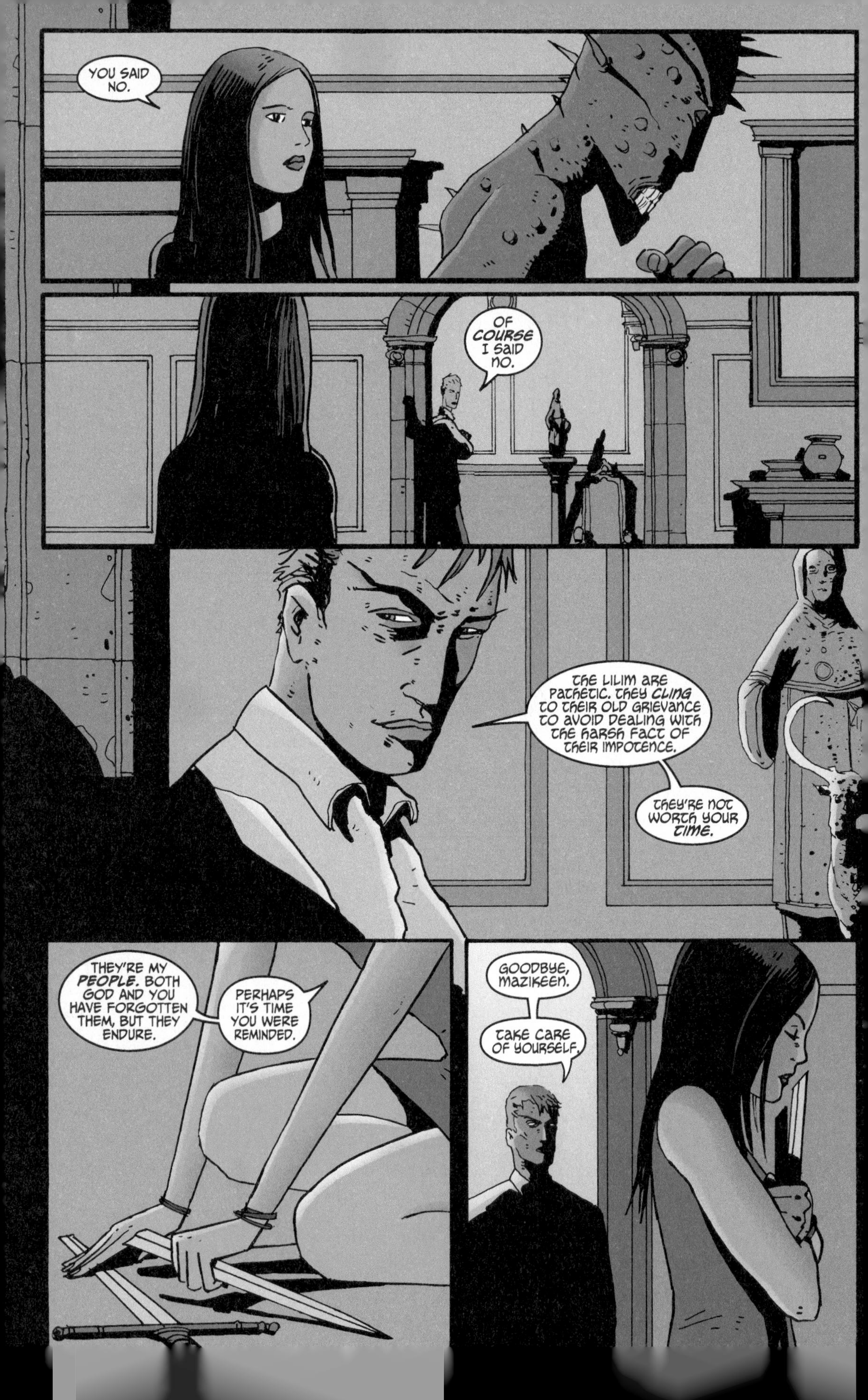
YOU SAID NO.
OF COURSE I SAID NO.
THE LILIM ARE PATHETIC. THEY CLING TO THEIR OLD GRIEVANCE TO AVOID DEALING WITH THE HARSH FACT OF THEIR IMPOTENCE.
THEY'RE NOT WORTH YOUR TIME.
THEY'RE MY PEOPLE. BOTH GOD AND YOU HAVE FORGOTTEN THEM, BUT THEY ENDURE.
PERHAPS IT'S TIME YOU WERE REMINDED.
GOODBYE, MAZIKEEN.
TAKE CARE OF YOURSELF.

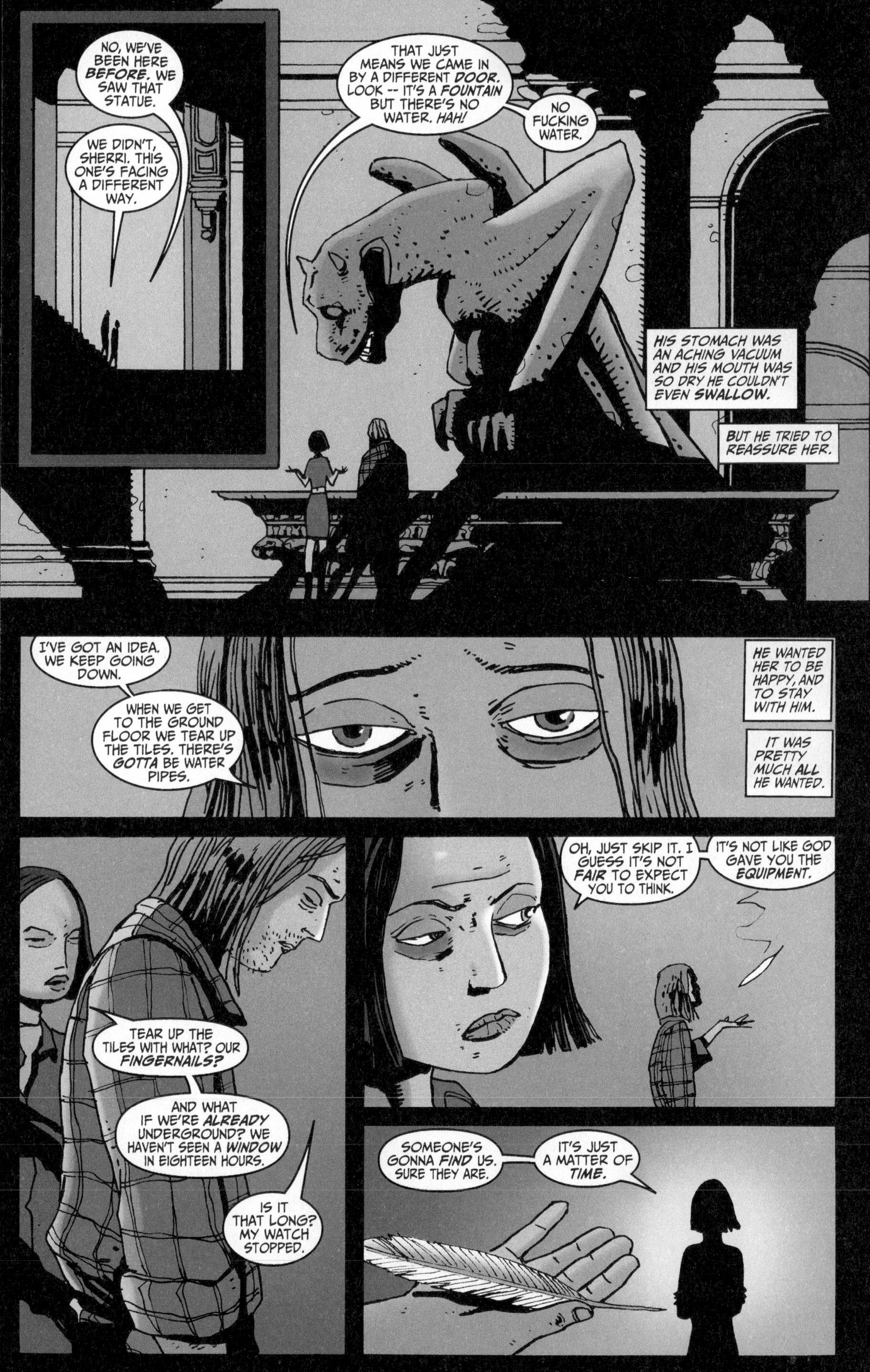
NO, WE'VE BEEN HERE BEFORE. WE SAW THAT STATUE.
WE DIDN'T, SHERRI. THIS ONE'S FACING A DIFFERENT WAY.
THAT JUST MEANS WE CAME IN BY A DIFFERENT DOOR. LOOK -- IT'S A FOUNTAIN BUT THERE'S NO WATER. HAH!
NO FUCKING WATER.
HIS STOMACH WAS AN ACHING VACUUM AND HIS MOUTH WAS SO DRY HE COULDN'T EVEN SWALLOW.
BUT HE TRIED TO REASSURE HER.
I'VE GOT AN IDEA. WE KEEP GOING DOWN.
WHEN WE GET TO THE GROUND FLOOR WE TEAR UP THE TILES. THERE'S GOTTA BE WATER PIPES.
HE WANTED HER TO BE HAPPY, AND TO STAY WITH HIM.
IT WAS PRETTY MUCH ALL HE WANTED.
TEAR UP THE TILES WITH WHAT? OUR FINGERNAILS?
AND WHAT IF WE'RE ALREADY UNDERGROUND? WE HAVEN'T SEEN A WINDOW IN EIGHTEEN HOURS.
IS IT THAT LONG? MY WATCH STOPPED.
OH, JUST SKIP IT. I GUESS IT'S NOT FAIR TO EXPECT YOU TO THINK.
IT'S NOT LIKE GOD GAVE YOU THE EQUIPMENT.
SOMEONE'S GONNA FIND US. SURE THEY ARE.
IT'S JUST A MATTER OF TIME.

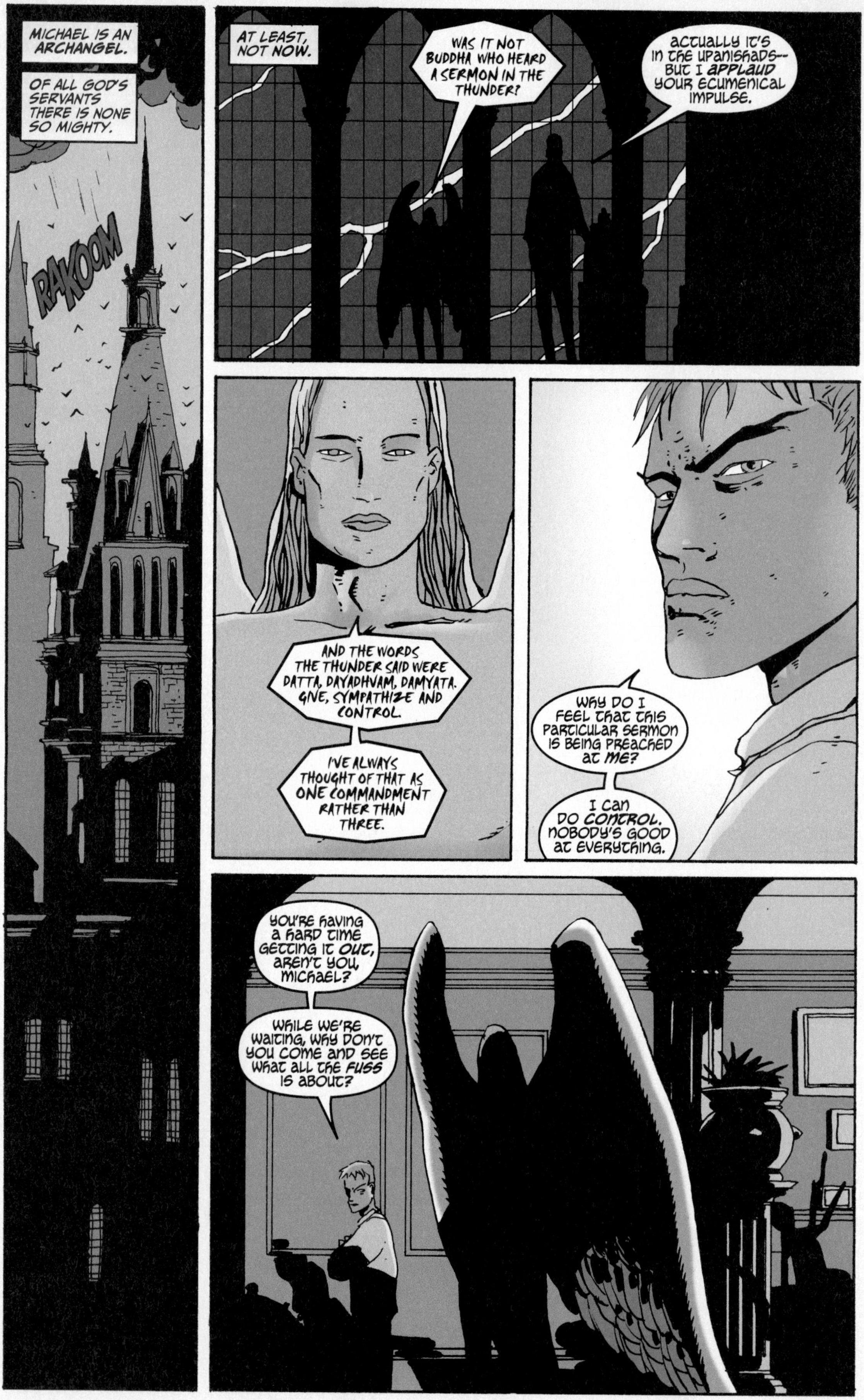
MICHAEL IS AN ARCHANGEL.
OF ALL GOD'S SERVANTS THERE IS NONE SO MIGHTY.
RAKOOM
AT LEAST, NOT NOW.
WAS IT NOT BUDDHA WHO HEARD A SERMON IN THE THUNDER?
ACTUALLY IT'S IN THE UPANISHADS-- BUT I APPLAUD YOUR ECUMENICAL IMPULSE.
AND THE WORDS THE THUNDER SAID WERE DATTA, DAYADHVAM, DAMYATA. GIVE, SYMPATHIZE AND CONTROL.
I'VE ALWAYS THOUGHT OF THAT AS ONE COMMANDMENT RATHER THAN THREE.
WHY DO I FEEL THAT THIS PARTICULAR SERMON IS BEING PREACHED AT ME?
I CAN DO CONTROL. NOBODY'S GOOD AT EVERYTHING.
YOU'RE HAVING A HARD TIME GETTING IT OUT, AREN'T YOU, MICHAEL?
WHILE WE'RE WAITING, WHY DON'T YOU COME AND SEE WHAT ALL THE FUSS IS ABOUT?

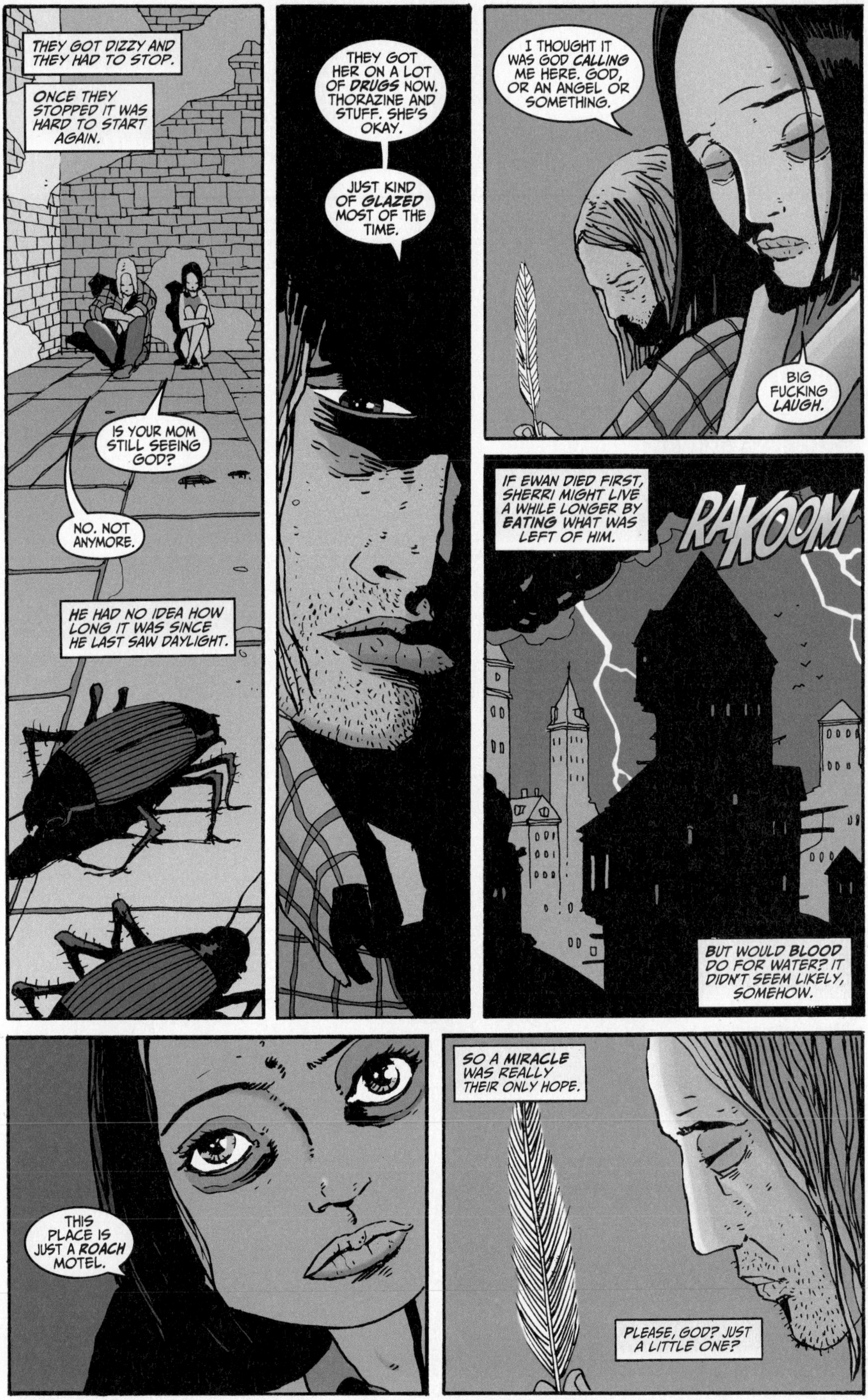
THEY GOT DIZZY AND THEY HAD TO STOP.
ONCE THEY STOPPED IT WAS HARD TO START AGAIN.
IS YOUR MOM STILL SEEING GOD?
NO. NOT ANYMORE.
HE HAD NO IDEA HOW LONG IT WAS SINCE HE LAST SAW DAYLIGHT.
THEY GOT HER ON A LOT OF DRUGS NOW. THORAZINE AND STUFF. SHE'S OKAY.
JUST KIND OF GLAZED MOST OF THE TIME.
I THOUGHT IT WAS GOD CALLING ME HERE. GOD, OR AN ANGEL OR SOMETHING.
BIG FUCKING LAUGH.
IF EWAN DIED FIRST, SHERRI MIGHT LIVE A WHILE LONGER BY EATING WHAT WAS LEFT OF HIM.
RAKOOM
BUT WOULD BLOOD DO FOR WATER? IT DIDN'T SEEM LIKELY, SOMEHOW.
THIS PLACE IS JUST A ROACH MOTEL.
SO A MIRACLE WAS REALLY THEIR ONLY HOPE.
PLEASE, GOD? JUST A LITTLE ONE?

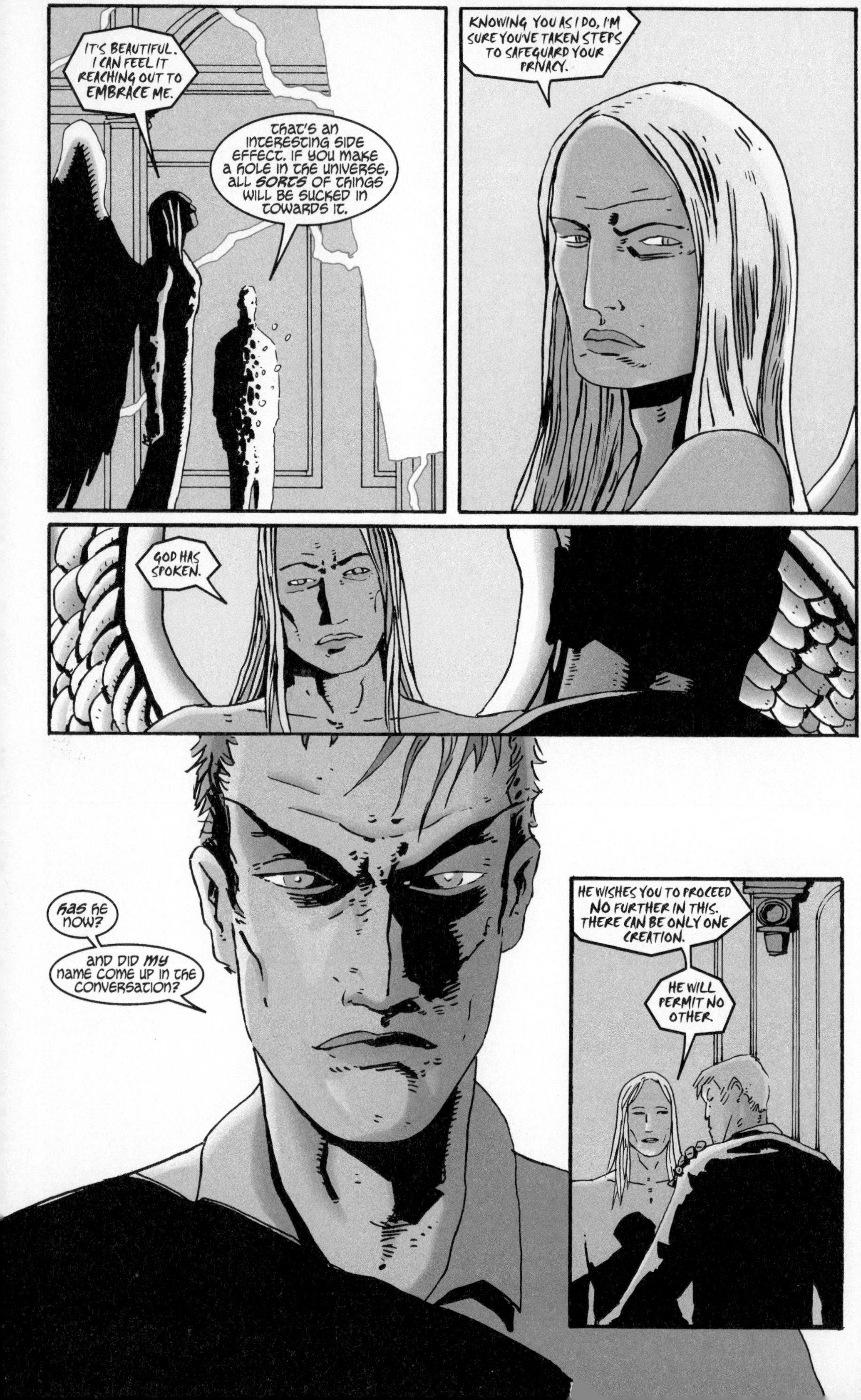
IT'S BEAUTIFUL. I CAN FEEL IT REACHING OUT TO EMBRACE ME.
THAT'S AN INTERESTING SIDE EFFECT. IF YOU MAKE A HOLE IN THE UNIVERSE, ALL SORTS OF THINGS WILL BE SUCKED IN TOWARDS IT.
KNOWING YOU AS I DO, I'M SURE YOU'VE TAKEN STEPS TO SAFEGUARD YOUR PRIVACY.
GOD HAS SPOKEN.
HAS HE NOW?
AND DID MY NAME COME UP IN THE CONVERSATION?
HE WISHES YOU TO PROCEED NO FURTHER IN THIS. THERE CAN BE ONLY ONE CREATION.
HE WILL PERMIT NO OTHER.

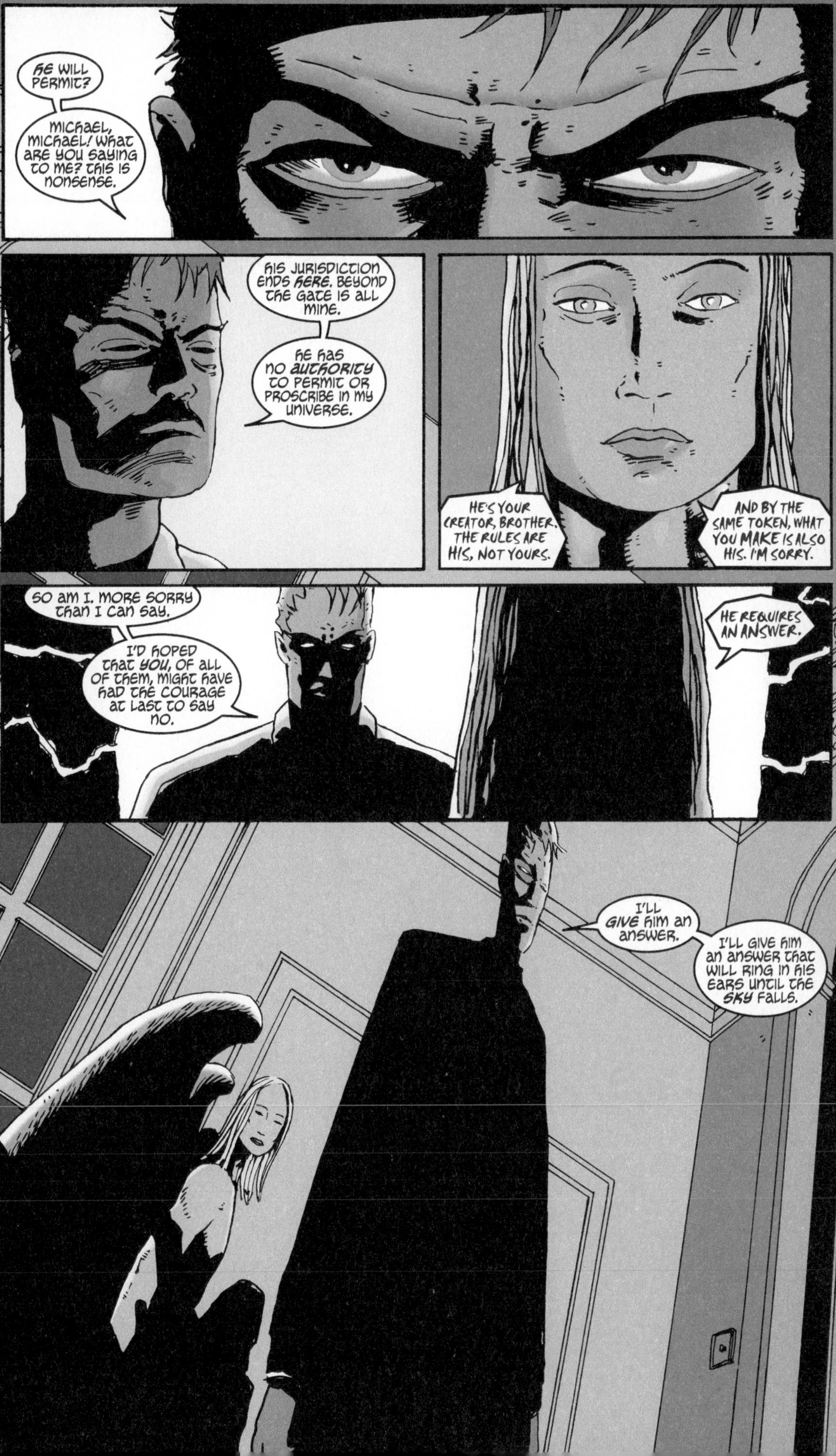
HE WILL PERMIT?
MICHAEL, MICHAEL! WHAT ARE YOU SAYING TO ME? THIS IS NONSENSE.
HIS JURISDICTION ENDS HERE. BEYOND THE GATE IS ALL MINE.
HE HAS NO AUTHORITY TO PERMIT OR PROSCRIBE IN MY UNIVERSE.
HE'S YOUR CREATOR, BROTHER. THE RULES ARE HIS, NOT YOURS.
AND BY THE SAME TOKEN, WHAT YOU MAKE IS ALSO HIS. I'M SORRY.
SO AM I. MORE SORRY THAN I CAN SAY.
I'D HOPED THAT YOU, OF ALL OF THEM, MIGHT HAVE HAD THE COURAGE AT LAST TO SAY NO.
HE REQUIRES AN ANSWER.
I'LL GIVE HIM AN ANSWER.
I'LL GIVE HIM AN ANSWER THAT WILL RING IN HIS EARS UNTIL THE SKY FALLS.

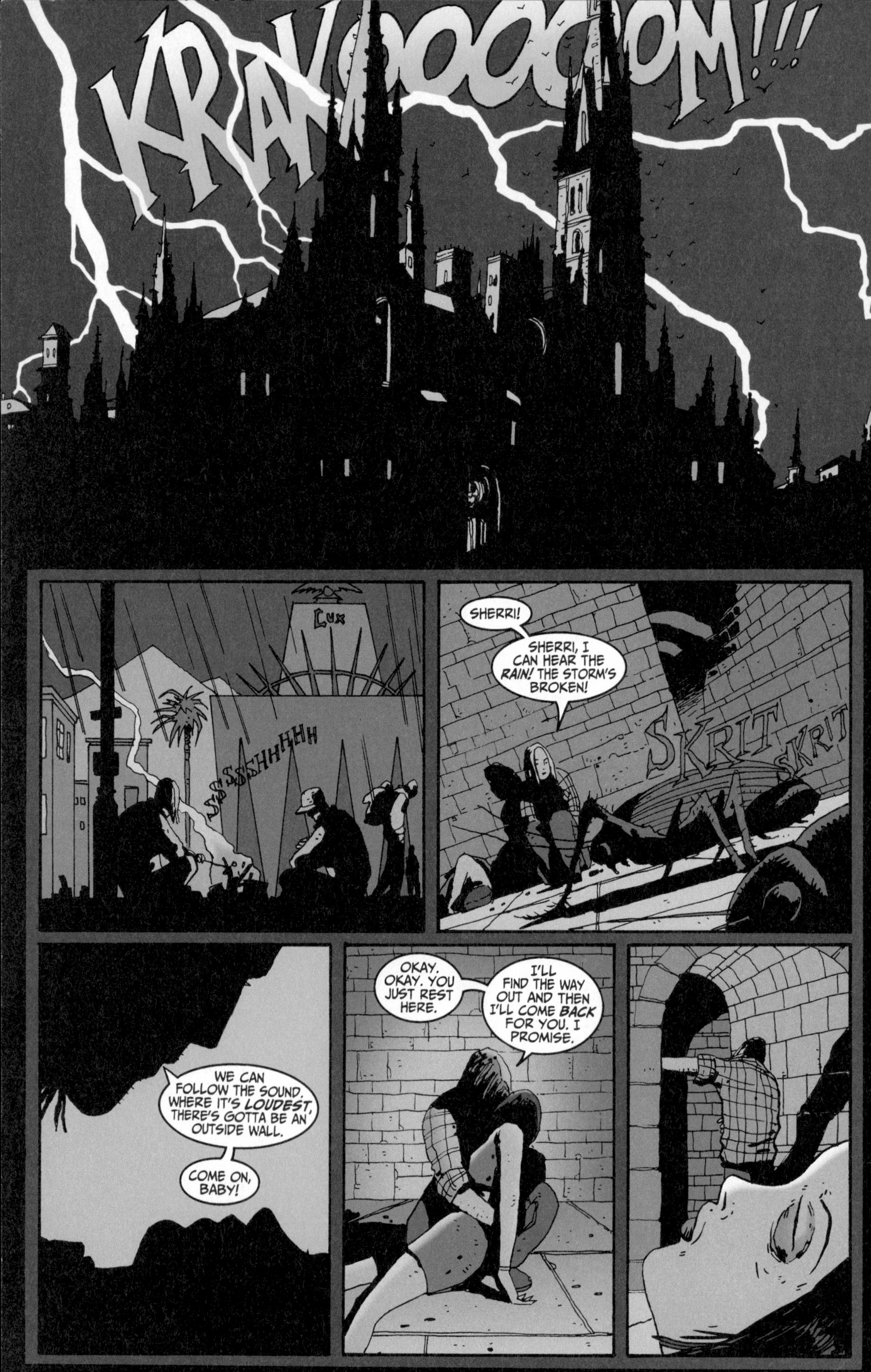
KRAKOOOOOM!!!
Lux
SSSSHHHHH
SHERRI!
SHERRI, I CAN HEAR THE *RAIN!* THE STORM'S BROKEN!
SKRIT
SKRIT
WE CAN FOLLOW THE SOUND. WHERE IT'S ***LOUDEST***, THERE'S GOTTA BE AN OUTSIDE WALL.
COME ON, BABY!
OKAY. OKAY. YOU JUST REST HERE.
I'LL FIND THE WAY OUT AND THEN I'LL COME ***BACK*** FOR YOU. I PROMISE.

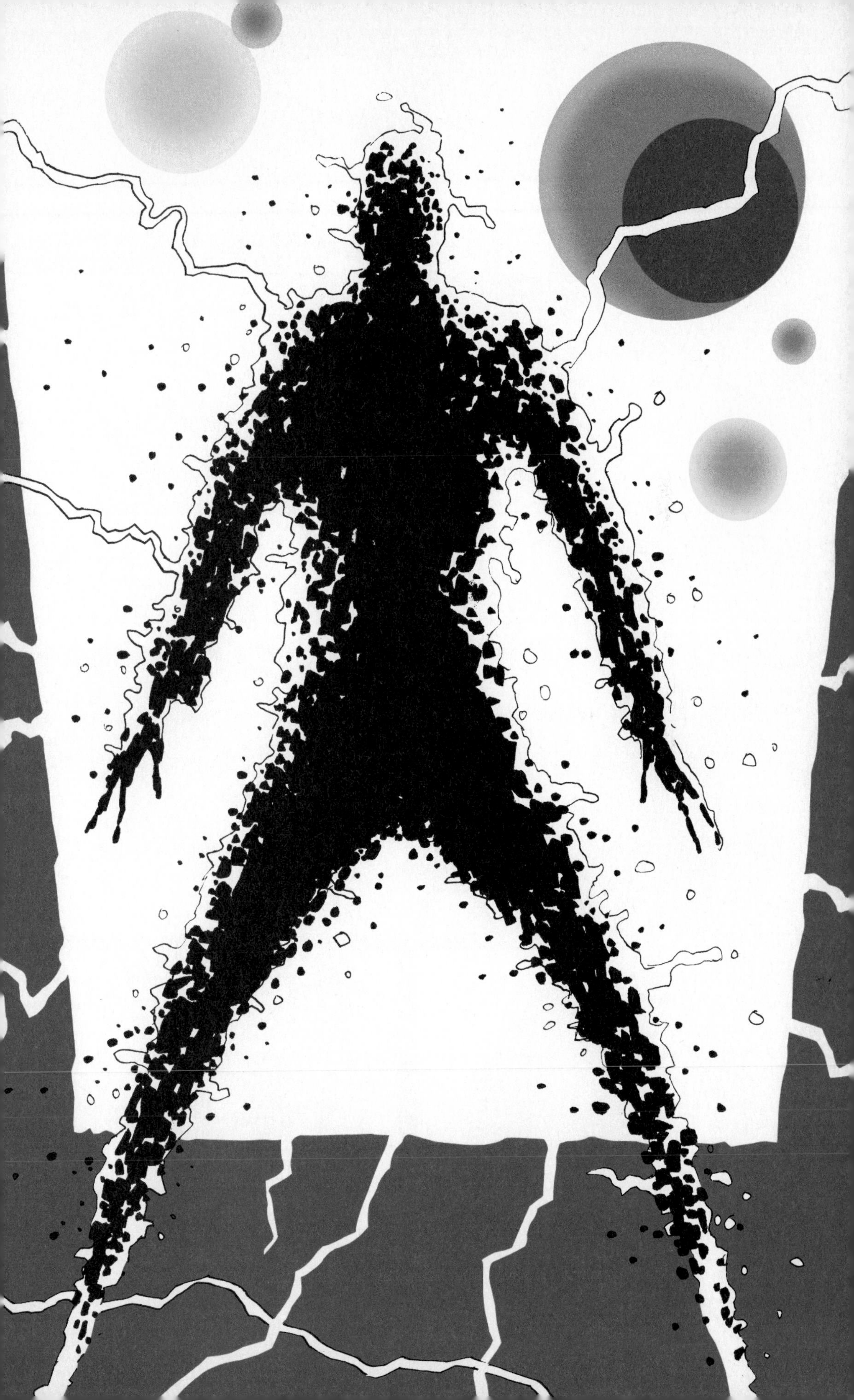

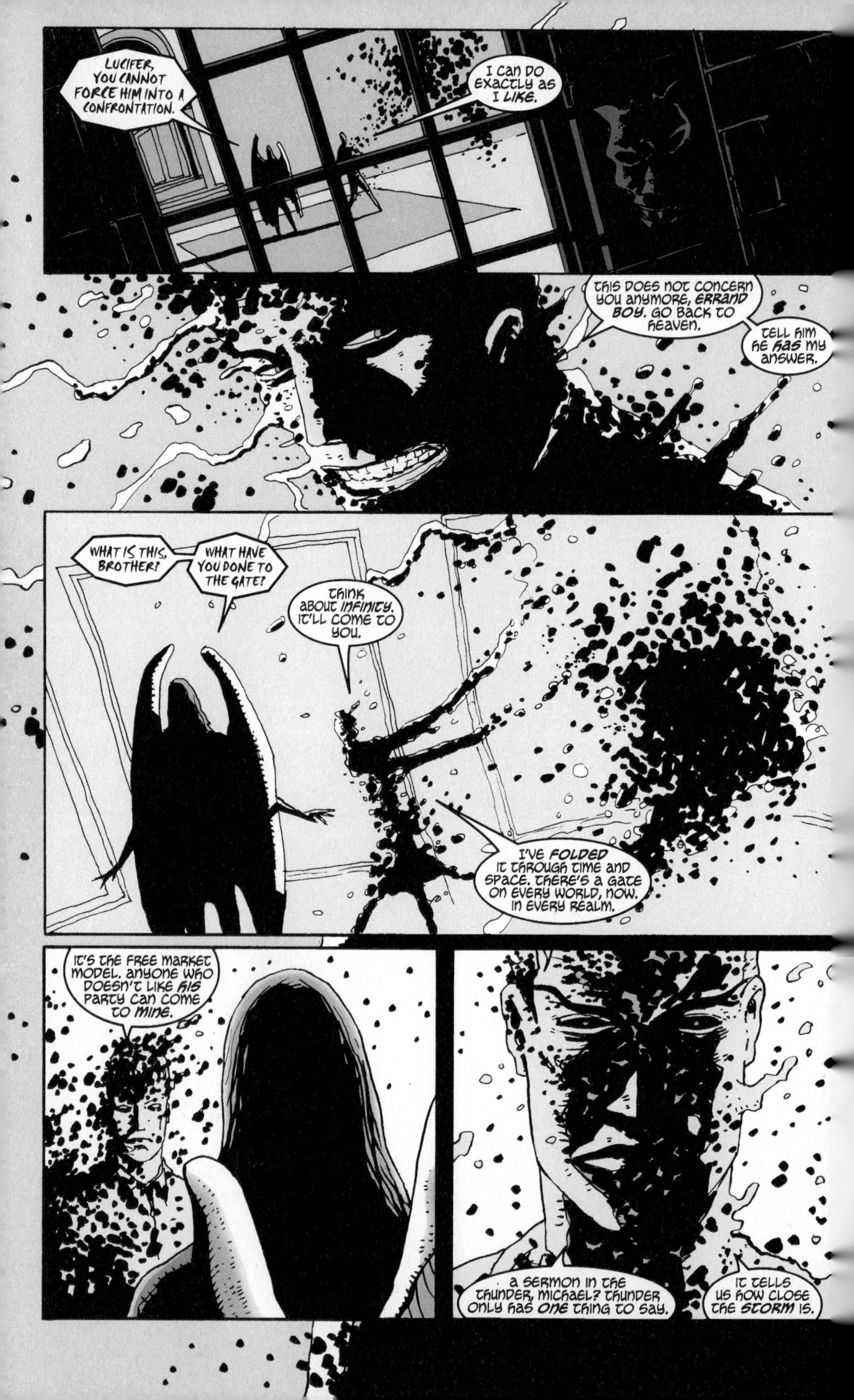
LUCIFER, YOU CANNOT FORCE HIM INTO A CONFRONTATION.
I CAN DO EXACTLY AS I LIKE.
THIS DOES NOT CONCERN YOU ANYMORE, ERRAND BOY. GO BACK TO HEAVEN.
TELL HIM HE HAS MY ANSWER.
WHAT IS THIS, BROTHER?
WHAT HAVE YOU DONE TO THE GATE?
THINK ABOUT INFINITY. IT'LL COME TO YOU.
I'VE FOLDED IT THROUGH TIME AND SPACE. THERE'S A GATE ON EVERY WORLD, NOW. IN EVERY REALM.
IT'S THE FREE MARKET MODEL. ANYONE WHO DOESN'T LIKE HIS PARTY CAN COME TO MINE.
A SERMON IN THE THUNDER, MICHAEL? THUNDER ONLY HAS ONE THING TO SAY.
IT TELLS US HOW CLOSE THE STORM IS.

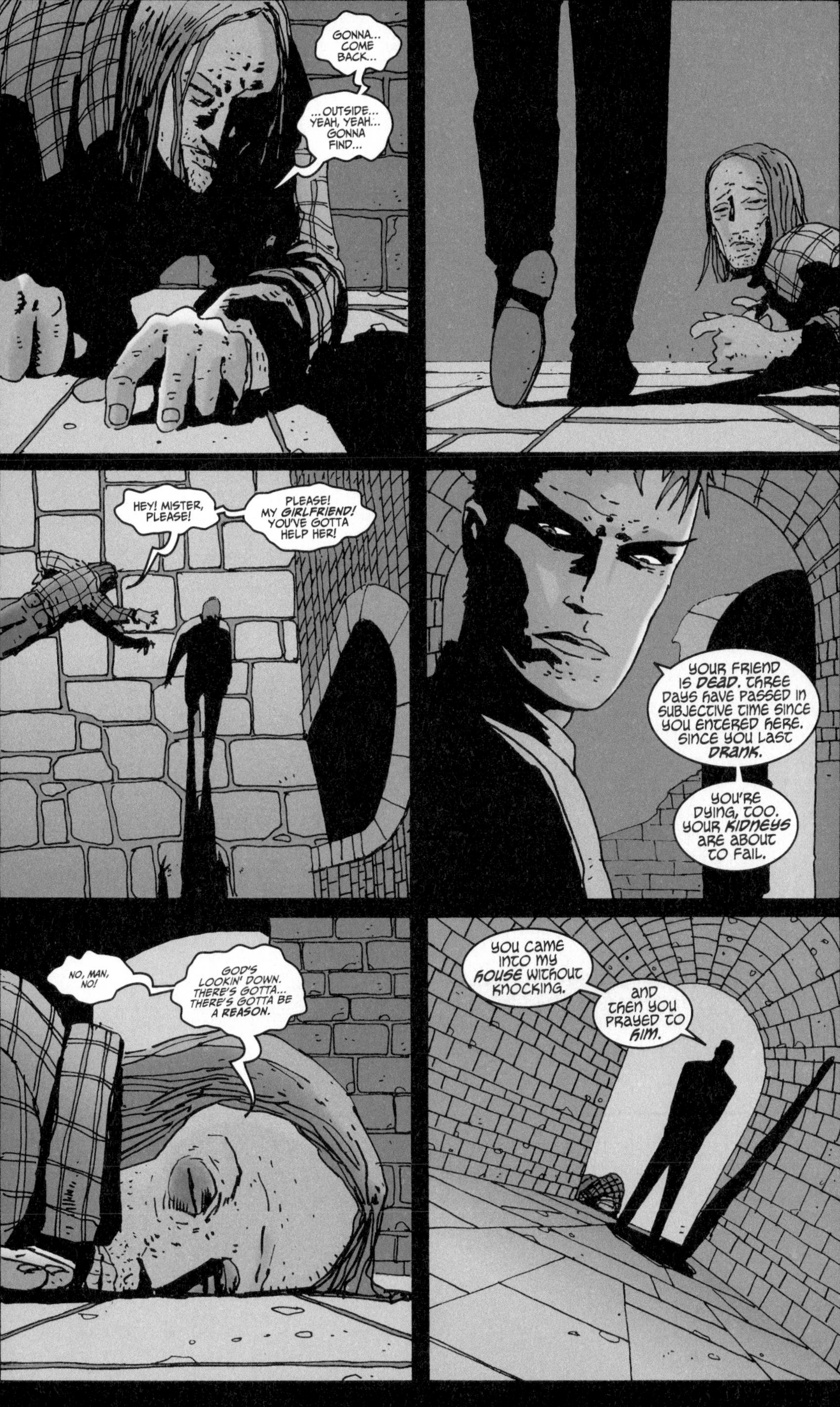
GONNA... COME BACK...
...OUTSIDE... YEAH, YEAH... GONNA FIND...
HEY! MISTER, PLEASE!
PLEASE! MY GIRLFRIEND! YOU'VE GOTTA HELP HER!
YOUR FRIEND IS DEAD. THREE DAYS HAVE PASSED IN SUBJECTIVE TIME SINCE YOU ENTERED HERE. SINCE YOU LAST DRANK.
YOU'RE DYING, TOO. YOUR KIDNEYS ARE ABOUT TO FAIL.
NO, MAN, NO!
GOD'S LOOKIN' DOWN. THERE'S GOTTA... THERE'S GOTTA BE A REASON.
YOU CAME INTO MY HOUSE WITHOUT KNOCKING.
AND THEN YOU PRAYED TO HIM.

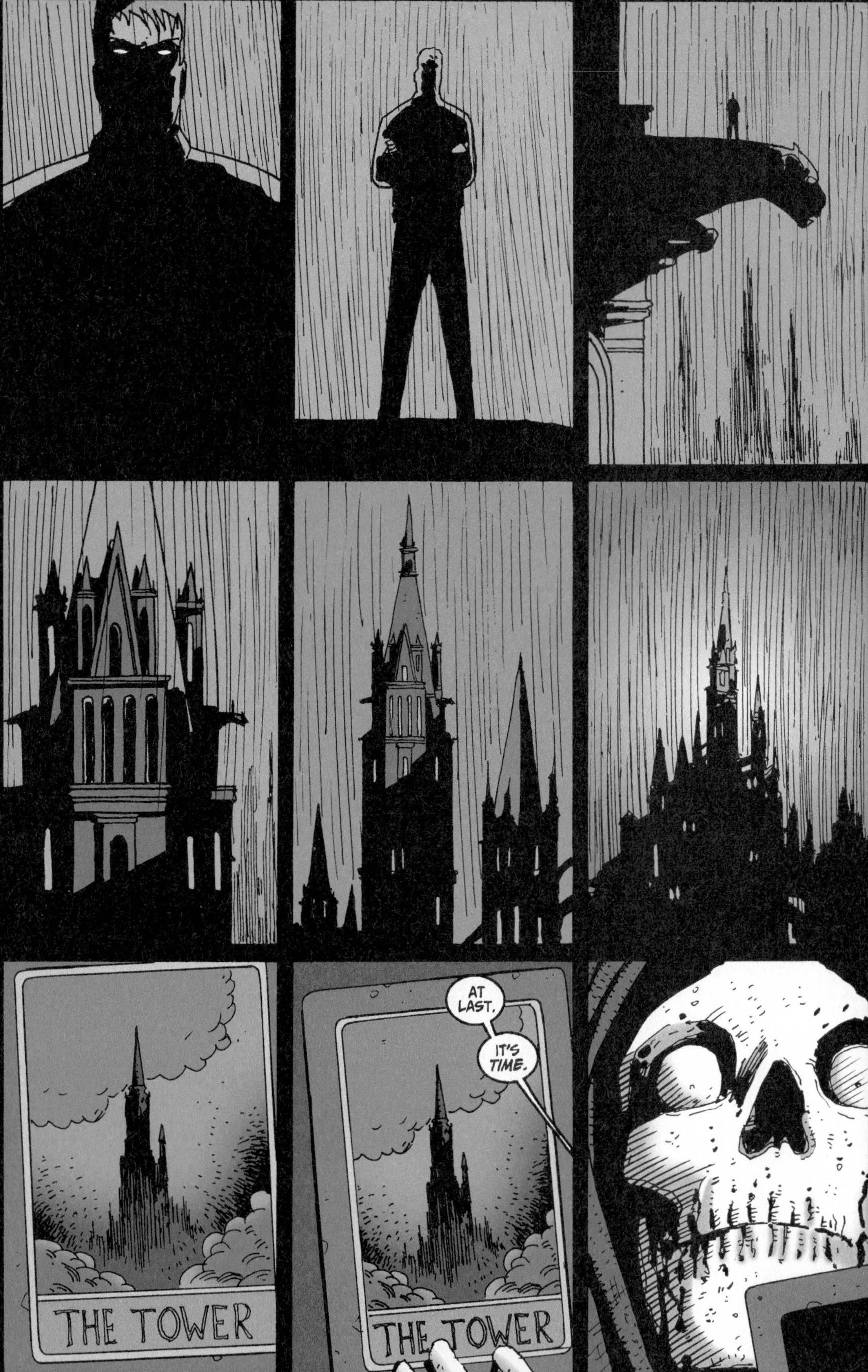
THE TOWER
AT LAST.
IT'S TIME.
THE TOWER
Next... PARADISO.

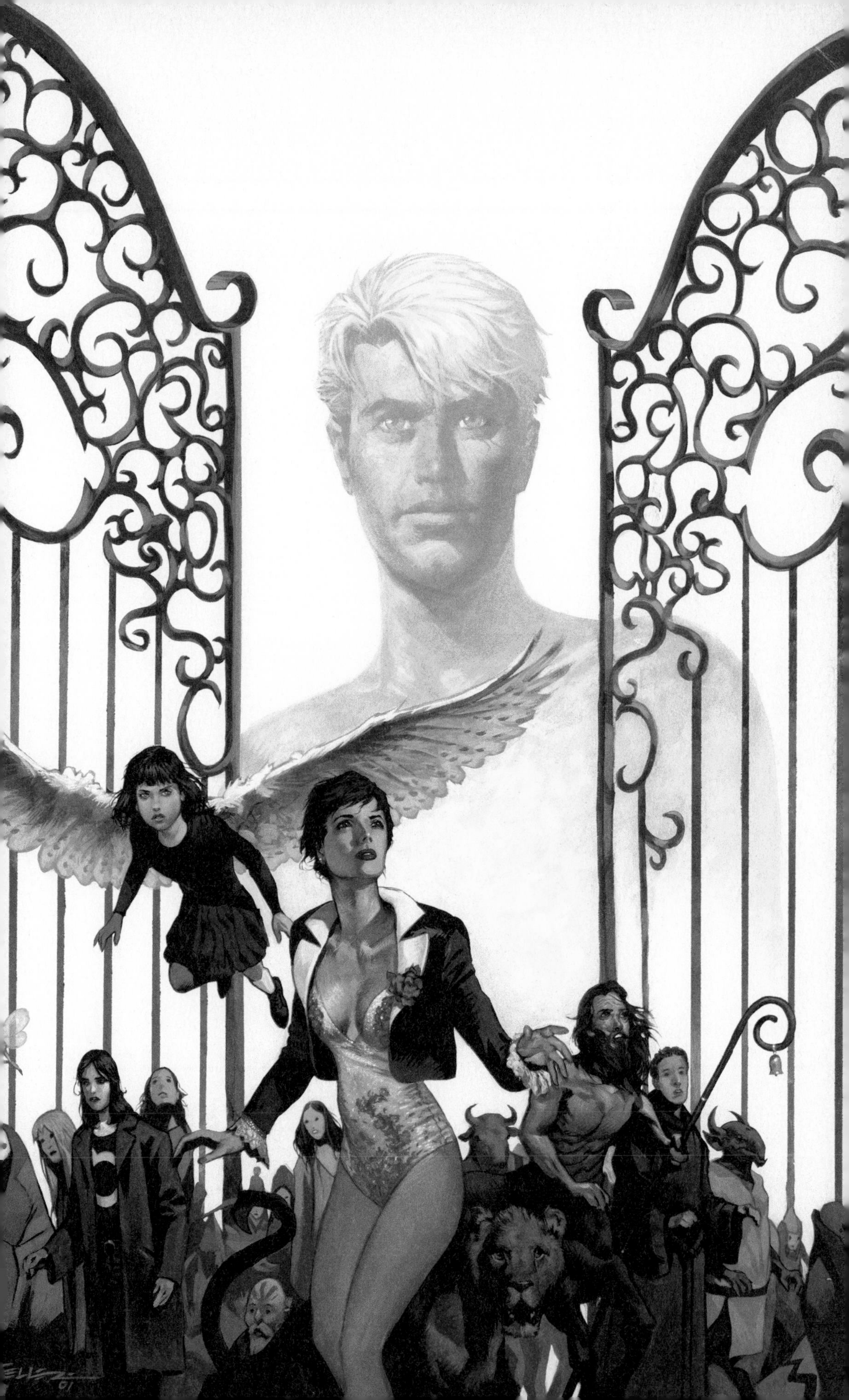

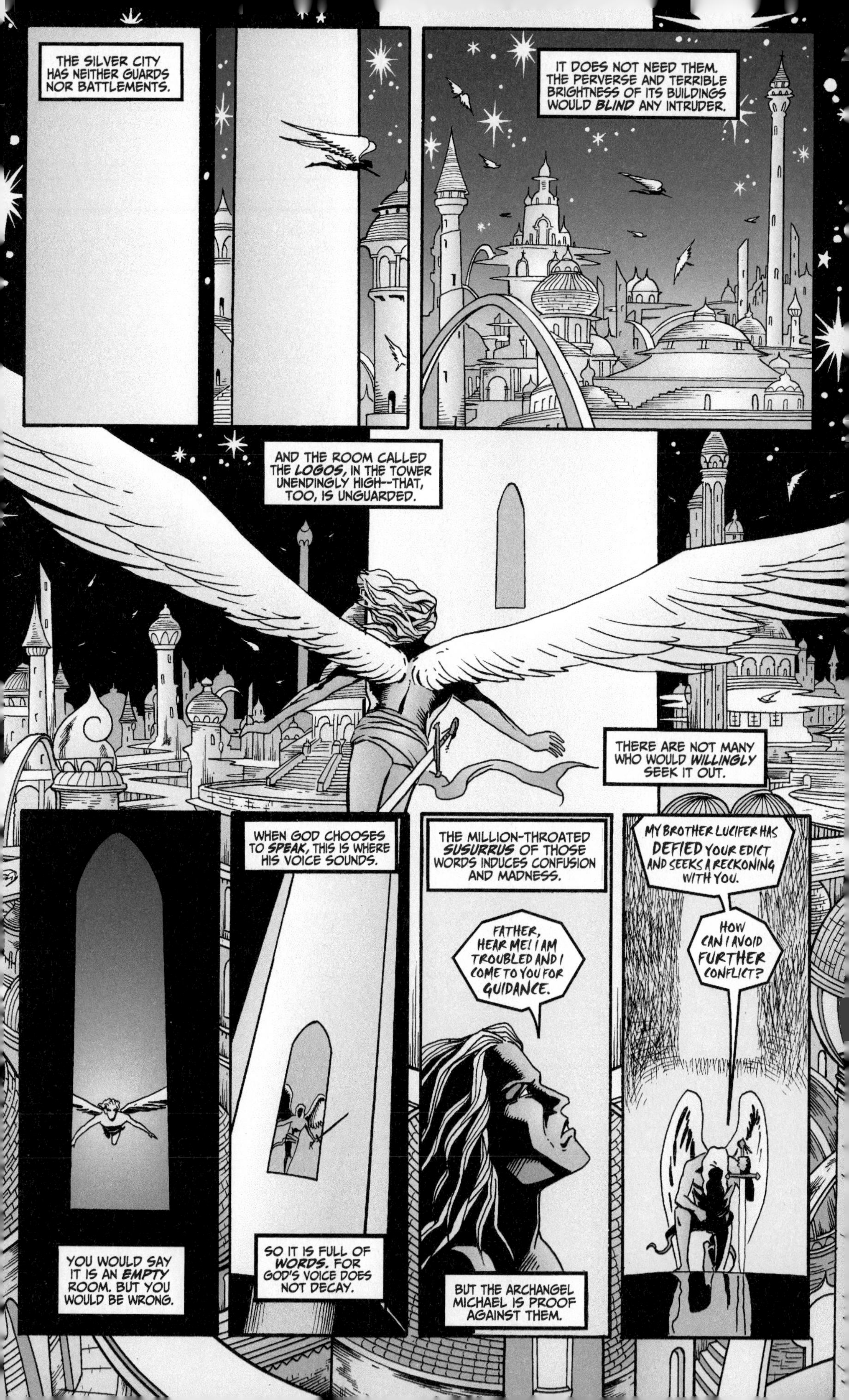
THE SILVER CITY HAS NEITHER GUARDS NOR BATTLEMENTS.
IT DOES NOT NEED THEM. THE PERVERSE AND TERRIBLE BRIGHTNESS OF ITS BUILDINGS WOULD BLIND ANY INTRUDER.
AND THE ROOM CALLED THE LOGOS, IN THE TOWER UNENDINGLY HIGH--THAT, TOO, IS UNGUARDED.
THERE ARE NOT MANY WHO WOULD WILLINGLY SEEK IT OUT.
YOU WOULD SAY IT IS AN EMPTY ROOM. BUT YOU WOULD BE WRONG.
WHEN GOD CHOOSES TO SPEAK, THIS IS WHERE HIS VOICE SOUNDS.
SO IT IS FULL OF WORDS. FOR GOD'S VOICE DOES NOT DECAY.
THE MILLION-THROATED SUSURRUS OF THOSE WORDS INDUCES CONFUSION AND MADNESS.
FATHER, HEAR ME! I AM TROUBLED AND I COME TO YOU FOR GUIDANCE.
BUT THE ARCHANGEL MICHAEL IS PROOF AGAINST THEM.
MY BROTHER LUCIFER HAS DEFIED YOUR EDICT AND SEEKS A RECKONING WITH YOU.
HOW CAN I AVOID FURTHER CONFLICT?

AND GOD *SPAKE* UNTO MICHAEL, IN THE TONGUE THAT ANGELS SPEAK.

AND MICHAEL SAW WHAT HAD BEEN, AND WHAT WAS, AND WHAT WOULD BE.

HE SAW THE WAR IN HEAVEN, WHEN LUCIFER'S WILL DROVE A THIRD OF THE HOST TO *REBEL* AGAINST THEIR CREATOR.

THE WAR IN WHICH HE HIMSELF HAD BEEN WOUNDED AND TAKEN PRISONER.

HE SAW LUCIFER RULING HELL-- AND *CHAFING* BECAUSE WHILE HE RULED HE WAS A *SUBJECT,* TOO.

BECAUSE ALL HIS POWER BROUGHT HIM NOT ONE *STEP* CLOSER TO HIS TRUE GOAL.

THAT IS WHY HE *LEFT,* OF COURSE. WHY HE GAVE AWAY THE KEY TO HELL AND RETIRED TO EARTH.

BECAUSE HE KNEW THAT HE WAS NOT FREE, AND IT HURT HIS DIGNITY TO *DANCE* ON THE END OF A LEASH.

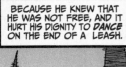

BUT THEN HEAVEN CALLED HIM BACK INTO ITS EMPLOY, USING THE ONLY BRIBE THAT WOULD EVER HAVE *WORKED* ON HIM.

A LETTER OF PASSAGE. A POTENTIAL *EXIT* FROM GOD'S CREATION.

HE SLEW THE VOICELESS GODS, AND WON HIS PRIZE-- THEN USED IT, NOT TO *LEAVE,* BUT TO OPEN A GATEWAY INTO THE VOID.

AND GOD WATCHED, SERENELY, FROM THE VANTAGE POINT OF ETERNITY. THIS, TOO WAS *FORESEEN.*

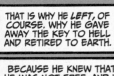

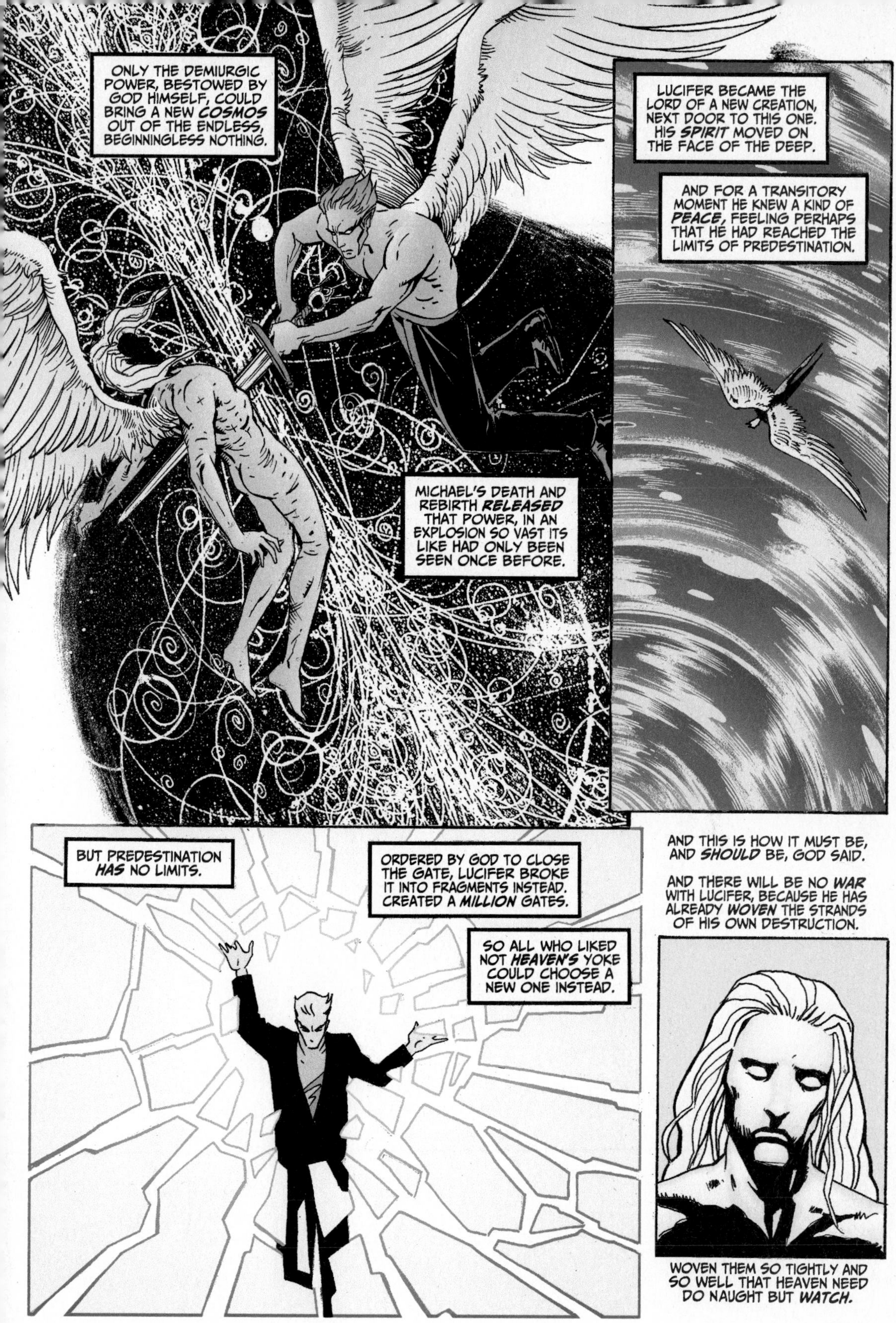
ONLY THE DEMIURGIC POWER, BESTOWED BY GOD HIMSELF, COULD BRING A NEW COSMOS OUT OF THE ENDLESS, BEGINNINGLESS NOTHING.
MICHAEL'S DEATH AND REBIRTH RELEASED THAT POWER, IN AN EXPLOSION SO VAST ITS LIKE HAD ONLY BEEN SEEN ONCE BEFORE.
LUCIFER BECAME THE LORD OF A NEW CREATION, NEXT DOOR TO THIS ONE. HIS SPIRIT MOVED ON THE FACE OF THE DEEP.
AND FOR A TRANSITORY MOMENT HE KNEW A KIND OF PEACE, FEELING PERHAPS THAT HE HAD REACHED THE LIMITS OF PREDESTINATION.
BUT PREDESTINATION HAS NO LIMITS.
ORDERED BY GOD TO CLOSE THE GATE, LUCIFER BROKE IT INTO FRAGMENTS INSTEAD. CREATED A MILLION GATES.
SO ALL WHO LIKED NOT HEAVEN'S YOKE COULD CHOOSE A NEW ONE INSTEAD.
AND THIS IS HOW IT MUST BE, AND SHOULD BE, GOD SAID.
AND THERE WILL BE NO WAR WITH LUCIFER, BECAUSE HE HAS ALREADY WOVEN THE STRANDS OF HIS OWN DESTRUCTION.
WOVEN THEM SO TIGHTLY AND SO WELL THAT HEAVEN NEED DO NAUGHT BUT WATCH.

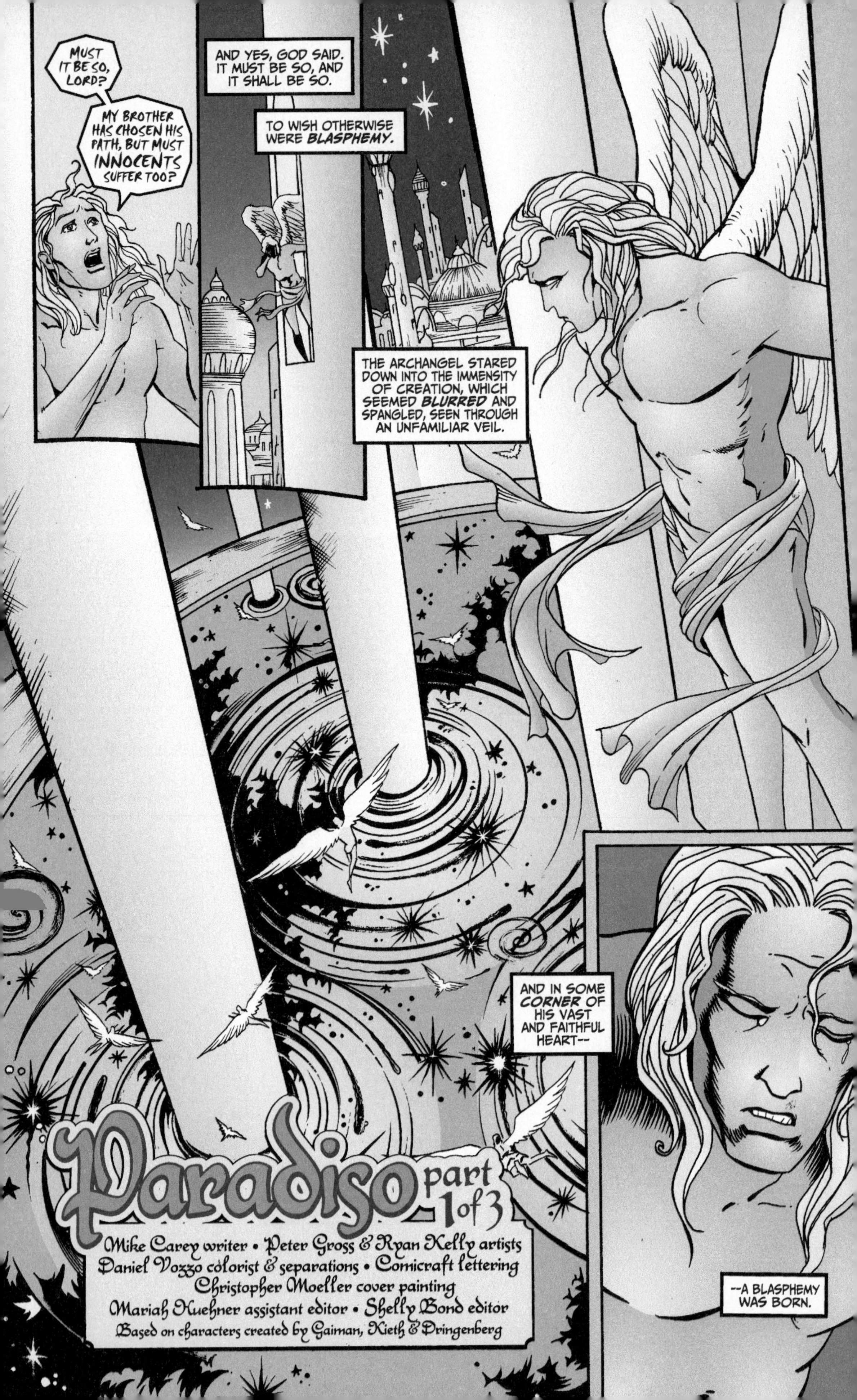

MUST IT BE SO, LORD?
MY BROTHER HAS CHOSEN HIS PATH, BUT MUST INNOCENTS SUFFER TOO?
AND YES, GOD SAID. IT MUST BE SO, AND IT SHALL BE SO.
TO WISH OTHERWISE WERE BLASPHEMY.
THE ARCHANGEL STARED DOWN INTO THE IMMENSITY OF CREATION, WHICH SEEMED BLURRED AND SPANGLED, SEEN THROUGH AN UNFAMILIAR VEIL.
AND IN SOME CORNER OF HIS VAST AND FAITHFUL HEART--
--A BLASPHEMY WAS BORN.
Paradiso part 1 of 3
Mike Carey writer • Peter Gross & Ryan Kelly artists
Daniel Vozzo colorist & separations • Comicraft lettering
Christopher Moeller cover painting
Mariah Huehner assistant editor • Shelly Bond editor
Based on characters created by Gaiman, Kieth & Dringenberg

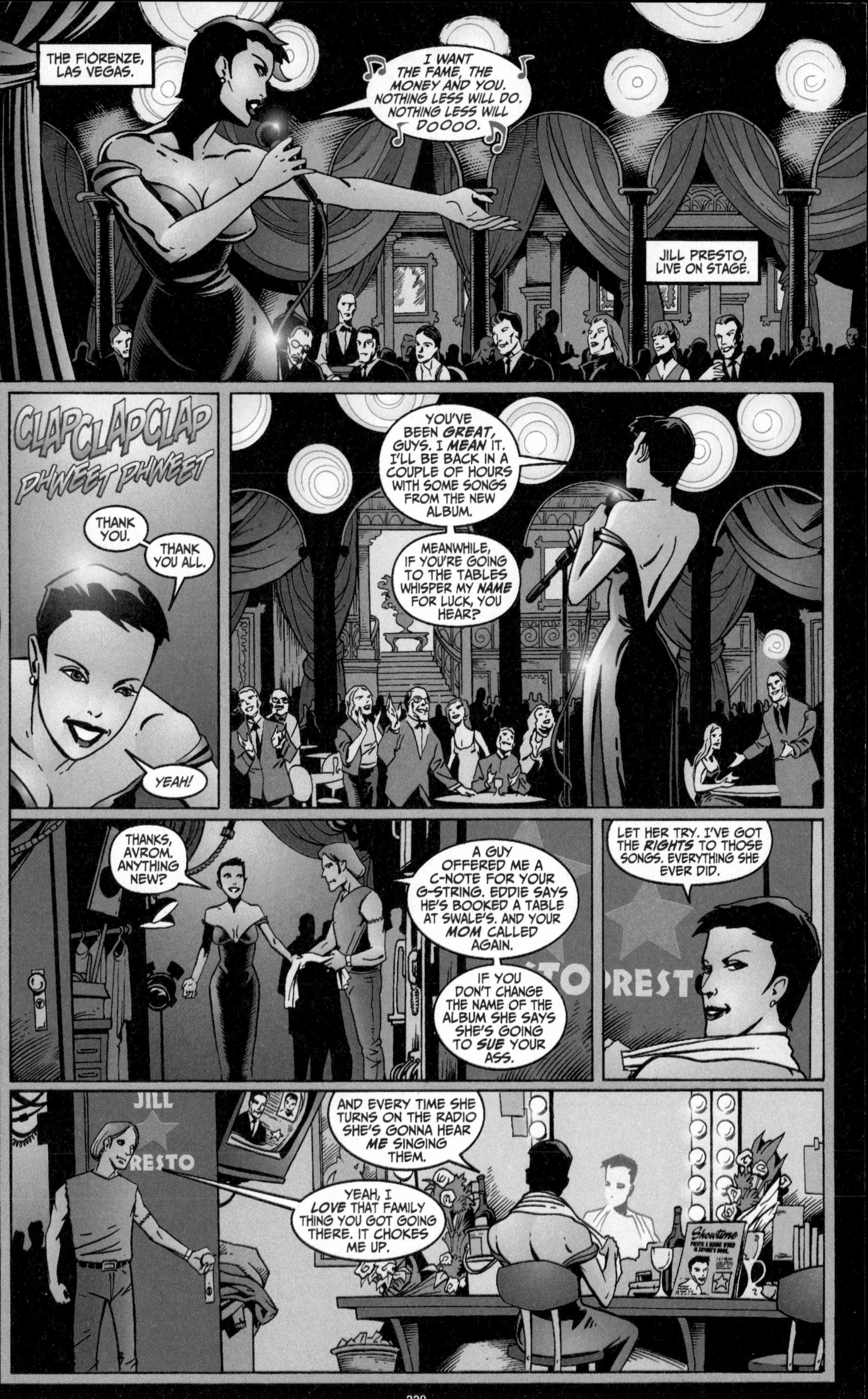
THE FIORENZE, LAS VEGAS.
I WANT THE FAME, THE MONEY AND YOU. NOTHING LESS WILL DO. NOTHING LESS WILL DOOOO.
JILL PRESTO, LIVE ON STAGE.
CLAPCLAPCLAP
PHWEET PHWEET
THANK YOU.
THANK YOU ALL.
YEAH!
YOU'VE BEEN GREAT, GUYS. I MEAN IT. I'LL BE BACK IN A COUPLE OF HOURS WITH SOME SONGS FROM THE NEW ALBUM.
MEANWHILE, IF YOU'RE GOING TO THE TABLES WHISPER MY NAME FOR LUCK, YOU HEAR?
THANKS, AVROM. ANYTHING NEW?
A GUY OFFERED ME A C-NOTE FOR YOUR G-STRING. EDDIE SAYS HE'S BOOKED A TABLE AT SWALE'S. AND YOUR MOM CALLED AGAIN.
IF YOU DON'T CHANGE THE NAME OF THE ALBUM SHE SAYS SHE'S GOING TO SUE YOUR ASS.
LET HER TRY. I'VE GOT THE RIGHTS TO THOSE SONGS. EVERYTHING SHE EVER DID.
JILL
RESTO
AND EVERY TIME SHE TURNS ON THE RADIO SHE'S GONNA HEAR ME SINGING THEM.
YEAH, I LOVE THAT FAMILY THING YOU GOT GOING THERE. IT CHOKES ME UP.
Showtime

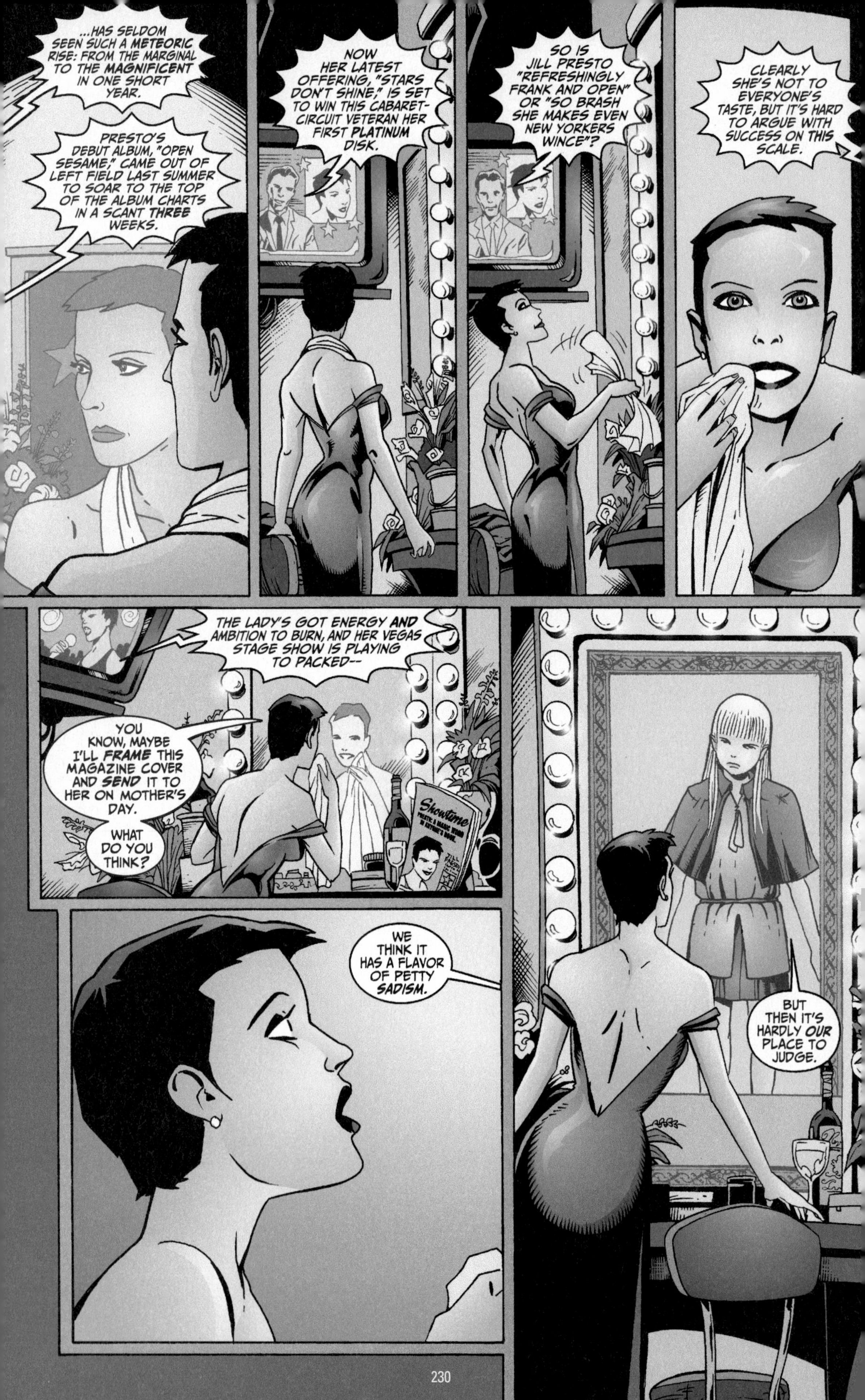
...HAS SELDOM SEEN SUCH A METEORIC RISE: FROM THE MARGINAL TO THE MAGNIFICENT IN ONE SHORT YEAR.
PRESTO'S DEBUT ALBUM, "OPEN SESAME," CAME OUT OF LEFT FIELD LAST SUMMER TO SOAR TO THE TOP OF THE ALBUM CHARTS IN A SCANT THREE WEEKS.
NOW HER LATEST OFFERING, "STARS DON'T SHINE," IS SET TO WIN THIS CABARET-CIRCUIT VETERAN HER FIRST PLATINUM DISK.
SO IS JILL PRESTO "REFRESHINGLY FRANK AND OPEN" OR "SO BRASH SHE MAKES EVEN NEW YORKERS WINCE"?
CLEARLY SHE'S NOT TO EVERYONE'S TASTE, BUT IT'S HARD TO ARGUE WITH SUCCESS ON THIS SCALE.
THE LADY'S GOT ENERGY AND AMBITION TO BURN, AND HER VEGAS STAGE SHOW IS PLAYING TO PACKED--
YOU KNOW, MAYBE I'LL FRAME THIS MAGAZINE COVER AND SEND IT TO HER ON MOTHER'S DAY.
WHAT DO YOU THINK?
Showtime
WE THINK IT HAS A FLAVOR OF PETTY SADISM.
BUT THEN IT'S HARDLY OUR PLACE TO JUDGE.

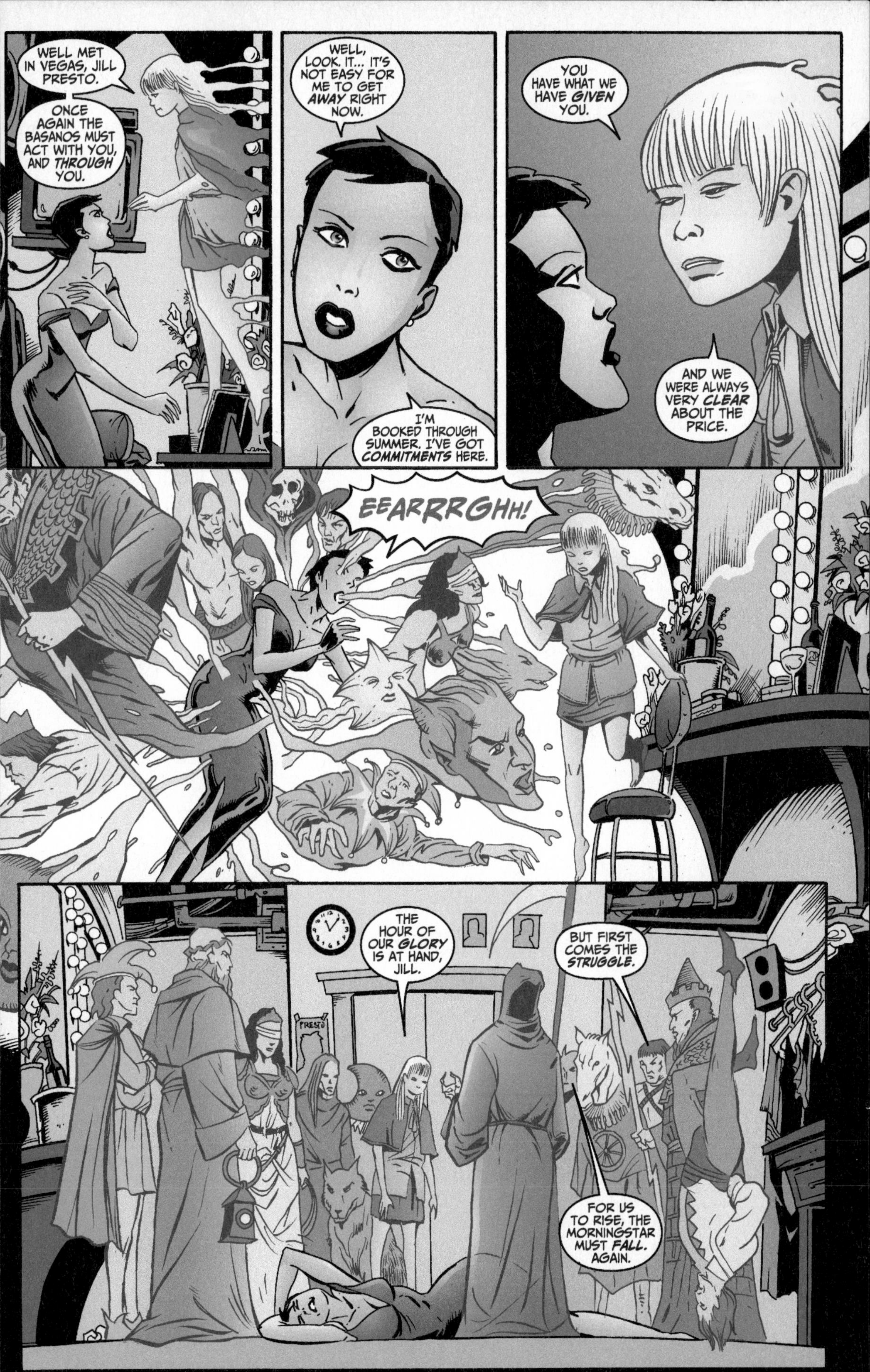
WELL MET IN VEGAS, JILL PRESTO.
ONCE AGAIN THE BASANOS MUST ACT WITH YOU, AND THROUGH YOU.
WELL, LOOK, IT... IT'S NOT EASY FOR ME TO GET AWAY RIGHT NOW.
I'M BOOKED THROUGH SUMMER. I'VE GOT COMMITMENTS HERE.
YOU HAVE WHAT WE HAVE GIVEN YOU.
AND WE WERE ALWAYS VERY CLEAR ABOUT THE PRICE.
EEARRRGHH!
THE HOUR OF OUR GLORY IS AT HAND, JILL.
BUT FIRST COMES THE STRUGGLE.
FOR US TO RISE, THE MORNINGSTAR MUST FALL. AGAIN.
PRESTO

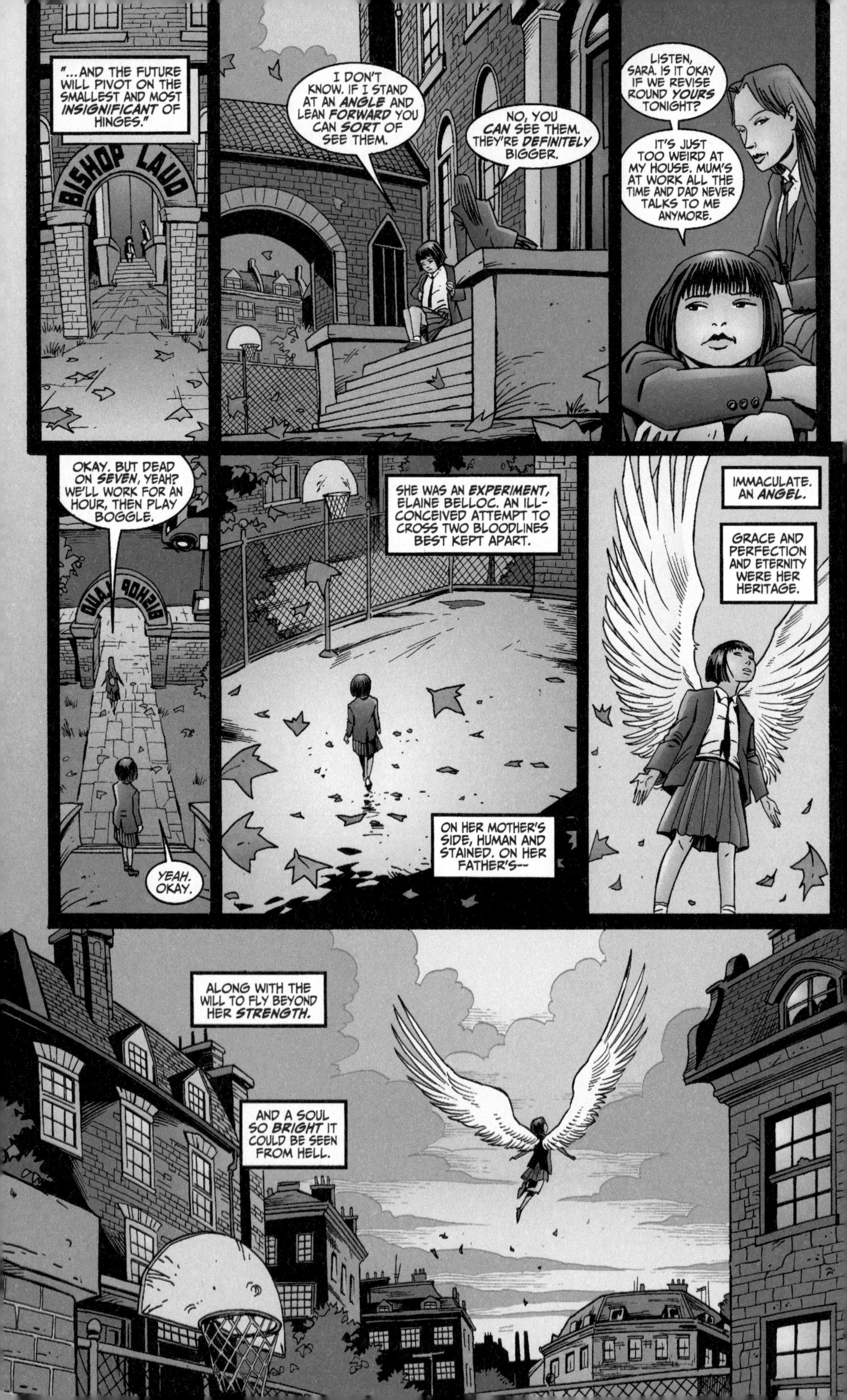
"...AND THE FUTURE WILL PIVOT ON THE SMALLEST AND MOST INSIGNIFICANT OF HINGES."
BISHOP LAUD
I DON'T KNOW. IF I STAND AT AN ANGLE AND LEAN FORWARD YOU CAN SORT OF SEE THEM.
NO, YOU CAN SEE THEM. THEY'RE DEFINITELY BIGGER.
LISTEN, SARA. IS IT OKAY IF WE REVISE ROUND YOURS TONIGHT?
IT'S JUST TOO WEIRD AT MY HOUSE. MUM'S AT WORK ALL THE TIME AND DAD NEVER TALKS TO ME ANYMORE.
OKAY. BUT DEAD ON SEVEN, YEAH? WE'LL WORK FOR AN HOUR, THEN PLAY BOGGLE.
YEAH. OKAY.
SHE WAS AN EXPERIMENT, ELAINE BELLOC. AN ILL-CONCEIVED ATTEMPT TO CROSS TWO BLOODLINES BEST KEPT APART.
ON HER MOTHER'S SIDE, HUMAN AND STAINED. ON HER FATHER'S--
IMMACULATE. AN ANGEL.
GRACE AND PERFECTION AND ETERNITY WERE HER HERITAGE.
ALONG WITH THE WILL TO FLY BEYOND HER STRENGTH.
AND A SOUL SO BRIGHT IT COULD BE SEEN FROM HELL.

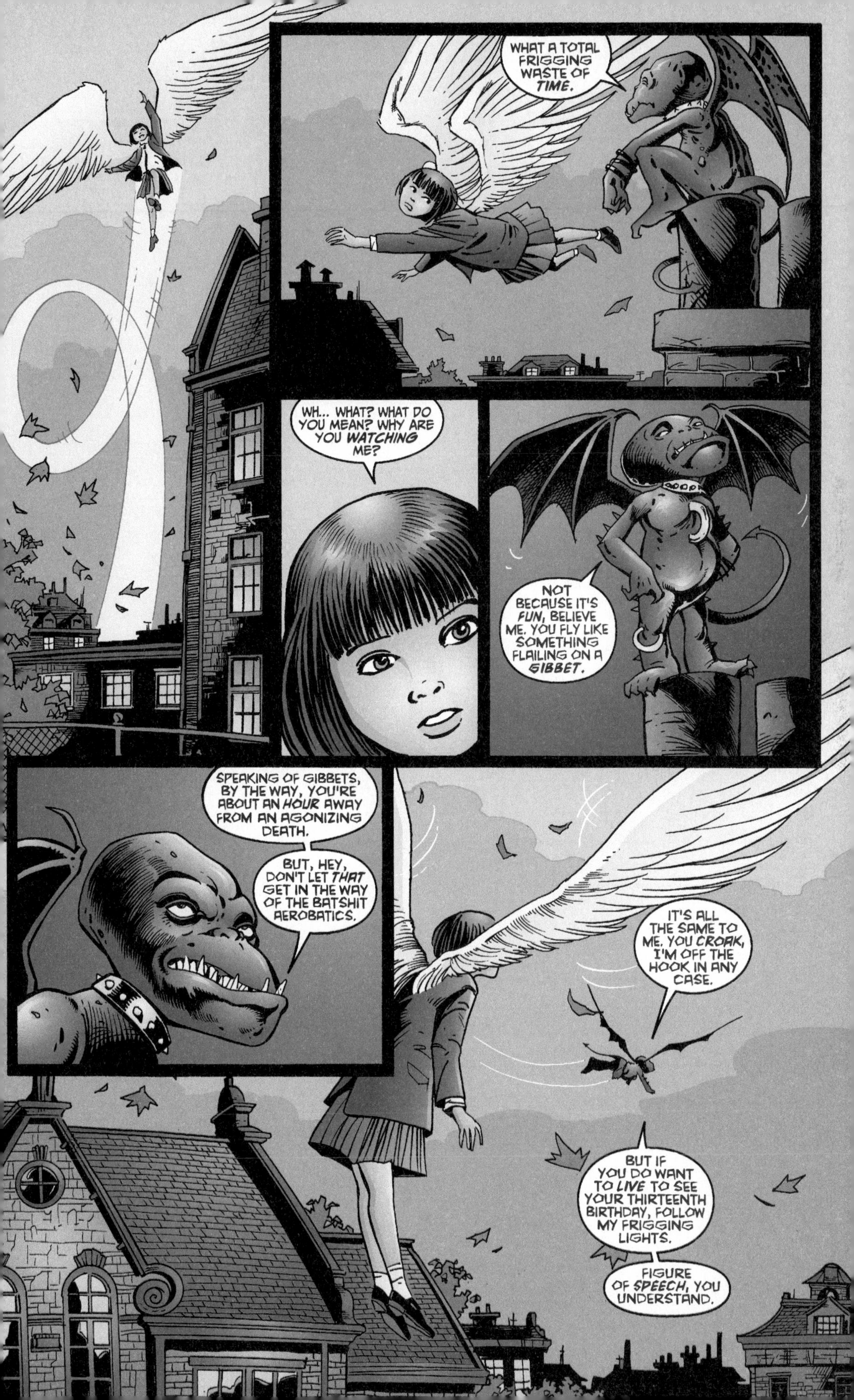
WHAT A TOTAL FRIGGING WASTE OF TIME.
WH... WHAT? WHAT DO YOU MEAN? WHY ARE YOU WATCHING ME?
NOT BECAUSE IT'S FUN, BELIEVE ME. YOU FLY LIKE SOMETHING FLAILING ON A GIBBET.
SPEAKING OF GIBBETS, BY THE WAY, YOU'RE ABOUT AN HOUR AWAY FROM AN AGONIZING DEATH.
BUT, HEY, DON'T LET THAT GET IN THE WAY OF THE BATSHIT AEROBATICS.
IT'S ALL THE SAME TO ME. YOU CROAK, I'M OFF THE HOOK IN ANY CASE.
BUT IF YOU DO WANT TO LIVE TO SEE YOUR THIRTEENTH BIRTHDAY, FOLLOW MY FRIGGING LIGHTS.
FIGURE OF SPEECH, YOU UNDERSTAND.

IT HAD BEGUN.

ACROSS THE CITIES AND THE DESERTS OF EARTH, ACROSS THE REALMS OF LIGHT AND THE REALMS OF PAIN, THE GATES WERE SCATTERED.

WELDED OPEN BY GOD'S OWN NAME.

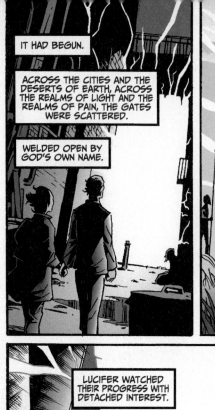

ALL WHO SOUGHT THEM FOUND THEM NOW, AS IRON *FILINGS* FIND A LODESTONE.

AS WITH THE SILVER CITY, THIS WAS A LAND WHOSE FRONTIERS WERE UNDEFENDED.

IN ONES, IN TWOS, AFRAID AND UNAFRAID, WITH OR WITHOUT BACKWARD GLANCES, THEY PASSED THROUGH--

--AND WERE *GONE*.

LUCIFER WATCHED THEIR PROGRESS WITH DETACHED INTEREST.

HE CARED *NOTHING* FOR THEM AS INDIVIDUALS.

BUT IN THEIR STEADY ACCUMULATION HE SAW THE GRADUAL *SHIFTING* OF A COSMIC CONSTANT.

IT CAME DOWN TO *THIS* AT LAST. AFTER THE ENDLESS SCRABBLING FOR PURCHASE AND PURPOSE.

THINGS WERE EITHER BLACK OR WHITE. HE WOULD BE *HIMSELF*.

OR HE WOULD BE *NOTHING*.

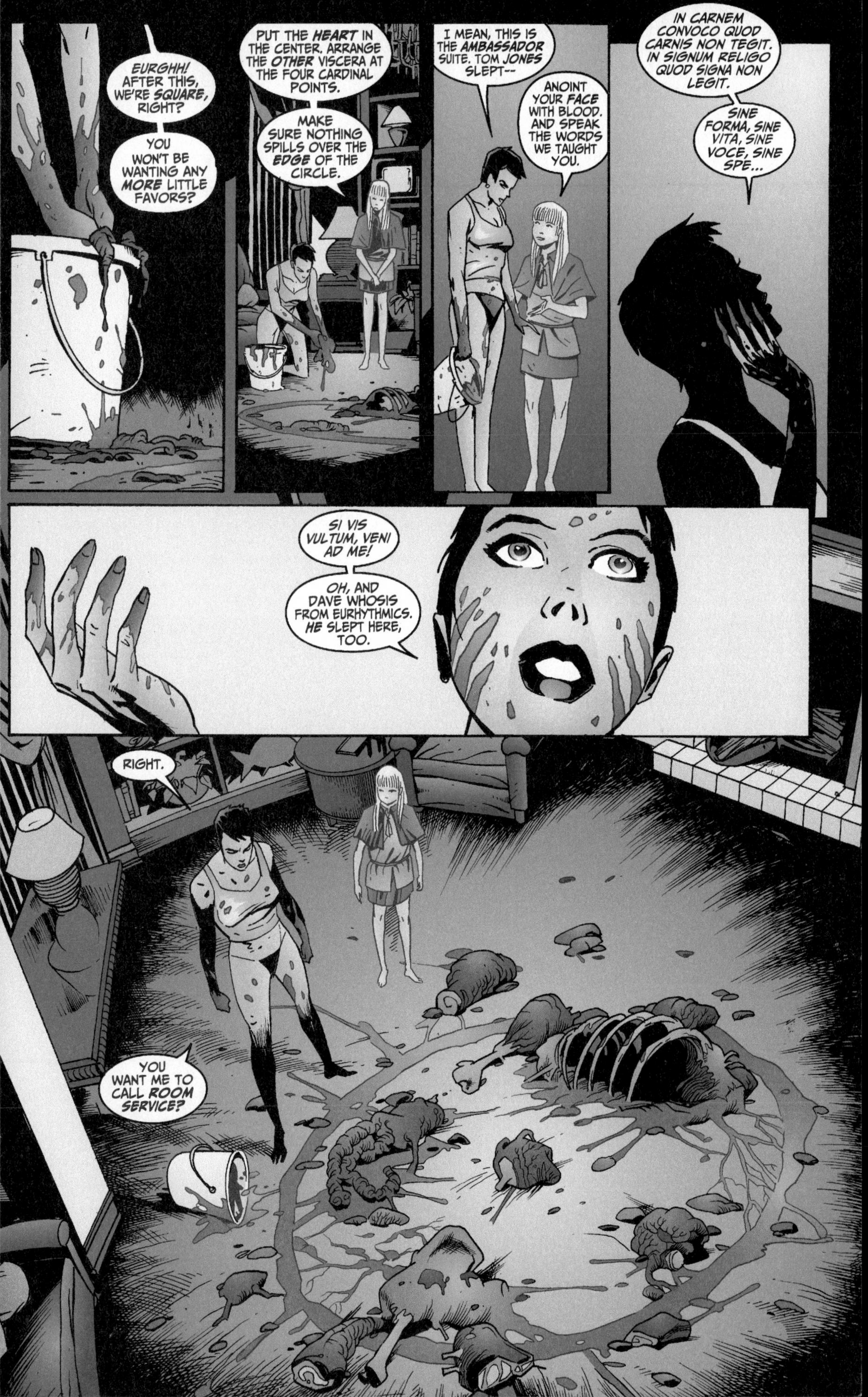
EURGHH! AFTER THIS, WE'RE SQUARE, RIGHT?
YOU WON'T BE WANTING ANY MORE LITTLE FAVORS?
PUT THE HEART IN THE CENTER. ARRANGE THE OTHER VISCERA AT THE FOUR CARDINAL POINTS.
MAKE SURE NOTHING SPILLS OVER THE EDGE OF THE CIRCLE.
I MEAN, THIS IS THE AMBASSADOR SUITE. TOM JONES SLEPT--
ANOINT YOUR FACE WITH BLOOD. AND SPEAK THE WORDS WE TAUGHT YOU.
IN CARNEM CONVOCO QUOD CARNIS NON TEGIT. IN SIGNUM RELIGO QUOD SIGNA NON LEGIT.
SINE FORMA, SINE VITA, SINE VOCE, SINE SPE...
SI VIS VULTUM, VENI AD ME!
OH, AND DAVE WHOSIS FROM EURHYTHMICS. HE SLEPT HERE, TOO.
RIGHT.
YOU WANT ME TO CALL ROOM SERVICE?

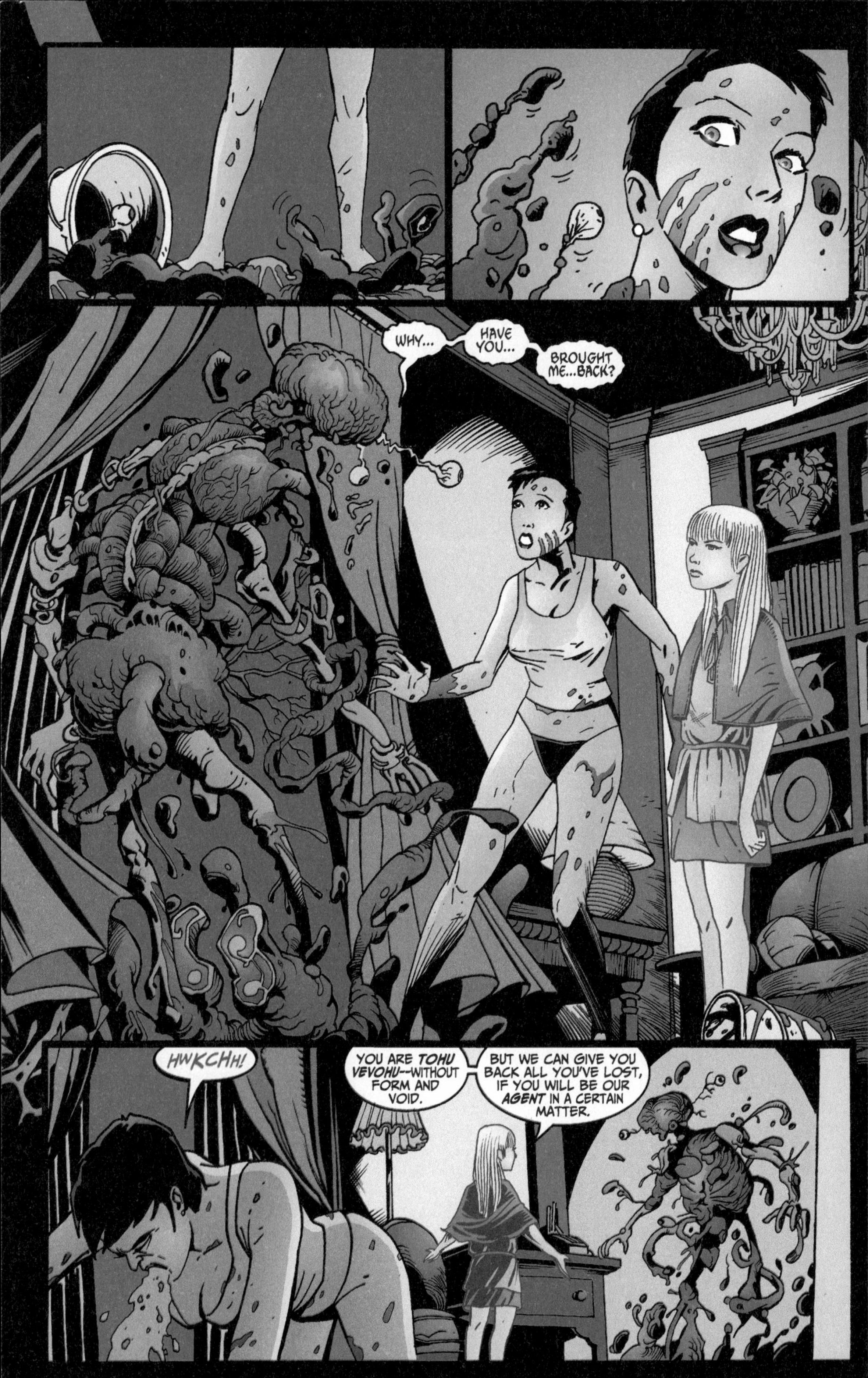
WHY...
HAVE YOU...
BROUGHT ME...BACK?
HWKCHH!
YOU ARE TOHU VEVOHU--WITHOUT FORM AND VOID.
BUT WE CAN GIVE YOU BACK ALL YOU'VE LOST, IF YOU WILL BE OUR AGENT IN A CERTAIN MATTER.

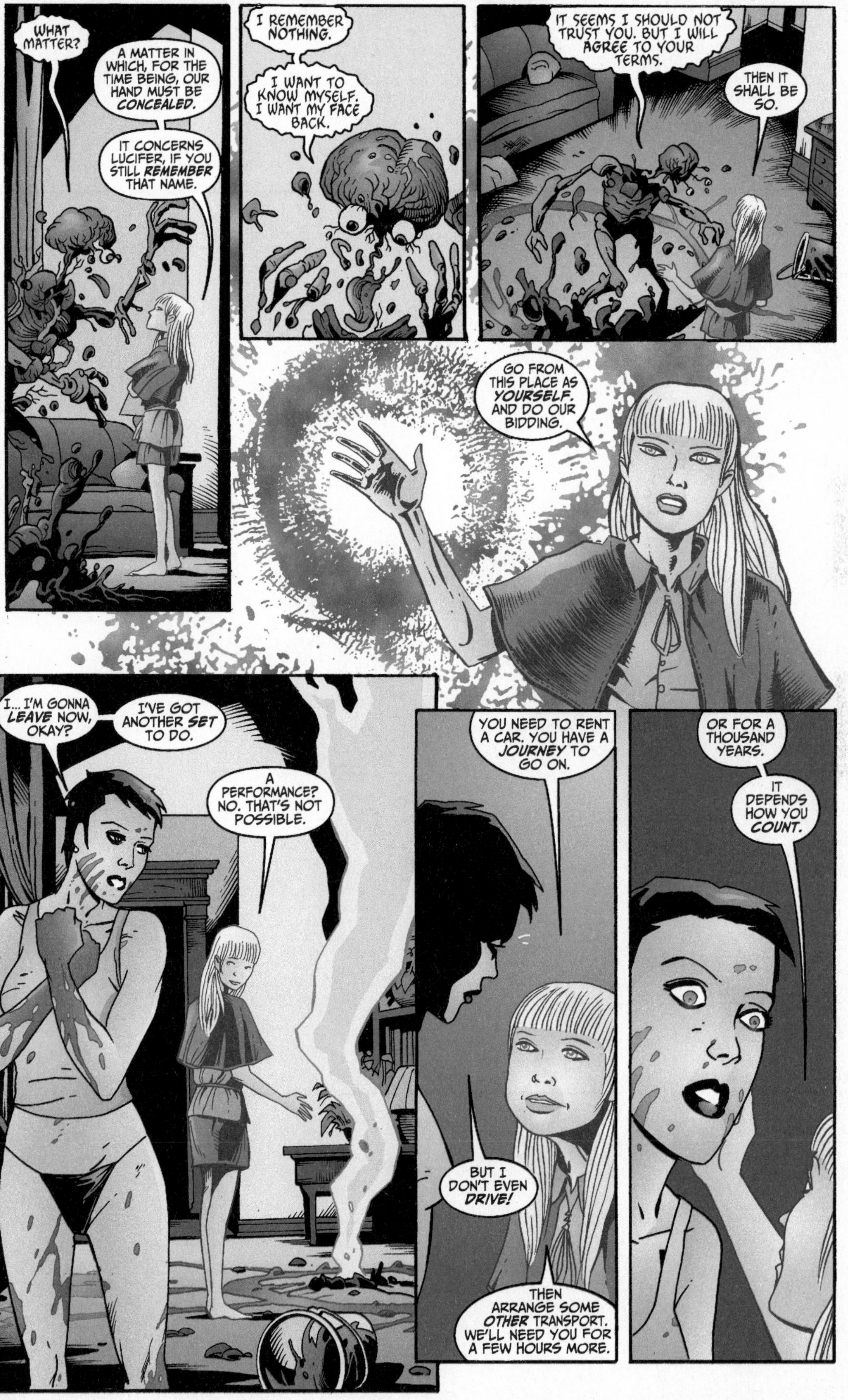
WHAT MATTER?
A MATTER IN WHICH, FOR THE TIME BEING, OUR HAND MUST BE CONCEALED.
IT CONCERNS LUCIFER, IF YOU STILL REMEMBER THAT NAME.
I REMEMBER NOTHING.
I WANT TO KNOW MYSELF. I WANT MY FACE BACK.
IT SEEMS I SHOULD NOT TRUST YOU. BUT I WILL AGREE TO YOUR TERMS.
THEN IT SHALL BE SO.
GO FROM THIS PLACE AS YOURSELF. AND DO OUR BIDDING.
I... I'M GONNA LEAVE NOW, OKAY?
I'VE GOT ANOTHER SET TO DO.
A PERFORMANCE? NO. THAT'S NOT POSSIBLE.
YOU NEED TO RENT A CAR. YOU HAVE A JOURNEY TO GO ON.
BUT I DON'T EVEN DRIVE!
THEN ARRANGE SOME OTHER TRANSPORT. WE'LL NEED YOU FOR A FEW HOURS MORE.
OR FOR A THOUSAND YEARS.
IT DEPENDS HOW YOU COUNT.

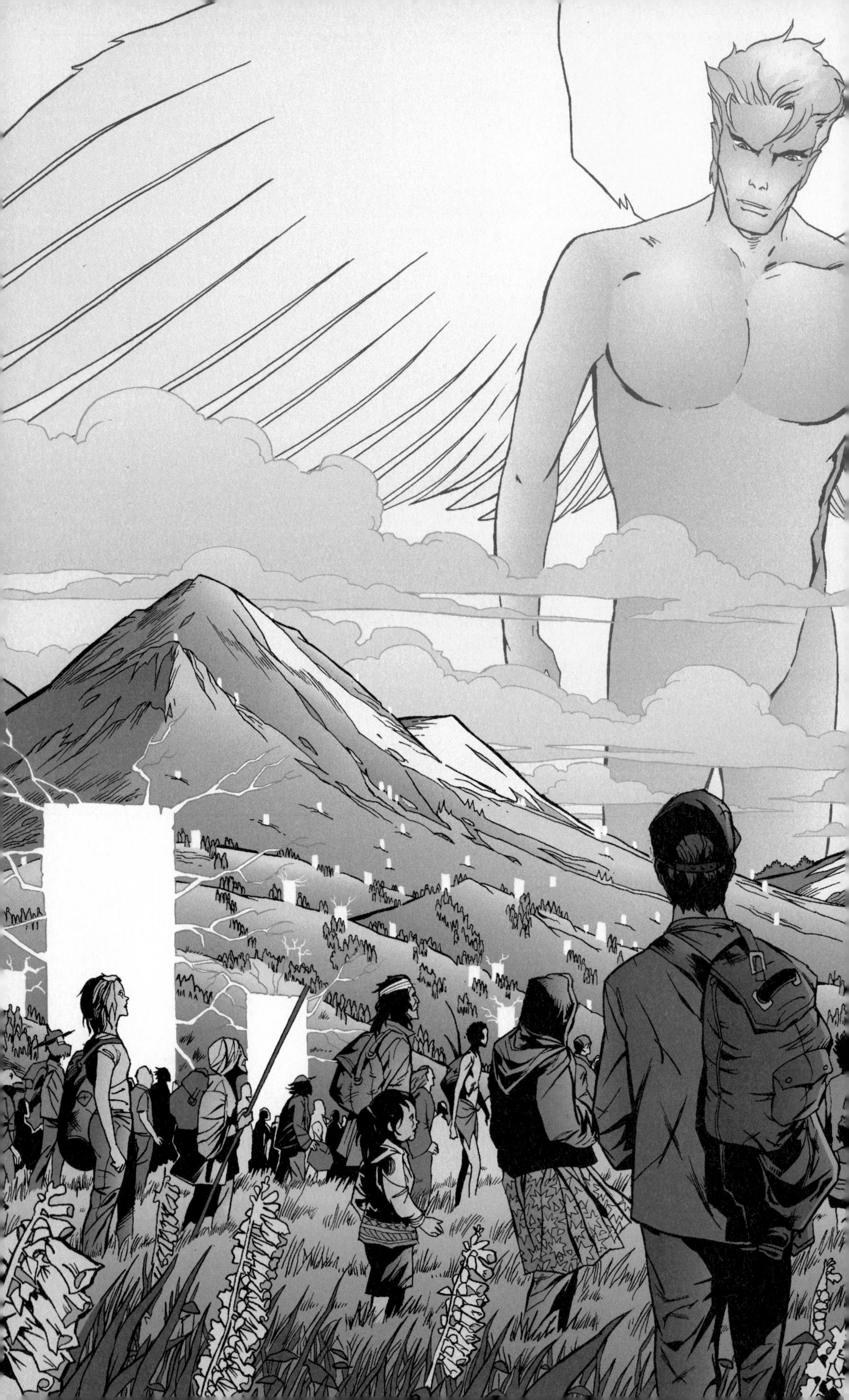

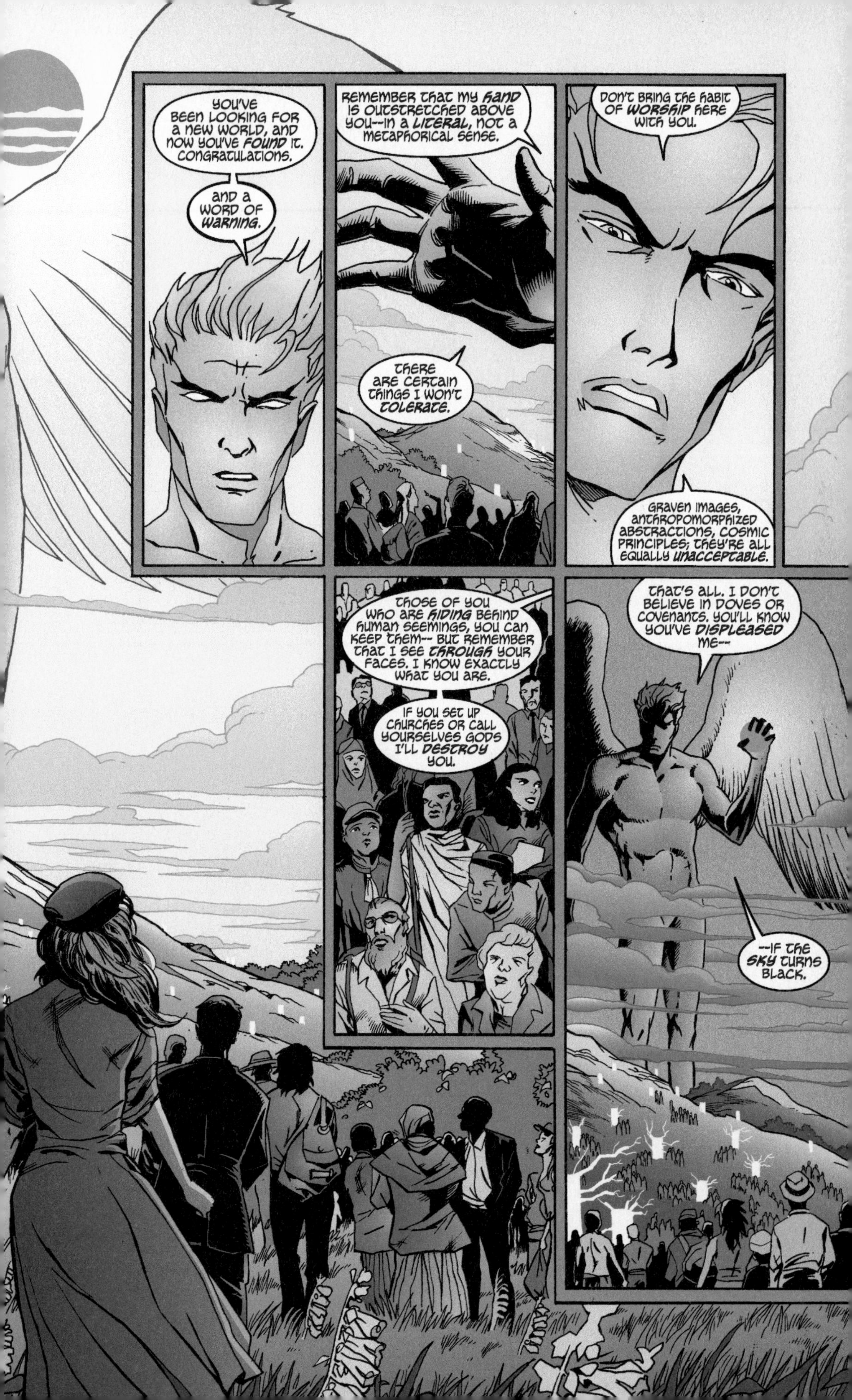
YOU'VE BEEN LOOKING FOR A NEW WORLD, AND NOW YOU'VE FOUND IT. CONGRATULATIONS.
AND A WORD OF WARNING.
REMEMBER THAT MY HAND IS OUTSTRETCHED ABOVE YOU--IN A LITERAL, NOT A METAPHORICAL SENSE.
THERE ARE CERTAIN THINGS I WON'T TOLERATE.
DON'T BRING THE HABIT OF WORSHIP HERE WITH YOU.
GRAVEN IMAGES, ANTHROPOMORPHIZED ABSTRACTIONS, COSMIC PRINCIPLES; THEY'RE ALL EQUALLY UNACCEPTABLE.
THOSE OF YOU WHO ARE HIDING BEHIND HUMAN SEEMINGS, YOU CAN KEEP THEM-- BUT REMEMBER THAT I SEE THROUGH YOUR FACES. I KNOW EXACTLY WHAT YOU ARE.
IF YOU SET UP CHURCHES OR CALL YOURSELVES GODS I'LL DESTROY YOU.
THAT'S ALL. I DON'T BELIEVE IN DOVES OR COVENANTS. YOU'LL KNOW YOU'VE DISPLEASED ME--
--IF THE SKY TURNS BLACK.

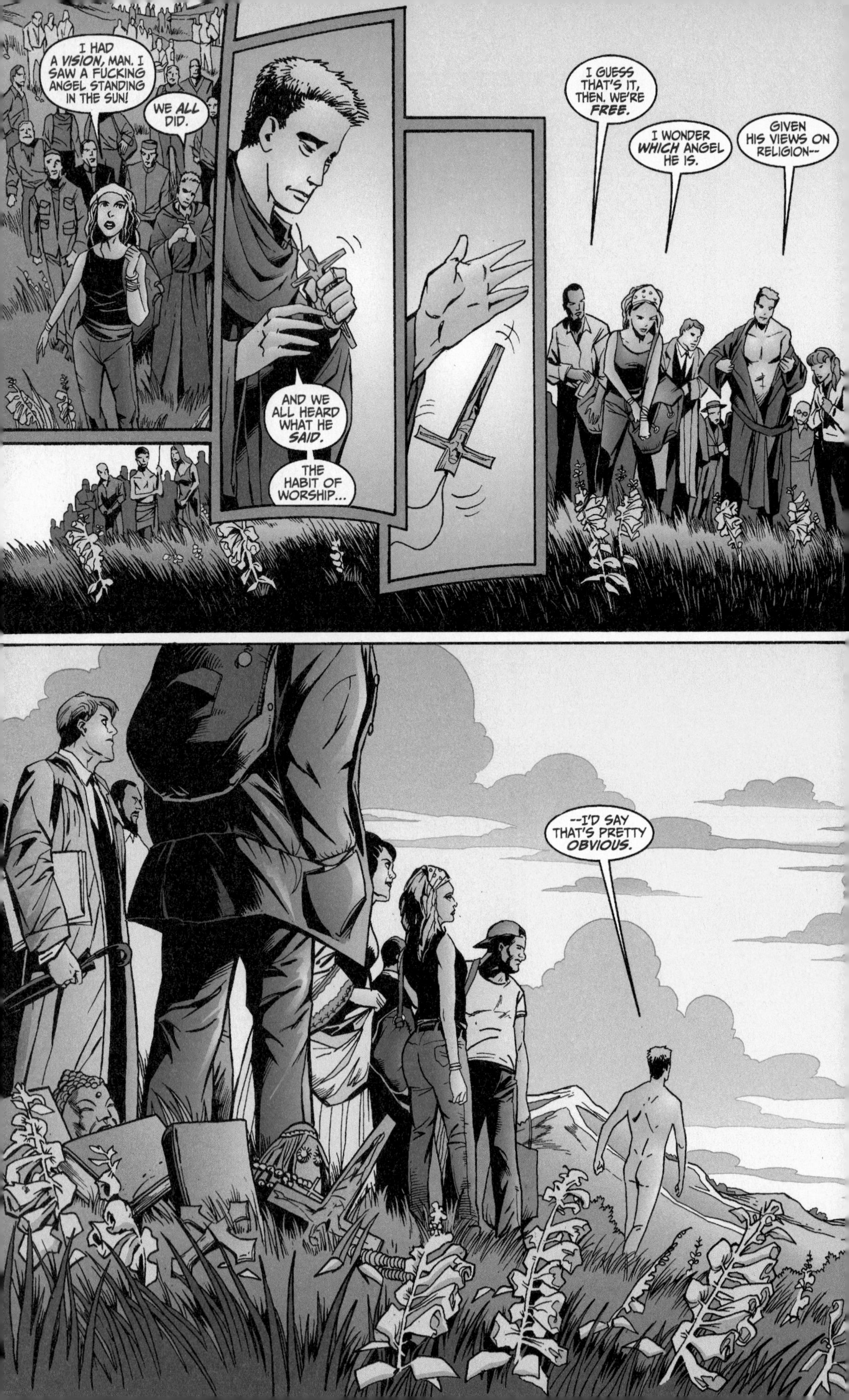
I HAD A VISION, MAN. I SAW A FUCKING ANGEL STANDING IN THE SUN!
WE ALL DID.
AND WE ALL HEARD WHAT HE SAID.
THE HABIT OF WORSHIP...
I GUESS THAT'S IT, THEN. WE'RE FREE.
I WONDER WHICH ANGEL HE IS.
GIVEN HIS VIEWS ON RELIGION--
--I'D SAY THAT'S PRETTY OBVIOUS.

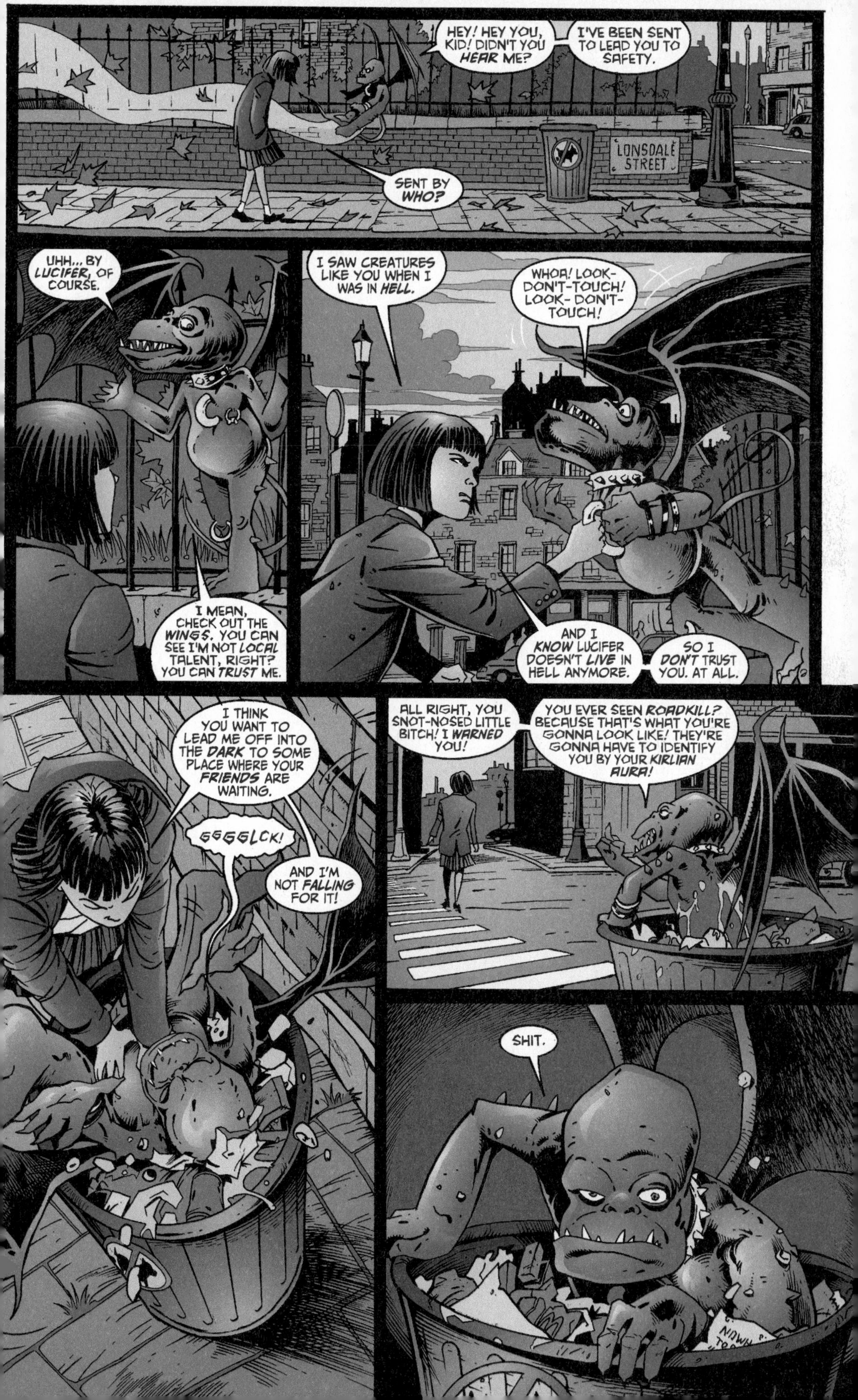
HEY! HEY YOU, KID! DIDN'T YOU HEAR ME?
I'VE BEEN SENT TO LEAD YOU TO SAFETY.
LONSDALE STREET
SENT BY WHO?
UHH... BY LUCIFER, OF COURSE.
I MEAN, CHECK OUT THE WINGS. YOU CAN SEE I'M NOT LOCAL TALENT, RIGHT? YOU CAN TRUST ME.
I SAW CREATURES LIKE YOU WHEN I WAS IN HELL.
WHOA! LOOK-DON'T-TOUCH! LOOK- DON'T-TOUCH!
AND I KNOW LUCIFER DOESN'T LIVE IN HELL ANYMORE.
SO I DON'T TRUST YOU. AT ALL.
I THINK YOU WANT TO LEAD ME OFF INTO THE DARK TO SOME PLACE WHERE YOUR FRIENDS ARE WAITING.
GGGGLCK!
AND I'M NOT FALLING FOR IT!
ALL RIGHT, YOU SNOT-NOSED LITTLE BITCH! I WARNED YOU!
YOU EVER SEEN ROADKILL? BECAUSE THAT'S WHAT YOU'RE GONNA LOOK LIKE! THEY'RE GONNA HAVE TO IDENTIFY YOU BY YOUR KIRLIAN AURA!
SHIT.

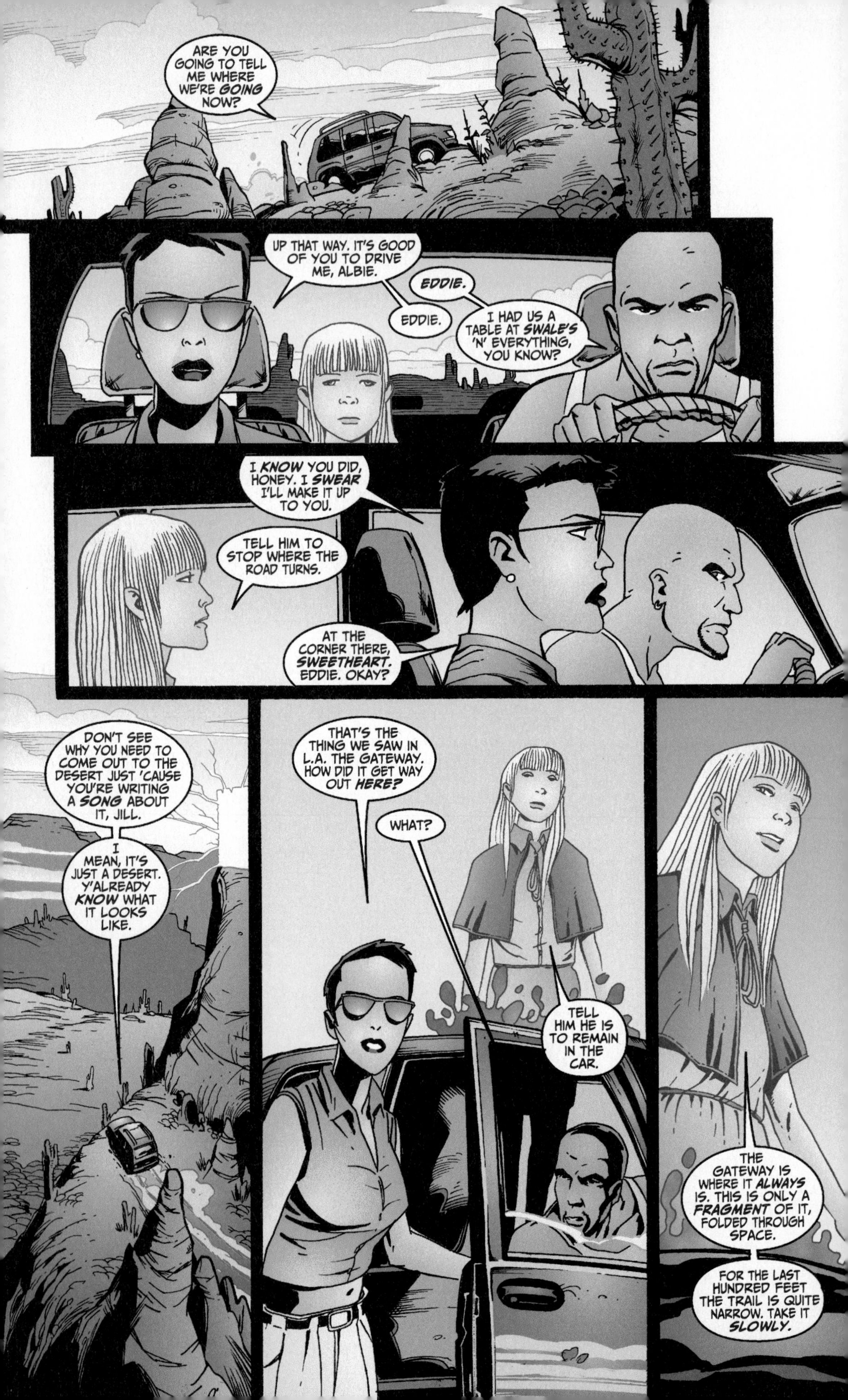
ARE YOU GOING TO TELL ME WHERE WE'RE GOING NOW?
UP THAT WAY. IT'S GOOD OF YOU TO DRIVE ME, ALBIE.
EDDIE.
EDDIE.
I HAD US A TABLE AT SWALE'S 'N' EVERYTHING, YOU KNOW?
I KNOW YOU DID, HONEY. I SWEAR I'LL MAKE IT UP TO YOU.
TELL HIM TO STOP WHERE THE ROAD TURNS.
AT THE CORNER THERE, SWEETHEART. EDDIE. OKAY?
DON'T SEE WHY YOU NEED TO COME OUT TO THE DESERT JUST 'CAUSE YOU'RE WRITING A SONG ABOUT IT, JILL.
I MEAN, IT'S JUST A DESERT. Y'ALREADY KNOW WHAT IT LOOKS LIKE.
THAT'S THE THING WE SAW IN L.A. THE GATEWAY. HOW DID IT GET WAY OUT HERE?
WHAT?
TELL HIM HE IS TO REMAIN IN THE CAR.
THE GATEWAY IS WHERE IT ALWAYS IS. THIS IS ONLY A FRAGMENT OF IT, FOLDED THROUGH SPACE.
FOR THE LAST HUNDRED FEET THE TRAIL IS QUITE NARROW. TAKE IT SLOWLY.

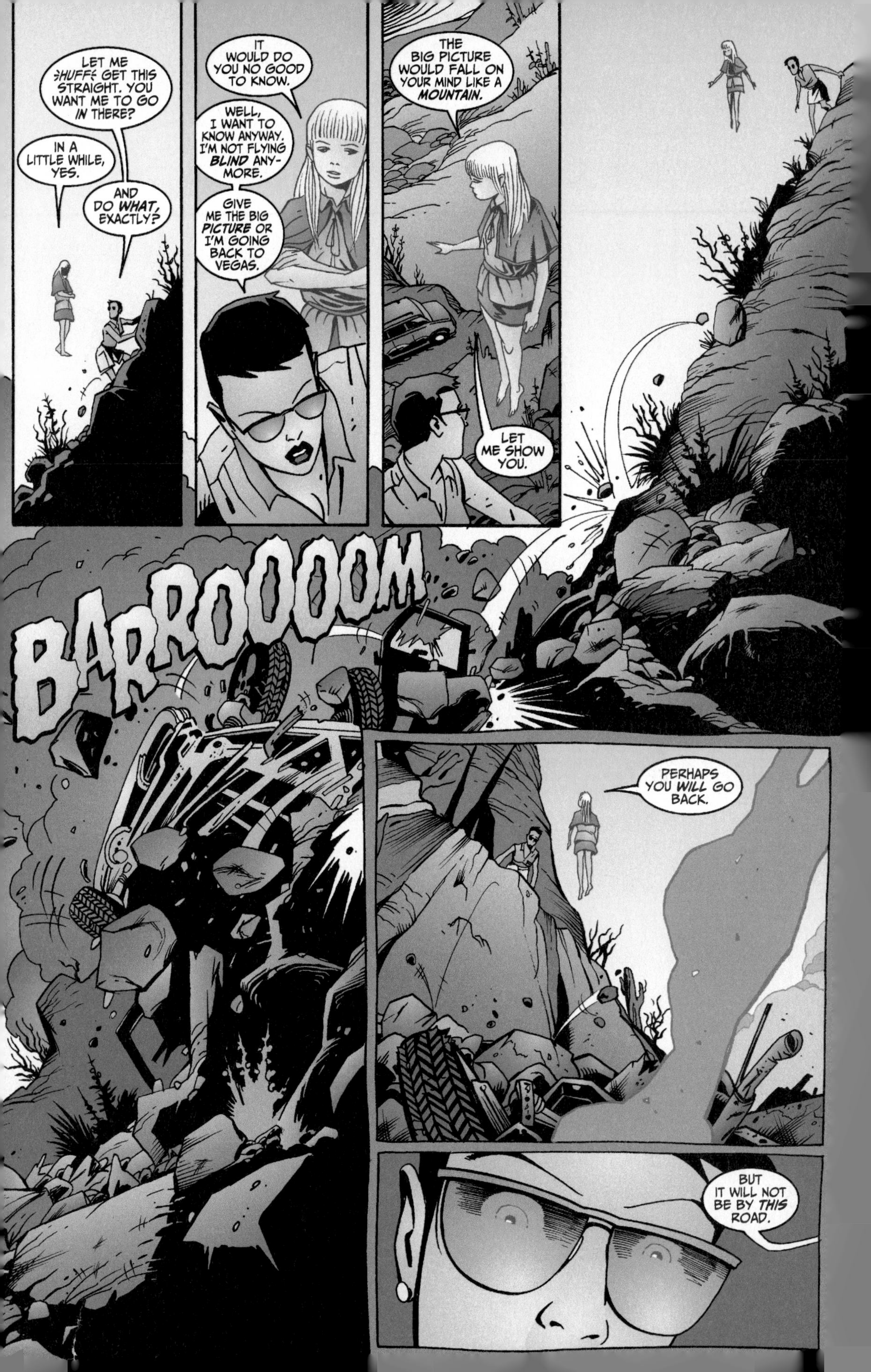
LET ME ≶HUFF≶ GET THIS STRAIGHT. YOU WANT ME TO GO *IN* THERE?
IN A LITTLE WHILE, YES.
AND DO *WHAT*, EXACTLY?
IT WOULD DO YOU NO GOOD TO KNOW.
WELL, I WANT TO KNOW ANYWAY. I'M NOT FLYING *BLIND* ANYMORE.
GIVE ME THE BIG *PICTURE* OR I'M GOING BACK TO VEGAS.
THE BIG PICTURE WOULD FALL ON YOUR MIND LIKE A *MOUNTAIN.*
LET ME SHOW YOU.
BARROOOOM
PERHAPS YOU *WILL* GO BACK.
BUT IT WILL NOT BE BY *THIS* ROAD.

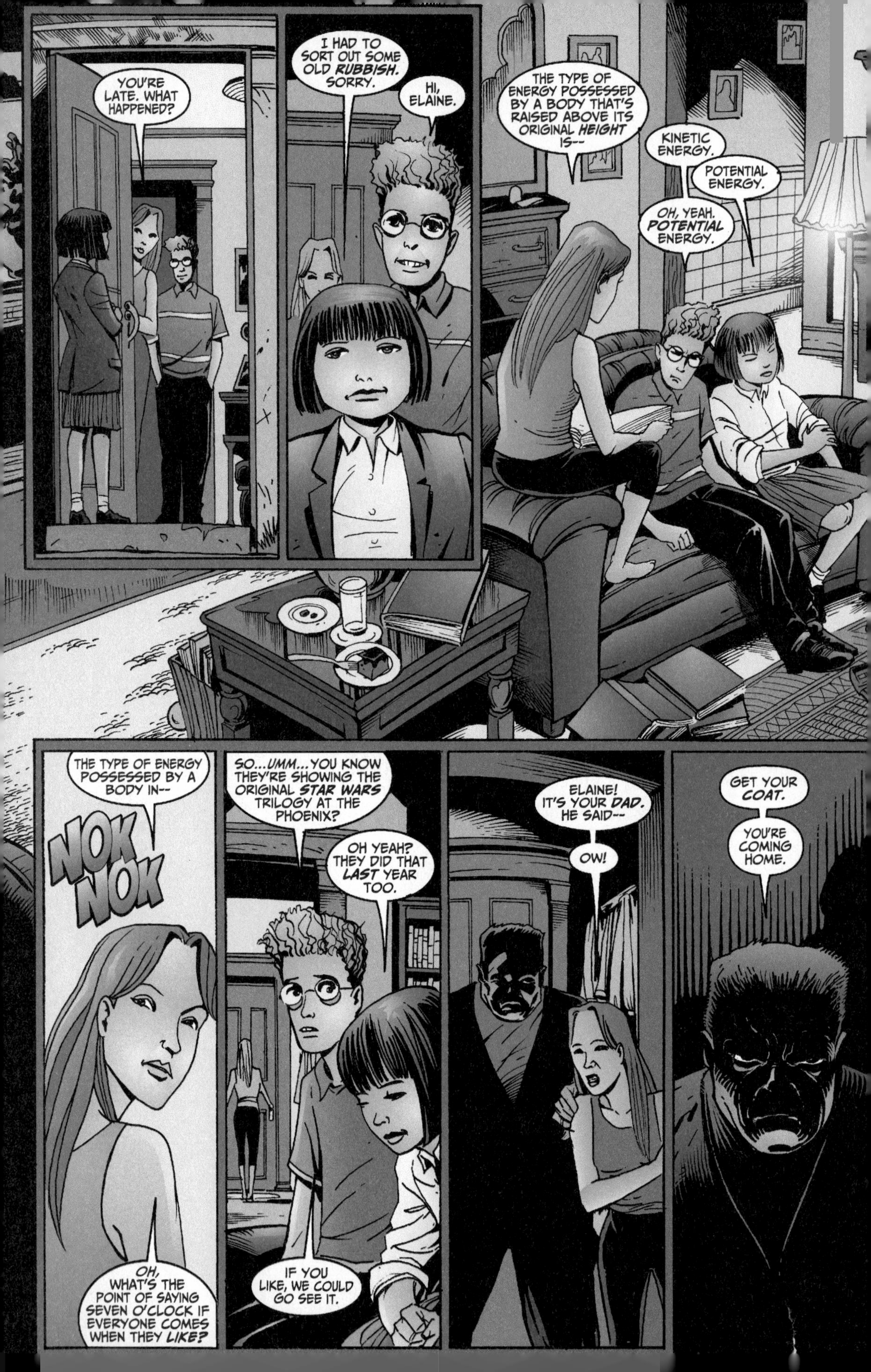
YOU'RE LATE. WHAT HAPPENED?
I HAD TO SORT OUT SOME OLD RUBBISH. SORRY.
HI, ELAINE.
THE TYPE OF ENERGY POSSESSED BY A BODY THAT'S RAISED ABOVE ITS ORIGINAL HEIGHT IS--
KINETIC ENERGY.
POTENTIAL ENERGY.
OH, YEAH. POTENTIAL ENERGY.
THE TYPE OF ENERGY POSSESSED BY A BODY IN--
NOK NOK
OH, WHAT'S THE POINT OF SAYING SEVEN O'CLOCK IF EVERYONE COMES WHEN THEY LIKE?
SO...UMM...YOU KNOW THEY'RE SHOWING THE ORIGINAL STAR WARS TRILOGY AT THE PHOENIX?
OH YEAH? THEY DID THAT LAST YEAR TOO.
IF YOU LIKE, WE COULD GO SEE IT.
ELAINE! IT'S YOUR DAD. HE SAID--
OW!
GET YOUR COAT.
YOU'RE COMING HOME.

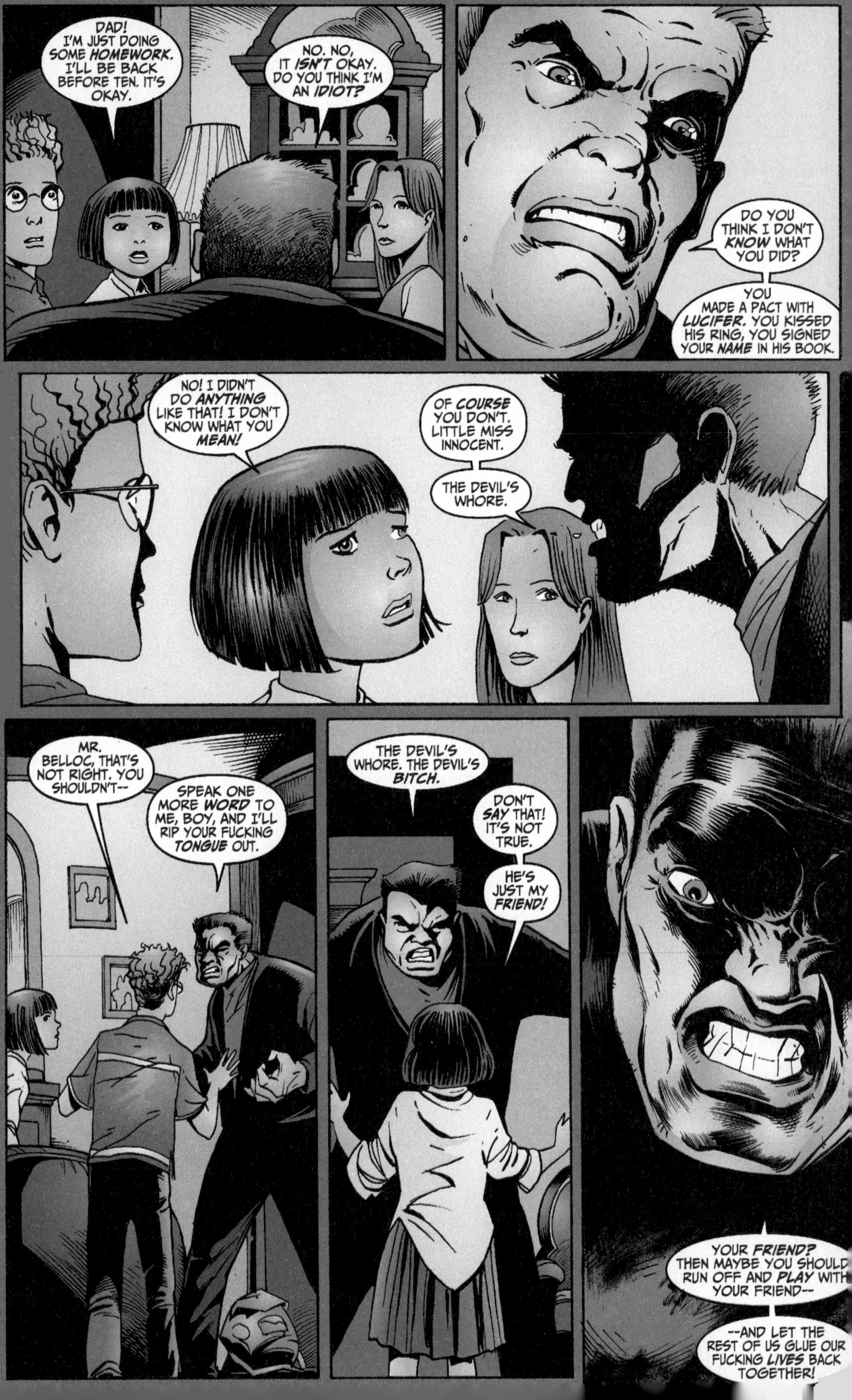
DAD! I'M JUST DOING SOME HOMEWORK. I'LL BE BACK BEFORE TEN. IT'S OKAY.
NO. NO, IT ISN'T OKAY. DO YOU THINK I'M AN IDIOT?
DO YOU THINK I DON'T KNOW WHAT YOU DID?
YOU MADE A PACT WITH LUCIFER. YOU KISSED HIS RING, YOU SIGNED YOUR NAME IN HIS BOOK.
NO! I DIDN'T DO ANYTHING LIKE THAT! I DON'T KNOW WHAT YOU MEAN!
OF COURSE YOU DON'T. LITTLE MISS INNOCENT.
THE DEVIL'S WHORE.
MR. BELLOC, THAT'S NOT RIGHT. YOU SHOULDN'T--
SPEAK ONE MORE WORD TO ME, BOY, AND I'LL RIP YOUR FUCKING TONGUE OUT.
THE DEVIL'S WHORE. THE DEVIL'S BITCH.
DON'T SAY THAT! IT'S NOT TRUE.
HE'S JUST MY FRIEND!
YOUR FRIEND? THEN MAYBE YOU SHOULD RUN OFF AND PLAY WITH YOUR FRIEND--
--AND LET THE REST OF US GLUE OUR FUCKING LIVES BACK TOGETHER!

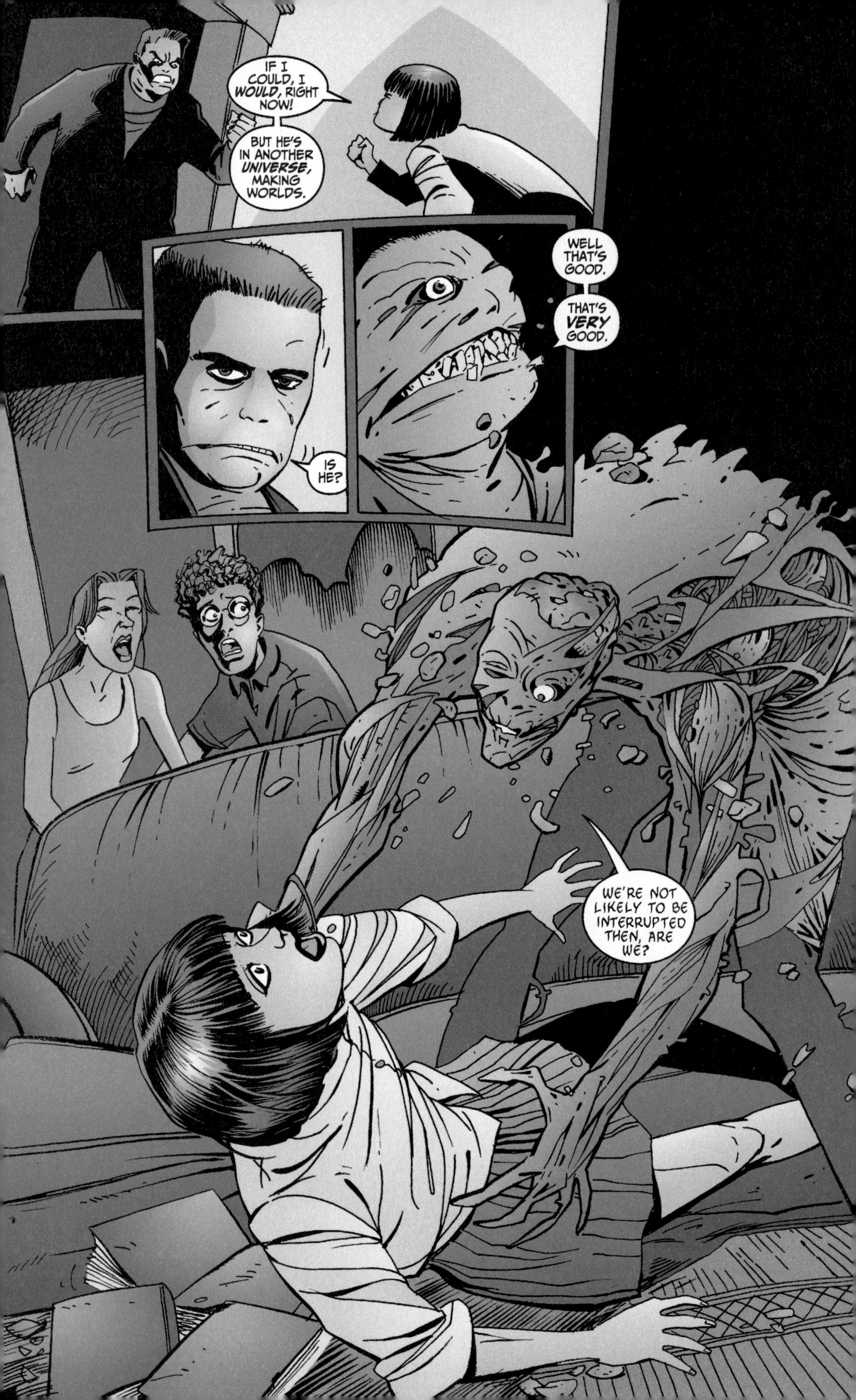
IF I COULD, I WOULD, RIGHT NOW!
BUT HE'S IN ANOTHER UNIVERSE, MAKING WORLDS.
IS HE?
WELL THAT'S GOOD.
THAT'S VERY GOOD.
WE'RE NOT LIKELY TO BE INTERRUPTED THEN, ARE WE?

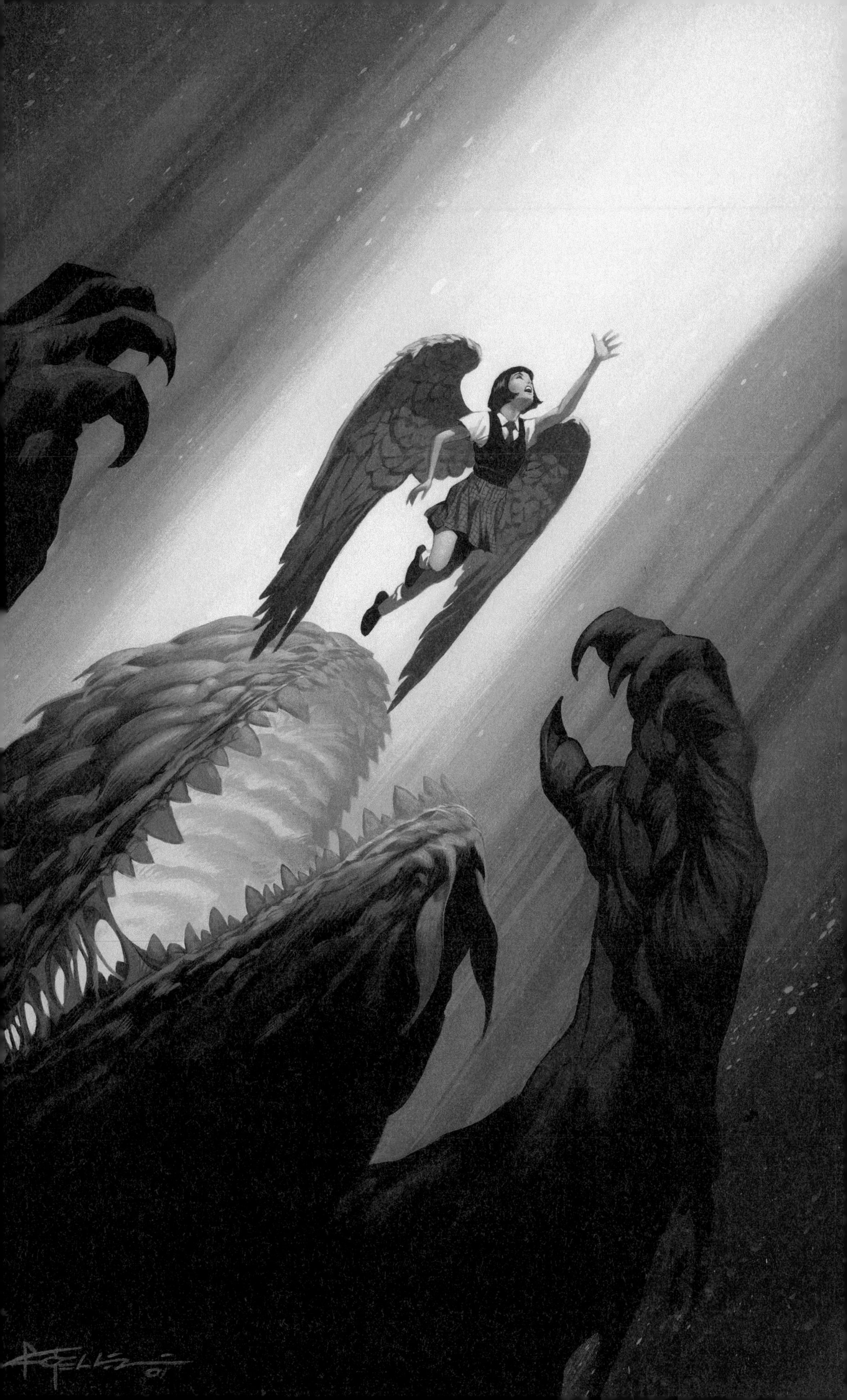

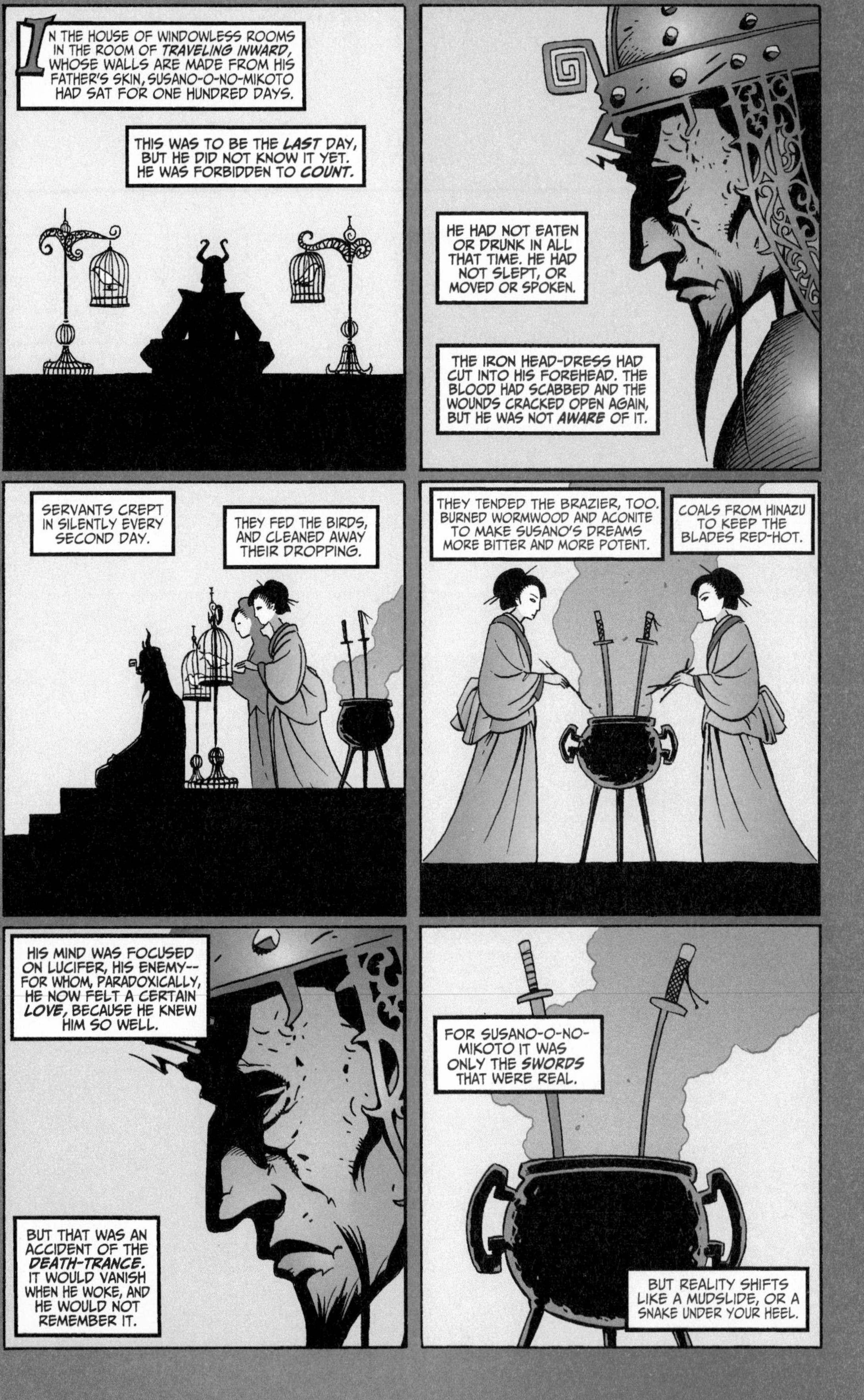

IN THE HOUSE OF WINDOWLESS ROOMS IN THE ROOM OF TRAVELING INWARD, WHOSE WALLS ARE MADE FROM HIS FATHER'S SKIN, SUSANO-O-NO-MIKOTO HAD SAT FOR ONE HUNDRED DAYS.
THIS WAS TO BE THE LAST DAY, BUT HE DID NOT KNOW IT YET. HE WAS FORBIDDEN TO COUNT.
HE HAD NOT EATEN OR DRUNK IN ALL THAT TIME. HE HAD NOT SLEPT, OR MOVED OR SPOKEN.
THE IRON HEAD-DRESS HAD CUT INTO HIS FOREHEAD. THE BLOOD HAD SCABBED AND THE WOUNDS CRACKED OPEN AGAIN, BUT HE WAS NOT AWARE OF IT.
SERVANTS CREPT IN SILENTLY EVERY SECOND DAY.
THEY FED THE BIRDS, AND CLEANED AWAY THEIR DROPPING.
THEY TENDED THE BRAZIER, TOO. BURNED WORMWOOD AND ACONITE TO MAKE SUSANO'S DREAMS MORE BITTER AND MORE POTENT.
COALS FROM HINAZU TO KEEP THE BLADES RED-HOT.
HIS MIND WAS FOCUSED ON LUCIFER, HIS ENEMY-- FOR WHOM, PARADOXICALLY, HE NOW FELT A CERTAIN LOVE, BECAUSE HE KNEW HIM SO WELL.
BUT THAT WAS AN ACCIDENT OF THE DEATH-TRANCE. IT WOULD VANISH WHEN HE WOKE, AND HE WOULD NOT REMEMBER IT.
FOR SUSANO-O-NO-MIKOTO IT WAS ONLY THE SWORDS THAT WERE REAL.
BUT REALITY SHIFTS LIKE A MUDSLIDE, OR A SNAKE UNDER YOUR HEEL.

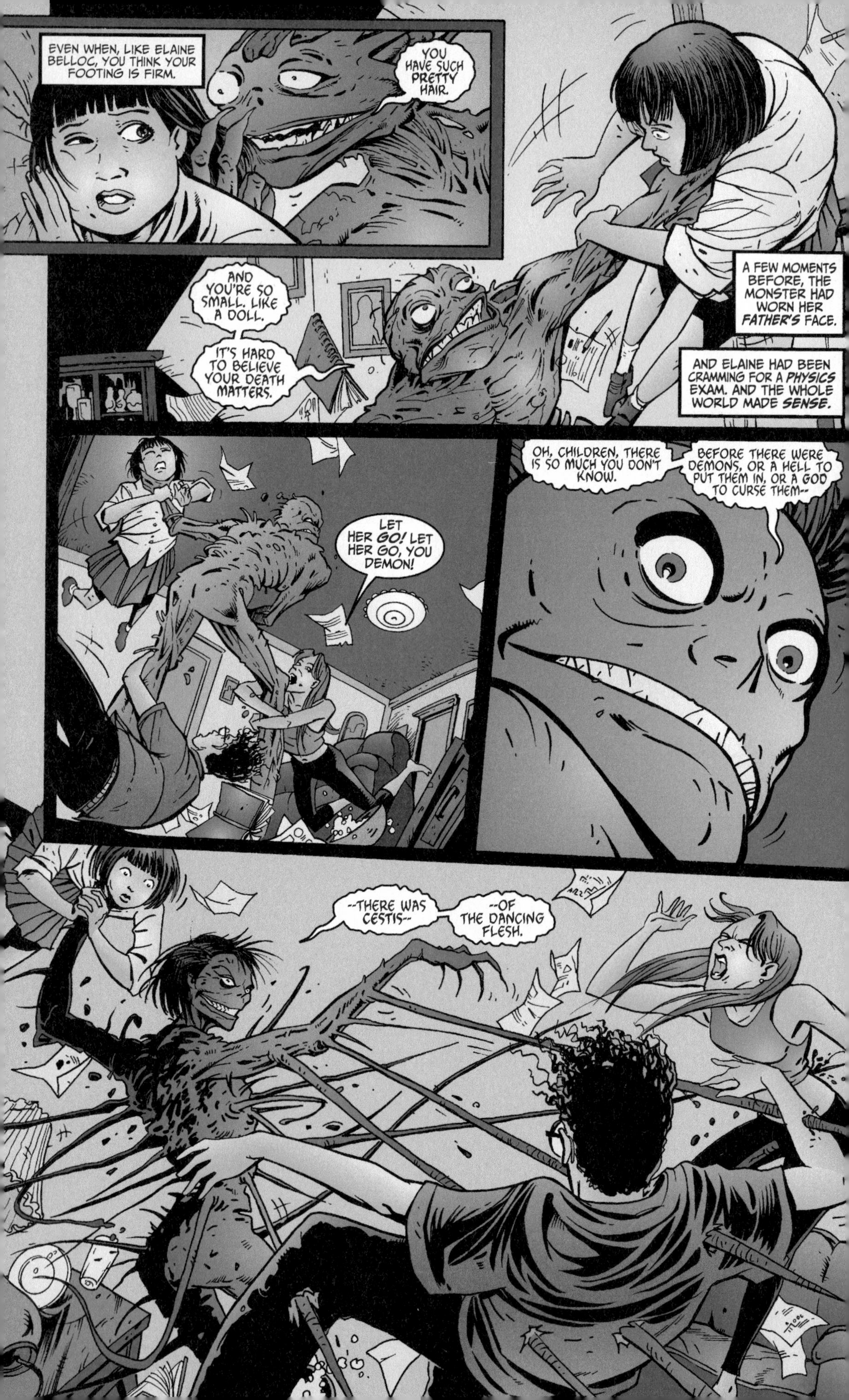
EVEN WHEN, LIKE ELAINE BELLOC, YOU THINK YOUR FOOTING IS FIRM.
YOU HAVE SUCH PRETTY HAIR.
AND YOU'RE SO SMALL. LIKE A DOLL.
IT'S HARD TO BELIEVE YOUR DEATH MATTERS.
A FEW MOMENTS BEFORE, THE MONSTER HAD WORN HER FATHER'S FACE.
AND ELAINE HAD BEEN CRAMMING FOR A PHYSICS EXAM. AND THE WHOLE WORLD MADE SENSE.
LET HER GO! LET HER GO, YOU DEMON!
OH, CHILDREN, THERE IS SO MUCH YOU DON'T KNOW.
BEFORE THERE WERE DEMONS, OR A HELL TO PUT THEM IN, OR A GOD TO CURSE THEM--
--THERE WAS CESTIS--
--OF THE DANCING FLESH.

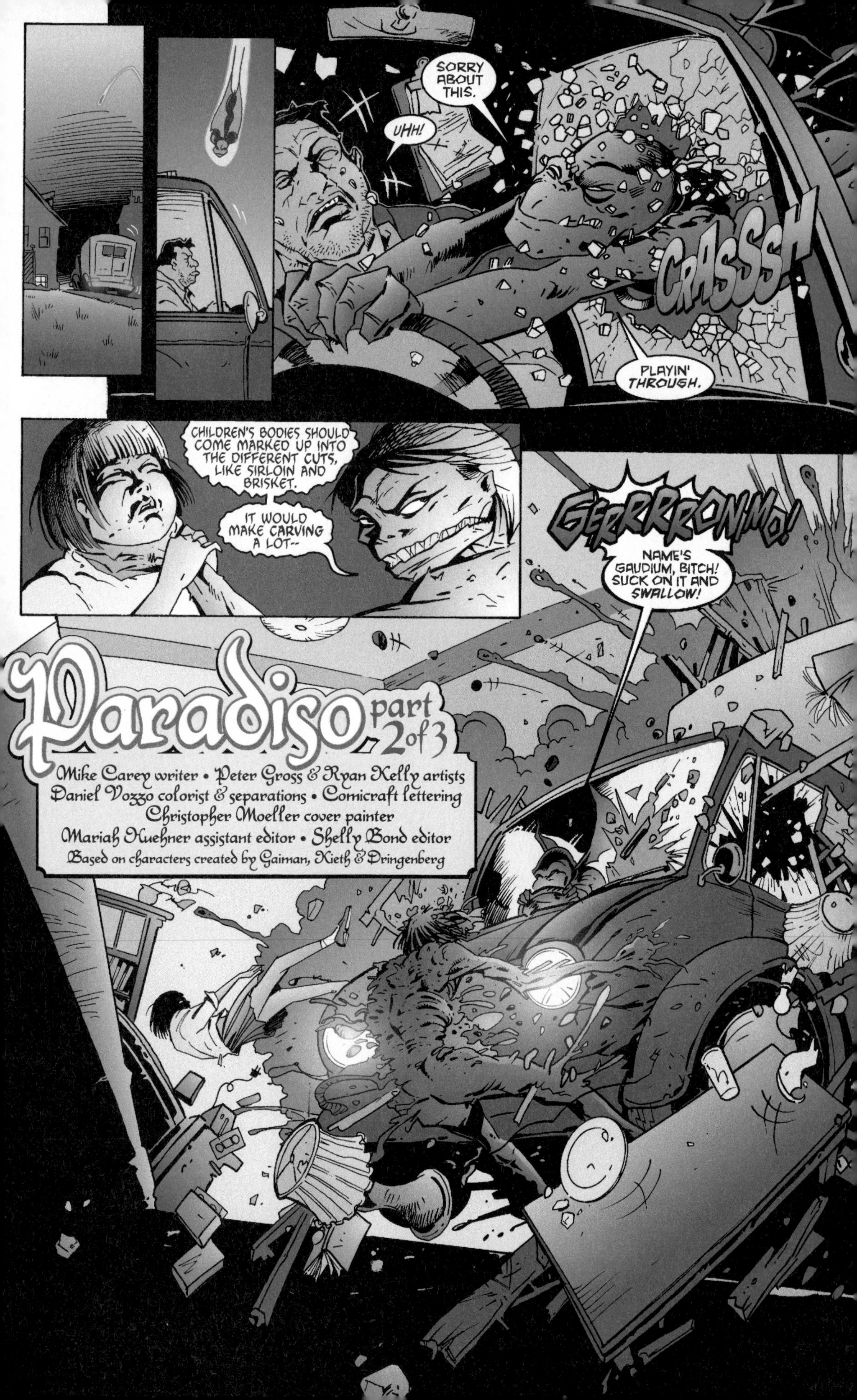

SORRY ABOUT THIS.
UHH!
CRASSSH
PLAYIN' THROUGH.
CHILDREN'S BODIES SHOULD COME MARKED UP INTO THE DIFFERENT CUTS, LIKE SIRLOIN AND BRISKET.
IT WOULD MAKE CARVING A LOT--
GERRRRONIMO!
NAME'S GAUDIUM, BITCH! SUCK ON IT AND SWALLOW!
Paradiso part 2 of 3
Mike Carey writer • Peter Gross & Ryan Kelly artists
Daniel Vozzo colorist & separations • Comicraft lettering
Christopher Moeller cover painter
Mariah Huehner assistant editor • Shelly Bond editor
Based on characters created by Gaiman, Kieth & Dringenberg

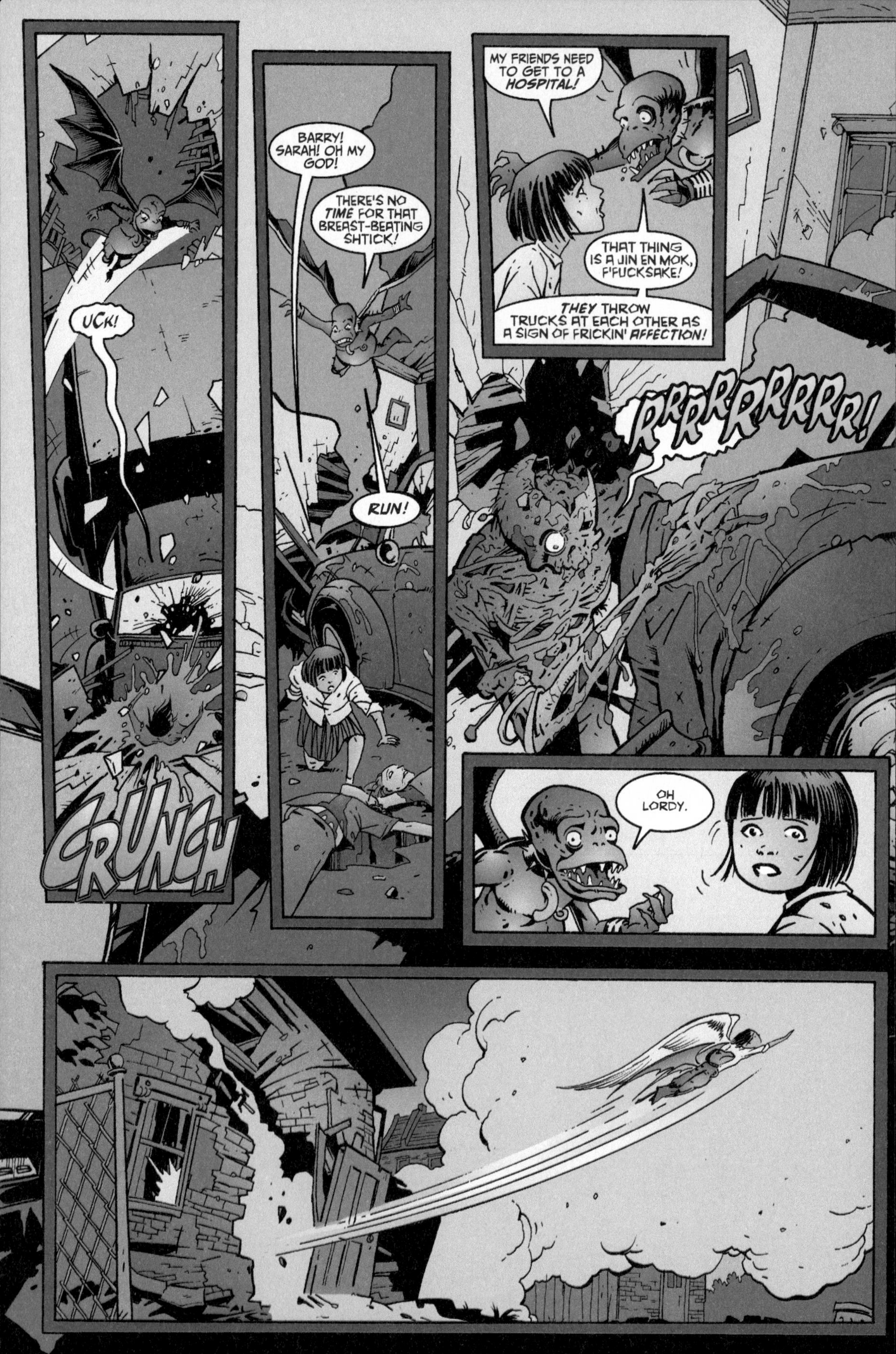
UCK!
CRUNCH
BARRY! SARAH! OH MY GOD!
THERE'S NO TIME FOR THAT BREAST-BEATING SHTICK!
RUN!
MY FRIENDS NEED TO GET TO A HOSPITAL!
THAT THING IS A JIN EN MOK, F'FUCKSAKE!
THEY THROW TRUCKS AT EACH OTHER AS A SIGN OF FRICKIN' AFFECTION!
RRRRRRRRRR!
OH LORDY.

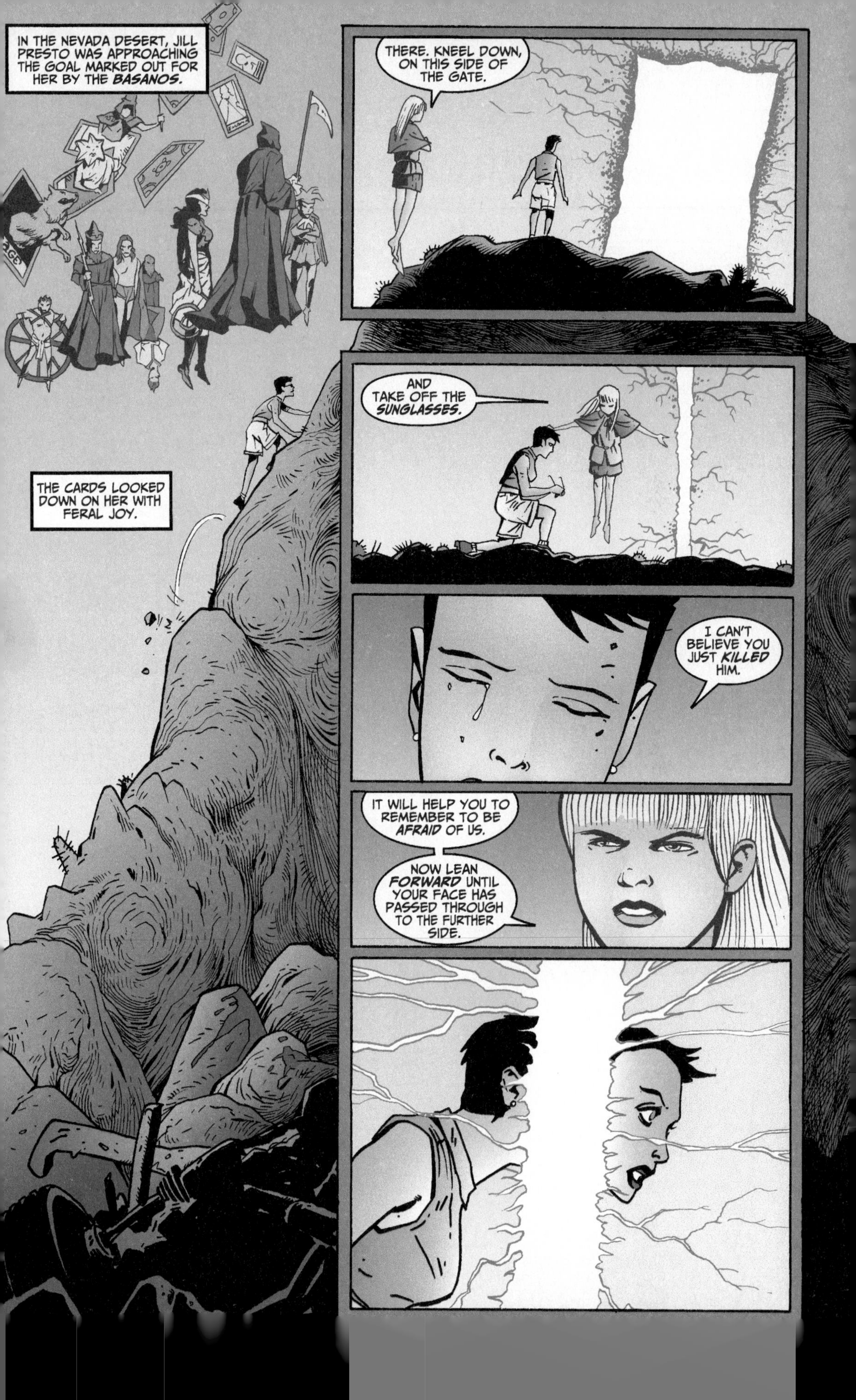
IN THE NEVADA DESERT, JILL PRESTO WAS APPROACHING THE GOAL MARKED OUT FOR HER BY THE BASANOS.
THE CARDS LOOKED DOWN ON HER WITH FERAL JOY.
THERE. KNEEL DOWN, ON THIS SIDE OF THE GATE.
AND TAKE OFF THE SUNGLASSES.
I CAN'T BELIEVE YOU JUST KILLED HIM.
IT WILL HELP YOU TO REMEMBER TO BE AFRAID OF US.
NOW LEAN FORWARD UNTIL YOUR FACE HAS PASSED THROUGH TO THE FURTHER SIDE.

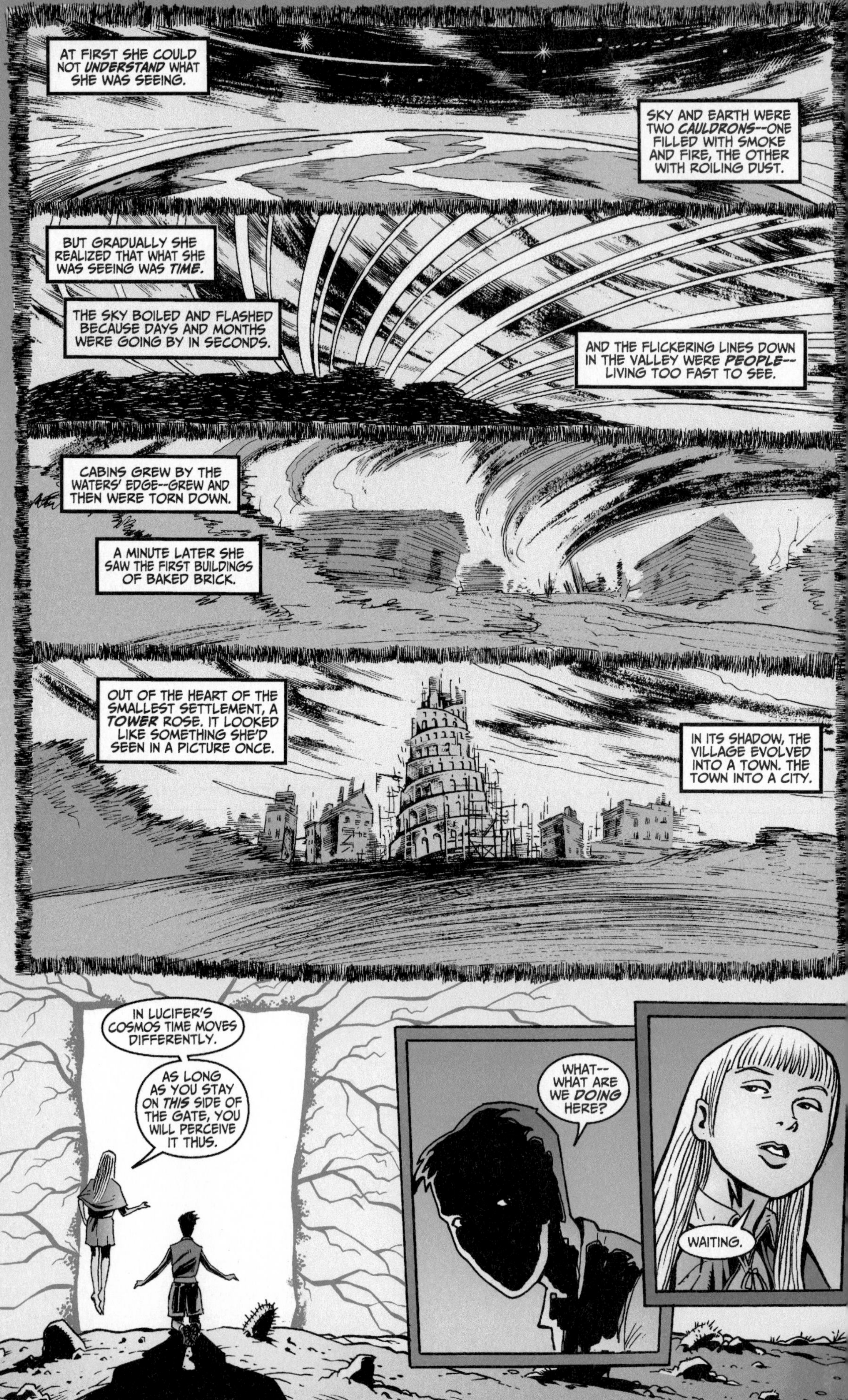

AT FIRST SHE COULD NOT UNDERSTAND WHAT SHE WAS SEEING.
SKY AND EARTH WERE TWO CAULDRONS--ONE FILLED WITH SMOKE AND FIRE, THE OTHER WITH ROILING DUST.
BUT GRADUALLY SHE REALIZED THAT WHAT SHE WAS SEEING WAS TIME.
THE SKY BOILED AND FLASHED BECAUSE DAYS AND MONTHS WERE GOING BY IN SECONDS.
AND THE FLICKERING LINES DOWN IN THE VALLEY WERE PEOPLE--LIVING TOO FAST TO SEE.
CABINS GREW BY THE WATERS' EDGE--GREW AND THEN WERE TORN DOWN.
A MINUTE LATER SHE SAW THE FIRST BUILDINGS OF BAKED BRICK.
OUT OF THE HEART OF THE SMALLEST SETTLEMENT, A TOWER ROSE. IT LOOKED LIKE SOMETHING SHE'D SEEN IN A PICTURE ONCE.
IN ITS SHADOW, THE VILLAGE EVOLVED INTO A TOWN. THE TOWN INTO A CITY.
IN LUCIFER'S COSMOS TIME MOVES DIFFERENTLY.
AS LONG AS YOU STAY ON THIS SIDE OF THE GATE, YOU WILL PERCEIVE IT THUS.
WHAT--WHAT ARE WE DOING HERE?
WAITING.

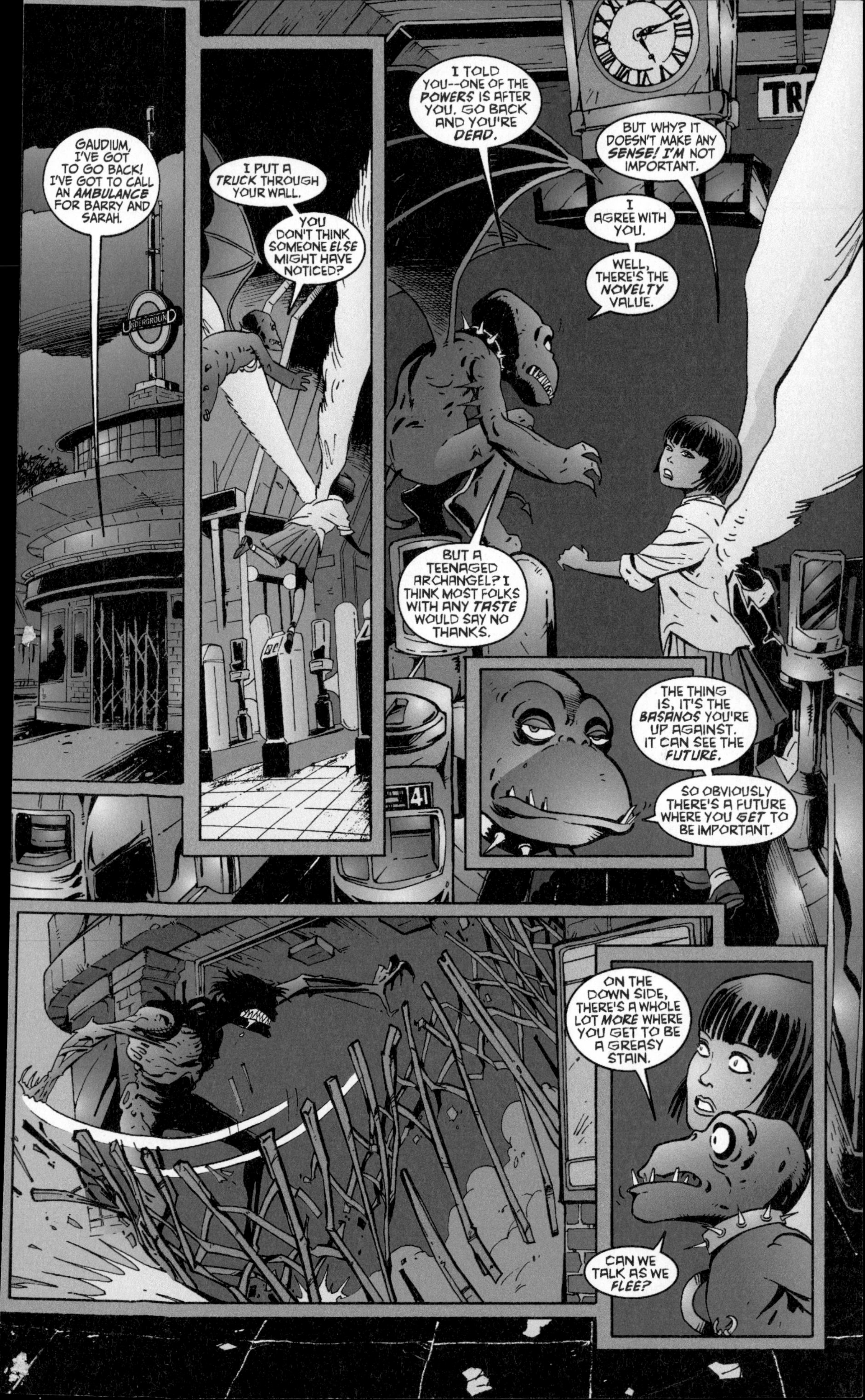
GAUDIUM, I'VE GOT TO GO BACK! I'VE GOT TO CALL AN AMBULANCE FOR BARRY AND SARAH.
UNDERGROUND
I PUT A TRUCK THROUGH YOUR WALL.
YOU DON'T THINK SOMEONE ELSE MIGHT HAVE NOTICED?
I TOLD YOU--ONE OF THE POWERS IS AFTER YOU. GO BACK AND YOU'RE DEAD.
TR
BUT WHY? IT DOESN'T MAKE ANY SENSE! I'M NOT IMPORTANT.
I AGREE WITH YOU.
WELL, THERE'S THE NOVELTY VALUE.
BUT A TEENAGED ARCHANGEL? I THINK MOST FOLKS WITH ANY TASTE WOULD SAY NO THANKS.
THE THING IS, IT'S THE BASANOS YOU'RE UP AGAINST. IT CAN SEE THE FUTURE.
SO OBVIOUSLY THERE'S A FUTURE WHERE YOU GET TO BE IMPORTANT.
41
ON THE DOWN SIDE, THERE'S A WHOLE LOT MORE WHERE YOU GET TO BE A GREASY STAIN.
CAN WE TALK AS WE FLEE?

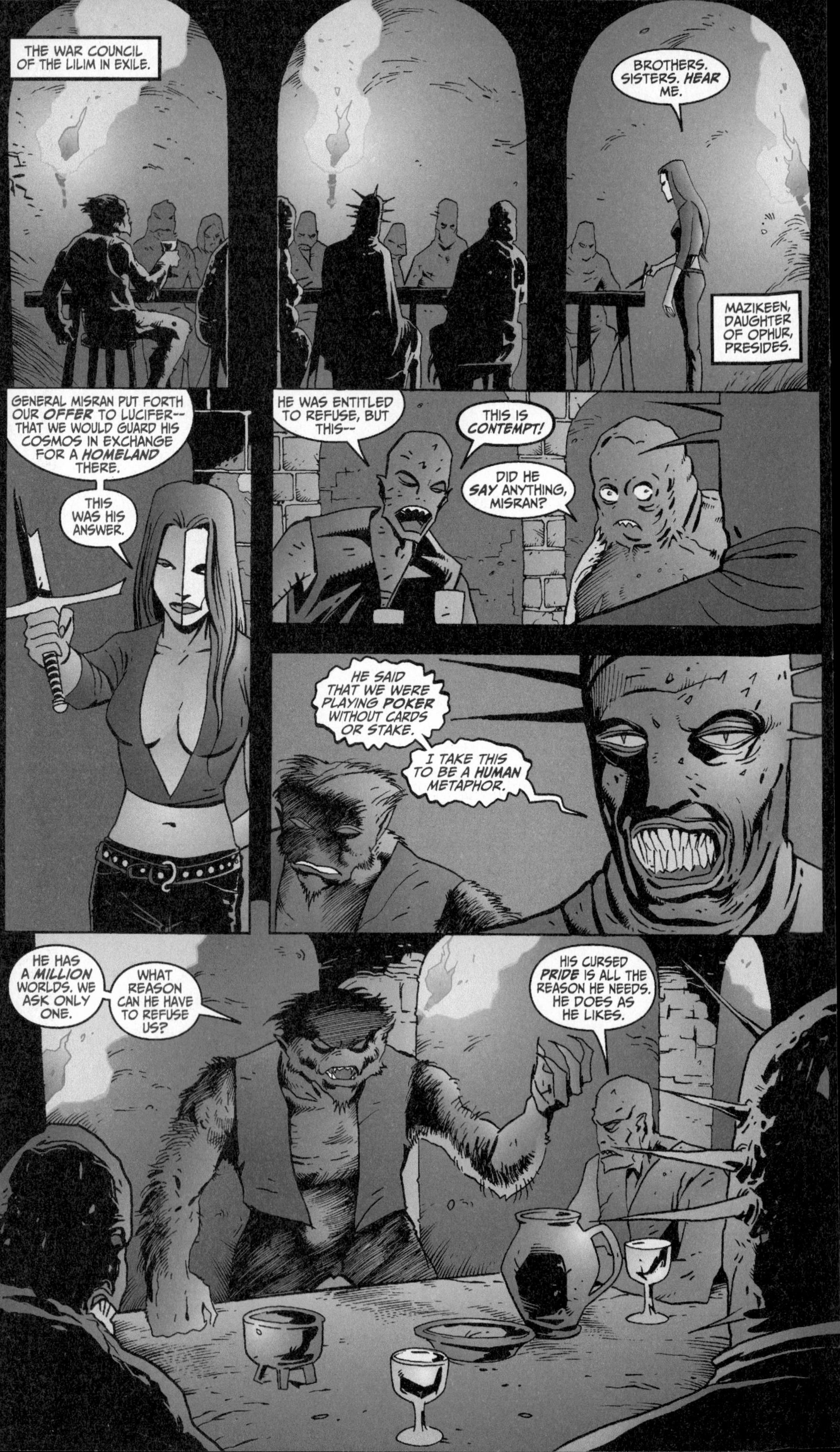
THE WAR COUNCIL OF THE LILIM IN EXILE.
BROTHERS. SISTERS. *HEAR* ME.
MAZIKEEN, DAUGHTER OF OPHUR, PRESIDES.
GENERAL MISRAN PUT FORTH OUR *OFFER* TO LUCIFER-- THAT WE WOULD GUARD HIS COSMOS IN EXCHANGE FOR A *HOMELAND* THERE.
THIS WAS HIS ANSWER.
HE WAS ENTITLED TO REFUSE, BUT THIS--
THIS IS *CONTEMPT!*
DID HE *SAY* ANYTHING, MISRAN?
HE SAID THAT WE WERE PLAYING *POKER* WITHOUT CARDS OR STAKE.
I TAKE THIS TO BE A *HUMAN* METAPHOR.
HE HAS A *MILLION* WORLDS. WE ASK ONLY ONE.
WHAT REASON CAN HE HAVE TO REFUSE US?
HIS CURSED *PRIDE* IS ALL THE REASON HE NEEDS. HE DOES AS HE LIKES.

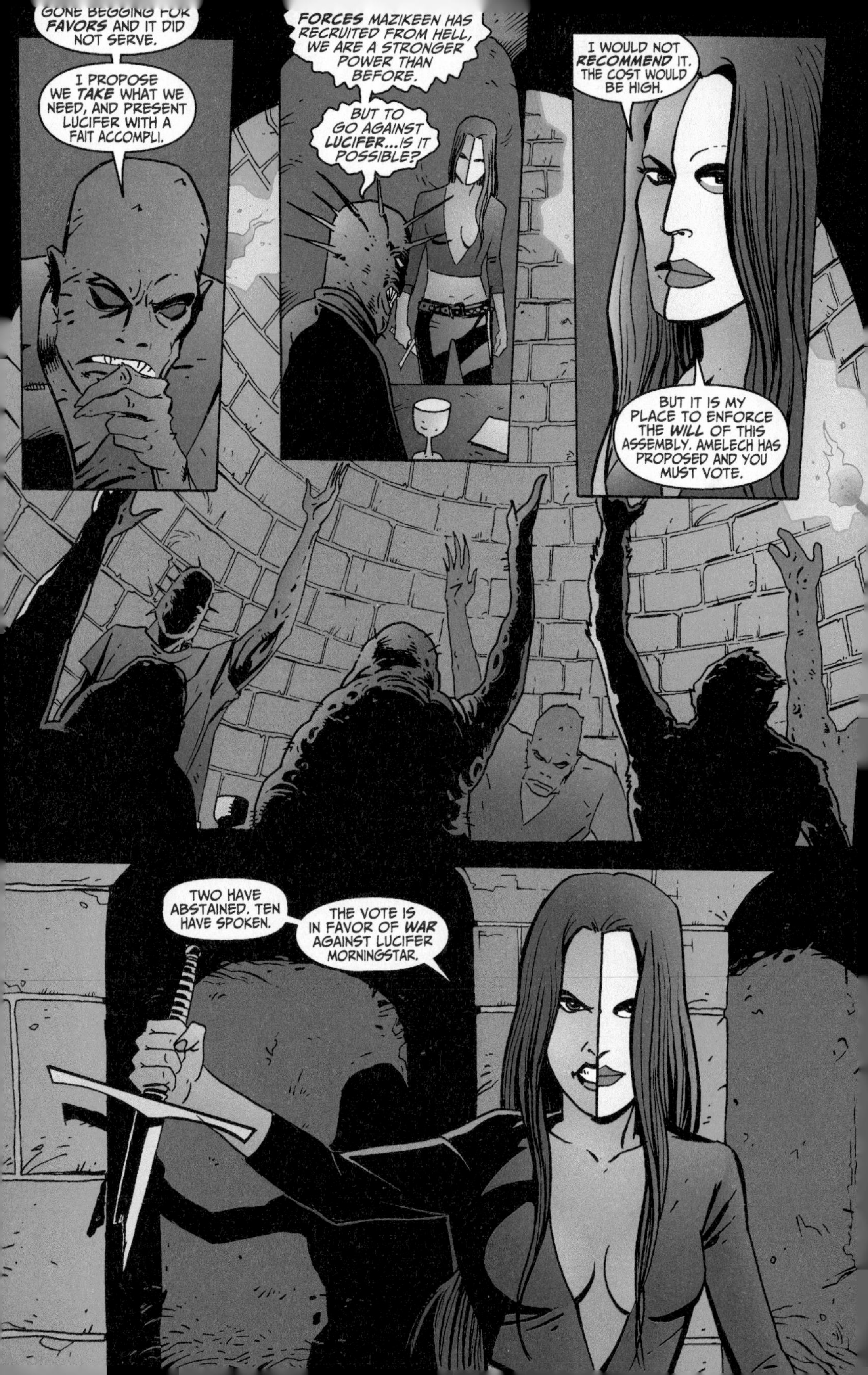
GONE BEGGING FOR FAVORS AND IT DID NOT SERVE.
I PROPOSE WE TAKE WHAT WE NEED, AND PRESENT LUCIFER WITH A FAIT ACCOMPLI.
FORCES MAZIKEEN HAS RECRUITED FROM HELL, WE ARE A STRONGER POWER THAN BEFORE.
BUT TO GO AGAINST LUCIFER...IS IT POSSIBLE?
I WOULD NOT RECOMMEND IT. THE COST WOULD BE HIGH.
BUT IT IS MY PLACE TO ENFORCE THE WILL OF THIS ASSEMBLY. AMELECH HAS PROPOSED AND YOU MUST VOTE.
TWO HAVE ABSTAINED. TEN HAVE SPOKEN.
THE VOTE IS IN FAVOR OF WAR AGAINST LUCIFER MORNINGSTAR.

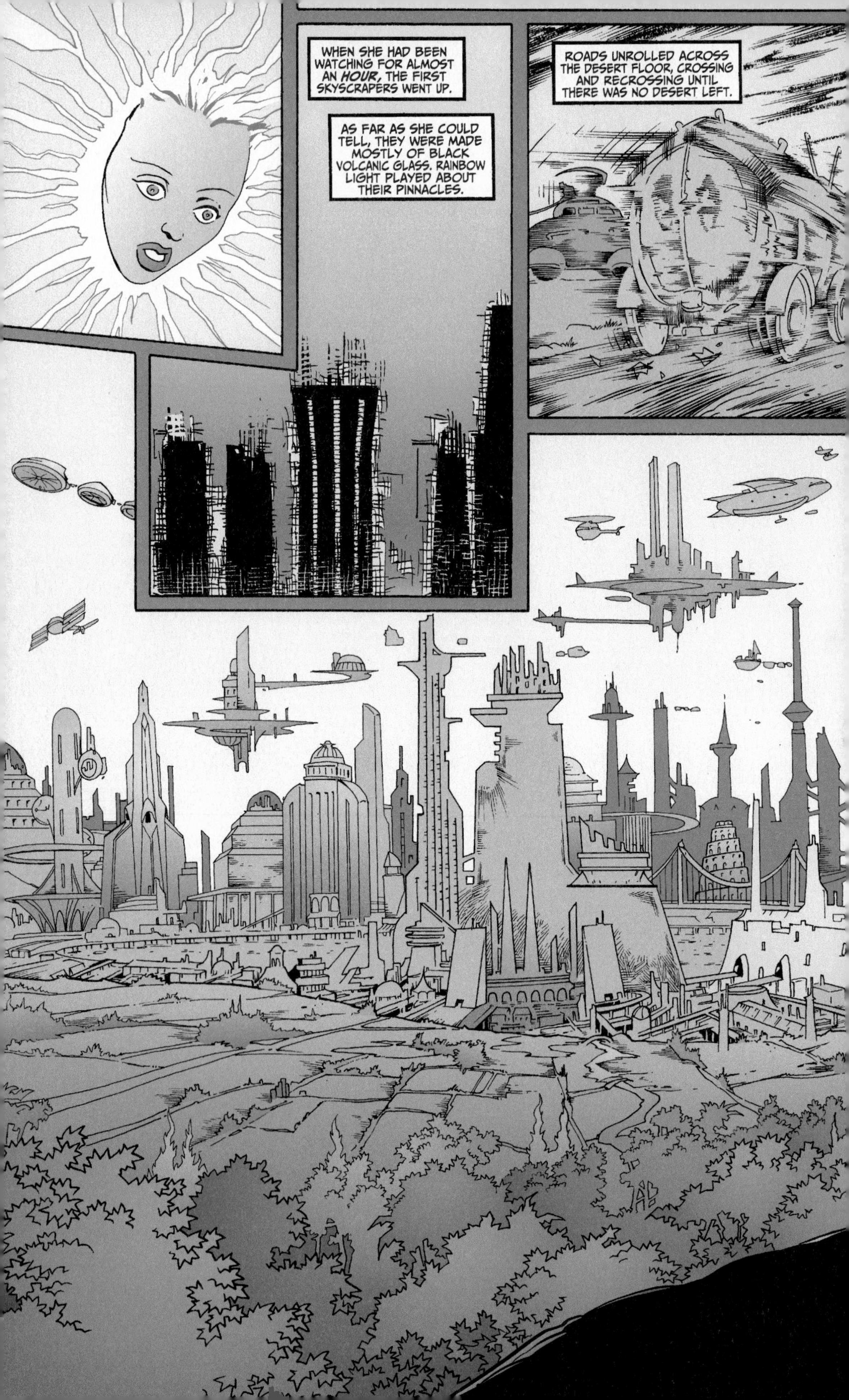
WHEN SHE HAD BEEN WATCHING FOR ALMOST AN *HOUR,* THE FIRST SKYSCRAPERS WENT UP.
AS FAR AS SHE COULD TELL, THEY WERE MADE MOSTLY OF BLACK VOLCANIC GLASS. RAINBOW LIGHT PLAYED ABOUT THEIR PINNACLES.
ROADS UNROLLED ACROSS THE DESERT FLOOR, CROSSING AND RECROSSING UNTIL THERE WAS NO DESERT LEFT.

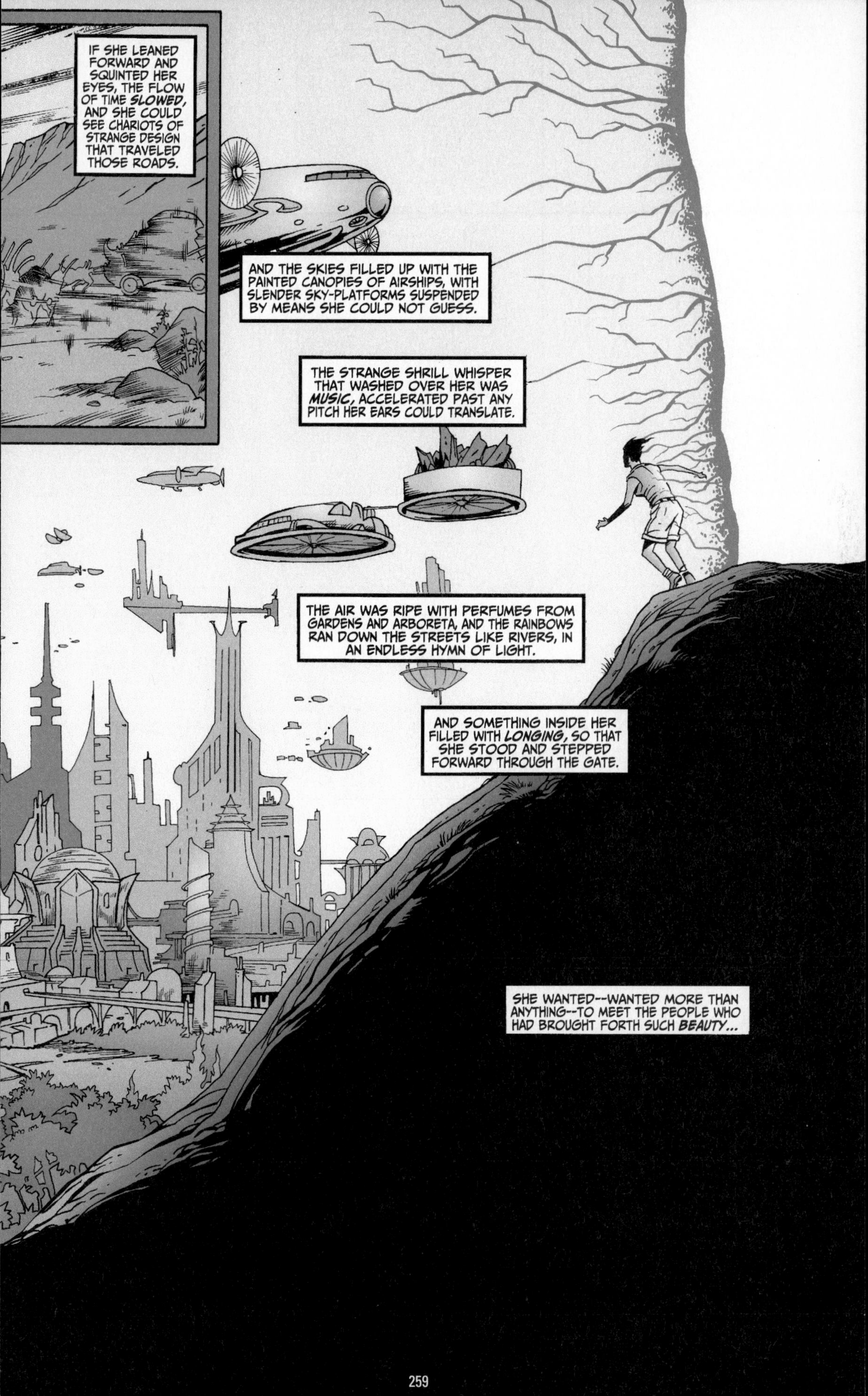
IF SHE LEANED FORWARD AND SQUINTED HER EYES, THE FLOW OF TIME *SLOWED*, AND SHE COULD SEE CHARIOTS OF STRANGE DESIGN THAT TRAVELED THOSE ROADS.
AND THE SKIES FILLED UP WITH THE PAINTED CANOPIES OF AIRSHIPS, WITH SLENDER SKY-PLATFORMS SUSPENDED BY MEANS SHE COULD NOT GUESS.
THE STRANGE SHRILL WHISPER THAT WASHED OVER HER WAS *MUSIC*, ACCELERATED PAST ANY PITCH HER EARS COULD TRANSLATE.
THE AIR WAS RIPE WITH PERFUMES FROM GARDENS AND ARBORETA, AND THE RAINBOWS RAN DOWN THE STREETS LIKE RIVERS, IN AN ENDLESS HYMN OF LIGHT.
AND SOMETHING INSIDE HER FILLED WITH *LONGING*, SO THAT SHE STOOD AND STEPPED FORWARD THROUGH THE GATE.
SHE WANTED--WANTED MORE THAN ANYTHING--TO MEET THE PEOPLE WHO HAD BROUGHT FORTH SUCH *BEAUTY*...

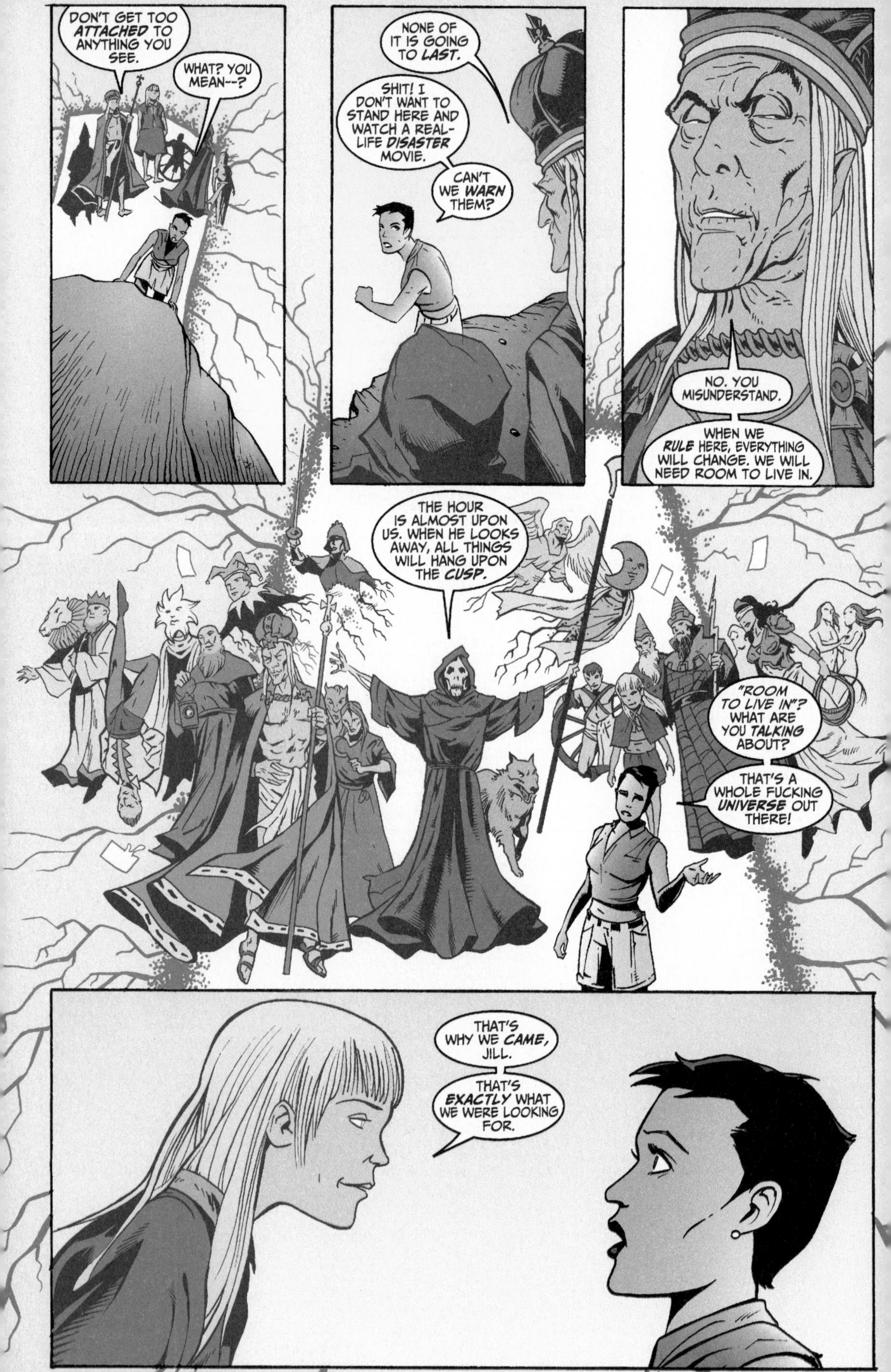
DON'T GET TOO ATTACHED TO ANYTHING YOU SEE.
WHAT? YOU MEAN--?
NONE OF IT IS GOING TO LAST.
SHIT! I DON'T WANT TO STAND HERE AND WATCH A REAL-LIFE DISASTER MOVIE.
CAN'T WE WARN THEM?
NO. YOU MISUNDERSTAND.
WHEN WE RULE HERE, EVERYTHING WILL CHANGE. WE WILL NEED ROOM TO LIVE IN.
THE HOUR IS ALMOST UPON US. WHEN HE LOOKS AWAY, ALL THINGS WILL HANG UPON THE CUSP.
"ROOM TO LIVE IN"? WHAT ARE YOU TALKING ABOUT?
THAT'S A WHOLE FUCKING UNIVERSE OUT THERE!
THAT'S WHY WE CAME, JILL.
THAT'S EXACTLY WHAT WE WERE LOOKING FOR.

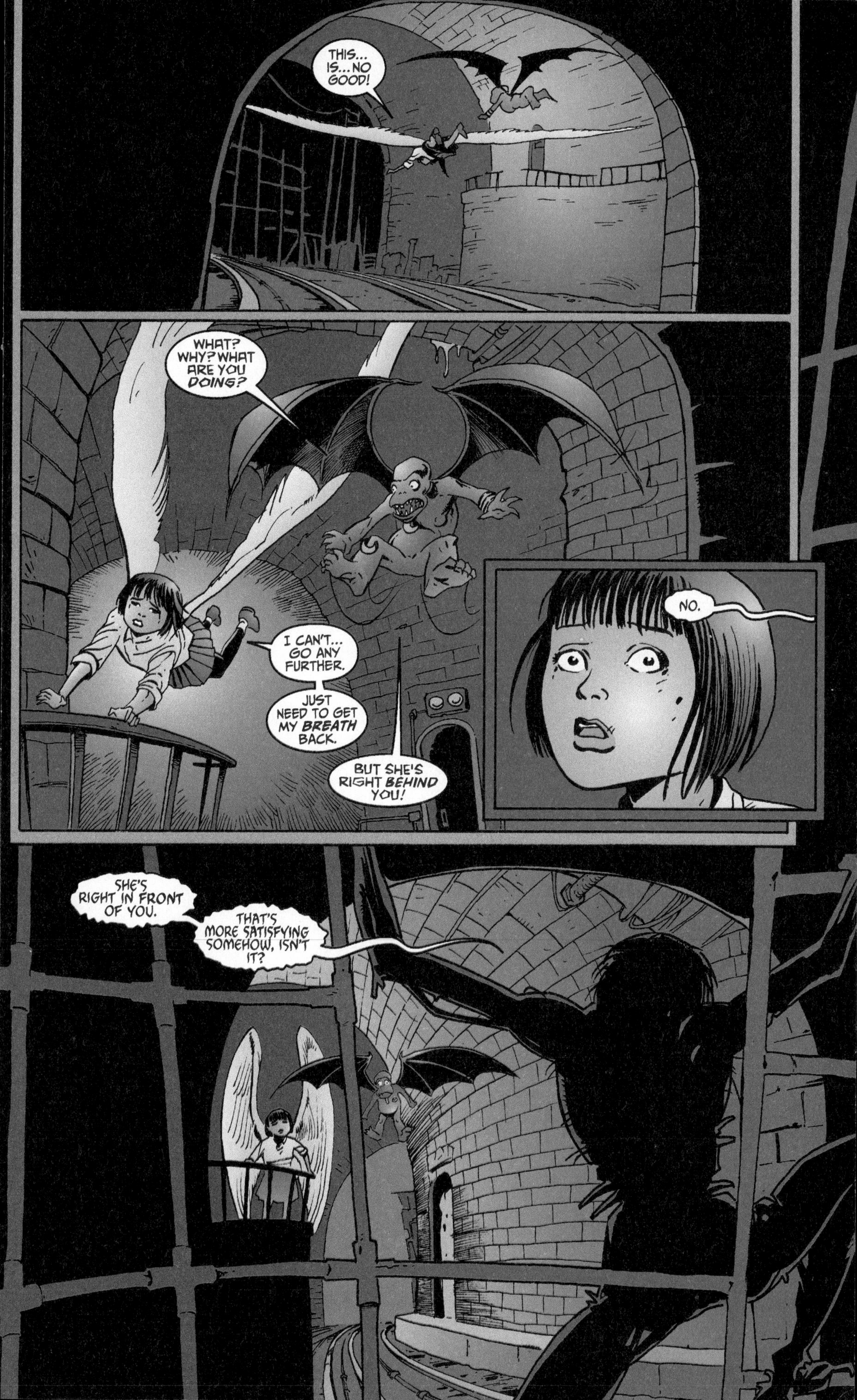
THIS... IS...NO GOOD!
WHAT? WHY? WHAT ARE YOU DOING?
I CAN'T... GO ANY FURTHER.
JUST NEED TO GET MY BREATH BACK.
BUT SHE'S RIGHT BEHIND YOU!
NO.
SHE'S RIGHT IN FRONT OF YOU.
THAT'S MORE SATISFYING SOMEHOW, ISN'T IT?

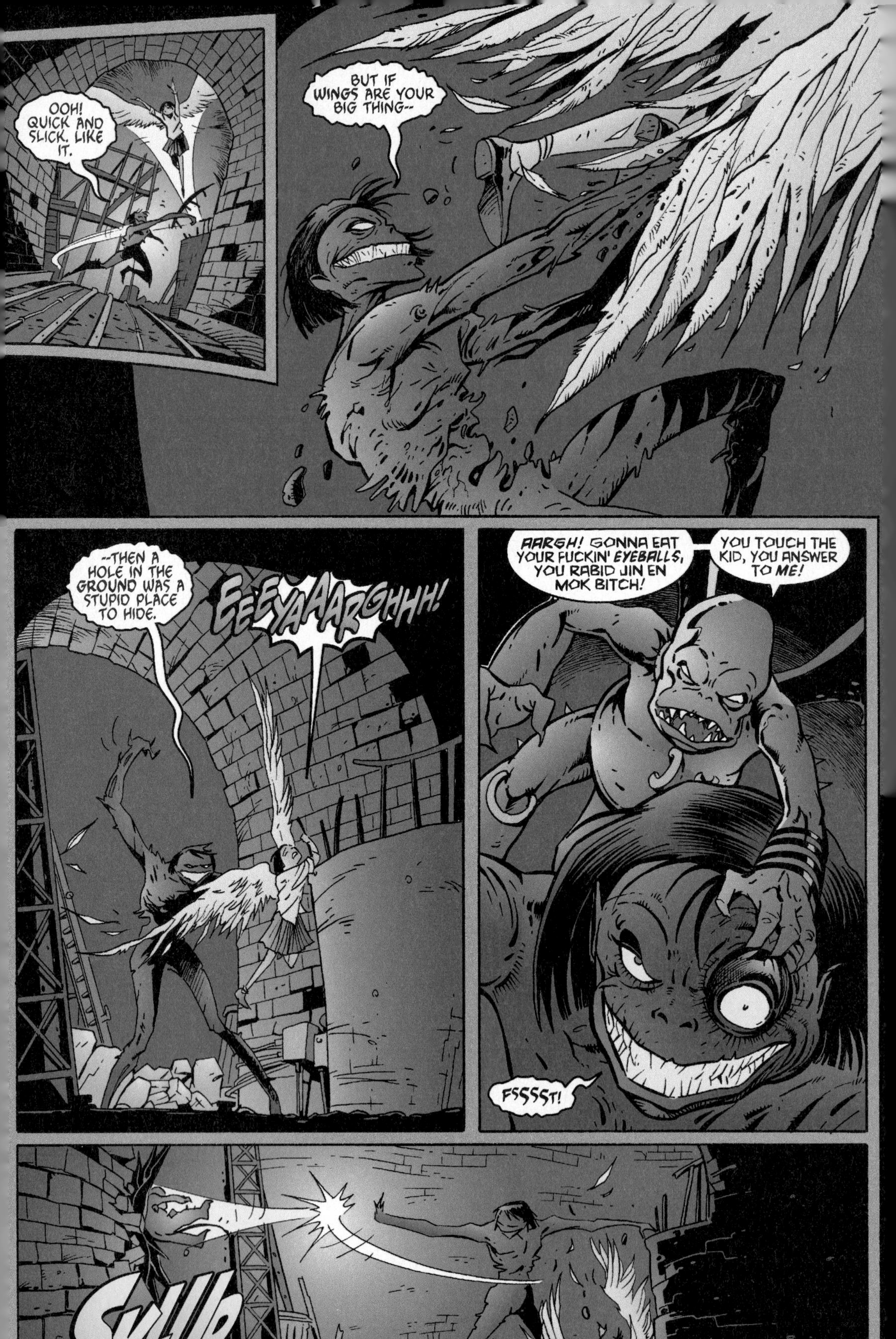
OOH! QUICK AND SLICK. LIKE IT.
BUT IF WINGS ARE YOUR BIG THING--
--THEN A HOLE IN THE GROUND WAS A STUPID PLACE TO HIDE.
EEEYAAARGHHH!
AARGH! GONNA EAT YOUR FUCKIN' EYEBALLS, YOU RABID JIN EN MOK BITCH!
YOU TOUCH THE KID, YOU ANSWER TO ME!
FSSSST!
SKLUP

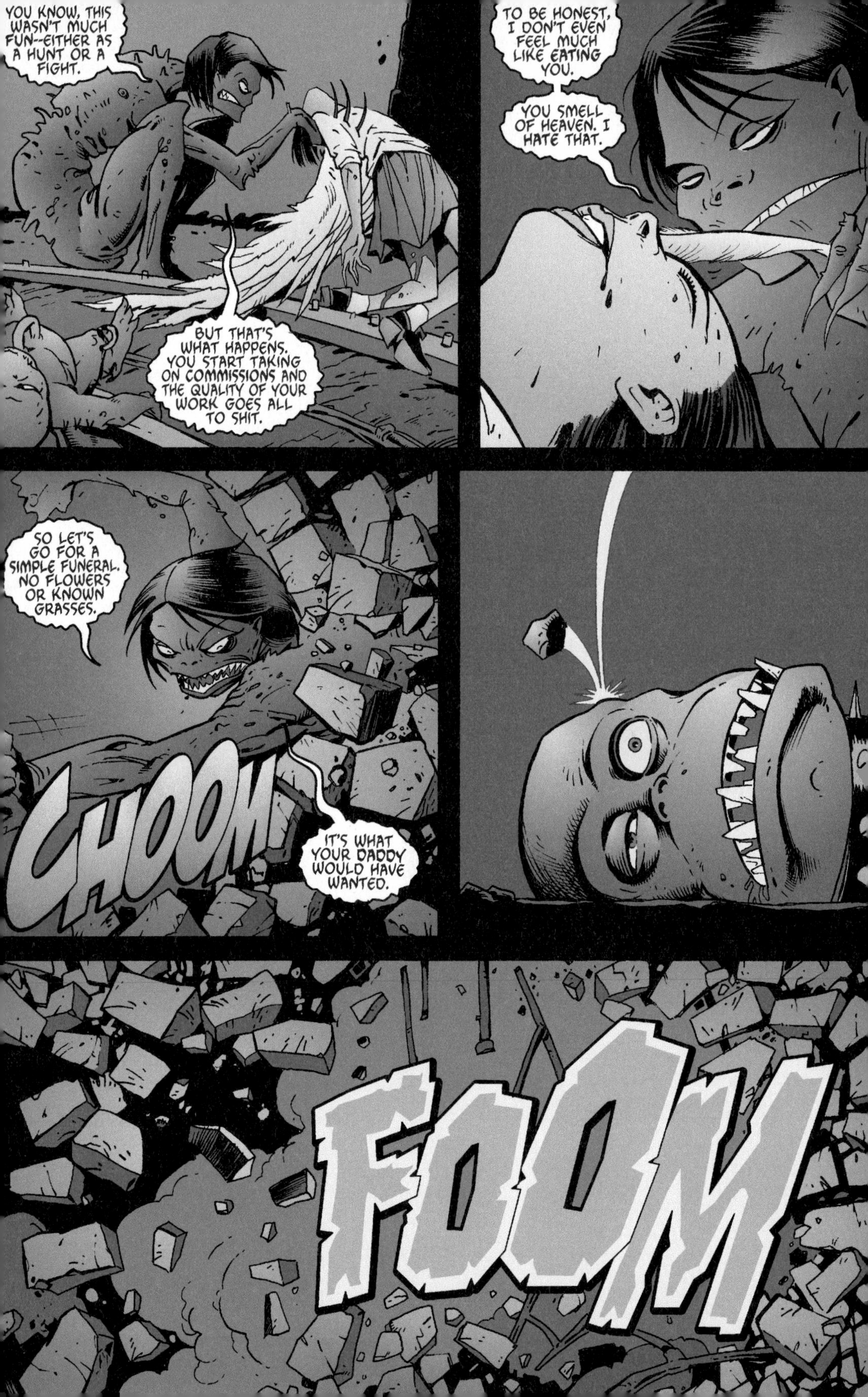
YOU KNOW, THIS WASN'T MUCH FUN--EITHER AS A HUNT OR A FIGHT.
BUT THAT'S WHAT HAPPENS. YOU START TAKING ON COMMISSIONS AND THE QUALITY OF YOUR WORK GOES ALL TO SHIT.
TO BE HONEST, I DON'T EVEN FEEL MUCH LIKE EATING YOU.
YOU SMELL OF HEAVEN. I HATE THAT.
SO LET'S GO FOR A SIMPLE FUNERAL. NO FLOWERS OR KNOWN GRASSES.
CHOOM
IT'S WHAT YOUR DADDY WOULD HAVE WANTED.
FOOM

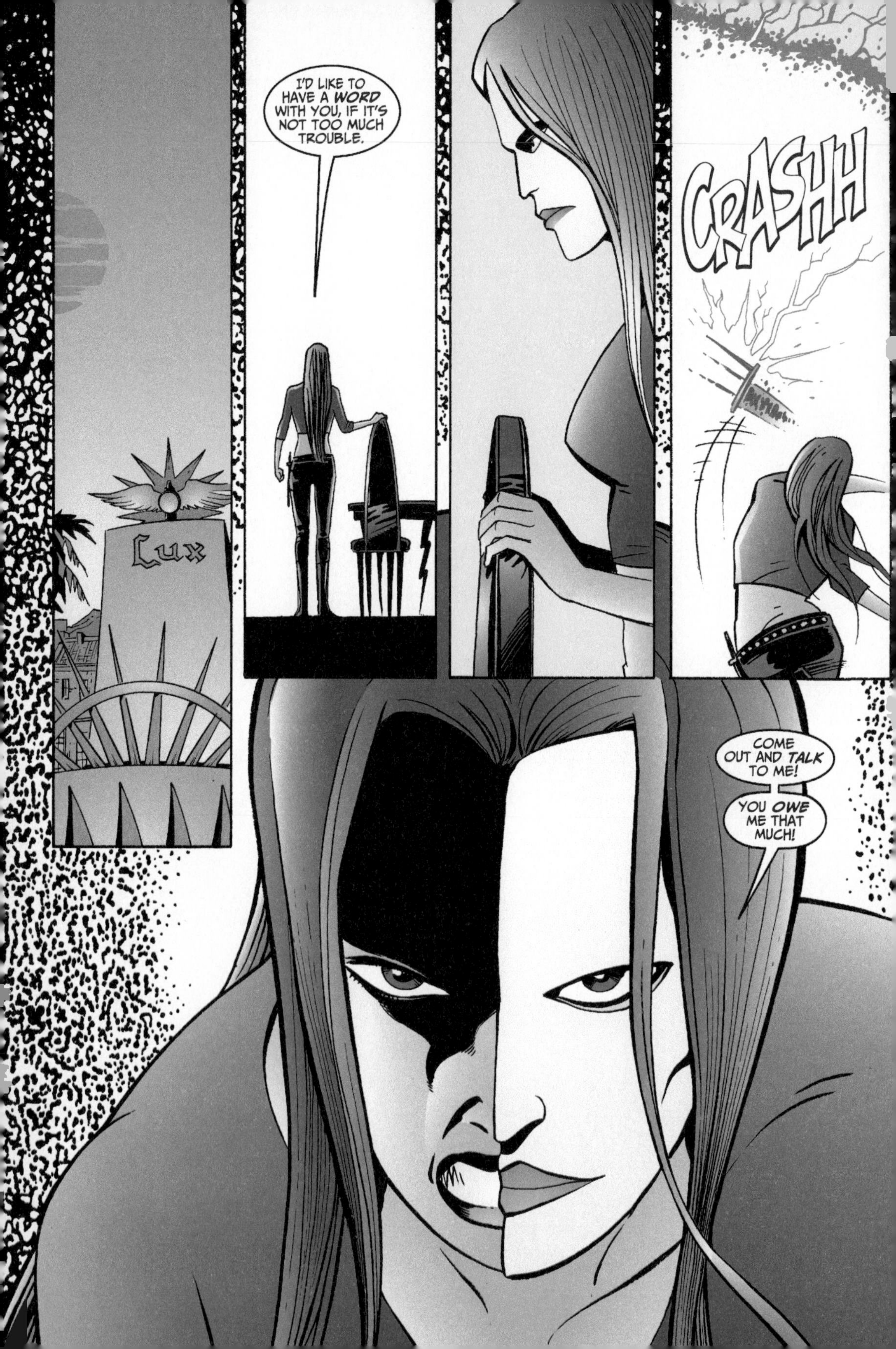
Lux
I'D LIKE TO HAVE A WORD WITH YOU, IF IT'S NOT TOO MUCH TROUBLE.
CRASHH
COME OUT AND TALK TO ME!
YOU OWE ME THAT MUCH!

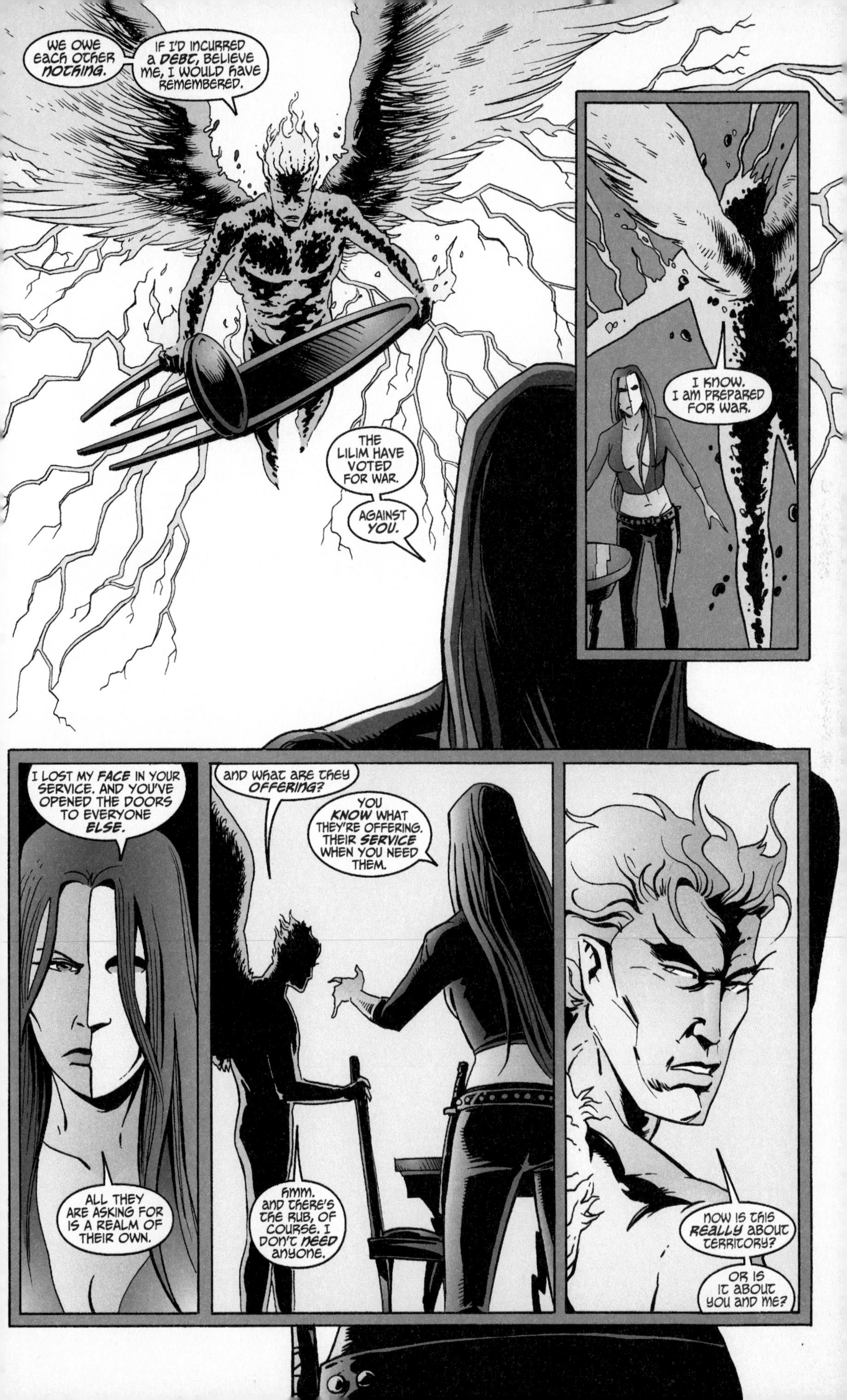

WE OWE EACH OTHER NOTHING.
IF I'D INCURRED A DEBT, BELIEVE ME, I WOULD HAVE REMEMBERED.
THE LILIM HAVE VOTED FOR WAR.
AGAINST YOU.
I KNOW. I AM PREPARED FOR WAR.
I LOST MY FACE IN YOUR SERVICE. AND YOU'VE OPENED THE DOORS TO EVERYONE ELSE.
ALL THEY ARE ASKING FOR IS A REALM OF THEIR OWN.
AND WHAT ARE THEY OFFERING?
YOU KNOW WHAT THEY'RE OFFERING. THEIR SERVICE WHEN YOU NEED THEM.
HMM. AND THERE'S THE RUB, OF COURSE. I DON'T NEED ANYONE.
NOW IS THIS REALLY ABOUT TERRITORY?
OR IS IT ABOUT YOU AND ME?

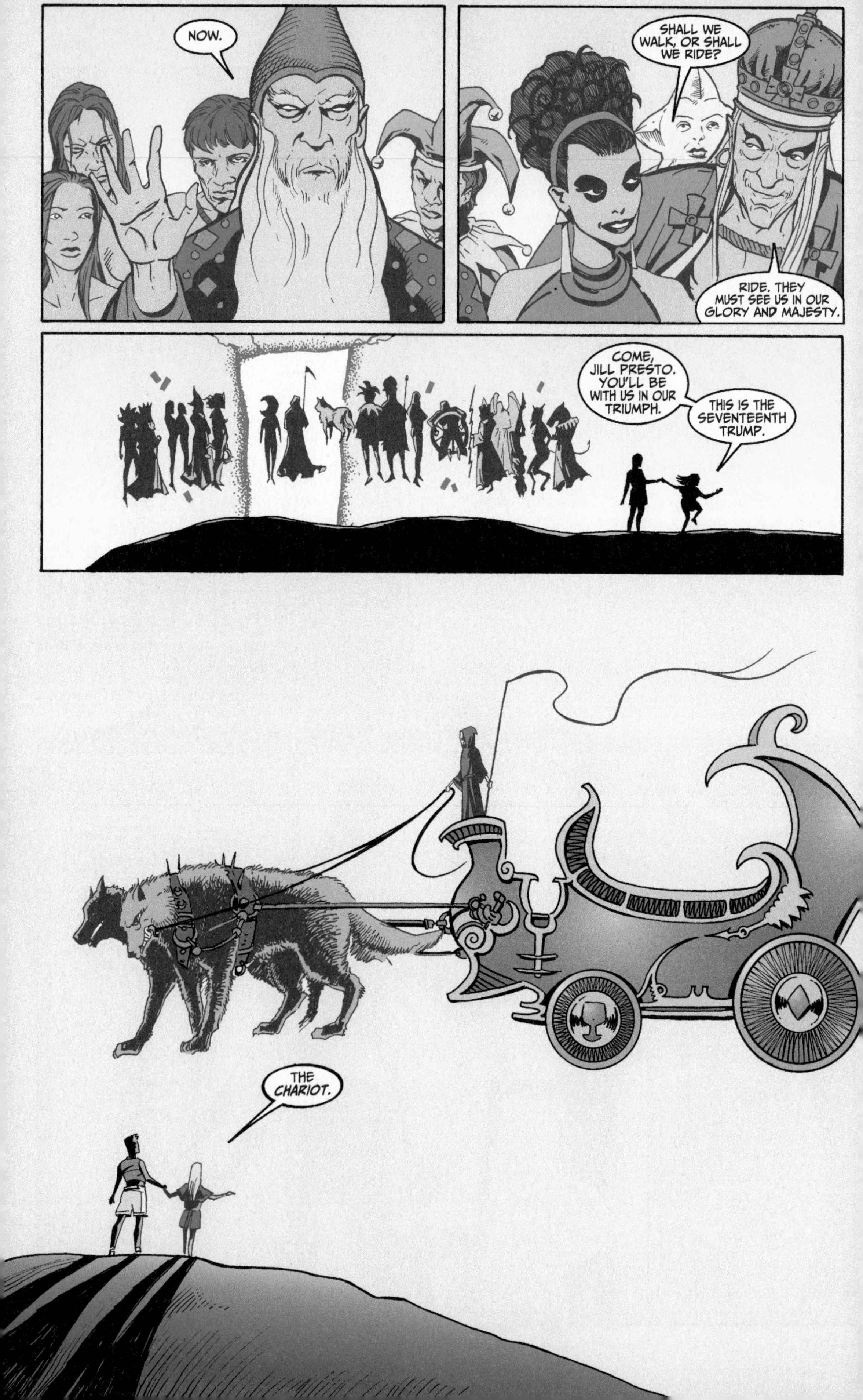
NOW.
SHALL WE WALK, OR SHALL WE RIDE?
RIDE. THEY MUST SEE US IN OUR GLORY AND MAJESTY.
COME, JILL PRESTO. YOU'LL BE WITH US IN OUR TRIUMPH.
THIS IS THE SEVENTEENTH TRUMP.
THE CHARIOT.

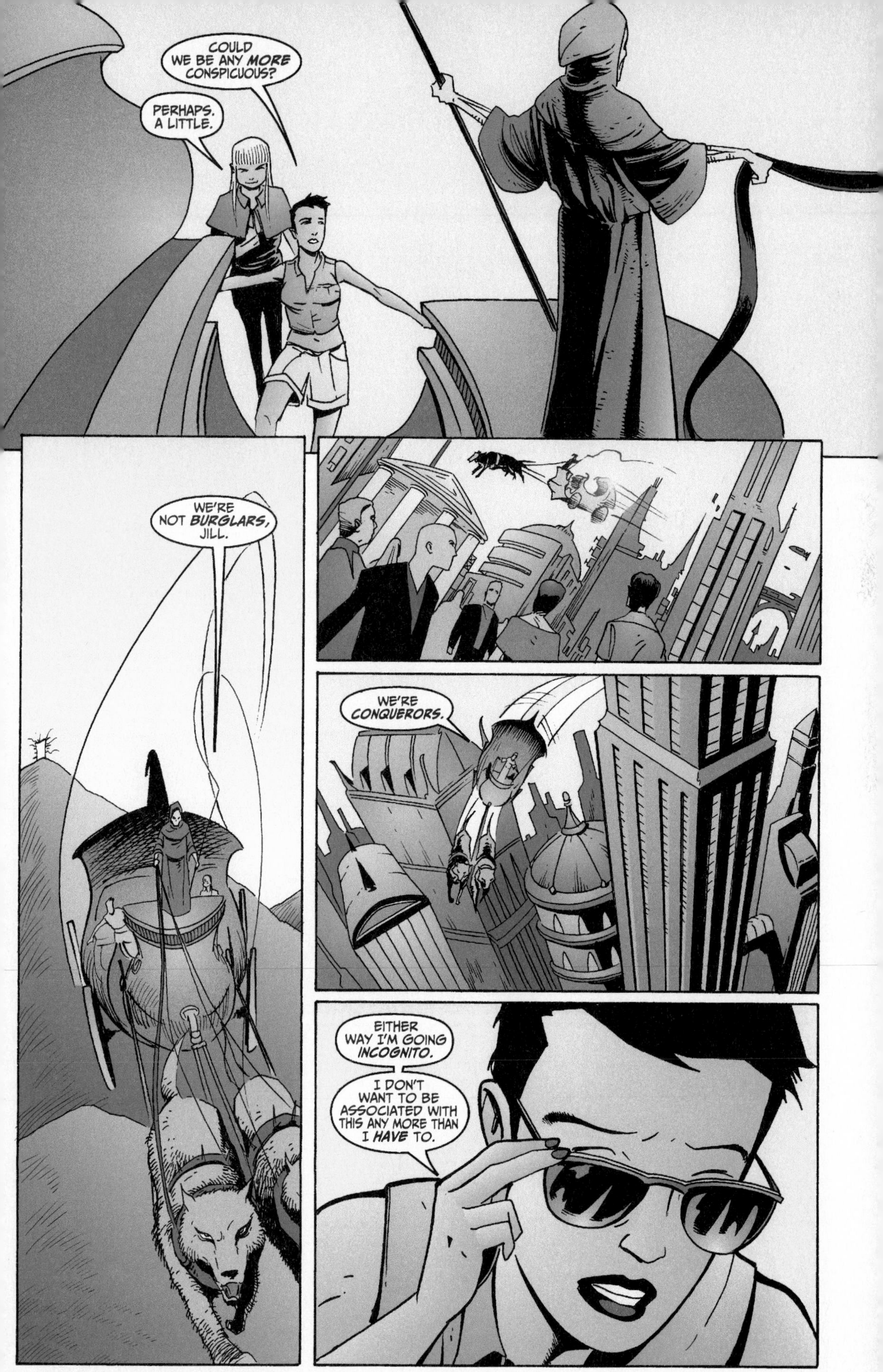

COULD WE BE ANY *MORE* CONSPICUOUS?
PERHAPS. A LITTLE.
WE'RE NOT *BURGLARS,* JILL.
WE'RE *CONQUERORS.*
EITHER WAY I'M GOING *INCOGNITO.*
I DON'T WANT TO BE ASSOCIATED WITH THIS ANY MORE THAN I *HAVE* TO.

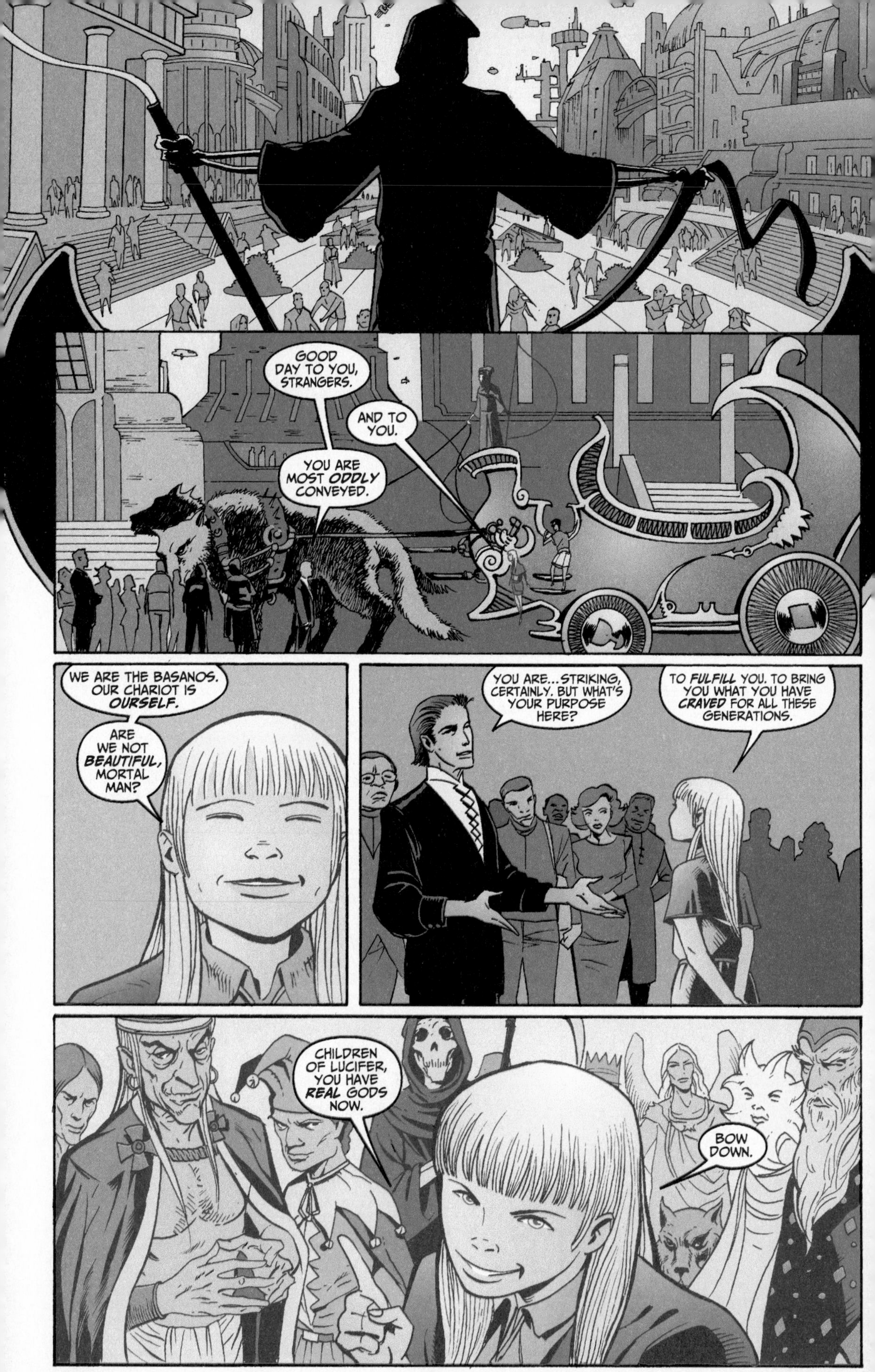
GOOD DAY TO YOU, STRANGERS.
AND TO YOU.
YOU ARE MOST ODDLY CONVEYED.
WE ARE THE BASANOS. OUR CHARIOT IS OURSELF.
ARE WE NOT BEAUTIFUL, MORTAL MAN?
YOU ARE...STRIKING, CERTAINLY. BUT WHAT'S YOUR PURPOSE HERE?
TO FULFILL YOU. TO BRING YOU WHAT YOU HAVE CRAVED FOR ALL THESE GENERATIONS.
CHILDREN OF LUCIFER, YOU HAVE REAL GODS NOW.
BOW DOWN.

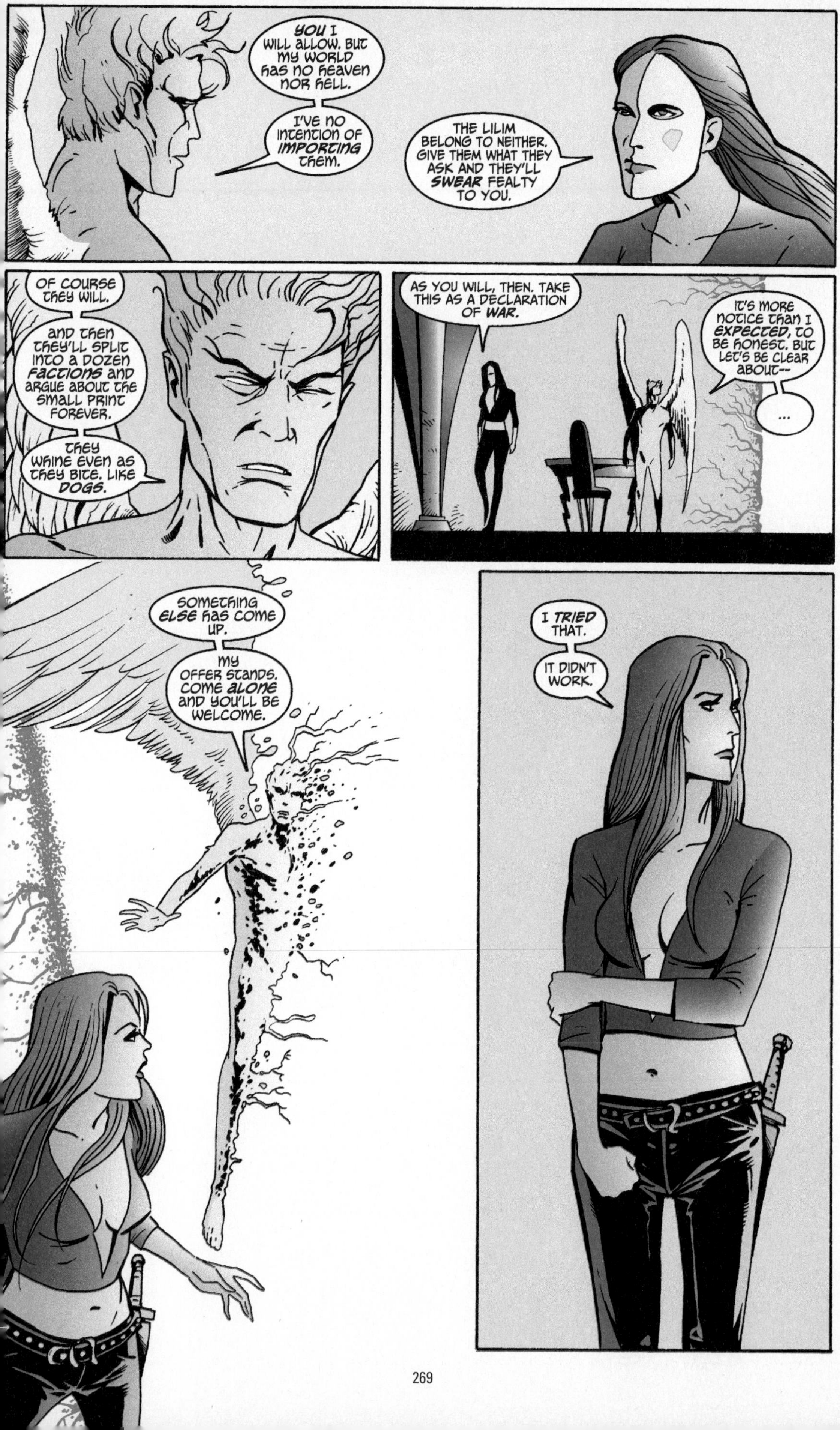
YOU I WILL ALLOW. BUT MY WORLD HAS NO HEAVEN NOR HELL.
I'VE NO INTENTION OF IMPORTING THEM.
THE LILIM BELONG TO NEITHER. GIVE THEM WHAT THEY ASK AND THEY'LL SWEAR FEALTY TO YOU.
OF COURSE THEY WILL.
AND THEN THEY'LL SPLIT INTO A DOZEN FACTIONS AND ARGUE ABOUT THE SMALL PRINT FOREVER.
THEY WHINE EVEN AS THEY BITE. LIKE DOGS.
AS YOU WILL, THEN. TAKE THIS AS A DECLARATION OF WAR.
IT'S MORE NOTICE THAN I EXPECTED, TO BE HONEST. BUT LET'S BE CLEAR ABOUT--
...
SOMETHING ELSE HAS COME UP.
MY OFFER STANDS. COME ALONE AND YOU'LL BE WELCOME.
I TRIED THAT.
IT DIDN'T WORK.

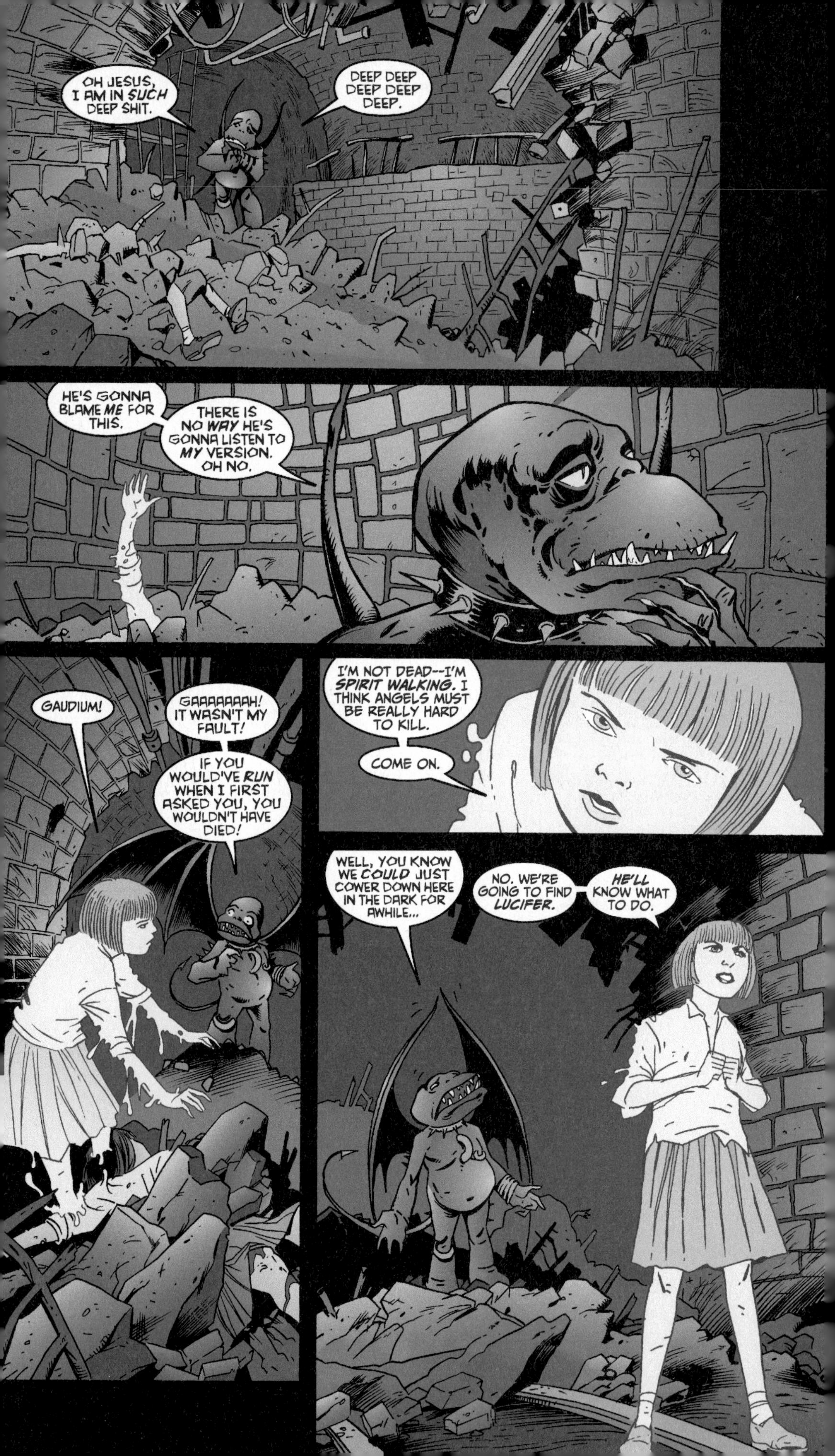
OH JESUS, I AM IN SUCH DEEP SHIT.
DEEP DEEP DEEP DEEP DEEP.
HE'S GONNA BLAME ME FOR THIS.
THERE IS NO WAY HE'S GONNA LISTEN TO MY VERSION. OH NO.
GAUDIUM!
GAAAAAAAH! IT WASN'T MY FAULT!
IF YOU WOULD'VE RUN WHEN I FIRST ASKED YOU, YOU WOULDN'T HAVE DIED!
I'M NOT DEAD--I'M SPIRIT WALKING. I THINK ANGELS MUST BE REALLY HARD TO KILL.
COME ON.
WELL, YOU KNOW WE COULD JUST COWER DOWN HERE IN THE DARK FOR AWHILE...
NO. WE'RE GOING TO FIND LUCIFER.
HE'LL KNOW WHAT TO DO.

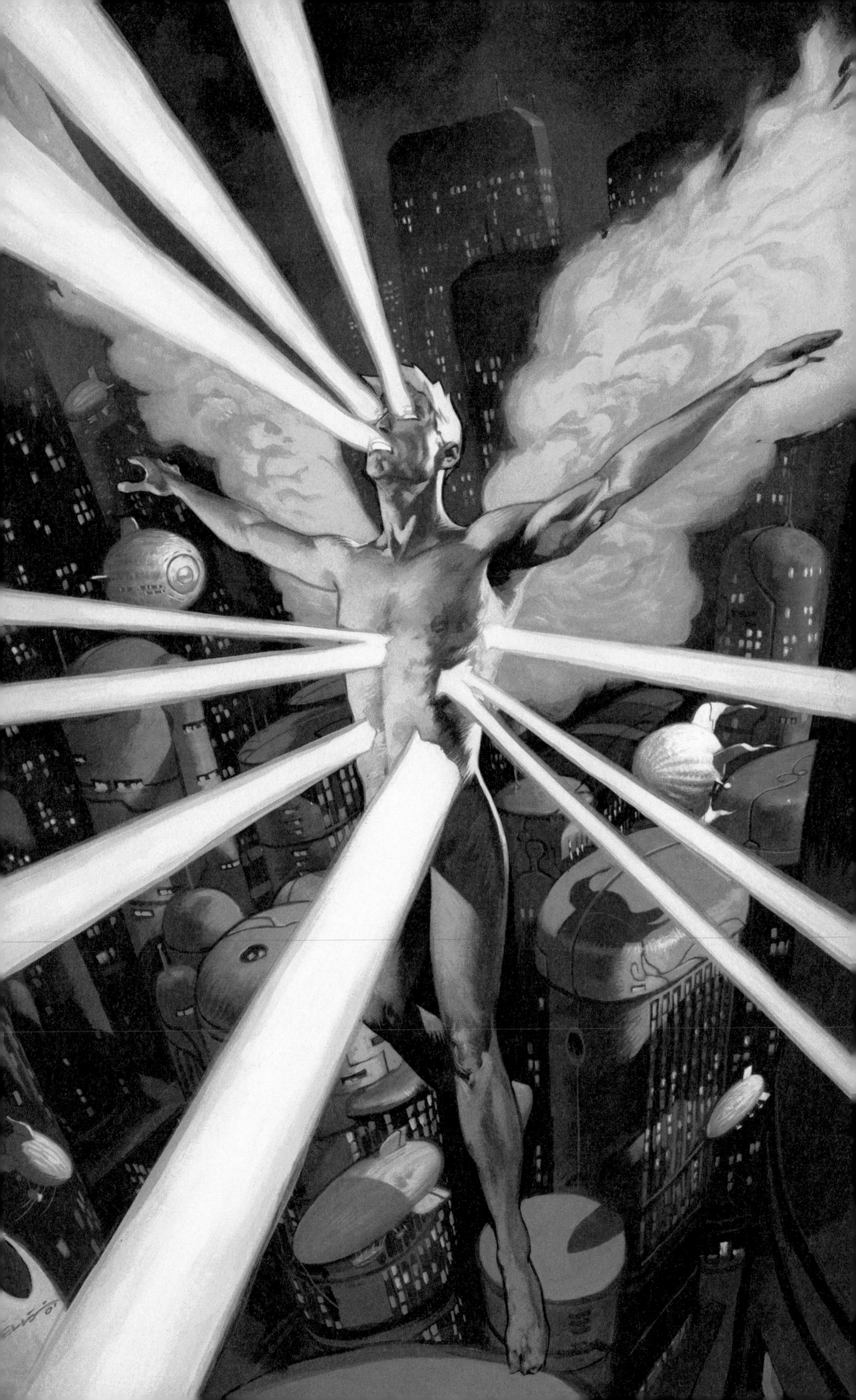

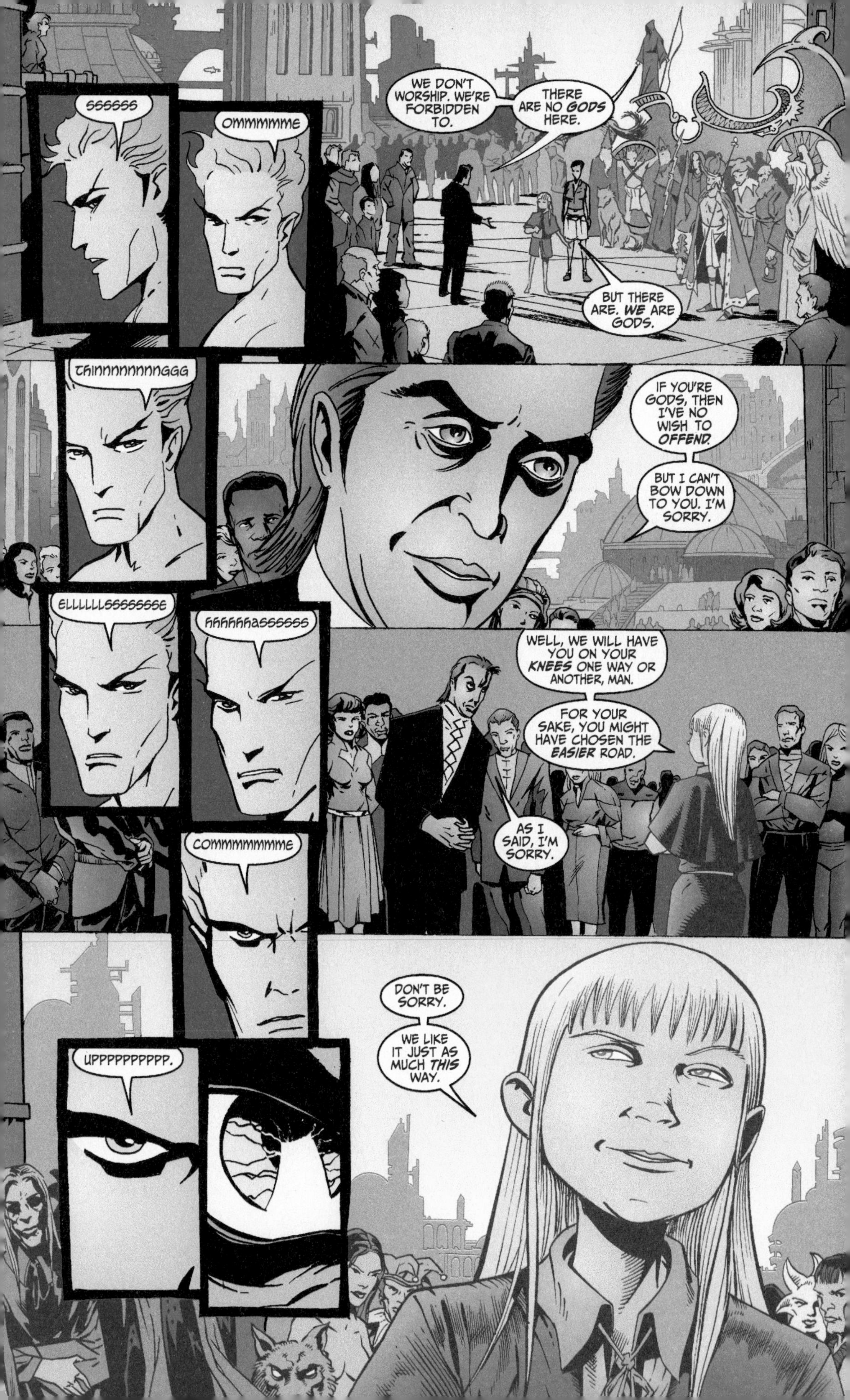
SSSSSS
OMMMMME
WE DON'T WORSHIP. WE'RE FORBIDDEN TO.
THERE ARE NO GODS HERE.
BUT THERE ARE. WE ARE GODS.
THINNNNNNNNNGGG
IF YOU'RE GODS, THEN I'VE NO WISH TO OFFEND.
BUT I CAN'T BOW DOWN TO YOU. I'M SORRY.
ELLLLLLLSSSSSSSE
HHHHHHASSSSSSS
WELL, WE WILL HAVE YOU ON YOUR KNEES ONE WAY OR ANOTHER, MAN.
FOR YOUR SAKE, YOU MIGHT HAVE CHOSEN THE EASIER ROAD.
AS I SAID, I'M SORRY.
COMMMMMMMME
UPPPPPPPPPP.
DON'T BE SORRY.
WE LIKE IT JUST AS MUCH THIS WAY.

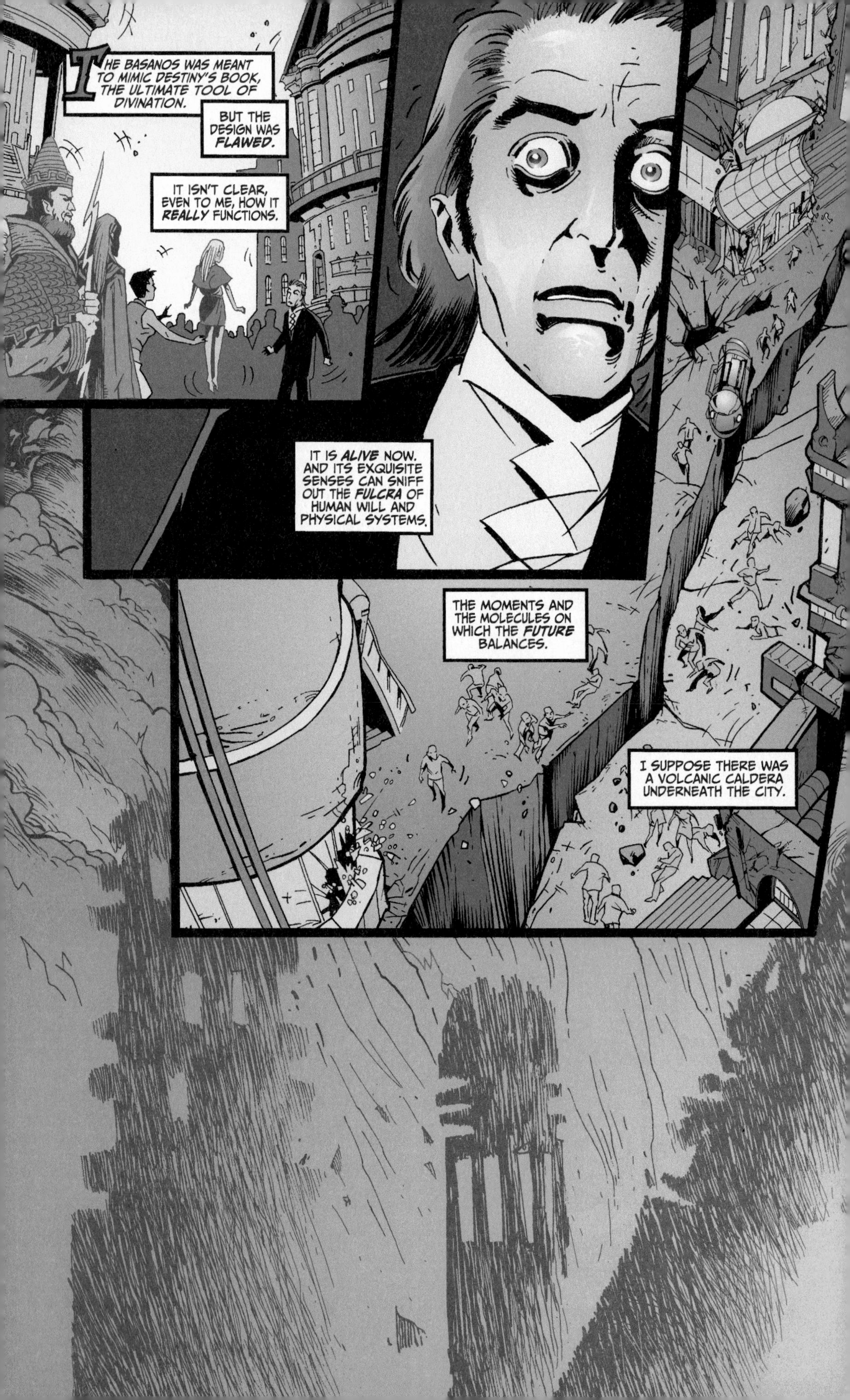
THE BASANOS WAS MEANT TO MIMIC DESTINY'S BOOK, THE ULTIMATE TOOL OF DIVINATION.
BUT THE DESIGN WAS FLAWED.
IT ISN'T CLEAR, EVEN TO ME, HOW IT REALLY FUNCTIONS.
IT IS ALIVE NOW. AND ITS EXQUISITE SENSES CAN SNIFF OUT THE FULCRA OF HUMAN WILL AND PHYSICAL SYSTEMS.
THE MOMENTS AND THE MOLECULES ON WHICH THE FUTURE BALANCES.
I SUPPOSE THERE WAS A VOLCANIC CALDERA UNDERNEATH THE CITY.

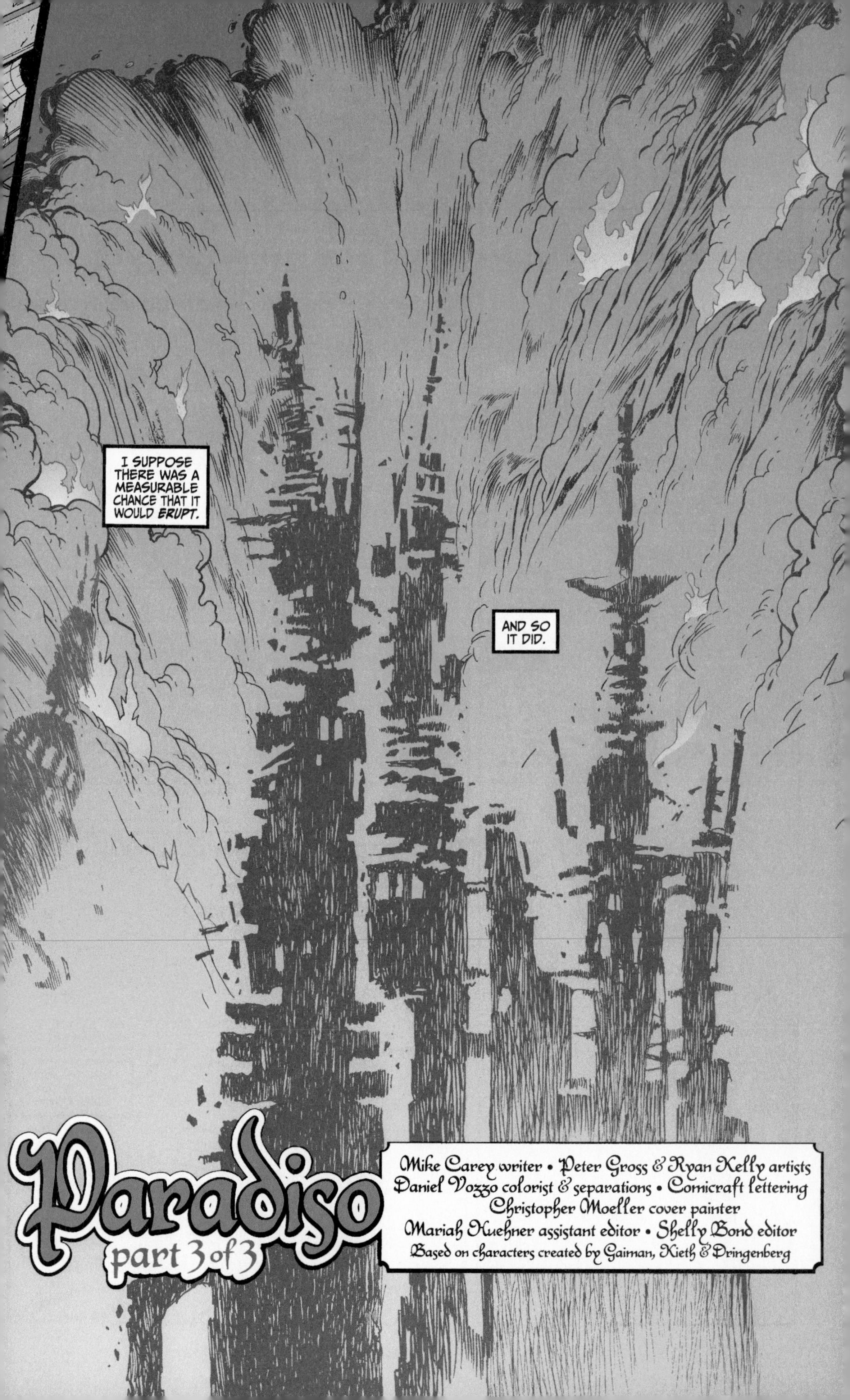
I SUPPOSE THERE WAS A MEASURABLE CHANCE THAT IT WOULD ERUPT.
AND SO IT DID.
Paradiso
part 3 of 3
Mike Carey writer • Peter Gross & Ryan Kelly artists
Daniel Vozzo colorist & separations • Comicraft lettering
Christopher Moeller cover painter
Mariah Huehner assistant editor • Shelly Bond editor
Based on characters created by Gaiman, Kieth & Dringenberg

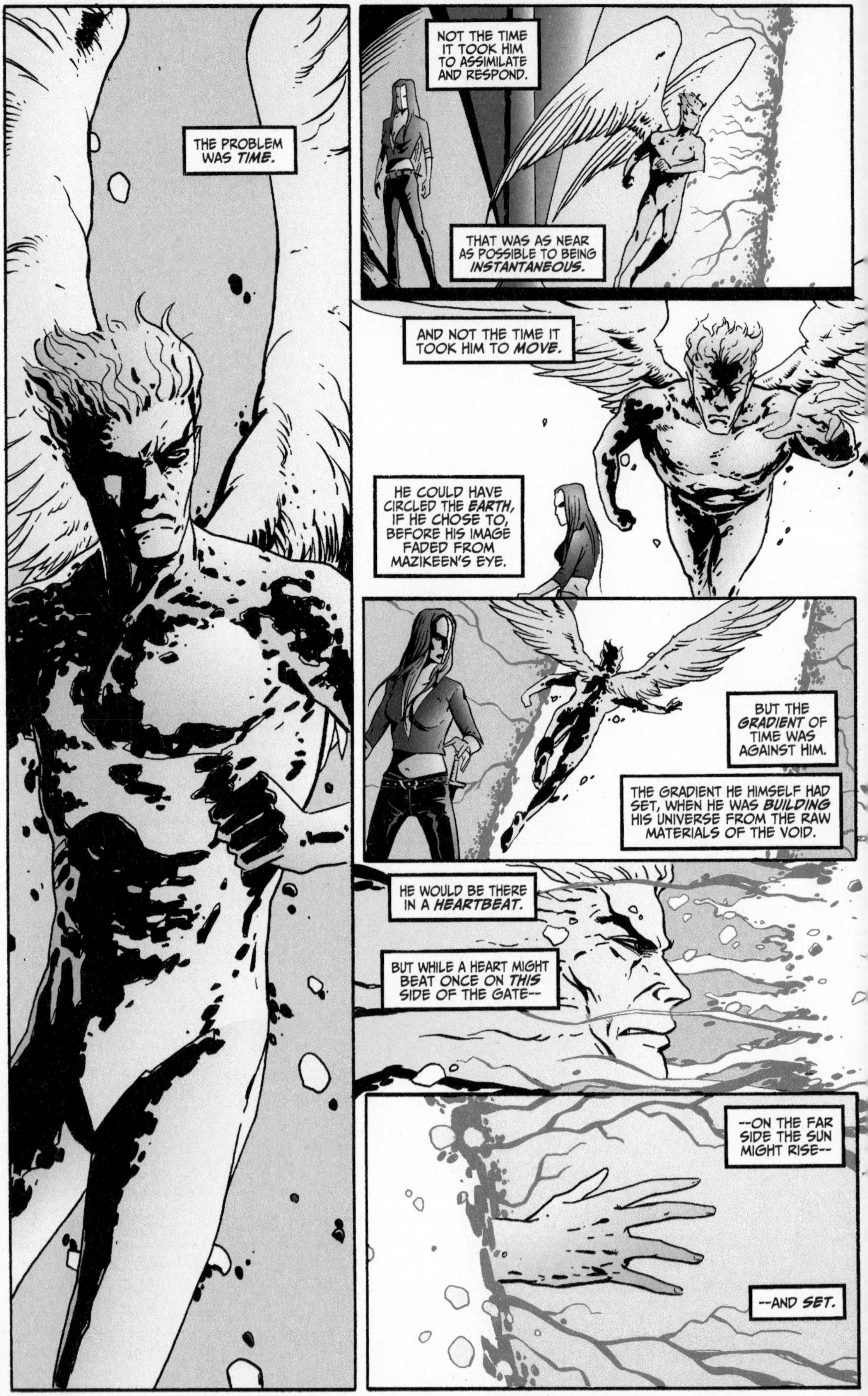
THE PROBLEM WAS *TIME.*
NOT THE TIME IT TOOK HIM TO ASSIMILATE AND RESPOND.
THAT WAS AS NEAR AS POSSIBLE TO BEING *INSTANTANEOUS.*
AND NOT THE TIME IT TOOK HIM TO *MOVE.*
HE COULD HAVE CIRCLED THE *EARTH,* IF HE CHOSE TO, BEFORE HIS IMAGE FADED FROM MAZIKEEN'S EYE.
BUT THE *GRADIENT* OF TIME WAS AGAINST HIM.
THE GRADIENT HE HIMSELF HAD SET, WHEN HE WAS *BUILDING* HIS UNIVERSE FROM THE RAW MATERIALS OF THE VOID.
HE WOULD BE THERE IN A *HEARTBEAT.*
BUT WHILE A HEART MIGHT BEAT ONCE ON *THIS* SIDE OF THE GATE--
--ON THE FAR SIDE THE SUN MIGHT RISE--
--AND *SET.*

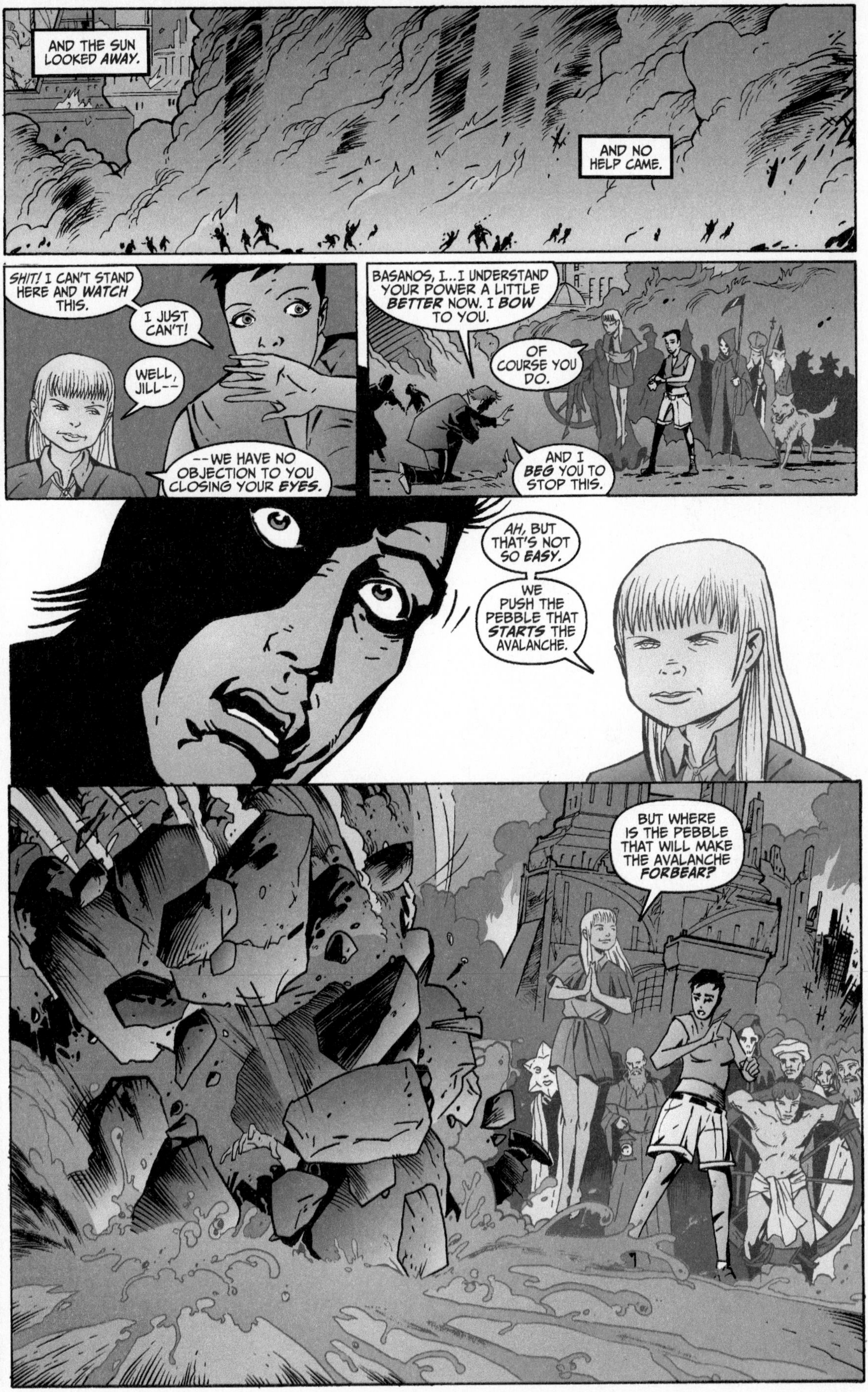
AND THE SUN LOOKED AWAY.
AND NO HELP CAME.
SHIT! I CAN'T STAND HERE AND WATCH THIS.
I JUST CAN'T!
WELL, JILL--
--WE HAVE NO OBJECTION TO YOU CLOSING YOUR EYES.
BASANOS, I...I UNDERSTAND YOUR POWER A LITTLE BETTER NOW. I BOW TO YOU.
OF COURSE YOU DO.
AND I BEG YOU TO STOP THIS.
AH, BUT THAT'S NOT SO EASY.
WE PUSH THE PEBBLE THAT STARTS THE AVALANCHE.
BUT WHERE IS THE PEBBLE THAT WILL MAKE THE AVALANCHE FORBEAR?

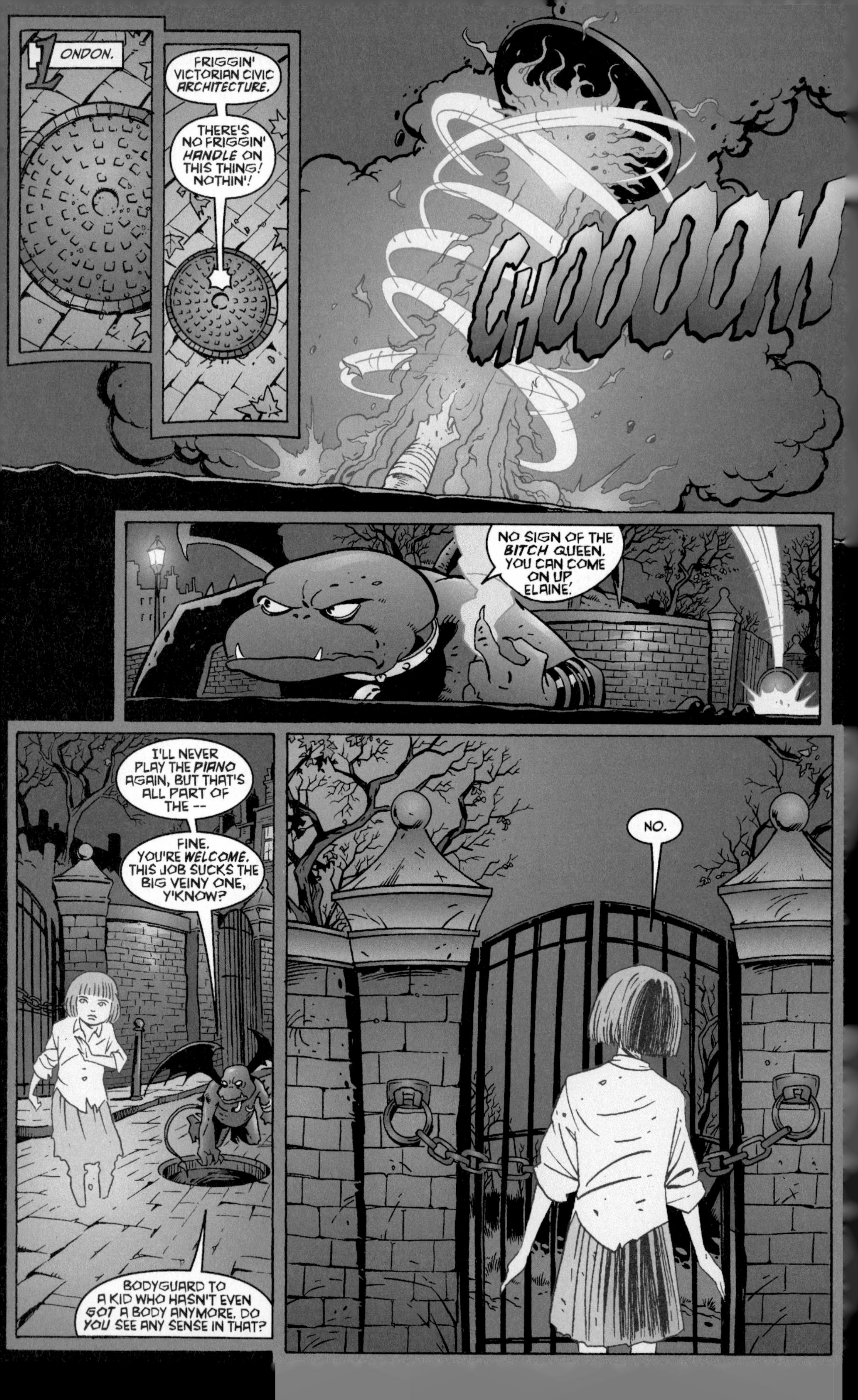
LONDON.
FRIGGIN' VICTORIAN CIVIC ARCHITECTURE.
THERE'S NO FRIGGIN' HANDLE ON THIS THING! NOTHIN'!
CHOOOOOM
NO SIGN OF THE BITCH QUEEN. YOU CAN COME ON UP ELAINE.
I'LL NEVER PLAY THE PIANO AGAIN, BUT THAT'S ALL PART OF THE --
FINE. YOU'RE WELCOME. THIS JOB SUCKS THE BIG VEINY ONE, Y'KNOW?
BODYGUARD TO A KID WHO HASN'T EVEN GOT A BODY ANYMORE. DO YOU SEE ANY SENSE IN THAT?
NO.

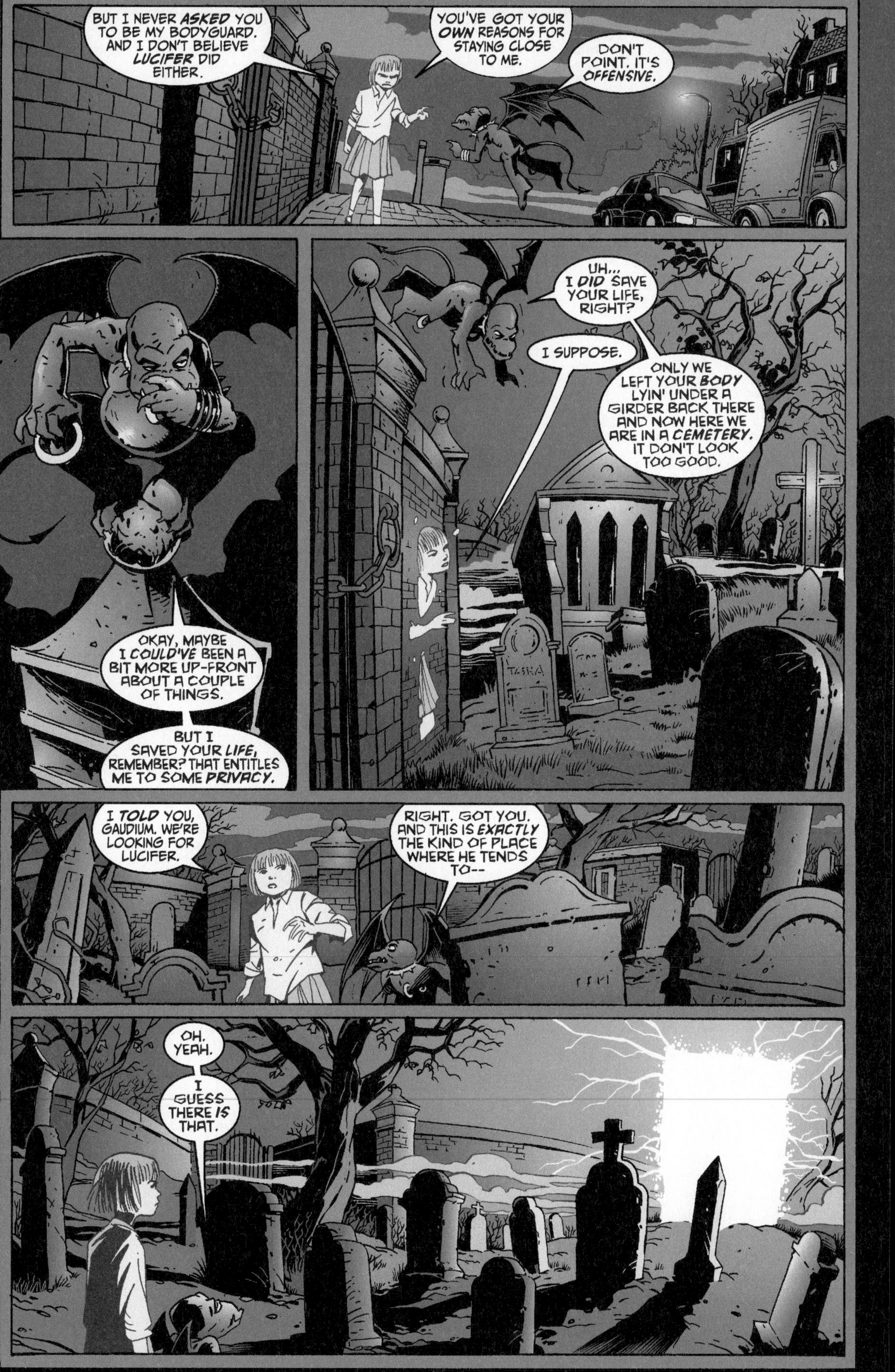
BUT I NEVER ASKED YOU TO BE MY BODYGUARD. AND I DON'T BELIEVE LUCIFER DID EITHER.
YOU'VE GOT YOUR OWN REASONS FOR STAYING CLOSE TO ME.
DON'T POINT. IT'S OFFENSIVE.
OKAY, MAYBE I COULD'VE BEEN A BIT MORE UP-FRONT ABOUT A COUPLE OF THINGS.
BUT I SAVED YOUR LIFE, REMEMBER? THAT ENTITLES ME TO SOME PRIVACY.
UH... I DID SAVE YOUR LIFE, RIGHT?
I SUPPOSE.
ONLY WE LEFT YOUR BODY LYIN' UNDER A GIRDER BACK THERE AND NOW HERE WE ARE IN A CEMETERY. IT DON'T LOOK TOO GOOD.
TASHA
I TOLD YOU, GAUDIUM. WE'RE LOOKING FOR LUCIFER.
RIGHT. GOT YOU. AND THIS IS EXACTLY THE KIND OF PLACE WHERE HE TENDS TO--
OH. YEAH.
I GUESS THERE IS THAT.

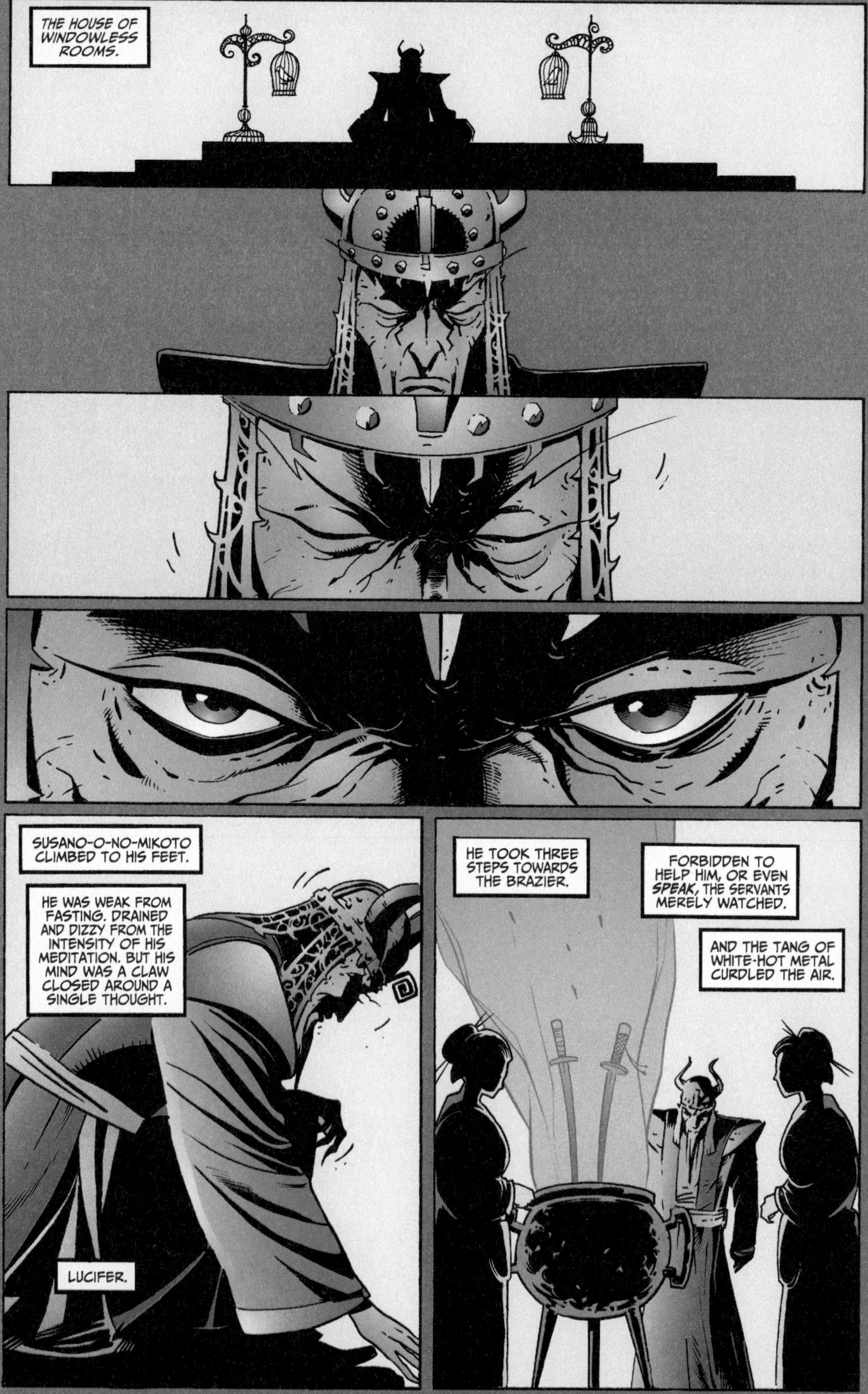
THE HOUSE OF WINDOWLESS ROOMS.
SUSANO-O-NO-MIKOTO CLIMBED TO HIS FEET.
HE WAS WEAK FROM FASTING. DRAINED AND DIZZY FROM THE INTENSITY OF HIS MEDITATION. BUT HIS MIND WAS A CLAW CLOSED AROUND A SINGLE THOUGHT.
LUCIFER.
HE TOOK THREE STEPS TOWARDS THE BRAZIER.
FORBIDDEN TO HELP HIM, OR EVEN SPEAK, THE SERVANTS MERELY WATCHED.
AND THE TANG OF WHITE-HOT METAL CURDLED THE AIR.

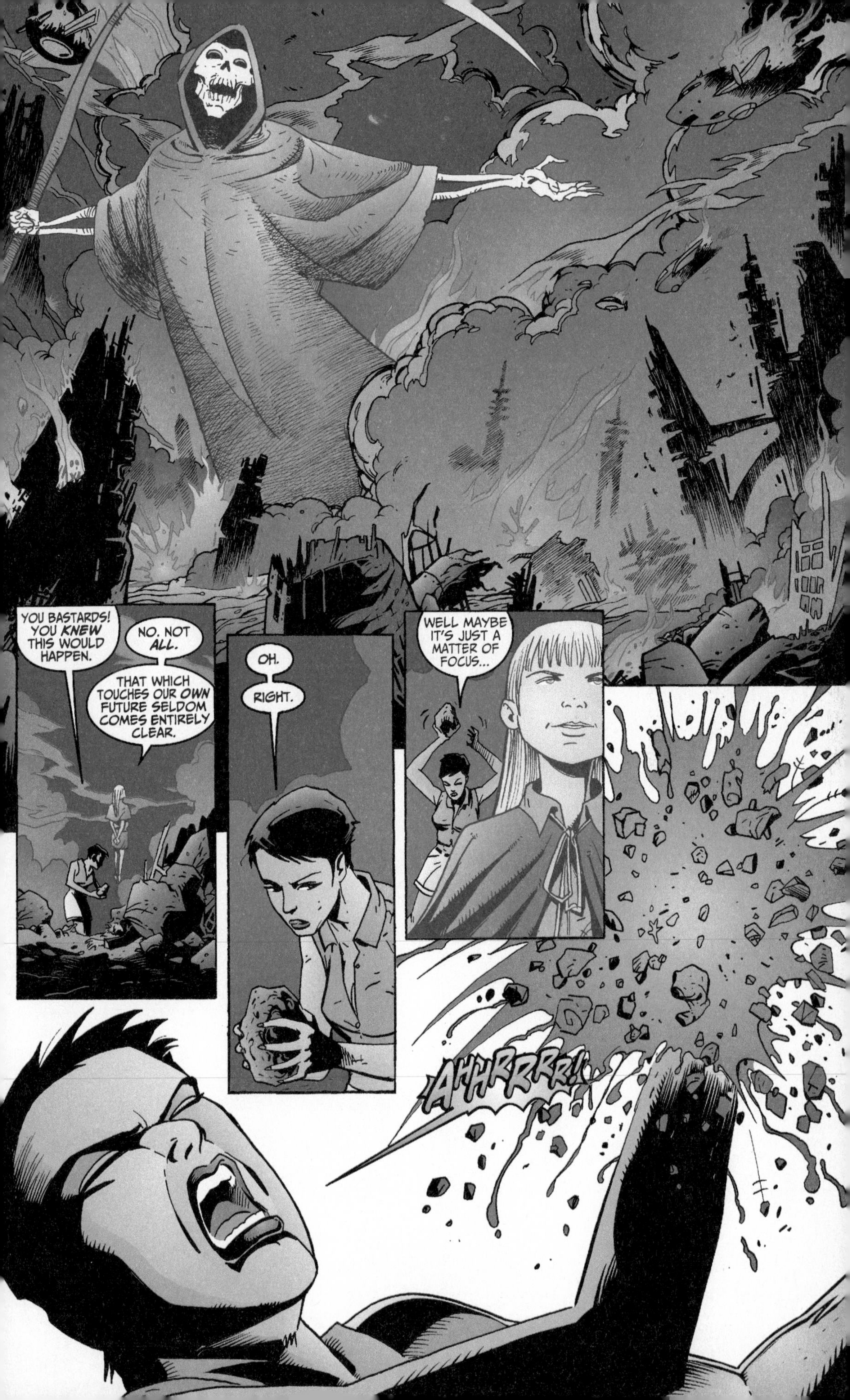

YOU BASTARDS! YOU KNEW THIS WOULD HAPPEN.
NO. NOT ALL.
THAT WHICH TOUCHES OUR OWN FUTURE SELDOM COMES ENTIRELY CLEAR.
OH.
RIGHT.
WELL MAYBE IT'S JUST A MATTER OF FOCUS...
AHHRRRR!!

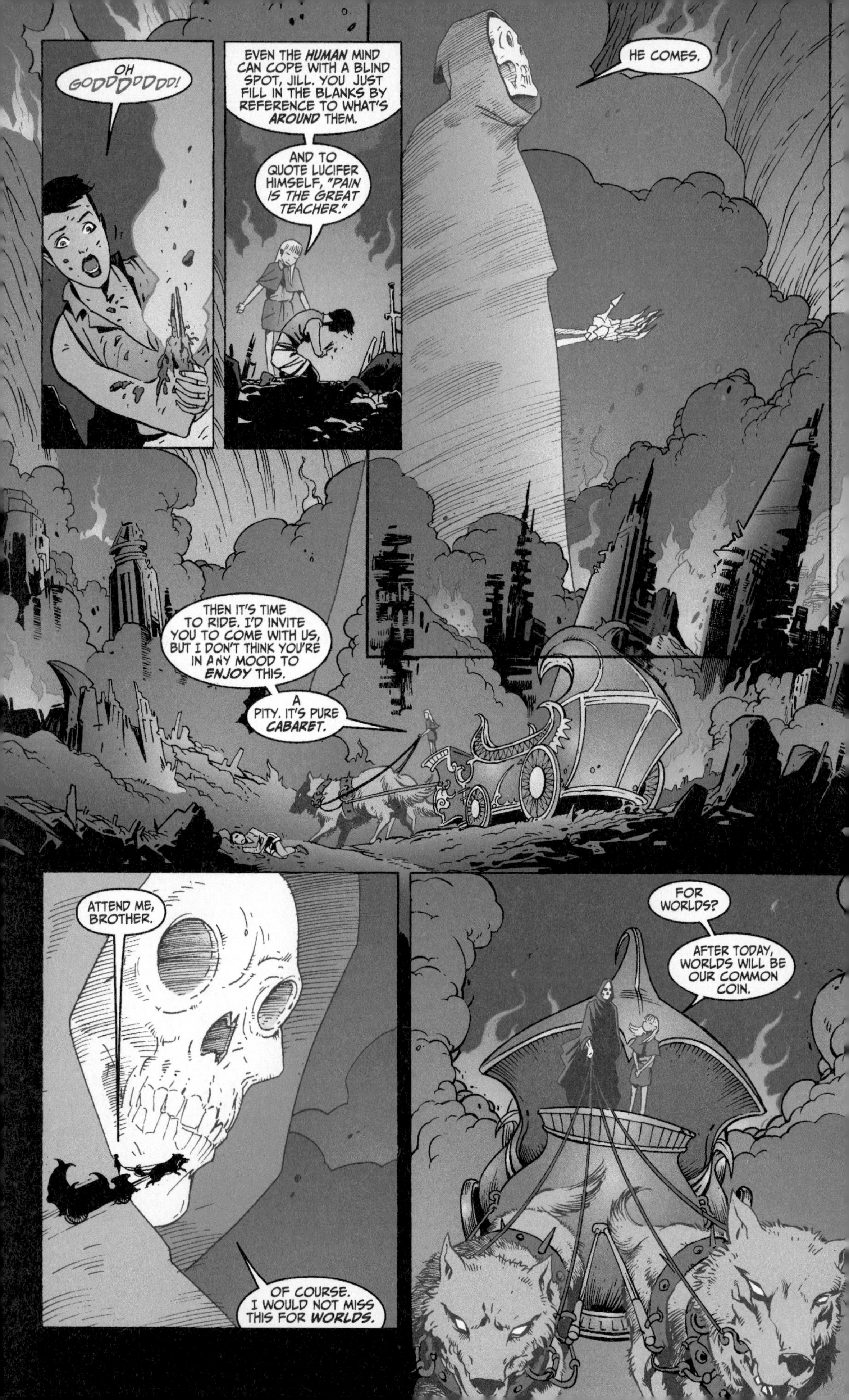
OH GODDDDDDD!
EVEN THE HUMAN MIND CAN COPE WITH A BLIND SPOT, JILL. YOU JUST FILL IN THE BLANKS BY REFERENCE TO WHAT'S AROUND THEM.
AND TO QUOTE LUCIFER HIMSELF, "PAIN IS THE GREAT TEACHER."
HE COMES.
THEN IT'S TIME TO RIDE. I'D INVITE YOU TO COME WITH US, BUT I DON'T THINK YOU'RE IN ANY MOOD TO ENJOY THIS.
A PITY. IT'S PURE CABARET.
ATTEND ME, BROTHER.
OF COURSE. I WOULD NOT MISS THIS FOR WORLDS.
FOR WORLDS?
AFTER TODAY, WORLDS WILL BE OUR COMMON COIN.

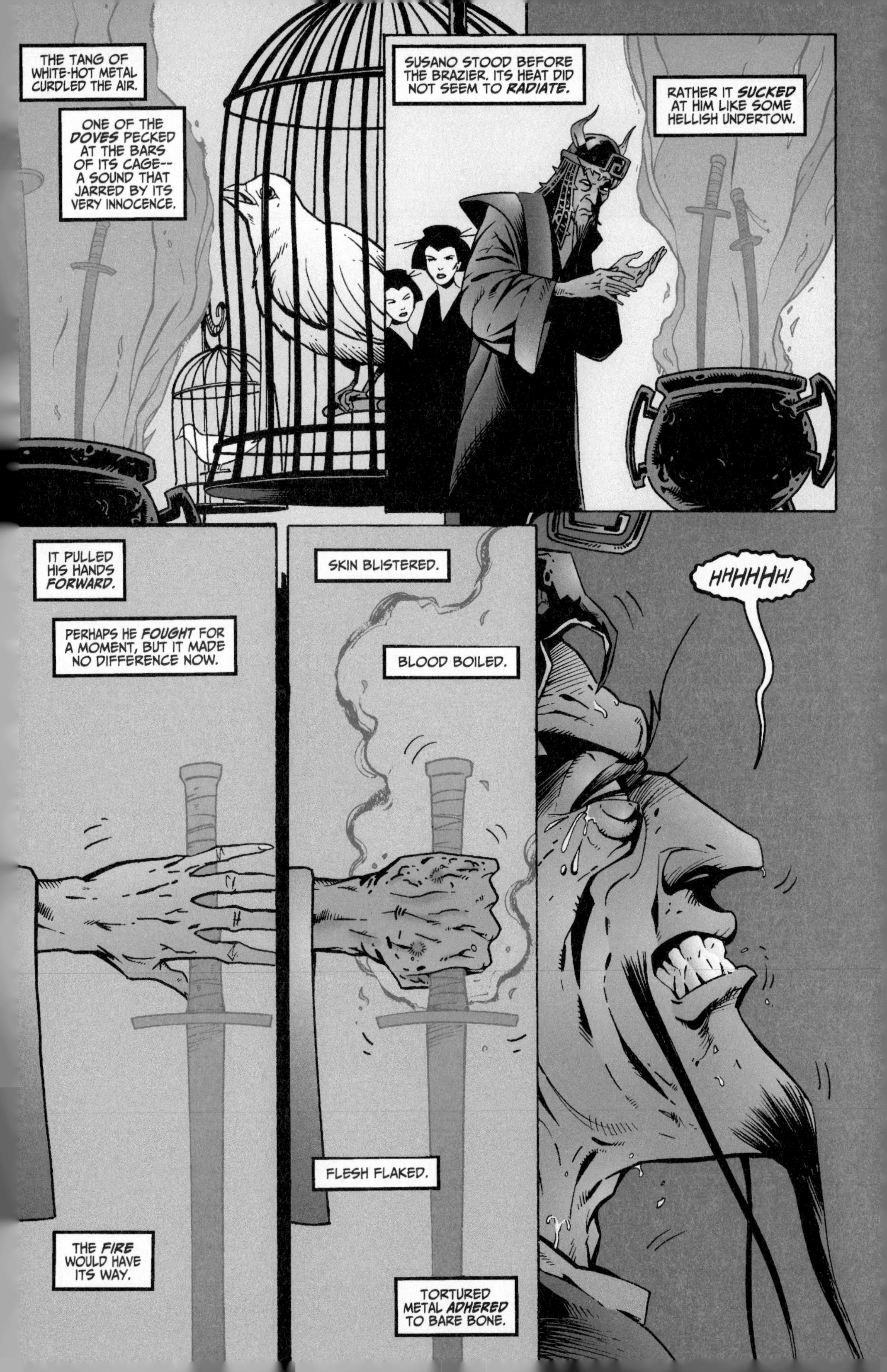

THE TANG OF WHITE-HOT METAL CURDLED THE AIR.
ONE OF THE DOVES PECKED AT THE BARS OF ITS CAGE-- A SOUND THAT JARRED BY ITS VERY INNOCENCE.
SUSANO STOOD BEFORE THE BRAZIER. ITS HEAT DID NOT SEEM TO RADIATE.
RATHER IT SUCKED AT HIM LIKE SOME HELLISH UNDERTOW.
IT PULLED HIS HANDS FORWARD.
PERHAPS HE FOUGHT FOR A MOMENT, BUT IT MADE NO DIFFERENCE NOW.
THE FIRE WOULD HAVE ITS WAY.
SKIN BLISTERED.
BLOOD BOILED.
FLESH FLAKED.
TORTURED METAL ADHERED TO BARE BONE.
HHHHHH!

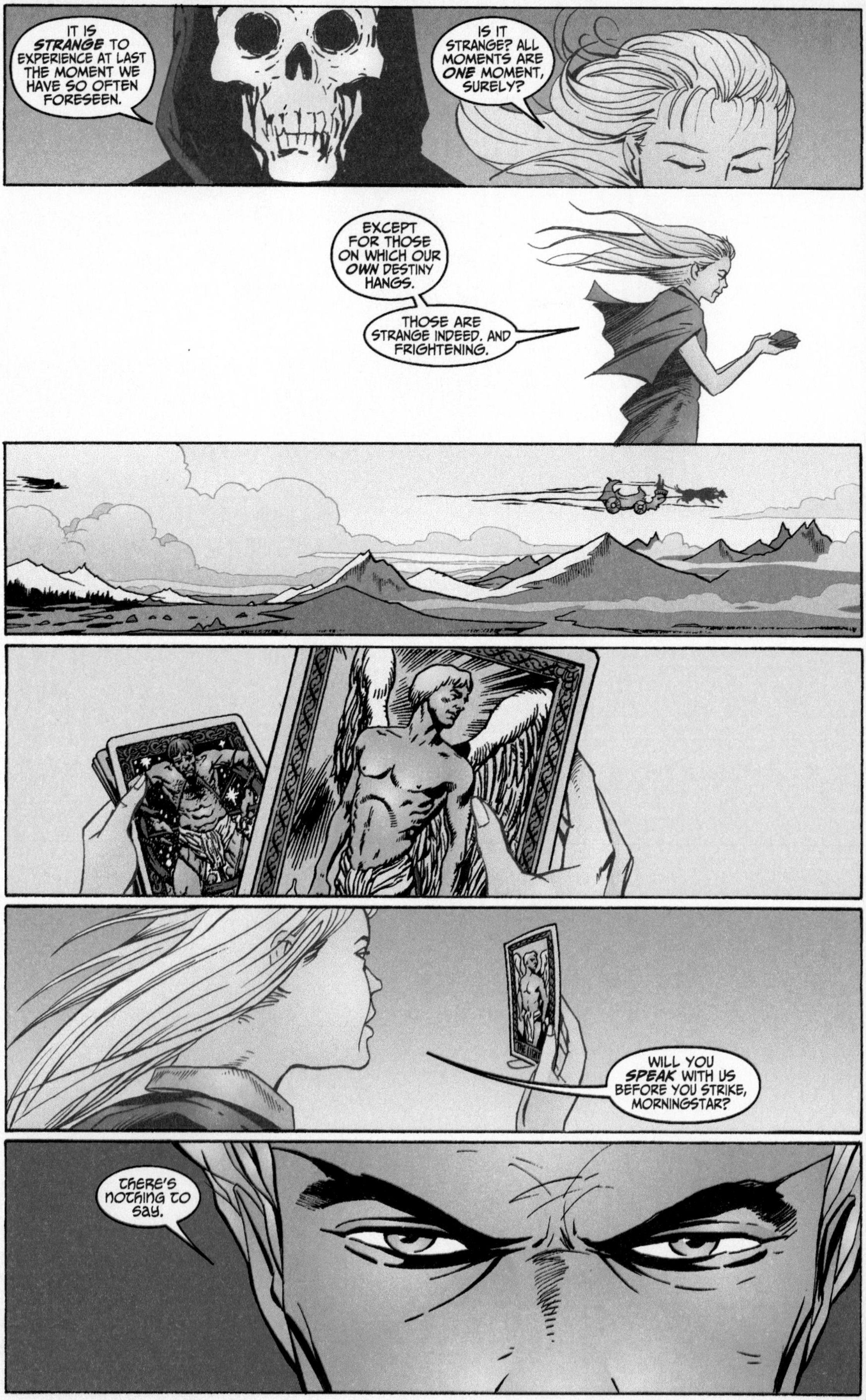
IT IS STRANGE TO EXPERIENCE AT LAST THE MOMENT WE HAVE SO OFTEN FORESEEN.
IS IT STRANGE? ALL MOMENTS ARE ONE MOMENT, SURELY?
EXCEPT FOR THOSE ON WHICH OUR OWN DESTINY HANGS.
THOSE ARE STRANGE INDEED. AND FRIGHTENING.
WILL YOU SPEAK WITH US BEFORE YOU STRIKE, MORNINGSTAR?
THERE'S NOTHING TO SAY.

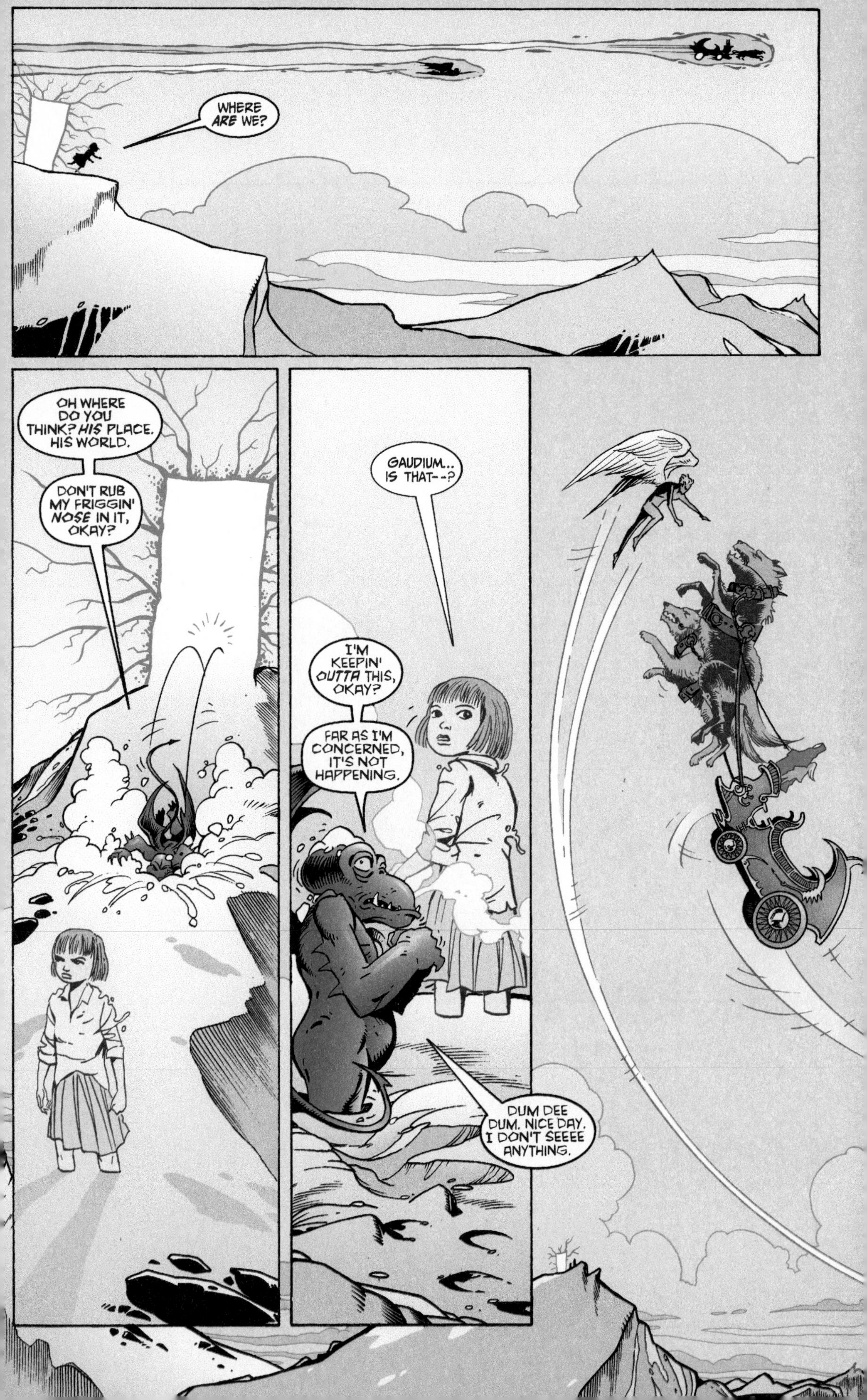
WHERE ARE WE?
OH WHERE DO YOU THINK? HIS PLACE. HIS WORLD.
DON'T RUB MY FRIGGIN' NOSE IN IT, OKAY?
GAUDIUM.. IS THAT--?
I'M KEEPIN' OUTTA THIS, OKAY?
FAR AS I'M CONCERNED, IT'S NOT HAPPENING.
DUM DEE DUM. NICE DAY. I DON'T SEEEE ANYTHING.

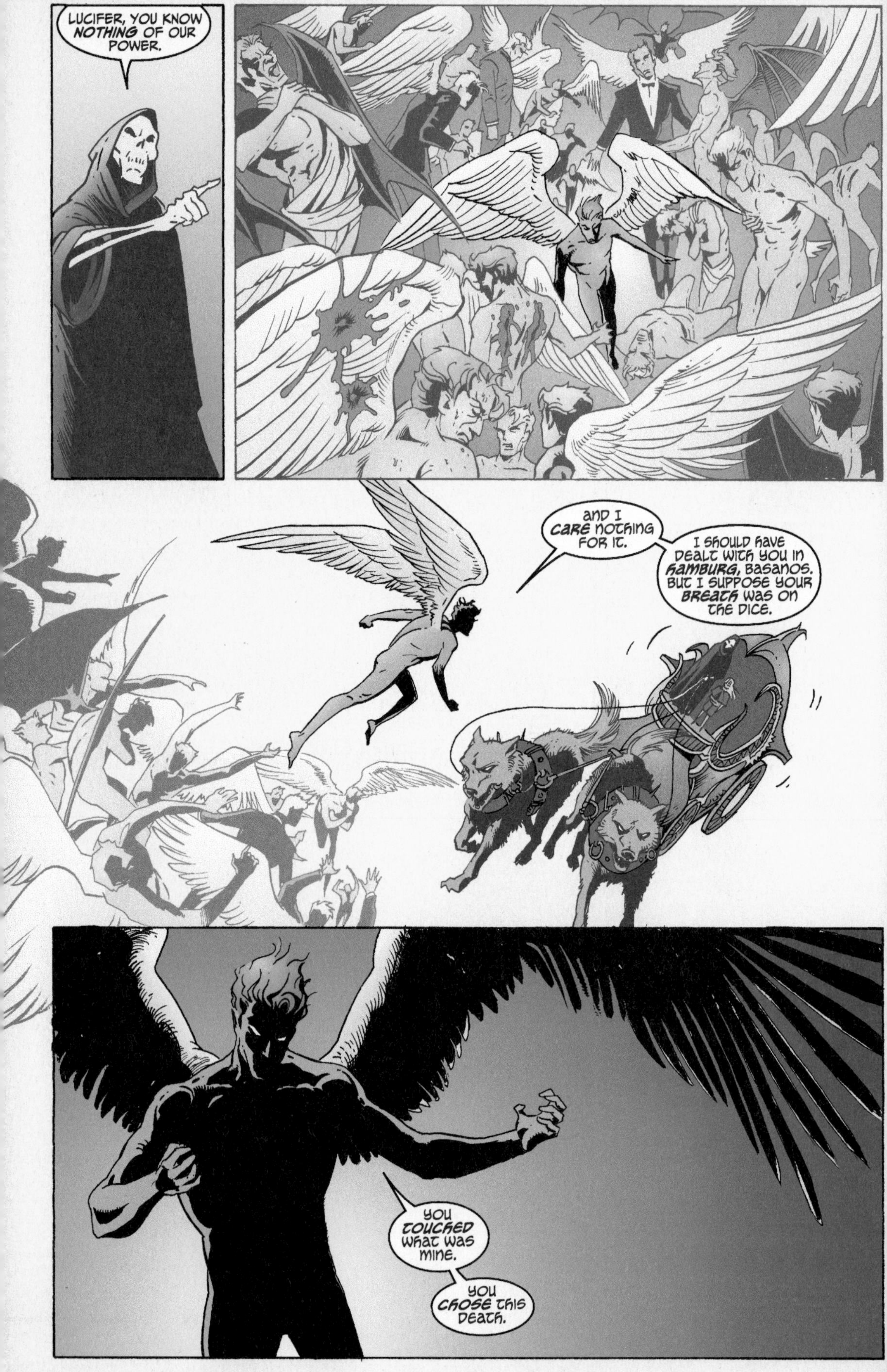
LUCIFER, YOU KNOW NOTHING OF OUR POWER.
AND I CARE NOTHING FOR IT.
I SHOULD HAVE DEALT WITH YOU IN HAMBURG, BASANOS. BUT I SUPPOSE YOUR BREATH WAS ON THE DICE.
YOU TOUCHED WHAT WAS MINE.
YOU CHOSE THIS DEATH.

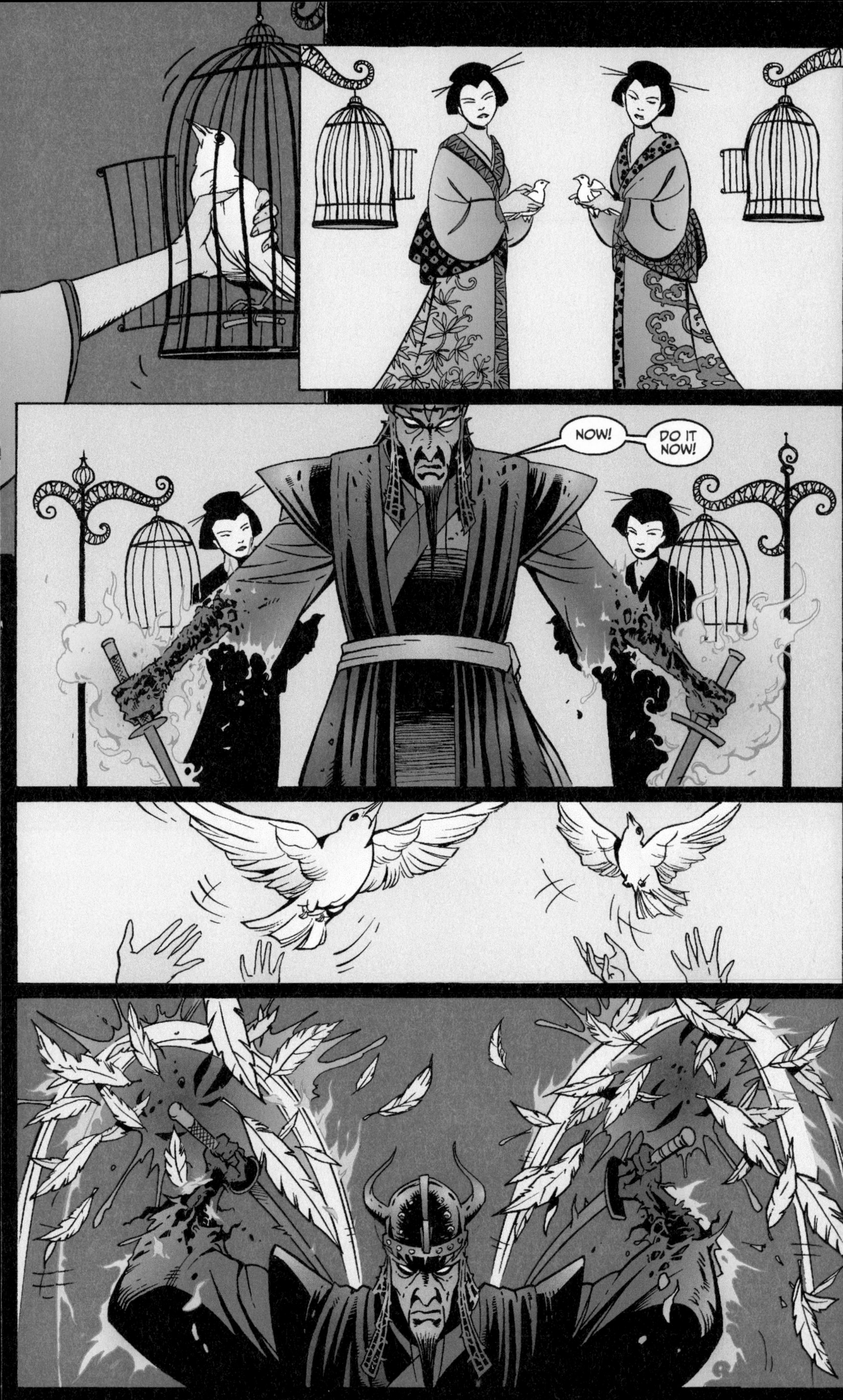
NOW!
DO IT NOW!

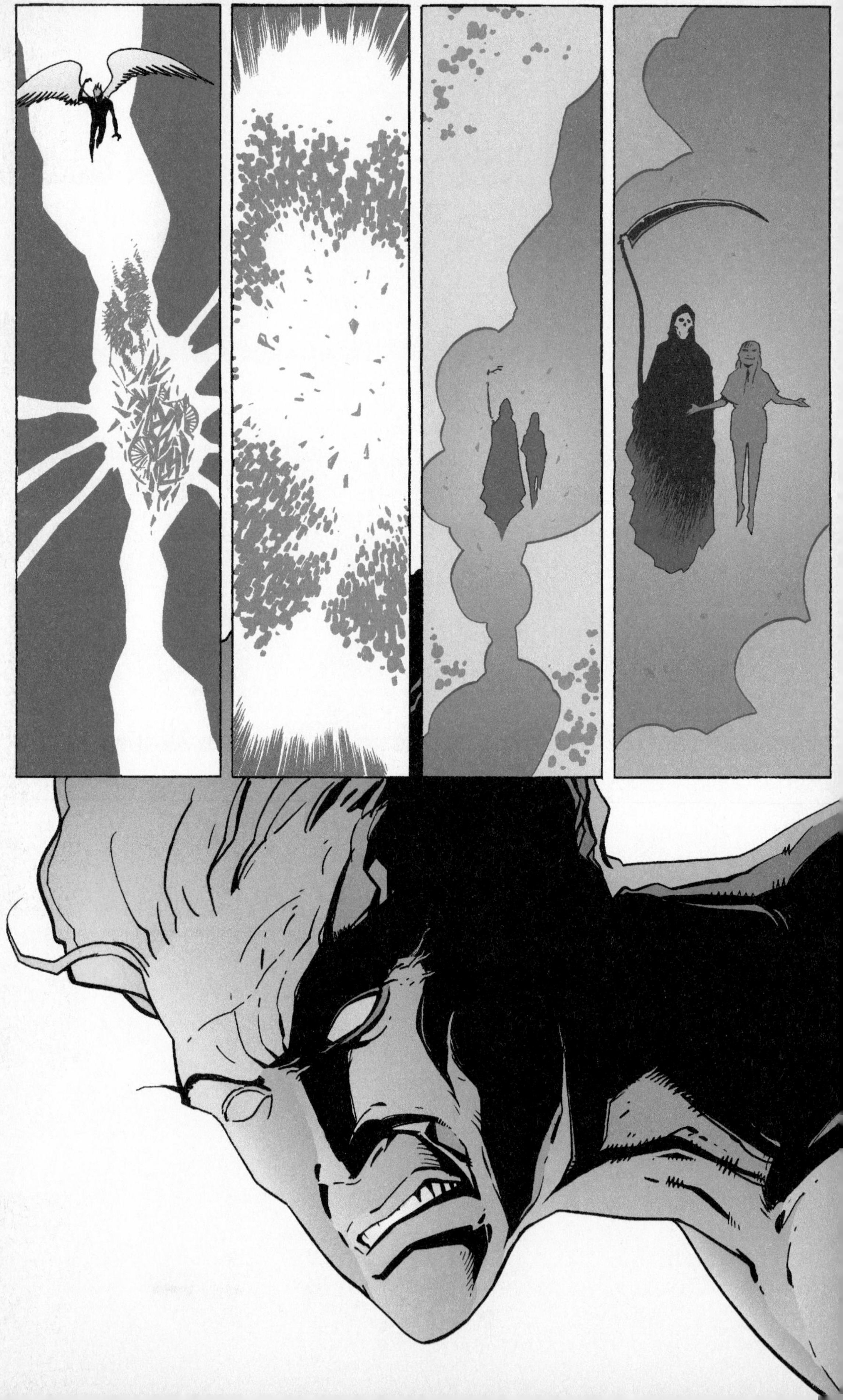

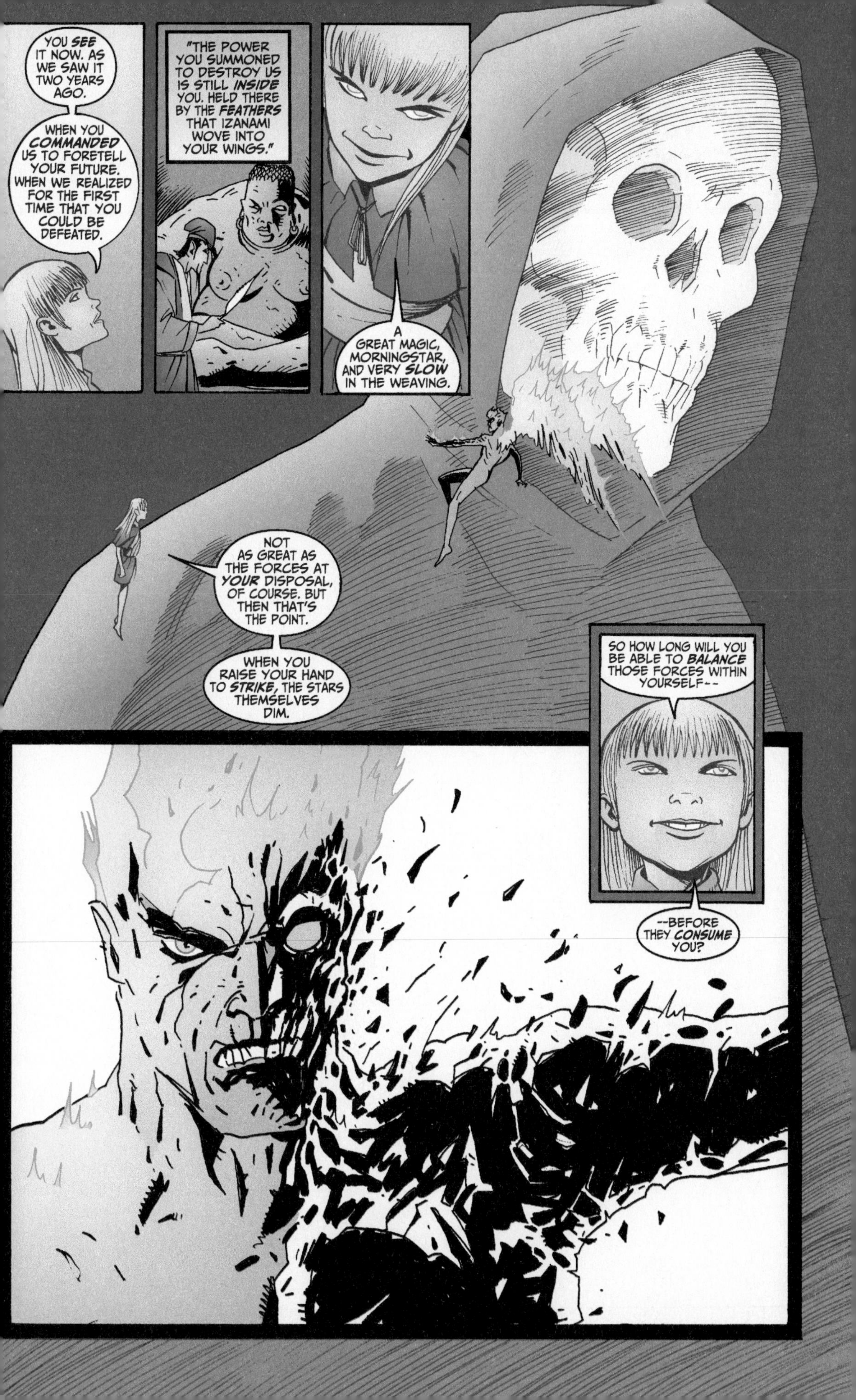
YOU SEE IT NOW. AS WE SAW IT TWO YEARS AGO.
WHEN YOU COMMANDED US TO FORETELL YOUR FUTURE. WHEN WE REALIZED FOR THE FIRST TIME THAT YOU COULD BE DEFEATED.
"THE POWER YOU SUMMONED TO DESTROY US IS STILL INSIDE YOU. HELD THERE BY THE FEATHERS THAT IZANAMI WOVE INTO YOUR WINGS."
A GREAT MAGIC, MORNINGSTAR, AND VERY SLOW IN THE WEAVING.
NOT AS GREAT AS THE FORCES AT YOUR DISPOSAL, OF COURSE. BUT THEN THAT'S THE POINT.
WHEN YOU RAISE YOUR HAND TO STRIKE, THE STARS THEMSELVES DIM.
SO HOW LONG WILL YOU BE ABLE TO BALANCE THOSE FORCES WITHIN YOURSELF--
--BEFORE THEY CONSUME YOU?

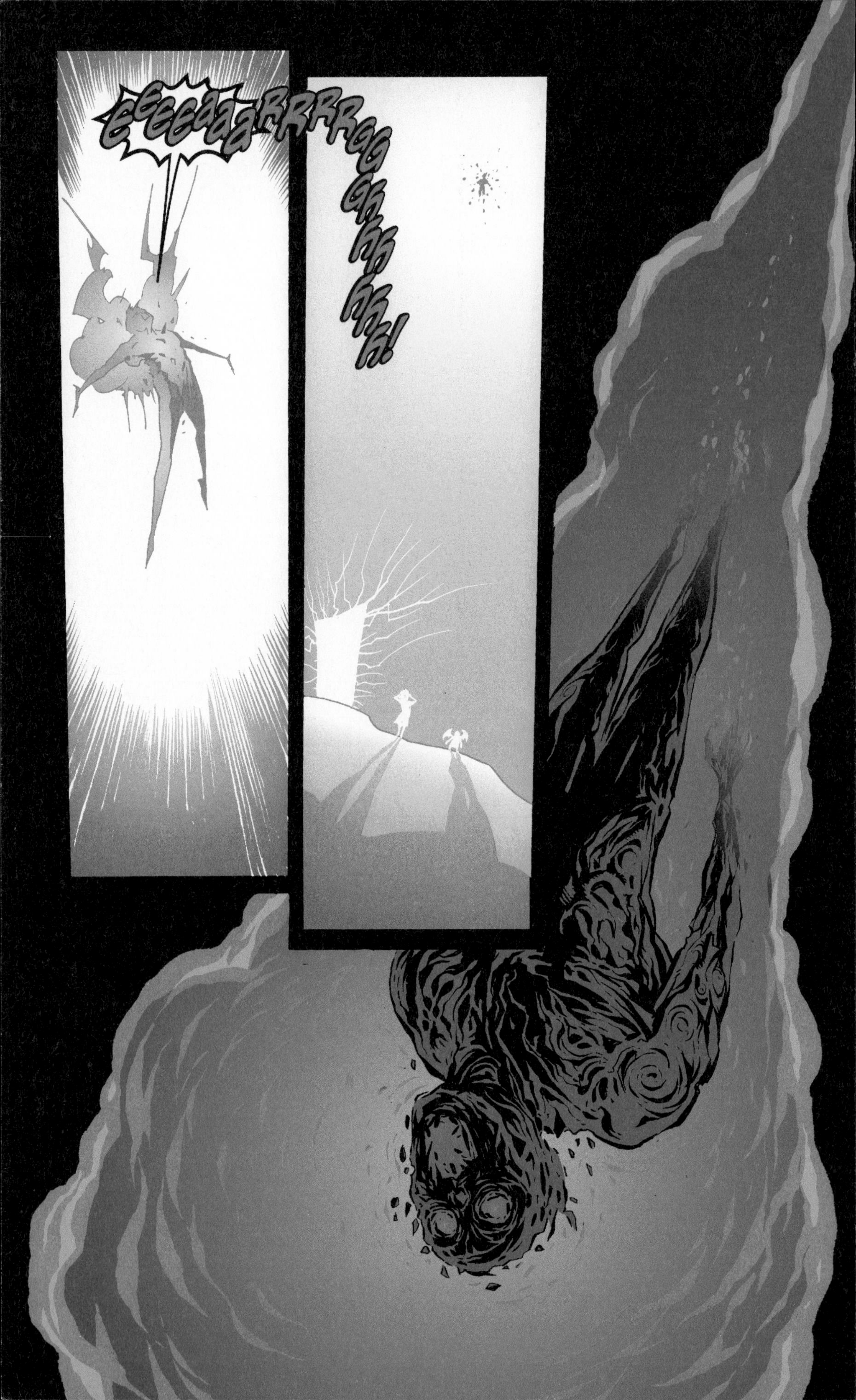
EEEEAAARRRRGGGHHHHHH!

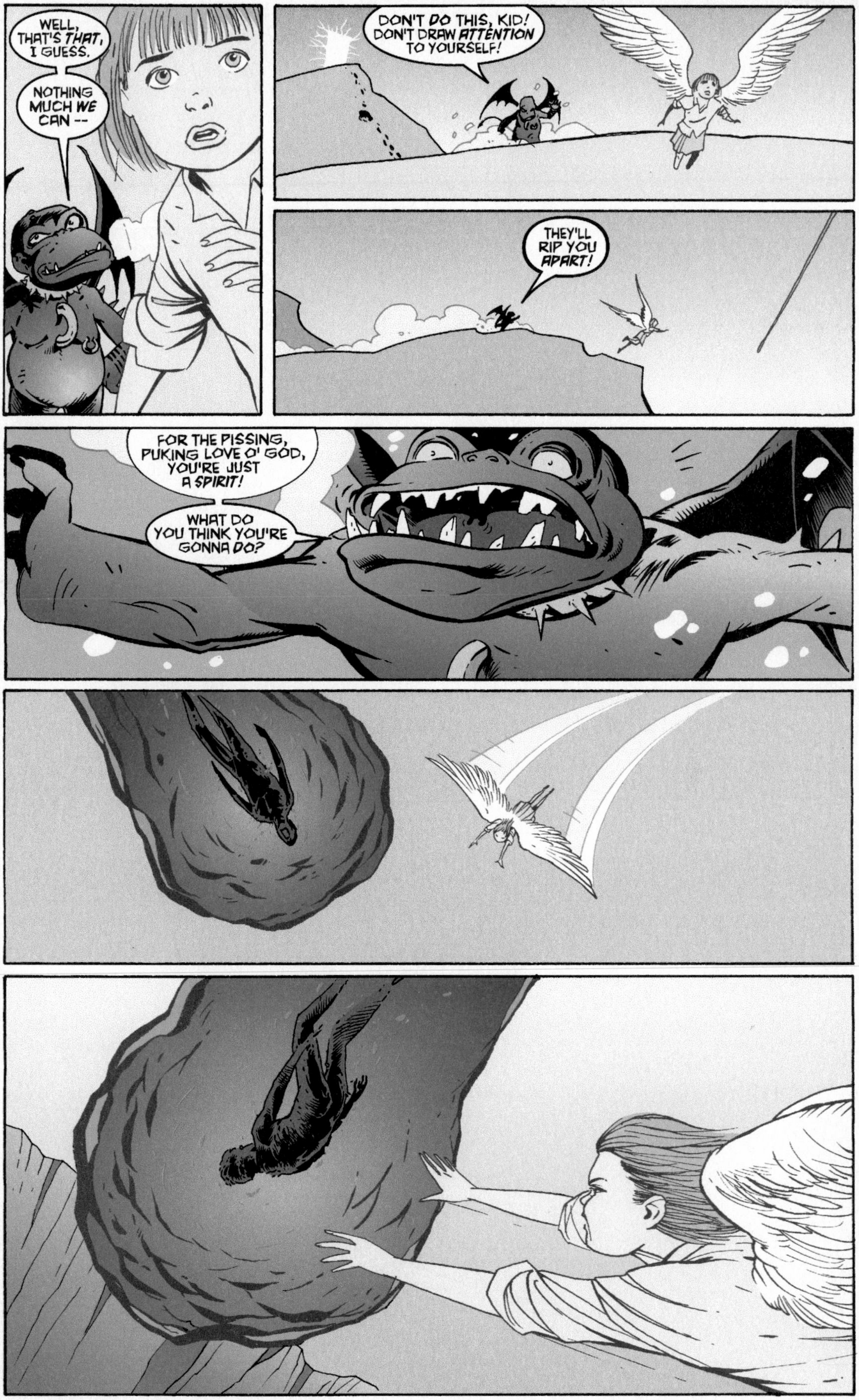
WELL, THAT'S THAT, I GUESS.
NOTHING MUCH WE CAN --
DON'T DO THIS, KID! DON'T DRAW ATTENTION TO YOURSELF!
THEY'LL RIP YOU APART!
FOR THE PISSING, PUKING LOVE O' GOD, YOU'RE JUST A SPIRIT!
WHAT DO YOU THINK YOU'RE GONNA DO?

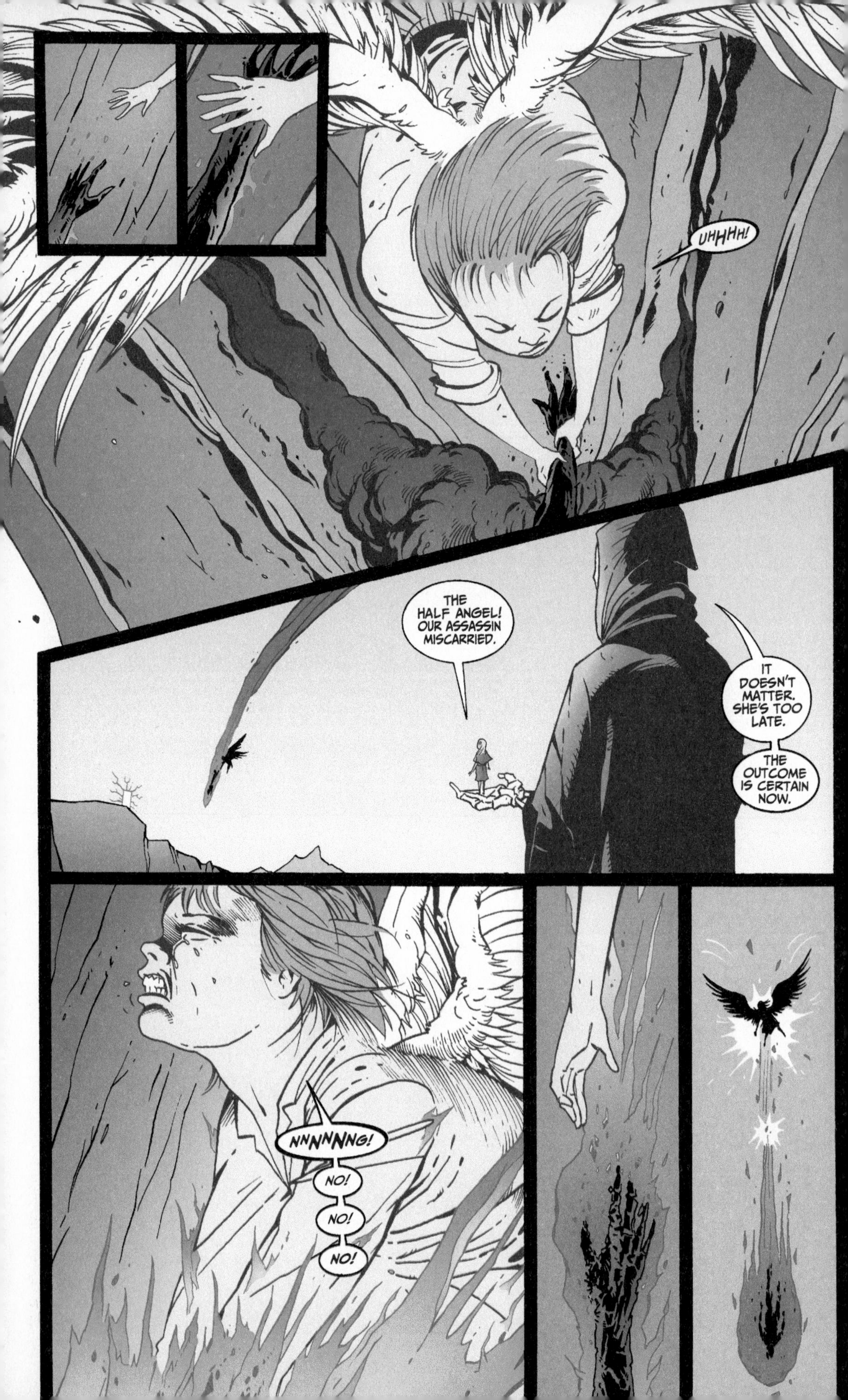
UHHHH!
THE HALF ANGEL! OUR ASSASSIN MISCARRIED.
IT DOESN'T MATTER. SHE'S TOO LATE.
THE OUTCOME IS CERTAIN NOW.
NNNNNNG!
NO!
NO!
NO!

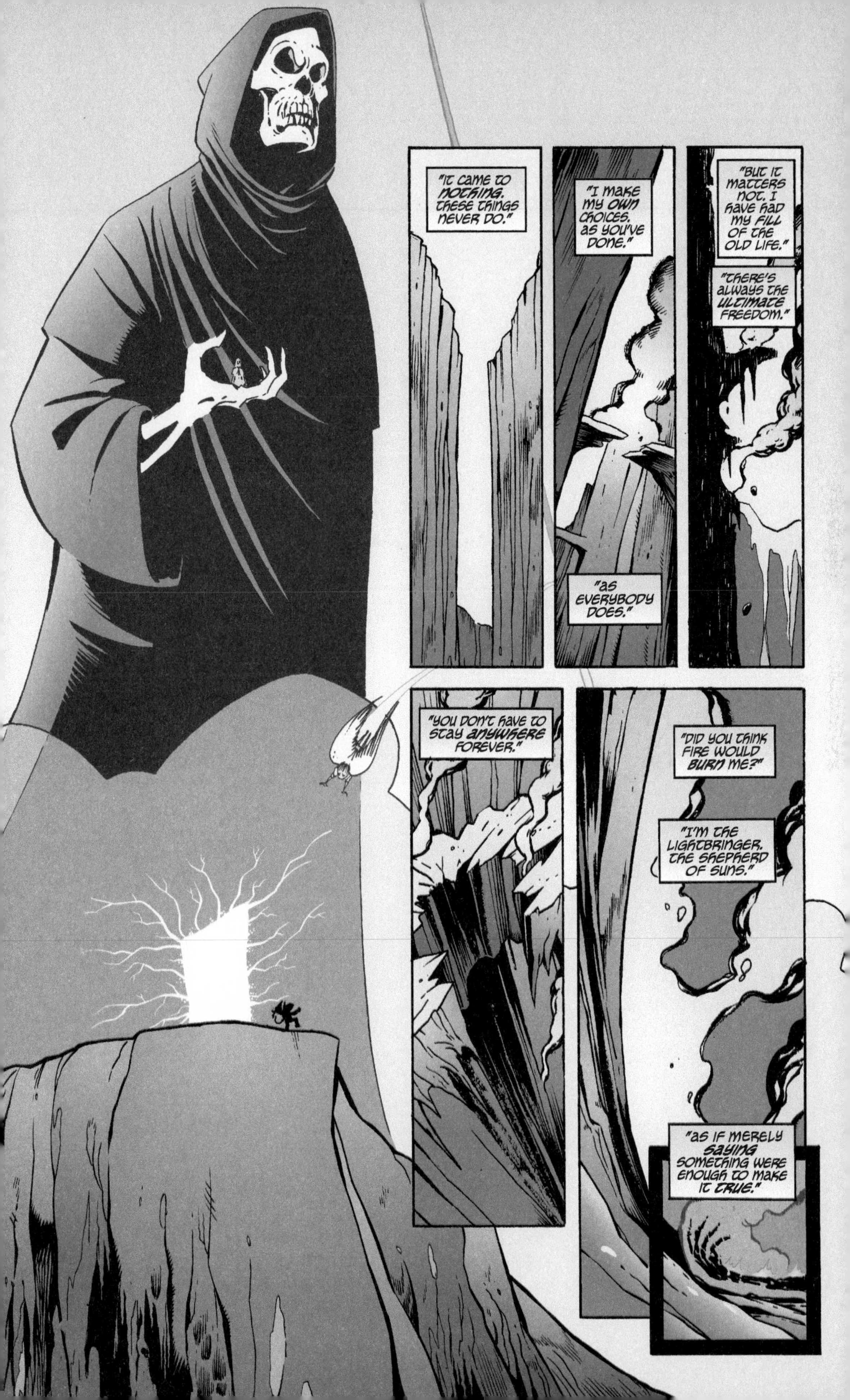
"IT CAME TO NOTHING. THESE THINGS NEVER DO."
"I MAKE MY OWN CHOICES. AS YOU'VE DONE."
"AS EVERYBODY DOES."
"BUT IT MATTERS NOT. I HAVE HAD MY FILL OF THE OLD LIFE."
"THERE'S ALWAYS THE ULTIMATE FREEDOM."
"YOU DON'T HAVE TO STAY ANYWHERE FOREVER."
"DID YOU THINK FIRE WOULD BURN ME?"
"I'M THE LIGHTBRINGER. THE SHEPHERD OF SUNS."
"AS IF MERELY SAYING SOMETHING WERE ENOUGH TO MAKE IT TRUE."

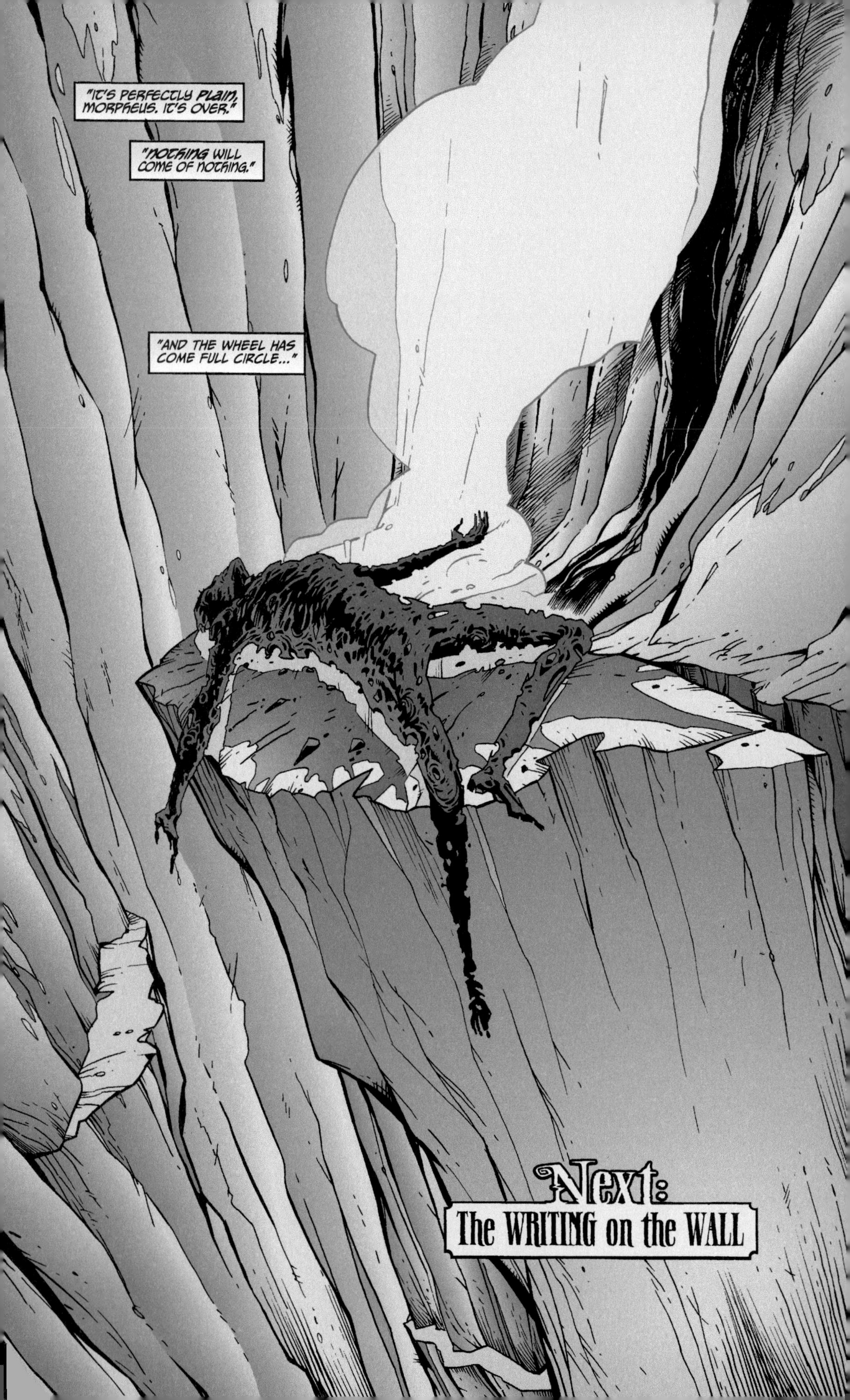
"IT'S PERFECTLY PLAIN, MORPHEUS. IT'S OVER."
"NOTHING WILL COME OF NOTHING."
"AND THE WHEEL HAS COME FULL CIRCLE..."
Next:
The WRITING on the WALL

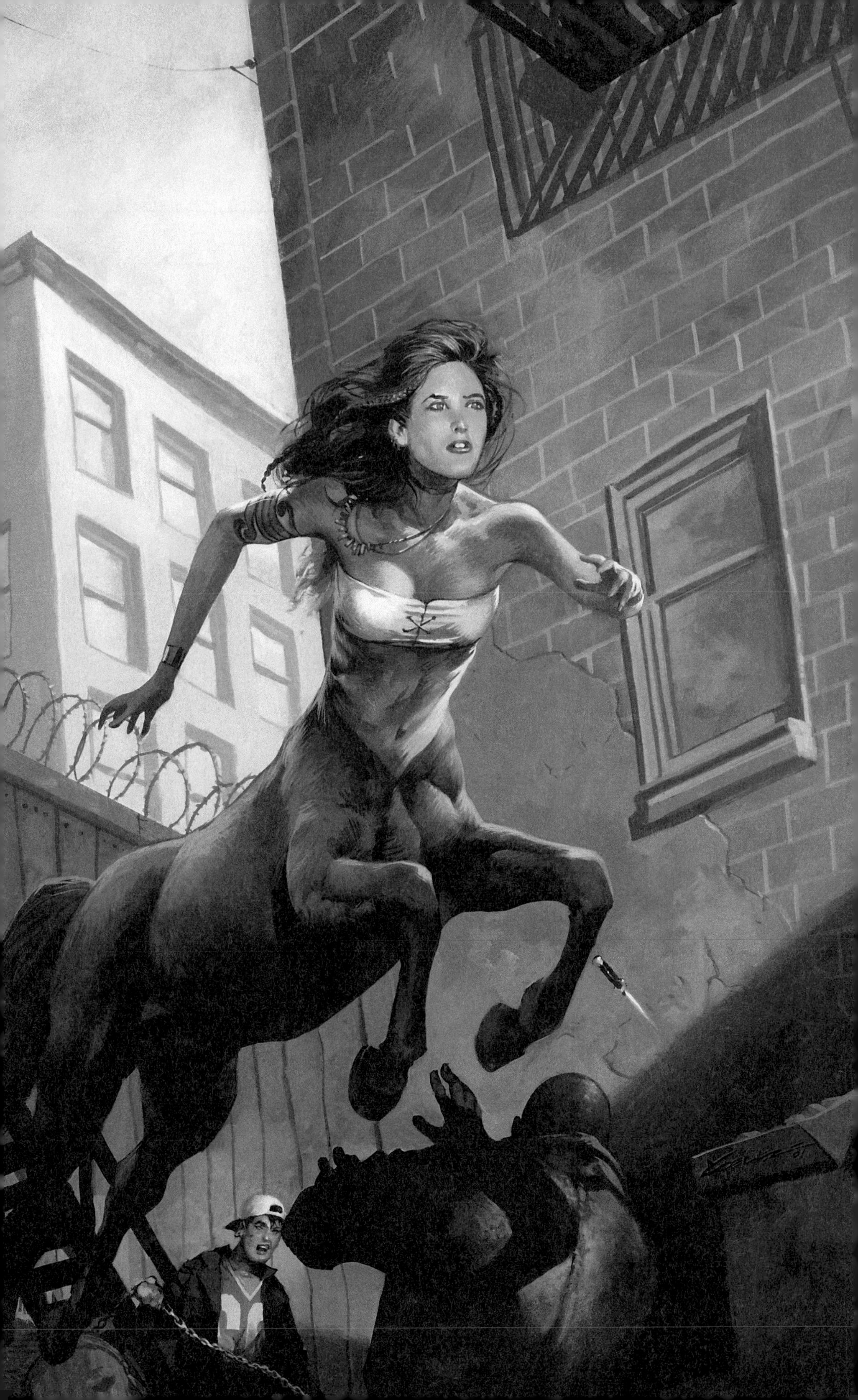

The Writing on the Wall

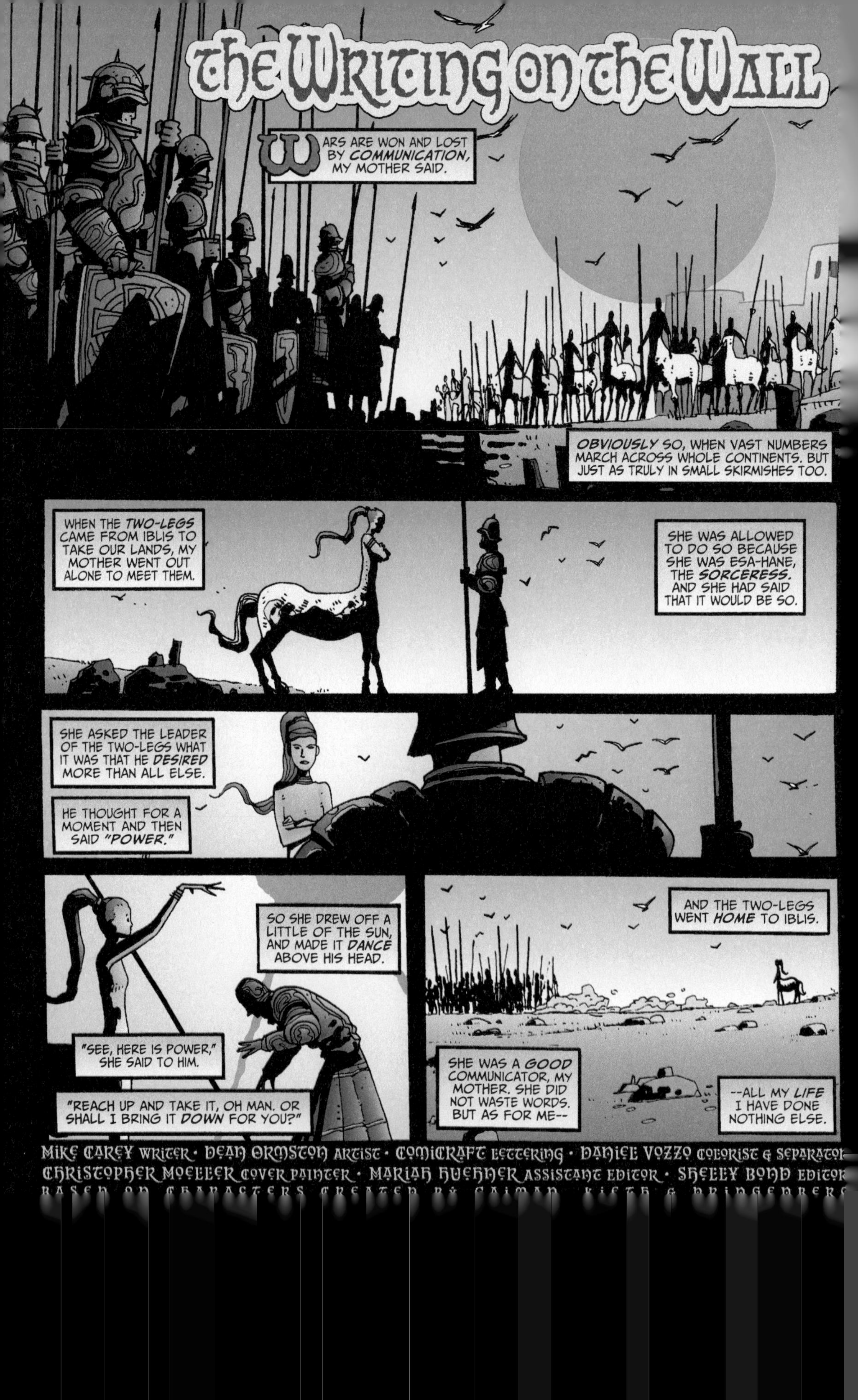
WARS ARE WON AND LOST BY COMMUNICATION, MY MOTHER SAID.
OBVIOUSLY SO, WHEN VAST NUMBERS MARCH ACROSS WHOLE CONTINENTS. BUT JUST AS TRULY IN SMALL SKIRMISHES TOO.
WHEN THE TWO-LEGS CAME FROM IBLIS TO TAKE OUR LANDS, MY MOTHER WENT OUT ALONE TO MEET THEM.
SHE WAS ALLOWED TO DO SO BECAUSE SHE WAS ESA-HANE, THE SORCERESS. AND SHE HAD SAID THAT IT WOULD BE SO.
SHE ASKED THE LEADER OF THE TWO-LEGS WHAT IT WAS THAT HE DESIRED MORE THAN ALL ELSE.
HE THOUGHT FOR A MOMENT AND THEN SAID "POWER."
SO SHE DREW OFF A LITTLE OF THE SUN, AND MADE IT DANCE ABOVE HIS HEAD.
"SEE, HERE IS POWER," SHE SAID TO HIM.
"REACH UP AND TAKE IT, OH MAN. OR SHALL I BRING IT DOWN FOR YOU?"
AND THE TWO-LEGS WENT HOME TO IBLIS.
SHE WAS A GOOD COMMUNICATOR, MY MOTHER. SHE DID NOT WASTE WORDS. BUT AS FOR ME--
--ALL MY LIFE I HAVE DONE NOTHING ELSE.

MIKE CAREY WRITER • DEAN ORMSTON ARTIST • COMICRAFT LETTERING • DANIEL VOZZO COLORIST & SEPARATOR
CHRISTOPHER MOELLER COVER PAINTER • MARIAH HUEHNER ASSISTANT EDITOR • SHELLEY BOND EDITOR

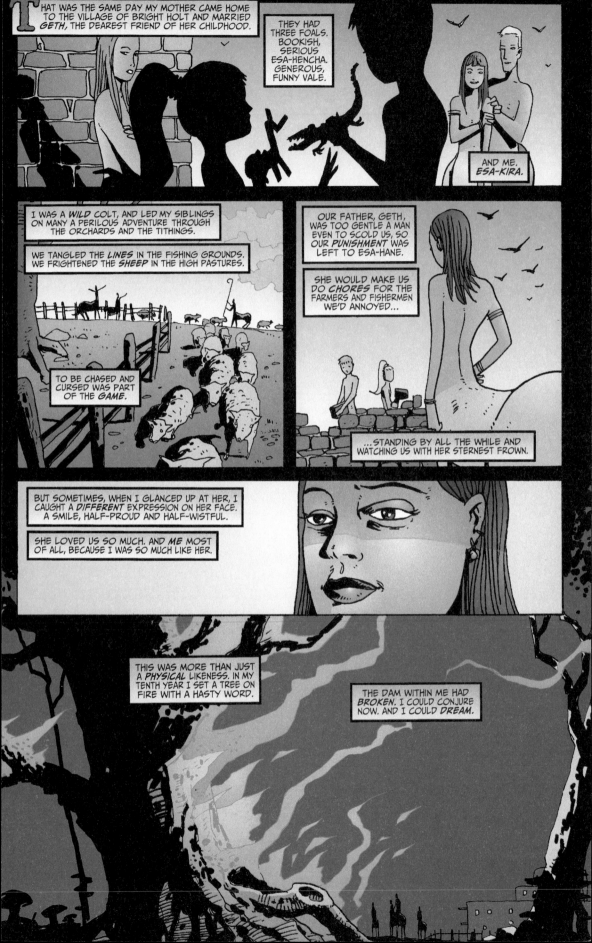

THAT WAS THE SAME DAY MY MOTHER CAME HOME TO THE VILLAGE OF BRIGHT HOLT AND MARRIED *GETH*, THE DEAREST FRIEND OF HER CHILDHOOD.

THEY HAD THREE FOALS. BOOKISH, SERIOUS ESA-HENCHA. GENEROUS, FUNNY VALE.

AND ME. ESA-KIRA.

I WAS A *WILD* COLT, AND LED MY SIBLINGS ON MANY A PERILOUS ADVENTURE THROUGH THE ORCHARDS AND THE TITHINGS.

WE TANGLED THE *LINES* IN THE FISHING GROUNDS. WE FRIGHTENED THE *SHEEP* IN THE HIGH PASTURES.

TO BE CHASED AND CURSED WAS PART OF THE *GAME*.

OUR FATHER, GETH, WAS TOO GENTLE A MAN EVEN TO SCOLD US, SO OUR *PUNISHMENT* WAS LEFT TO ESA-HANE.

SHE WOULD MAKE US *DO CHORES* FOR THE FARMERS AND FISHERMEN WE'D ANNOYED...

...STANDING BY ALL THE WHILE AND WATCHING US WITH HER STERNEST FROWN.

BUT SOMETIMES, WHEN I GLANCED UP AT HER, I CAUGHT A *DIFFERENT* EXPRESSION ON HER FACE. A SMILE, HALF-PROUD AND HALF-WISTFUL.

SHE LOVED US SO MUCH. AND *ME* MOST OF ALL, BECAUSE I WAS SO MUCH LIKE HER.

THIS WAS MORE THAN JUST A *PHYSICAL* LIKENESS. IN MY TENTH YEAR I SET A TREE ON FIRE WITH A HASTY WORD.

THE DAM WITHIN ME HAD *BROKEN*. I COULD CONJURE NOW. AND I COULD *DREAM*.

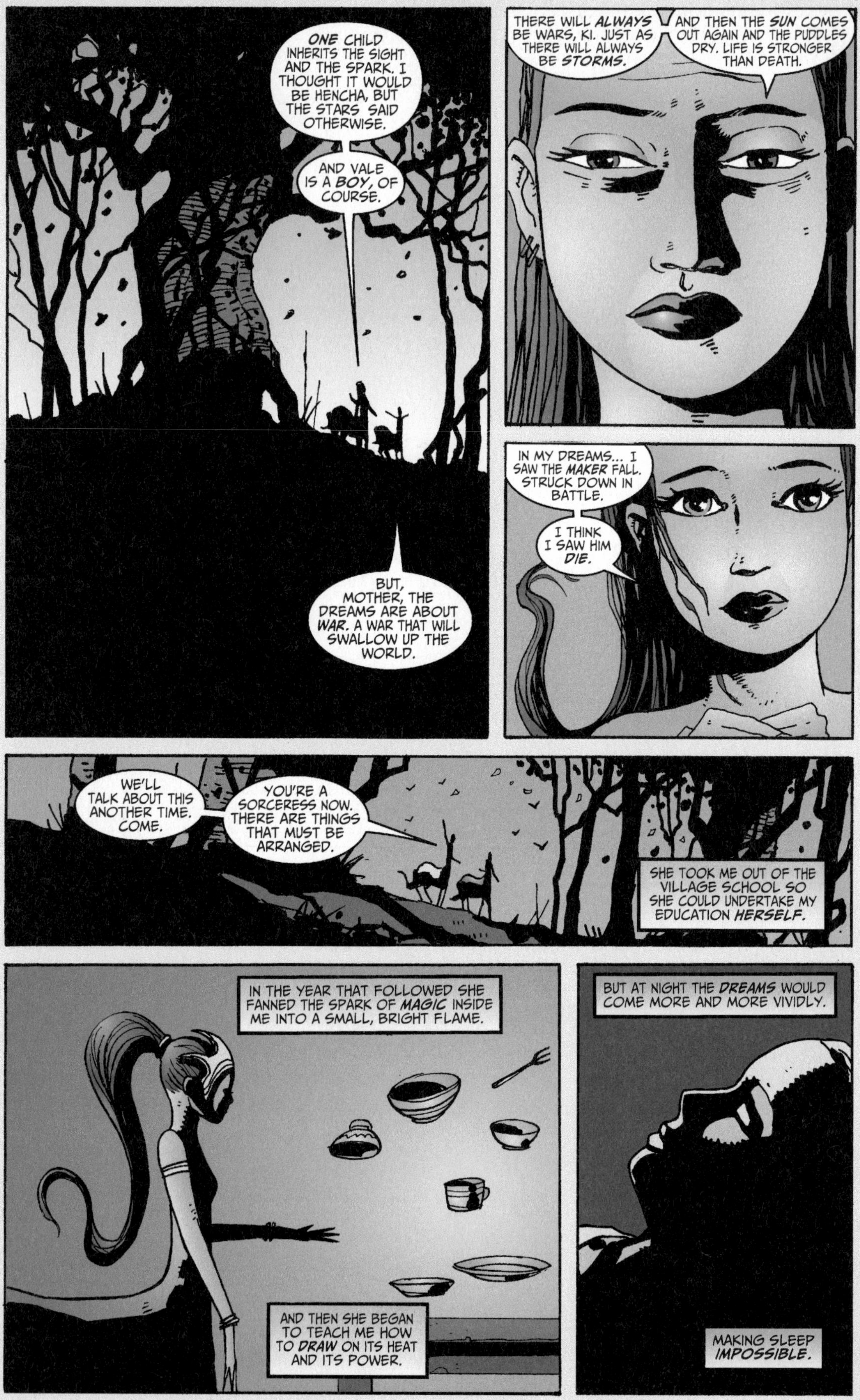

ONE CHILD INHERITS THE SIGHT AND THE SPARK. I THOUGHT IT WOULD BE HENCHA, BUT THE STARS SAID OTHERWISE.
AND VALE IS A BOY, OF COURSE.
BUT, MOTHER, THE DREAMS ARE ABOUT WAR. A WAR THAT WILL SWALLOW UP THE WORLD.
THERE WILL ALWAYS BE WARS, KI. JUST AS THERE WILL ALWAYS BE STORMS.
AND THEN THE SUN COMES OUT AGAIN AND THE PUDDLES DRY. LIFE IS STRONGER THAN DEATH.
IN MY DREAMS... I SAW THE MAKER FALL. STRUCK DOWN IN BATTLE.
I THINK I SAW HIM DIE.
WE'LL TALK ABOUT THIS ANOTHER TIME. COME.
YOU'RE A SORCERESS NOW. THERE ARE THINGS THAT MUST BE ARRANGED.
SHE TOOK ME OUT OF THE VILLAGE SCHOOL SO SHE COULD UNDERTAKE MY EDUCATION HERSELF.
IN THE YEAR THAT FOLLOWED SHE FANNED THE SPARK OF MAGIC INSIDE ME INTO A SMALL, BRIGHT FLAME.
AND THEN SHE BEGAN TO TEACH ME HOW TO DRAW ON ITS HEAT AND ITS POWER.
BUT AT NIGHT THE DREAMS WOULD COME MORE AND MORE VIVIDLY.
MAKING SLEEP IMPOSSIBLE.

THE MAKER IN HIS WRATH AND HIS MAJESTY, ASSAILING THE *CHARIOT* OF HIS FOES.

AND THEN STRUCK DOWN *HIMSELF* BY A MAGICAL ATTACK FROM BEHIND.

HIS BODY BURNING AND FALLING. HIS *SCREAM* IN MY MIND LIKE A RAIN OF GLASS SPLINTERS.

MOTHER, WHAT SHOULD I *DO?* THE MAKER NEEDS TO BE WARNED. HE MAY NOT KNOW HE IS IN DANGER!

KI...

IN *MY* DREAMS THE MAKER APPEARS AS A ROCK. WHAT DOES THAT MEAN?

UMM... THAT HE'S THE *FOUNDATION* OF OUR WORLD AND OUR LIFE?

THAT HE'S THE ONLY THING WE CAN *DEPEND* ON?

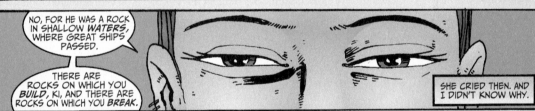

NO, FOR HE WAS A ROCK IN SHALLOW *WATERS,* WHERE GREAT SHIPS PASSED.

THERE ARE ROCKS ON WHICH YOU *BUILD,* KI, AND THERE ARE ROCKS ON WHICH YOU *BREAK.*

SHE CRIED THEN. AND I DIDN'T KNOW WHY.

IDIOT.

I WAS HER *DAUGHTER*--HER SECOND SELF. SHE DIDN'T NEED THE SIGHT OR THE SPARK TO KNOW WHAT WAS IN MY MIND.

I WAS *THIRTEEN* YEARS OLD. THERE WAS A BOY CALLED ENU IN BIRCH FASTNESS WHO HAD ASKED FOR MY HAND, BUT MOTHER SAID I WAS TOO YOUNG.

TOO YOUNG! THE NEXT MORNING I ROSE WITH THE SUN.

AND SET OFF THROUGH THE DEW AND THE THOUSANDFOLD BIRDSONG TO *SAVE* THE MAKER.

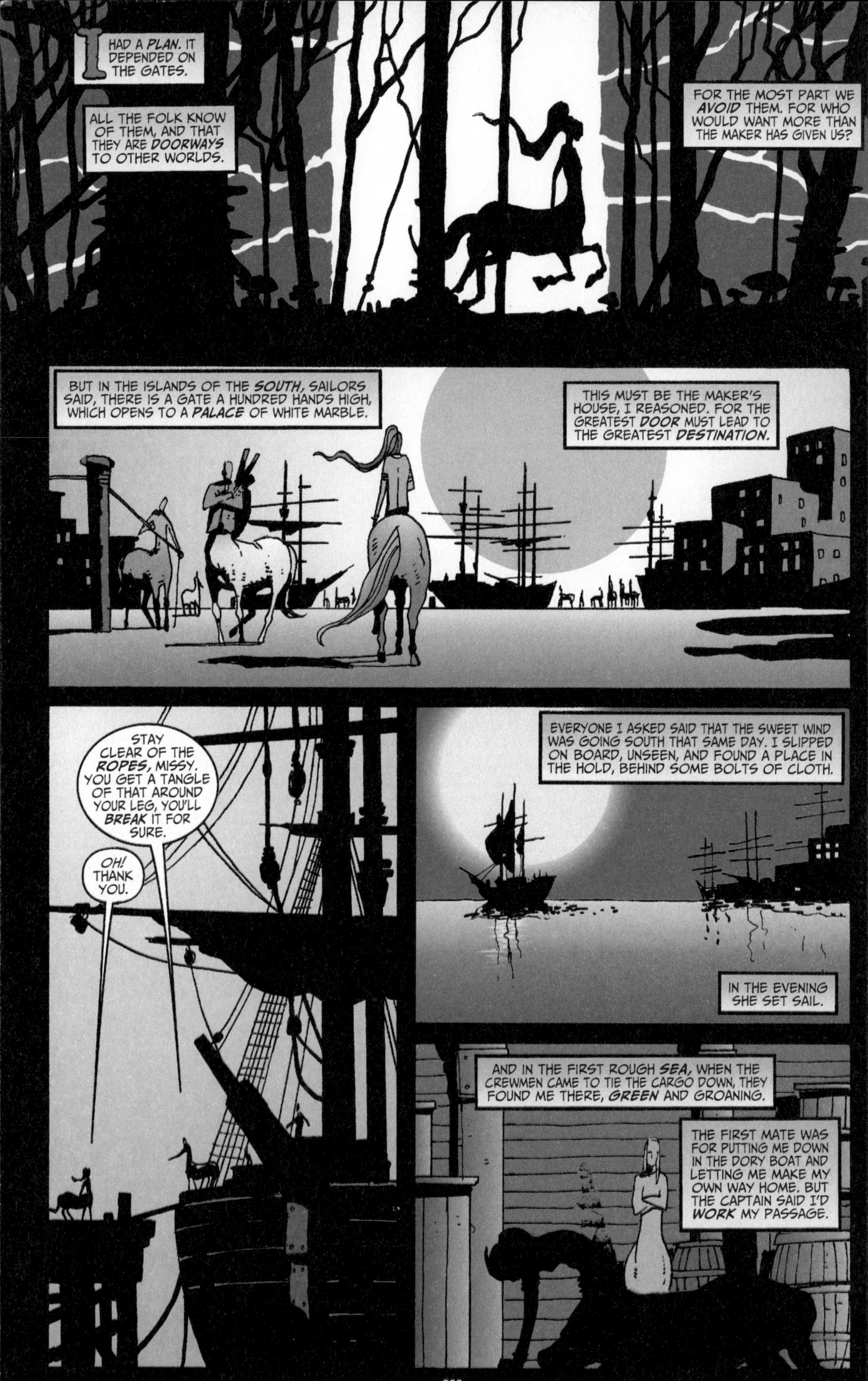
I HAD A PLAN. IT DEPENDED ON THE GATES.
ALL THE FOLK KNOW OF THEM, AND THAT THEY ARE DOORWAYS TO OTHER WORLDS.
FOR THE MOST PART WE AVOID THEM. FOR WHO WOULD WANT MORE THAN THE MAKER HAS GIVEN US?
BUT IN THE ISLANDS OF THE SOUTH, SAILORS SAID, THERE IS A GATE A HUNDRED HANDS HIGH, WHICH OPENS TO A PALACE OF WHITE MARBLE.
THIS MUST BE THE MAKER'S HOUSE, I REASONED. FOR THE GREATEST DOOR MUST LEAD TO THE GREATEST DESTINATION.
STAY CLEAR OF THE ROPES, MISSY. YOU GET A TANGLE OF THAT AROUND YOUR LEG, YOU'LL BREAK IT FOR SURE.
OH! THANK YOU.
EVERYONE I ASKED SAID THAT THE SWEET WIND WAS GOING SOUTH THAT SAME DAY. I SLIPPED ON BOARD, UNSEEN, AND FOUND A PLACE IN THE HOLD, BEHIND SOME BOLTS OF CLOTH.
IN THE EVENING SHE SET SAIL.
AND IN THE FIRST ROUGH SEA, WHEN THE CREWMEN CAME TO TIE THE CARGO DOWN, THEY FOUND ME THERE, GREEN AND GROANING.
THE FIRST MATE WAS FOR PUTTING ME DOWN IN THE DORY BOAT AND LETTING ME MAKE MY OWN WAY HOME. BUT THE CAPTAIN SAID I'D WORK MY PASSAGE.

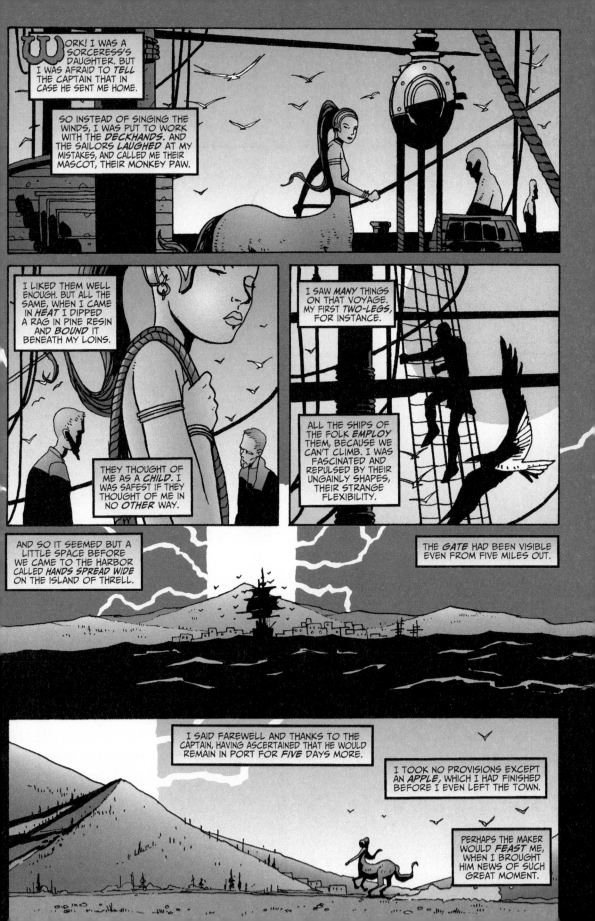

WORK! I WAS A SORCERESS'S DAUGHTER. BUT I WAS AFRAID TO *TELL* THE CAPTAIN THAT IN CASE HE SENT ME HOME.

SO INSTEAD OF SINGING THE WINDS, I WAS PUT TO WORK WITH THE *DECKHANDS.* AND THE SAILORS *LAUGHED* AT MY MISTAKES, AND CALLED ME THEIR MASCOT, THEIR MONKEY PAW.

I LIKED THEM WELL ENOUGH. BUT ALL THE SAME, WHEN I CAME IN *HEAT* I DIPPED A RAG IN PINE RESIN AND *BOUND* IT BENEATH MY LOINS.

THEY THOUGHT OF ME AS A *CHILD.* I WAS SAFEST IF THEY THOUGHT OF ME IN NO *OTHER* WAY.

I SAW *MANY* THINGS ON THAT VOYAGE. MY FIRST *TWO-LEGS,* FOR INSTANCE.

ALL THE SHIPS OF THE FOLK *EMPLOY* THEM, BECAUSE WE CAN'T CLIMB. I WAS FASCINATED AND REPULSED BY THEIR UNGAINLY SHAPES, THEIR STRANGE FLEXIBILITY.

AND SO IT SEEMED BUT A LITTLE SPACE BEFORE WE CAME TO THE HARBOR CALLED *HANDS SPREAD WIDE* ON THE ISLAND OF THRELL.

THE *GATE* HAD BEEN VISIBLE EVEN FROM FIVE MILES OUT.

I SAID FAREWELL AND THANKS TO THE CAPTAIN, HAVING ASCERTAINED THAT HE WOULD REMAIN IN PORT FOR *FIVE* DAYS MORE.

I TOOK NO PROVISIONS EXCEPT AN *APPLE,* WHICH I HAD FINISHED BEFORE I EVEN LEFT THE TOWN.

PERHAPS THE MAKER WOULD *FEAST* ME, WHEN I BROUGHT HIM NEWS OF SUCH GREAT MOMENT.

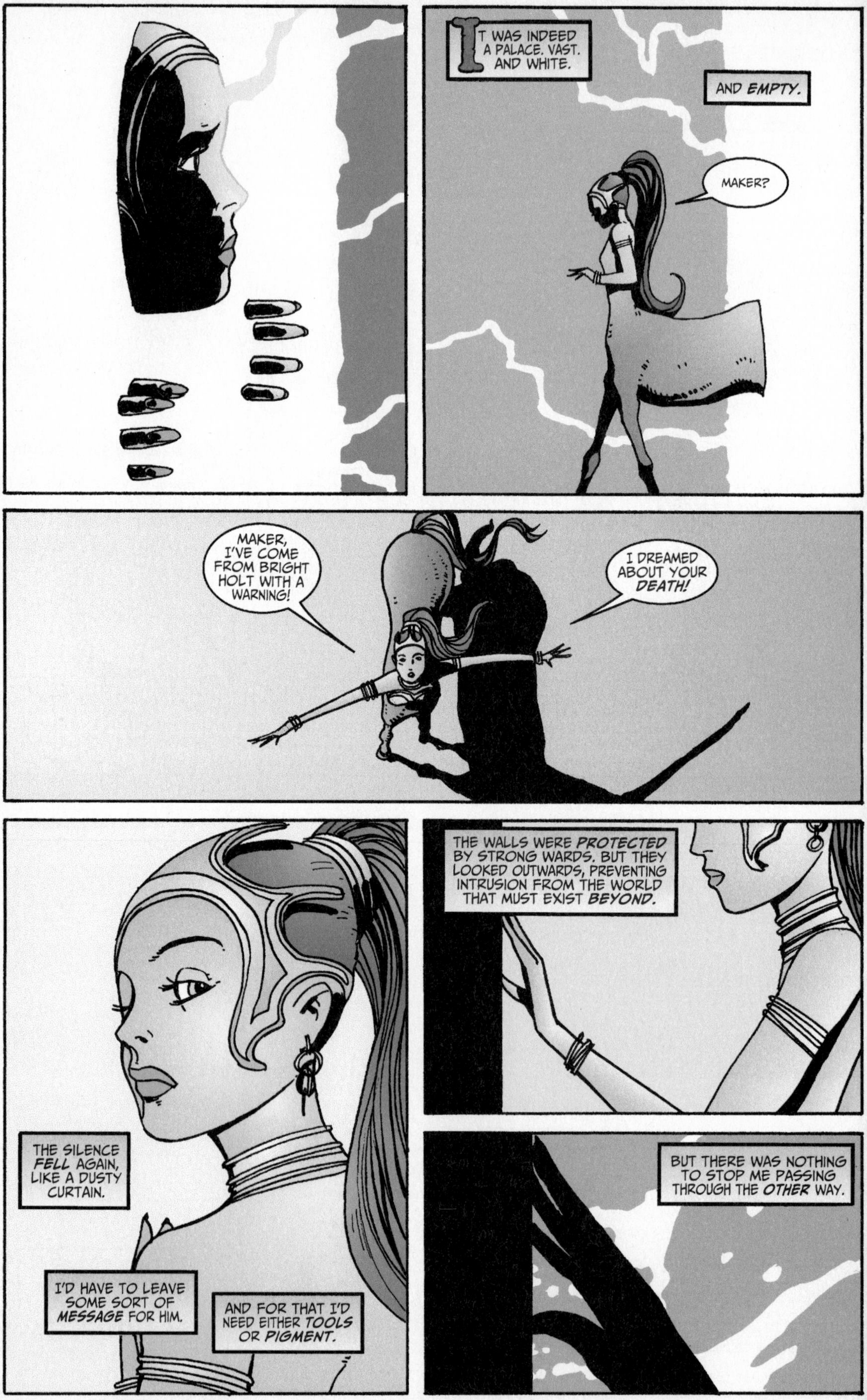
IT WAS INDEED A PALACE. VAST. AND WHITE.
AND EMPTY.
MAKER?
MAKER, I'VE COME FROM BRIGHT HOLT WITH A WARNING!
I DREAMED ABOUT YOUR DEATH!
THE SILENCE FELL AGAIN, LIKE A DUSTY CURTAIN.
I'D HAVE TO LEAVE SOME SORT OF MESSAGE FOR HIM.
AND FOR THAT I'D NEED EITHER TOOLS OR PIGMENT.
THE WALLS WERE PROTECTED BY STRONG WARDS. BUT THEY LOOKED OUTWARDS, PREVENTING INTRUSION FROM THE WORLD THAT MUST EXIST BEYOND.
BUT THERE WAS NOTHING TO STOP ME PASSING THROUGH THE OTHER WAY.

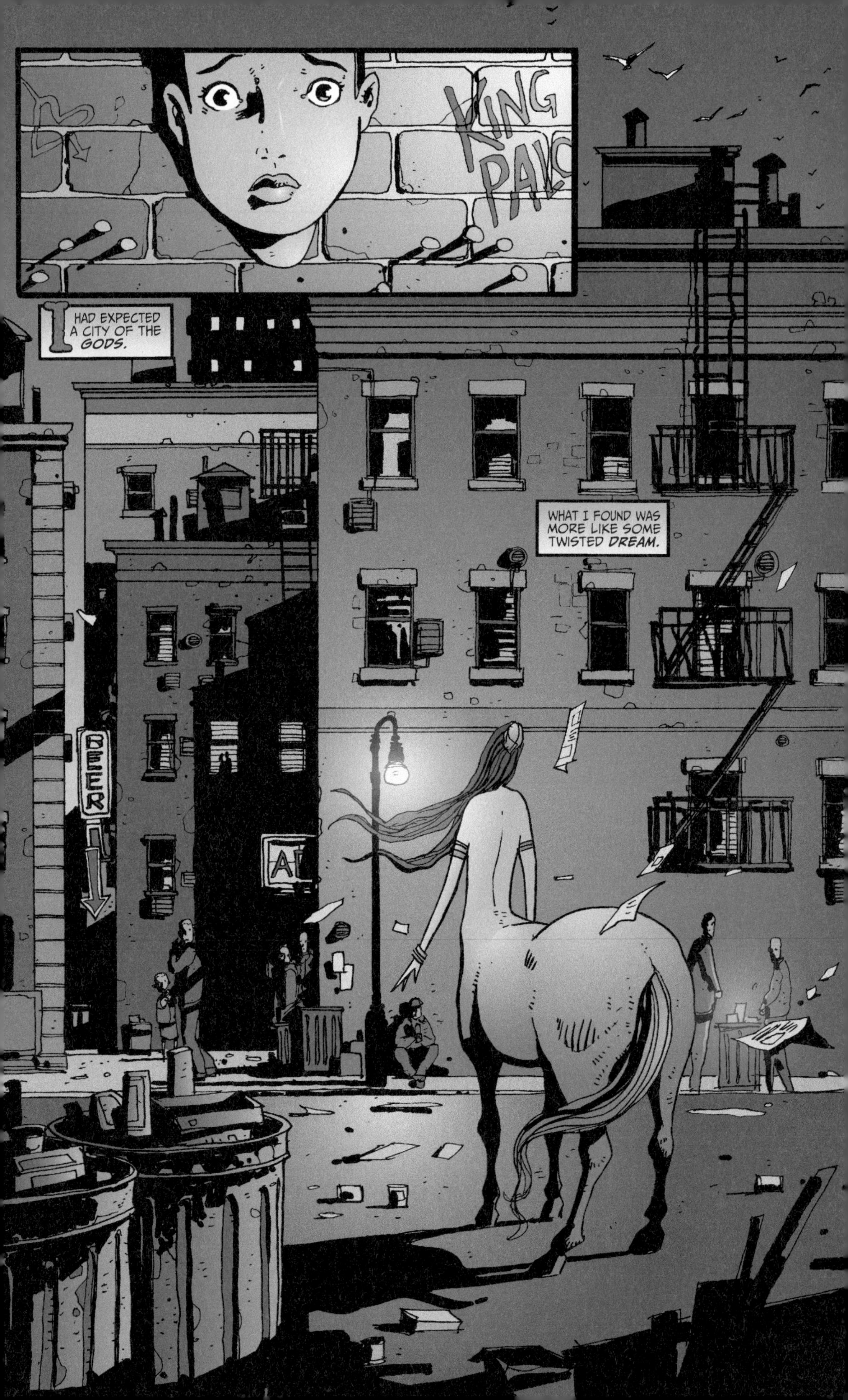
KING
I HAD EXPECTED A CITY OF THE GODS.
WHAT I FOUND WAS MORE LIKE SOME TWISTED DREAM.
BEER

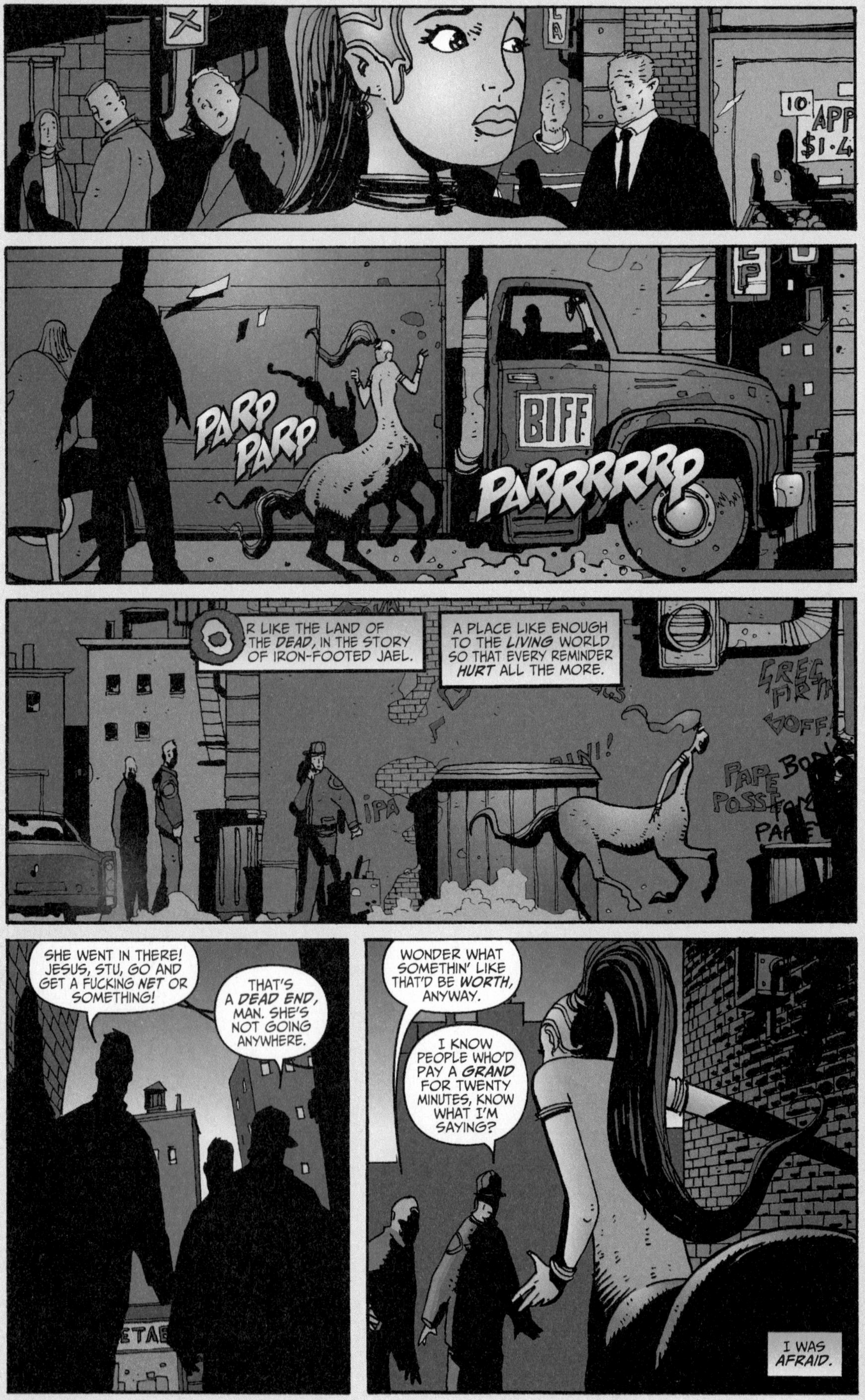
PARP PARP
PARRRRRP
BIFF
R LIKE THE LAND OF THE DEAD, IN THE STORY OF IRON-FOOTED JAEL.
A PLACE LIKE ENOUGH TO THE LIVING WORLD SO THAT EVERY REMINDER HURT ALL THE MORE.
SHE WENT IN THERE! JESUS, STU, GO AND GET A FUCKING NET OR SOMETHING!
THAT'S A DEAD END, MAN. SHE'S NOT GOING ANYWHERE.
WONDER WHAT SOMETHIN' LIKE THAT'D BE WORTH, ANYWAY.
I KNOW PEOPLE WHO'D PAY A GRAND FOR TWENTY MINUTES, KNOW WHAT I'M SAYING?
I WAS AFRAID.

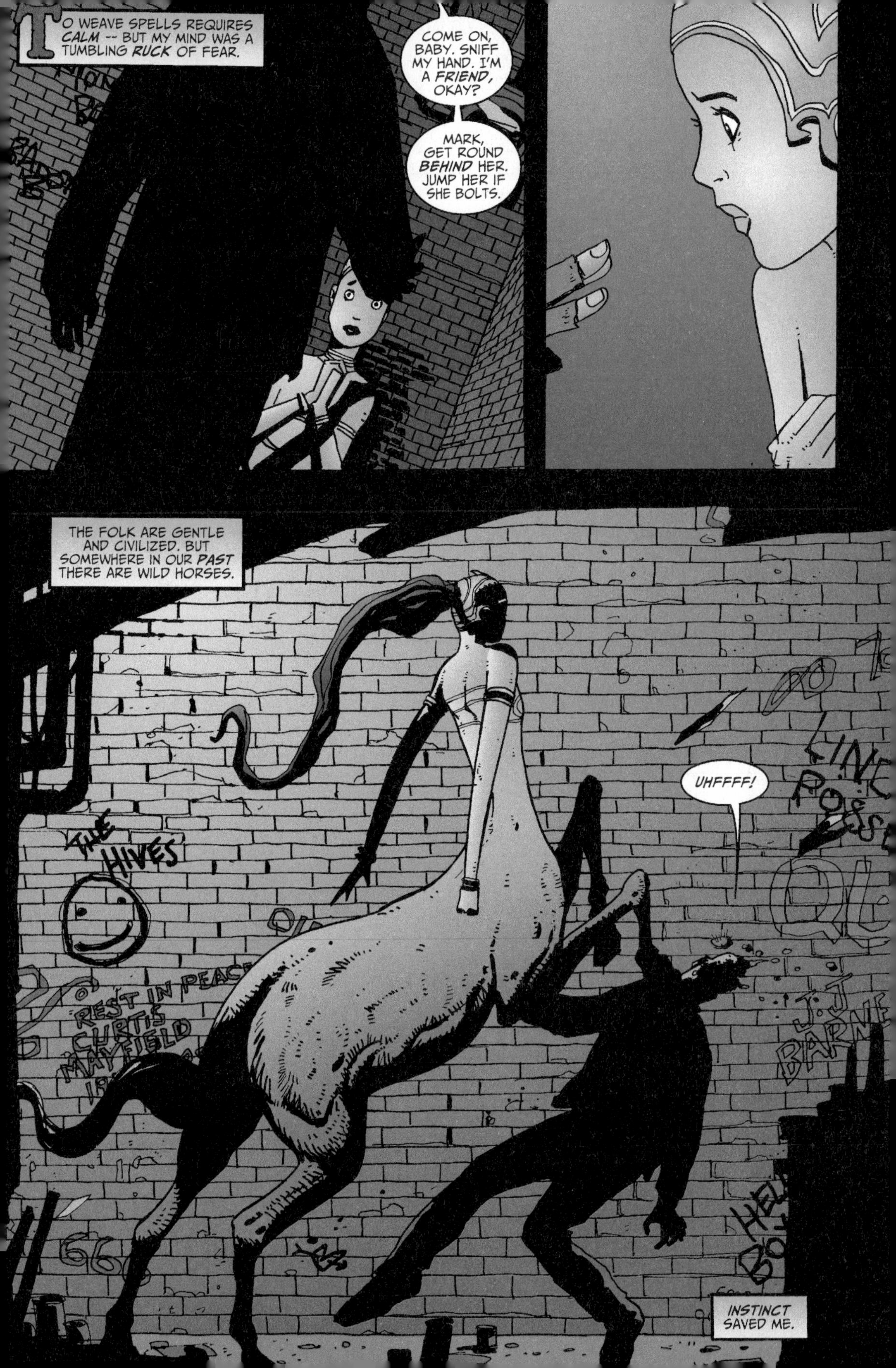
TO WEAVE SPELLS REQUIRES CALM -- BUT MY MIND WAS A TUMBLING RUCK OF FEAR.
COME ON, BABY. SNIFF MY HAND. I'M A FRIEND, OKAY?
MARK, GET ROUND BEHIND HER. JUMP HER IF SHE BOLTS.
THE FOLK ARE GENTLE AND CIVILIZED. BUT SOMEWHERE IN OUR PAST THERE ARE WILD HORSES.
UHFFFF!
THE HIVES
REST IN PEACE CURTIS MAYFIELD
INSTINCT SAVED ME.

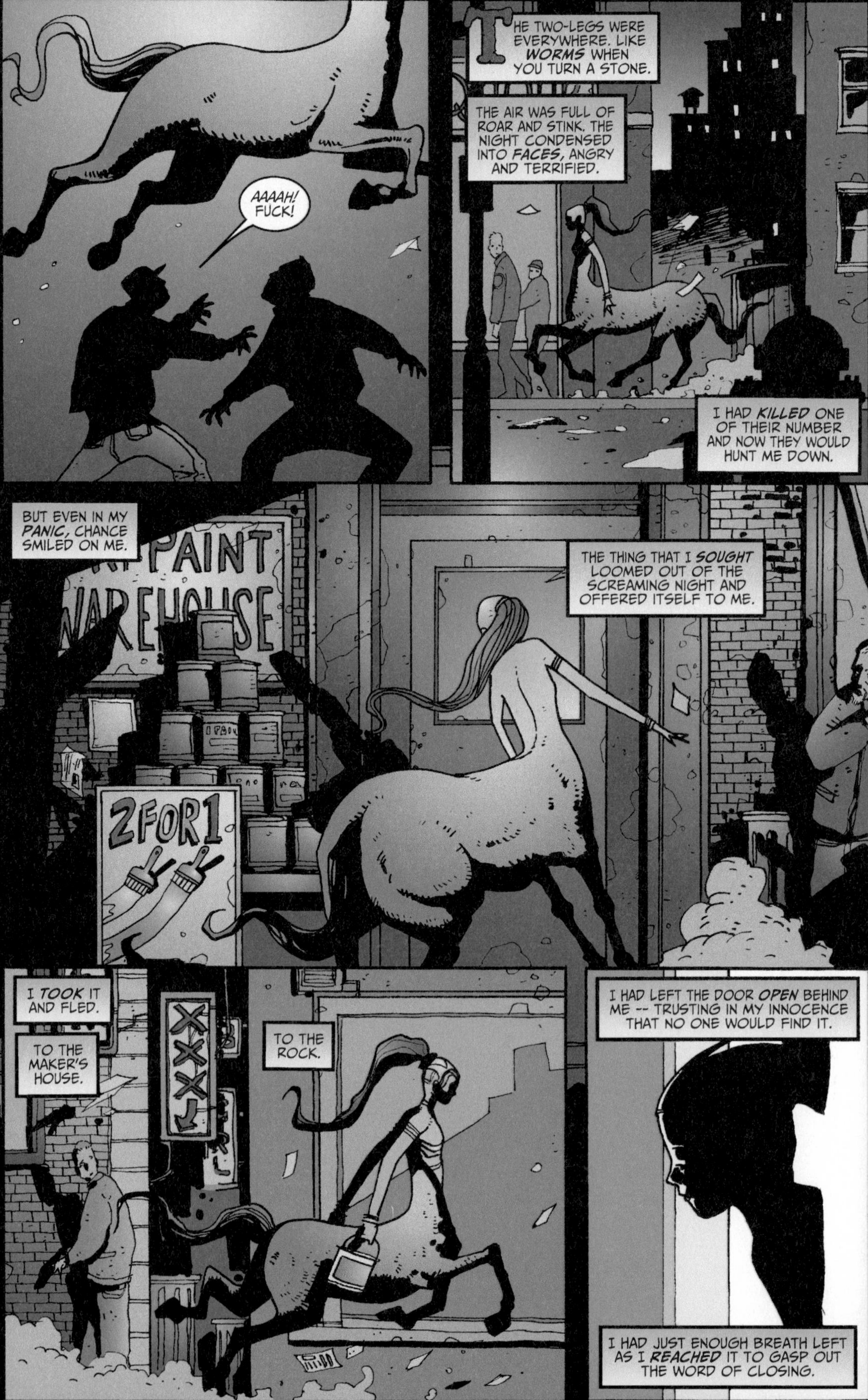
AAAAH! FUCK!
THE TWO-LEGS WERE EVERYWHERE. LIKE WORMS WHEN YOU TURN A STONE.
THE AIR WAS FULL OF ROAR AND STINK. THE NIGHT CONDENSED INTO FACES, ANGRY AND TERRIFIED.
I HAD KILLED ONE OF THEIR NUMBER AND NOW THEY WOULD HUNT ME DOWN.
BUT EVEN IN MY PANIC, CHANCE SMILED ON ME.
PAINT
WAREHOUSE
THE THING THAT I SOUGHT LOOMED OUT OF THE SCREAMING NIGHT AND OFFERED ITSELF TO ME.
2FOR1
I TOOK IT AND FLED.
TO THE MAKER'S HOUSE.
XXX
TO THE ROCK.
I HAD LEFT THE DOOR OPEN BEHIND ME -- TRUSTING IN MY INNOCENCE THAT NO ONE WOULD FIND IT.
I HAD JUST ENOUGH BREATH LEFT AS I REACHED IT TO GASP OUT THE WORD OF CLOSING.

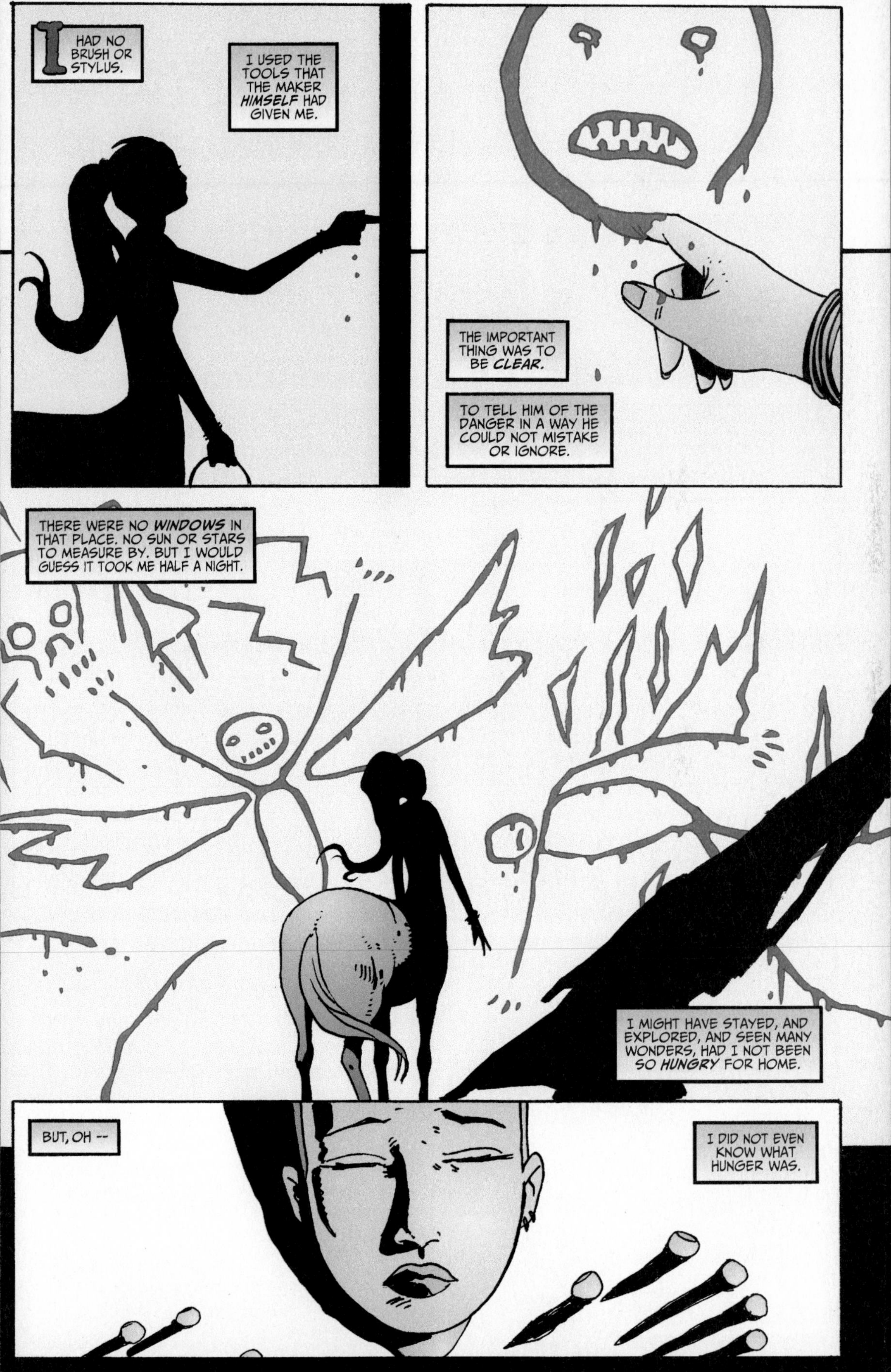
I HAD NO BRUSH OR STYLUS.
I USED THE TOOLS THAT THE MAKER *HIMSELF* HAD GIVEN ME.
THE IMPORTANT THING WAS TO BE *CLEAR.*
TO TELL HIM OF THE DANGER IN A WAY HE COULD NOT MISTAKE OR IGNORE.
THERE WERE NO *WINDOWS* IN THAT PLACE. NO SUN OR STARS TO MEASURE BY. BUT I WOULD GUESS IT TOOK ME HALF A NIGHT.
I MIGHT HAVE STAYED, AND EXPLORED, AND SEEN MANY WONDERS, HAD I NOT BEEN SO *HUNGRY* FOR HOME.
BUT, OH --
I DID NOT EVEN KNOW WHAT HUNGER WAS.

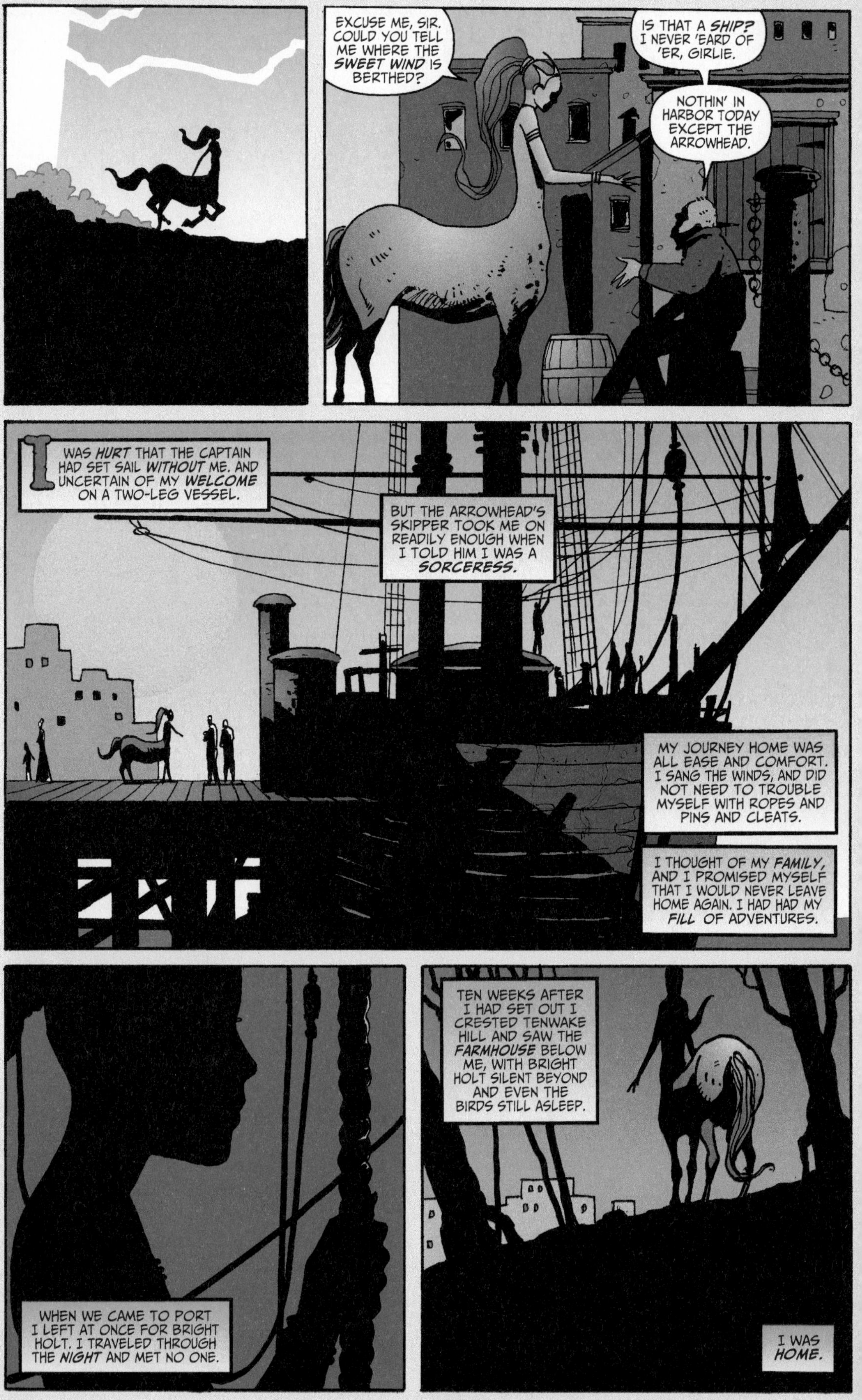
EXCUSE ME, SIR. COULD YOU TELL ME WHERE THE *SWEET WIND* IS BERTHED?
IS THAT A *SHIP?* I NEVER 'EARD OF 'ER, GIRLIE.
NOTHIN' IN HARBOR TODAY EXCEPT THE ARROWHEAD.
I WAS *HURT* THAT THE CAPTAIN HAD SET SAIL *WITHOUT* ME. AND UNCERTAIN OF MY *WELCOME* ON A TWO-LEG VESSEL.
BUT THE ARROWHEAD'S SKIPPER TOOK ME ON READILY ENOUGH WHEN I TOLD HIM I WAS A *SORCERESS.*
MY JOURNEY HOME WAS ALL EASE AND COMFORT. I SANG THE WINDS, AND DID NOT NEED TO TROUBLE MYSELF WITH ROPES AND PINS AND CLEATS.
I THOUGHT OF MY *FAMILY,* AND I PROMISED MYSELF THAT I WOULD NEVER LEAVE HOME AGAIN. I HAD HAD MY *FILL* OF ADVENTURES.
WHEN WE CAME TO PORT I LEFT AT ONCE FOR BRIGHT HOLT. I TRAVELED THROUGH THE *NIGHT* AND MET NO ONE.
TEN WEEKS AFTER I HAD SET OUT I CRESTED TENWAKE HILL AND SAW THE *FARMHOUSE* BELOW ME, WITH BRIGHT HOLT SILENT BEYOND AND EVEN THE BIRDS STILL ASLEEP.
I WAS *HOME.*

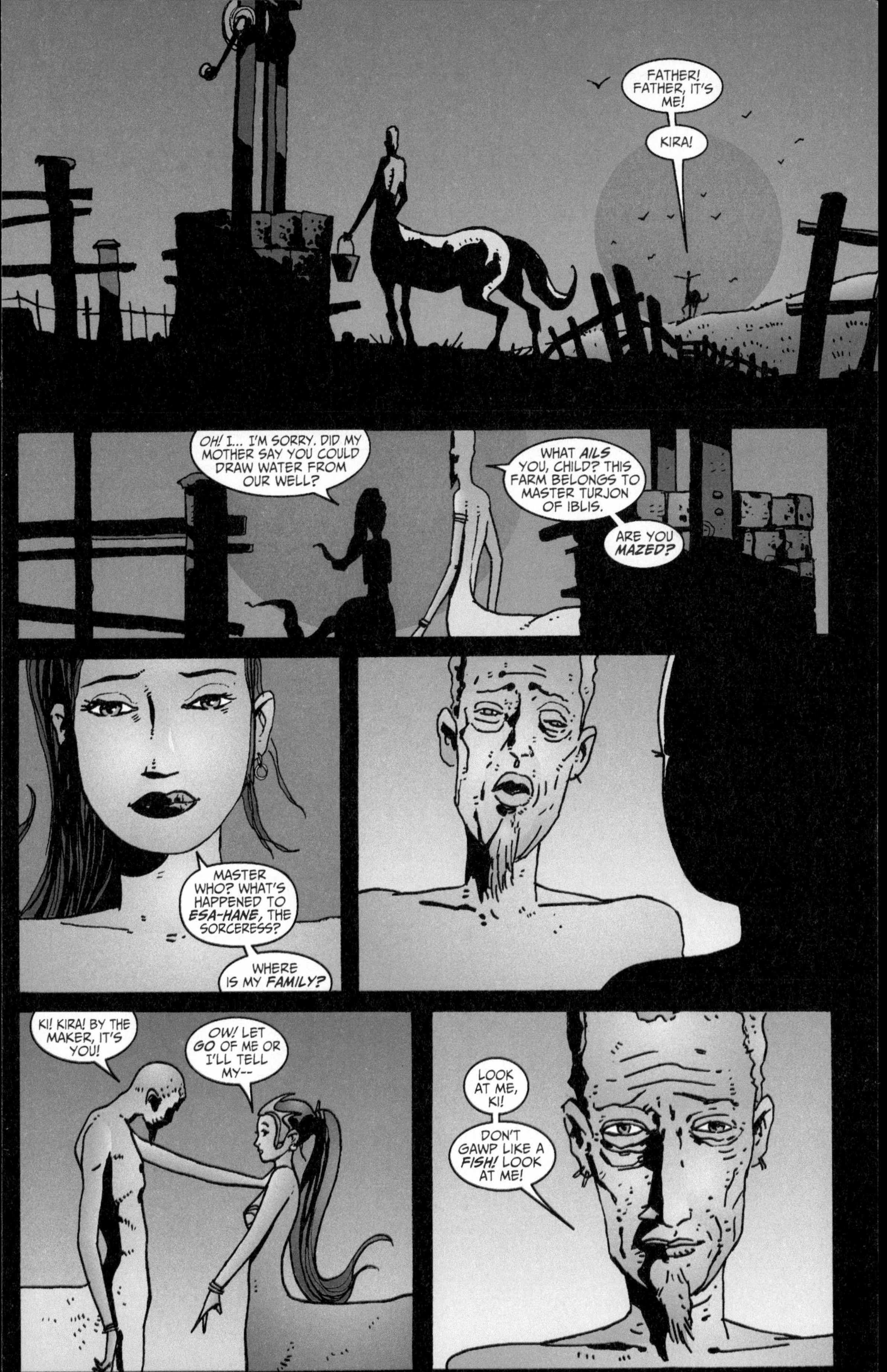
FATHER! FATHER, IT'S ME!
KIRA!
OH! I... I'M SORRY. DID MY MOTHER SAY YOU COULD DRAW WATER FROM OUR WELL?
WHAT AILS YOU, CHILD? THIS FARM BELONGS TO MASTER TURJON OF IBLIS.
ARE YOU MAZED?
MASTER WHO? WHAT'S HAPPENED TO ESA-HANE, THE SORCERESS?
WHERE IS MY FAMILY?
KI! KIRA! BY THE MAKER, IT'S YOU!
OW! LET GO OF ME OR I'LL TELL MY--
LOOK AT ME, KI!
DON'T GAWP LIKE A FISH! LOOK AT ME!

VALE?

OH, SWEET FATES!

WHAT *HAPPENED* TO YOU?

ONLY TIME, KI. *TIME* HAPPENS TO EVERYONE-- EXCEPT *YOU*, IT SEEMS.

COME, DON'T CRY. DON'T--

I HAD BEEN GONE FOR *SIXTY YEARS.*

AND MY MOTHER HAD DIED ONLY TEN YEARS AFTER I LEFT. DIED CALLING MY *NAME*, WITH THE DOCTOR STANDING HELPLESS BECAUSE SHE WASN'T EVEN *SICK.*

WE THOUGHT YOU WERE *DEAD.*

OH, KI, WE THOUGHT YOU WERE DEAD AND BURIED.

MY FATHER THREW HIMSELF ON HER *FUNERAL* PYRE, AS A GOOD HUSBAND *SHOULD.*

THEN THE TWO-LEGS CAME BACK FROM IBLIS AND TOOK THE VILLAGE. THERE WAS NO LONGER A SORCERESS TO *STOP* THEM.

THE BOY, ENU, WHO HAD ALMOST BEEN MY SWEETHEART, HAD DIED IN THAT BATTLE. HENCHA WAS SOLD INTO *SLAVERY* TO THE SEVEN CLOUDS CLAN.

AND VALE LIVED ON AS A *LABORER* ON THE FARM OUR FAMILY HAD OWNED FOR THREE HUNDRED YEARS.

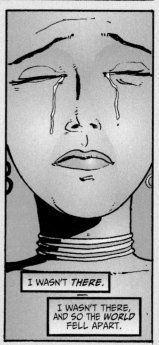

I WASN'T *THERE.*

I WASN'T THERE, AND SO THE *WORLD* FELL APART.

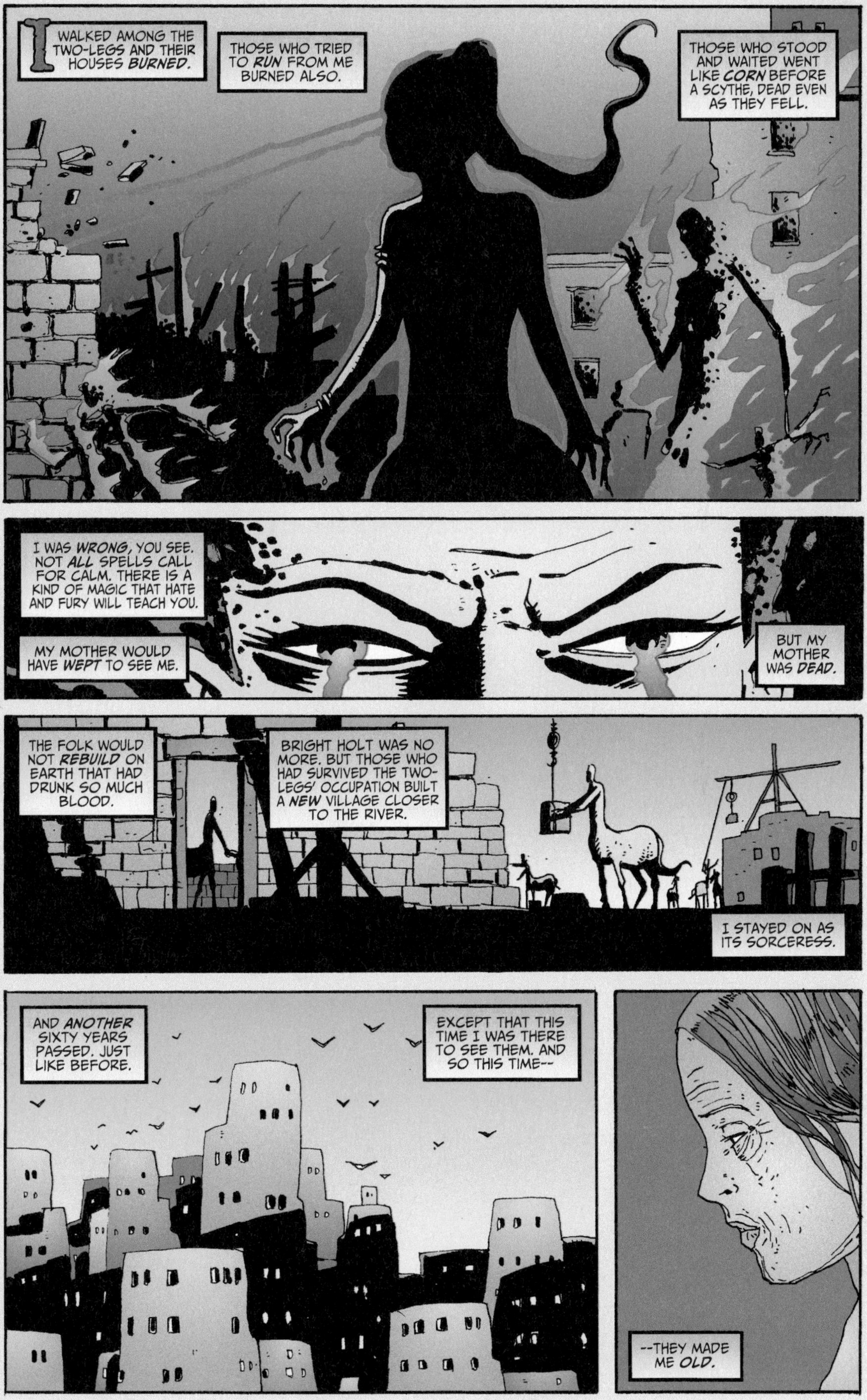
I WALKED AMONG THE TWO-LEGS AND THEIR HOUSES BURNED.
THOSE WHO TRIED TO RUN FROM ME BURNED ALSO.
THOSE WHO STOOD AND WAITED WENT LIKE CORN BEFORE A SCYTHE, DEAD EVEN AS THEY FELL.
I WAS WRONG, YOU SEE. NOT ALL SPELLS CALL FOR CALM. THERE IS A KIND OF MAGIC THAT HATE AND FURY WILL TEACH YOU.
MY MOTHER WOULD HAVE WEPT TO SEE ME.
BUT MY MOTHER WAS DEAD.
THE FOLK WOULD NOT REBUILD ON EARTH THAT HAD DRUNK SO MUCH BLOOD.
BRIGHT HOLT WAS NO MORE. BUT THOSE WHO HAD SURVIVED THE TWO-LEGS' OCCUPATION BUILT A NEW VILLAGE CLOSER TO THE RIVER.
I STAYED ON AS ITS SORCERESS.
AND ANOTHER SIXTY YEARS PASSED. JUST LIKE BEFORE.
EXCEPT THAT THIS TIME I WAS THERE TO SEE THEM. AND SO THIS TIME--
--THEY MADE ME OLD.

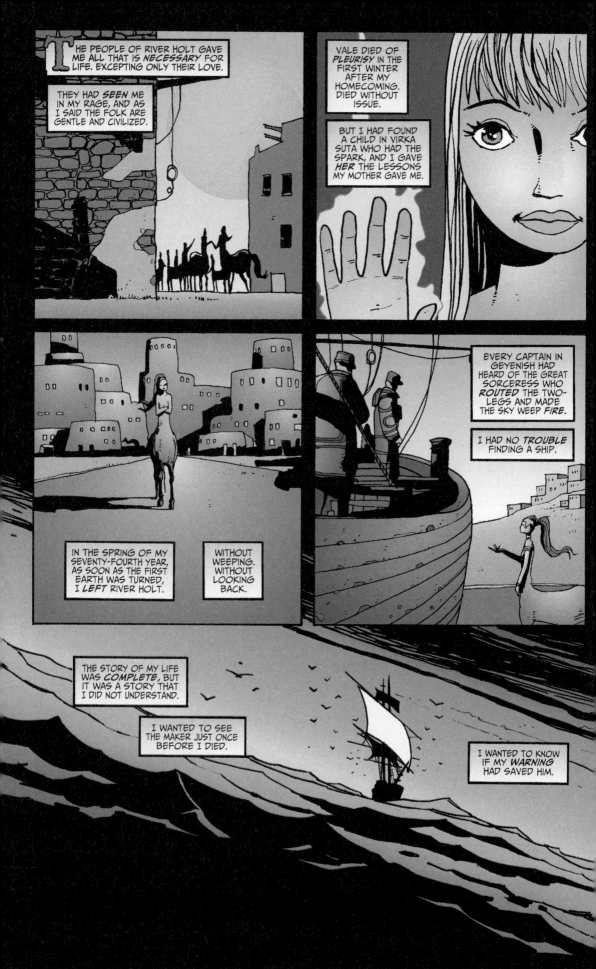

THE PEOPLE OF RIVER HOLT GAVE ME ALL THAT IS *NECESSARY* FOR LIFE. EXCEPTING ONLY THEIR LOVE.

THEY HAD *SEEN* ME IN MY RAGE, AND AS I SAID THE FOLK ARE GENTLE AND CIVILIZED.

VALE DIED OF *PLEURISY* IN THE FIRST WINTER AFTER MY HOMECOMING. DIED WITHOUT ISSUE.

BUT I HAD FOUND A CHILD IN VIRKA SUTA WHO HAD THE SPARK, AND I GAVE *HER* THE LESSONS MY MOTHER GAVE ME.

IN THE SPRING OF MY SEVENTY-FOURTH YEAR, AS SOON AS THE FIRST EARTH WAS TURNED, I *LEFT* RIVER HOLT.

WITHOUT WEEPING. WITHOUT LOOKING BACK.

EVERY CAPTAIN IN GEYENISH HAD HEARD OF THE GREAT SORCERESS WHO *ROUTED* THE TWO-LEGS AND MADE THE SKY WEEP *FIRE.*

I HAD NO *TROUBLE* FINDING A SHIP.

THE STORY OF MY LIFE WAS *COMPLETE,* BUT IT WAS A STORY THAT I DID NOT UNDERSTAND.

I WANTED TO SEE THE MAKER JUST ONCE BEFORE I DIED.

I WANTED TO KNOW IF MY *WARNING* HAD SAVED HIM.

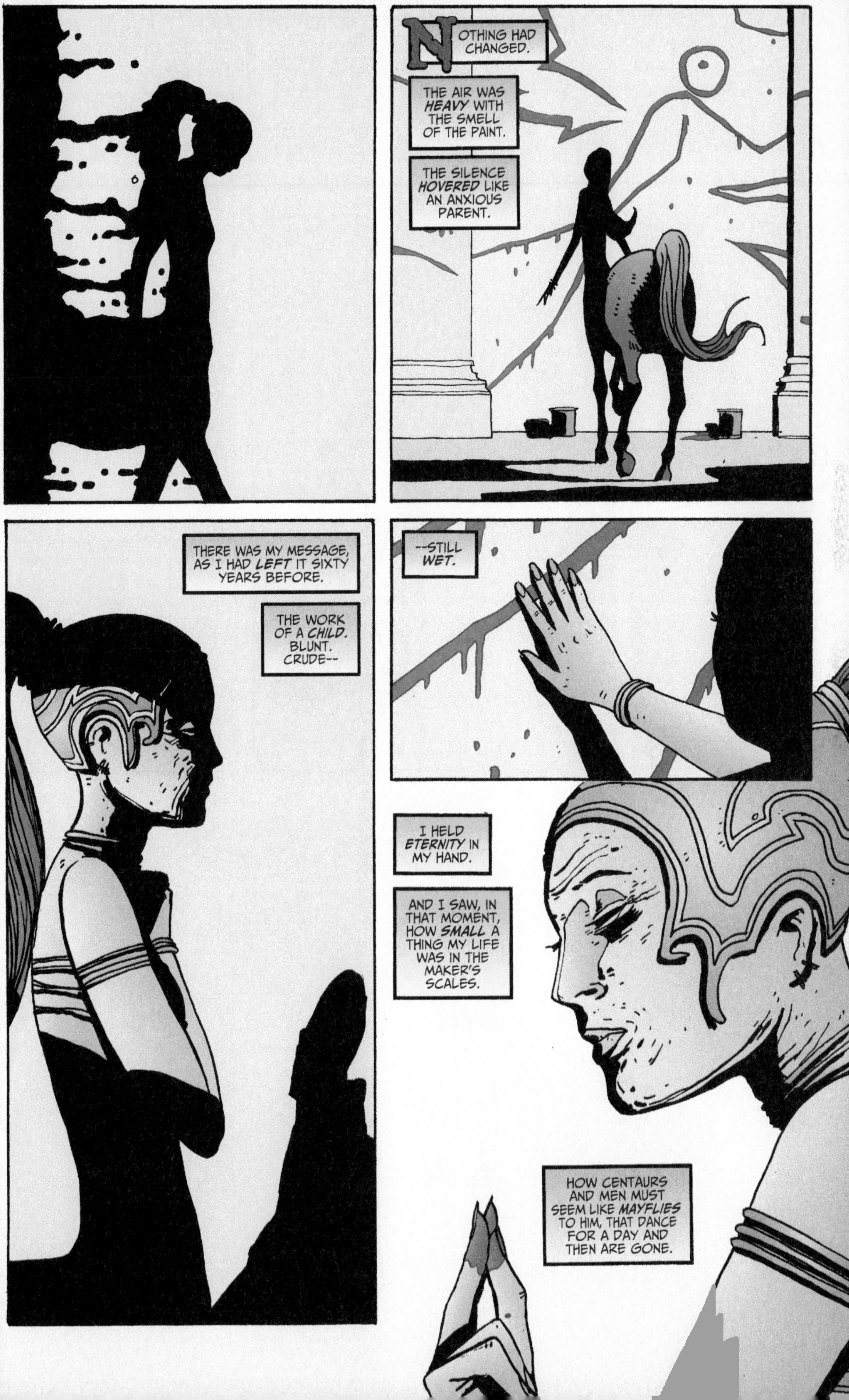
NOTHING HAD CHANGED.
THE AIR WAS HEAVY WITH THE SMELL OF THE PAINT.
THE SILENCE HOVERED LIKE AN ANXIOUS PARENT.
THERE WAS MY MESSAGE, AS I HAD LEFT IT SIXTY YEARS BEFORE.
THE WORK OF A CHILD. BLUNT. CRUDE--
--STILL WET.
I HELD ETERNITY IN MY HAND.
AND I SAW, IN THAT MOMENT, HOW SMALL A THING MY LIFE WAS IN THE MAKER'S SCALES.
HOW CENTAURS AND MEN MUST SEEM LIKE MAYFLIES TO HIM, THAT DANCE FOR A DAY AND THEN ARE GONE.

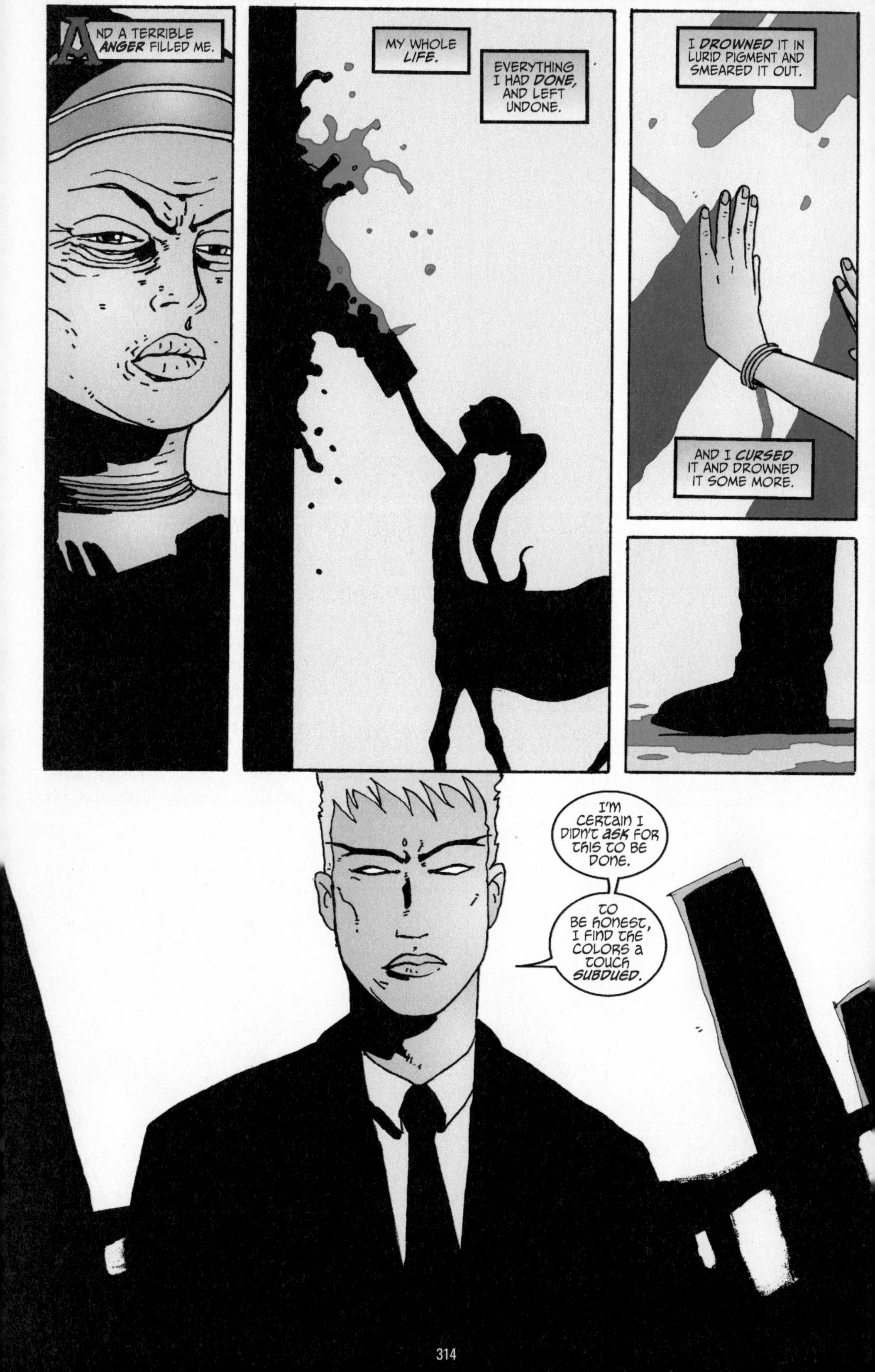
AND A TERRIBLE ANGER FILLED ME.
MY WHOLE LIFE.
EVERYTHING I HAD DONE, AND LEFT UNDONE.
I DROWNED IT IN LURID PIGMENT AND SMEARED IT OUT.
AND I CURSED IT AND DROWNED IT SOME MORE.
I'M CERTAIN I DIDN'T ASK FOR THIS TO BE DONE.
TO BE HONEST, I FIND THE COLORS A TOUCH SUBDUED.

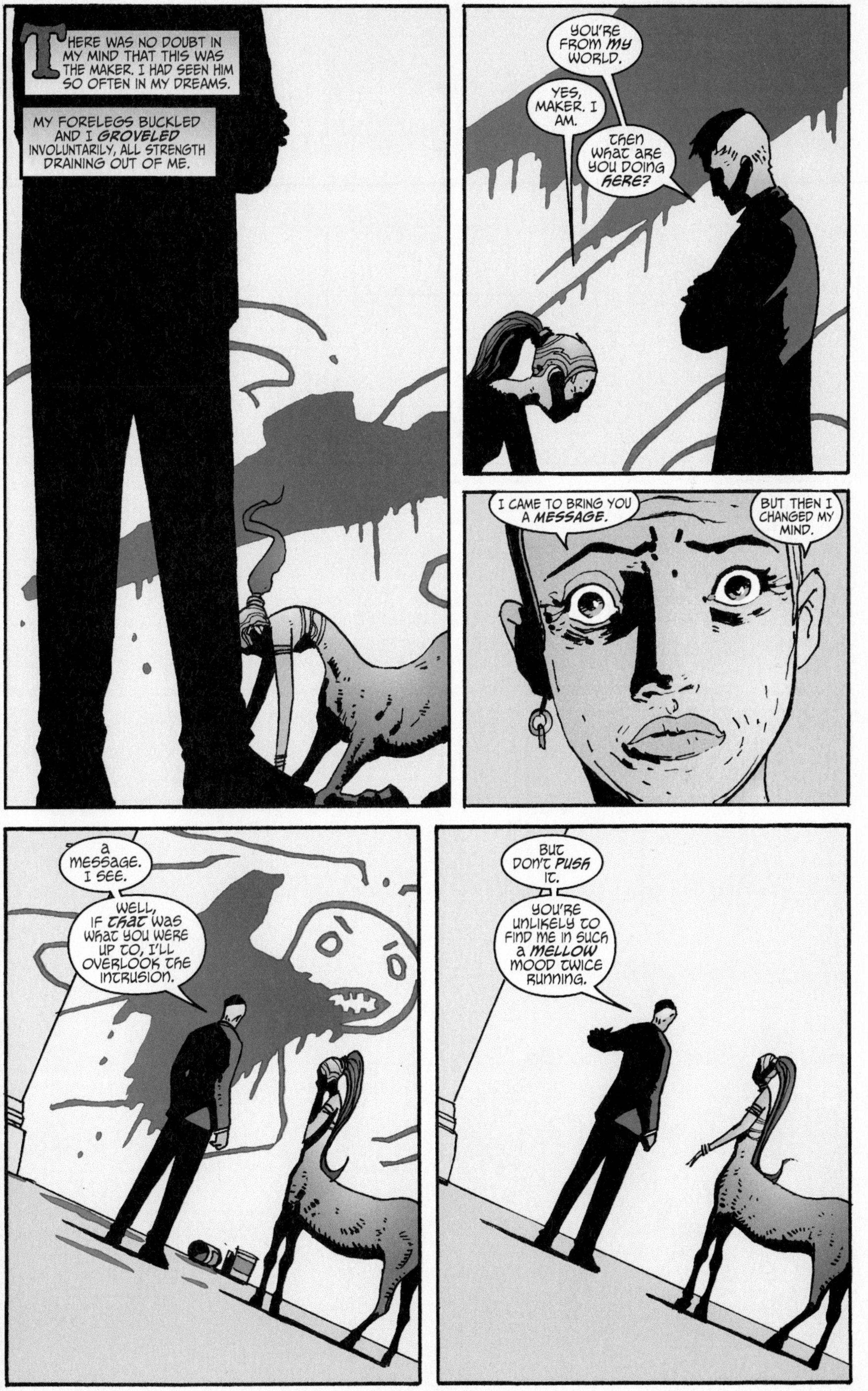
THERE WAS NO DOUBT IN MY MIND THAT THIS WAS THE MAKER. I HAD SEEN HIM SO OFTEN IN MY DREAMS.
MY FORELEGS BUCKLED AND I GROVELED INVOLUNTARILY, ALL STRENGTH DRAINING OUT OF ME.
YOU'RE FROM MY WORLD.
YES, MAKER. I AM.
THEN WHAT ARE YOU DOING HERE?
I CAME TO BRING YOU A MESSAGE.
BUT THEN I CHANGED MY MIND.
A MESSAGE. I SEE.
WELL, IF THAT WAS WHAT YOU WERE UP TO, I'LL OVERLOOK THE INTRUSION.
BUT DON'T PUSH IT.
YOU'RE UNLIKELY TO FIND ME IN SUCH A MELLOW MOOD TWICE RUNNING.

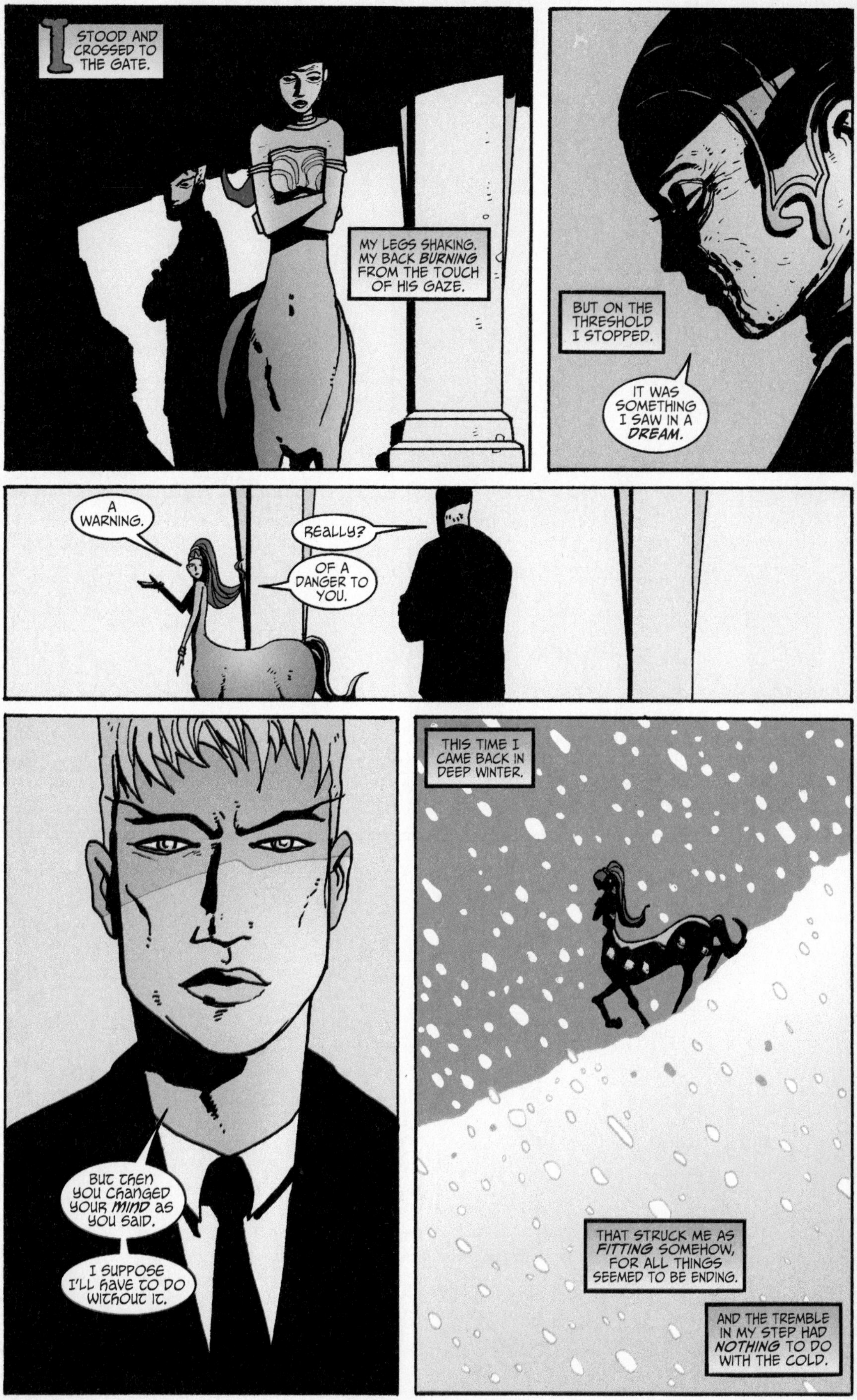
I STOOD AND CROSSED TO THE GATE.
MY LEGS SHAKING. MY BACK *BURNING* FROM THE TOUCH OF HIS GAZE.
BUT ON THE THRESHOLD I STOPPED.
IT WAS SOMETHING I SAW IN A *DREAM.*
A WARNING.
REALLY?
OF A DANGER TO YOU.
BUT THEN YOU CHANGED YOUR *MIND* AS YOU SAID.
I SUPPOSE I'LL HAVE TO DO WITHOUT IT.
THIS TIME I CAME BACK IN DEEP WINTER.
THAT STRUCK ME AS *FITTING* SOMEHOW, FOR ALL THINGS SEEMED TO BE ENDING.
AND THE TREMBLE IN MY STEP HAD *NOTHING* TO DO WITH THE COLD.

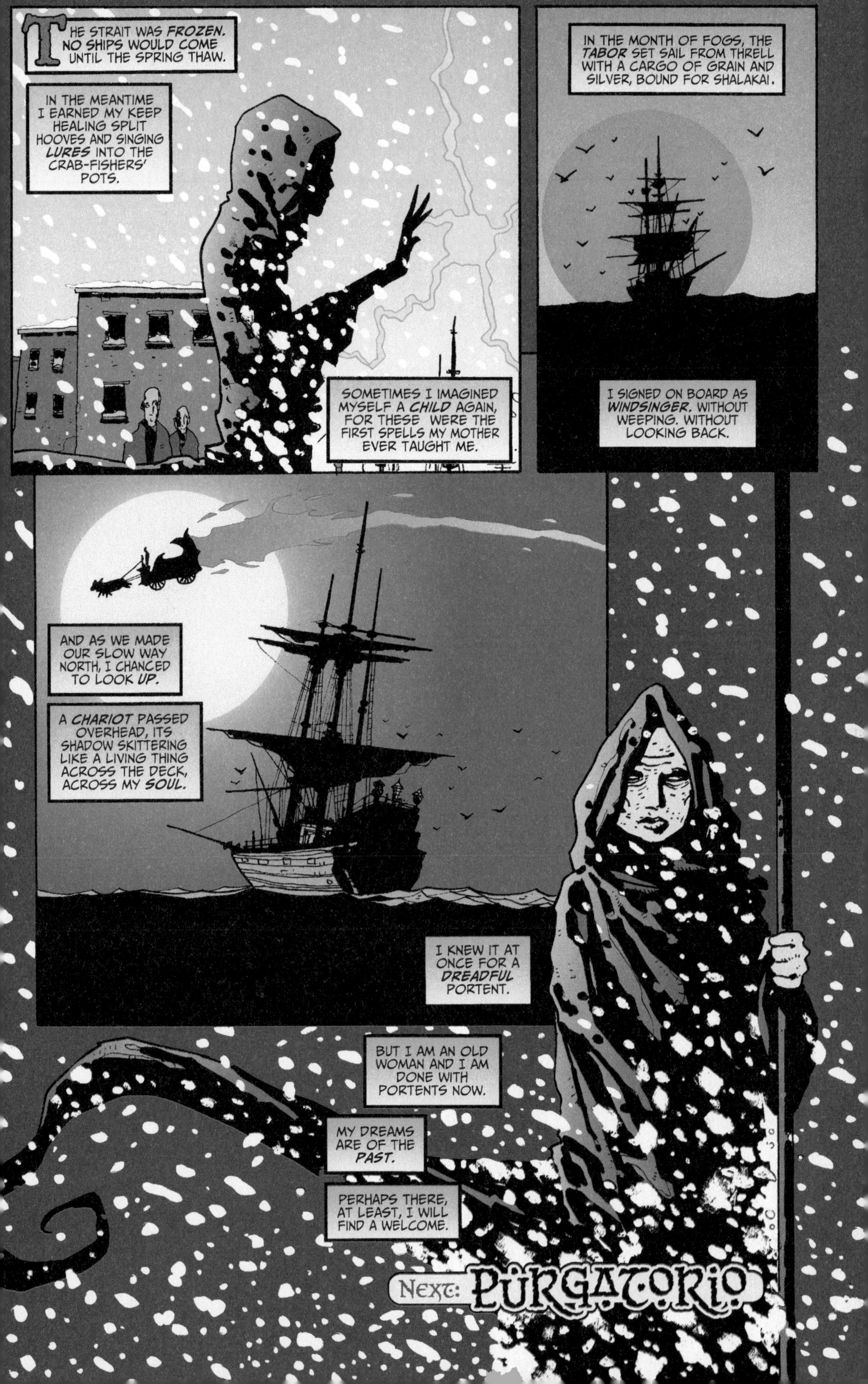
THE STRAIT WAS FROZEN. NO SHIPS WOULD COME UNTIL THE SPRING THAW.
IN THE MEANTIME I EARNED MY KEEP HEALING SPLIT HOOVES AND SINGING LURES INTO THE CRAB-FISHERS' POTS.
SOMETIMES I IMAGINED MYSELF A CHILD AGAIN, FOR THESE WERE THE FIRST SPELLS MY MOTHER EVER TAUGHT ME.
IN THE MONTH OF FOGS, THE TABOR SET SAIL FROM THRELL WITH A CARGO OF GRAIN AND SILVER, BOUND FOR SHALAKAI.
I SIGNED ON BOARD AS WINDSINGER. WITHOUT WEEPING. WITHOUT LOOKING BACK.
AND AS WE MADE OUR SLOW WAY NORTH, I CHANCED TO LOOK UP.
A CHARIOT PASSED OVERHEAD, ITS SHADOW SKITTERING LIKE A LIVING THING ACROSS THE DECK, ACROSS MY SOUL.
I KNEW IT AT ONCE FOR A DREADFUL PORTENT.
BUT I AM AN OLD WOMAN AND I AM DONE WITH PORTENTS NOW.
MY DREAMS ARE OF THE PAST.
PERHAPS THERE, AT LEAST, I WILL FIND A WELCOME.
Next: PURGATORIO

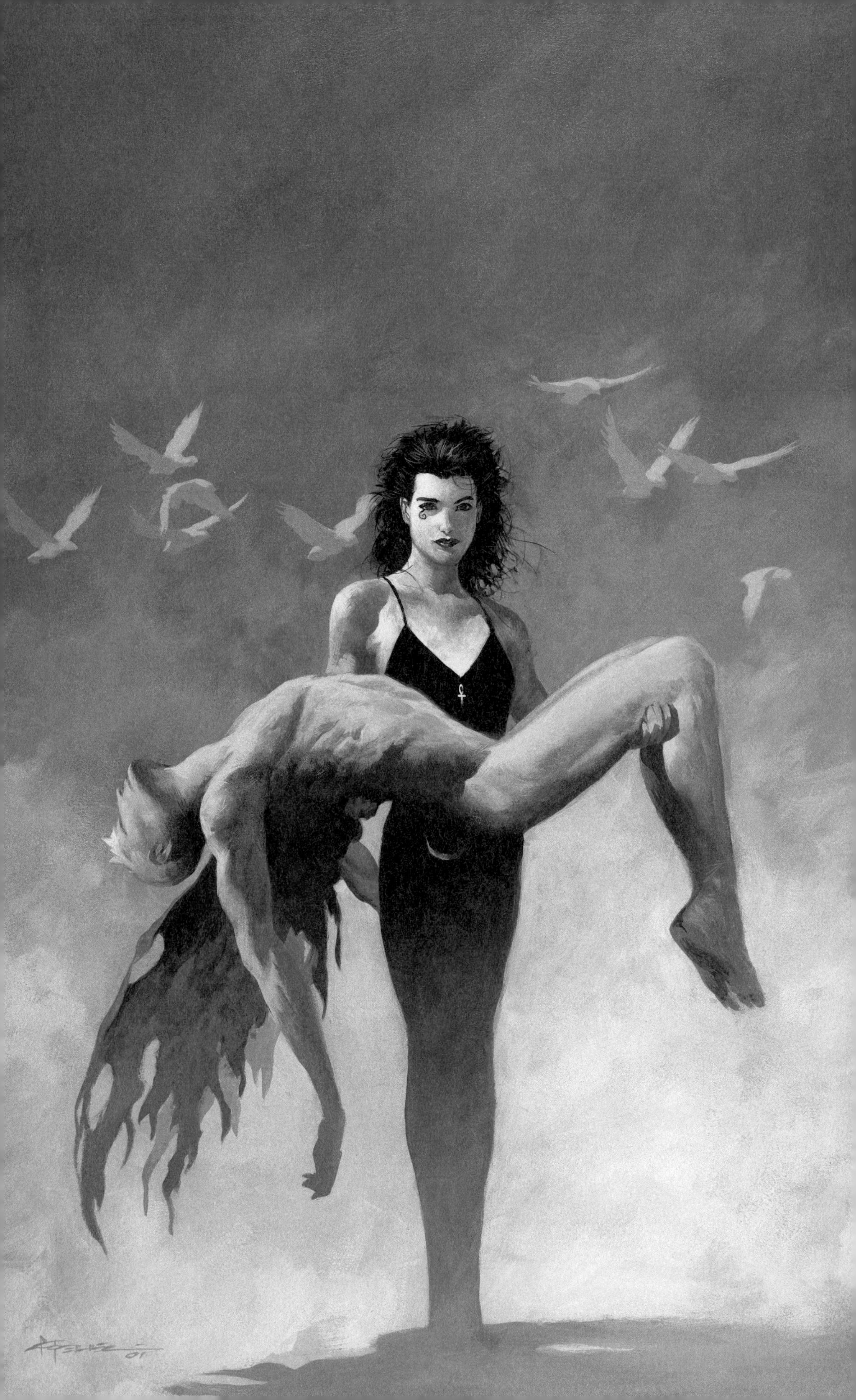

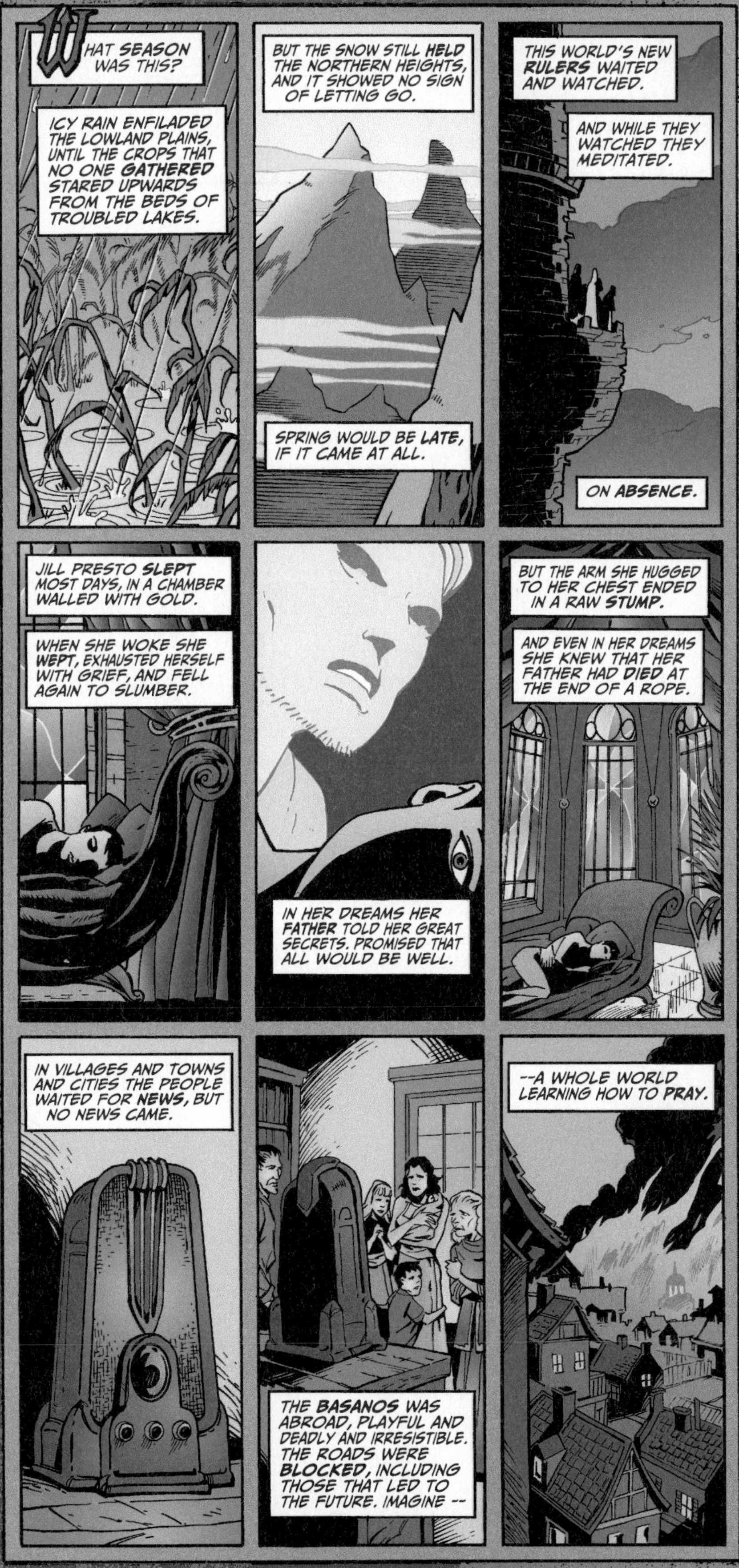
WHAT SEASON WAS THIS?
ICY RAIN ENFILADED THE LOWLAND PLAINS, UNTIL THE CROPS THAT NO ONE GATHERED STARED UPWARDS FROM THE BEDS OF TROUBLED LAKES.
BUT THE SNOW STILL HELD THE NORTHERN HEIGHTS, AND IT SHOWED NO SIGN OF LETTING GO.
SPRING WOULD BE LATE, IF IT CAME AT ALL.
THIS WORLD'S NEW RULERS WAITED AND WATCHED.
AND WHILE THEY WATCHED THEY MEDITATED.
ON ABSENCE.
JILL PRESTO SLEPT MOST DAYS, IN A CHAMBER WALLED WITH GOLD.
WHEN SHE WOKE SHE WEPT, EXHAUSTED HERSELF WITH GRIEF, AND FELL AGAIN TO SLUMBER.
IN HER DREAMS HER FATHER TOLD HER GREAT SECRETS. PROMISED THAT ALL WOULD BE WELL.
BUT THE ARM SHE HUGGED TO HER CHEST ENDED IN A RAW STUMP.
AND EVEN IN HER DREAMS SHE KNEW THAT HER FATHER HAD DIED AT THE END OF A ROPE.
IN VILLAGES AND TOWNS AND CITIES THE PEOPLE WAITED FOR NEWS, BUT NO NEWS CAME.
THE BASANOS WAS ABROAD, PLAYFUL AND DEADLY AND IRRESISTIBLE. THE ROADS WERE BLOCKED, INCLUDING THOSE THAT LED TO THE FUTURE. IMAGINE --
--A WHOLE WORLD LEARNING HOW TO PRAY.

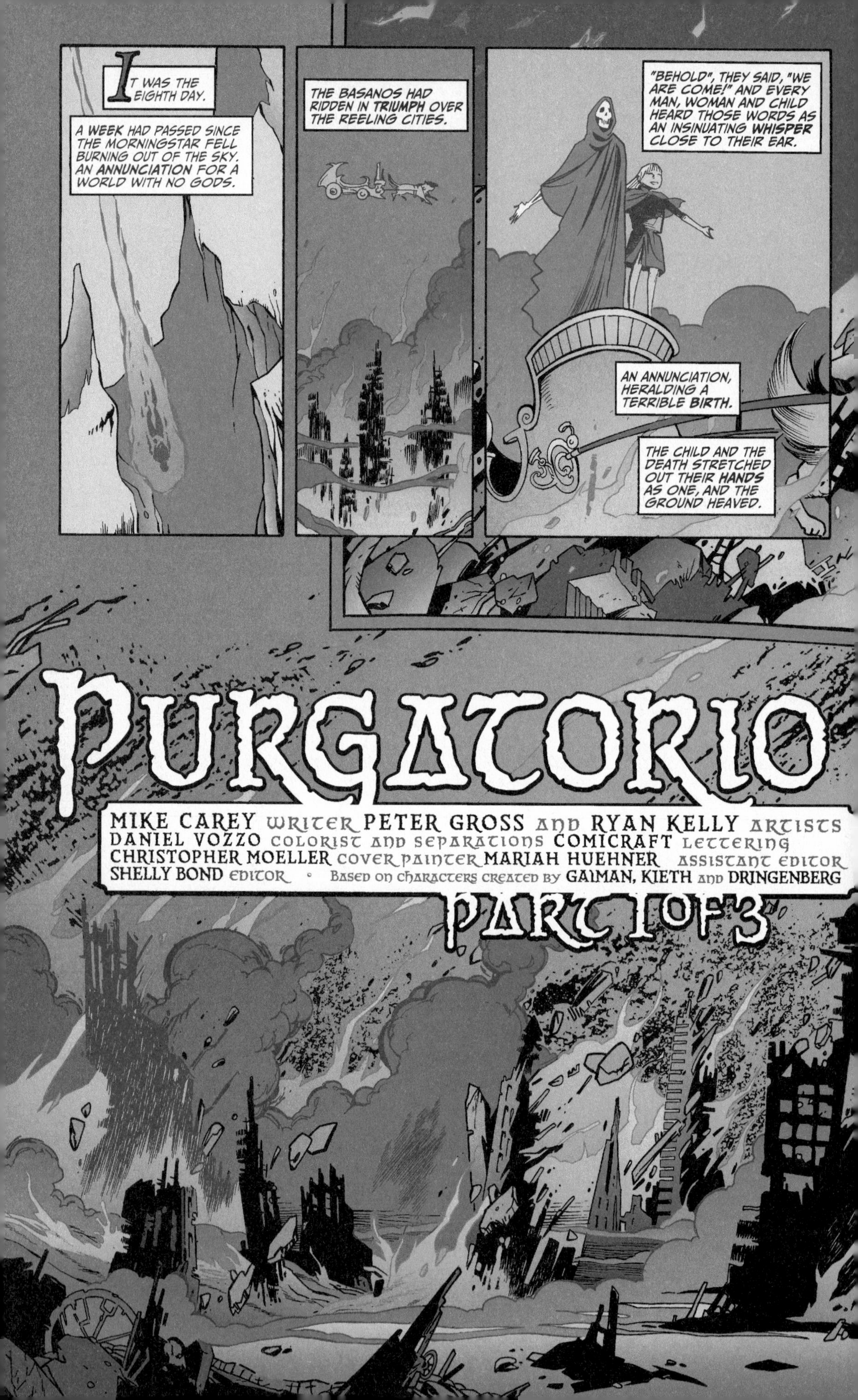
IT WAS THE EIGHTH DAY.
A WEEK HAD PASSED SINCE THE MORNINGSTAR FELL BURNING OUT OF THE SKY. AN ANNUNCIATION FOR A WORLD WITH NO GODS.
THE BASANOS HAD RIDDEN IN TRIUMPH OVER THE REELING CITIES.
"BEHOLD", THEY SAID, "WE ARE COME!" AND EVERY MAN, WOMAN AND CHILD HEARD THOSE WORDS AS AN INSINUATING WHISPER CLOSE TO THEIR EAR.
AN ANNUNCIATION, HERALDING A TERRIBLE BIRTH.
THE CHILD AND THE DEATH STRETCHED OUT THEIR HANDS AS ONE, AND THE GROUND HEAVED.
PURGATORIO
MIKE CAREY WRITER PETER GROSS AND RYAN KELLY ARTISTS
DANIEL VOZZO COLORIST AND SEPARATIONS COMICRAFT LETTERING
CHRISTOPHER MOELLER COVER PAINTER MARIAH HUEHNER ASSISTANT EDITOR
SHELLY BOND EDITOR • BASED ON CHARACTERS CREATED BY GAIMAN, KIETH AND DRINGENBERG
PART 1 OF 3

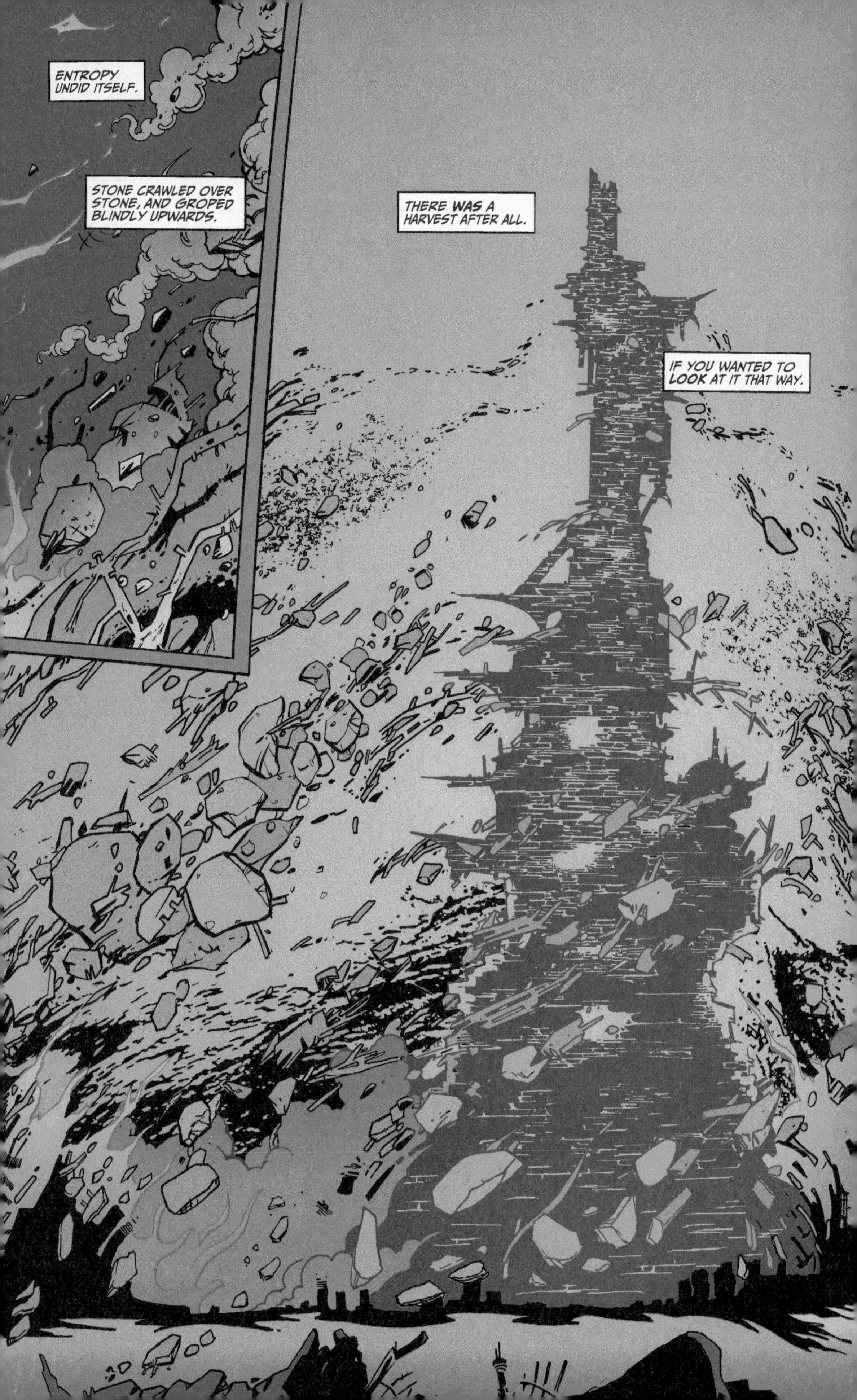
ENTROPY UNDID ITSELF.
STONE CRAWLED OVER STONE, AND GROPED BLINDLY UPWARDS.
THERE WAS A HARVEST AFTER ALL.
IF YOU WANTED TO LOOK AT IT THAT WAY.

I KNOW. I KNOW IT'S BEEN *DONE*. BUT IT'S NOT LIKE IT'S A *LONG* LIST.

STEVIE WONDER. THAT *PUNK* GUY WHO HAD POLIO.

HARPO MARX.

I'M SORRY.

I'M JUST NOT THAT *STRONG*.

HHHHHHH!

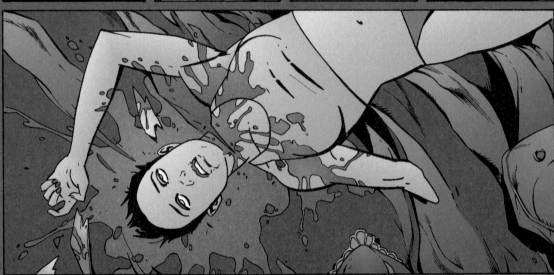

IN THE INTERESTS OF SECURITY AND STABILITY, JILL PRESTO, CERTAIN BASIC *FREEDOMS* HAVE BEEN SUSPENDED.

I ASSURE YOU, IT'S ONLY *TEMPORARY*.

MAGICIAN

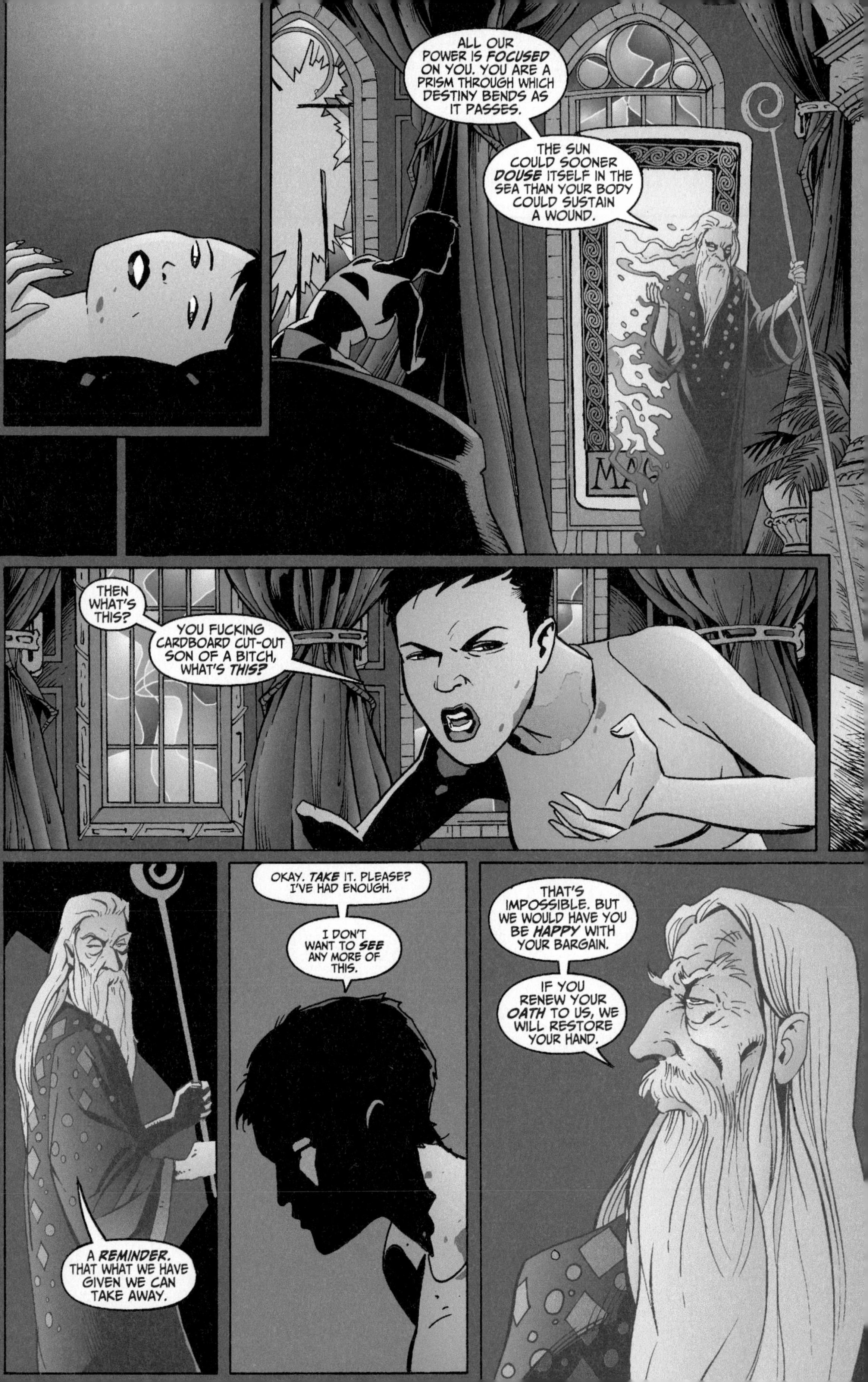
ALL OUR POWER IS FOCUSED ON YOU. YOU ARE A PRISM THROUGH WHICH DESTINY BENDS AS IT PASSES.
THE SUN COULD SOONER DOUSE ITSELF IN THE SEA THAN YOUR BODY COULD SUSTAIN A WOUND.
THEN WHAT'S THIS?
YOU FUCKING CARDBOARD CUT-OUT SON OF A BITCH, WHAT'S THIS?
A REMINDER. THAT WHAT WE HAVE GIVEN WE CAN TAKE AWAY.
OKAY. TAKE IT. PLEASE? I'VE HAD ENOUGH.
I DON'T WANT TO SEE ANY MORE OF THIS.
THAT'S IMPOSSIBLE. BUT WE WOULD HAVE YOU BE HAPPY WITH YOUR BARGAIN.
IF YOU RENEW YOUR OATH TO US, WE WILL RESTORE YOUR HAND.

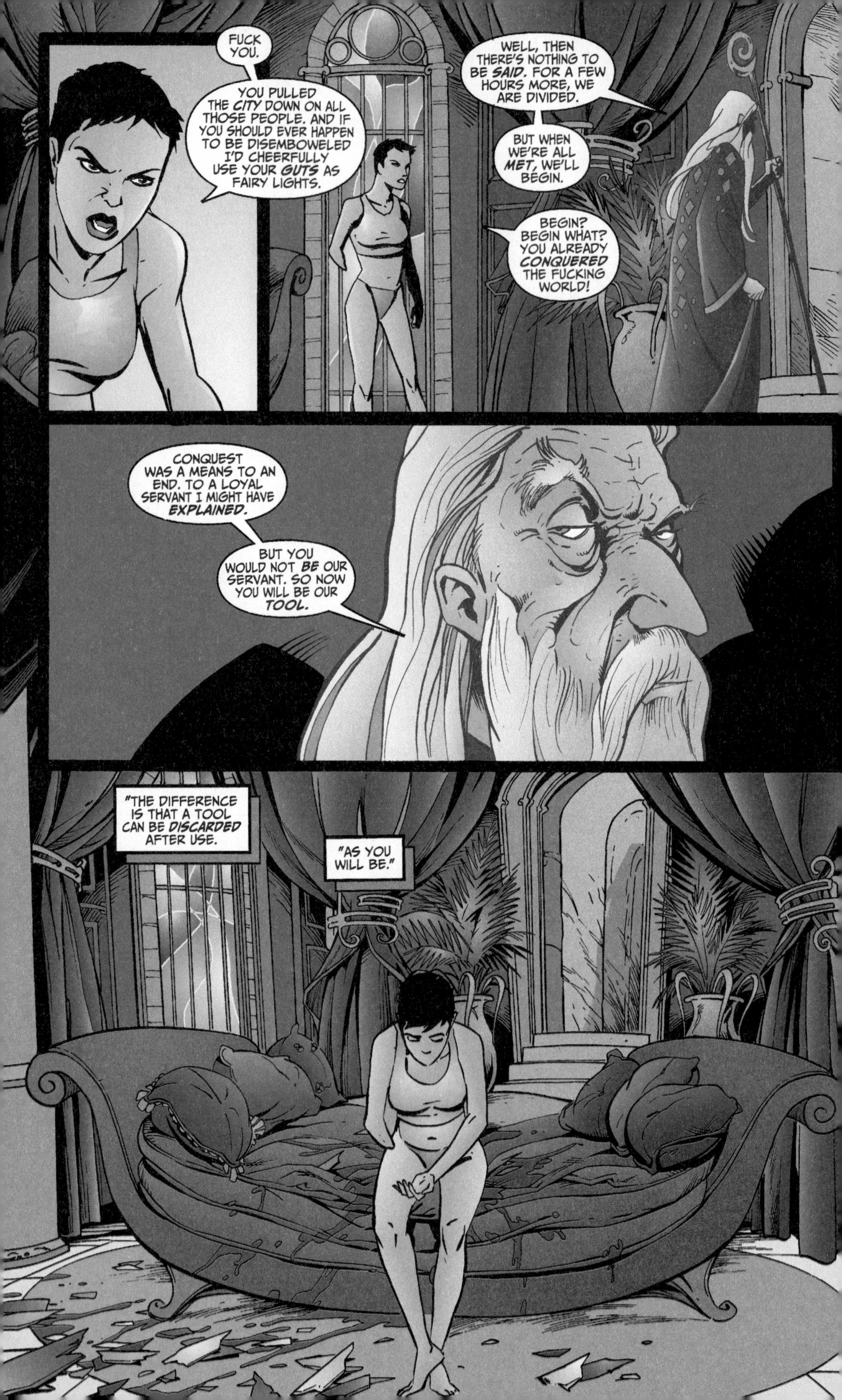
FUCK YOU.
YOU PULLED THE CITY DOWN ON ALL THOSE PEOPLE. AND IF YOU SHOULD EVER HAPPEN TO BE DISEMBOWELED I'D CHEERFULLY USE YOUR GUTS AS FAIRY LIGHTS.
WELL, THEN THERE'S NOTHING TO BE SAID. FOR A FEW HOURS MORE, WE ARE DIVIDED.
BUT WHEN WE'RE ALL MET, WE'LL BEGIN.
BEGIN? BEGIN WHAT? YOU ALREADY CONQUERED THE FUCKING WORLD!
CONQUEST WAS A MEANS TO AN END. TO A LOYAL SERVANT I MIGHT HAVE EXPLAINED.
BUT YOU WOULD NOT BE OUR SERVANT. SO NOW YOU WILL BE OUR TOOL.
"THE DIFFERENCE IS THAT A TOOL CAN BE DISCARDED AFTER USE.
"AS YOU WILL BE."

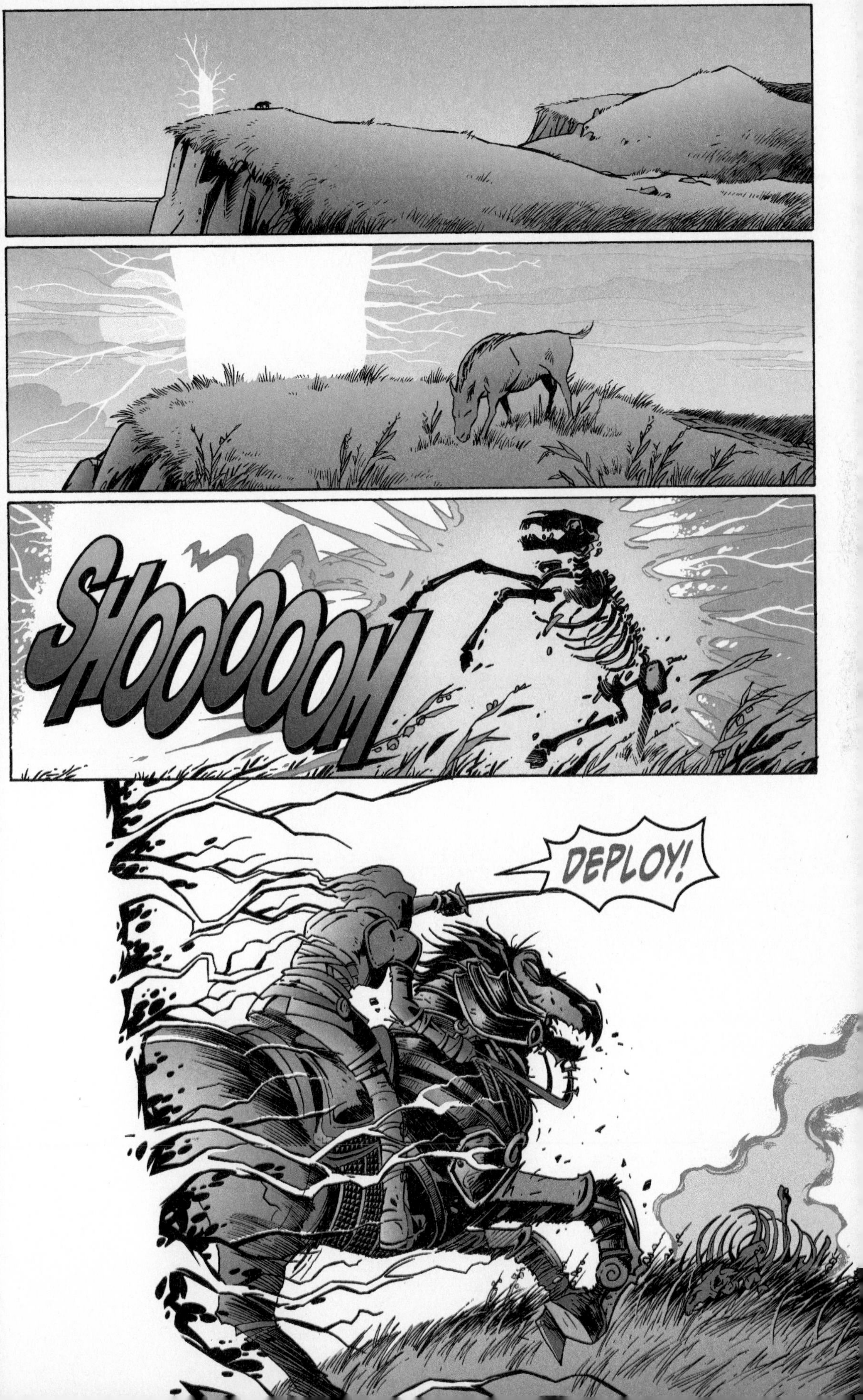
SHOOOOOM
DEPLOY!

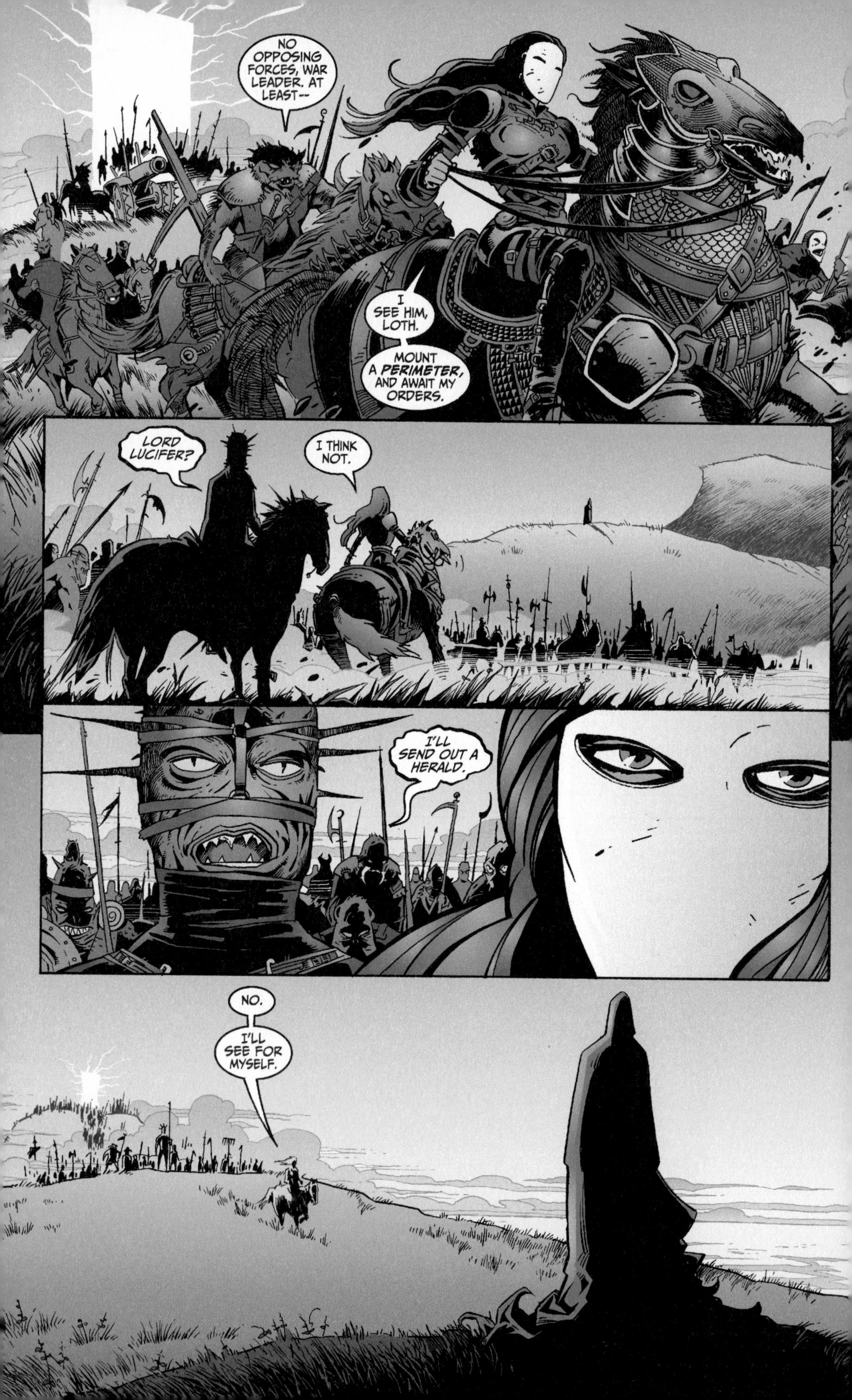
NO OPPOSING FORCES, WAR LEADER. AT LEAST--
I SEE HIM, LOTH.
MOUNT A *PERIMETER,* AND AWAIT MY ORDERS.
LORD LUCIFER?
I THINK NOT.
I'LL SEND OUT A HERALD.
NO.
I'LL SEE FOR MYSELF.

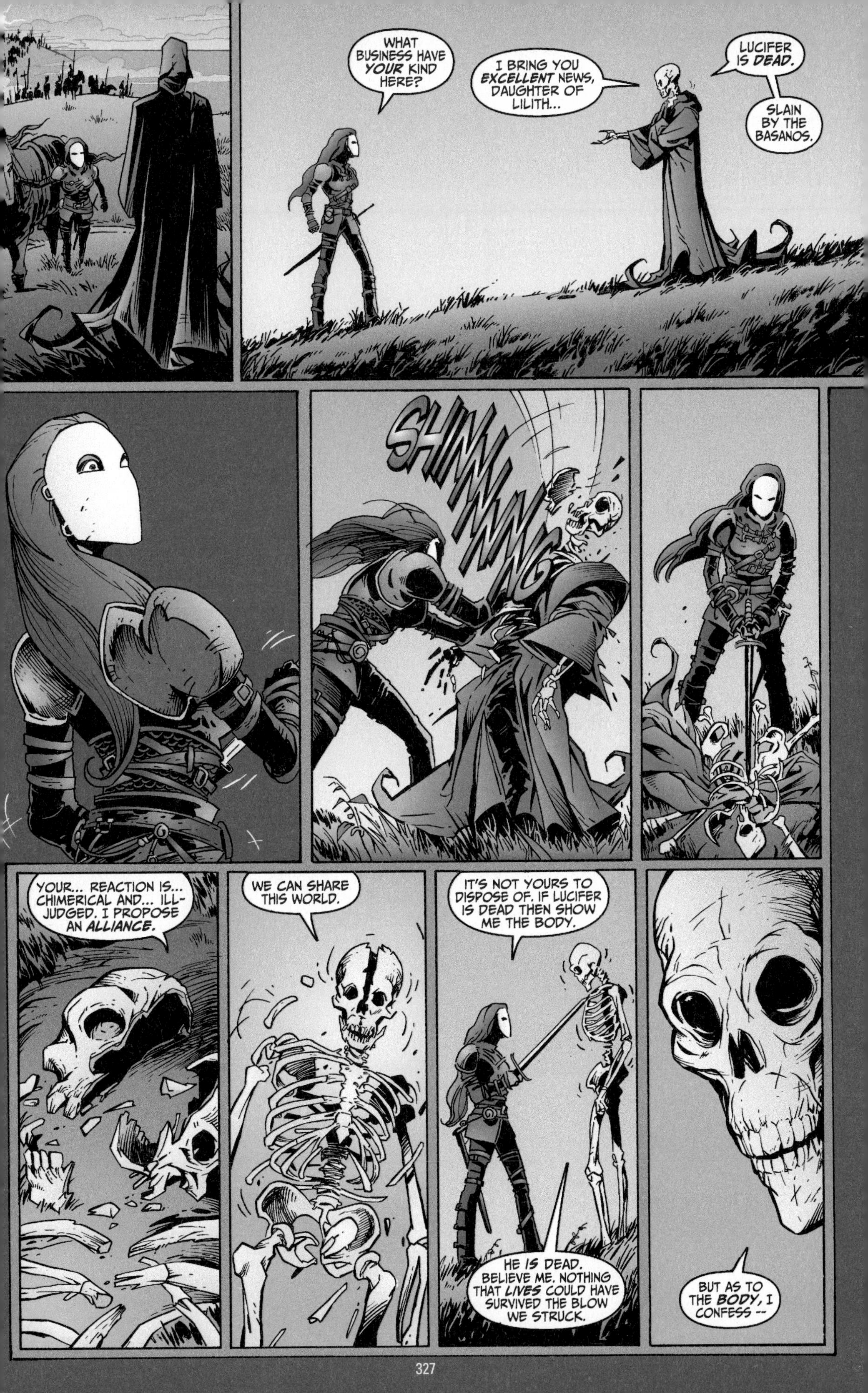
WHAT BUSINESS HAVE YOUR KIND HERE?
I BRING YOU EXCELLENT NEWS, DAUGHTER OF LILITH...
LUCIFER IS DEAD.
SLAIN BY THE BASANOS.
SHINNNNNG
YOUR... REACTION IS... CHIMERICAL AND... ILL-JUDGED. I PROPOSE AN ALLIANCE.
WE CAN SHARE THIS WORLD.
IT'S NOT YOURS TO DISPOSE OF. IF LUCIFER IS DEAD THEN SHOW ME THE BODY.
HE IS DEAD. BELIEVE ME. NOTHING THAT LIVES COULD HAVE SURVIVED THE BLOW WE STRUCK.
BUT AS TO THE BODY, I CONFESS --

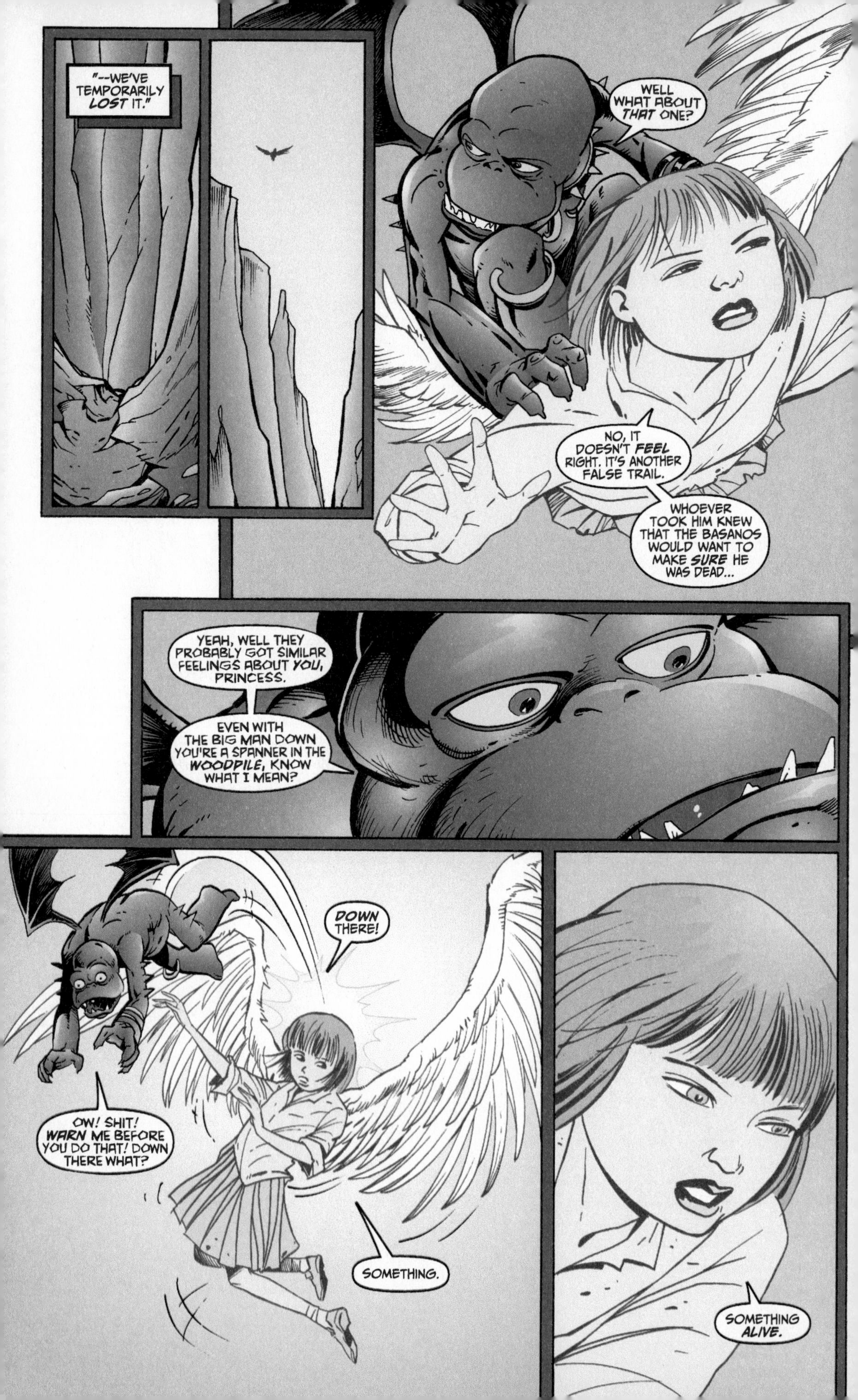
"--WE'VE TEMPORARILY LOST IT."
WELL WHAT ABOUT THAT ONE?
NO, IT DOESN'T FEEL RIGHT. IT'S ANOTHER FALSE TRAIL.
WHOEVER TOOK HIM KNEW THAT THE BASANOS WOULD WANT TO MAKE SURE HE WAS DEAD...
YEAH, WELL THEY PROBABLY GOT SIMILAR FEELINGS ABOUT YOU, PRINCESS.
EVEN WITH THE BIG MAN DOWN YOU'RE A SPANNER IN THE WOODPILE, KNOW WHAT I MEAN?
DOWN THERE!
OW! SHIT! WARN ME BEFORE YOU DO THAT! DOWN THERE WHAT?
SOMETHING.
SOMETHING ALIVE.

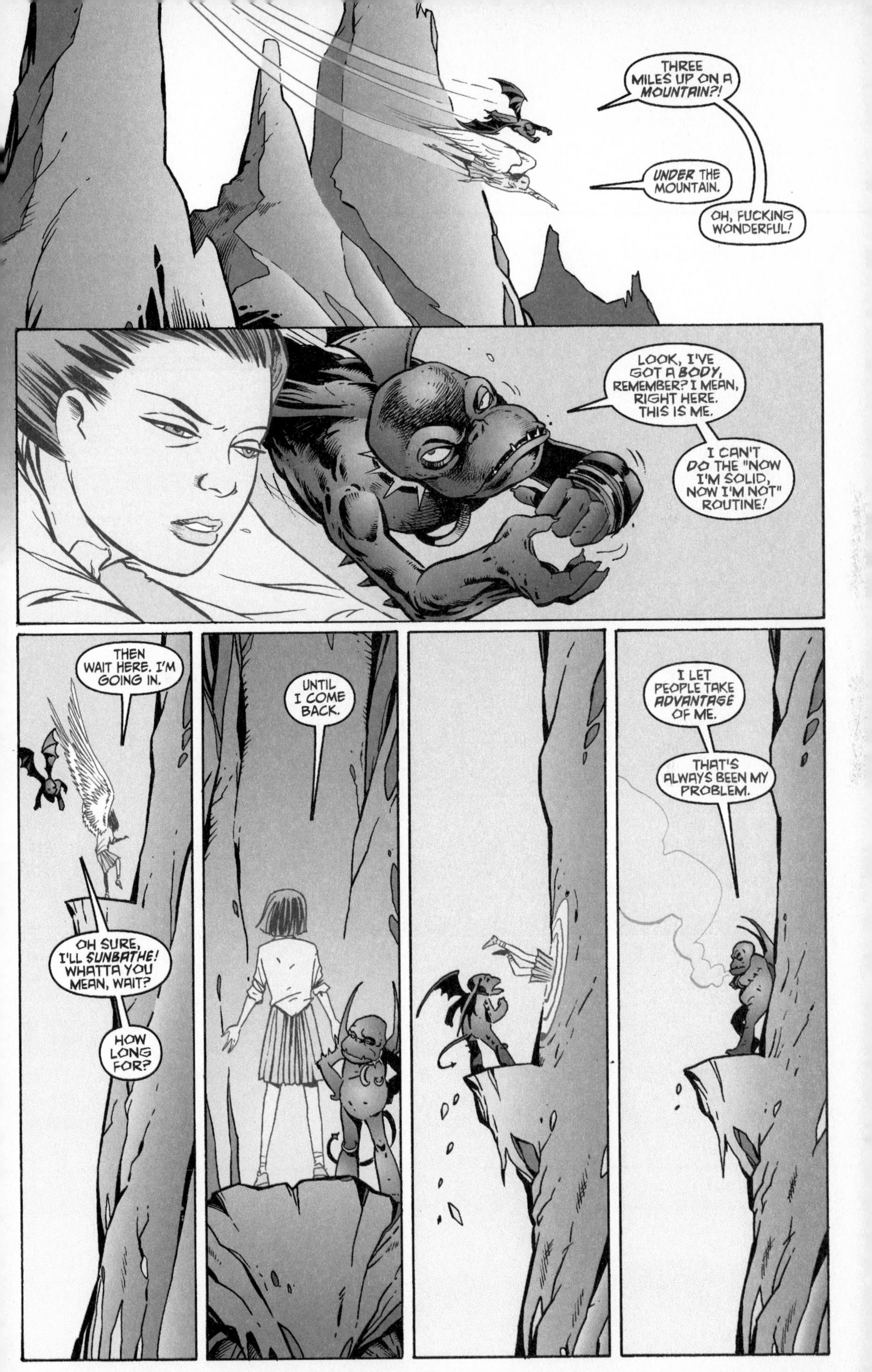
THREE MILES UP ON A MOUNTAIN?!
UNDER THE MOUNTAIN.
OH, FUCKING WONDERFUL!
LOOK, I'VE GOT A BODY, REMEMBER? I MEAN, RIGHT HERE. THIS IS ME.
I CAN'T DO THE "NOW I'M SOLID, NOW I'M NOT" ROUTINE!
THEN WAIT HERE. I'M GOING IN.
OH SURE, I'LL SUNBATHE! WHATTA YOU MEAN, WAIT?
HOW LONG FOR?
UNTIL I COME BACK.
I LET PEOPLE TAKE ADVANTAGE OF ME.
THAT'S ALWAYS BEEN MY PROBLEM.

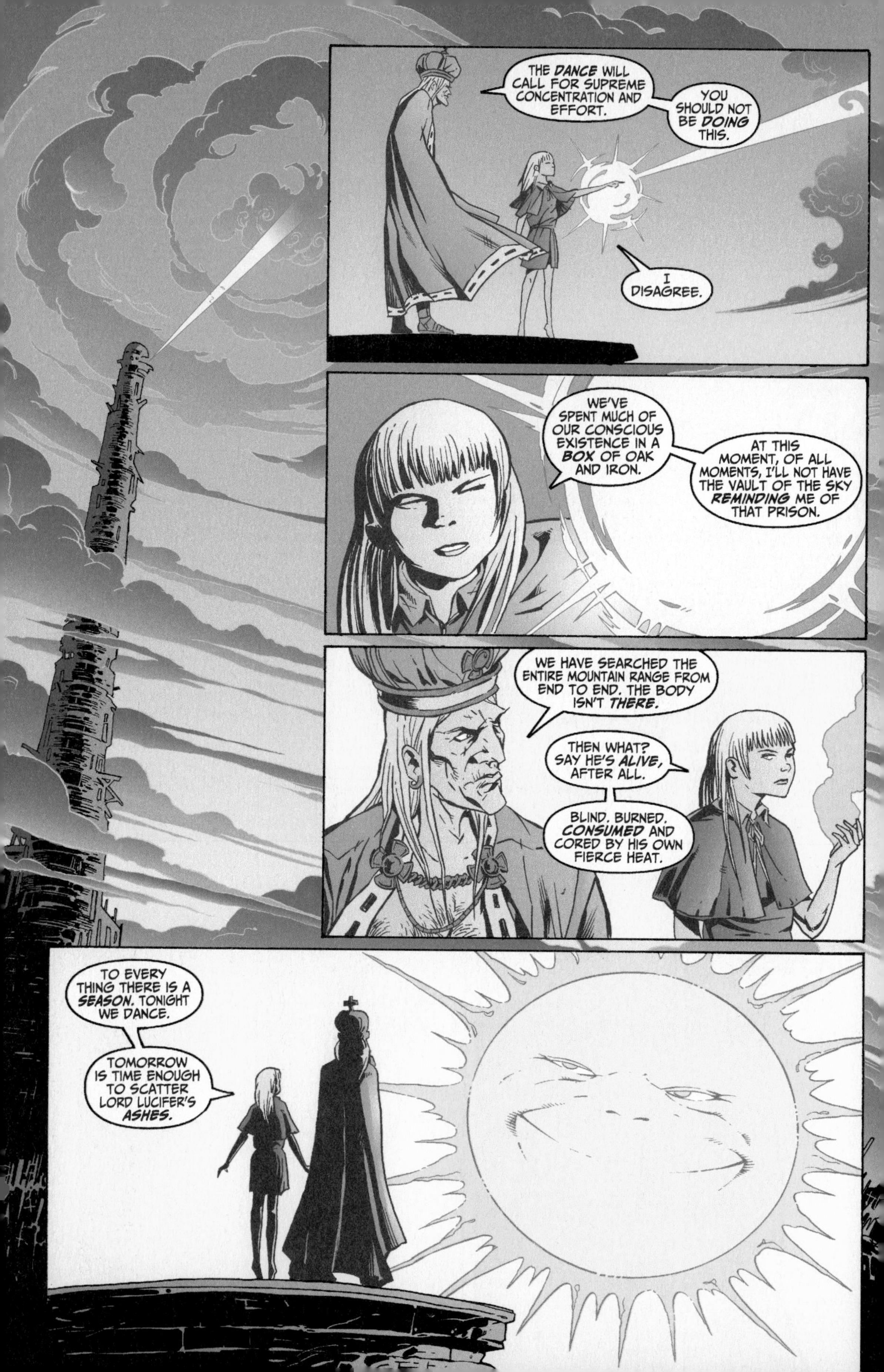
THE DANCE WILL CALL FOR SUPREME CONCENTRATION AND EFFORT.
YOU SHOULD NOT BE DOING THIS.
I DISAGREE.
WE'VE SPENT MUCH OF OUR CONSCIOUS EXISTENCE IN A BOX OF OAK AND IRON.
AT THIS MOMENT, OF ALL MOMENTS, I'LL NOT HAVE THE VAULT OF THE SKY REMINDING ME OF THAT PRISON.
WE HAVE SEARCHED THE ENTIRE MOUNTAIN RANGE FROM END TO END. THE BODY ISN'T THERE.
THEN WHAT? SAY HE'S ALIVE, AFTER ALL.
BLIND. BURNED. CONSUMED AND CORED BY HIS OWN FIERCE HEAT.
TO EVERY THING THERE IS A SEASON. TONIGHT WE DANCE.
TOMORROW IS TIME ENOUGH TO SCATTER LORD LUCIFER'S ASHES.

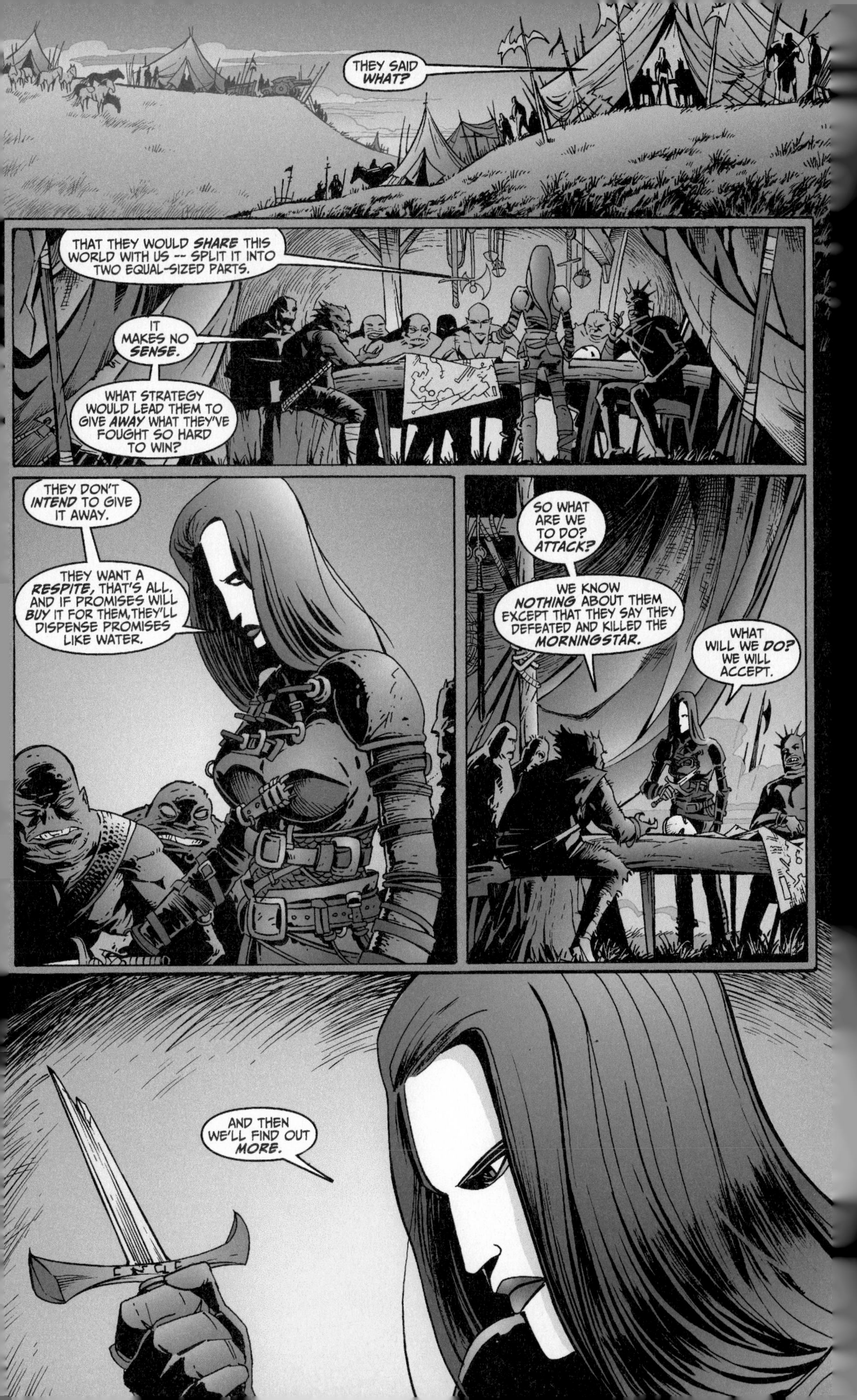
THEY SAID WHAT?
THAT THEY WOULD SHARE THIS WORLD WITH US -- SPLIT IT INTO TWO EQUAL-SIZED PARTS.
IT MAKES NO SENSE.
WHAT STRATEGY WOULD LEAD THEM TO GIVE AWAY WHAT THEY'VE FOUGHT SO HARD TO WIN?
THEY DON'T INTEND TO GIVE IT AWAY.
THEY WANT A RESPITE, THAT'S ALL. AND IF PROMISES WILL BUY IT FOR THEM, THEY'LL DISPENSE PROMISES LIKE WATER.
SO WHAT ARE WE TO DO? ATTACK?
WE KNOW NOTHING ABOUT THEM EXCEPT THAT THEY SAY THEY DEFEATED AND KILLED THE MORNINGSTAR.
WHAT WILL WE DO? WE WILL ACCEPT.
AND THEN WE'LL FIND OUT MORE.

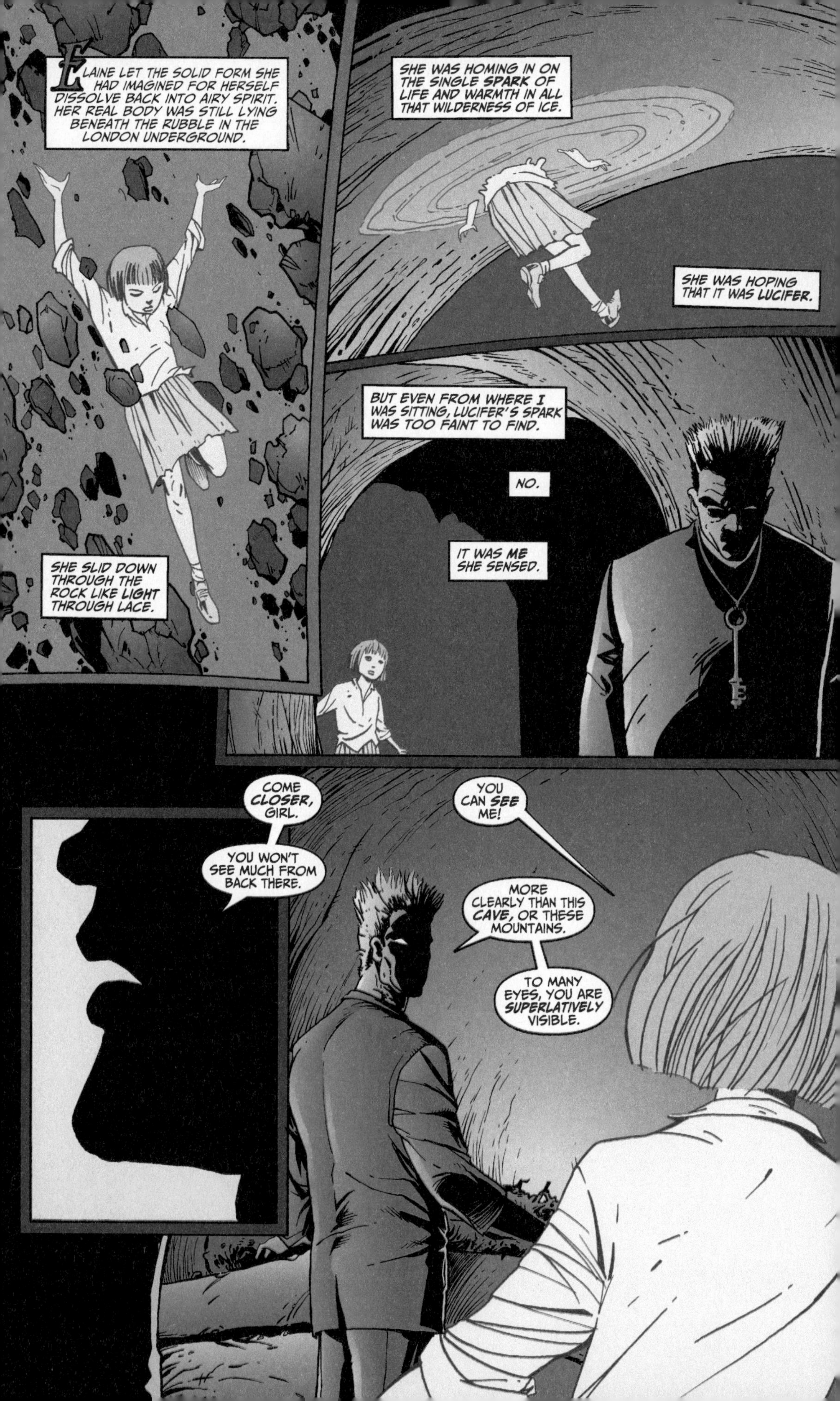
ELAINE LET THE SOLID FORM SHE HAD IMAGINED FOR HERSELF DISSOLVE BACK INTO AIRY SPIRIT. HER REAL BODY WAS STILL LYING BENEATH THE RUBBLE IN THE LONDON UNDERGROUND.
SHE SLID DOWN THROUGH THE ROCK LIKE LIGHT THROUGH LACE.
SHE WAS HOMING IN ON THE SINGLE SPARK OF LIFE AND WARMTH IN ALL THAT WILDERNESS OF ICE.
SHE WAS HOPING THAT IT WAS LUCIFER.
BUT EVEN FROM WHERE I WAS SITTING, LUCIFER'S SPARK WAS TOO FAINT TO FIND.
NO.
IT WAS ME SHE SENSED.
COME CLOSER, GIRL.
YOU WON'T SEE MUCH FROM BACK THERE.
YOU CAN SEE ME!
MORE CLEARLY THAN THIS CAVE, OR THESE MOUNTAINS.
TO MANY EYES, YOU ARE SUPERLATIVELY VISIBLE.

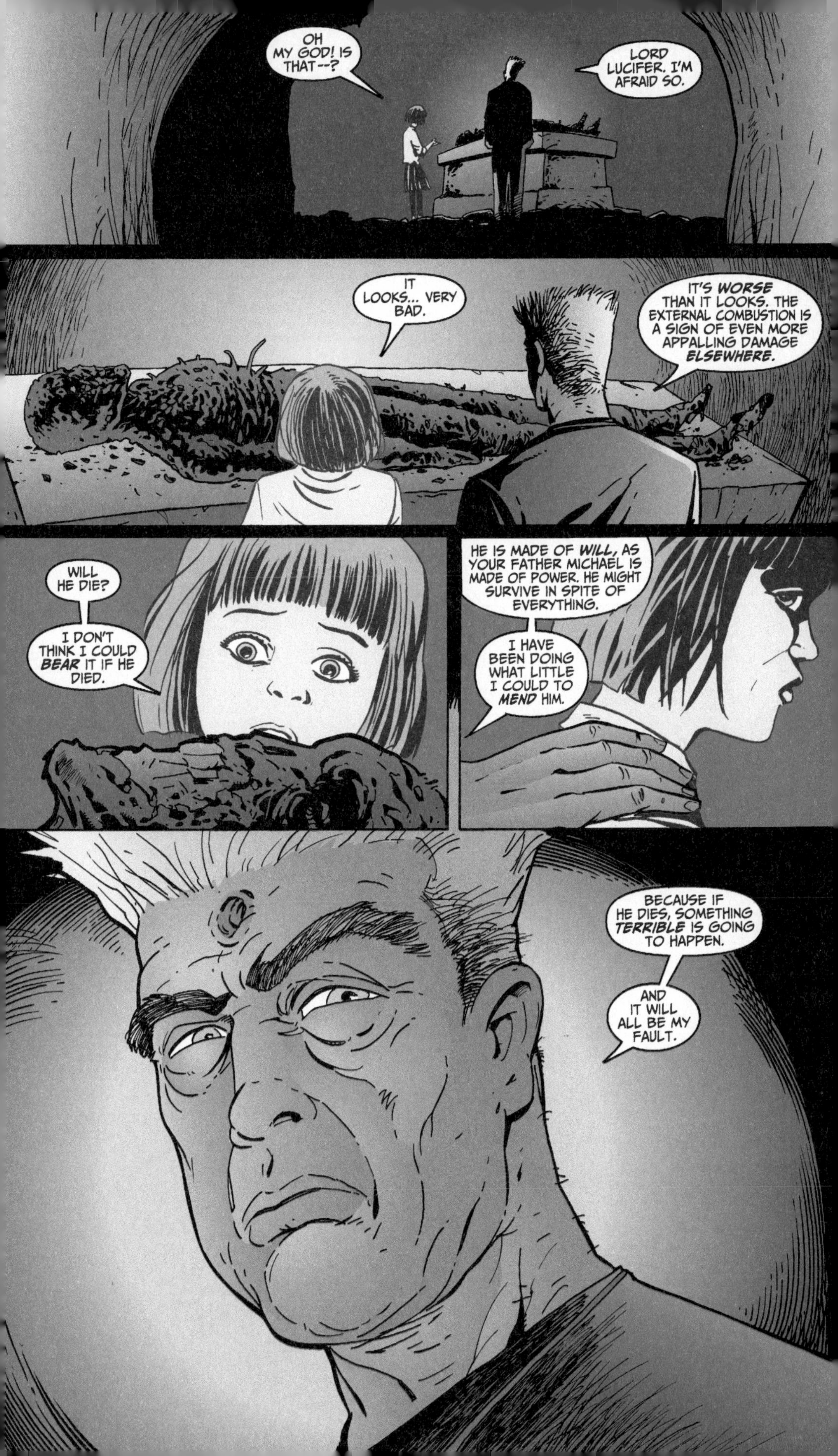

OH MY GOD! IS THAT--?
LORD LUCIFER. I'M AFRAID SO.
IT LOOKS... VERY BAD.
IT'S WORSE THAN IT LOOKS. THE EXTERNAL COMBUSTION IS A SIGN OF EVEN MORE APPALLING DAMAGE ELSEWHERE.
WILL HE DIE?
I DON'T THINK I COULD BEAR IT IF HE DIED.
HE IS MADE OF WILL, AS YOUR FATHER MICHAEL IS MADE OF POWER. HE MIGHT SURVIVE IN SPITE OF EVERYTHING.
I HAVE BEEN DOING WHAT LITTLE I COULD TO MEND HIM.
BECAUSE IF HE DIES, SOMETHING TERRIBLE IS GOING TO HAPPEN.
AND IT WILL ALL BE MY FAULT.

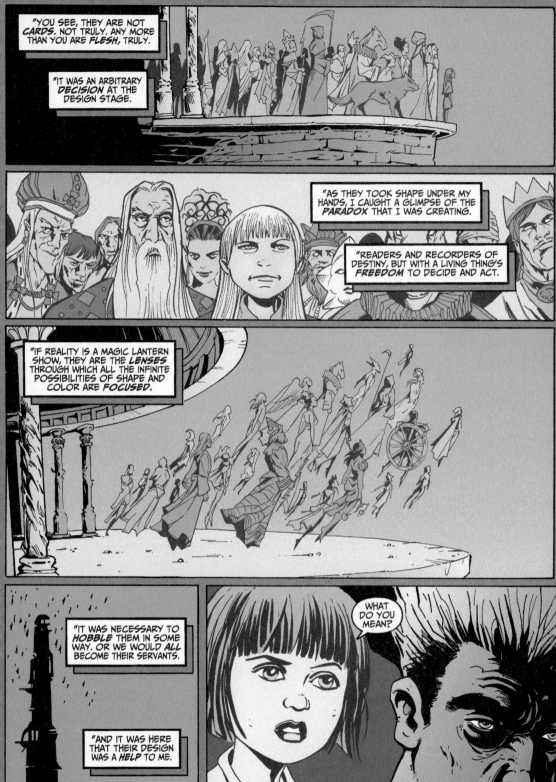

"YOU SEE, THEY ARE NOT *CARDS*. NOT TRULY. ANY MORE THAN YOU ARE *FLESH*, TRULY.

"IT WAS AN ARBITRARY *DECISION* AT THE DESIGN STAGE.

"AS THEY TOOK SHAPE UNDER MY HANDS, I CAUGHT A GLIMPSE OF THE *PARADOX* THAT I WAS CREATING.

"READERS AND RECORDERS OF DESTINY, BUT WITH A LIVING THING'S *FREEDOM* TO DECIDE AND ACT.

"IF REALITY IS A MAGIC LANTERN SHOW, THEY ARE THE *LENSES* THROUGH WHICH ALL THE INFINITE POSSIBILITIES OF SHAPE AND COLOR ARE *FOCUSED*.

"IT WAS NECESSARY TO *HOBBLE* THEM IN SOME WAY. OR WE WOULD *ALL* BECOME THEIR SERVANTS.

"AND IT WAS HERE THAT THEIR DESIGN WAS A *HELP* TO ME.

WHAT DO YOU MEAN?

IT SEEMED... EASY, AND SENSIBLE, TO DENY THEM SOME OF THE *OTHER* PREROGATIVES OF LIVING THINGS.

TO MAKE THEM FINITE, IN THAT RESPECT AT LEAST.

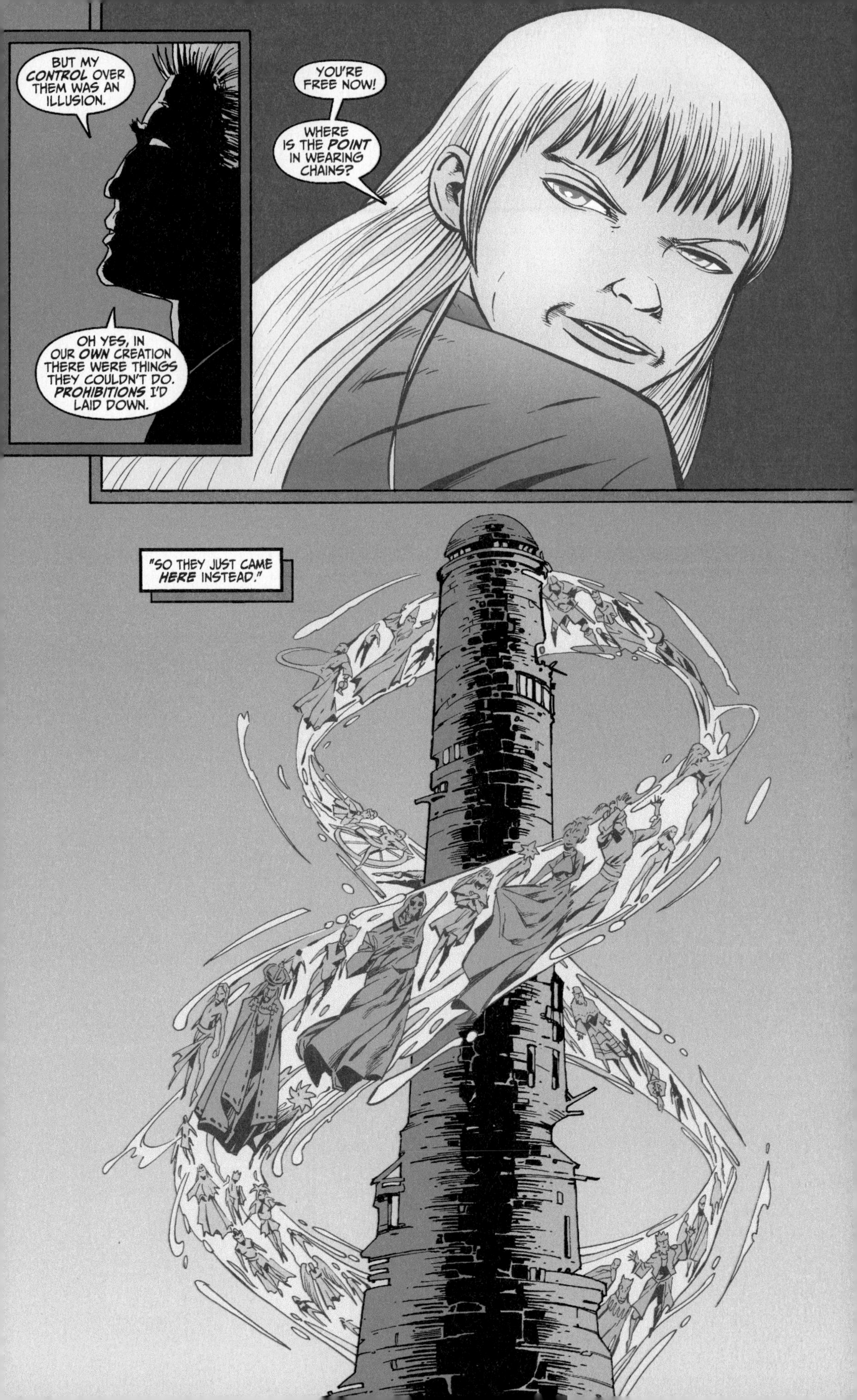
BUT MY CONTROL OVER THEM WAS AN ILLUSION.
OH YES, IN OUR OWN CREATION THERE WERE THINGS THEY COULDN'T DO. PROHIBITIONS I'D LAID DOWN.
YOU'RE FREE NOW!
WHERE IS THE POINT IN WEARING CHAINS?
"SO THEY JUST CAME HERE INSTEAD."

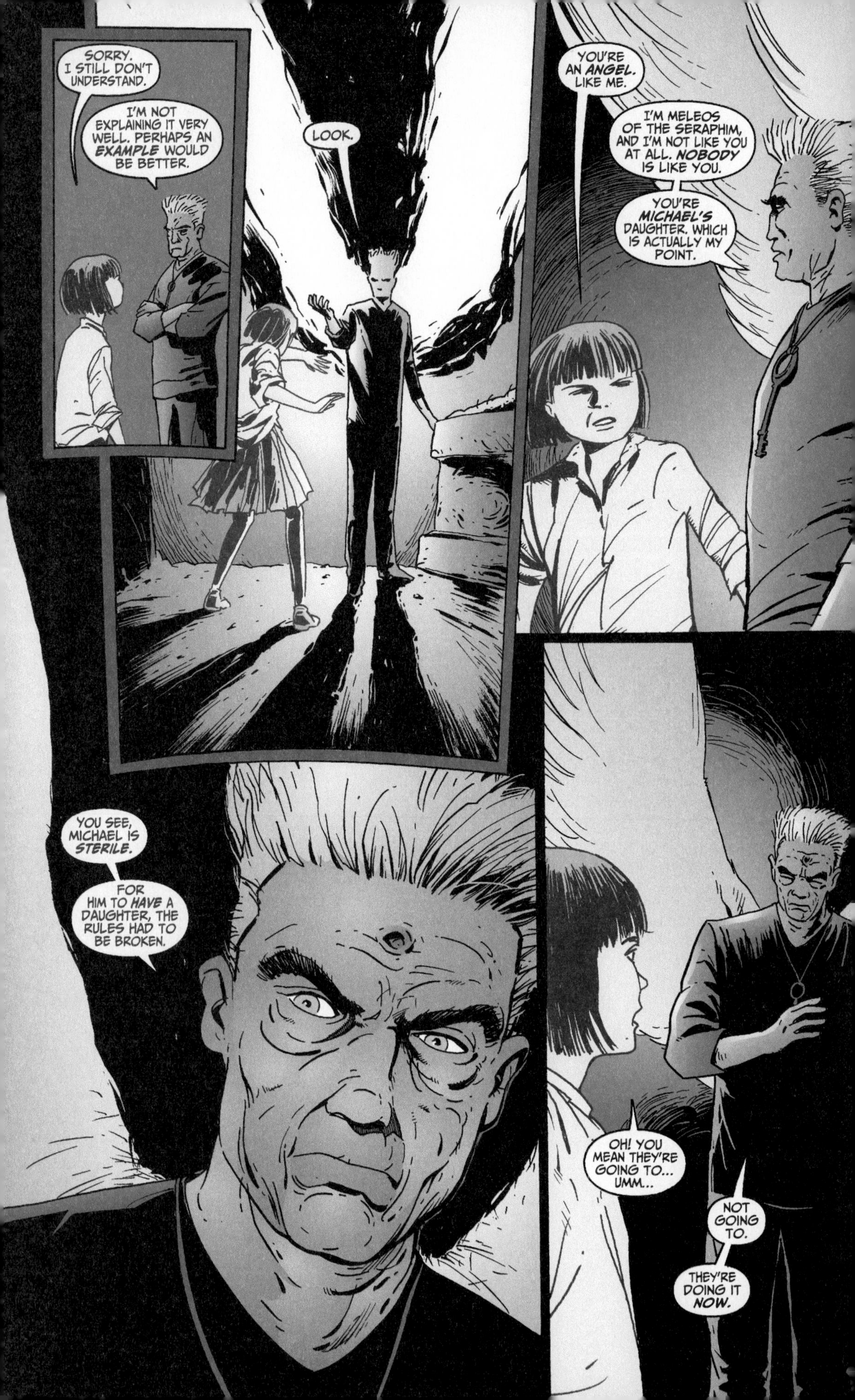
SORRY. I STILL DON'T UNDERSTAND.
I'M NOT EXPLAINING IT VERY WELL. PERHAPS AN **EXAMPLE** WOULD BE BETTER.
LOOK.
YOU'RE AN **ANGEL.** LIKE ME.
I'M MELEOS OF THE SERAPHIM, AND I'M NOT LIKE YOU AT ALL. **NOBODY** IS LIKE YOU.
YOU'RE **MICHAEL'S** DAUGHTER. WHICH IS ACTUALLY MY POINT.
YOU SEE, MICHAEL IS **STERILE.**
FOR HIM TO **HAVE** A DAUGHTER, THE RULES HAD TO BE BROKEN.
OH! YOU MEAN THEY'RE GOING TO... UMM...
NOT GOING TO.
THEY'RE DOING IT **NOW.**

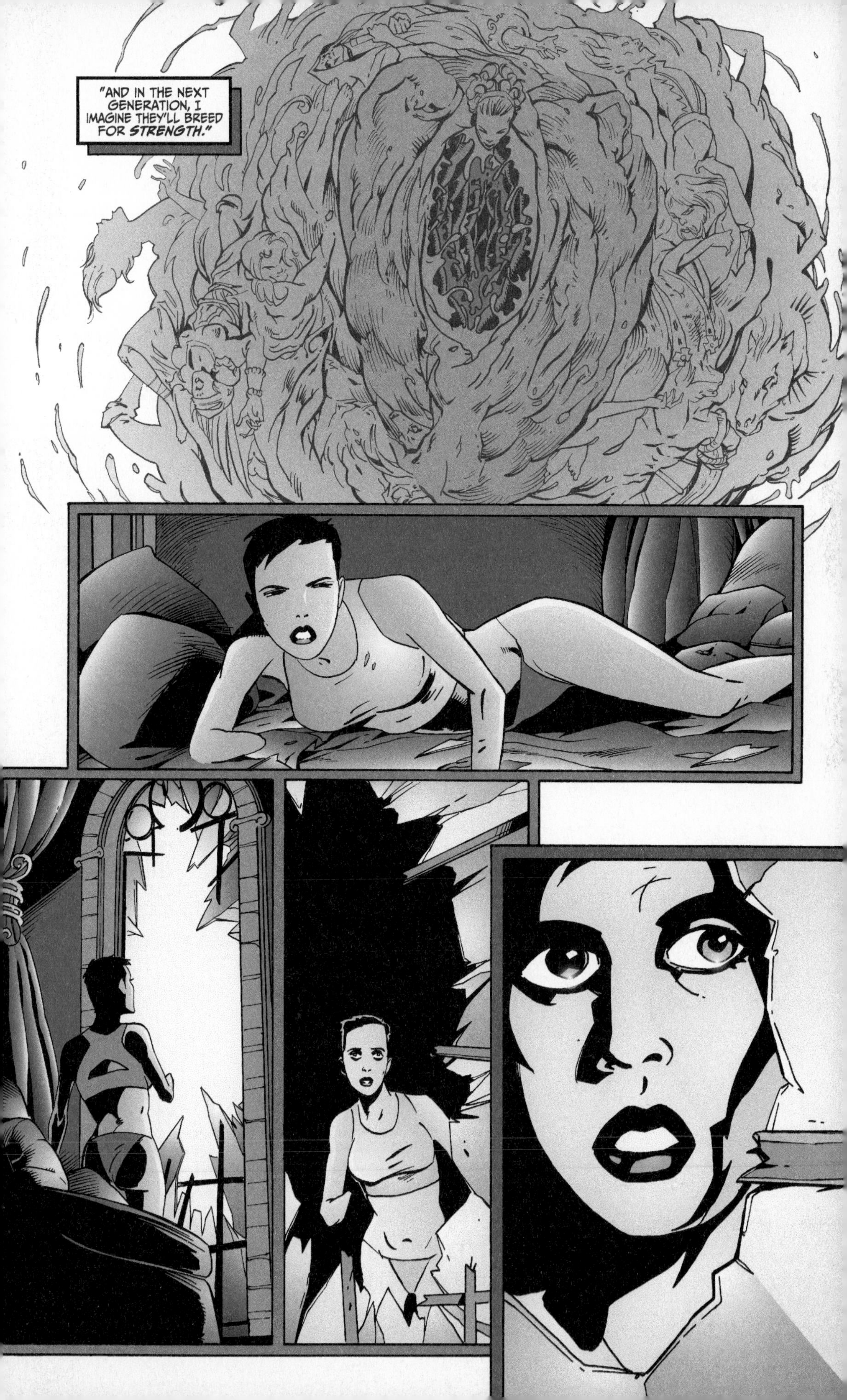
"AND IN THE NEXT GENERATION, I IMAGINE THEY'LL BREED FOR STRENGTH."

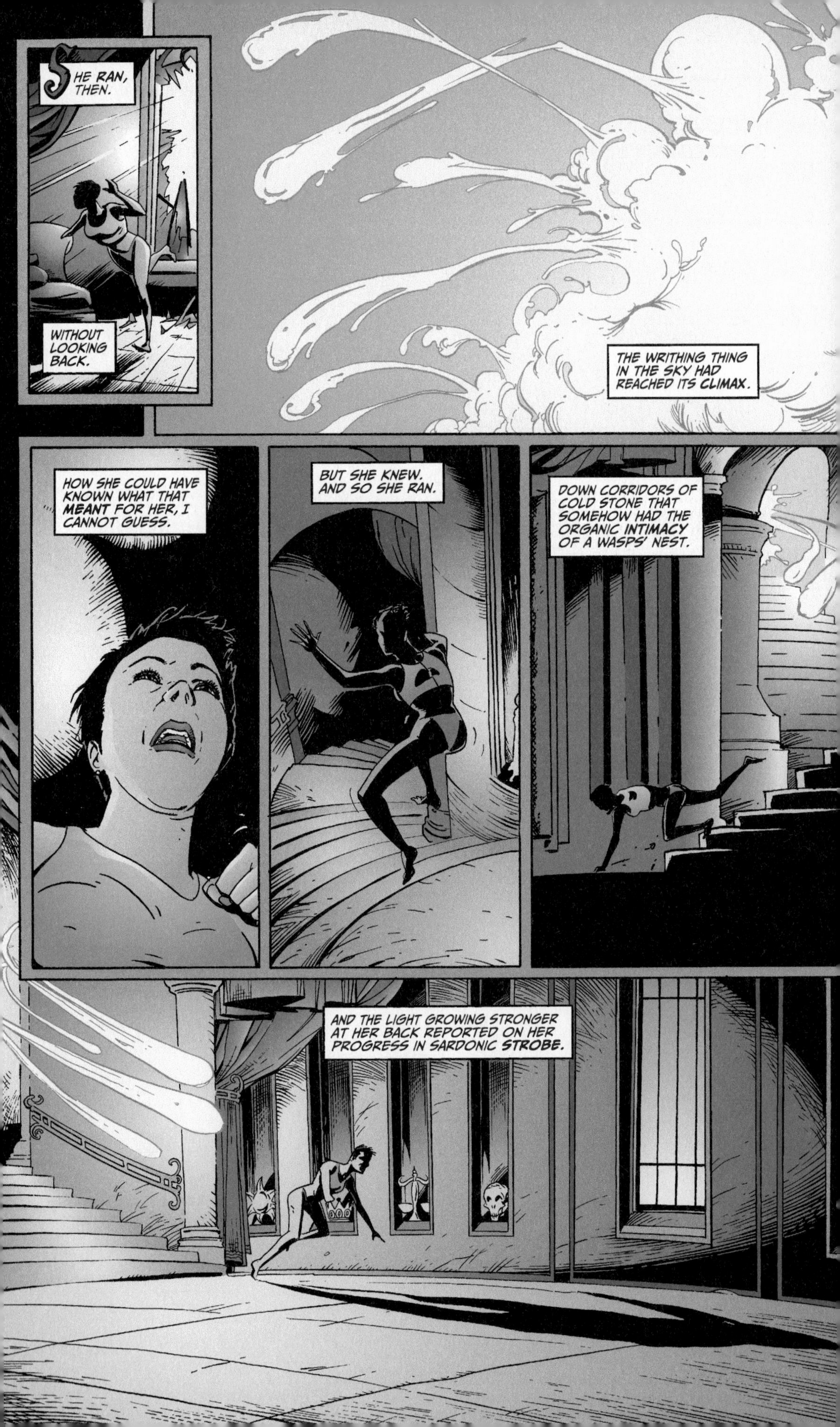
SHE RAN, THEN.
WITHOUT LOOKING BACK.
THE WRITHING THING IN THE SKY HAD REACHED ITS CLIMAX.
HOW SHE COULD HAVE KNOWN WHAT THAT MEANT FOR HER, I CANNOT GUESS.
BUT SHE KNEW. AND SO SHE RAN.
DOWN CORRIDORS OF COLD STONE THAT SOMEHOW HAD THE ORGANIC INTIMACY OF A WASPS' NEST.
AND THE LIGHT GROWING STRONGER AT HER BACK REPORTED ON HER PROGRESS IN SARDONIC STROBE.

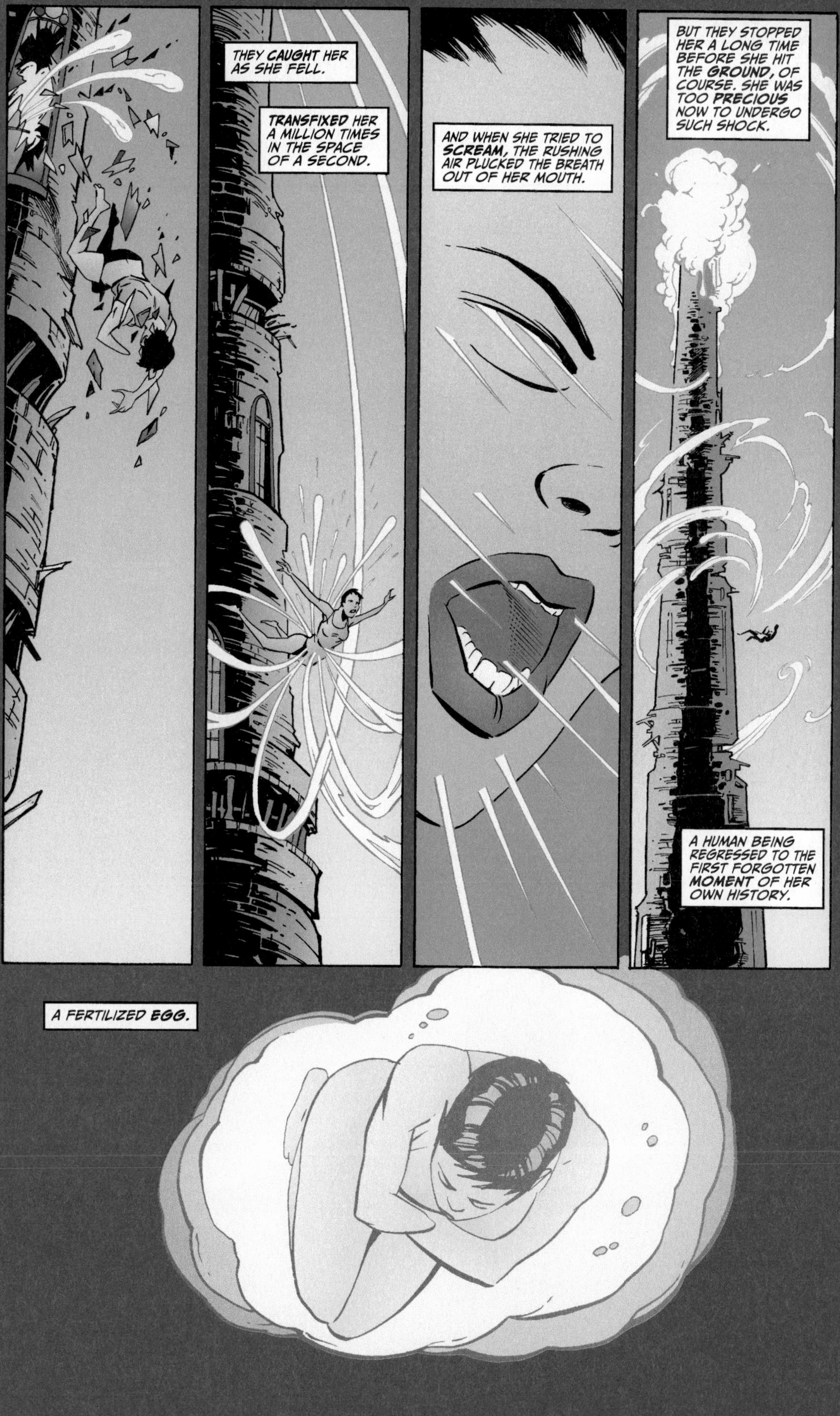
THEY CAUGHT HER AS SHE FELL.
TRANSFIXED HER A MILLION TIMES IN THE SPACE OF A SECOND.
AND WHEN SHE TRIED TO SCREAM, THE RUSHING AIR PLUCKED THE BREATH OUT OF HER MOUTH.
BUT THEY STOPPED HER A LONG TIME BEFORE SHE HIT THE GROUND, OF COURSE. SHE WAS TOO PRECIOUS NOW TO UNDERGO SUCH SHOCK.
A HUMAN BEING REGRESSED TO THE FIRST FORGOTTEN MOMENT OF HER OWN HISTORY.
A FERTILIZED EGG.

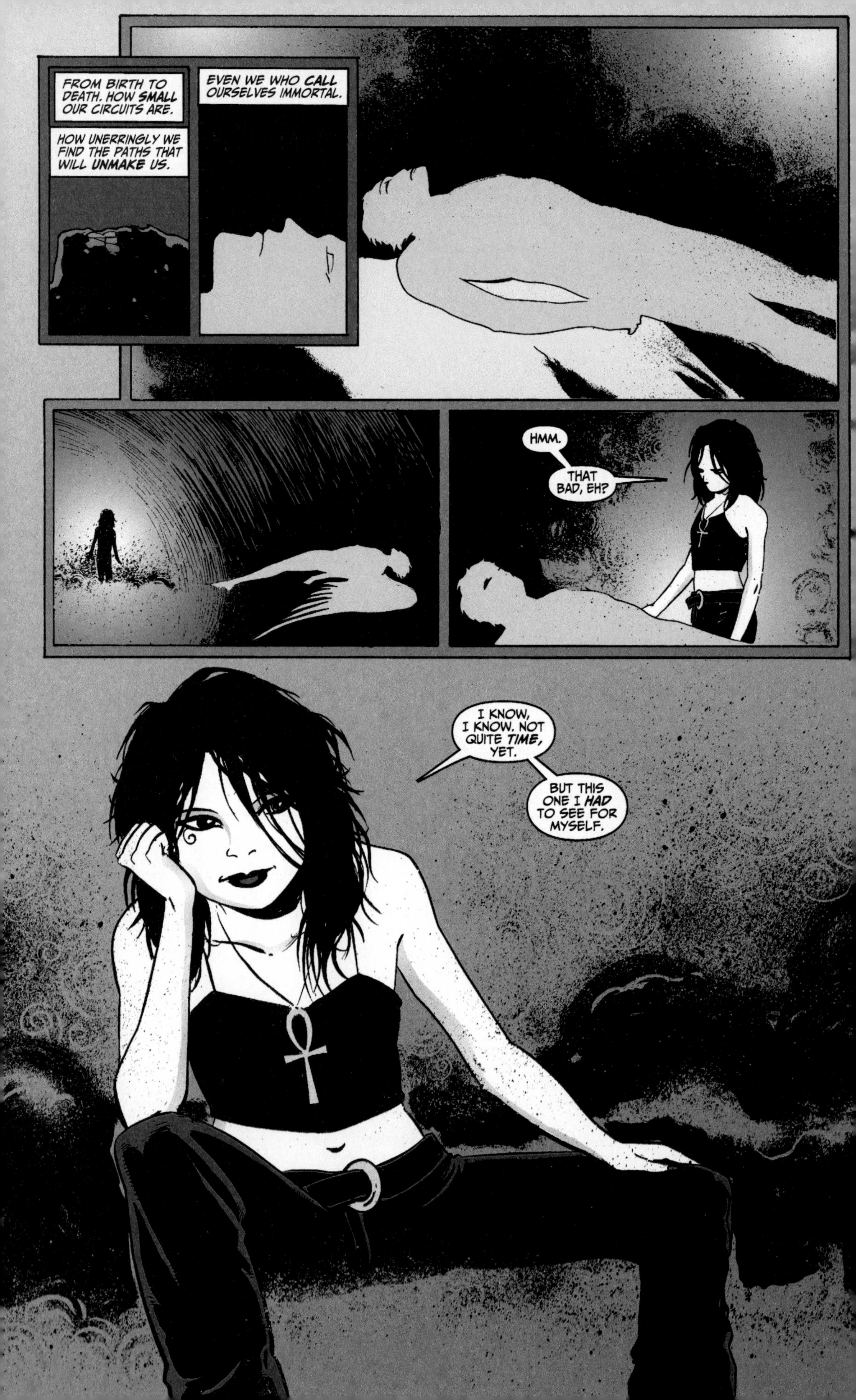
FROM BIRTH TO DEATH. HOW SMALL OUR CIRCUITS ARE.
HOW UNERRINGLY WE FIND THE PATHS THAT WILL UNMAKE US.
EVEN WE WHO CALL OURSELVES IMMORTAL.
HMM.
THAT BAD, EH?
I KNOW, I KNOW. NOT QUITE TIME, YET.
BUT THIS ONE I HAD TO SEE FOR MYSELF.

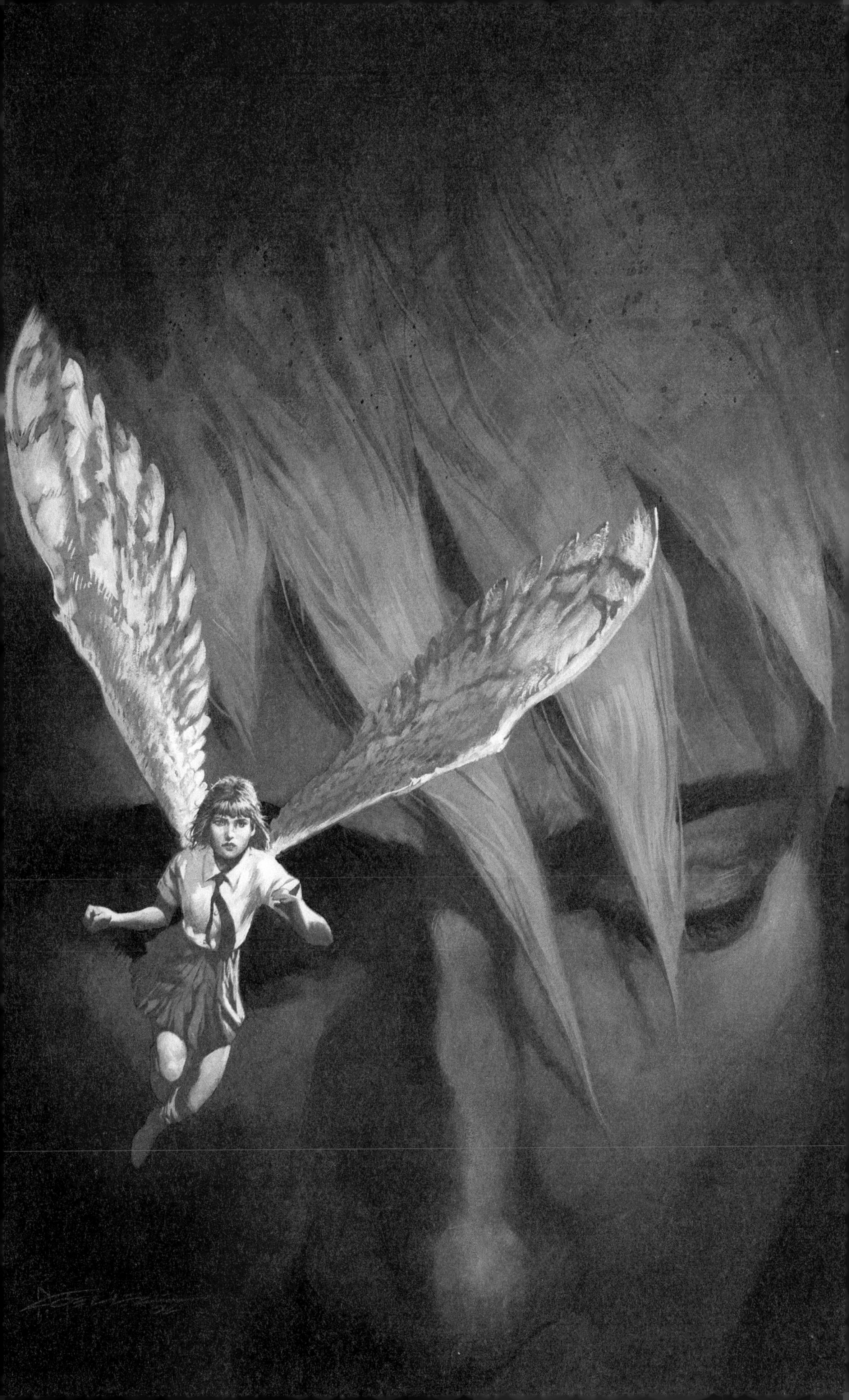

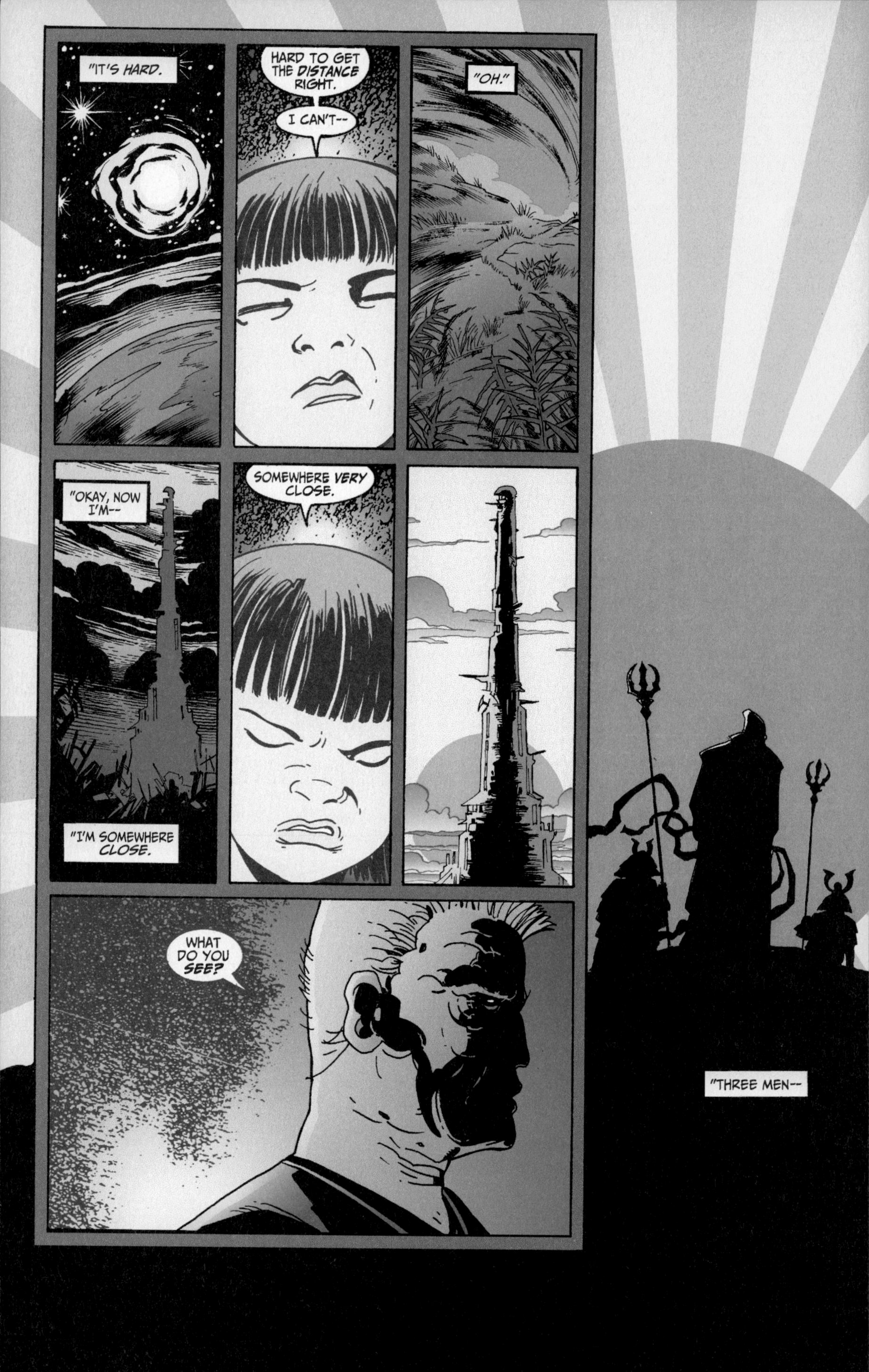
"IT'S HARD.
HARD TO GET THE DISTANCE RIGHT.
I CAN'T--
"OH."
"OKAY, NOW I'M--
"I'M SOMEWHERE CLOSE.
SOMEWHERE VERY CLOSE.
WHAT DO YOU SEE?
"THREE MEN--

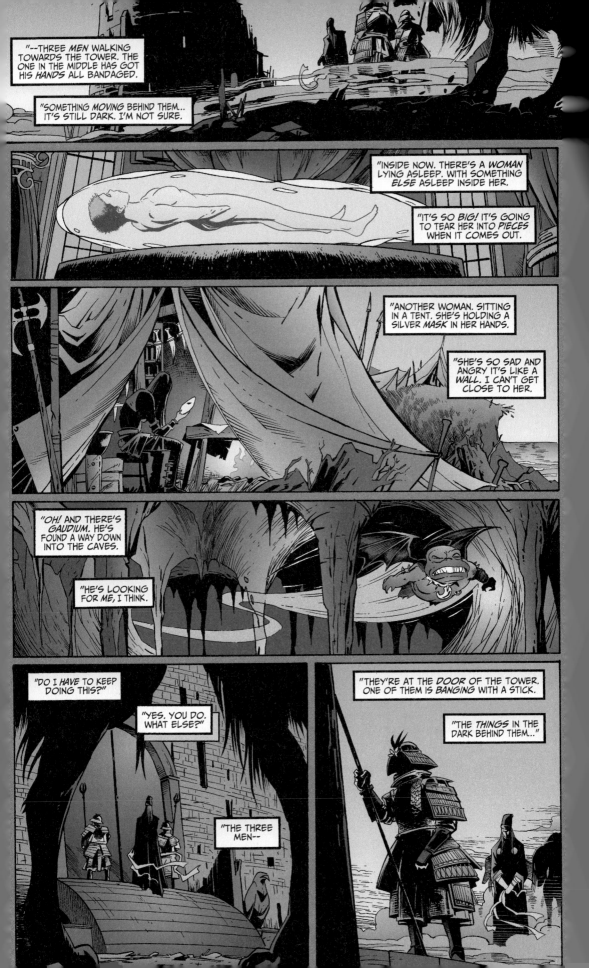

"--THREE *MEN* WALKING TOWARDS THE TOWER. THE ONE IN THE MIDDLE HAS GOT HIS *HANDS* ALL BANDAGED.

"SOMETHING *MOVING* BEHIND THEM... IT'S STILL DARK. I'M NOT SURE.

"INSIDE NOW. THERE'S A *WOMAN* LYING ASLEEP. WITH SOMETHING *ELSE* ASLEEP INSIDE HER.

"IT'S SO *BIG!* IT'S GOING TO TEAR HER INTO *PIECES* WHEN IT COMES OUT.

"ANOTHER WOMAN. SITTING IN A TENT. SHE'S HOLDING A SILVER *MASK* IN HER HANDS.

"SHE'S SO SAD AND ANGRY IT'S LIKE A *WALL.* I CAN'T GET CLOSE TO HER.

"OH! AND THERE'S *GAUDIUM.* HE'S FOUND A WAY DOWN INTO THE CAVES.

"HE'S LOOKING FOR *ME,* I THINK.

"DO I *HAVE* TO KEEP DOING THIS?"

"YES. YOU DO. WHAT ELSE?"

"THE THREE MEN--

"THEY'RE AT THE *DOOR* OF THE TOWER. ONE OF THEM IS *BANGING* WITH A STICK.

"THE *THINGS* IN THE DARK BEHIND THEM..."

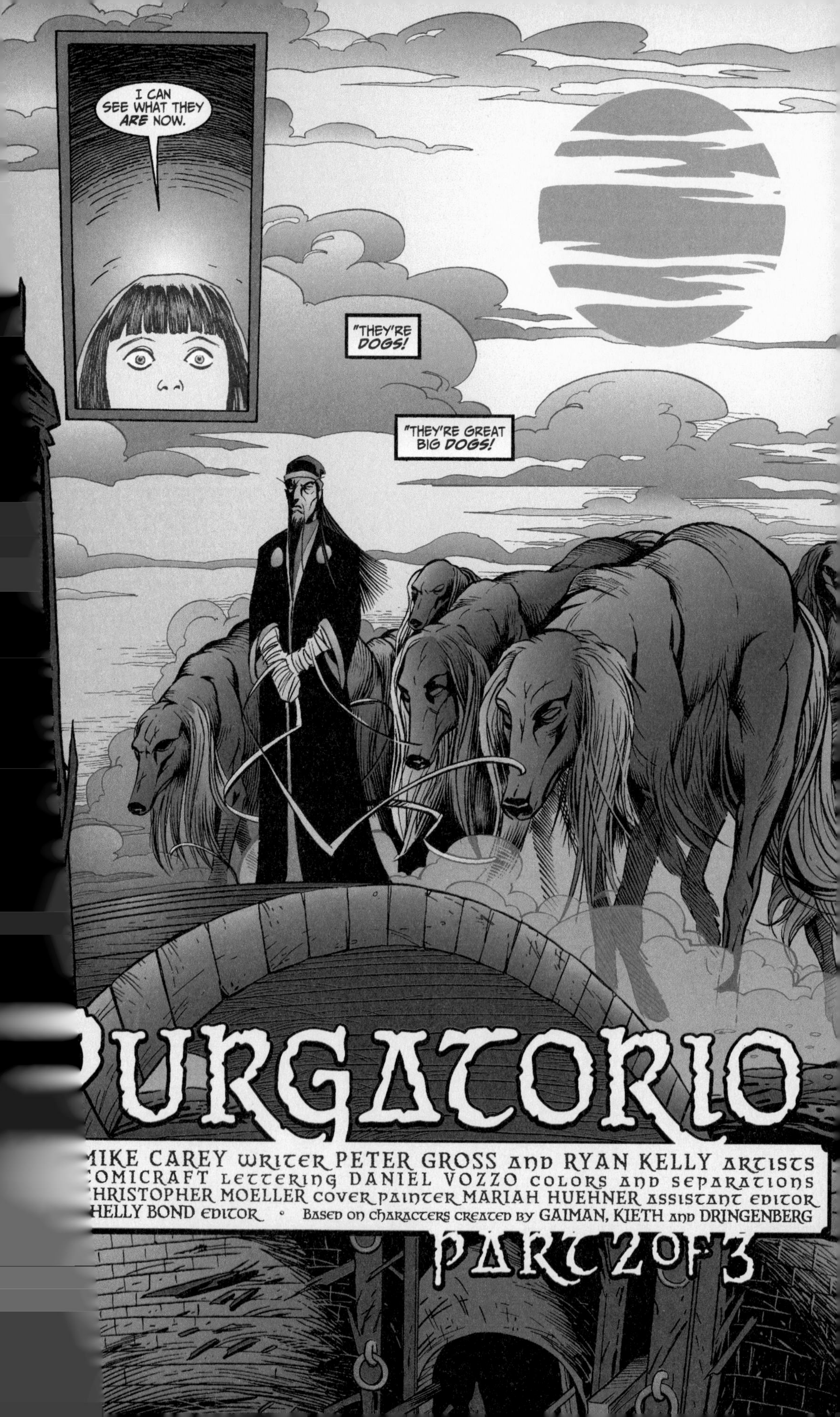
I CAN SEE WHAT THEY ARE NOW.
"THEY'RE DOGS!
"THEY'RE GREAT BIG DOGS!
PURGATORIO
MIKE CAREY WRITER PETER GROSS AND RYAN KELLY ARTISTS
OMICRAFT LETTERING DANIEL VOZZO COLORS AND SEPARATIONS
HRISTOPHER MOELLER COVER PAINTER MARIAH HUEHNER ASSISTANT EDITOR
HELLY BOND EDITOR • BASED ON CHARACTERS CREATED BY GAIMAN, KIETH AND DRINGENBERG
PART 2 OF 3

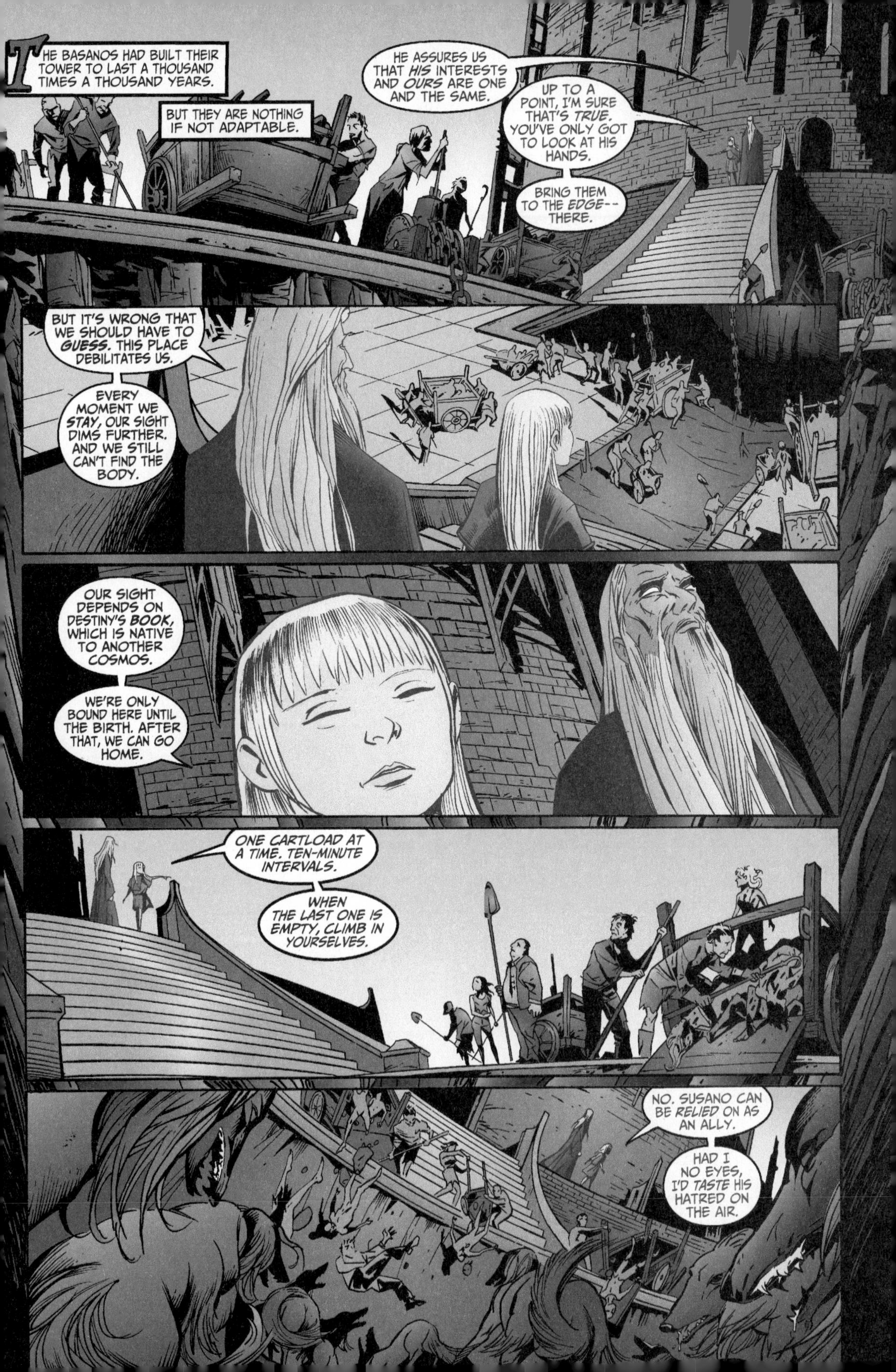
THE BASANOS HAD BUILT THEIR TOWER TO LAST A THOUSAND TIMES A THOUSAND YEARS.
BUT THEY ARE NOTHING IF NOT ADAPTABLE.
HE ASSURES US THAT *HIS* INTERESTS AND *OURS* ARE ONE AND THE SAME.
UP TO A POINT, I'M SURE THAT'S *TRUE.* YOU'VE ONLY GOT TO LOOK AT HIS HANDS.
BRING THEM TO THE *EDGE*-- THERE.
BUT IT'S WRONG THAT WE SHOULD HAVE TO *GUESS.* THIS PLACE DEBILITATES US.
EVERY MOMENT WE *STAY,* OUR SIGHT DIMS FURTHER. AND WE STILL CAN'T FIND THE BODY.
OUR SIGHT DEPENDS ON DESTINY'S *BOOK,* WHICH IS NATIVE TO ANOTHER COSMOS.
WE'RE ONLY BOUND HERE UNTIL THE BIRTH. AFTER THAT, WE CAN GO HOME.
ONE CARTLOAD AT A TIME. TEN-MINUTE INTERVALS.
WHEN THE LAST ONE IS EMPTY, CLIMB IN YOURSELVES.
NO. SUSANO CAN BE *RELIED* ON AS AN ALLY.
HAD I NO EYES, I'D *TASTE* HIS HATRED ON THE AIR.

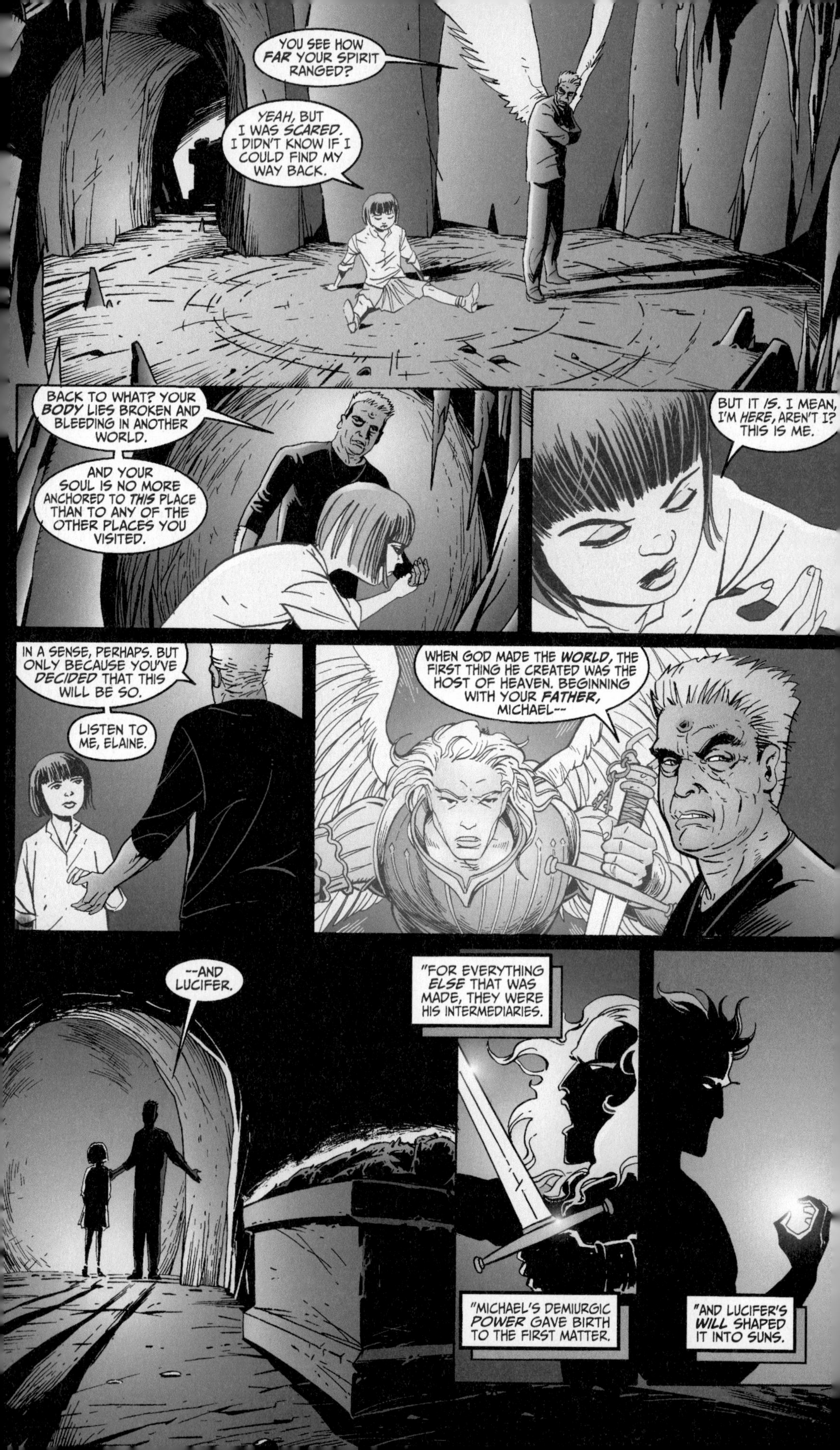

YOU SEE HOW FAR YOUR SPIRIT RANGED?
YEAH, BUT I WAS SCARED. I DIDN'T KNOW IF I COULD FIND MY WAY BACK.
BACK TO WHAT? YOUR BODY LIES BROKEN AND BLEEDING IN ANOTHER WORLD.
AND YOUR SOUL IS NO MORE ANCHORED TO THIS PLACE THAN TO ANY OF THE OTHER PLACES YOU VISITED.
BUT IT IS. I MEAN, I'M HERE, AREN'T I? THIS IS ME.
IN A SENSE, PERHAPS. BUT ONLY BECAUSE YOU'VE DECIDED THAT THIS WILL BE SO.
LISTEN TO ME, ELAINE.
WHEN GOD MADE THE WORLD, THE FIRST THING HE CREATED WAS THE HOST OF HEAVEN. BEGINNING WITH YOUR FATHER, MICHAEL--
--AND LUCIFER.
"FOR EVERYTHING ELSE THAT WAS MADE, THEY WERE HIS INTERMEDIARIES.
"MICHAEL'S DEMIURGIC POWER GAVE BIRTH TO THE FIRST MATTER.
"AND LUCIFER'S WILL SHAPED IT INTO SUNS.

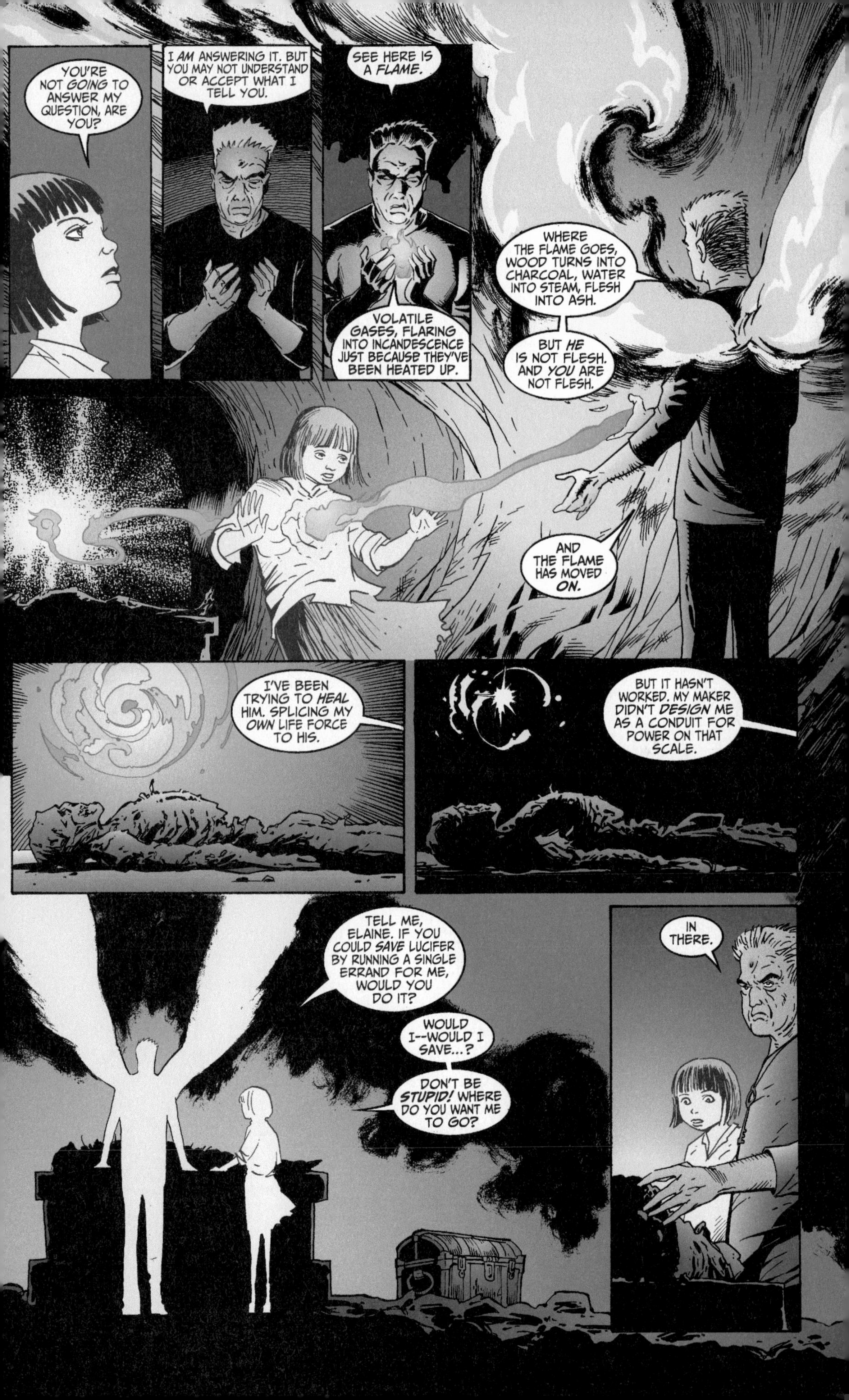
YOU'RE NOT GOING TO ANSWER MY QUESTION, ARE YOU?
I AM ANSWERING IT. BUT YOU MAY NOT UNDERSTAND OR ACCEPT WHAT I TELL YOU.
SEE HERE IS A FLAME.
VOLATILE GASES, FLARING INTO INCANDESCENCE JUST BECAUSE THEY'VE BEEN HEATED UP.
WHERE THE FLAME GOES, WOOD TURNS INTO CHARCOAL, WATER INTO STEAM, FLESH INTO ASH.
BUT HE IS NOT FLESH. AND YOU ARE NOT FLESH.
AND THE FLAME HAS MOVED ON.
I'VE BEEN TRYING TO HEAL HIM. SPLICING MY OWN LIFE FORCE TO HIS.
BUT IT HASN'T WORKED. MY MAKER DIDN'T DESIGN ME AS A CONDUIT FOR POWER ON THAT SCALE.
TELL ME, ELAINE. IF YOU COULD SAVE LUCIFER BY RUNNING A SINGLE ERRAND FOR ME, WOULD YOU DO IT?
WOULD I--WOULD I SAVE...?
DON'T BE STUPID! WHERE DO YOU WANT ME TO GO?
IN THERE.

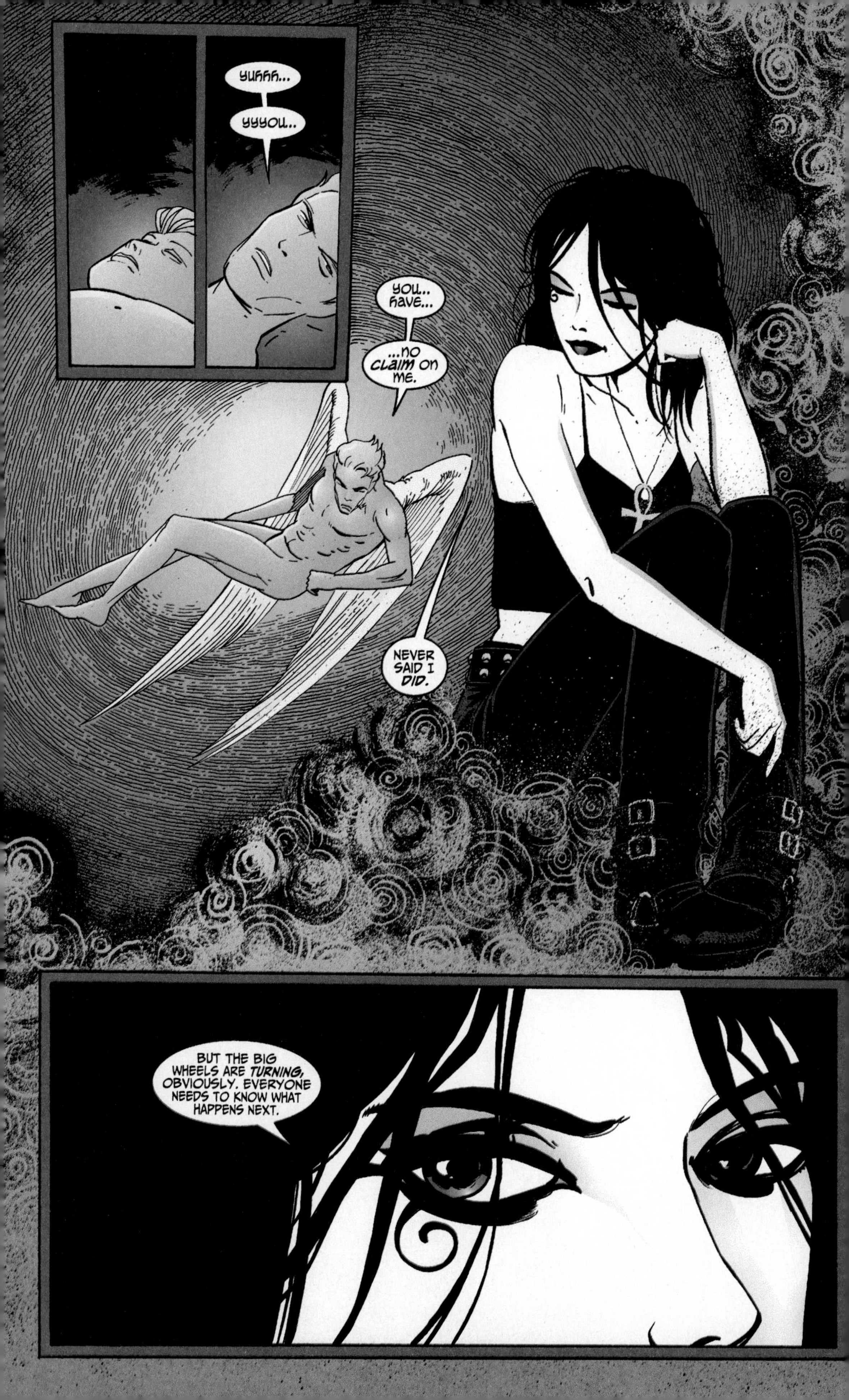
YUHHH...
YYYOU...
YOU... HAVE...
...NO CLAIM ON ME.
NEVER SAID I DID.
BUT THE BIG WHEELS ARE TURNING, OBVIOUSLY. EVERYONE NEEDS TO KNOW WHAT HAPPENS NEXT.

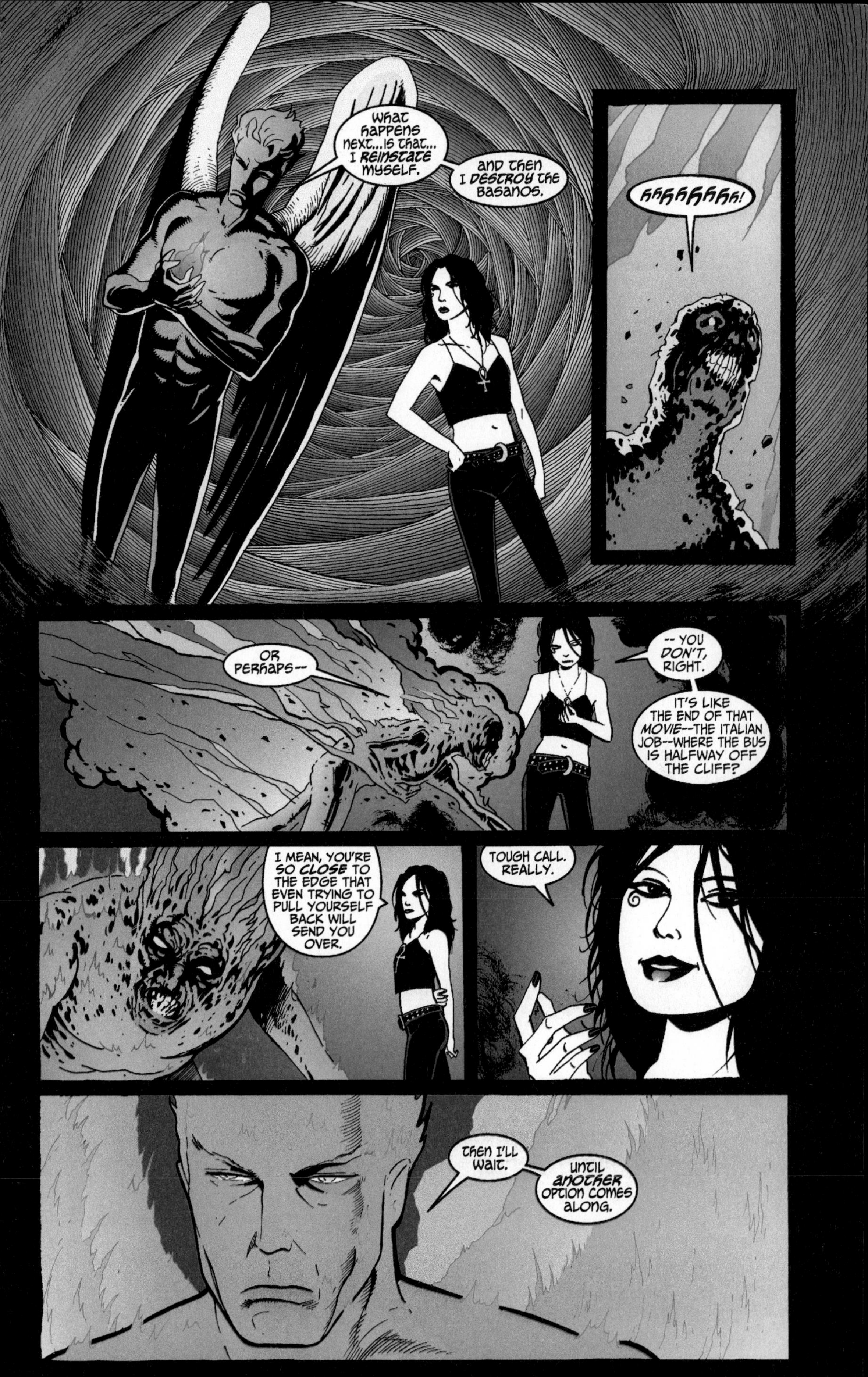
WHAT HAPPENS NEXT...IS THAT... I REINSTATE MYSELF.
AND THEN I DESTROY THE BASANOS.
AHHHHHHH!
OR PERHAPS--
--YOU DON'T, RIGHT.
IT'S LIKE THE END OF THAT MOVIE--THE ITALIAN JOB--WHERE THE BUS IS HALFWAY OFF THE CLIFF?
I MEAN, YOU'RE SO CLOSE TO THE EDGE THAT EVEN TRYING TO PULL YOURSELF BACK WILL SEND YOU OVER.
TOUGH CALL. REALLY.
THEN I'LL WAIT.
UNTIL ANOTHER OPTION COMES ALONG.

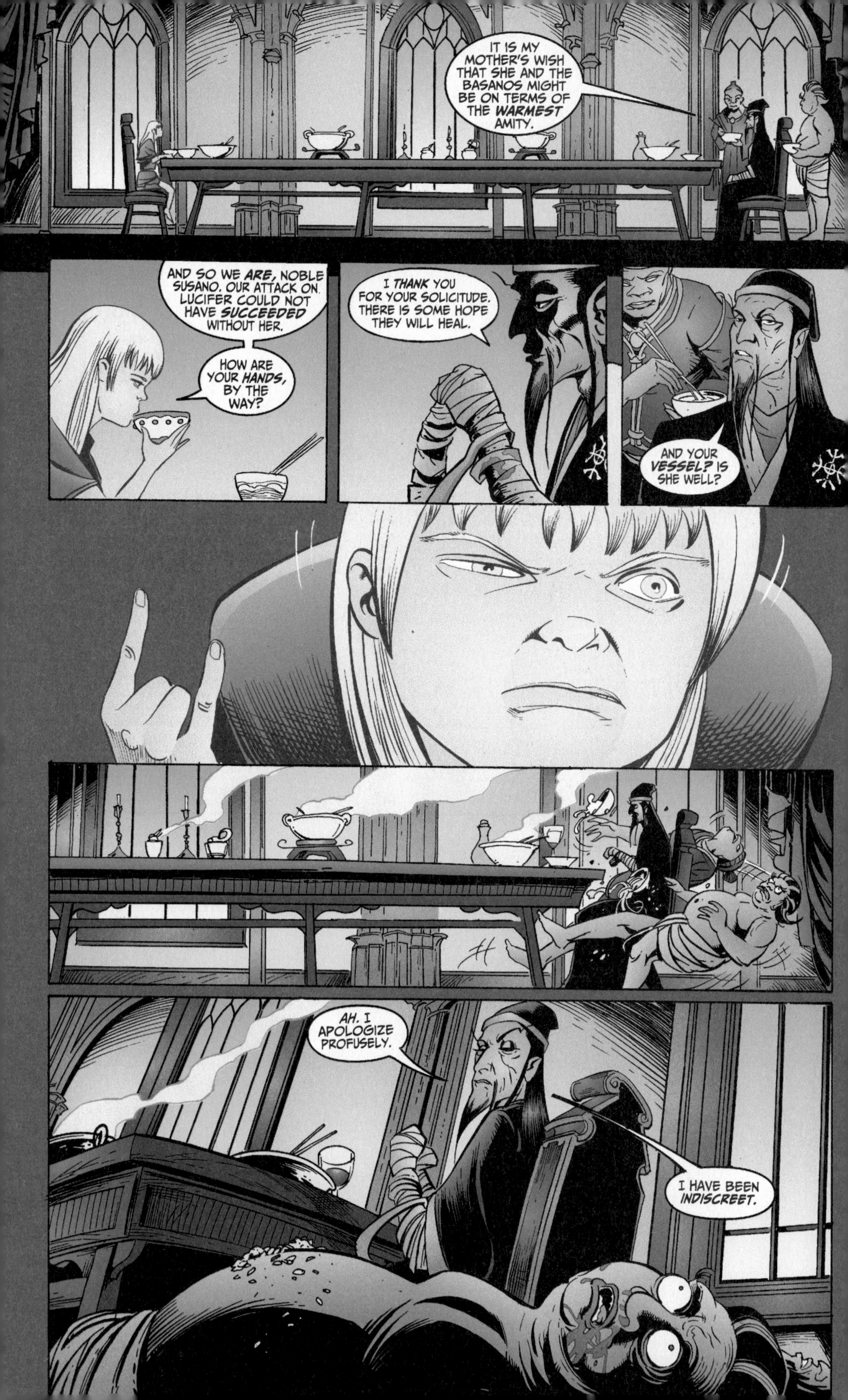
IT IS MY MOTHER'S WISH THAT SHE AND THE BASANOS MIGHT BE ON TERMS OF THE WARMEST AMITY.
AND SO WE ARE, NOBLE SUSANO. OUR ATTACK ON LUCIFER COULD NOT HAVE SUCCEEDED WITHOUT HER.
HOW ARE YOUR HANDS, BY THE WAY?
I THANK YOU FOR YOUR SOLICITUDE. THERE IS SOME HOPE THEY WILL HEAL.
AND YOUR VESSEL? IS SHE WELL?
AH. I APOLOGIZE PROFUSELY.
I HAVE BEEN INDISCREET.

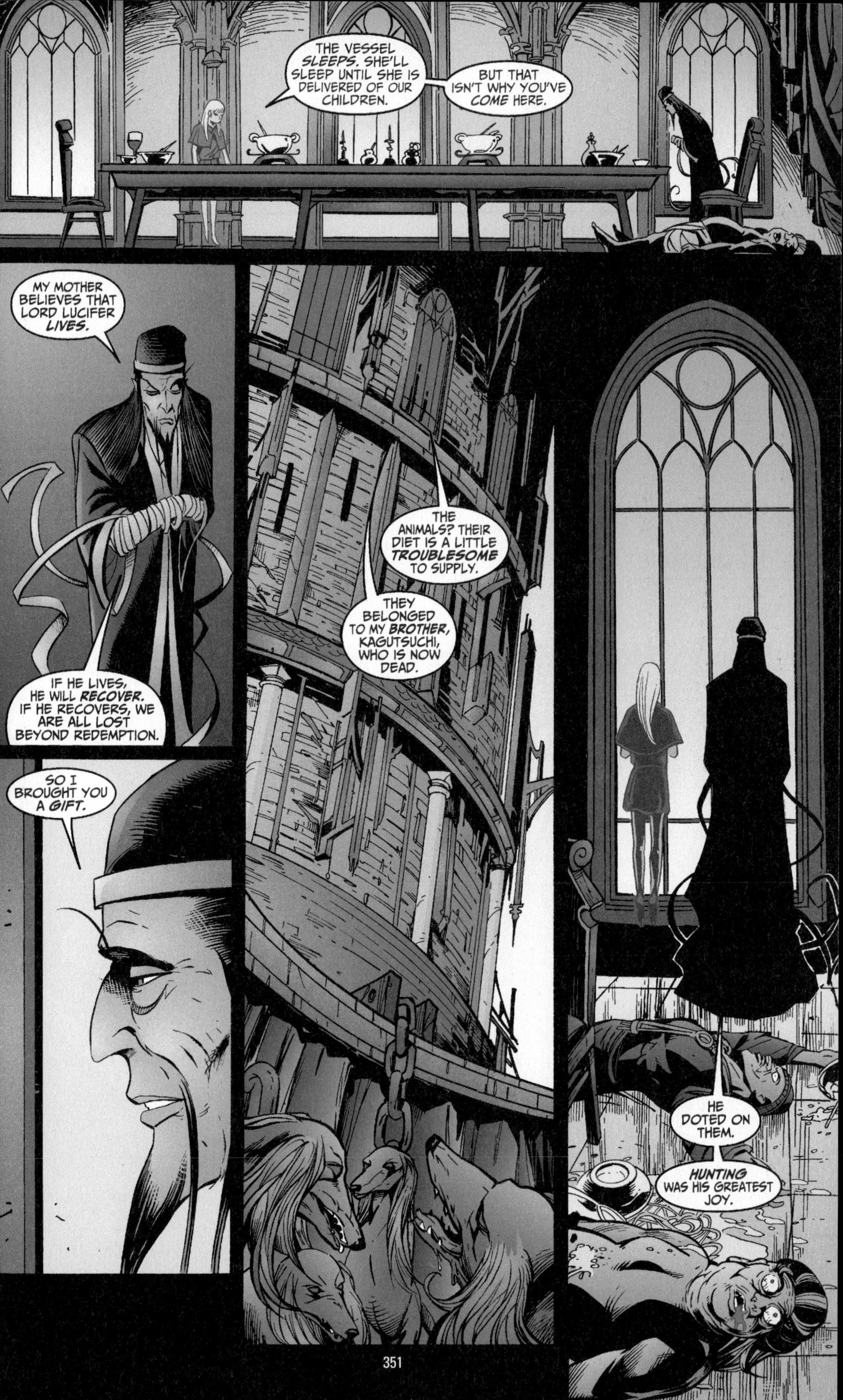
THE VESSEL SLEEPS. SHE'LL SLEEP UNTIL SHE IS DELIVERED OF OUR CHILDREN.
BUT THAT ISN'T WHY YOU'VE COME HERE.
MY MOTHER BELIEVES THAT LORD LUCIFER LIVES.
IF HE LIVES, HE WILL RECOVER. IF HE RECOVERS, WE ARE ALL LOST BEYOND REDEMPTION.
SO I BROUGHT YOU A GIFT.
THE ANIMALS? THEIR DIET IS A LITTLE TROUBLESOME TO SUPPLY.
THEY BELONGED TO MY BROTHER, KAGUTSUCHI, WHO IS NOW DEAD.
HE DOTED ON THEM.
HUNTING WAS HIS GREATEST JOY.

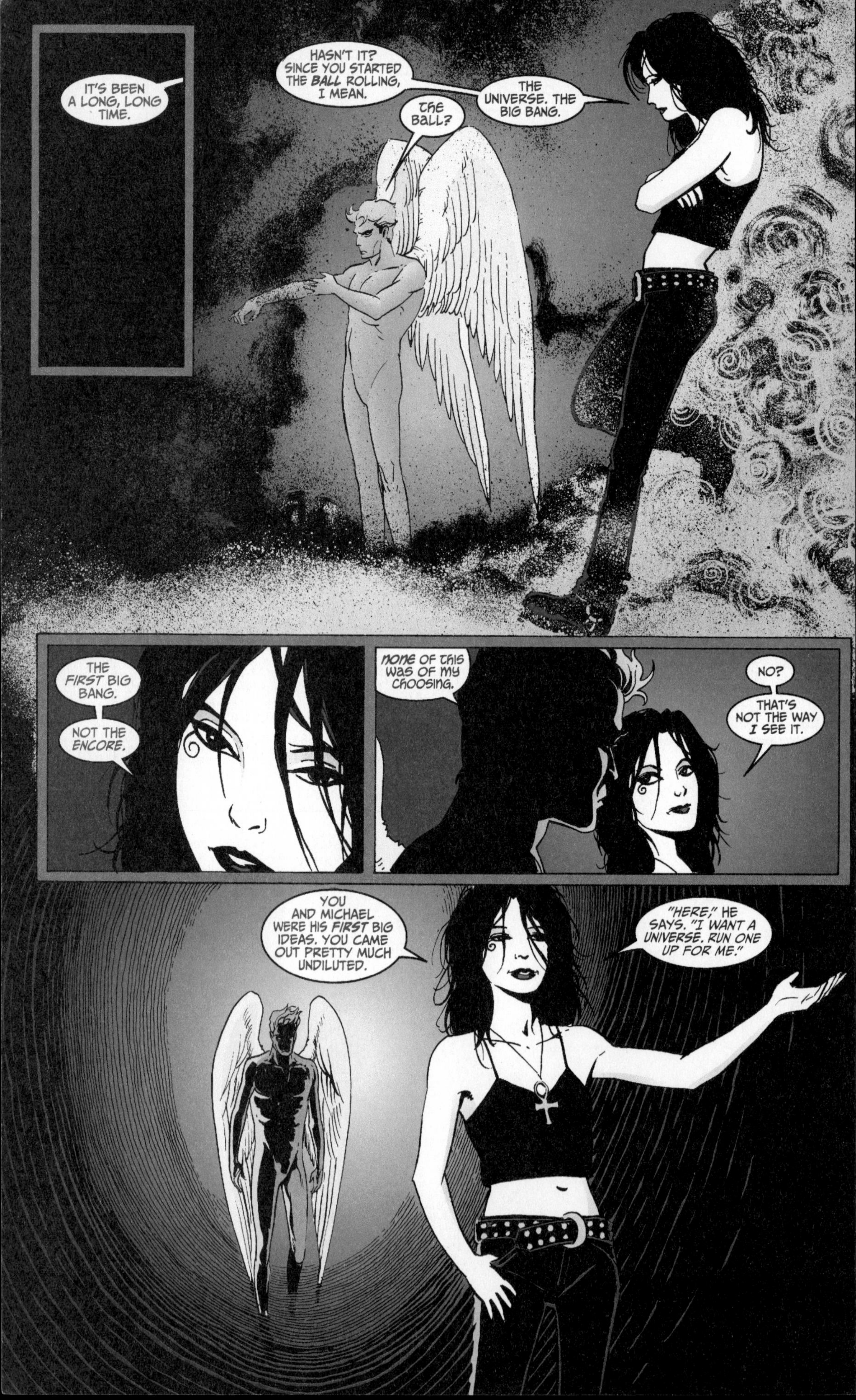
IT'S BEEN A LONG, LONG TIME.
HASN'T IT? SINCE YOU STARTED THE BALL ROLLING, I MEAN.
THE BALL?
THE UNIVERSE. THE BIG BANG.
THE FIRST BIG BANG.
NOT THE ENCORE.
NONE OF THIS WAS OF MY CHOOSING.
NO?
THAT'S NOT THE WAY I SEE IT.
YOU AND MICHAEL WERE HIS FIRST BIG IDEAS. YOU CAME OUT PRETTY MUCH UNDILUTED.
"HERE," HE SAYS. "I WANT A UNIVERSE. RUN ONE UP FOR ME."

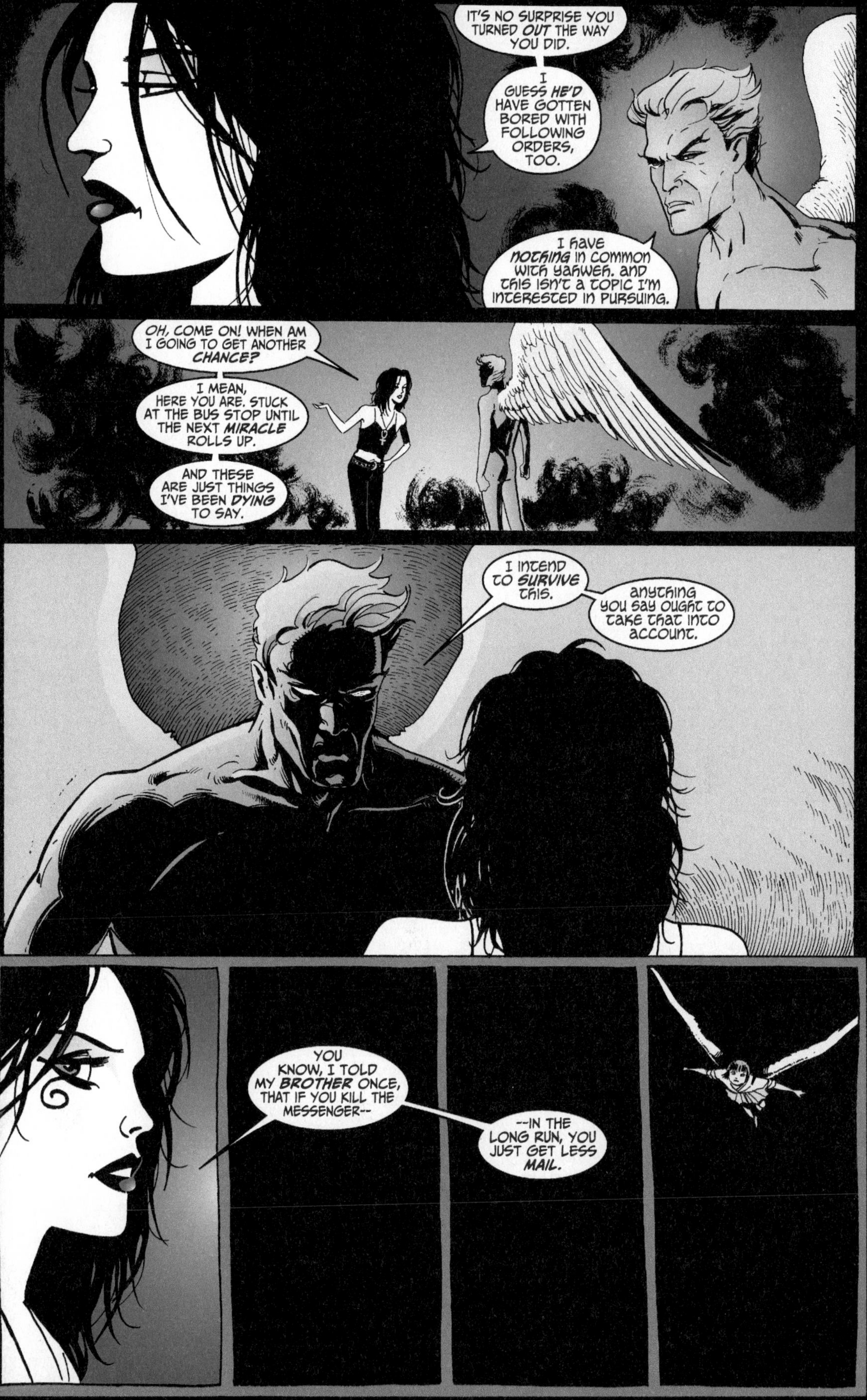
IT'S NO SURPRISE YOU TURNED OUT THE WAY YOU DID.
I GUESS HE'D HAVE GOTTEN BORED WITH FOLLOWING ORDERS, TOO.
I HAVE NOTHING IN COMMON WITH YAHWEH. AND THIS ISN'T A TOPIC I'M INTERESTED IN PURSUING.
OH, COME ON! WHEN AM I GOING TO GET ANOTHER CHANCE?
I MEAN, HERE YOU ARE. STUCK AT THE BUS STOP UNTIL THE NEXT MIRACLE ROLLS UP.
AND THESE ARE JUST THINGS I'VE BEEN DYING TO SAY.
I INTEND TO SURVIVE THIS.
ANYTHING YOU SAY OUGHT TO TAKE THAT INTO ACCOUNT.
YOU KNOW, I TOLD MY BROTHER ONCE, THAT IF YOU KILL THE MESSENGER--
--IN THE LONG RUN, YOU JUST GET LESS MAIL.

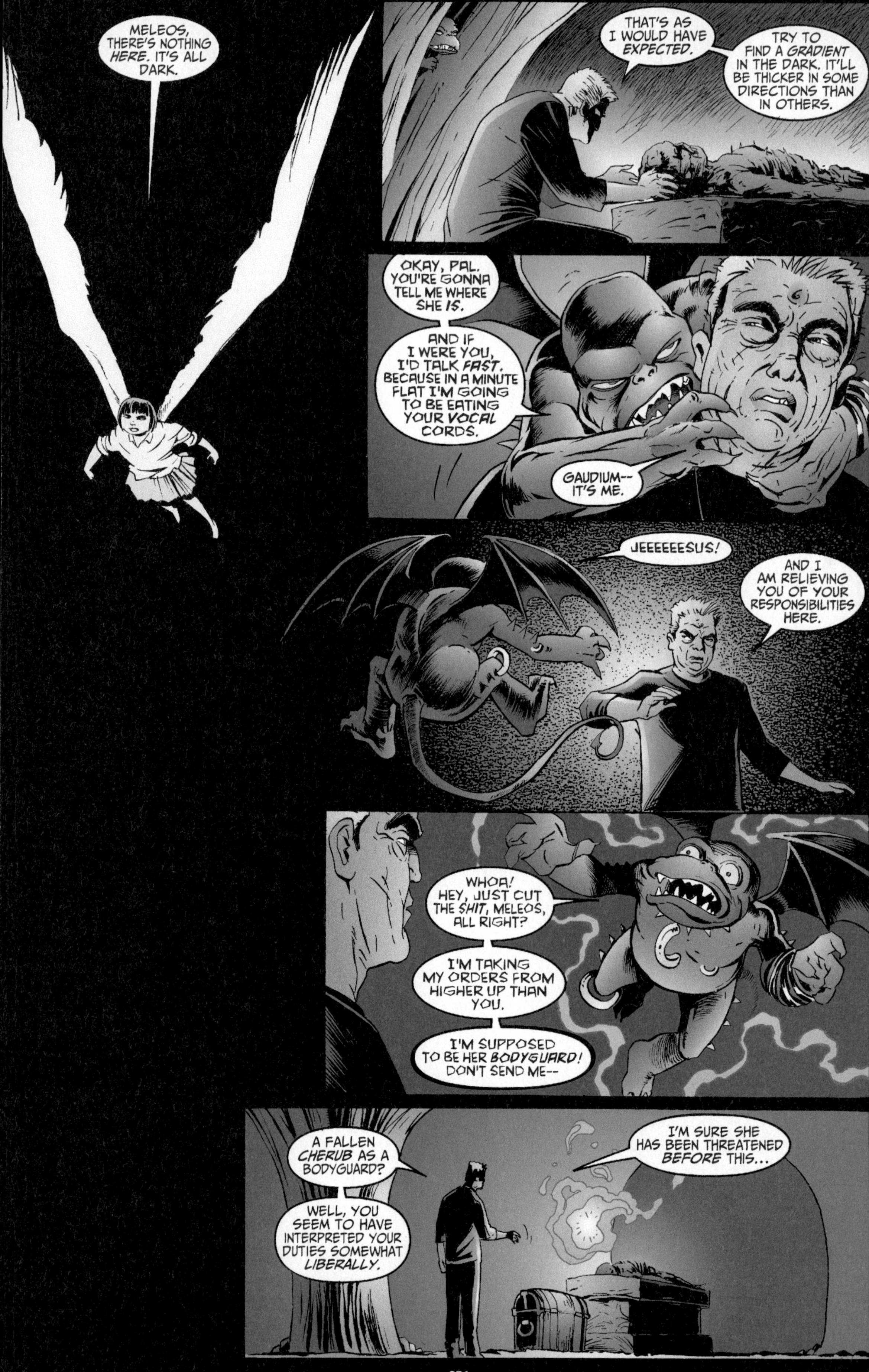
MELEOS, THERE'S NOTHING HERE. IT'S ALL DARK.
THAT'S AS I WOULD HAVE EXPECTED.
TRY TO FIND A GRADIENT IN THE DARK. IT'LL BE THICKER IN SOME DIRECTIONS THAN IN OTHERS.
OKAY, PAL. YOU'RE GONNA TELL ME WHERE SHE IS.
AND IF I WERE YOU, I'D TALK FAST. BECAUSE IN A MINUTE FLAT I'M GOING TO BE EATING YOUR VOCAL CORDS.
GAUDIUM-- IT'S ME.
JEEEEEESUS!
AND I AM RELIEVING YOU OF YOUR RESPONSIBILITIES HERE.
WHOA! HEY, JUST CUT THE SHIT, MELEOS, ALL RIGHT?
I'M TAKING MY ORDERS FROM HIGHER UP THAN YOU.
I'M SUPPOSED TO BE HER BODYGUARD! DON'T SEND ME--
A FALLEN CHERUB AS A BODYGUARD?
WELL, YOU SEEM TO HAVE INTERPRETED YOUR DUTIES SOMEWHAT LIBERALLY.
I'M SURE SHE HAS BEEN THREATENED BEFORE THIS...

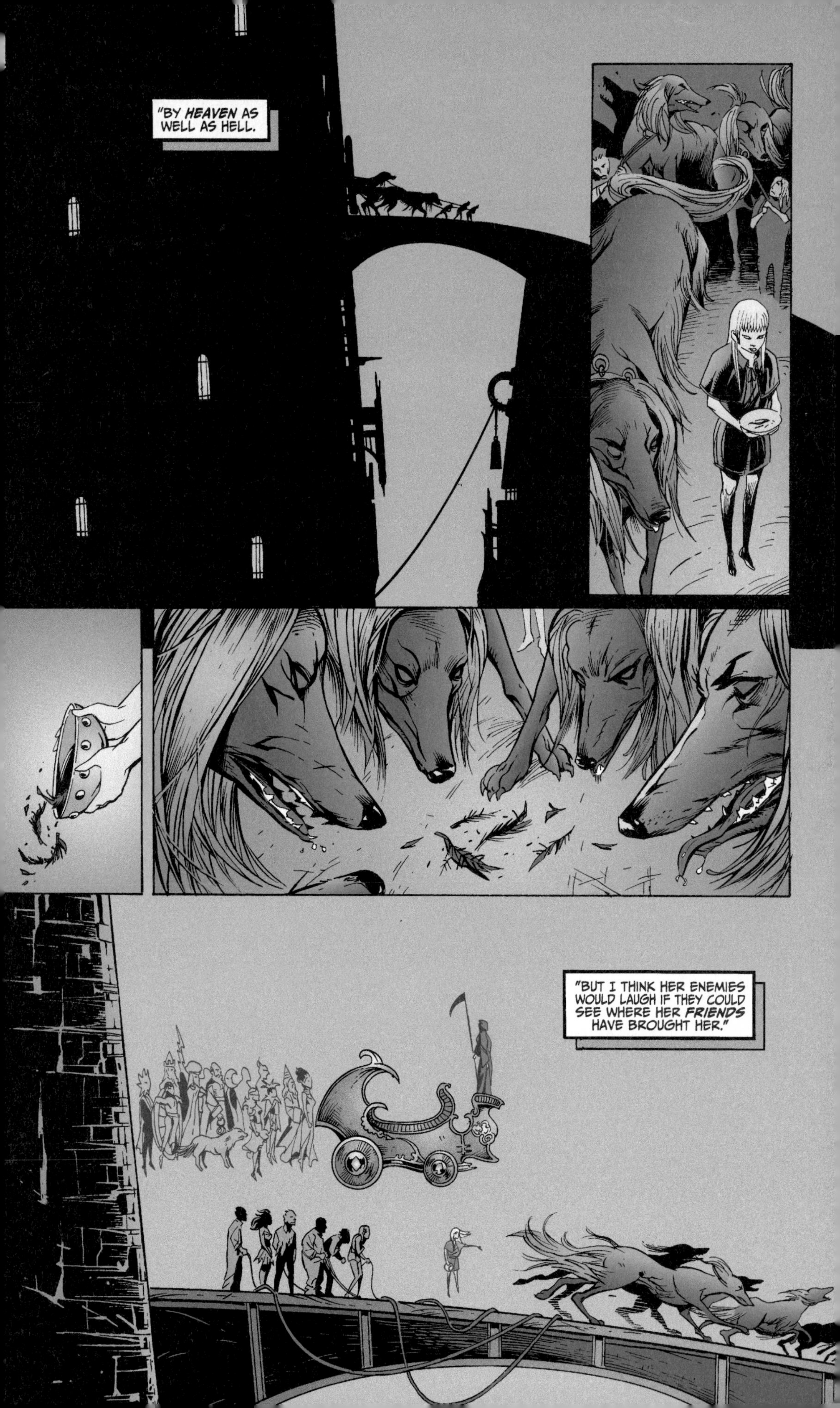
"BY HEAVEN AS WELL AS HELL.
"BUT I THINK HER ENEMIES WOULD LAUGH IF THEY COULD SEE WHERE HER FRIENDS HAVE BROUGHT HER."

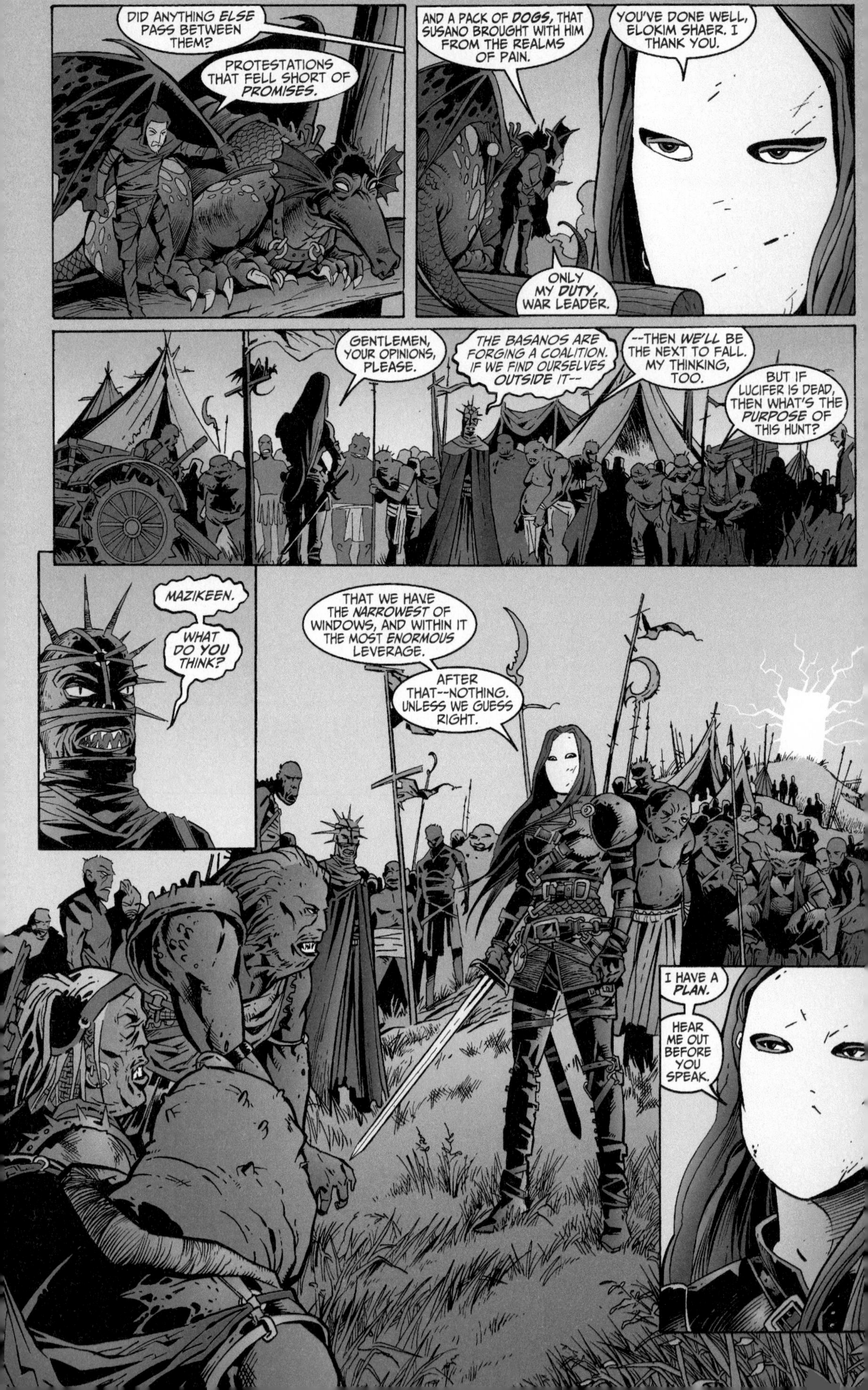
DID ANYTHING ELSE PASS BETWEEN THEM?
PROTESTATIONS THAT FELL SHORT OF PROMISES.
AND A PACK OF DOGS, THAT SUSANO BROUGHT WITH HIM FROM THE REALMS OF PAIN.
YOU'VE DONE WELL, ELOKIM SHAER. I THANK YOU.
ONLY MY DUTY, WAR LEADER.
GENTLEMEN, YOUR OPINIONS, PLEASE.
THE BASANOS ARE FORGING A COALITION. IF WE FIND OURSELVES OUTSIDE IT--
--THEN WE'LL BE THE NEXT TO FALL. MY THINKING, TOO.
BUT IF LUCIFER IS DEAD, THEN WHAT'S THE PURPOSE OF THIS HUNT?
MAZIKEEN.
WHAT DO YOU THINK?
THAT WE HAVE THE NARROWEST OF WINDOWS, AND WITHIN IT THE MOST ENORMOUS LEVERAGE.
AFTER THAT--NOTHING. UNLESS WE GUESS RIGHT.
I HAVE A PLAN.
HEAR ME OUT BEFORE YOU SPEAK.

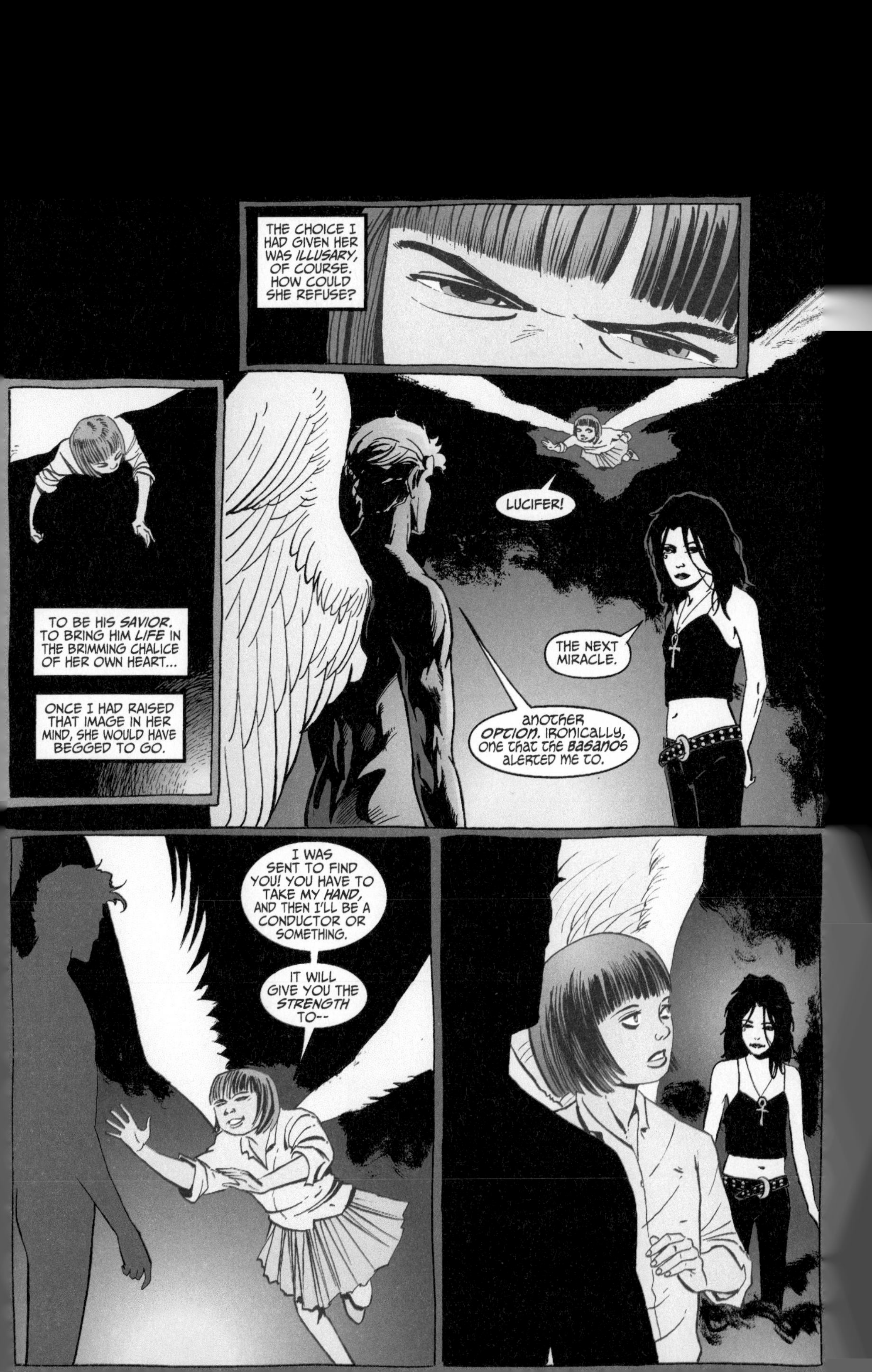
THE CHOICE I HAD GIVEN HER WAS ILLUSARY, OF COURSE. HOW COULD SHE REFUSE?
TO BE HIS SAVIOR. TO BRING HIM LIFE IN THE BRIMMING CHALICE OF HER OWN HEART...
ONCE I HAD RAISED THAT IMAGE IN HER MIND, SHE WOULD HAVE BEGGED TO GO.
LUCIFER!
THE NEXT MIRACLE.
ANOTHER OPTION. IRONICALLY, ONE THAT THE BASANOS ALERTED ME TO.
I WAS SENT TO FIND YOU! YOU HAVE TO TAKE MY HAND, AND THEN I'LL BE A CONDUCTOR OR SOMETHING.
IT WILL GIVE YOU THE STRENGTH TO--

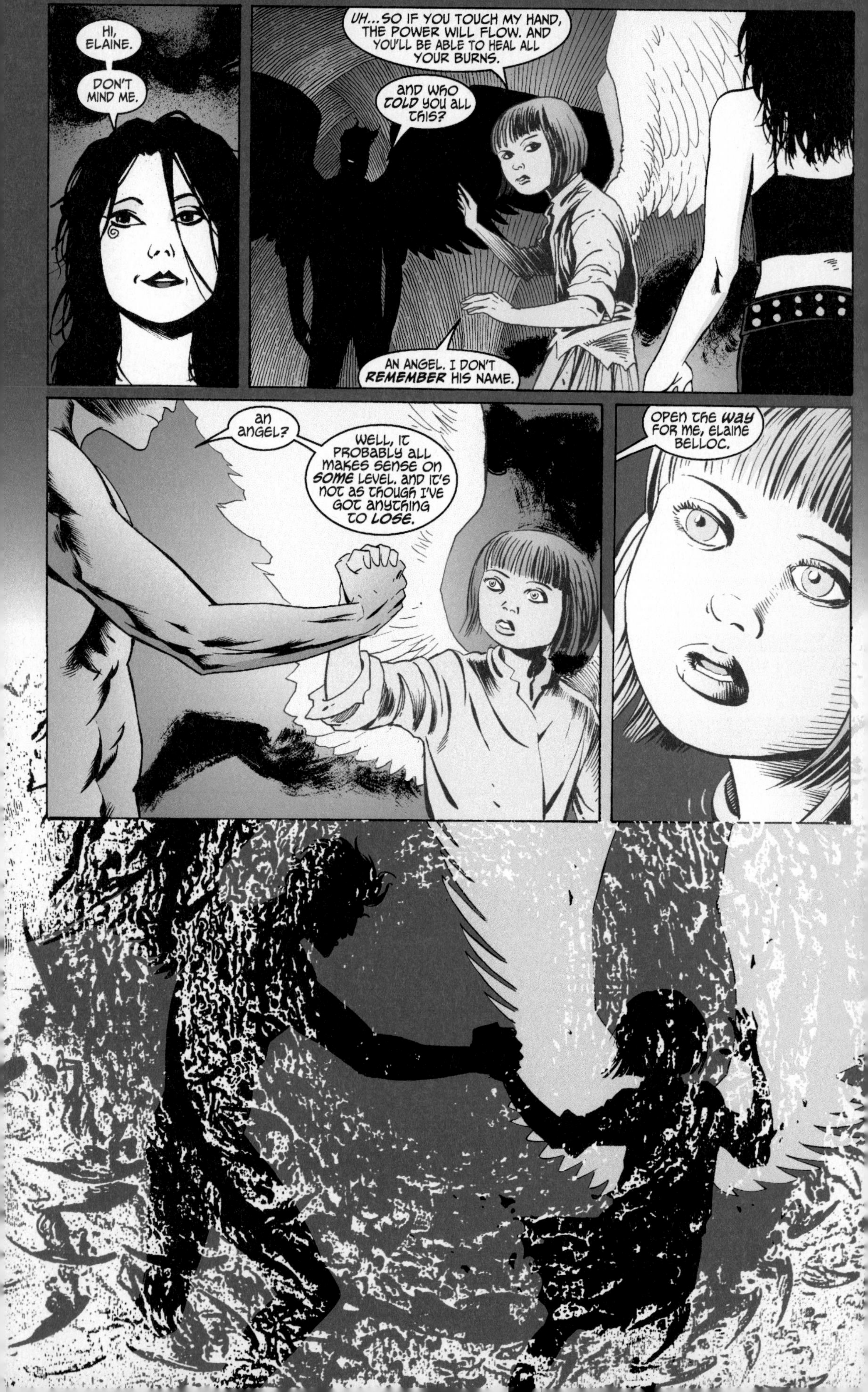
HI, ELAINE.
DON'T MIND ME.
UH...SO IF YOU TOUCH MY HAND, THE POWER WILL FLOW. AND YOU'LL BE ABLE TO HEAL ALL YOUR BURNS.
and WHO TOLD YOU all THIS?
AN ANGEL. I DON'T REMEMBER HIS NAME.
an angel?
WELL, IT PROBABLY ALL MAKES SENSE ON SOME LEVEL. AND IT'S NOT AS THOUGH I'VE GOT ANYTHING TO LOSE.
OPEN THE WAY FOR ME, ELAINE BELLOC.

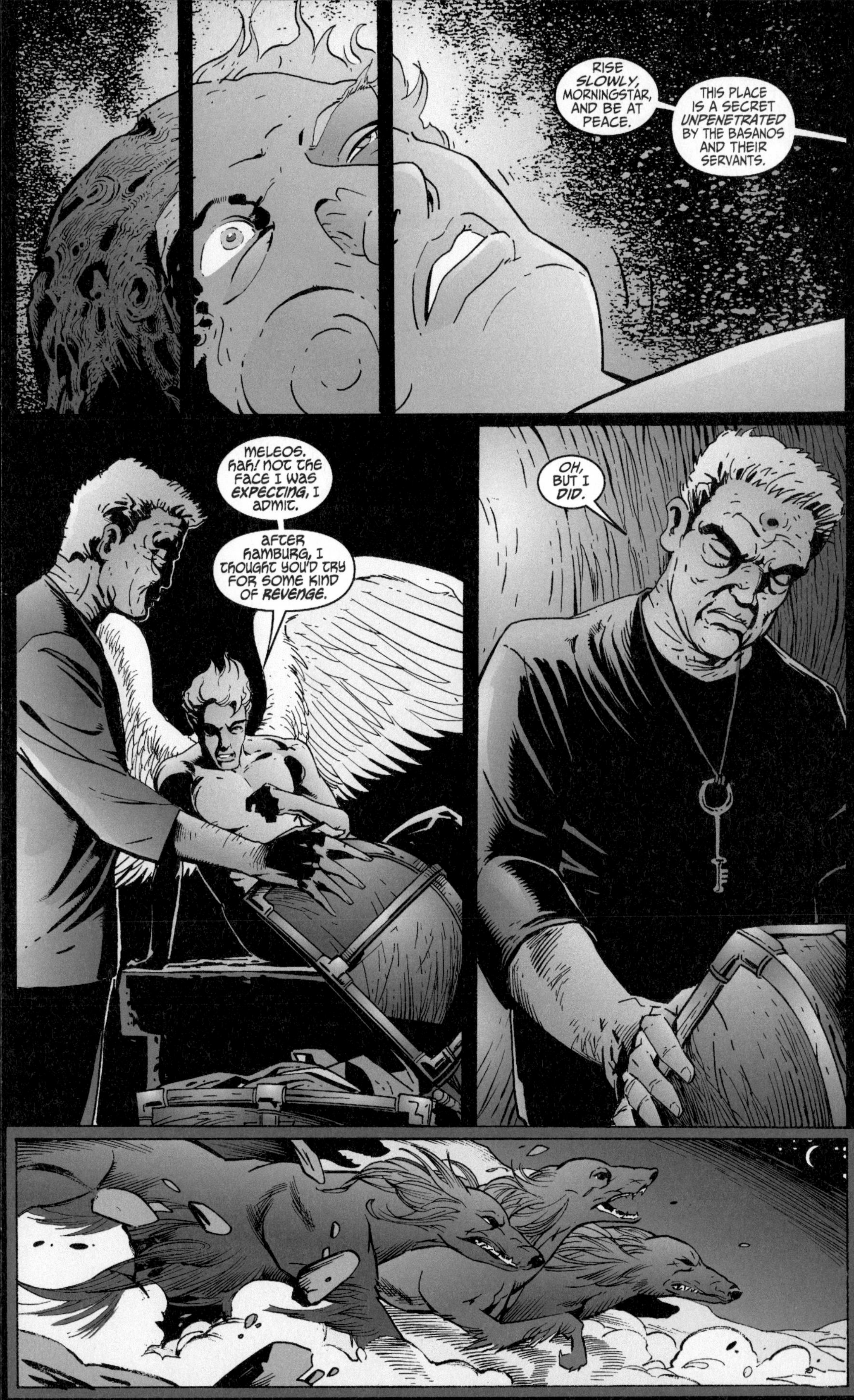
RISE SLOWLY, MORNINGSTAR, AND BE AT PEACE.
THIS PLACE IS A SECRET UNPENETRATED BY THE BASANOS AND THEIR SERVANTS.
MELEOS. HAH! NOT THE FACE I WAS EXPECTING, I ADMIT.
AFTER HAMBURG, I THOUGHT YOU'D TRY FOR SOME KIND OF REVENGE.
OH, BUT I DID.

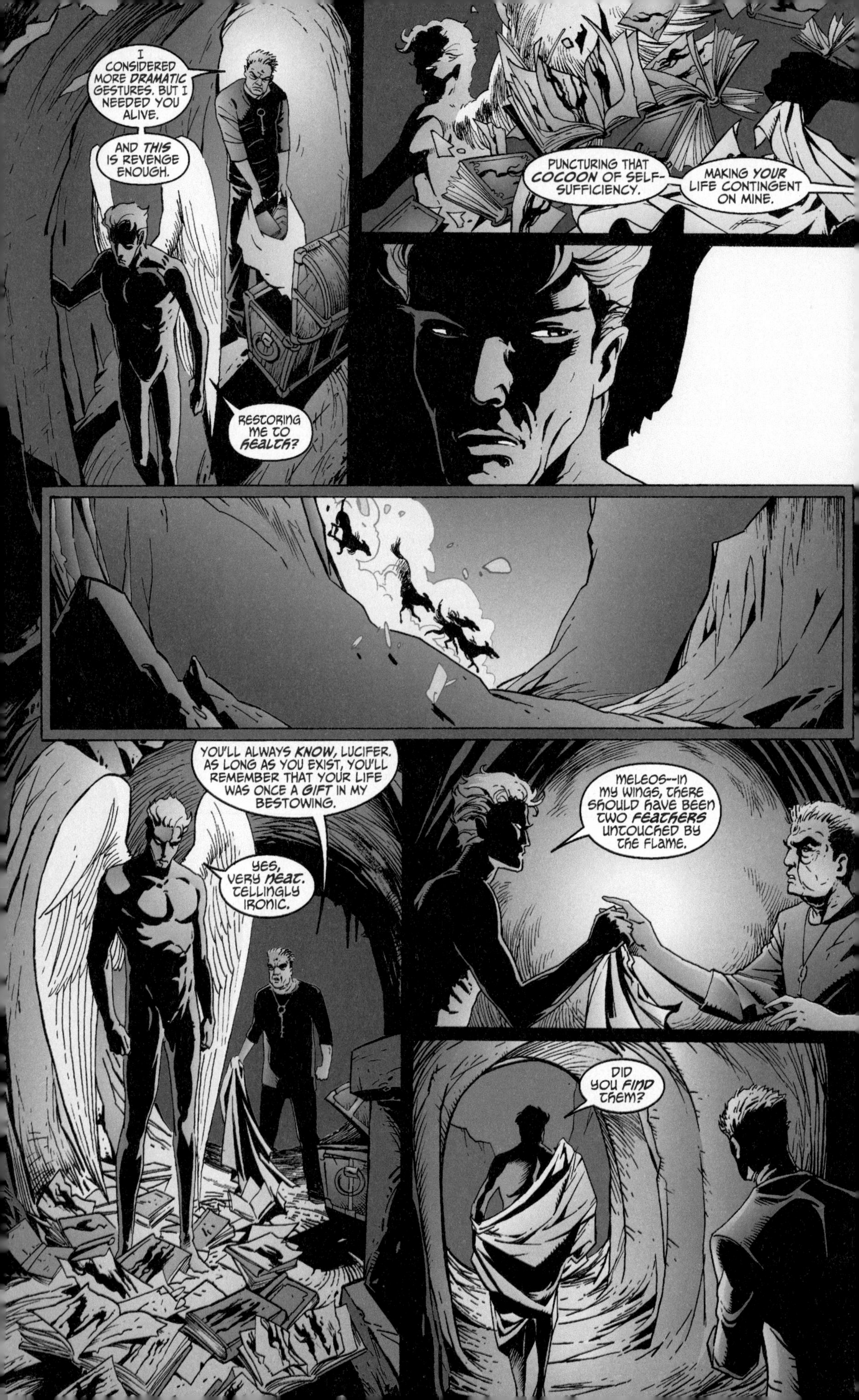
I CONSIDERED MORE DRAMATIC GESTURES. BUT I NEEDED YOU ALIVE.
AND THIS IS REVENGE ENOUGH.
RESTORING ME TO HEALTH?
PUNCTURING THAT COCOON OF SELF-SUFFICIENCY.
MAKING YOUR LIFE CONTINGENT ON MINE.
YOU'LL ALWAYS KNOW, LUCIFER. AS LONG AS YOU EXIST, YOU'LL REMEMBER THAT YOUR LIFE WAS ONCE A GIFT IN MY BESTOWING.
YES, VERY NEAT. TELLINGLY IRONIC.
MELEOS--IN MY WINGS, THERE SHOULD HAVE BEEN TWO FEATHERS UNTOUCHED BY THE FLAME.
DID YOU FIND THEM?

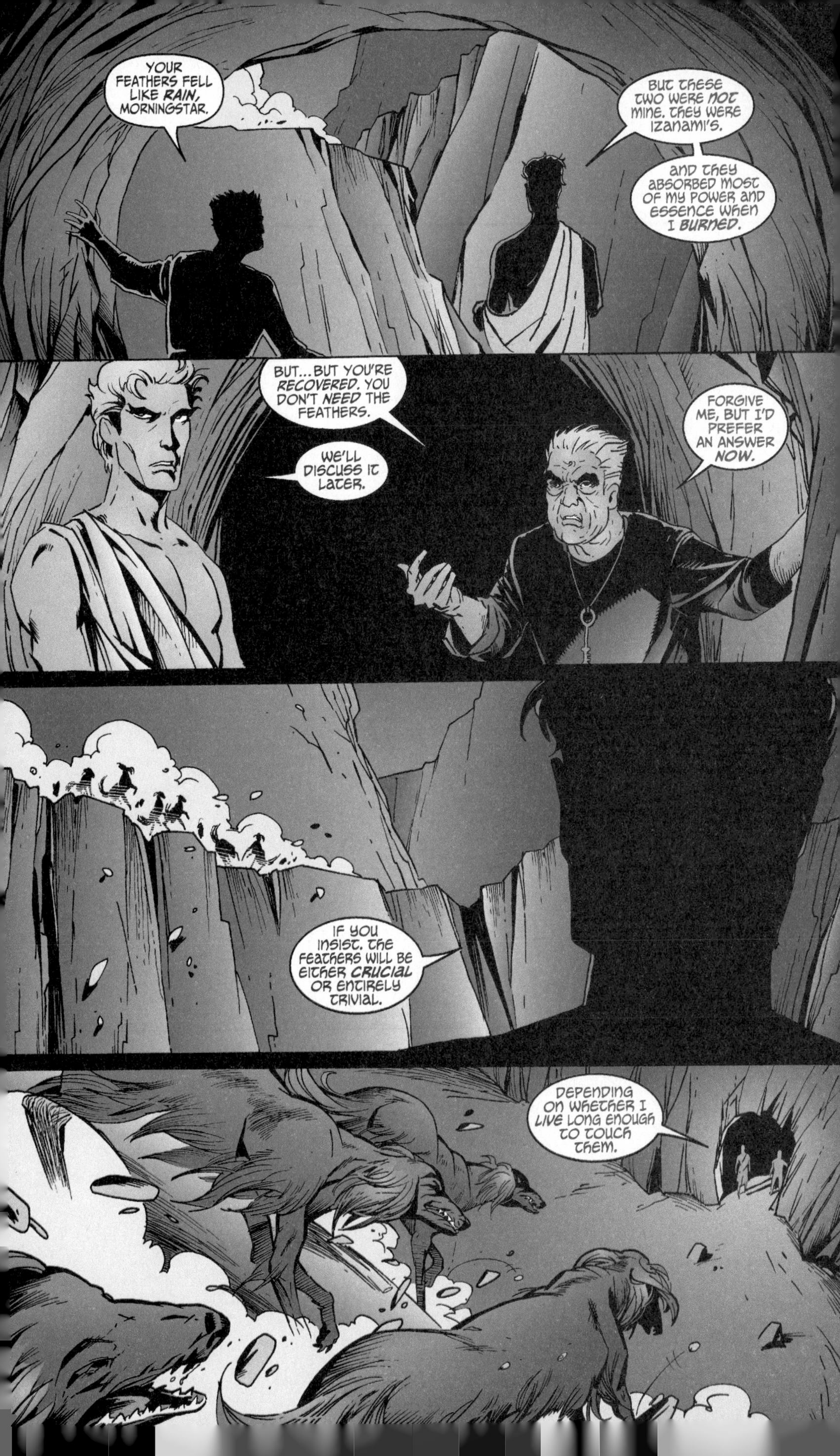
YOUR FEATHERS FELL LIKE RAIN, MORNINGSTAR.
BUT THESE TWO WERE NOT MINE. THEY WERE IZANAMI'S.
AND THEY ABSORBED MOST OF MY POWER AND ESSENCE WHEN I BURNED.
BUT...BUT YOU'RE RECOVERED. YOU DON'T NEED THE FEATHERS.
WE'LL DISCUSS IT LATER.
FORGIVE ME, BUT I'D PREFER AN ANSWER NOW.
IF YOU INSIST. THE FEATHERS WILL BE EITHER CRUCIAL OR ENTIRELY TRIVIAL.
DEPENDING ON WHETHER I LIVE LONG ENOUGH TO TOUCH THEM.

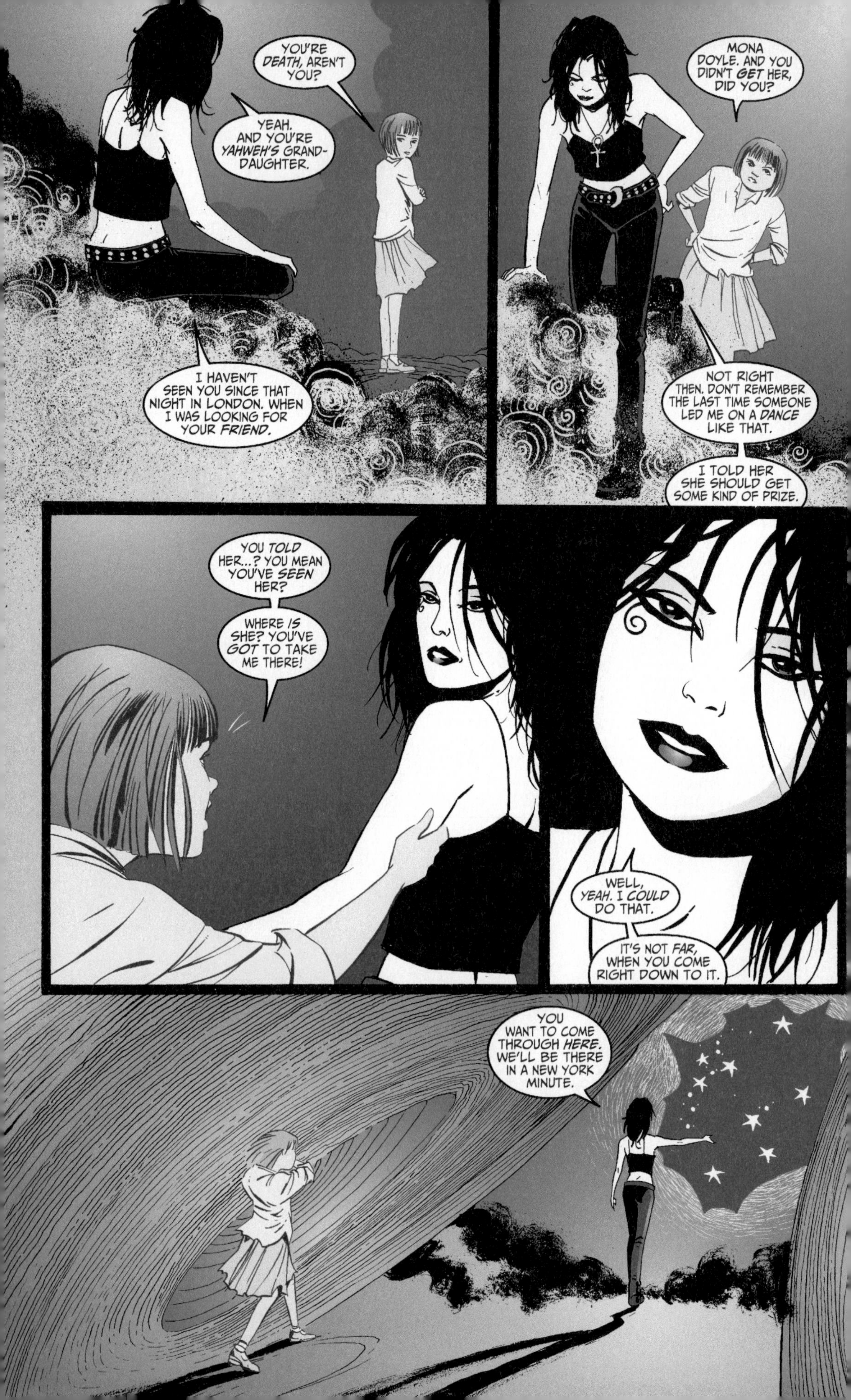
YOU'RE *DEATH*, AREN'T YOU?
YEAH. AND YOU'RE *YAHWEH'S* GRAND-DAUGHTER.
I HAVEN'T SEEN YOU SINCE THAT NIGHT IN LONDON. WHEN I WAS LOOKING FOR YOUR *FRIEND.*
MONA DOYLE. AND YOU DIDN'T *GET* HER, DID YOU?
NOT RIGHT THEN. DON'T REMEMBER THE LAST TIME SOMEONE LED ME ON A *DANCE* LIKE THAT.
I TOLD HER SHE SHOULD GET SOME KIND OF PRIZE.
YOU *TOLD* HER...? YOU MEAN YOU'VE *SEEN* HER?
WHERE *IS* SHE? YOU'VE *GOT* TO TAKE ME THERE!
WELL, *YEAH.* I *COULD* DO THAT.
IT'S NOT *FAR,* WHEN YOU COME RIGHT DOWN TO IT.
YOU WANT TO COME THROUGH *HERE.* WE'LL BE THERE IN A NEW YORK MINUTE.

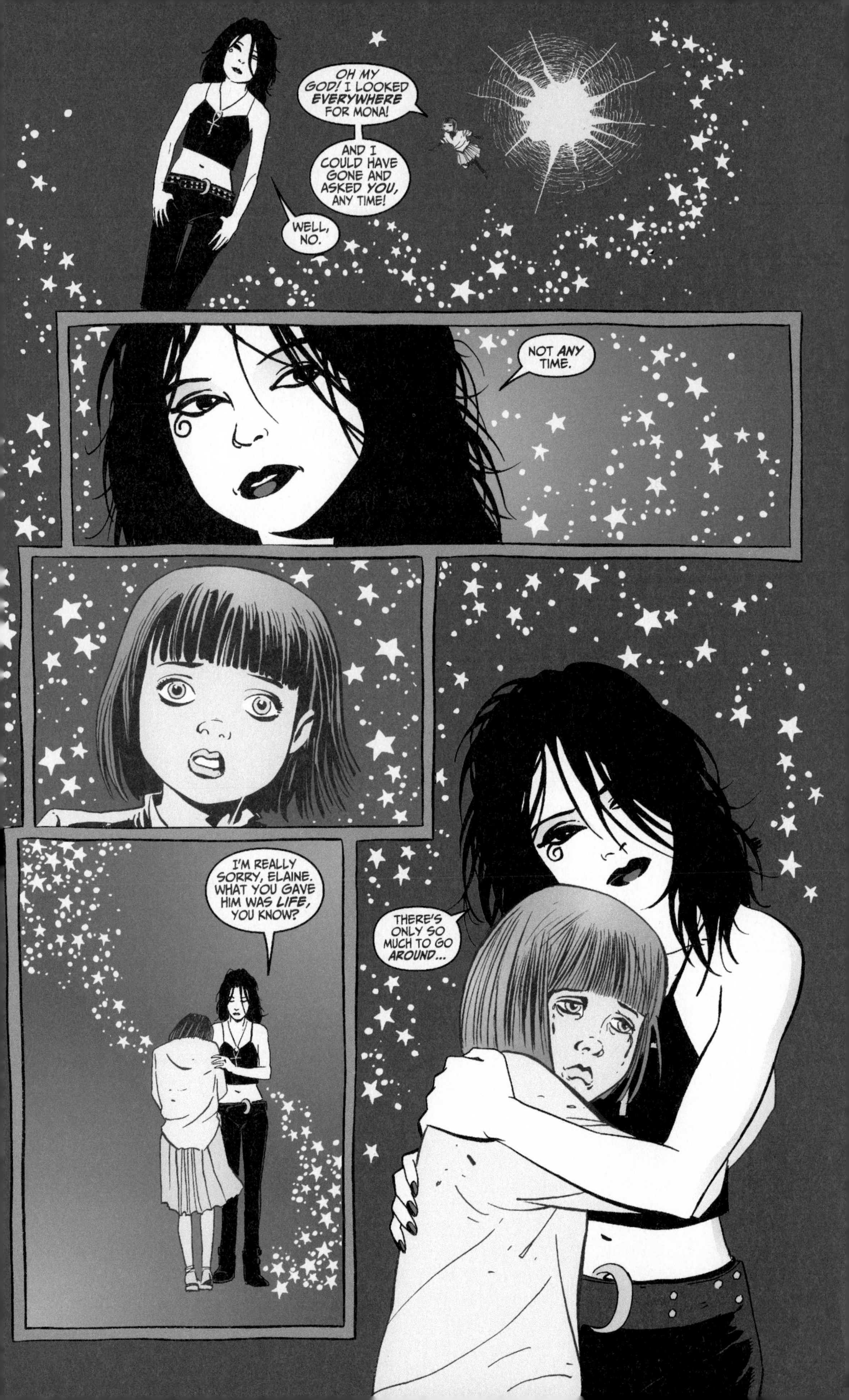
OH MY GOD! I LOOKED EVERYWHERE FOR MONA!
AND I COULD HAVE GONE AND ASKED YOU, ANY TIME!
WELL, NO.
NOT ANY TIME.
I'M REALLY SORRY, ELAINE. WHAT YOU GAVE HIM WAS LIFE, YOU KNOW?
THERE'S ONLY SO MUCH TO GO AROUND...

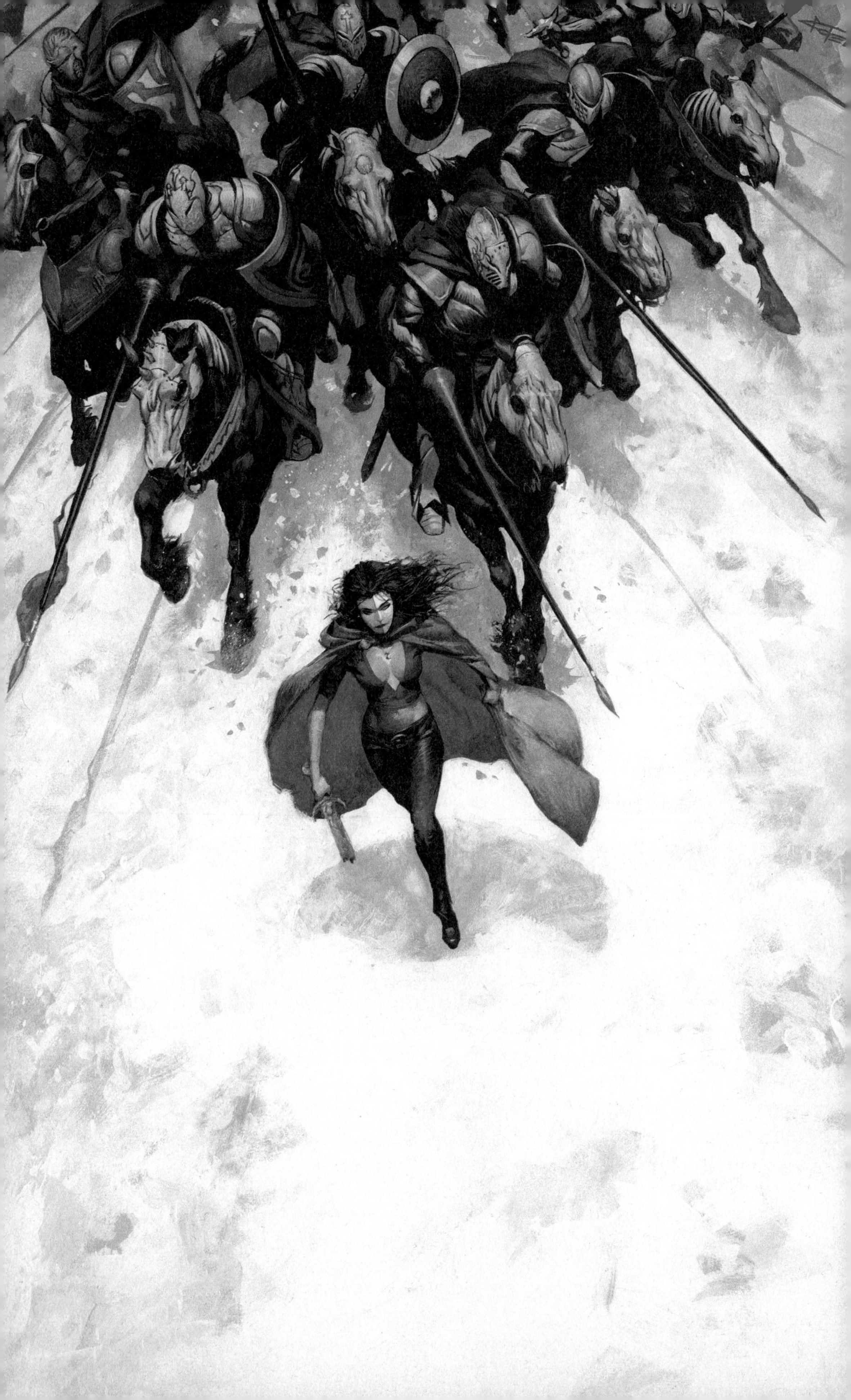

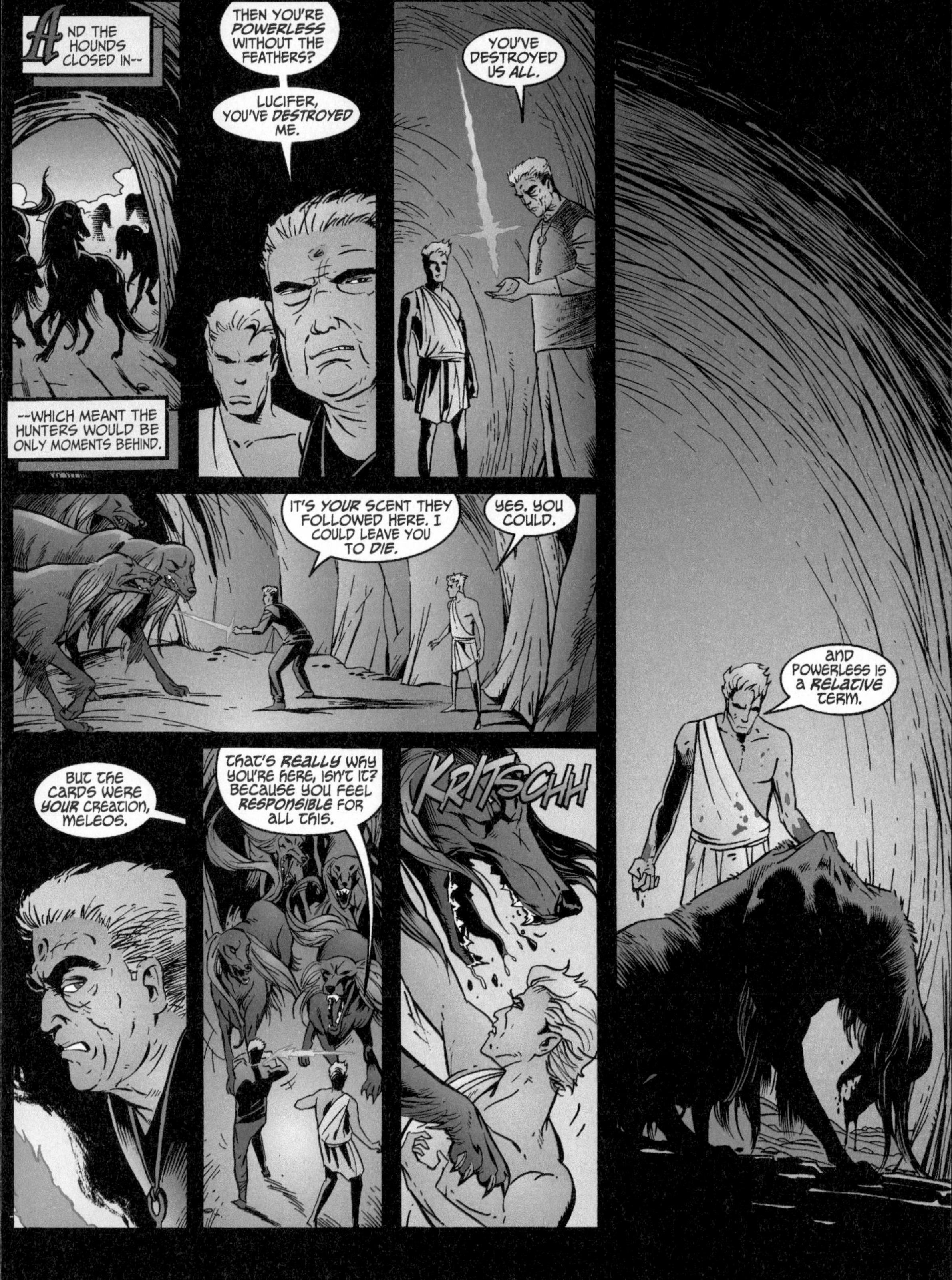
AND THE HOUNDS CLOSED IN--
--WHICH MEANT THE HUNTERS WOULD BE ONLY MOMENTS BEHIND.
THEN YOU'RE POWERLESS WITHOUT THE FEATHERS?
LUCIFER, YOU'VE DESTROYED ME.
YOU'VE DESTROYED US ALL.
IT'S YOUR SCENT THEY FOLLOWED HERE. I COULD LEAVE YOU TO DIE.
YES. YOU COULD.
BUT THE CARDS WERE YOUR CREATION, MELEOS.
THAT'S REALLY WHY YOU'RE HERE, ISN'T IT? BECAUSE YOU FEEL RESPONSIBLE FOR ALL THIS.
KRITSCHH
AND POWERLESS IS A RELATIVE TERM.

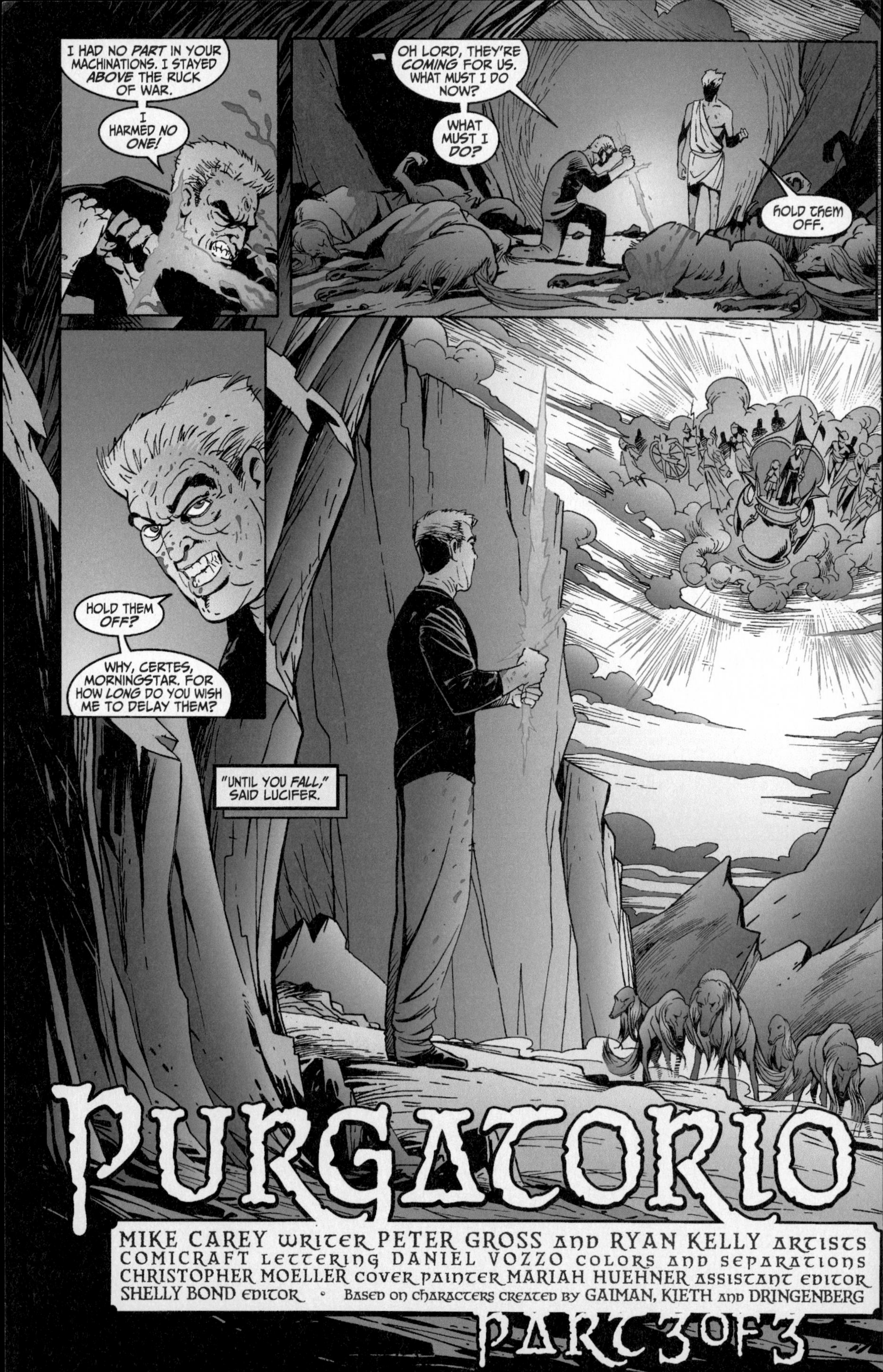
I HAD NO PART IN YOUR MACHINATIONS. I STAYED ABOVE THE RUCK OF WAR.
I HARMED NO ONE!
OH LORD, THEY'RE COMING FOR US. WHAT MUST I DO NOW?
WHAT MUST I DO?
HOLD THEM OFF.
HOLD THEM OFF?
WHY, CERTES, MORNINGSTAR. FOR HOW LONG DO YOU WISH ME TO DELAY THEM?
"UNTIL YOU FALL," SAID LUCIFER.
PURGATORIO
MIKE CAREY WRITER PETER GROSS AND RYAN KELLY ARTISTS
COMICRAFT LETTERING DANIEL VOZZO COLORS AND SEPARATIONS
CHRISTOPHER MOELLER COVER PAINTER MARIAH HUEHNER ASSISTANT EDITOR
SHELLY BOND EDITOR • BASED ON CHARACTERS CREATED BY GAIMAN, KIETH AND DRINGENBERG
PART 3 OF 3

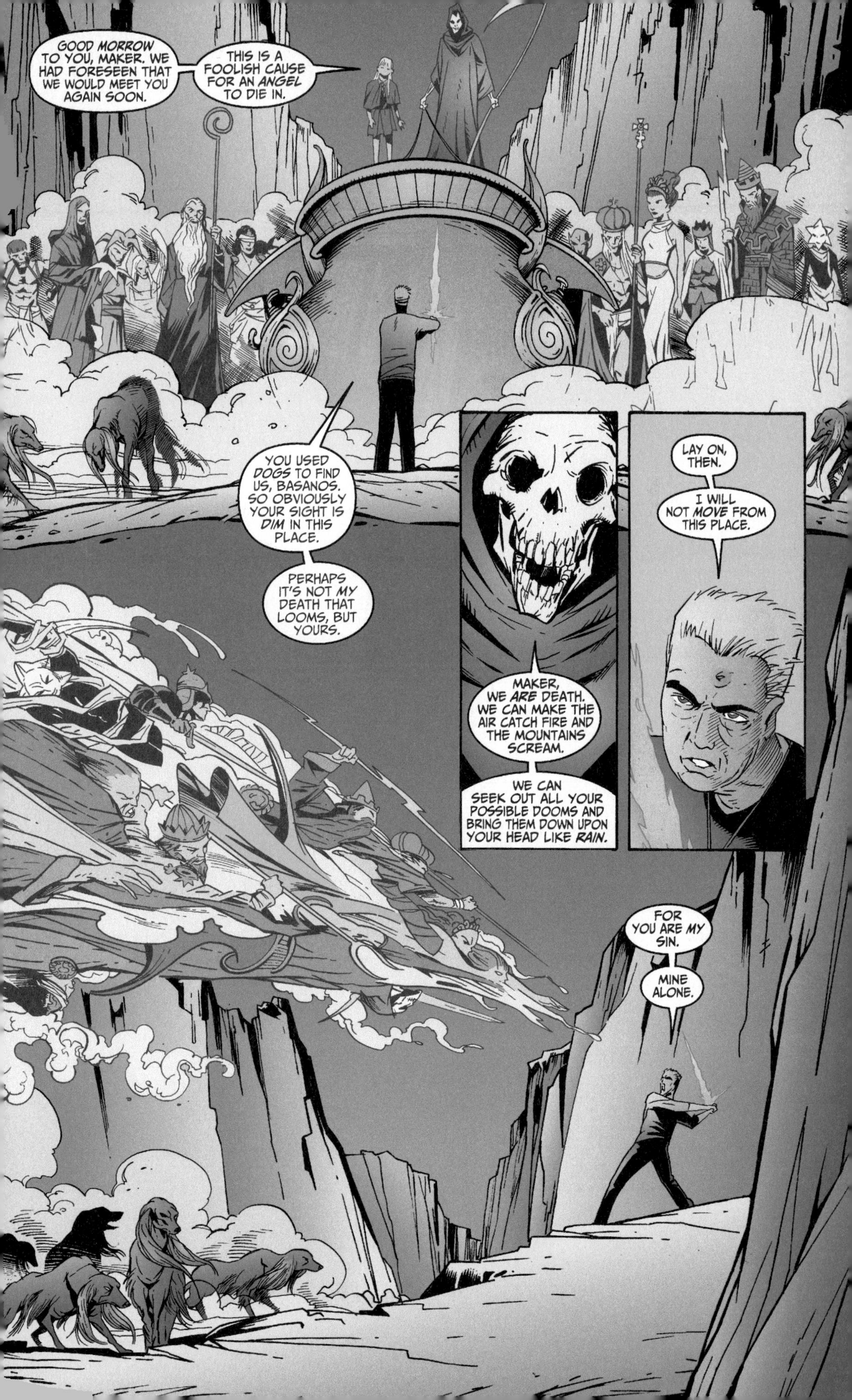
GOOD MORROW TO YOU, MAKER. WE HAD FORESEEN THAT WE WOULD MEET YOU AGAIN SOON.
THIS IS A FOOLISH CAUSE FOR AN ANGEL TO DIE IN.
YOU USED DOGS TO FIND US, BASANOS. SO OBVIOUSLY YOUR SIGHT IS DIM IN THIS PLACE.
PERHAPS IT'S NOT MY DEATH THAT LOOMS, BUT YOURS.
MAKER, WE ARE DEATH. WE CAN MAKE THE AIR CATCH FIRE AND THE MOUNTAINS SCREAM.
WE CAN SEEK OUT ALL YOUR POSSIBLE DOOMS AND BRING THEM DOWN UPON YOUR HEAD LIKE RAIN.
LAY ON, THEN.
I WILL NOT MOVE FROM THIS PLACE.
FOR YOU ARE MY SIN.
MINE ALONE.

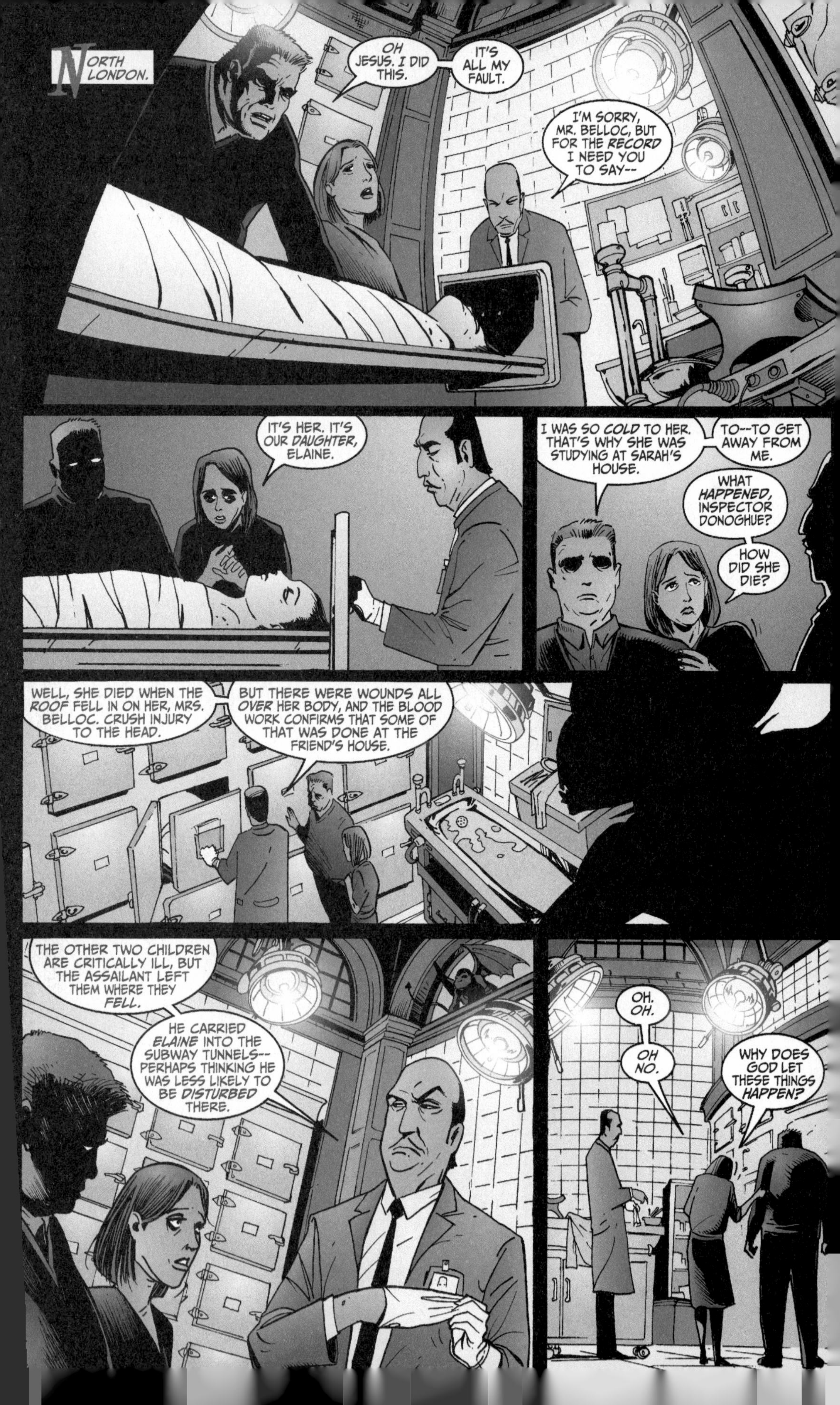
NORTH LONDON.
OH JESUS. I DID THIS.
IT'S ALL MY FAULT.
I'M SORRY, MR. BELLOC, BUT FOR THE RECORD I NEED YOU TO SAY--
IT'S HER. IT'S OUR DAUGHTER, ELAINE.
I WAS SO COLD TO HER. THAT'S WHY SHE WAS STUDYING AT SARAH'S HOUSE.
TO--TO GET AWAY FROM ME.
WHAT HAPPENED, INSPECTOR DONOGHUE?
HOW DID SHE DIE?
WELL, SHE DIED WHEN THE ROOF FELL IN ON HER, MRS. BELLOC. CRUSH INJURY TO THE HEAD.
BUT THERE WERE WOUNDS ALL OVER HER BODY, AND THE BLOOD WORK CONFIRMS THAT SOME OF THAT WAS DONE AT THE FRIEND'S HOUSE.
THE OTHER TWO CHILDREN ARE CRITICALLY ILL, BUT THE ASSAILANT LEFT THEM WHERE THEY FELL.
HE CARRIED ELAINE INTO THE SUBWAY TUNNELS--PERHAPS THINKING HE WAS LESS LIKELY TO BE DISTURBED THERE.
OH. OH.
OH NO.
WHY DOES GOD LET THESE THINGS HAPPEN?

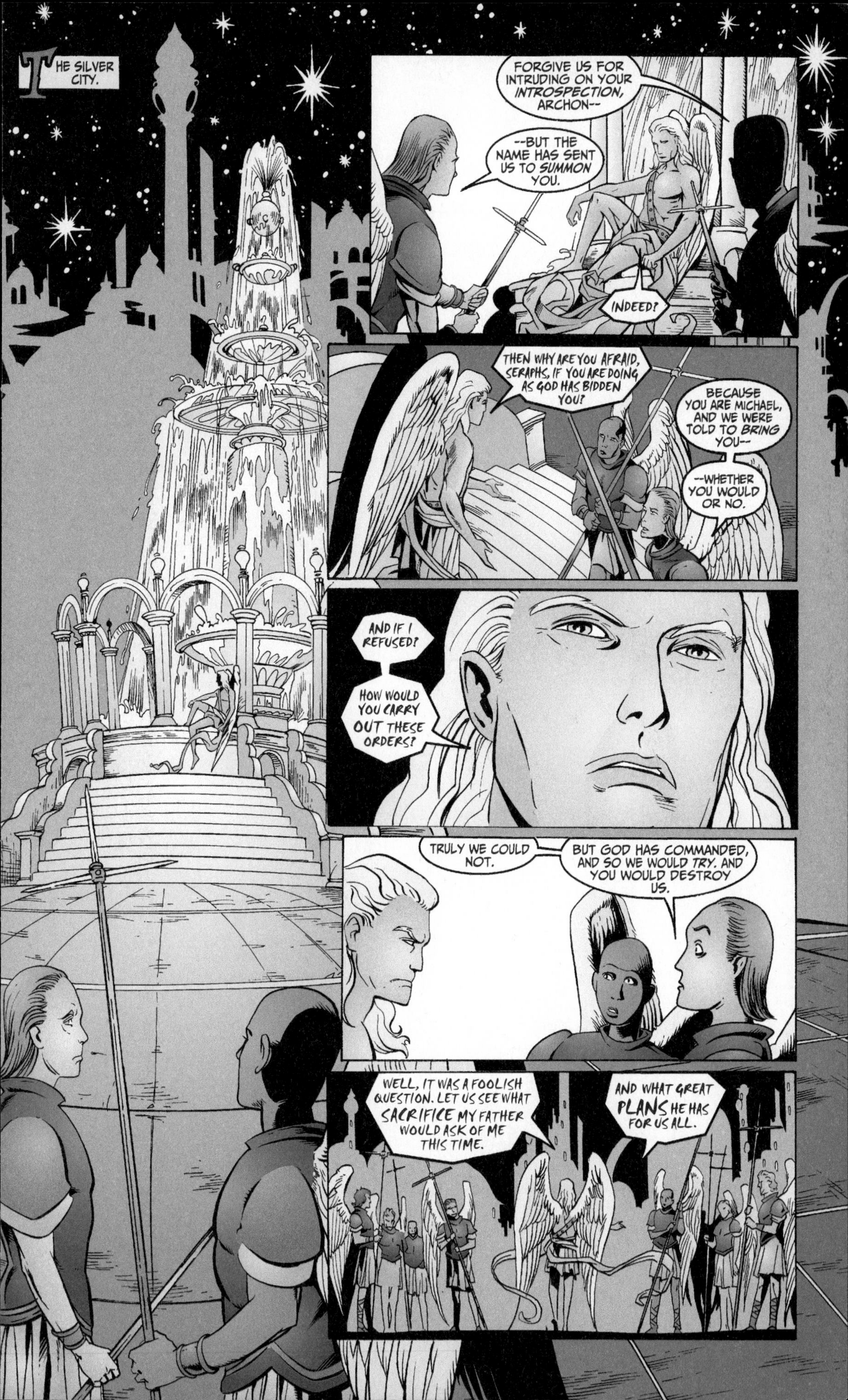
THE SILVER CITY.
FORGIVE US FOR INTRUDING ON YOUR INTROSPECTION, ARCHON--
--BUT THE NAME HAS SENT US TO SUMMON YOU.
INDEED?
THEN WHY ARE YOU AFRAID, SERAPHS, IF YOU ARE DOING AS GOD HAS BIDDEN YOU?
BECAUSE YOU ARE MICHAEL, AND WE WERE TOLD TO BRING YOU--
--WHETHER YOU WOULD OR NO.
AND IF I REFUSED?
HOW WOULD YOU CARRY OUT THESE ORDERS?
TRULY WE COULD NOT.
BUT GOD HAS COMMANDED, AND SO WE WOULD TRY. AND YOU WOULD DESTROY US.
WELL, IT WAS A FOOLISH QUESTION. LET US SEE WHAT SACRIFICE MY FATHER WOULD ASK OF ME THIS TIME.
AND WHAT GREAT PLANS HE HAS FOR US ALL.

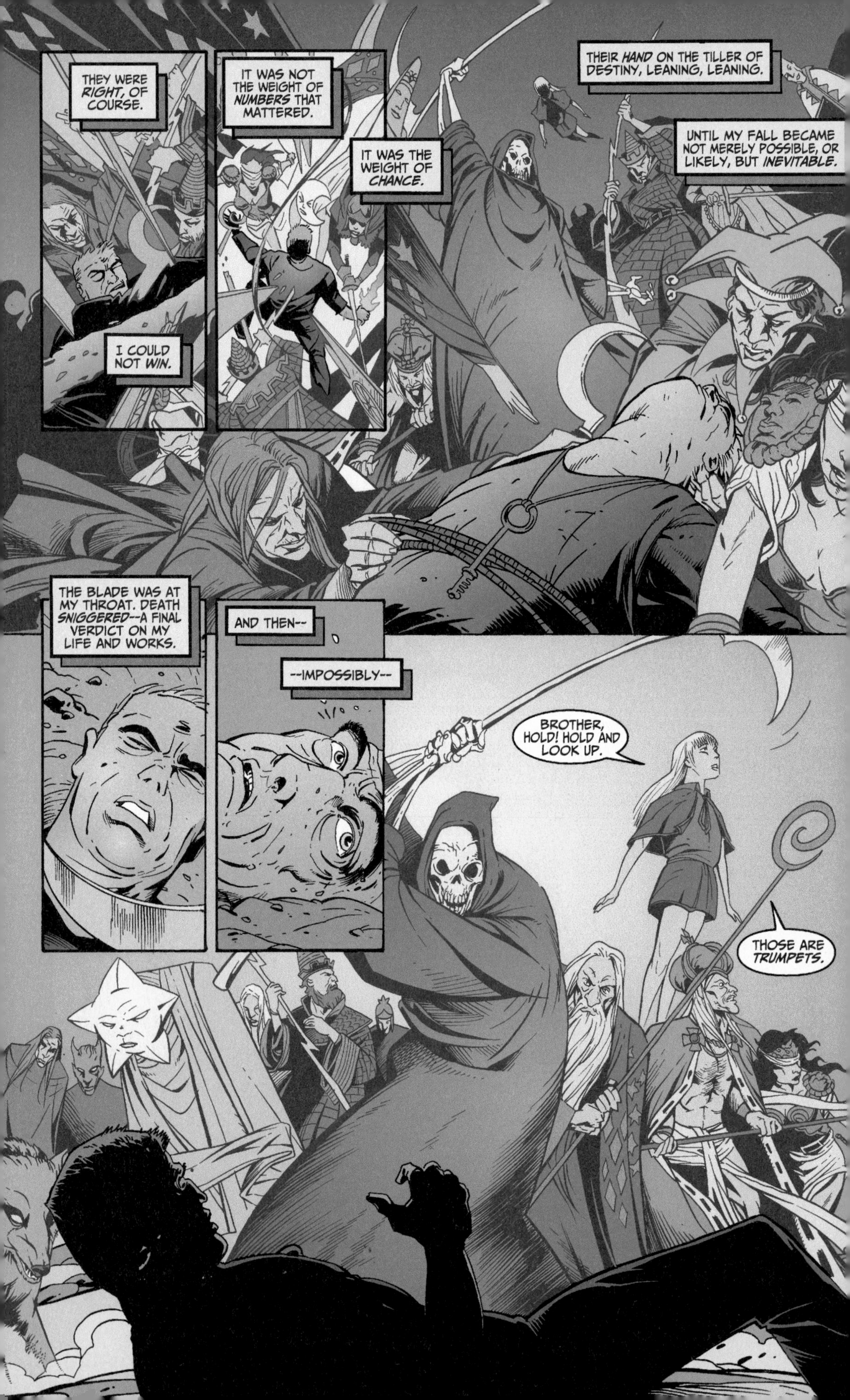
THEY WERE *RIGHT*, OF COURSE.
I COULD NOT *WIN*.
IT WAS NOT THE WEIGHT OF *NUMBERS* THAT MATTERED.
IT WAS THE WEIGHT OF *CHANCE*.
THEIR *HAND* ON THE TILLER OF DESTINY, LEANING, LEANING.
UNTIL MY FALL BECAME NOT MERELY POSSIBLE, OR LIKELY, BUT *INEVITABLE*.
THE BLADE WAS AT MY THROAT. DEATH *SNIGGERED*--A FINAL VERDICT ON MY LIFE AND WORKS.
AND THEN--
--IMPOSSIBLY--
BROTHER, HOLD! HOLD AND LOOK UP.
THOSE ARE *TRUMPETS*.

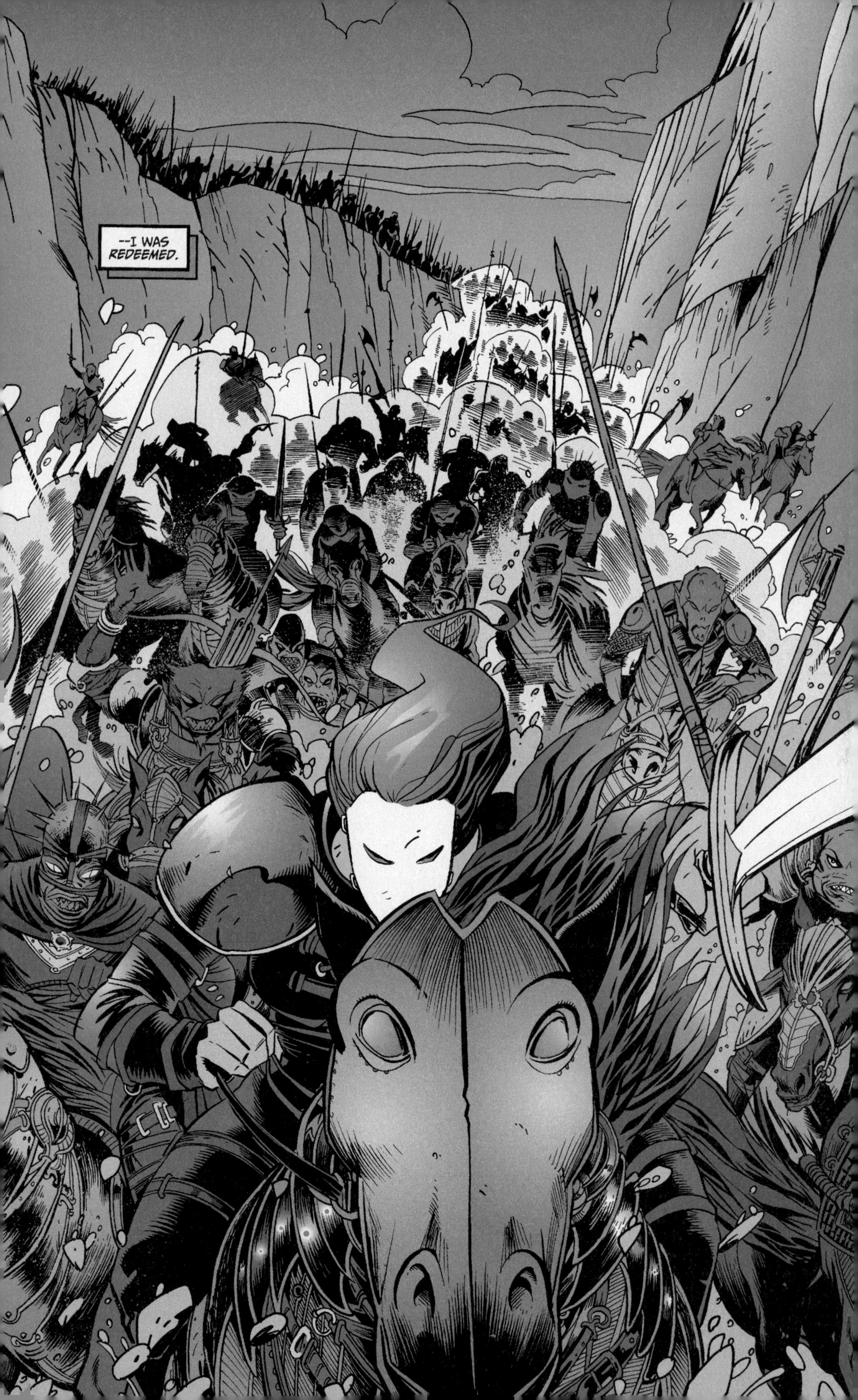
--I WAS REDEEMED.

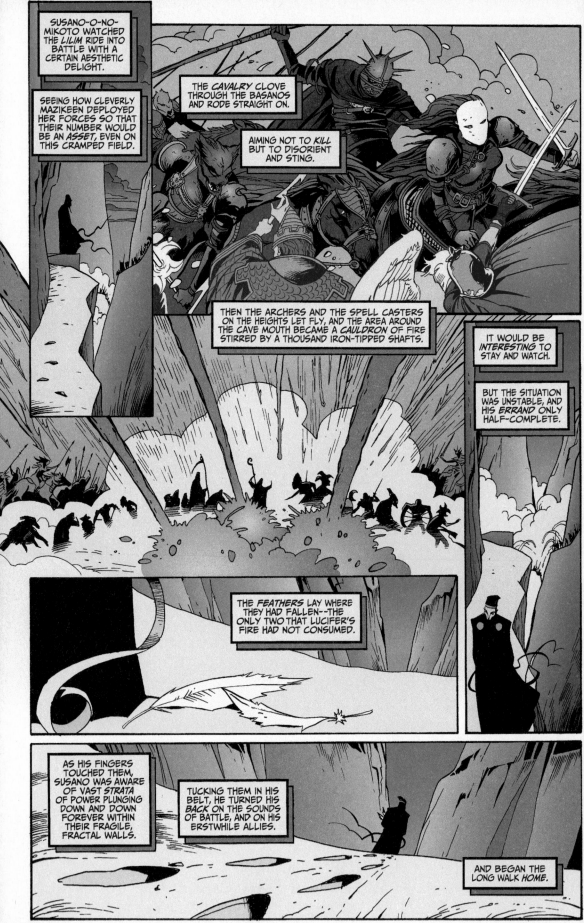

SUSANO-O-NO-MIKOTO WATCHED THE *LILIM* RIDE INTO BATTLE WITH A CERTAIN AESTHETIC DELIGHT.

SEEING HOW CLEVERLY MAZIKEEN DEPLOYED HER FORCES SO THAT THEIR NUMBER WOULD BE AN *ASSET*, EVEN ON THIS CRAMPED FIELD.

THE *CAVALRY* CLOVE THROUGH THE BASANOS AND RODE STRAIGHT ON.

AIMING NOT TO *KILL* BUT TO DISORIENT AND STING.

THEN THE ARCHERS AND THE SPELL CASTERS ON THE HEIGHTS LET FLY, AND THE AREA AROUND THE CAVE MOUTH BECAME A *CAULDRON* OF FIRE STIRRED BY A THOUSAND IRON-TIPPED SHAFTS.

IT WOULD BE *INTERESTING* TO STAY AND WATCH.

BUT THE SITUATION WAS UNSTABLE, AND HIS *ERRAND* ONLY HALF-COMPLETE.

THE *FEATHERS* LAY WHERE THEY HAD FALLEN--THE ONLY TWO THAT LUCIFER'S FIRE HAD NOT CONSUMED.

AS HIS FINGERS TOUCHED THEM, SUSANO WAS AWARE OF VAST *STRATA* OF POWER PLUNGING DOWN AND DOWN FOREVER WITHIN THEIR FRAGILE, FRACTAL WALLS.

TUCKING THEM IN HIS BELT, HE TURNED HIS *BACK* ON THE SOUNDS OF BATTLE, AND ON HIS ERSTWHILE ALLIES.

AND BEGAN THE LONG WALK *HOME*.

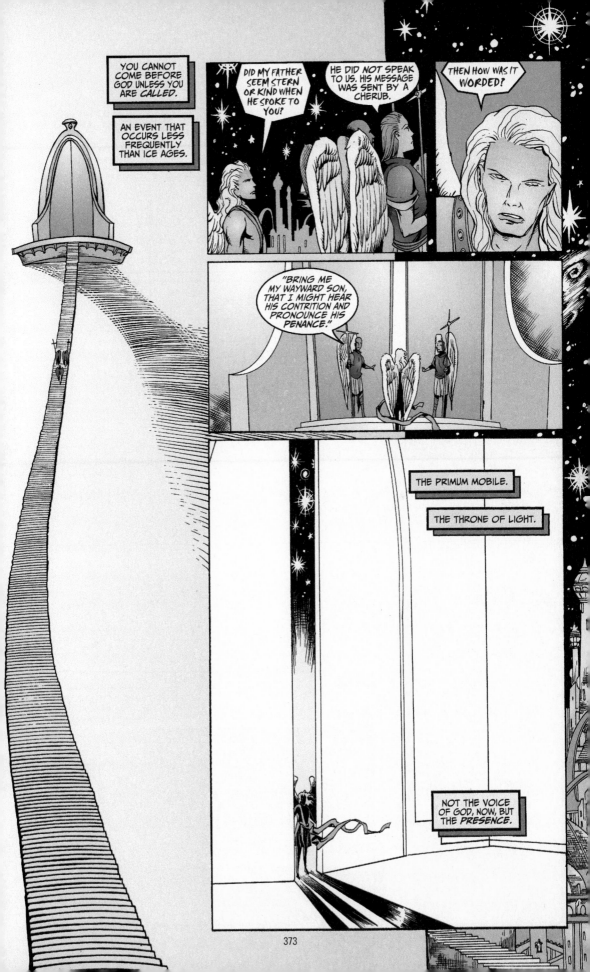

YOU CANNOT COME BEFORE GOD UNLESS YOU ARE *CALLED*.

AN EVENT THAT OCCURS LESS FREQUENTLY THAN ICE AGES.

DID MY FATHER SEEM STERN OR KIND WHEN HE SPOKE TO YOU?

HE DID *NOT* SPEAK TO US. HIS MESSAGE WAS SENT BY A CHERUB.

THEN HOW WAS IT WORDED?

"BRING ME MY WAYWARD SON, THAT I MIGHT HEAR HIS CONTRITION AND PRONOUNCE HIS PENANCE."

THE PRIMUM MOBILE.

THE THRONE OF LIGHT.

NOT THE VOICE OF GOD, NOW, BUT THE *PRESENCE*.

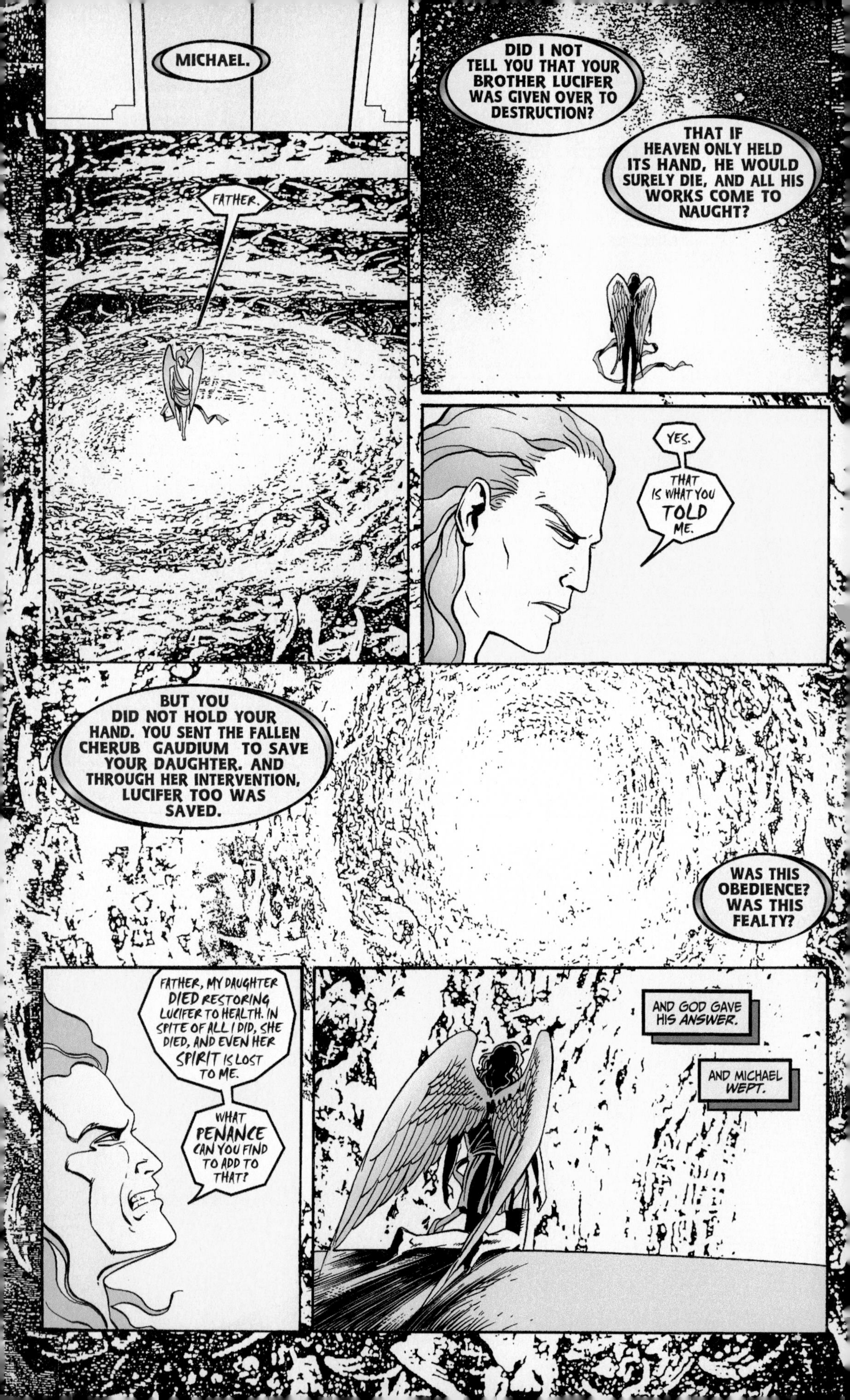

MICHAEL.
FATHER.
DID I NOT TELL YOU THAT YOUR BROTHER LUCIFER WAS GIVEN OVER TO DESTRUCTION?
THAT IF HEAVEN ONLY HELD ITS HAND, HE WOULD SURELY DIE, AND ALL HIS WORKS COME TO NAUGHT?
YES.
THAT IS WHAT YOU TOLD ME.
BUT YOU DID NOT HOLD YOUR HAND. YOU SENT THE FALLEN CHERUB GAUDIUM TO SAVE YOUR DAUGHTER. AND THROUGH HER INTERVENTION, LUCIFER TOO WAS SAVED.
WAS THIS OBEDIENCE? WAS THIS FEALTY?
FATHER, MY DAUGHTER DIED RESTORING LUCIFER TO HEALTH. IN SPITE OF ALL I DID, SHE DIED, AND EVEN HER SPIRIT IS LOST TO ME.
WHAT PENANCE CAN YOU FIND TO ADD TO THAT?
AND GOD GAVE HIS ANSWER.
AND MICHAEL WEPT.

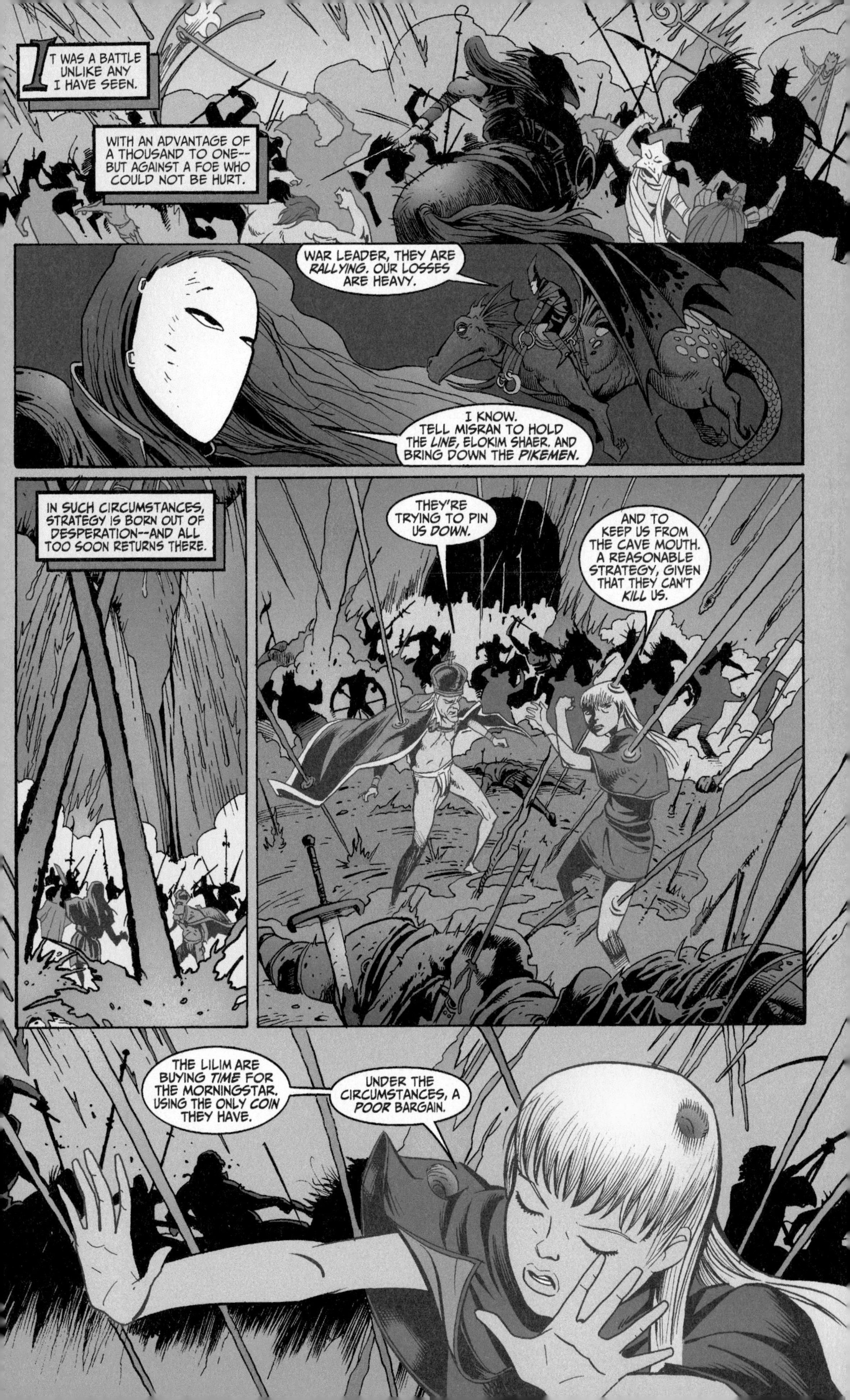
IT WAS A BATTLE UNLIKE ANY I HAVE SEEN.
WITH AN ADVANTAGE OF A THOUSAND TO ONE-- BUT AGAINST A FOE WHO COULD NOT BE HURT.
WAR LEADER, THEY ARE RALLYING. OUR LOSSES ARE HEAVY.
I KNOW. TELL MISRAN TO HOLD THE LINE, ELOKIM SHAER. AND BRING DOWN THE PIKEMEN.
IN SUCH CIRCUMSTANCES, STRATEGY IS BORN OUT OF DESPERATION--AND ALL TOO SOON RETURNS THERE.
THEY'RE TRYING TO PIN US DOWN.
AND TO KEEP US FROM THE CAVE MOUTH. A REASONABLE STRATEGY, GIVEN THAT THEY CAN'T KILL US.
THE LILIM ARE BUYING TIME FOR THE MORNINGSTAR. USING THE ONLY COIN THEY HAVE.
UNDER THE CIRCUMSTANCES, A POOR BARGAIN.

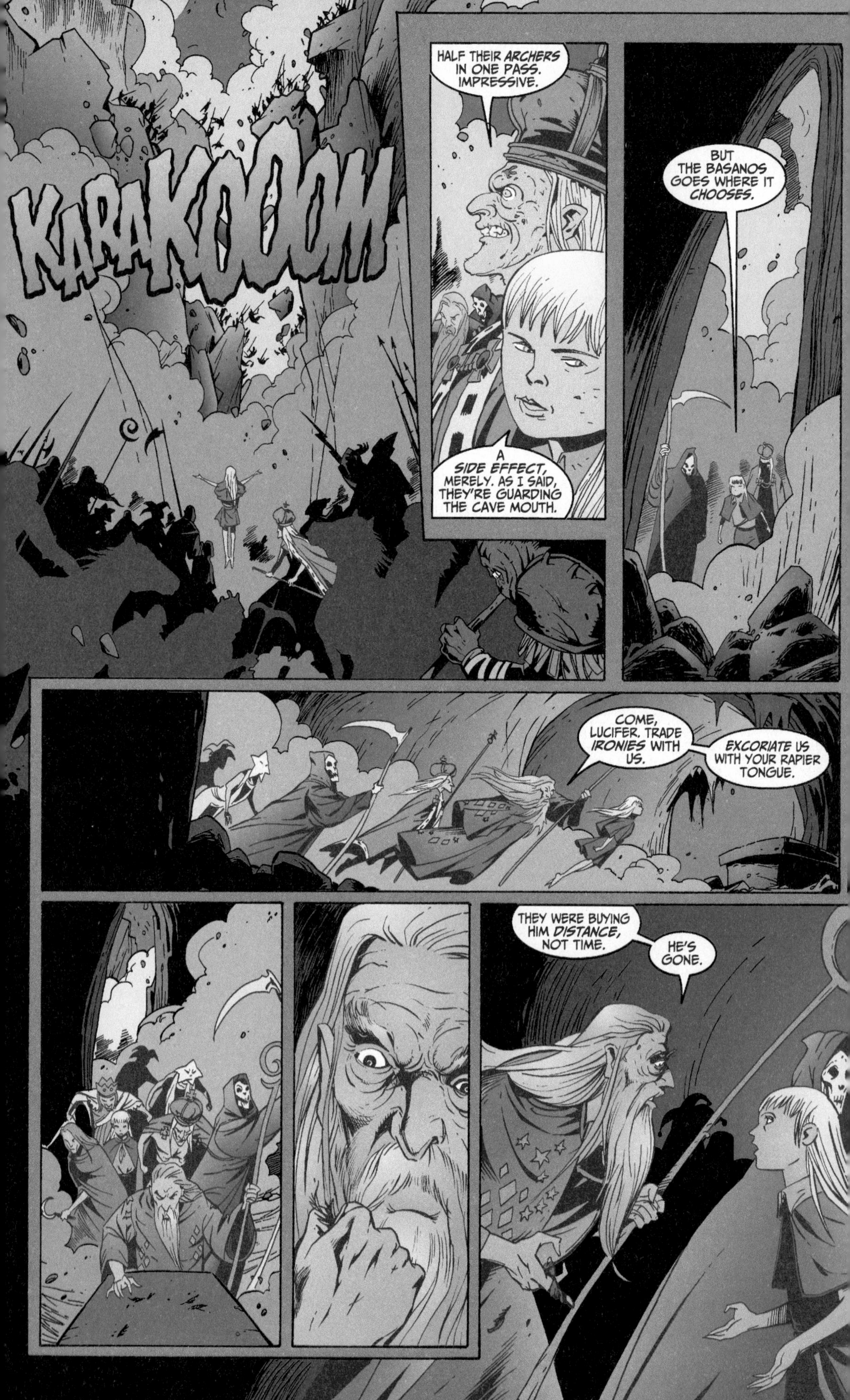
KARAKOOOM
HALF THEIR ARCHERS IN ONE PASS. IMPRESSIVE.
A SIDE EFFECT, MERELY. AS I SAID, THEY'RE GUARDING THE CAVE MOUTH.
BUT THE BASANOS GOES WHERE IT CHOOSES.
COME, LUCIFER. TRADE IRONIES WITH US.
EXCORIATE US WITH YOUR RAPIER TONGUE.
THEY WERE BUYING HIM DISTANCE, NOT TIME.
HE'S GONE.

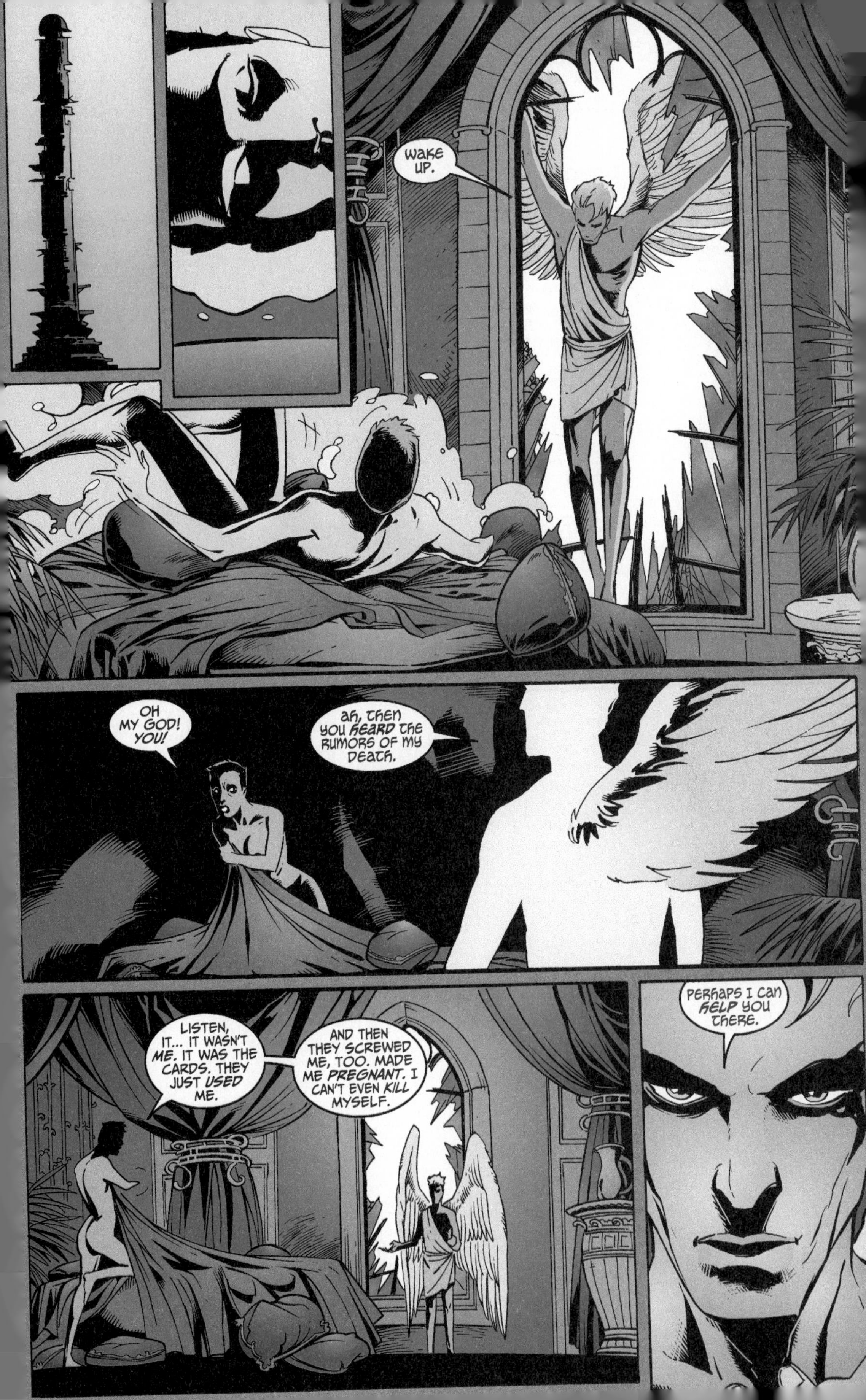
WAKE UP.
OH MY GOD! YOU!
AH, THEN YOU HEARD THE RUMORS OF MY DEATH.
LISTEN, IT... IT WASN'T ME. IT WAS THE CARDS. THEY JUST USED ME.
AND THEN THEY SCREWED ME, TOO. MADE ME PREGNANT. I CAN'T EVEN KILL MYSELF.
PERHAPS I CAN HELP YOU THERE.

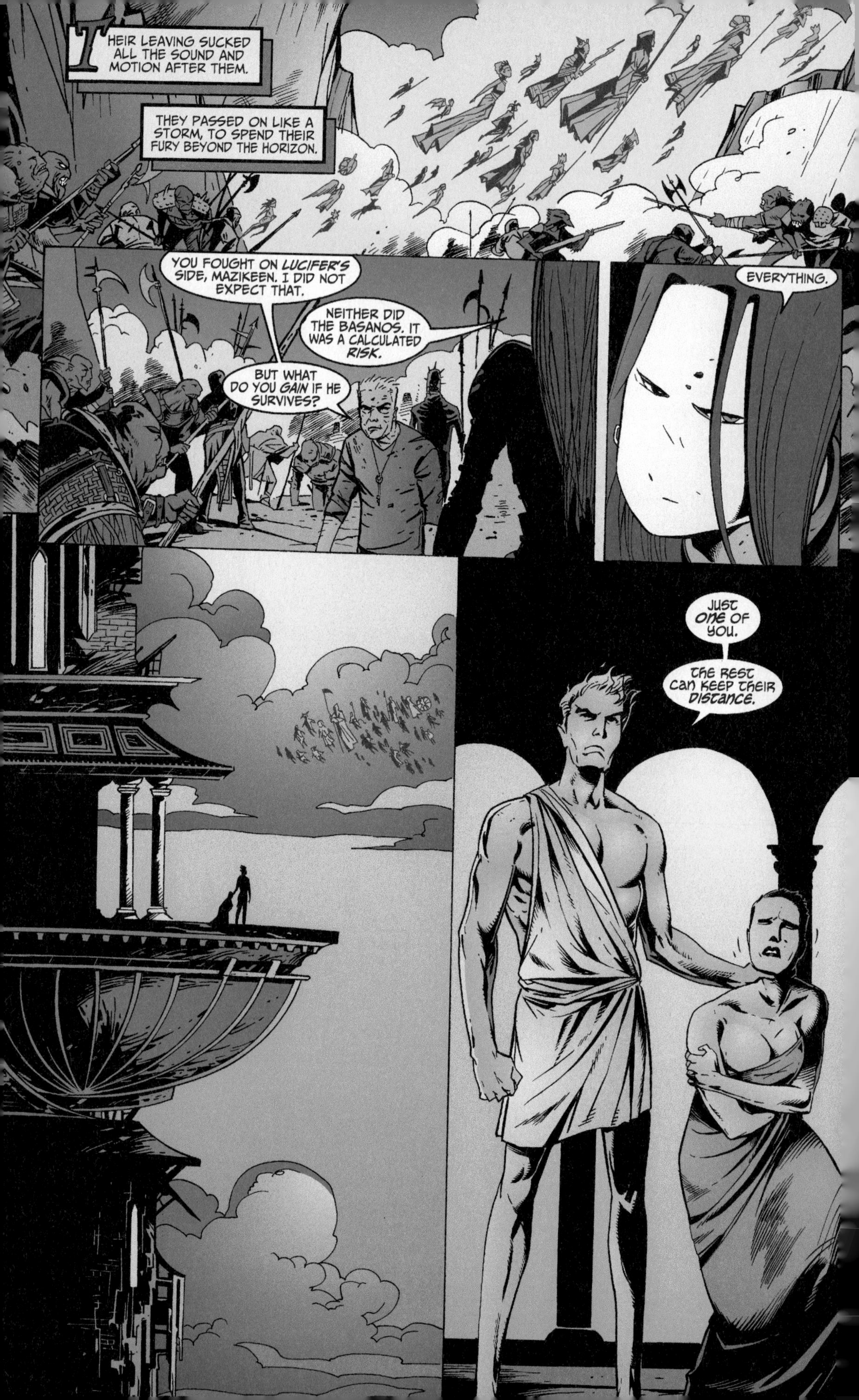
THEIR LEAVING SUCKED ALL THE SOUND AND MOTION AFTER THEM.
THEY PASSED ON LIKE A STORM, TO SPEND THEIR FURY BEYOND THE HORIZON.
YOU FOUGHT ON LUCIFER'S SIDE, MAZIKEEN. I DID NOT EXPECT THAT.
NEITHER DID THE BASANOS. IT WAS A CALCULATED RISK.
BUT WHAT DO YOU GAIN IF HE SURVIVES?
EVERYTHING.
JUST ONE OF YOU.
THE REST CAN KEEP THEIR DISTANCE.

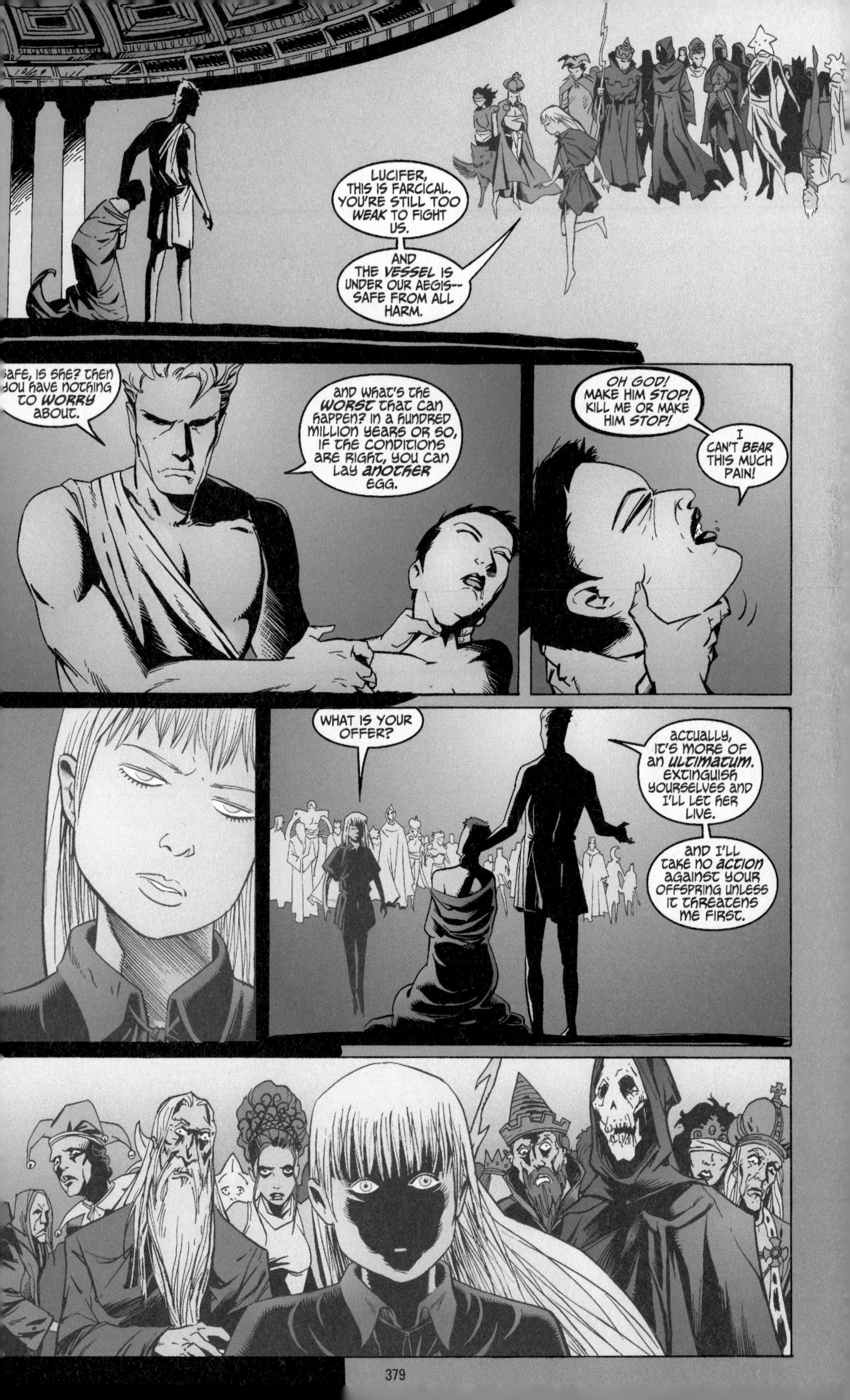
LUCIFER, THIS IS FARCICAL. YOU'RE STILL TOO WEAK TO FIGHT US.
AND THE VESSEL IS UNDER OUR AEGIS-- SAFE FROM ALL HARM.
SAFE, IS SHE? THEN YOU HAVE NOTHING TO WORRY ABOUT.
AND WHAT'S THE WORST THAT CAN HAPPEN? IN A HUNDRED MILLION YEARS OR SO, IF THE CONDITIONS ARE RIGHT, YOU CAN LAY ANOTHER EGG.
OH GOD! MAKE HIM STOP! KILL ME OR MAKE HIM STOP!
I CAN'T BEAR THIS MUCH PAIN!
WHAT IS YOUR OFFER?
ACTUALLY, IT'S MORE OF AN ULTIMATUM. EXTINGUISH YOURSELVES AND I'LL LET HER LIVE.
AND I'LL TAKE NO ACTION AGAINST YOUR OFFSPRING UNLESS IT THREATENS ME FIRST.

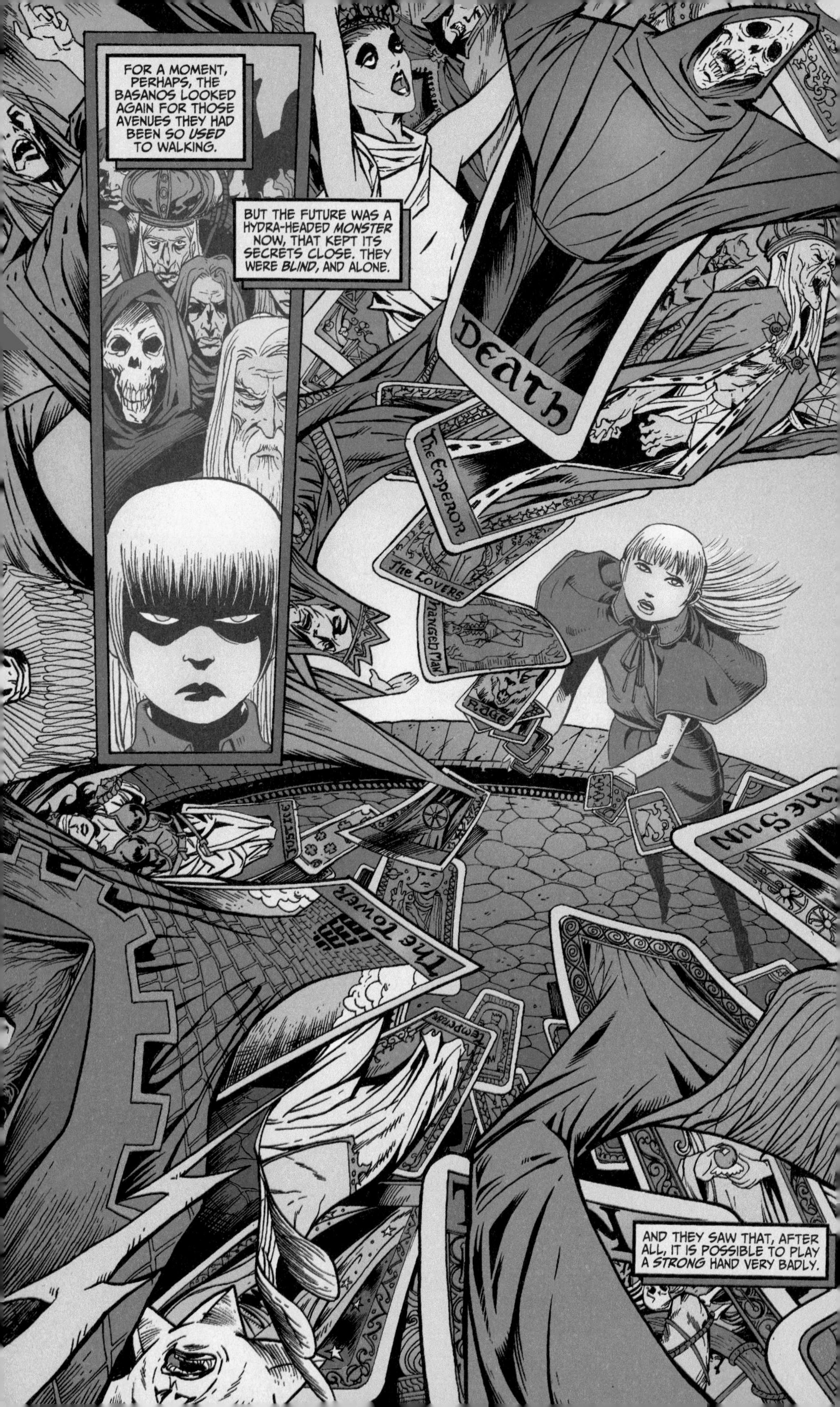
FOR A MOMENT, PERHAPS, THE BASANOS LOOKED AGAIN FOR THOSE AVENUES THEY HAD BEEN SO USED TO WALKING.
BUT THE FUTURE WAS A HYDRA-HEADED MONSTER NOW, THAT KEPT ITS SECRETS CLOSE. THEY WERE BLIND, AND ALONE.
DEATH
THE EMPEROR
THE LOVERS
HANGED MAN
RAGE
JUSTICE
THE TOWER
THE SUN
TEMPERANCE
AND THEY SAW THAT, AFTER ALL, IT IS POSSIBLE TO PLAY A STRONG HAND VERY BADLY.

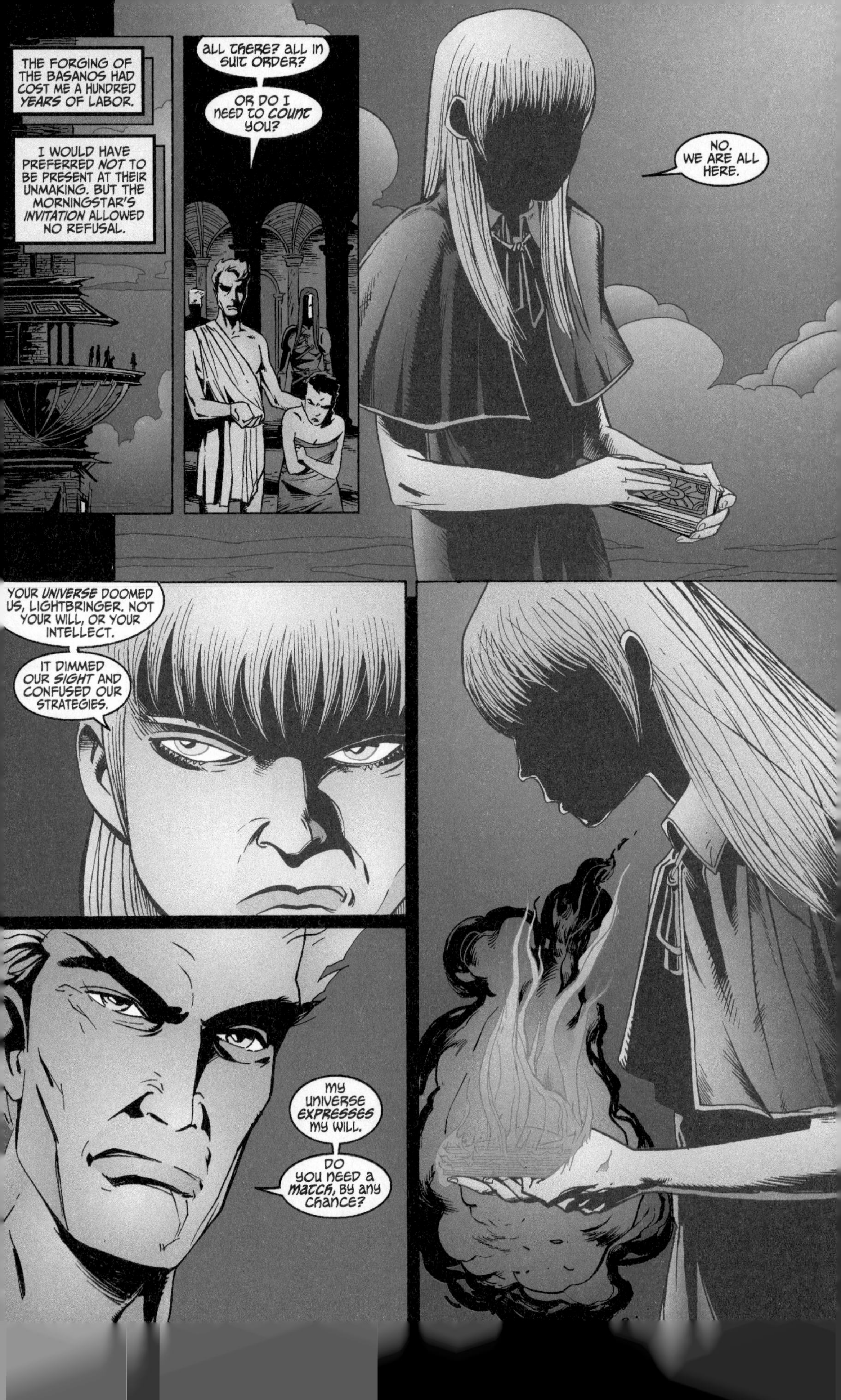
THE FORGING OF THE BASANOS HAD COST ME A HUNDRED *YEARS* OF LABOR.
I WOULD HAVE PREFERRED *NOT* TO BE PRESENT AT THEIR UNMAKING. BUT THE MORNINGSTAR'S *INVITATION* ALLOWED NO REFUSAL.
ALL THERE? ALL IN SUIT ORDER?
OR DO I NEED TO *COUNT* YOU?
NO. WE ARE ALL HERE.
YOUR *UNIVERSE* DOOMED US, LIGHTBRINGER. NOT YOUR WILL, OR YOUR INTELLECT.
IT DIMMED OUR *SIGHT* AND CONFUSED OUR STRATEGIES.
MY UNIVERSE *EXPRESSES* MY WILL.
DO YOU NEED A *MATCH*, BY ANY CHANCE?

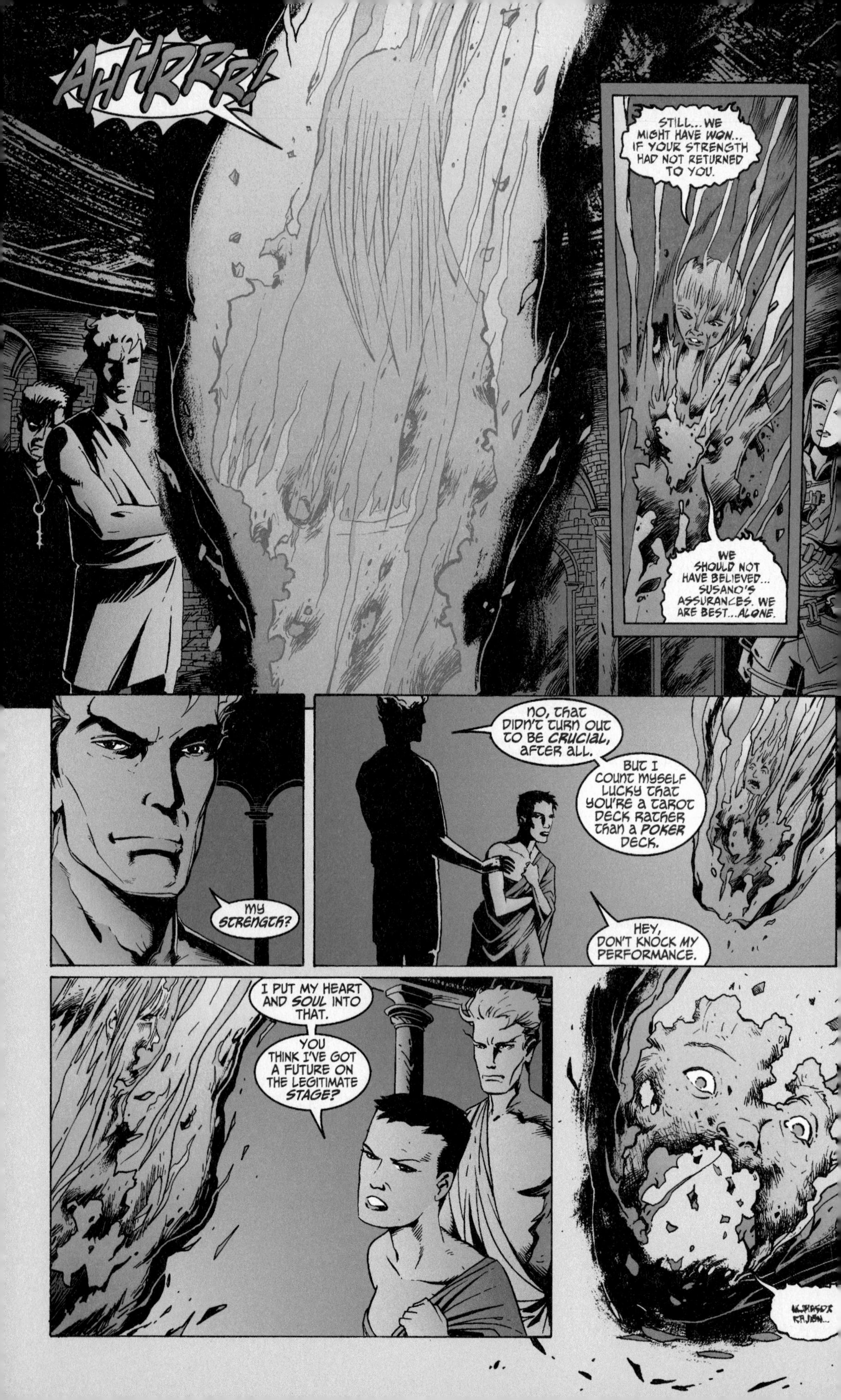
AHHRRR!
STILL... WE MIGHT HAVE WON... IF YOUR STRENGTH HAD NOT RETURNED TO YOU.
WE SHOULD NOT HAVE BELIEVED... SUSANO'S ASSURANCES. WE ARE BEST... ALONE.
MY STRENGTH?
NO, THAT DIDN'T TURN OUT TO BE CRUCIAL, AFTER ALL.
BUT I COUNT MYSELF LUCKY THAT YOU'RE A TAROT DECK RATHER THAN A POKER DECK.
HEY, DON'T KNOCK MY PERFORMANCE.
I PUT MY HEART AND SOUL INTO THAT.
YOU THINK I'VE GOT A FUTURE ON THE LEGITIMATE STAGE?

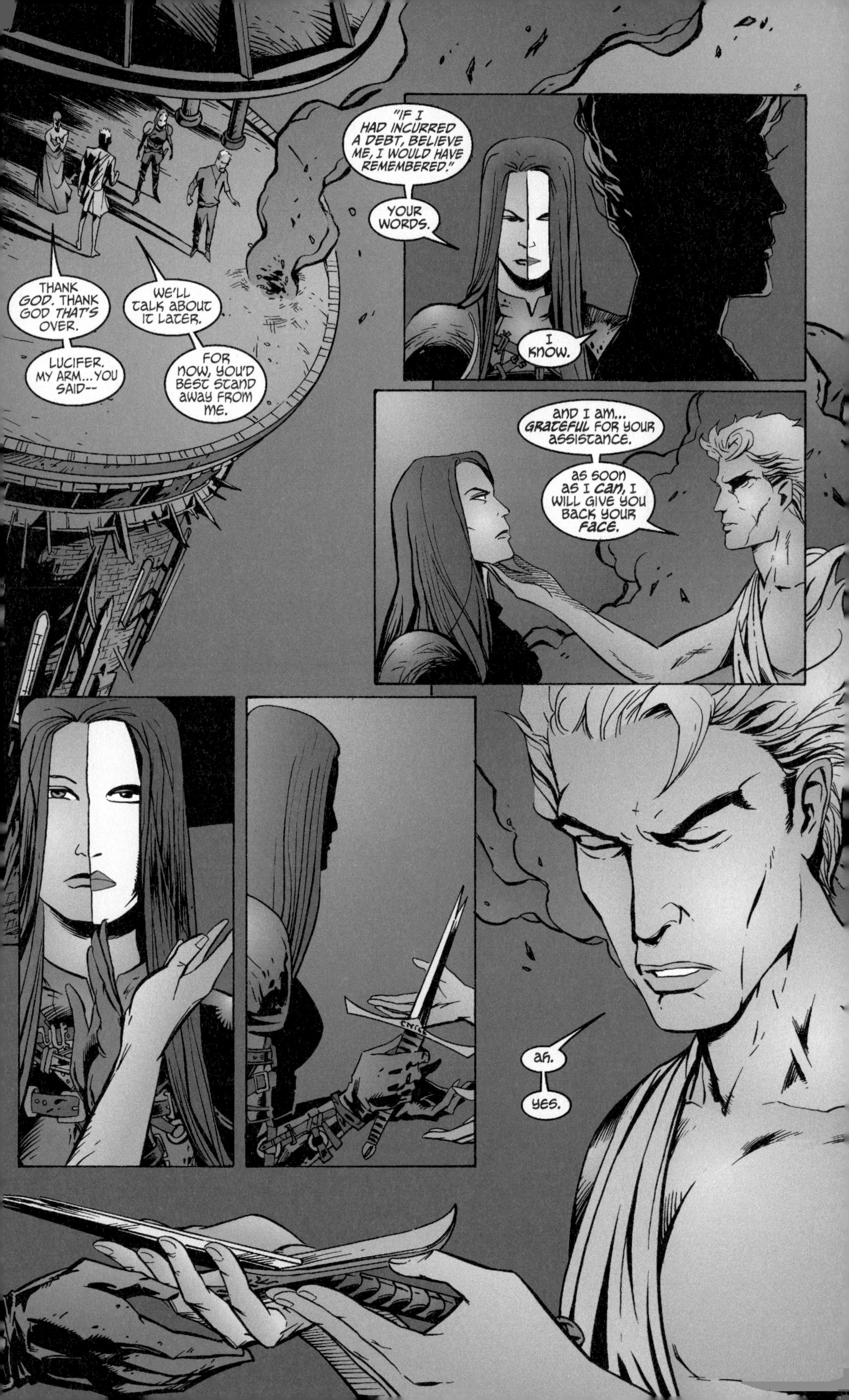
THANK GOD. THANK GOD THAT'S OVER.
LUCIFER. MY ARM... YOU SAID--
WE'LL TALK ABOUT IT LATER.
FOR NOW, YOU'D BEST STAND AWAY FROM ME.
"IF I HAD INCURRED A DEBT, BELIEVE ME, I WOULD HAVE REMEMBERED."
YOUR WORDS.
I KNOW.
AND I AM... GRATEFUL FOR YOUR ASSISTANCE.
AS SOON AS I CAN, I WILL GIVE YOU BACK YOUR FACE.
AH.
YES.

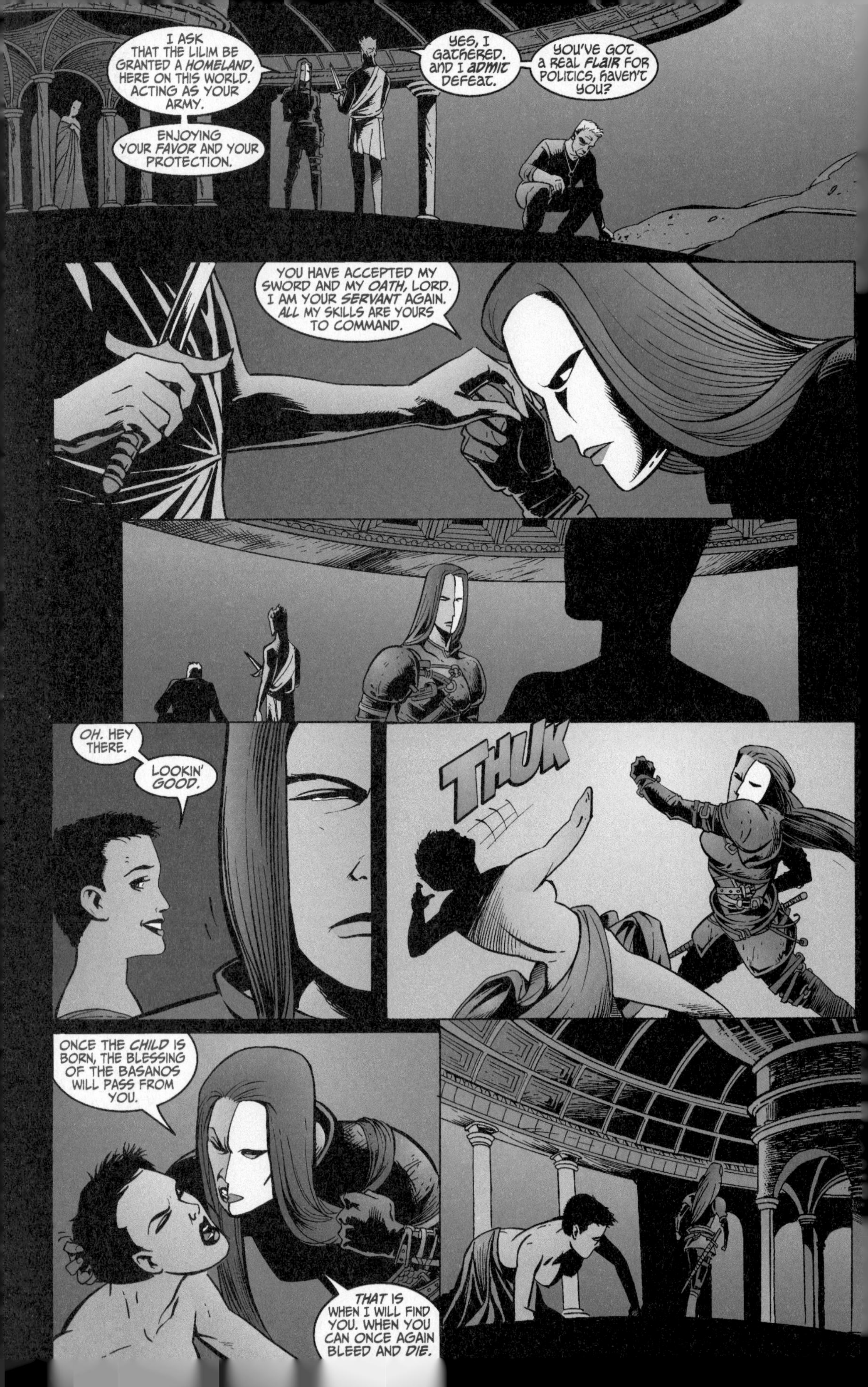
I ASK THAT THE LILIM BE GRANTED A *HOMELAND*, HERE ON THIS WORLD. ACTING AS YOUR ARMY.
ENJOYING YOUR *FAVOR* AND YOUR PROTECTION.
YES, I GATHERED. AND I *ADMIT* DEFEAT.
YOU'VE GOT A REAL *FLAIR* FOR POLITICS, HAVEN'T YOU?
YOU HAVE ACCEPTED MY SWORD AND MY *OATH*, LORD. I AM YOUR *SERVANT* AGAIN. *ALL* MY SKILLS ARE YOURS TO COMMAND.
OH. HEY THERE.
LOOKIN' *GOOD*.
THUK
ONCE THE *CHILD* IS BORN, THE BLESSING OF THE BASANOS WILL PASS FROM YOU.
THAT IS WHEN I WILL FIND YOU. WHEN YOU CAN ONCE AGAIN BLEED AND *DIE*.

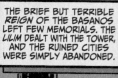

THE BRIEF BUT TERRIBLE *REIGN* OF THE BASANOS LEFT FEW MEMORIALS. THE *LILIM* DEALT WITH THE TOWER, AND THE RUINED CITIES WERE SIMPLY ABANDONED.

LUCIFER HAD OUTLAWED WORSHIP, BUT HE SAID NOTHING EITHER WAY ABOUT *SUPERSTITION*.

AS FOR THE MORNINGSTAR HIMSELF, HE HAD *OTHER* MATTERS TO SETTLE BEFORE HE LEFT.

HE SPOKE LONG AND LATE WITH THE MORTAL WOMAN, JILL PRESTO. I WAS NOT *PRIVY* TO THEIR COUNSELS.

THE GENERALS OF THE LILIM IN EXILE WERE ALSO SUMMONED TO HIM, AND DECAMPED SOON AFTER.

IT WAS ASSUMED THAT THEY HAD BEEN ENTRUSTED WITH AN ERRAND OF SOME DELICACY OR MOMENT.

ON THE MORNING OF HIS DEPARTURE, WE SPOKE ONE FINAL TIME--OF DEBT AND OBLIGATION, AND OF THE CHILD, ELAINE BELLOC.

HE HAD A *MESSAGE* FOR HER FATHER. SINCE I WAS INSTRUMENTAL IN HER DEATH HE BADE ME *CARRY* IT FOR HIM.

AND THEN HE *LEFT* THAT PLACE.

AND I *CEASED* TO BE HIS CHRONICLER.

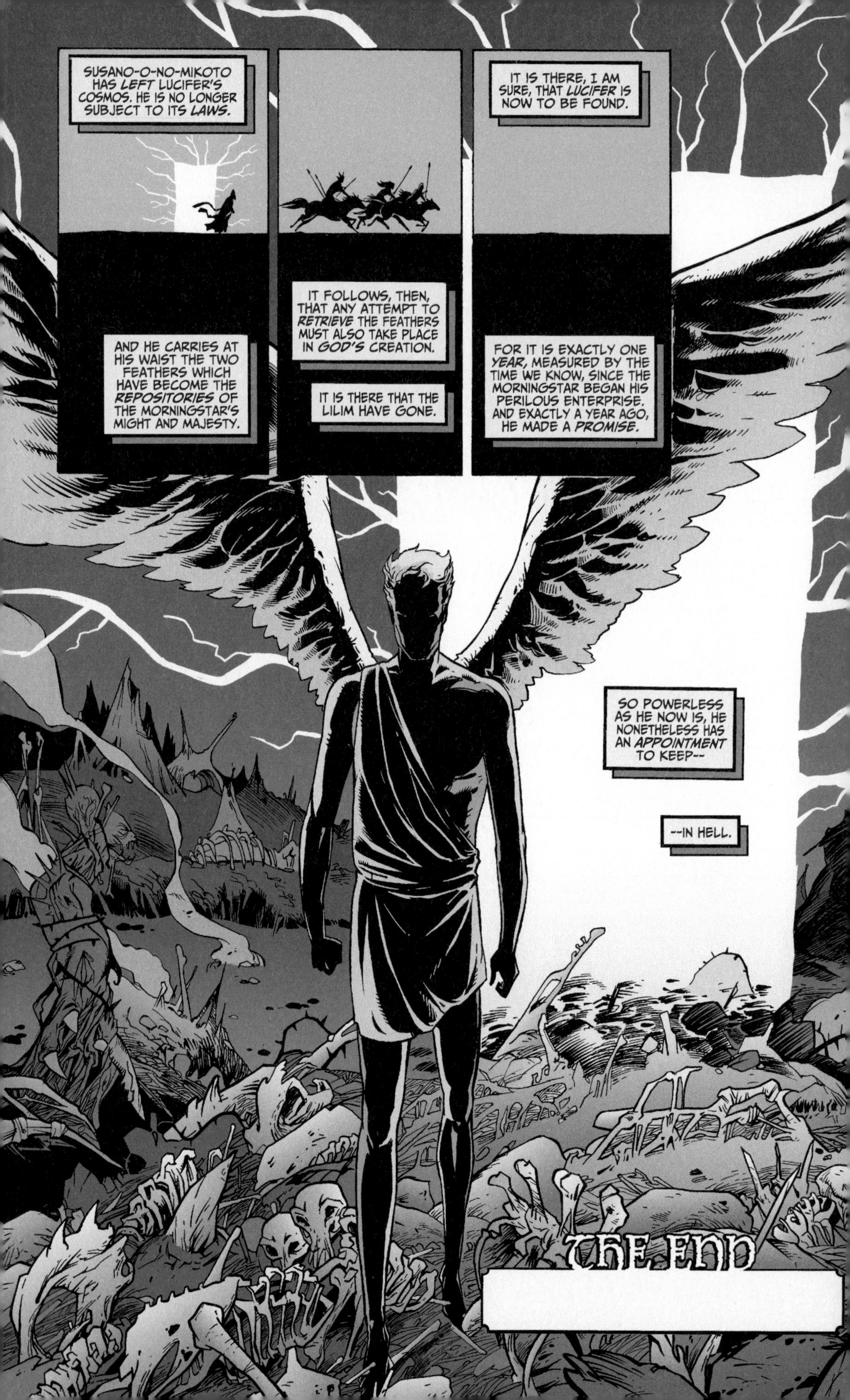
SUSANO-O-NO-MIKOTO HAS LEFT LUCIFER'S COSMOS. HE IS NO LONGER SUBJECT TO ITS LAWS.
AND HE CARRIES AT HIS WAIST THE TWO FEATHERS WHICH HAVE BECOME THE REPOSITORIES OF THE MORNINGSTAR'S MIGHT AND MAJESTY.
IT FOLLOWS, THEN, THAT ANY ATTEMPT TO RETRIEVE THE FEATHERS MUST ALSO TAKE PLACE IN GOD'S CREATION.
IT IS THERE THAT THE LILIM HAVE GONE.
IT IS THERE, I AM SURE, THAT LUCIFER IS NOW TO BE FOUND.
FOR IT IS EXACTLY ONE YEAR, MEASURED BY THE TIME WE KNOW, SINCE THE MORNINGSTAR BEGAN HIS PERILOUS ENTERPRISE. AND EXACTLY A YEAR AGO, HE MADE A PROMISE.
SO POWERLESS AS HE NOW IS, HE NONETHELESS HAS AN APPOINTMENT TO KEEP--
--IN HELL.
THE END

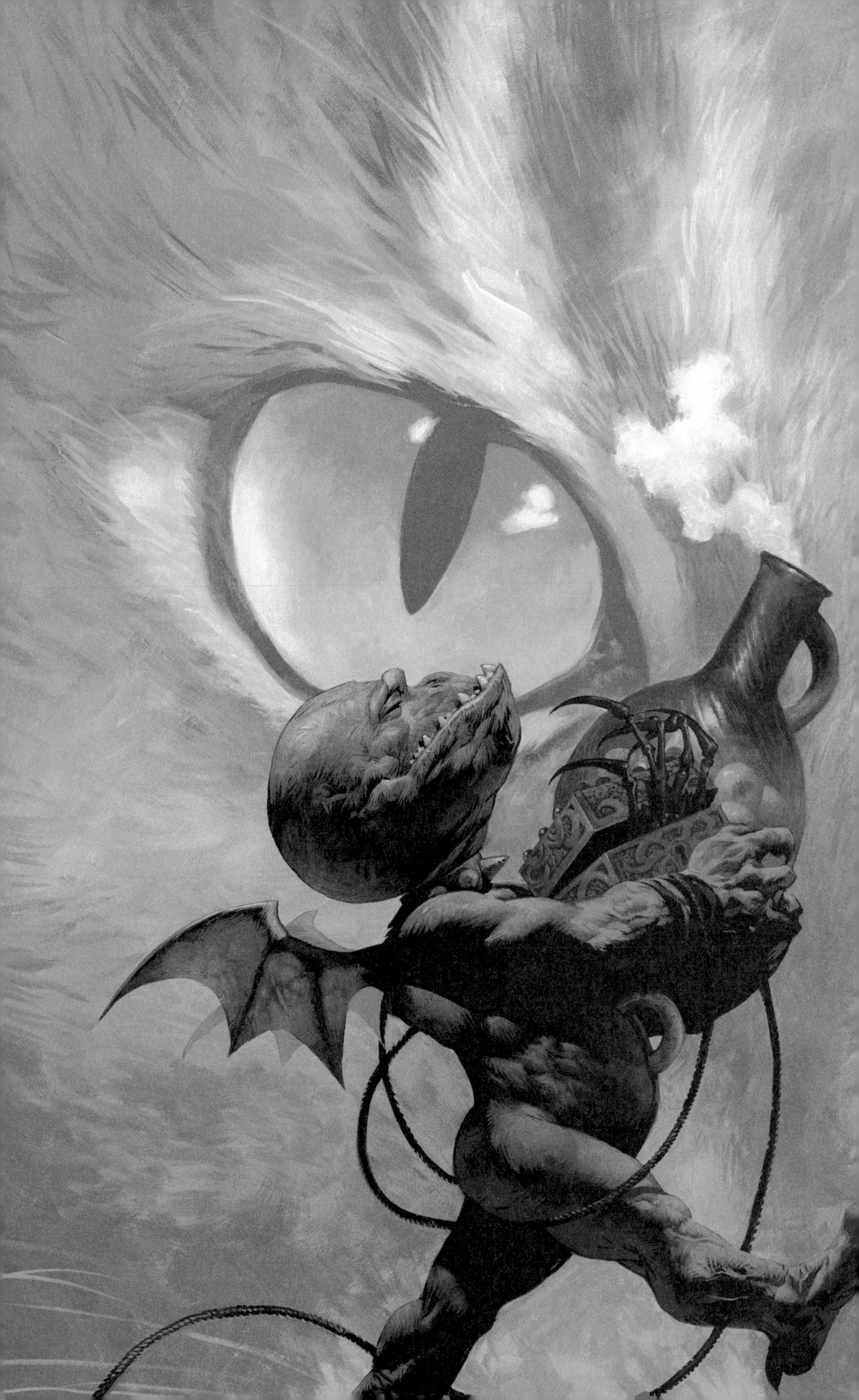

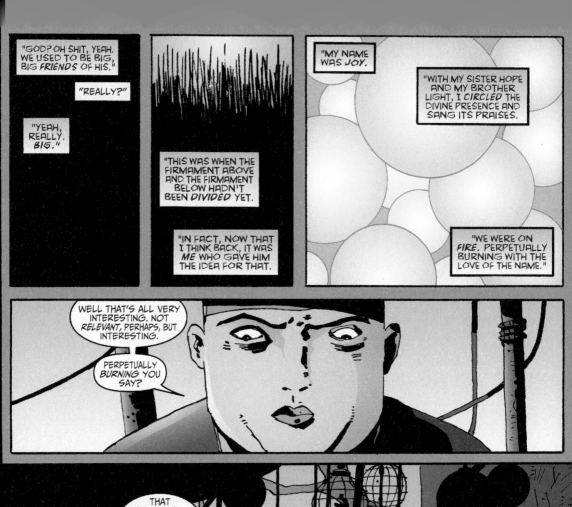

"GOD? OH SHIT, YEAH. WE USED TO BE BIG, BIG *FRIENDS* OF HIS."

"REALLY?"

"YEAH, REALLY. *BIG.*"

"THIS WAS WHEN THE FIRMAMENT ABOVE AND THE FIRMAMENT BELOW HADN'T BEEN *DIVIDED* YET."

"IN FACT, NOW THAT I THINK BACK, IT WAS *ME* WHO GAVE HIM THE IDEA FOR THAT."

"MY NAME WAS *JOY*.

"WITH MY SISTER HOPE AND MY BROTHER LIGHT, I *CIRCLED* THE DIVINE PRESENCE AND SANG ITS PRAISES.

"WE WERE ON *FIRE*. PERPETUALLY BURNING WITH THE LOVE OF THE NAME."

WELL THAT'S ALL VERY INTERESTING. NOT *RELEVANT*, PERHAPS, BUT INTERESTING.

PERPETUALLY *BURNING* YOU SAY?

THAT PROBABLY EXPLAINS WHY YOU LOOK LIKE THE KNOCKINGS THAT COME OUT OF MY PIPE.

LISTEN, PALLY? THIS HERE IS A FUCKING *MARKET*, RIGHT?

WE CAN TAKE OUR TRADE WHEREVER WE *LIKE*, SO LESS OF THE SMART MOUTH.

YOU'RE FALLEN CHERUBS. YOU HAVE THE *TAINT* OF HELL.

MOST FAIRIES WILL *SHUN* YOU.

OH YEAH? WELL THAT'S WHERE YOU'RE--

HEY, SPERA, ARE YOU *NUTS* OR SOMETHING?

KEEP YOUR THIEVING PAWS TO YOURSELF!

OW!

WHAT'D YOU *HIT* ME FOR, GAUDIUM?

YOUR OWN *GOOD*. THEY GOT LAWS HERE.

YOU STEAL SO MUCH AS A *PIN* FROM THIS GUY, HE CAN MAKE YOU WIPE HIS ASS WITH YOUR *TONGUE* FOR THE NEXT FIFTY YEARS.

MAYBE YOU SHOULD TELL HIM THAT *YOU* DO THAT STUFF FOR FREE.

IN FRONT OF A *STRANGER* YOU'RE SAYING THIS TO ME?

AHEM.

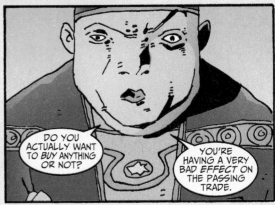

DO YOU ACTUALLY WANT TO *BUY* ANYTHING OR NOT?

YOU'RE HAVING A VERY BAD *EFFECT* ON THE PASSING TRADE.

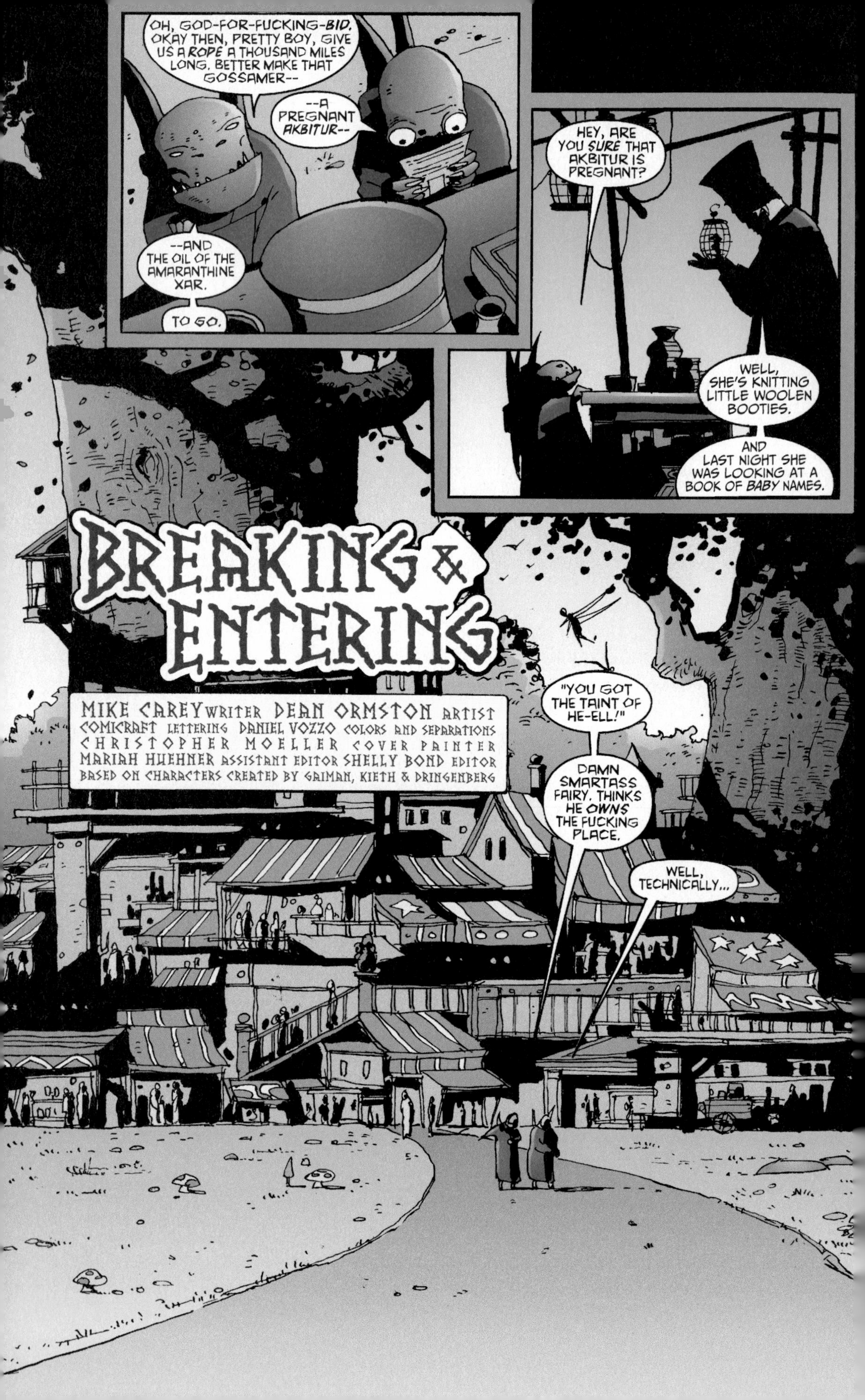

OH, GOD-FOR-FUCKING-BID. OKAY THEN, PRETTY BOY, GIVE US A ROPE A THOUSAND MILES LONG. BETTER MAKE THAT GOSSAMER--
--A PREGNANT AKBITUR--
--AND THE OIL OF THE AMARANTHINE XAR.
TO GO.
HEY, ARE YOU SURE THAT AKBITUR IS PREGNANT?
WELL, SHE'S KNITTING LITTLE WOOLEN BOOTIES.
AND LAST NIGHT SHE WAS LOOKING AT A BOOK OF BABY NAMES.
BREAKING & ENTERING
MIKE CAREY WRITER DEAN ORMSTON ARTIST
COMICRAFT LETTERING DANIEL VOZZO COLORS AND SEPARATIONS
CHRISTOPHER MOELLER COVER PAINTER
MARIAH HUEHNER ASSISTANT EDITOR SHELLY BOND EDITOR
BASED ON CHARACTERS CREATED BY GAIMAN, KIETH & DRINGENBERG
"YOU GOT THE TAINT OF HE-ELL!"
DAMN SMARTASS FAIRY. THINKS HE OWNS THE FUCKING PLACE.
WELL, TECHNICALLY...

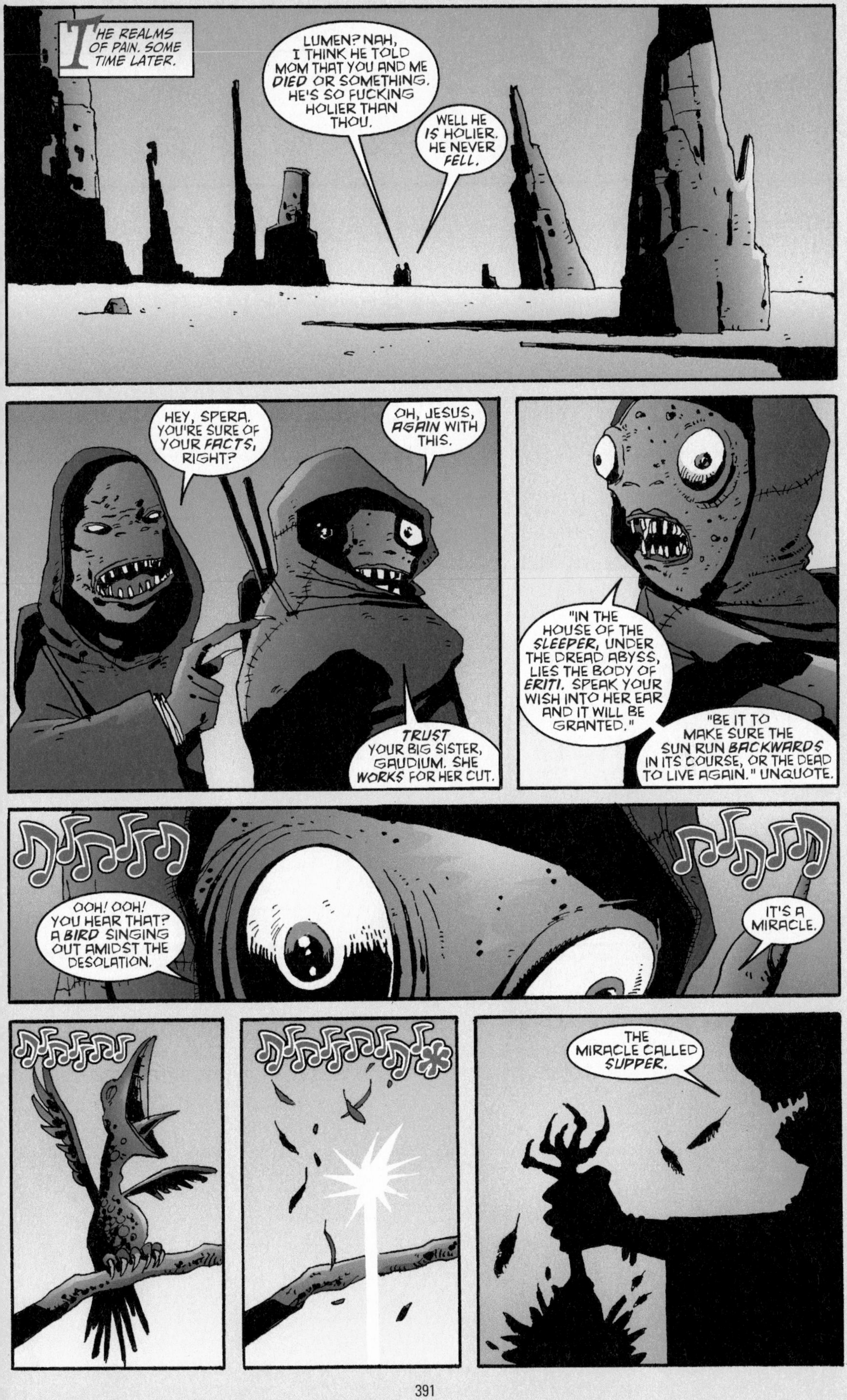
THE REALMS OF PAIN. SOME TIME LATER.
LUMEN? NAH, I THINK HE TOLD MOM THAT YOU AND ME DIED OR SOMETHING. HE'S SO FUCKING HOLIER THAN THOU.
WELL HE IS HOLIER. HE NEVER FELL.
HEY, SPERA. YOU'RE SURE OF YOUR FACTS, RIGHT?
OH, JESUS, AGAIN WITH THIS.
TRUST YOUR BIG SISTER, GAUDIUM. SHE WORKS FOR HER CUT.
"IN THE HOUSE OF THE SLEEPER, UNDER THE DREAD ABYSS, LIES THE BODY OF ERITI. SPEAK YOUR WISH INTO HER EAR AND IT WILL BE GRANTED."
"BE IT TO MAKE SURE THE SUN RUN BACKWARDS IN ITS COURSE, OR THE DEAD TO LIVE AGAIN." UNQUOTE.
OOH! OOH! YOU HEAR THAT? A BIRD SINGING OUT AMIDST THE DESOLATION.
IT'S A MIRACLE.
THE MIRACLE CALLED SUPPER.

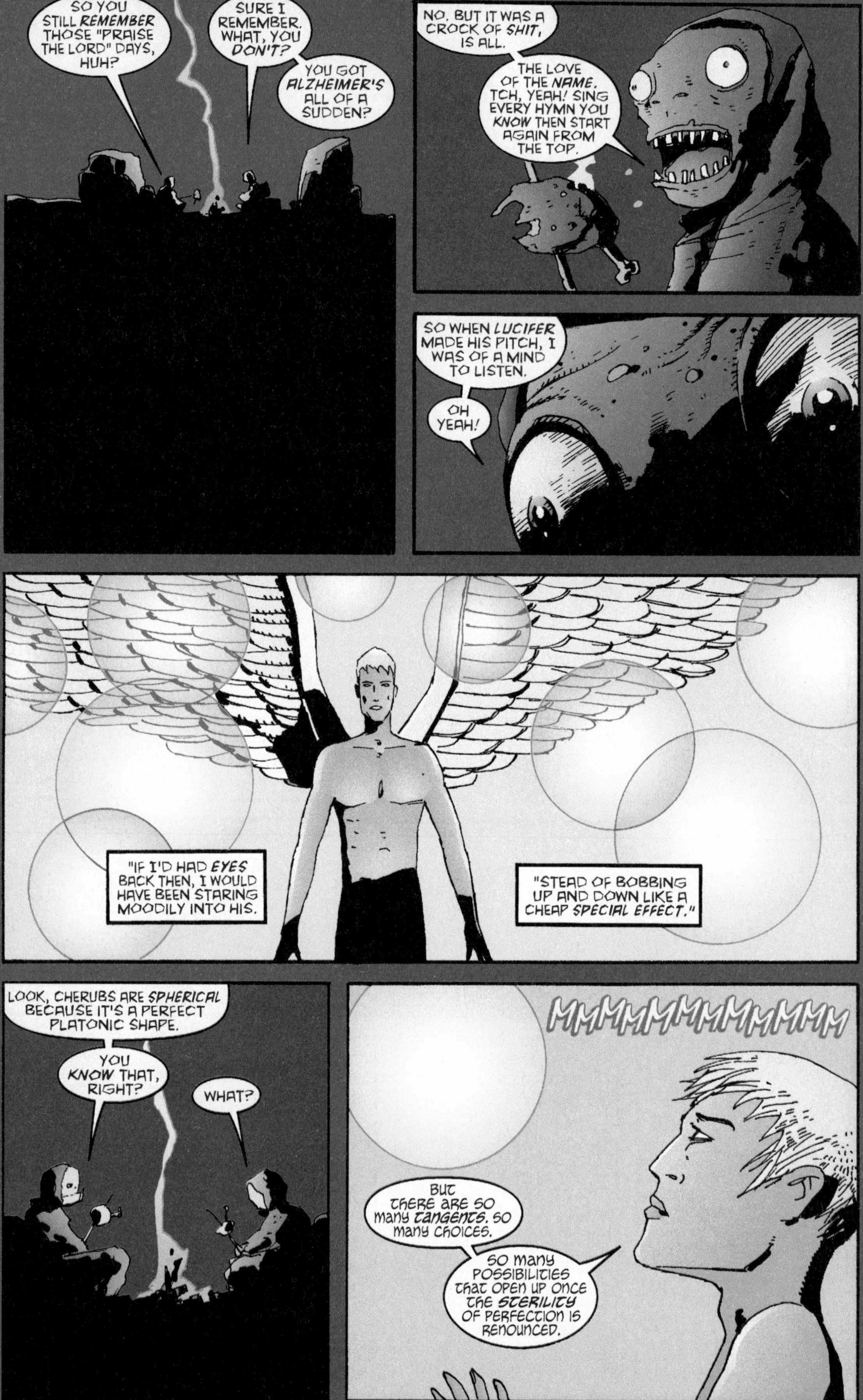
SO YOU STILL REMEMBER THOSE "PRAISE THE LORD" DAYS, HUH?
SURE I REMEMBER. WHAT, YOU DON'T?
YOU GOT ALZHEIMER'S ALL OF A SUDDEN?
NO. BUT IT WAS A CROCK OF SHIT, IS ALL.
THE LOVE OF THE NAME. TCH, YEAH! SING EVERY HYMN YOU KNOW THEN START AGAIN FROM THE TOP.
SO WHEN LUCIFER MADE HIS PITCH, I WAS OF A MIND TO LISTEN.
OH YEAH!
"IF I'D HAD EYES BACK THEN, I WOULD HAVE BEEN STARING MOODILY INTO HIS.
"STEAD OF BOBBING UP AND DOWN LIKE A CHEAP SPECIAL EFFECT."
LOOK, CHERUBS ARE SPHERICAL BECAUSE IT'S A PERFECT PLATONIC SHAPE.
YOU KNOW THAT, RIGHT?
WHAT?
MMMMMMMMMMMMMM
BUT THERE ARE SO MANY TANGENTS. SO MANY CHOICES.
SO MANY POSSIBILITIES THAT OPEN UP ONCE THE STERILITY OF PERFECTION IS RENOUNCED.

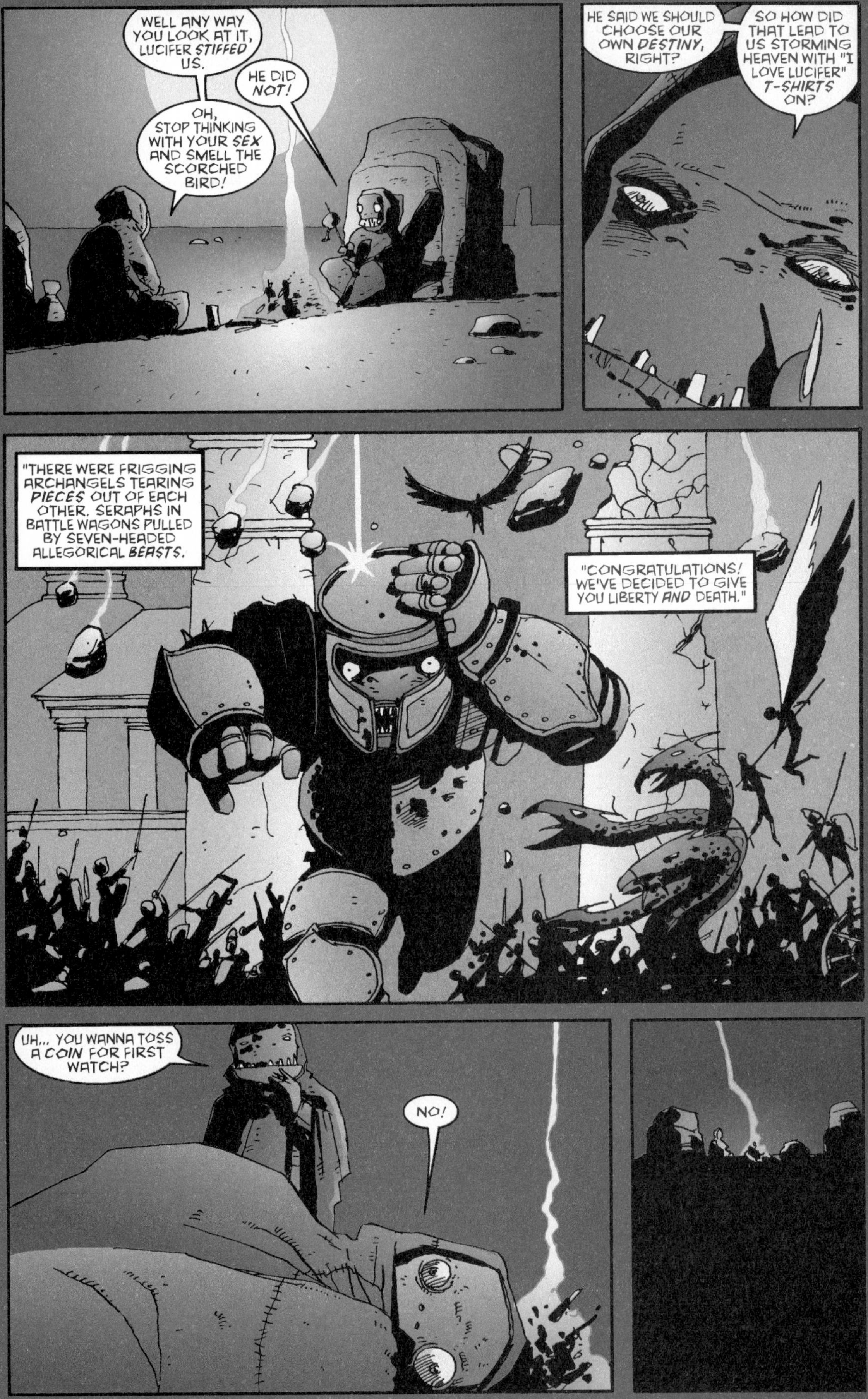
WELL ANY WAY YOU LOOK AT IT, LUCIFER STIFFED US.
HE DID NOT!
OH, STOP THINKING WITH YOUR SEX AND SMELL THE SCORCHED BIRD!
HE SAID WE SHOULD CHOOSE OUR OWN DESTINY, RIGHT?
SO HOW DID THAT LEAD TO US STORMING HEAVEN WITH "I LOVE LUCIFER" T-SHIRTS ON?
"THERE WERE FRIGGING ARCHANGELS TEARING PIECES OUT OF EACH OTHER. SERAPHS IN BATTLE WAGONS PULLED BY SEVEN-HEADED ALLEGORICAL BEASTS.
"CONGRATULATIONS! WE'VE DECIDED TO GIVE YOU LIBERTY AND DEATH."
UH... YOU WANNA TOSS A COIN FOR FIRST WATCH?
NO!

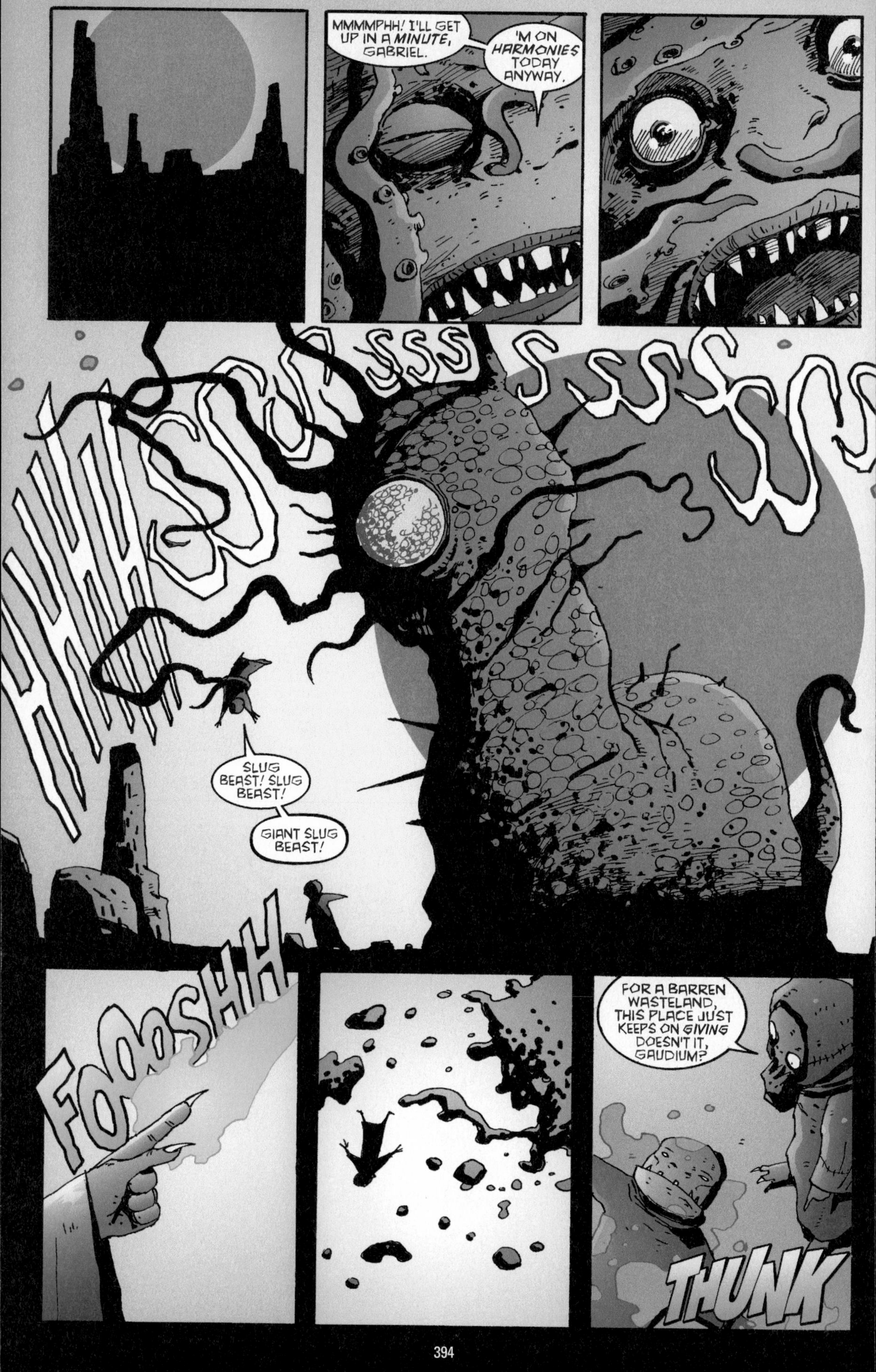

MMMMPHH! I'LL GET UP IN A MINUTE, GABRIEL.
'M ON HARMONIES TODAY ANYWAY.
HHHHSSSSSSSSSSSSS
SLUG BEAST! SLUG BEAST!
GIANT SLUG BEAST!
FOOOSHH
FOR A BARREN WASTELAND, THIS PLACE JUST KEEPS ON GIVING DOESN'T IT, GAUDIUM?
THUNK

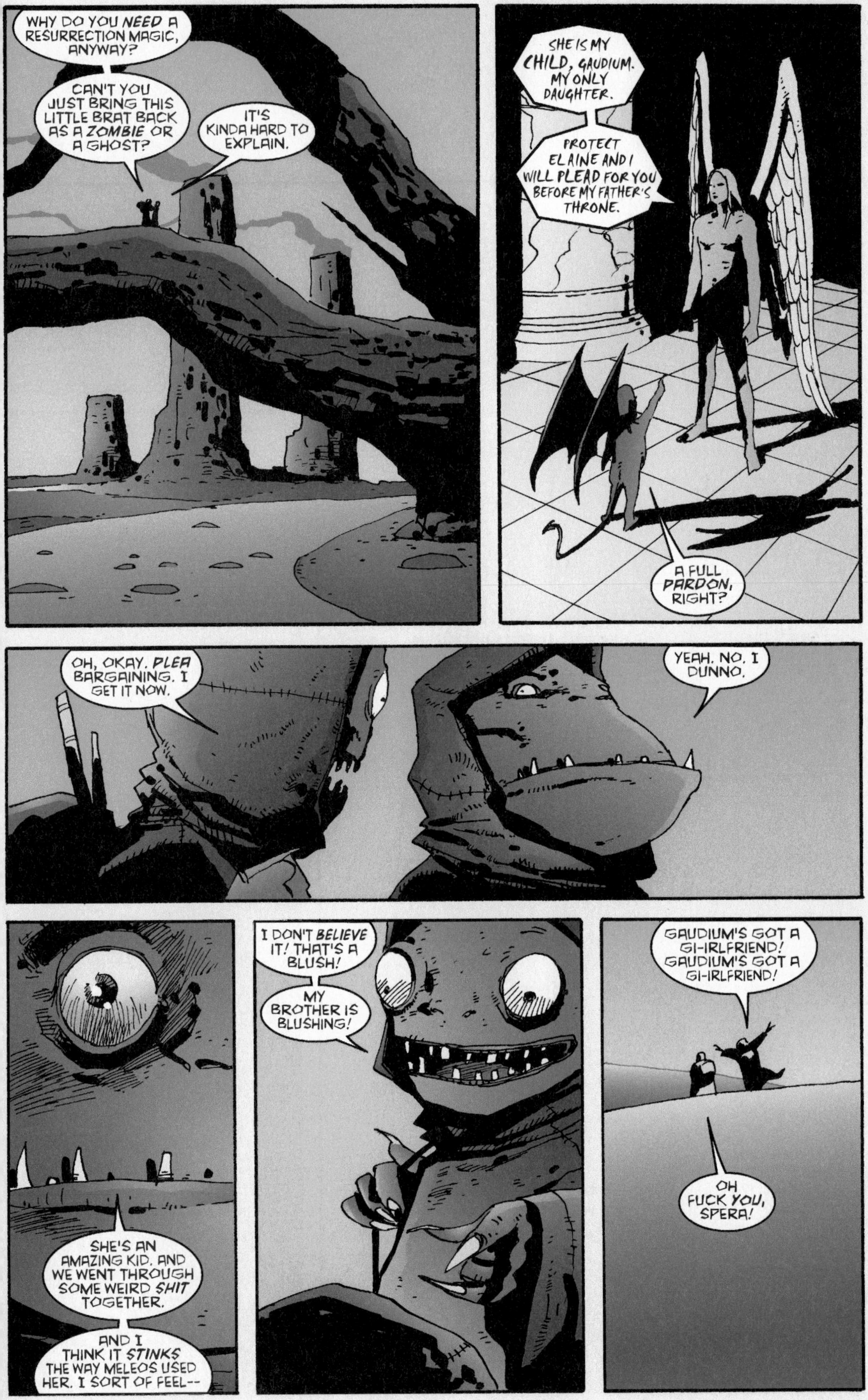
WHY DO YOU NEED A RESURRECTION MAGIC, ANYWAY?
CAN'T YOU JUST BRING THIS LITTLE BRAT BACK AS A ZOMBIE OR A GHOST?
IT'S KINDA HARD TO EXPLAIN.
SHE IS MY CHILD, GAUDIUM. MY ONLY DAUGHTER.
PROTECT ELAINE AND I WILL PLEAD FOR YOU BEFORE MY FATHER'S THRONE.
A FULL PARDON, RIGHT?
OH, OKAY. PLEA BARGAINING. I GET IT NOW.
YEAH. NO. I DUNNO.
SHE'S AN AMAZING KID. AND WE WENT THROUGH SOME WEIRD SHIT TOGETHER.
AND I THINK IT STINKS THE WAY MELEOS USED HER. I SORT OF FEEL--
I DON'T BELIEVE IT! THAT'S A BLUSH!
MY BROTHER IS BLUSHING!
GAUDIUM'S GOT A GI-IRLFRIEND! GAUDIUM'S GOT A GI-IRLFRIEND!
OH FUCK YOU, SPERA!

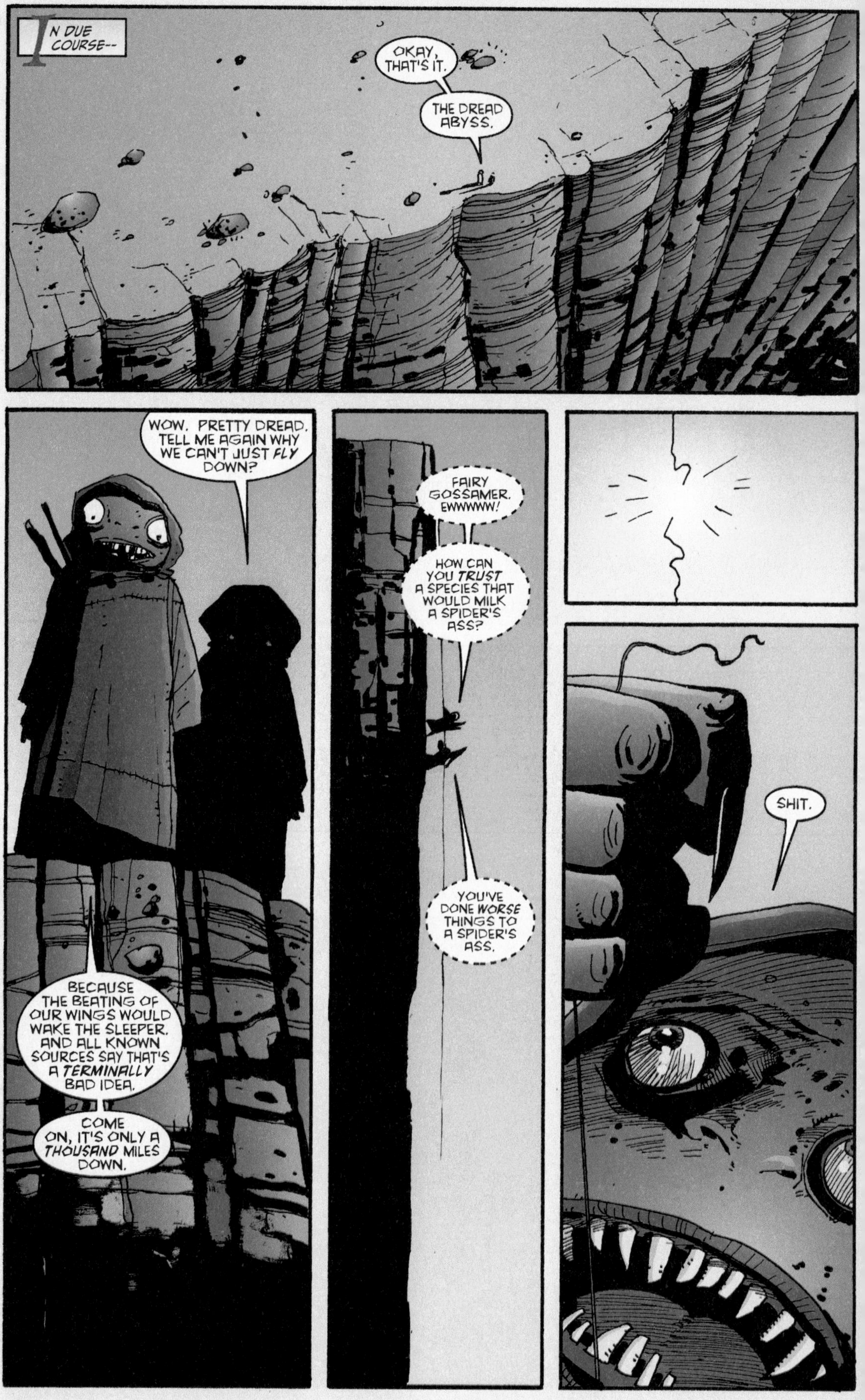
IN DUE COURSE--
OKAY, THAT'S IT.
THE DREAD ABYSS.
WOW. PRETTY DREAD. TELL ME AGAIN WHY WE CAN'T JUST FLY DOWN?
BECAUSE THE BEATING OF OUR WINGS WOULD WAKE THE SLEEPER. AND ALL KNOWN SOURCES SAY THAT'S A TERMINALLY BAD IDEA.
COME ON, IT'S ONLY A THOUSAND MILES DOWN.
FAIRY GOSSAMER. EWWWWW!
HOW CAN YOU TRUST A SPECIES THAT WOULD MILK A SPIDER'S ASS?
YOU'VE DONE WORSE THINGS TO A SPIDER'S ASS.
SHIT.

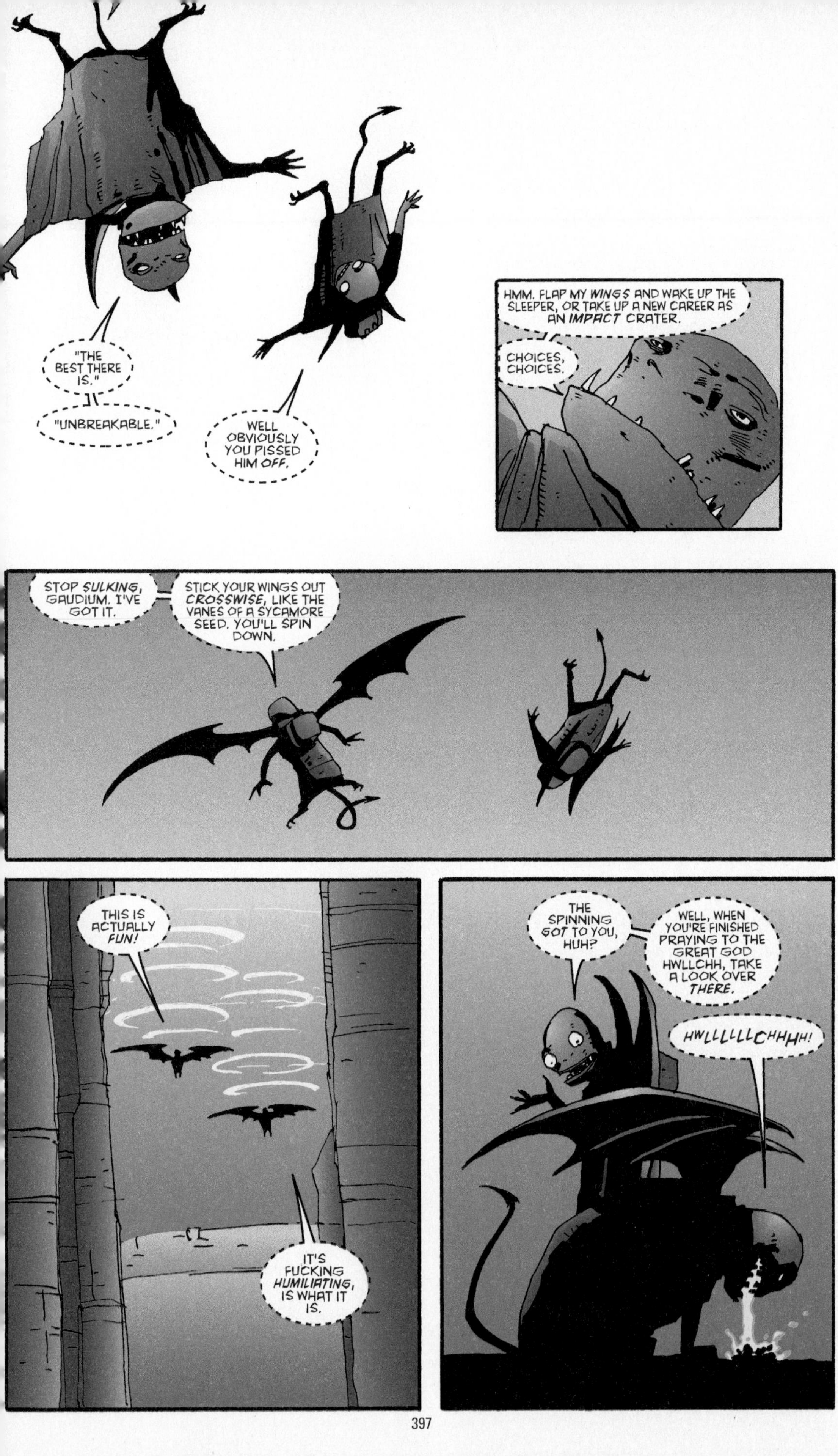
"THE BEST THERE IS."
"UNBREAKABLE."
WELL OBVIOUSLY YOU PISSED HIM OFF.
HMM. FLAP MY WINGS AND WAKE UP THE SLEEPER, OR TAKE UP A NEW CAREER AS AN IMPACT CRATER.
CHOICES, CHOICES.
STOP SULKING, GAUDIUM. I'VE GOT IT.
STICK YOUR WINGS OUT CROSSWISE, LIKE THE VANES OF A SYCAMORE SEED. YOU'LL SPIN DOWN.
THIS IS ACTUALLY FUN!
IT'S FUCKING HUMILIATING, IS WHAT IT IS.
THE SPINNING GOT TO YOU, HUH?
WELL, WHEN YOU'RE FINISHED PRAYING TO THE GREAT GOD HWLLCHH, TAKE A LOOK OVER THERE.
HWLLLLLLCHHHH!

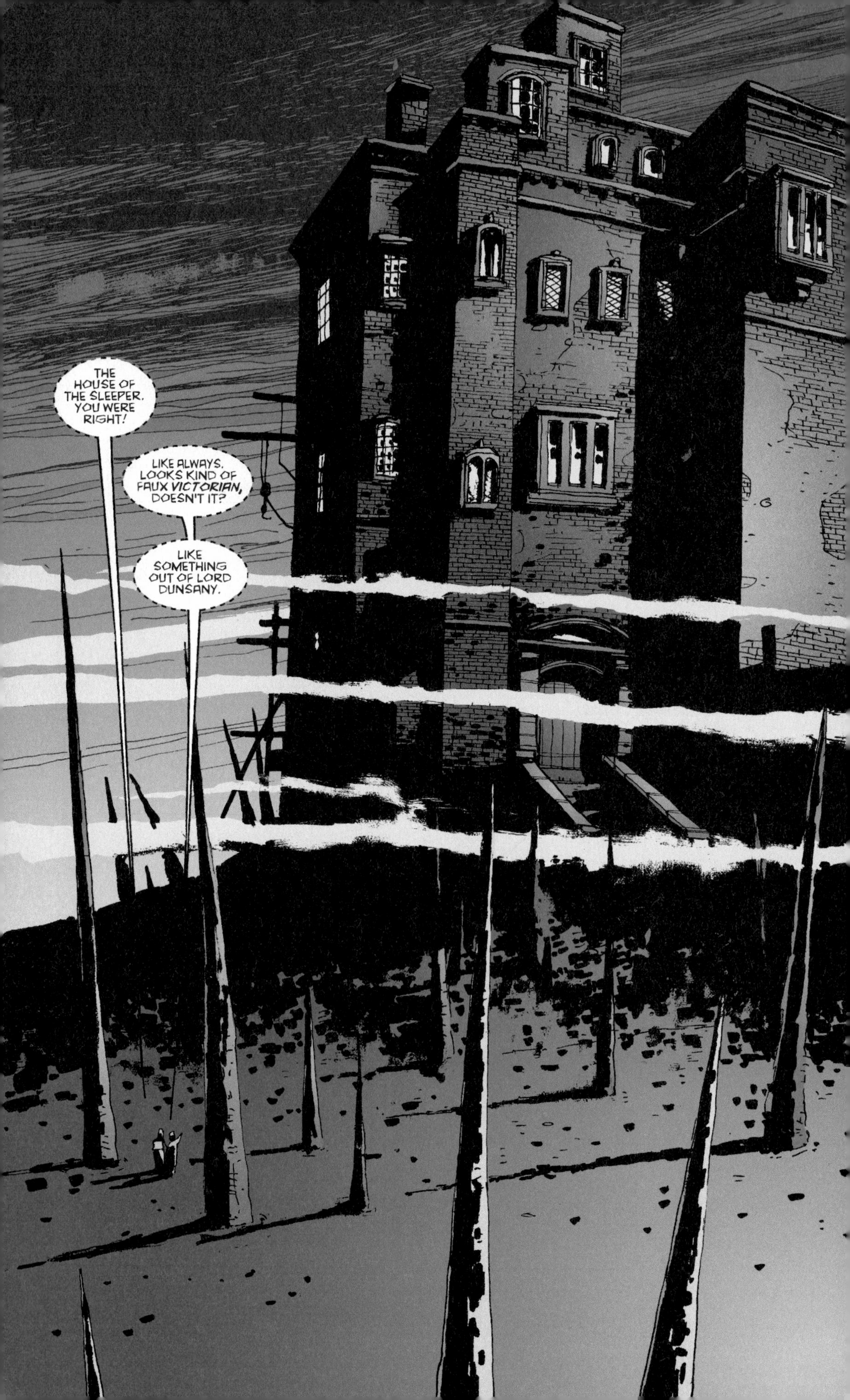
THE HOUSE OF THE SLEEPER. YOU WERE RIGHT!
LIKE ALWAYS. LOOKS KIND OF FAUX VICTORIAN, DOESN'T IT?
LIKE SOMETHING OUT OF LORD DUNSANY.

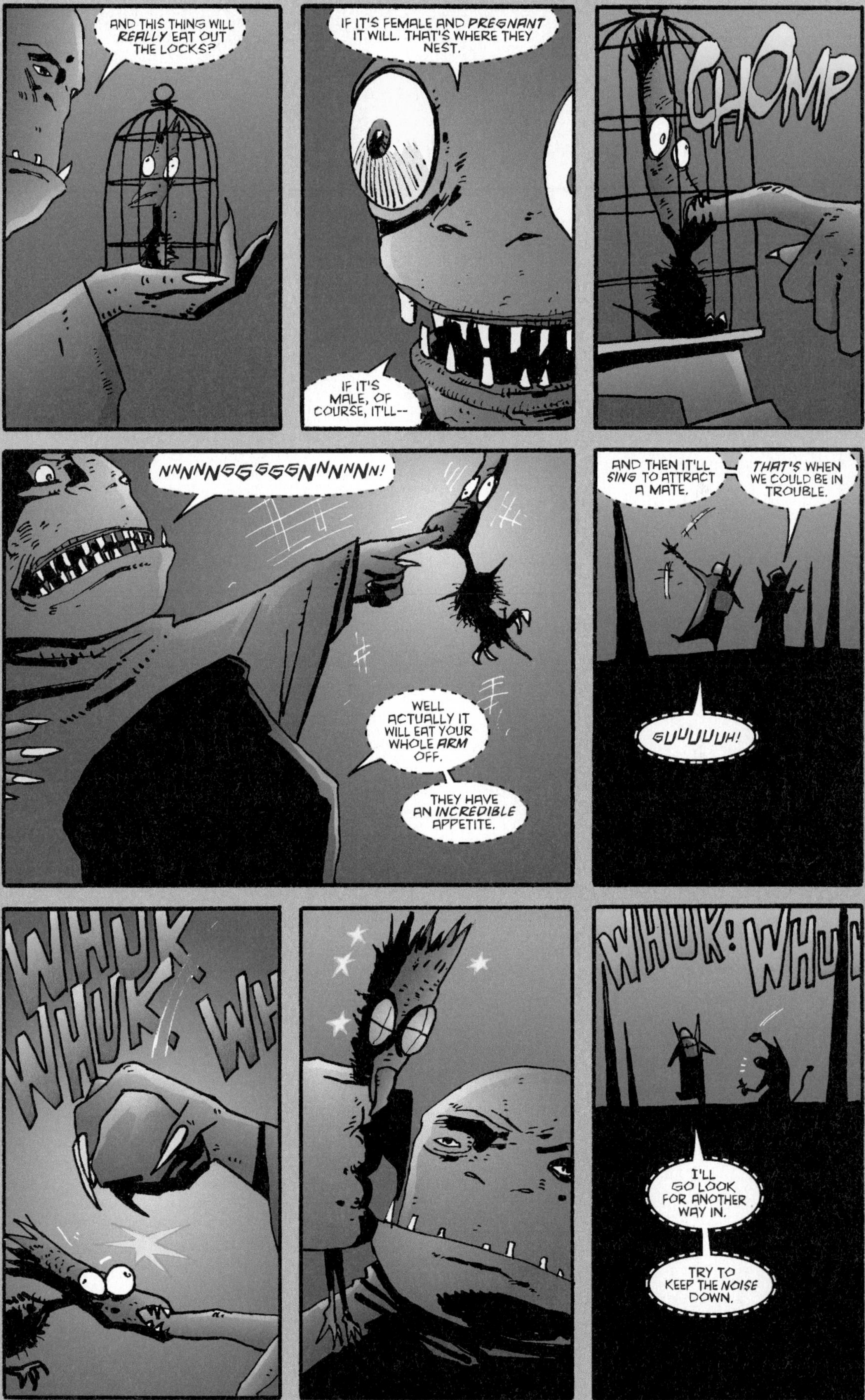
AND THIS THING WILL REALLY EAT OUT THE LOCKS?
IF IT'S FEMALE AND PREGNANT IT WILL. THAT'S WHERE THEY NEST.
IF IT'S MALE, OF COURSE, IT'LL--
CHOMP
NNNNNGGGGGNNNNNN!
WELL ACTUALLY IT WILL EAT YOUR WHOLE ARM OFF.
THEY HAVE AN INCREDIBLE APPETITE.
AND THEN IT'LL SING TO ATTRACT A MATE.
THAT'S WHEN WE COULD BE IN TROUBLE.
GUUUUUH!
WHUK WHUK. WH
WHUK! WHU
I'LL GO LOOK FOR ANOTHER WAY IN.
TRY TO KEEP THE NOISE DOWN.

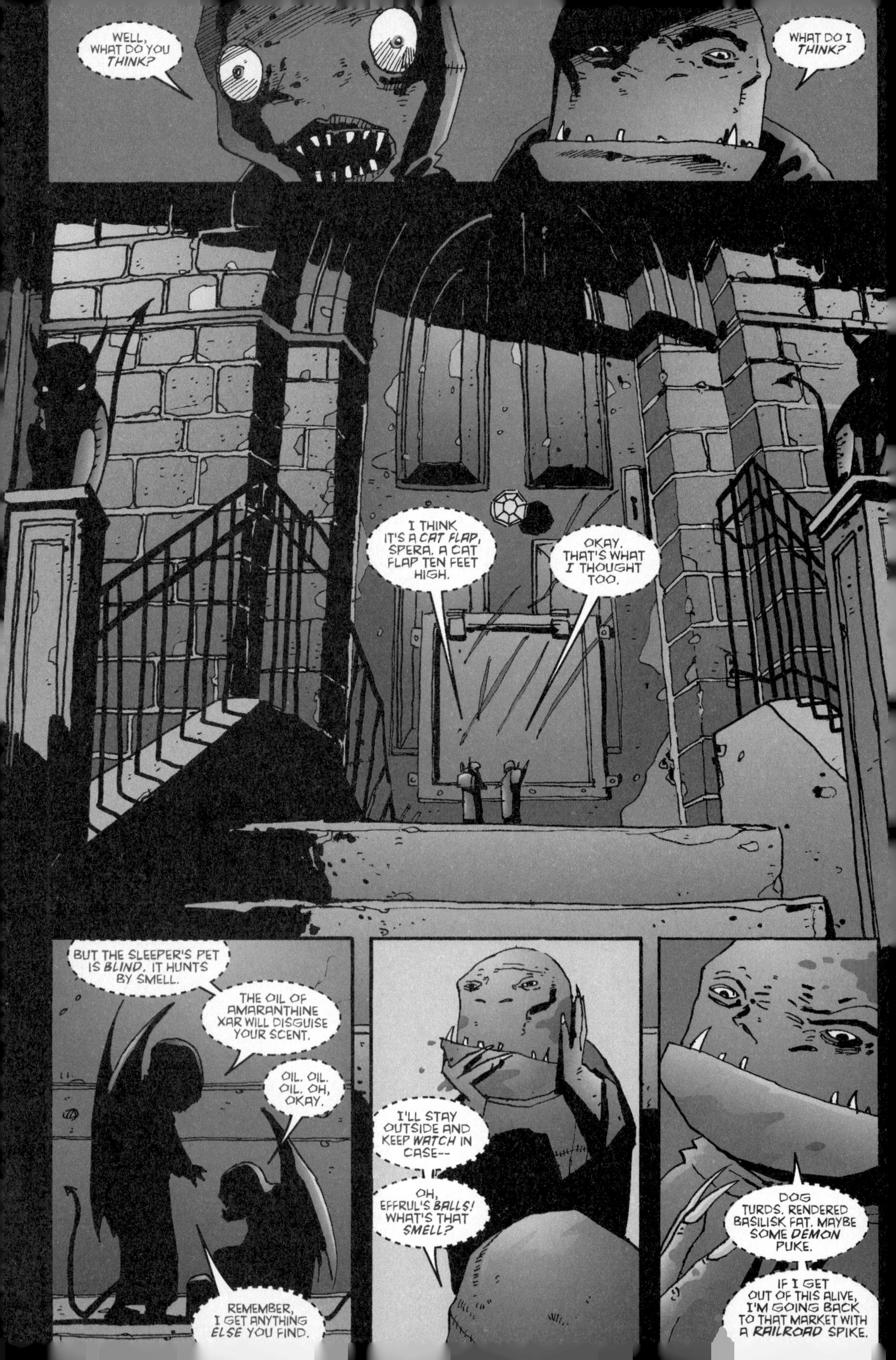

WELL, WHAT DO YOU THINK?
WHAT DO I THINK?
I THINK IT'S A CAT FLAP, SPERA. A CAT FLAP TEN FEET HIGH.
OKAY. THAT'S WHAT I THOUGHT TOO.
BUT THE SLEEPER'S PET IS BLIND. IT HUNTS BY SMELL.
THE OIL OF AMARANTHINE XAR WILL DISGUISE YOUR SCENT.
OIL. OIL. OIL. OH, OKAY.
REMEMBER, I GET ANYTHING ELSE YOU FIND.
I'LL STAY OUTSIDE AND KEEP WATCH IN CASE--
OH, EFFRUL'S BALLS! WHAT'S THAT SMELL?
DOG TURDS. RENDERED BASILISK FAT. MAYBE SOME DEMON PUKE.
IF I GET OUT OF THIS ALIVE, I'M GOING BACK TO THAT MARKET WITH A RAILROAD SPIKE.

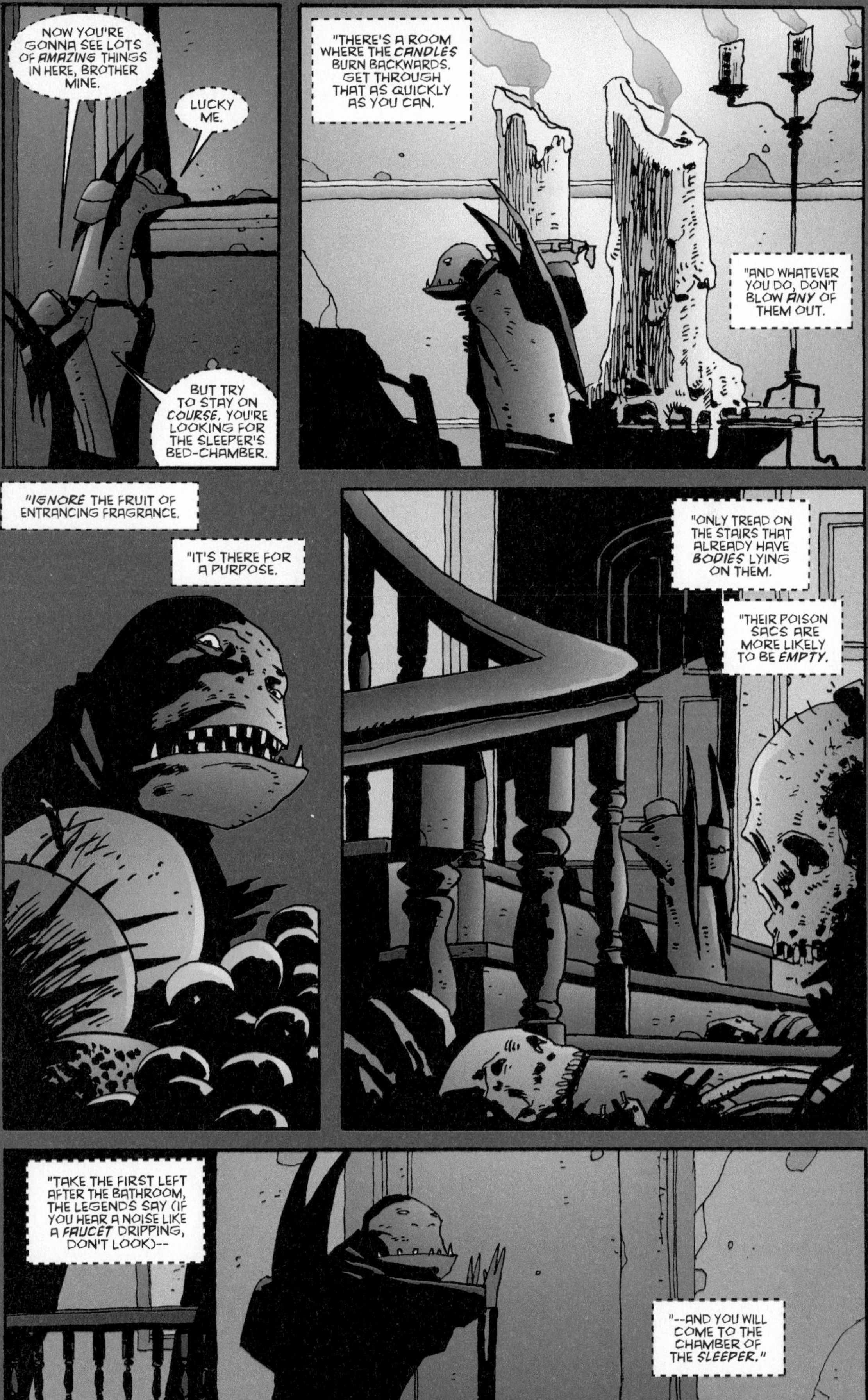
NOW YOU'RE GONNA SEE LOTS OF AMAZING THINGS IN HERE, BROTHER MINE.
LUCKY ME.
BUT TRY TO STAY ON COURSE. YOU'RE LOOKING FOR THE SLEEPER'S BED-CHAMBER.
"THERE'S A ROOM WHERE THE CANDLES BURN BACKWARDS. GET THROUGH THAT AS QUICKLY AS YOU CAN.
"AND WHATEVER YOU DO, DON'T BLOW ANY OF THEM OUT.
"IGNORE THE FRUIT OF ENTRANCING FRAGRANCE.
"IT'S THERE FOR A PURPOSE.
"ONLY TREAD ON THE STAIRS THAT ALREADY HAVE BODIES LYING ON THEM.
"THEIR POISON SACS ARE MORE LIKELY TO BE EMPTY.
"TAKE THE FIRST LEFT AFTER THE BATHROOM, THE LEGENDS SAY (IF YOU HEAR A NOISE LIKE A FAUCET DRIPPING, DON'T LOOK)--
"--AND YOU WILL COME TO THE CHAMBER OF THE SLEEPER."

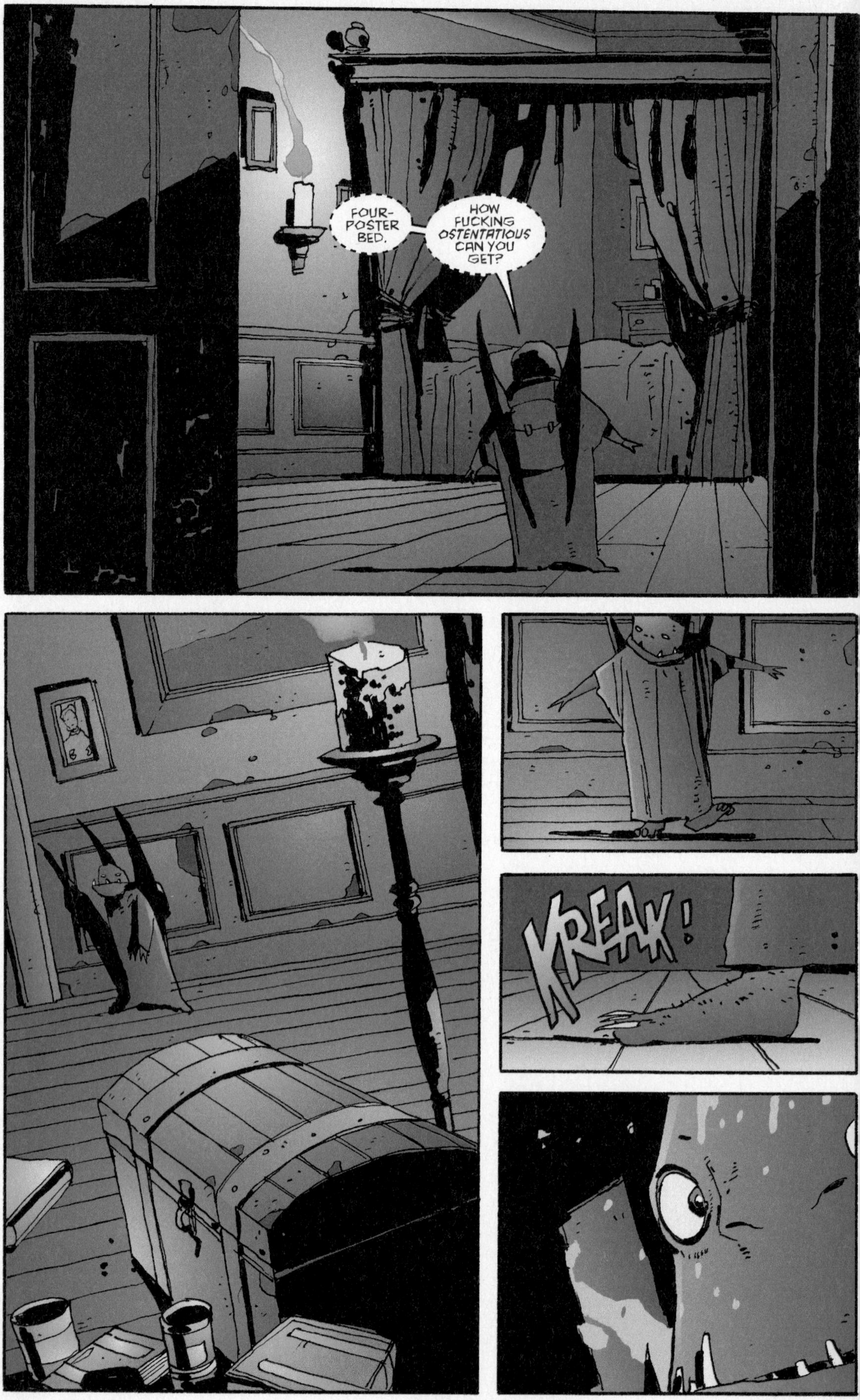
FOUR-POSTER BED.
HOW FUCKING OSTENTATIOUS CAN YOU GET?
KREAK!

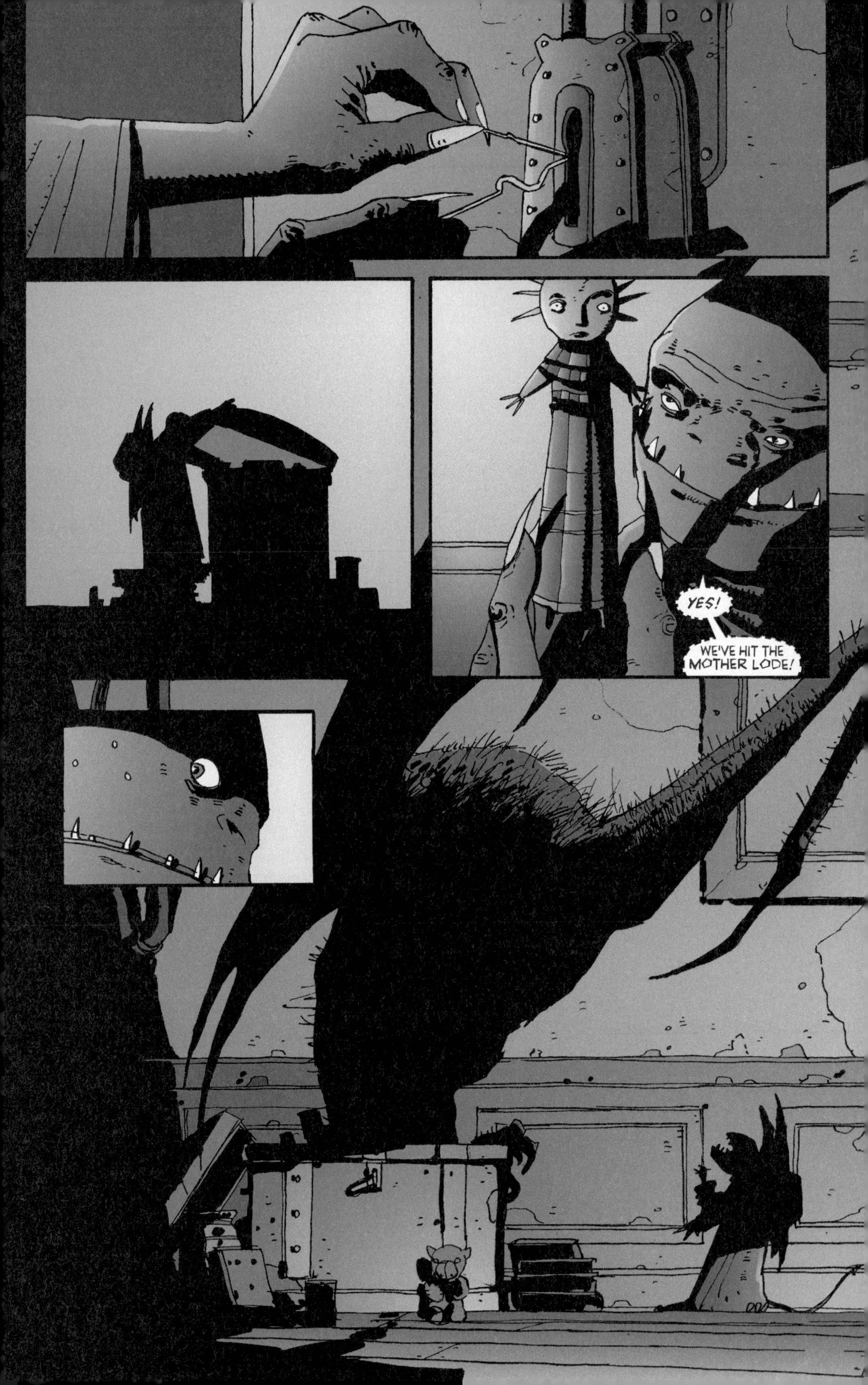
YES!
WE'VE HIT THE MOTHER LODE!

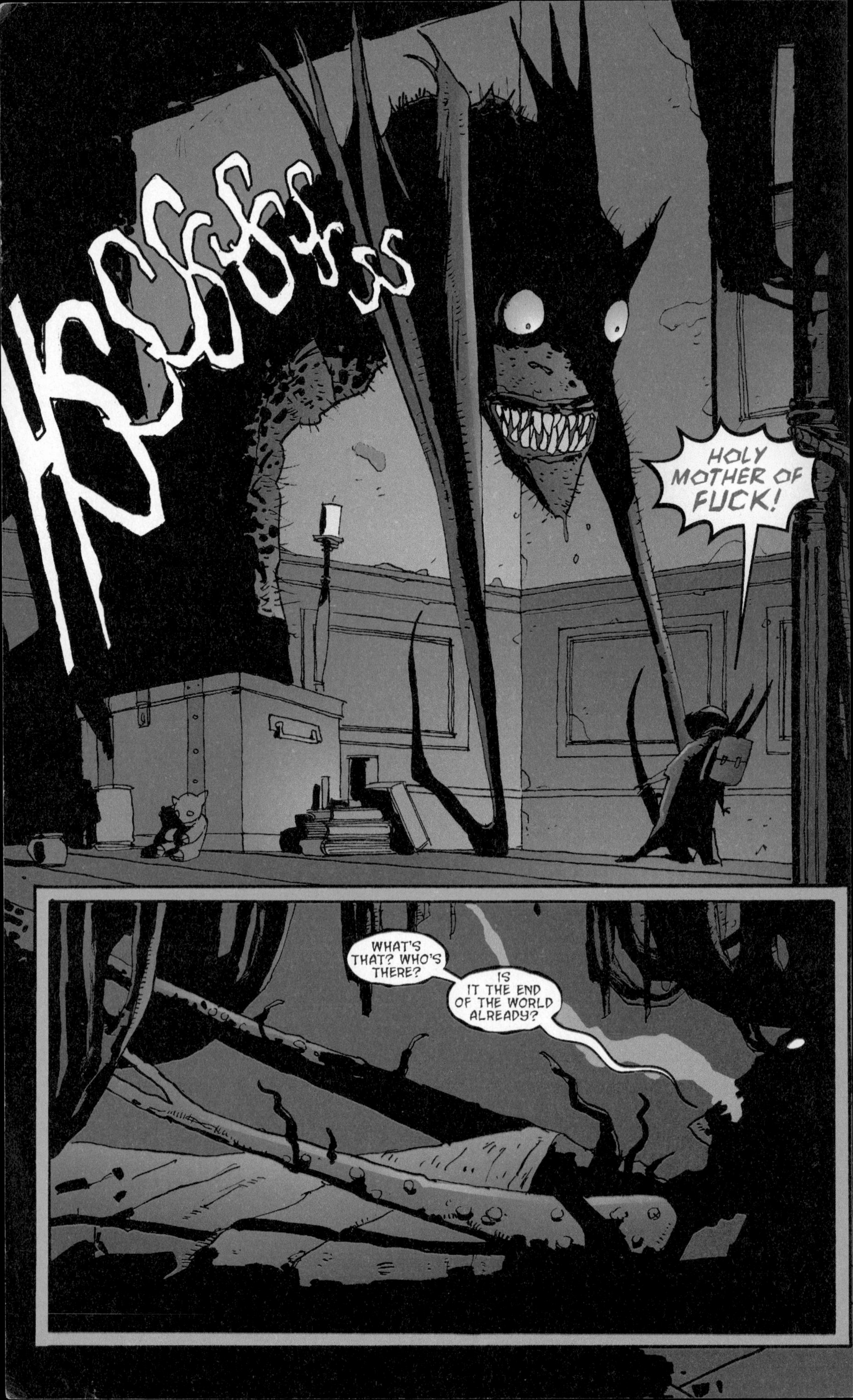
HSSSSSss
HOLY MOTHER OF FUCK!
WHAT'S THAT? WHO'S THERE?
IS IT THE END OF THE WORLD ALREADY?

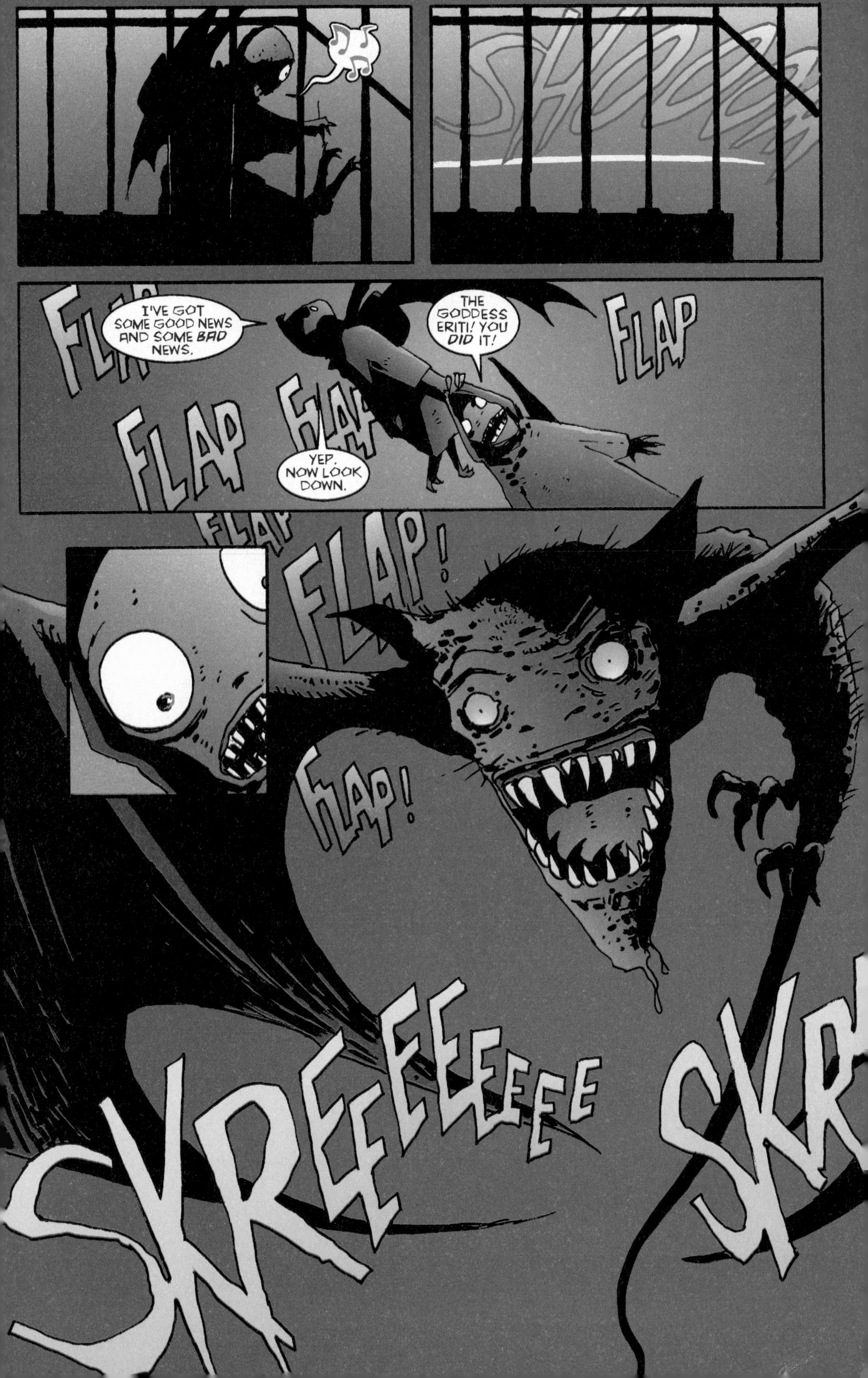
SHOOM
FLAP
I'VE GOT SOME GOOD NEWS AND SOME BAD NEWS.
THE GODDESS ERITI! YOU DID IT!
FLAP
FLAP
FLAP
YEP. NOW LOOK DOWN.
FLAP
FLAP!
FLAP!
SKREEEEEEEEE
SKR

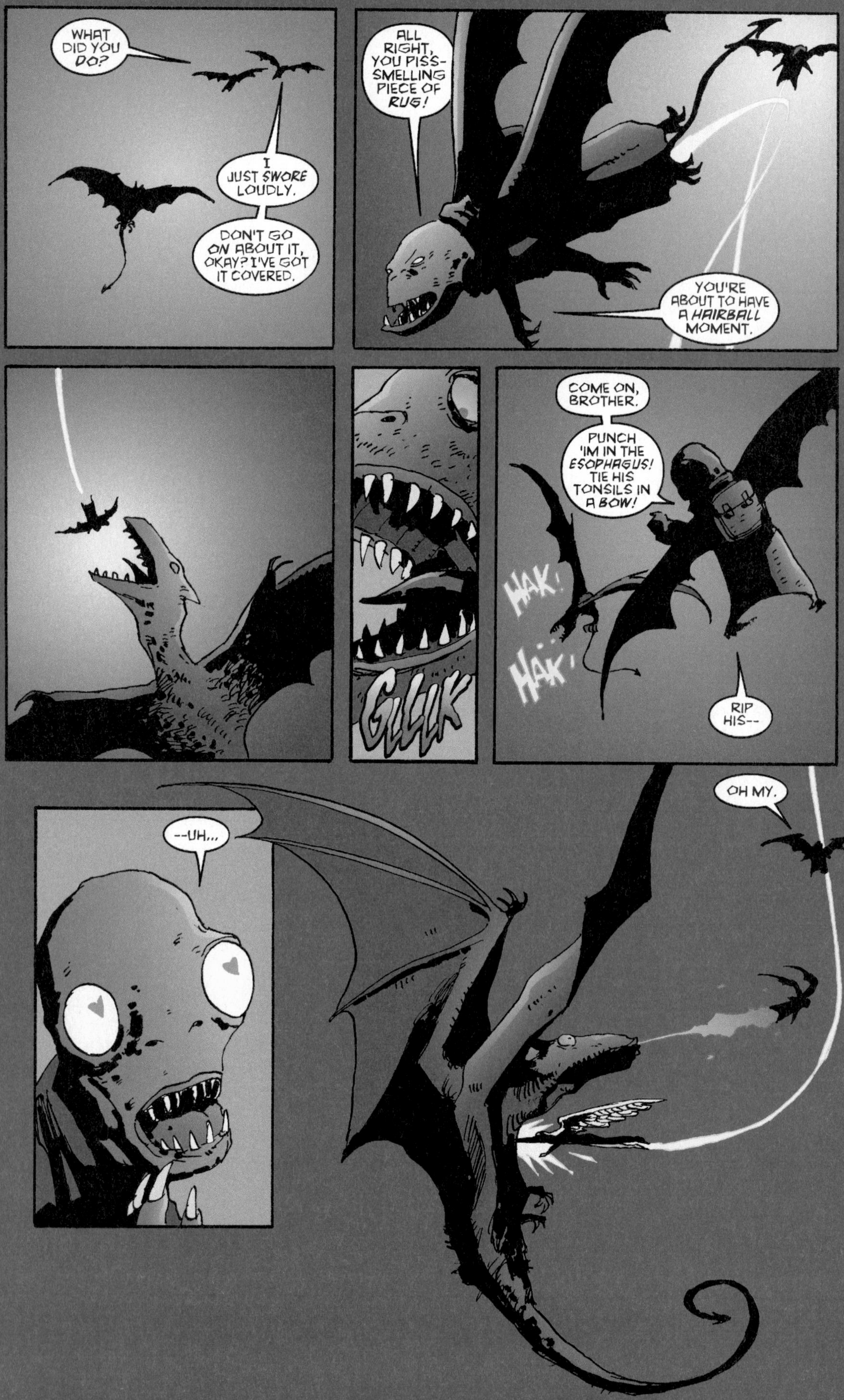
WHAT DID YOU DO?
I JUST SWORE LOUDLY.
DON'T GO ON ABOUT IT, OKAY? I'VE GOT IT COVERED.
ALL RIGHT, YOU PISS-SMELLING PIECE OF RUG!
YOU'RE ABOUT TO HAVE A HAIRBALL MOMENT.
GLLLK
COME ON, BROTHER.
PUNCH 'IM IN THE ESOPHAGUS! TIE HIS TONSILS IN A BOW!
HAK!
HAK!
RIP HIS--
--UH...
OH MY.

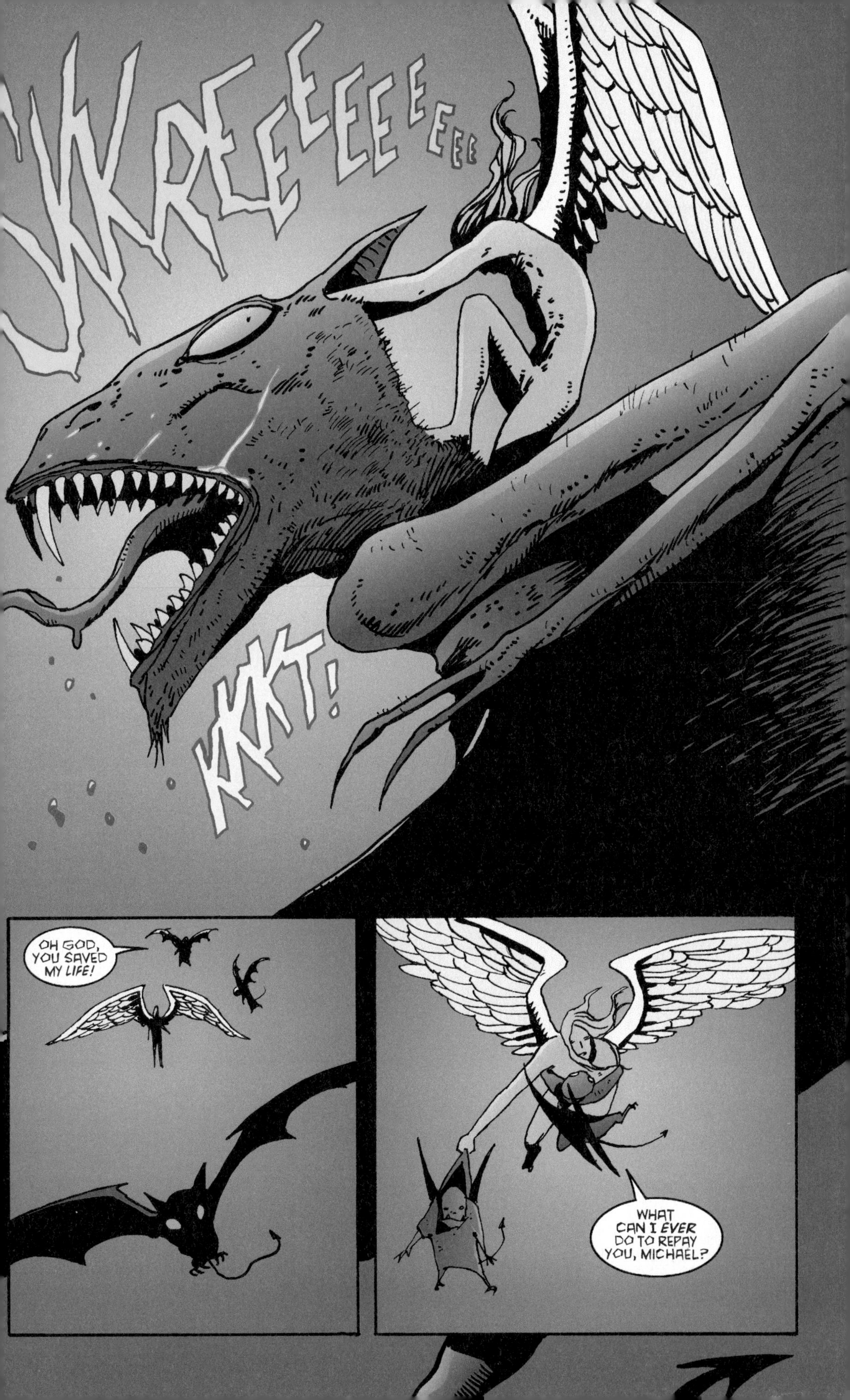
WREEEEEEEE
KKKT!
OH GOD, YOU SAVED MY LIFE!
WHAT CAN I EVER DO TO REPAY YOU, MICHAEL?

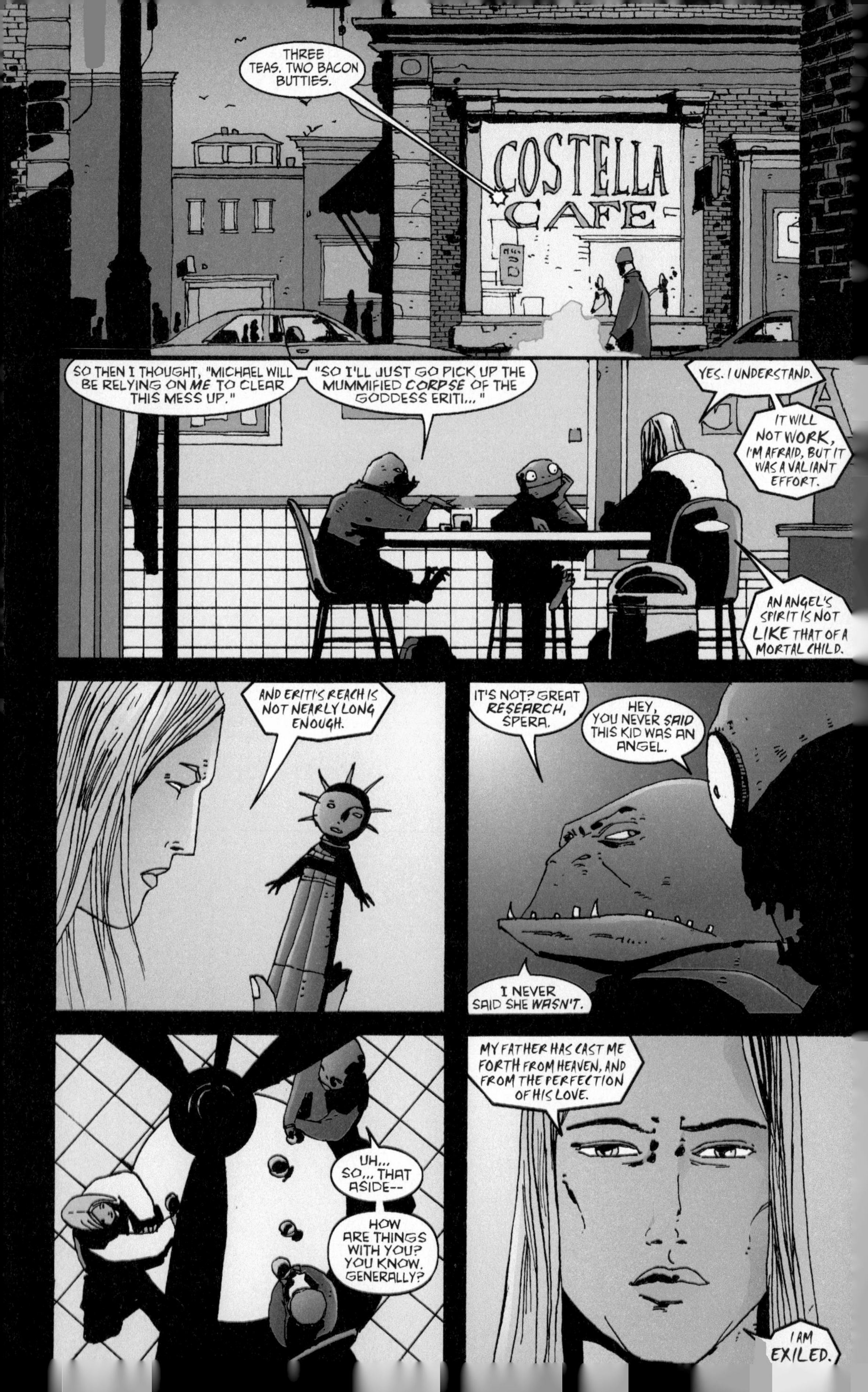
THREE TEAS. TWO BACON BUTTIES.
COSTELLA CAFE
SO THEN I THOUGHT, "MICHAEL WILL BE RELYING ON ME TO CLEAR THIS MESS UP."
"SO I'LL JUST GO PICK UP THE MUMMIFIED CORPSE OF THE GODDESS ERITI..."
YES. I UNDERSTAND.
IT WILL NOT WORK, I'M AFRAID, BUT IT WAS A VALIANT EFFORT.
AN ANGEL'S SPIRIT IS NOT LIKE THAT OF A MORTAL CHILD.
AND ERITI'S REACH IS NOT NEARLY LONG ENOUGH.
IT'S NOT? GREAT RESEARCH, SPERA.
HEY, YOU NEVER SAID THIS KID WAS AN ANGEL.
I NEVER SAID SHE WASN'T.
UH... SO... THAT ASIDE--
HOW ARE THINGS WITH YOU? YOU KNOW. GENERALLY?
MY FATHER HAS CAST ME FORTH FROM HEAVEN, AND FROM THE PERFECTION OF HIS LOVE.
I AM EXILED.

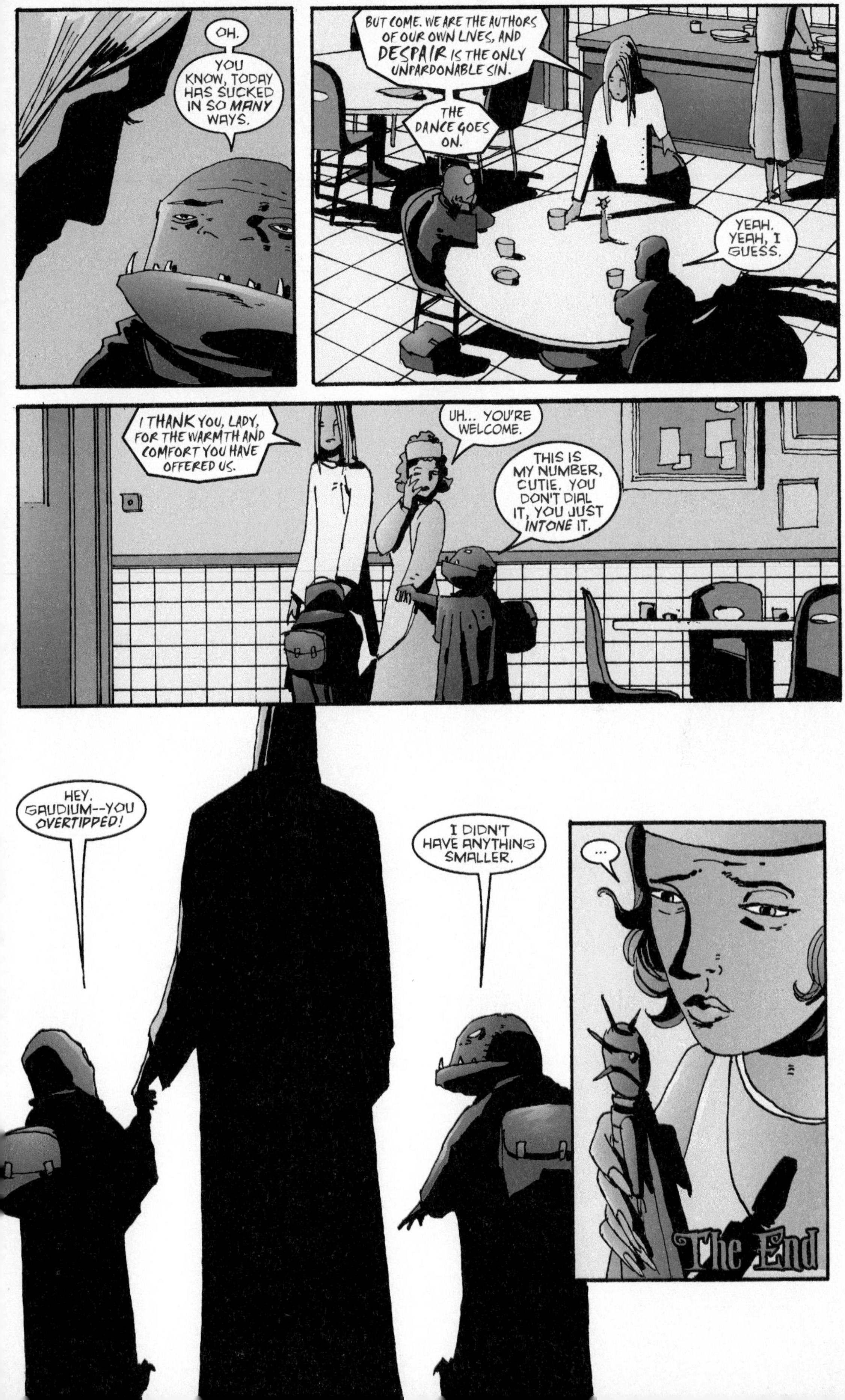
OH.
YOU KNOW, TODAY HAS SUCKED IN SO MANY WAYS.
BUT COME. WE ARE THE AUTHORS OF OUR OWN LIVES, AND DESPAIR IS THE ONLY UNPARDONABLE SIN.
THE DANCE GOES ON.
YEAH. YEAH, I GUESS.
I THANK YOU, LADY, FOR THE WARMTH AND COMFORT YOU HAVE OFFERED US.
UH... YOU'RE WELCOME.
THIS IS MY NUMBER, CUTIE. YOU DON'T DIAL IT, YOU JUST INTONE IT.
HEY. GAUDIUM--YOU OVERTIPPED!
I DIDN'T HAVE ANYTHING SMALLER.
...
The End

The Road to Hell

Sketches by **Dean Ormston** and layouts by **Peter Gross**

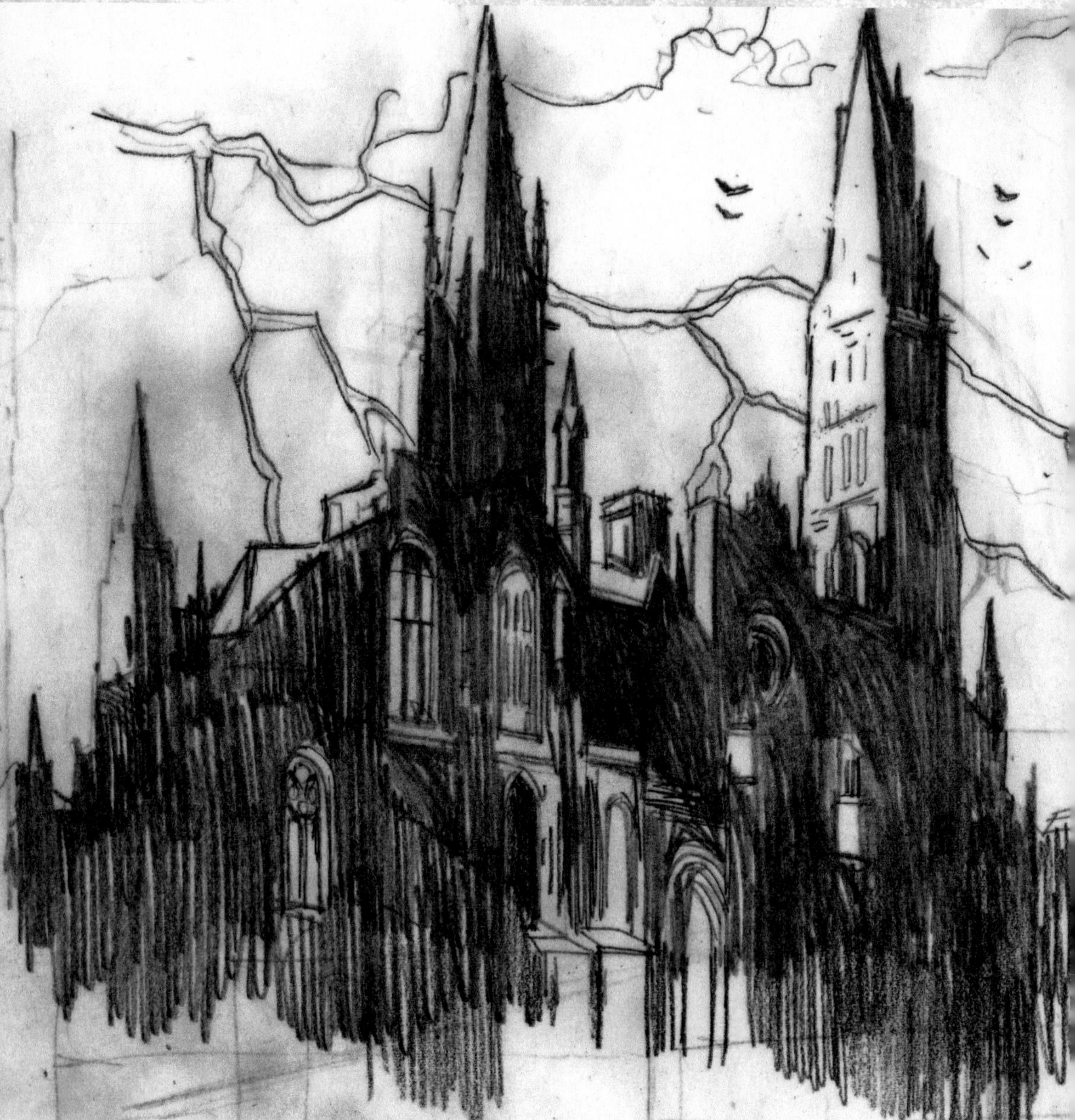

TITLE: LUCIFER #15 PAGE 1

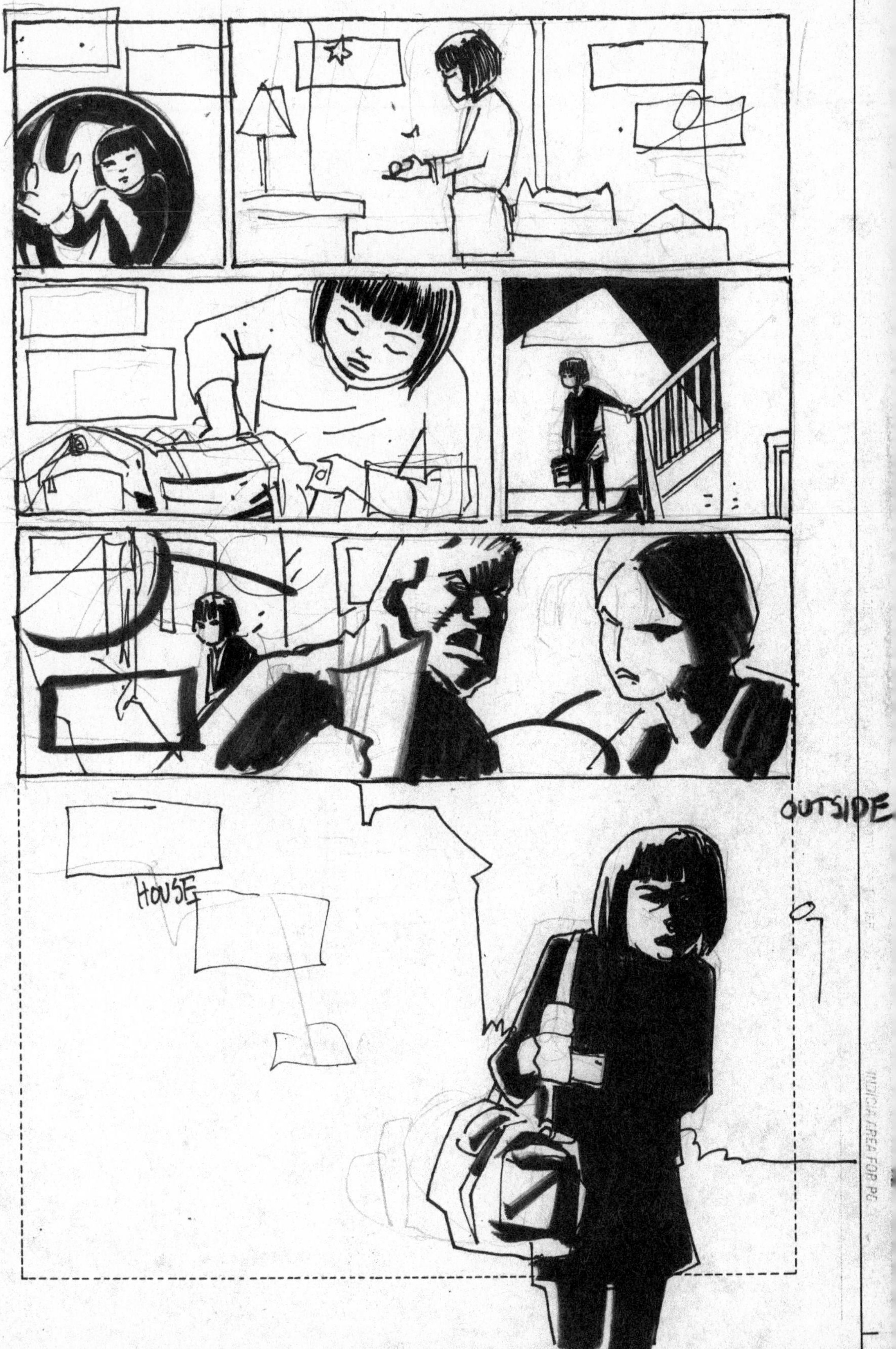
HOUSE
OUTSIDE

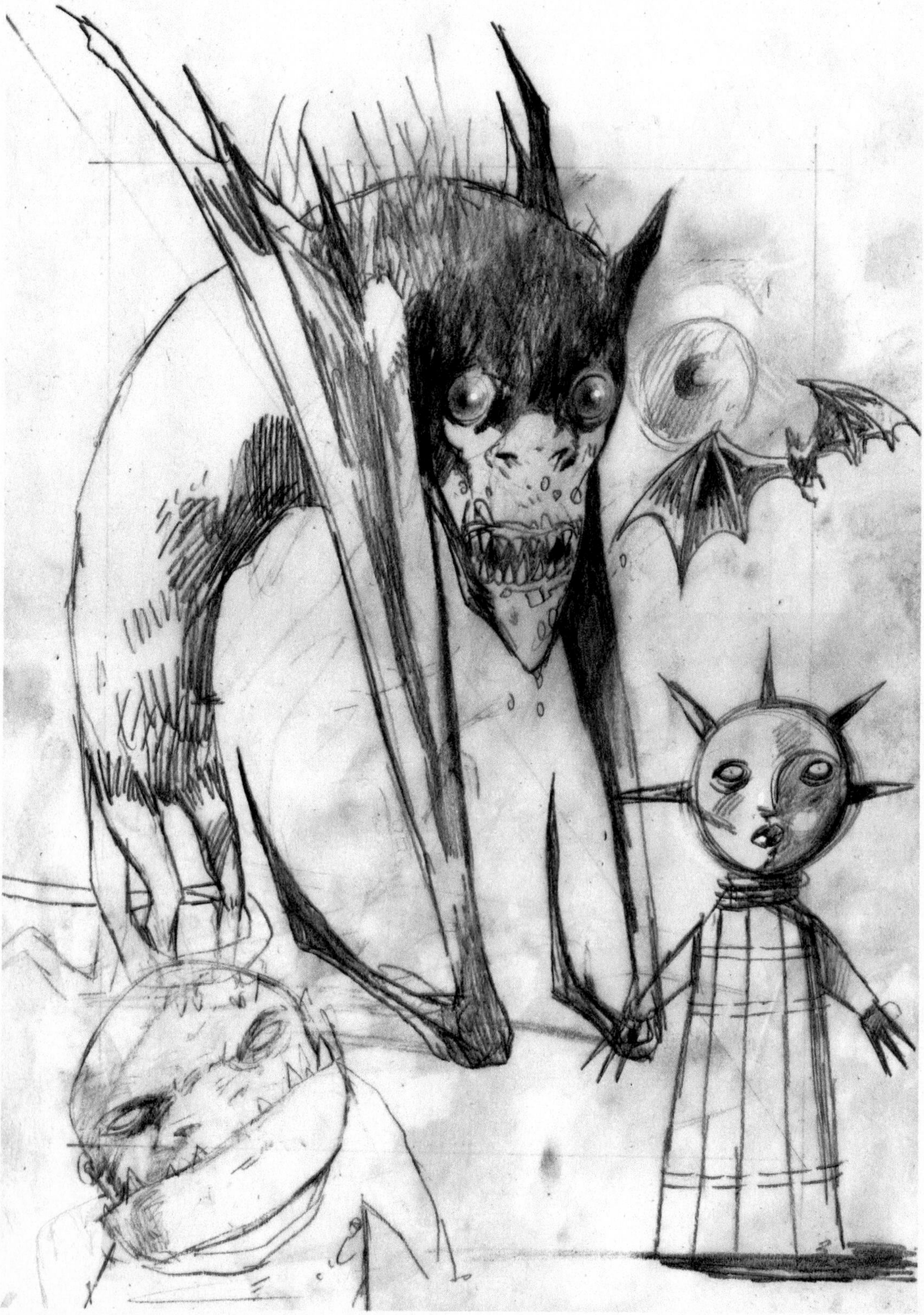

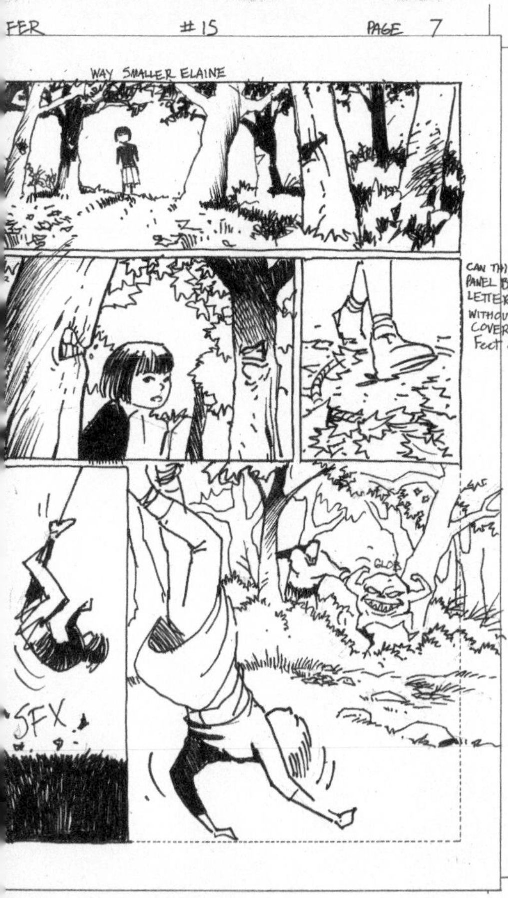
FER #15 PAGE 7
WAY SMALLER ELAINE
CAN THIS PANEL BE LETTERED WITHOUT COVERING Feet or Rope?
GLOB
SFX

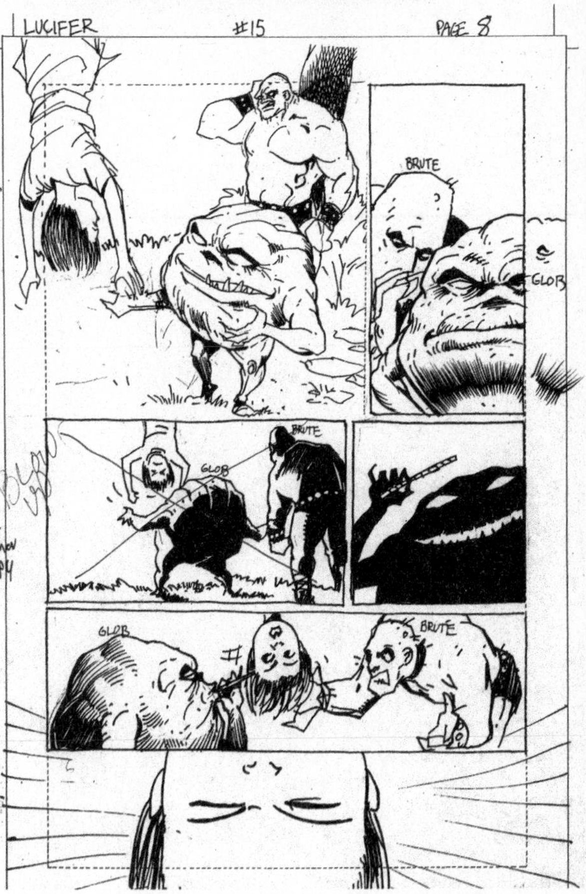
LUCIFER #15 PAGE 8
BRUTE
GLOB
See other copy
GLOB
BRUTE
GLOB
BRUTE

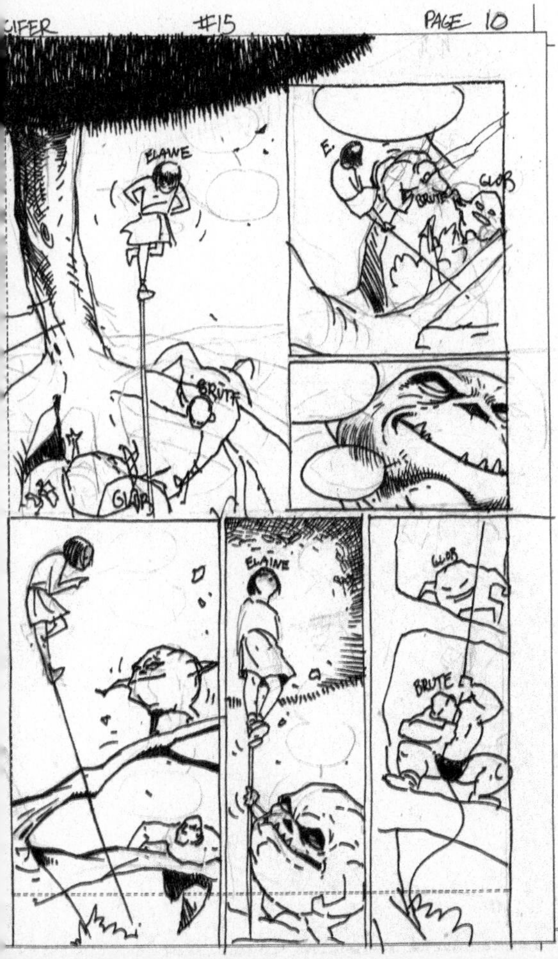
IFER #15 PAGE 10
ELAINE
E.
BRUTE
GLOB
BRUTE
GLOB
ELAINE
GLOB
BRUTE

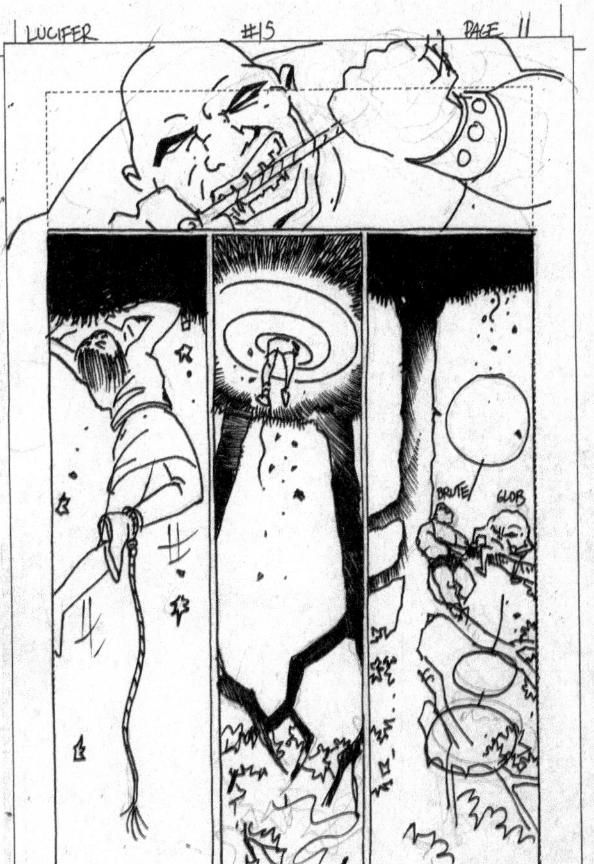
LUCIFER #15 PAGE 11
BRUTE
GLOB

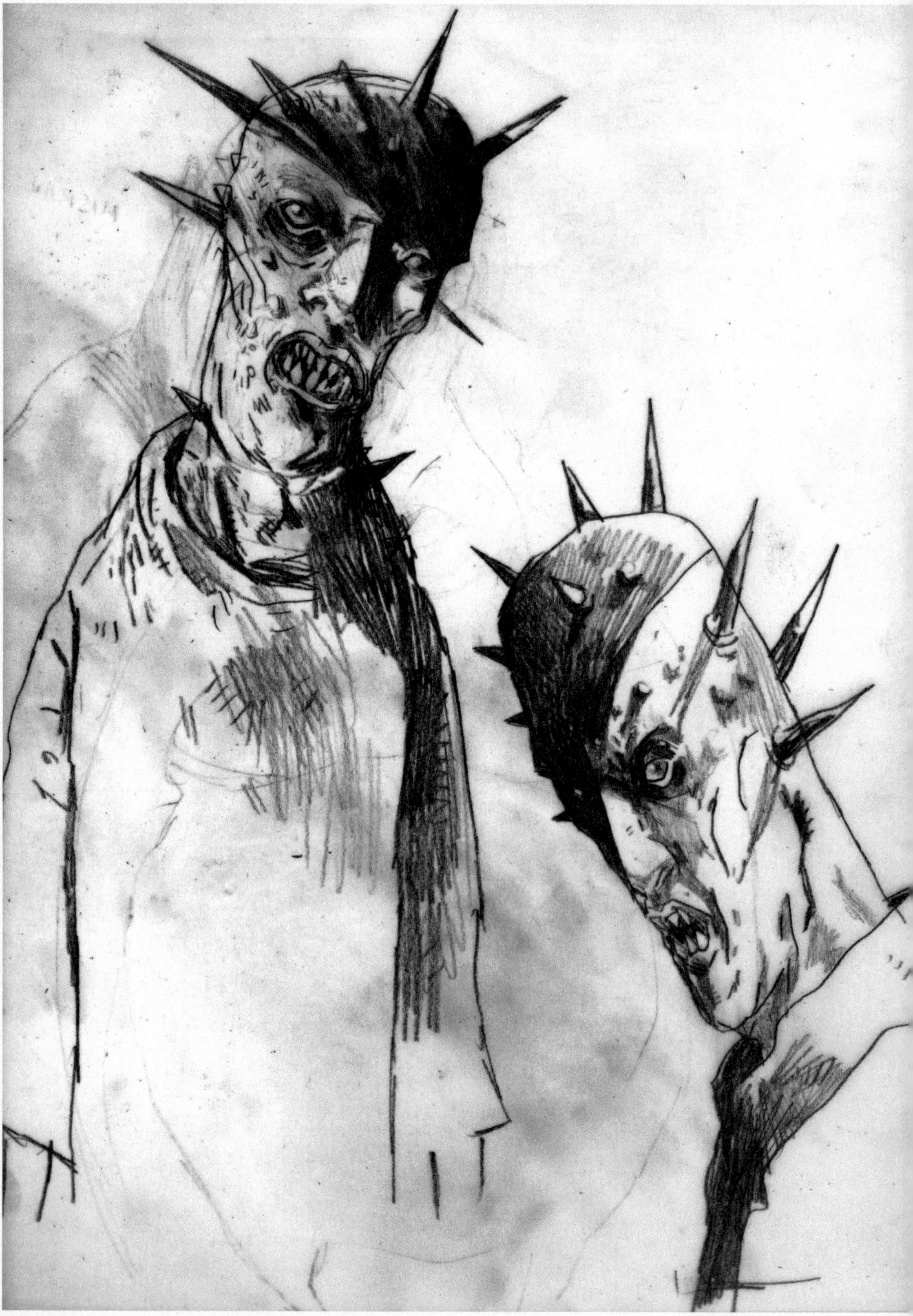

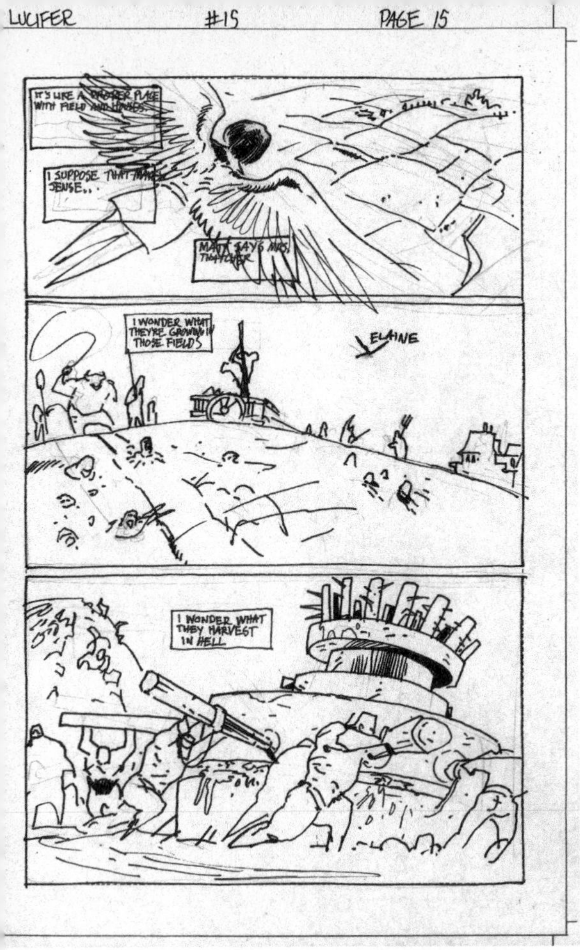
LUCIFER
#15
PAGE 15
I WONDER WHAT THEY'RE GROWING IN THOSE FIELDS
ELAINE
I WONDER WHAT THEY HARVEST IN HELL

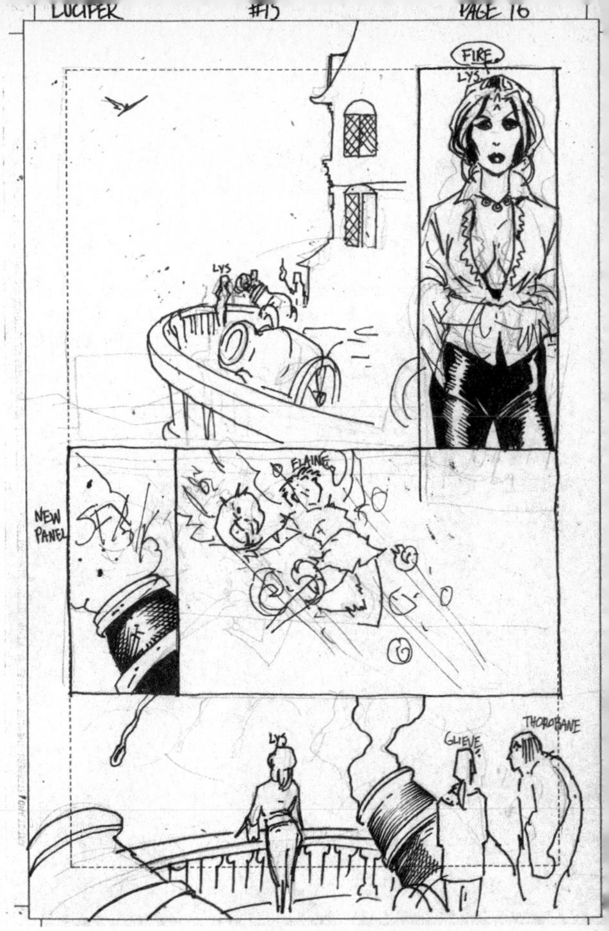
LUCIFER
#15
PAGE 16
FIRE
LYS
LYS
NEW PANEL
ELAINE
LYS
GLIEVE
THOROBANE

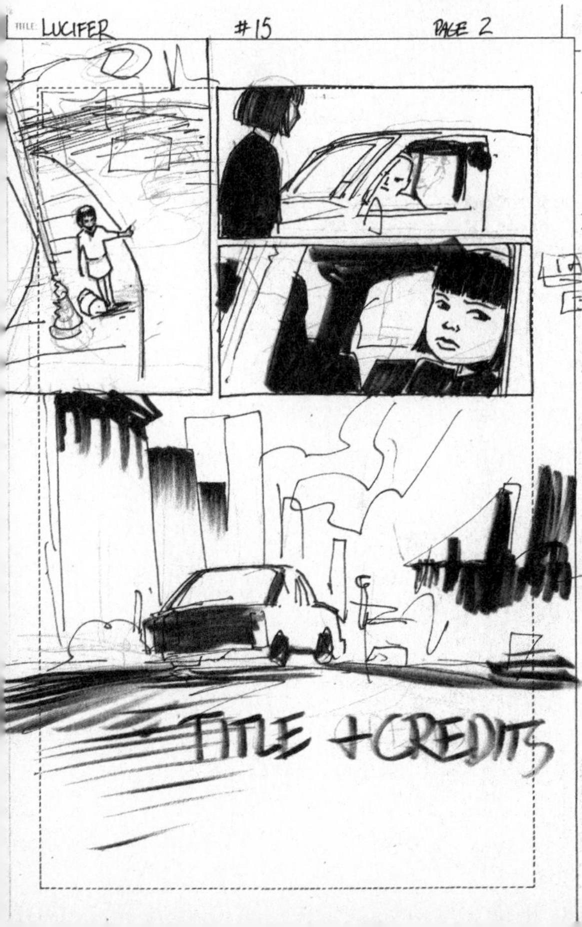
LUCIFER
#15
PAGE 2
TITLE + CREDITS

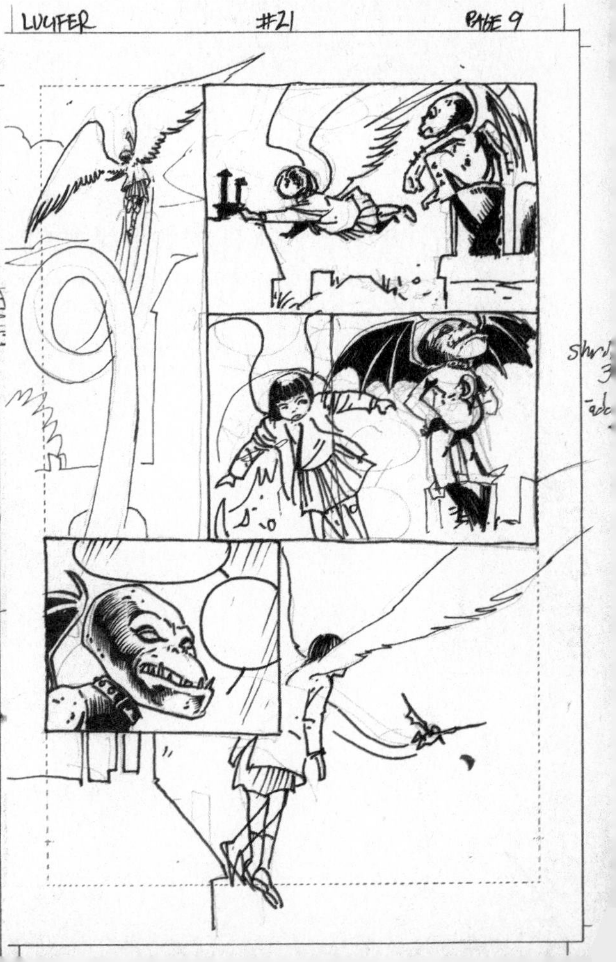
LUCIFER
#21
PAGE 9

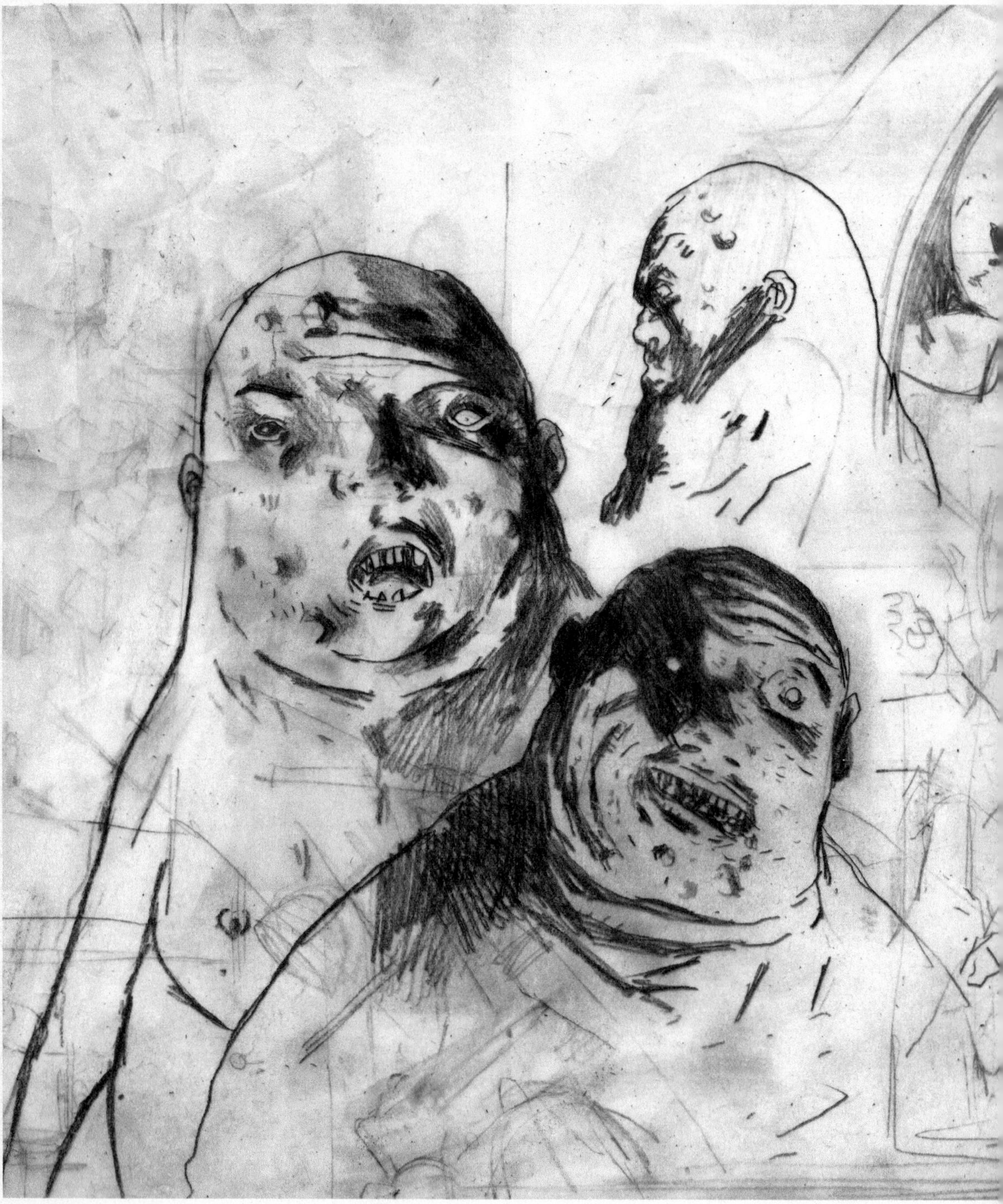